"This is the book I've been waiting for! Laura George is both an engaging writer and a meticulous researcher, leading the reader to a clear understanding of complex concepts such as integral theory, quantum physics, and the esoteric destiny of America. But there is more: *The Light* offers a comprehensive recipe for what 'Team Light' must do to help birth the next level of human consciousness through Truth, Love, and Light. What a treasure."

  – **Rev. Deborah Moldow**, founder of Garden of Light and Director of the
  Evolutionary Leaders Circle of the Source of Synergy Foundation

"Intriguing and fascinating ideas about consciousness, spirituality, and humanity! *The Light* gives us a lot of things to think about, especially about the merger of science and spirituality. I share Rev. George's hope for an evolutionary trajectory that brings humanity together and fosters greater compassion and understanding about the universe."

  – **Andrew Newberg, M.D.**, neuroscientist, professor, and author of
  How God Changes Your Brain, *Why We Believe What We Believe*, and
  Neurotheology: How Science Can Enlighten Us About Spirituality

"Bravo to Reverend Laura George for articulating the dawning spiritual epoch in her new book, *The Light*."

  – **Alex Grey**, artist and co-founder of the Chapel of Sacred Mirrors

"Laura George does research like few I know. The result, always, is a deeper look into the subject than anything you can find anywhere else. She stands alone in what she investigates and how. Her charts, her discoveries are awesome! Her description of the New Human, what we left behind, and what we are turning out to be is the best I've seen. Highly recommended for anyone who questions Light and Truth."

  – **PMH Atwater, L.H.D.**, researcher of near-death states and spiritual
  transformations, and author of *The Big Book of Near-Death Experiences*,
  Future Memory, *Beyond the Light*, and *Children of the Fifth World*

"*The Light* is faithful to its role in the Oracle *Truth* and *Love* trilogy. This masterful work illuminates how to avoid demonization/glorification traps, repress less, and raise more vibration for humanity – individually and collectively. An uplifting and heartful guide, Laura brings the 'Dove of Peace' and 'Crow of Sacred Law' per-spective that inspires us to shine as we face our great challenges, present and future."

  – **W. Cliff Kayser, III**, Vice President of Polarity Partnerships, LLC, Senior
  Fellow at the Institute for Polarities of Democracy, and co-author of *And:*
  Making a Difference by Leveraging Polarity, Paradox, or Dilemma (Vol. II)

THE PENTACLE

The Oracle Institute chose the Pentacle as a symbol for its humanitarian work after researching, designing, and considering dozens of potential logos. We selected the Pentacle because of its noble history and the fact that the Truth about this ancient symbol – like all Truth – needs to be revealed.

The oldest known use of the Pentacle dates to 3000 BCE, when it was used by the Sumerians and Babylonians to depict angles and provide directional orientation. Scholars believe that these civilizations also used the Pentacle for astrological purposes, assigning the five points to the planets: Mercury, Mars, Jupiter, Saturn, and Venus.

The great Greek mathematician Pythagoras was fascinated by the Pentacle. He recognized in its geometry a division of lines which resulted in the "golden ratio," an emblem of perfection that was incorporated into Greek art and architecture. Pythagoras was the first person to refer to the harmony and balance of the Cosmos, and his followers embraced the mystical concept of the soul's eternal existence through the process of transmigration. His followers also ascribed the points of the Pentacle to the five classical elements: earth, air, fire, water, and ideas.

Later, Roman Emperor Constantine used the symbol as a seal and amulet. When the Roman Catholic Church formed, some Christians adopted the Pentacle as a representation of the five wounds of Jesus, which pierced his two hands, two feet, and side. Other faiths associated the Pentacle with the five senses: touch, taste, smell, hearing, and sight.

In medieval times, the Pentacle was associated with the legends of King Arthur and the Knights of the Round Table, who were said to possess five virtues: friendship, generosity, chastity, courtesy, and piety. During the Renaissance, Leonardo da Vinci revived the Pentacle when he illustrated that the proportions of the human body symmetrically align within this sublime shape.

Today, at the close of the Fourth Spiritual Paradigm, the Pentacle reminds us of the five primary religions: Hinduism, Judaism, Christianity, Buddhism, and Islam. May these now ancient religions update their teachings and unify their wisdom traditions in order to guide humanity toward the utopian state described by their prophets as "heaven on earth."

And at the dawn of the Fifth Spiritual Paradigm, may we recall the most glorious and enduring use of the Pentacle – as a symbol for Venus, the goddess of Love. We, at The Oracle Institute, believe that it is this aspect of the Godhead and of our own divine nature which will inspire each of us to seek the perennial promise of the Pentacle:

Spiritual Enlightenment

THE LIGHT:
And the New Human

Book III of a Foundational Trilogy

Written in Association with:
The Oracle Institute

Contributed by Tau Lama
(Rev. Laura M. George, J.D.)

Book I of The Oracle Trilogy:
The Truth: About the Five Primary Religions

Book II of The Oracle Trilogy:
The Love: Of the Fifth Spiritual Paradigm

Oracle Institute Press, LLC

Published by:
Oracle Institute Press, LLC

A Division of:
The Oracle Institute
www.TheOracleInstitute.org

The Peace Pentagon
88 Oracle Way
Independence, VA 24348

Publisher's Cataloging-in-Publication Data

Names: George, Laura M., author.
Title: The light : and the new human / Rev. Laura M. George, J.D.
Series: Oracle Institute Foundational Trilogy
Description: Includes bibliographical references and index. | Independence, VA: Oracle Institute Press, LLC, 2022.
Identifiers: LCCN: 2022942375 | ISBN: 978-1-937465-32-2 (paperback) | ISBN: 978-1-937465-33-9 (ebook)
Subjects: LCSH Religion--Philosophy. | Religion and politics. | Religion and sociology. | Evolutionary psychology. | Social change. | Internationalism | United States--Civilization--21st century. | United States--Social conditions--21st century. | Mysticism. | Mind and body. | Self-help. | Feminism. | BISAC RELIGION / Philosophy | PHILOSOPHY / Metaphysics | BODY, MIND & SPIRIT / Mysticism | SELF-HELP / Spiritual | PSYCHOLOGY / Social Psychology | SOCIAL SCIENCE / Feminism & Feminist Theory
Classification: LCC BL51 .G46 2022 | DDC 201--dc23

Interior Design:
Deborah Eckbreth

Cover Fine Art:
Anthony Coviello

ORACLE PRESS BOOKS

The Truth: About the Five Primary Religions
Book I of the Oracle Foundational Trilogy

The Love: Of the Fifth Spiritual Paradigm
Book II of the Oracle Foundational Trilogy

The Light: And the New Human
Book III of the Oracle Foundational Trilogy

The Earth Constitution Solution: Design for a Living Planet
By Glen T. Martin, Ph.D. of Earth Constitution Institute

Evolutionary Relationships: Unleashing the Power of Mutual Awakening
By Patricia Albere of Evolutionary Collective

Trusting Doubt: A Former Evangelical Looks at Old Beliefs in a New Light
By Valerie Tarico, Ph.D.

Deas and Other Imaginings: Ten Spiritual Folk Tales for Children
By Valerie Tarico, Ph.D.

Divine Attunement: Music as a Path to Wisdom
By Yuval Ron, of the interfaith Yuval Ron Ensemble

Dying to Learn: First Book of the Initiate
By Oberto "Falco" Airaudi, founder of Damanhur

Reborn to Live: Second Book of the Initiate
By Oberto "Falco" Airaudi. founder of Damanhur

Seven Scarlet Doors: Third Book of the Initiate
By Oberto "Falco" Airaudi. founder of Damanhur

Bral Talej Divination Cards
By Shama Viola of Damanhur

DEDICATION

To my daughter Erin,
whose spiritual awakening is proving to be
as difficult as my own.

May she, and everyone who reads this book,
find comfort in the realization:
All paths lead back to the true Self and to God.

One more thing:
I revoke the dedication to J.C. in my first book.
Had I only known *The Truth* back then ...

TABLE OF CONTENTS

CHAPTER EIGHT

INTRODUCTION

Thoughts that have important consequences are always simple.
All my thinking could be summed up with these words:
Since corrupt people unite among themselves to constitute a force,
honest people must do the same. It's as simple as that.

Leo Tolstoy, *War and Peace*

L ike every New Human, I have been on a spiritual quest for answers, and
after twenty years of dedicated exploration, I finally feel ready to share
intimate aspects of my journey, including what I have learned during the
course of my esoteric studies. I therefore humbly offer my discoveries of God,
which (as opposed to *whom*) I most often will refer to as the "Light."

At this stage of my enlightenment adventure, I cringe at anthropomorphic
depictions of God and wince whenever a pronoun is used. None of them work:
neither "He," nor "She," nor "It." Truly, our vocabulary is limited, painfully so.
May the Light infuse me with the wisdom to write this book, which constitutes
the final installment of The Oracle Institute foundational trilogy.

For those who haven't read the first two book in this series, *The Truth: About
the Five Primary Religions* and *The Love: Of the Fifth Spiritual Paradigm*, no
worries. In the first chapter of *The Light: And the New Human*, I will quickly
review the five paradigms humanity has passed through to date and introduce
a vocabulary that will assist us in our pursuit of the Light and the identification
of what it means to be a New Human.

While the New Human, as we shall define such a person, is exceptional,
the truth is that we need *everyone* at full alert – ready, willing, and able to help
build a New World. There is much work to do if we are to survive and surmount
the myriad unprecedented challenges facing us. It is easy to feel overwhelmed:
global warming, wealth inequality, overpopulation, the Sixth Great Extinction,
threat of nuclear war, rise of artificial intelligence ... and now authoritarianism.
Truly, we are living in a dual and dangerous plane, one that is marked by ever-
increasing polarization and conflicting worldviews.

Now don't go getting all "New Agey" on me before you hear me out. I am
aware that most of what takes place on this planet is a grand illusion and that
non-duality is the goal. However, unless you are a spiritual master and have the
ability (and time) to indefinitely maintain the sublime state of *samadhi* (blissful
meditation), you will suffer under the delusion of duality.

Consequently, there is such a thing as evil. In fact, every one of our heroes fought evil, which is why we admire them. Jesus opposed the hypocrites of his day, Gandhi shamed the British into leaving India, and Martin Luther King, Jr. battled racism. Moreover, many of our heroes were killed pursuing their causes, including the three just mentioned. So with all due respect to monks on mountaintops (a.k.a. Lightholders) who enjoy prolonged periods of exaltation, what we need now are Lightworkers and Spiritual Warriors ... and lots of them!

We also need to collectively birth a new spiritual paradigm, one worthy of our 21st Century minds and hearts. Clearly, the next paradigm is breech, which means there will be plenty of pain to go around. To date, no paradigm shift has ever gone smoothly, without major sacrifice for those trapped in the crossfire between an old and a new belief system. Such is the history of epochal change: It leaves chaos in its wake until an orderly, new cosmic course is established.

Currently, we are witnessing a death match between the passing paradigm which was founded on "God the Father," and a new paradigm which promises the return of "God the Mother." If all goes well, the Godhead will shift into a gender-balanced equilibrium beyond ancient polytheism – a synergistic space energized with both Divine Masculine and Divine Feminine forces.

The cover of this book depicts a pregnant woman bearing a New Human. She integrates Ishtar, Isis, Sophia, the Holy Shekinah, and Shakti energy that has been suppressed for over two thousand years while humanity experimented with and suffered through "Daddy Deism" and attendant patriarchal afflictions. The woman is set against the backdrop of a pentacle in classic "Vitruvian" pose, made famous by Leonardo da Vinci. Therefore, she also represents the perfect woman – the "Daughter of Man" – in juxtaposition to the "Son of Man," a tragically misinterpreted construct of orthodox Judeo-Christianity.

Today, my patience is at an end, as I suspect yours is too. New Humans demand a Godhead that includes the Sacred Feminine and acknowledges her full partnership in protecting, preserving, and inspiring future New Humans. Mystics have always understood that the Godhead includes the Holy Mother alongside the Holy Father. For example, the Tree of Life in the *Kabballah* has two branches: one masculine, one feminine. The top two *sephirot* on the pillars are *Hokmah* (the Father) and *Binah* (the Mother), and above them – as the penultimate *sefirah* – lies *Keter* (the Crown), wherein the duality of the Divine Masculine and Feminine merge into a sublime, non-dual, genderful, genderless, allthingness, nothingness, Source of All Being: The Light!

To honor the return of the Sacred Feminine, we will not shirk from our duty to discern how and why she was suppressed for millennia. Neither will we avoid a sophisticated inquiry into what it means for New Humans to live in a dual and perilous plane alongside old humans, who fail to grasp the most basic and simplistic Law of the Universe – the Law of Gender.

Additionally, we will awaken the Divine Feminine by using the pronouns "she" and "her" to shorten sentence structure when referring to New Humans, while we will continue to use the standard pronouns "he" and "him" when referring to old humans. At first, the use of female pronouns may feel strange, even awkward. Yet, this gender-altered convention will arouse the feminine in each of us and generate relevant subliminal impact.

> *A New Human may incarnate a male, female, or transgender body.*
> *Such a person has balanced **her** masculine and feminine energies, as*
> *well as **her** left and right brain functions. Conversely, an old human*
> *is someone who still suffers from **his** fears and foibles.*

In most esoteric traditions, the masculine side of the Light is viewed as the "Creative" force in the Universe, while the feminine side is the "Wisdom" force. New Humans are creative and wise, strong and gentle, strategic and passionate. They also are ego-balanced, worldcentric, and conscious players in what I call the "God Game." New Humans are systems-thinkers who hold the big picture in their mind's eye, while also placing themselves in another person's shoes (including old humans) and expressing deep compassion. In sum, New Humans reliably and consistently seek the **Truth**, share the **Love**, and follow the **Light**.

So what will happen once there are enough New Humans on our beloved planet to reach the elusive Tipping Point into the next spiritual paradigm? We will enter an era in which the Golden Rule finally manifests for Team Human. I believe it is our destiny to build this prophesied paradise while still on Earth. First, however, we must locate the Light within ourselves, allow it to shine, and then utilize it to guide others to the threshold of a glorious New World. To wit: I offer this solemn text, a lettered vision quest to my sisters and brothers.

> *May this book inspire everyone who reads it, and*
> *May this book energize the Fifth Spiritual Paradigm.*
> *For the good of All and according to the free will of All.*
> *So it mote be.*

CHAPTER

DUALITY AND DISSONANCE: FRACTURING OF THE LIGHT

There is only Light and the Light is all.
Everything else is but a picture made of Light. ...
When you stand motionless, only watching,
you discover yourself as the Light beyond the watcher. ...
Consciousness does not shine by itself.
It shines by a Light beyond it.

In non-duality there is bliss; in duality – experience.
What comes and goes is experience with its
duality of pain and pleasure. ...
There is no such thing as an expression of reality.
You are introducing a duality where none exists.

Sri Nisargadatta Maharaj, *I Am That*

Duality has existed since the Big Bang, a perennial interplay between the Light and the Dark, good and evil, the Godhead and humanity. Moreover, duality is here to stay in the short run, and by "short run," I unfortunately mean hundreds (if not thousands) of years. Simply put, duality is the reality on the Earth Plane for the vast majority of humans, despite the wisdom contained in the opening quote. Here's another sad fact: Most people won't understand the quote, including some "New Humans" – who are the primary subject of this book.

To the chagrin of many of my "woke" friends, there is no way to start our exploration into the Light or the New Human except by categorizing people. How else will we know who views God as Light (i.e., an energy) and who thinks God is a guy in the sky? How else will we explore the myriad spiritual beliefs that exist today and their impact on society? How else will we know who is an "old" or a "new" human?

> *There may be said to be two classes of people in the world;*
> *those who constantly divide the people of the world into two classes,*
> *and those who do not.*[1]

Robert Benchley

The above quote is better known. In fact, I hear it often, since it's a favorite mantra of friends who accuse me of over-simplifying the world on the one hand by grouping humans, or being too judgmental on the other. Judging others is a definite no-no in the New Age belief system (and supposedly in Christianity). The inherent paradox of judging a person for judging others is a common characteristic of the New Age community and an inconsistency that is understood by students of **Spiral Dynamics**.[2] In the next chapter, we will address the issue of judgement vs. discernment.

For now, I will confess (a holdover habit from being raised Catholic): I do categorize people. I do this not to judge them, but to help myself comprehend the radical differences in how people relate to and operate within the world. Certainly, we can agree as a starting point that *Homo sapiens* is a complicated species. My goodness, the New Human (a.k.a. *Homo universalis*; a term coined by visionary Barbara Marx Hubbard) is even more complex!

By way of contrast, let us consider the variety that exists among canines. Essentially, a dog is a dog is a dog. Sure, there are breeds (and usually mutts) that are more intelligent than others, more aggressive, or more protective. Sometimes we place our own dogs into two categories depending on their behavior: "good dog" and "bad dog." Despite these differences, it still is reasonable to lump all breeds of dogs together and speak of canines as a homogeneous species with a relatively uniform set of loving and loyal traits, making them "man's best friend" in the animal kingdom.

Not so with human beings. Our IQs, innate gifts, educational levels, gender, race, and proximate cultures create vast differences right off the bat. Add to such asymmetry our individual worldviews and belief systems, and the differences become too extensive to treat humans as a monolithic group. That's why Ken Wilber – dubbed the "Einstein of Consciousness" – wrote the book and created the model known as the **Spectrum of Consciousness**.

> *Throughout this book, whenever consciousness is referred to as a spectrum, or as being comprised of numerous bands or vibratory levels, the meaning remains strictly metaphorical. ...*
>
> *Since there exists today a veritable plethora of psycho-therapeutic techniques, methods, schools, philosophies and disciplines, the problem – and it is a very real one, for therapist and layman alike – is to discover a semblance of order, an inner logic, a thread of continuity in this vast complexity of different and frequently contradictory psychological systems. Using the Spectrum of Consciousness as a model, this hidden semblance of order may in fact be demonstrated.*[3]
>
> Ken Wilber, *The Spectrum of Consciousness*

Consequently, if we wish to define what a New Human looks and acts like – morally, culturally, spiritually – we must accept and then analyze the broad number of exterior, objective factors, as well as the nearly limitless interior, subjective structures and states that impact human behavior. Indeed, we cannot approach any advanced spiritual topic or meaningful discussion of paradigm shift without a thoughtful blueprint for grouping humans.

For the purposes of this book, we will not categorize humans by their IQ, education, gender, race, wealth, or buying habits – as marketing experts do. Instead, we will explore: *Why do people believe what they believe?* We will look at why duality exists on the **Earth Plane** (the physical, material, seen world) and how it impacts our spiritual quest for non-duality and the Light in the **Ethereal Plane** (multiple dimensions of the unseen world). And we will learn why dissonance is required – *massive dissonance* – for people to question their belief system and substitute a new one, thereby vertically ascending the Spectrum of Consciousness.

Let's begin with a simple categorization, an observation I made years ago: In terms of basic focus, there actually are three kinds of people in the world: (i) those who choose to live in the past; (ii) those who predominantly live in the present (not to be confused with the "timeless now" discussed later); and (iii) those who prefer to live in the future. In short, this book is for those who live in the future – people who incarnated to shift the paradigm and build a brilliant New World, people who may be called New Humans.

Some of you may not have read the first two books in The Oracle Institute foundational trilogy, of which *The Light* is the third installment. *The Truth: About the Five Primary Religions* is the award-winning premier text in the trilogy, and it covers our past attempts to understand and define the **Godhead**.[4] *The Truth* focuses on mankind's religious history from the dawn of time through the start of the New Millennium, and it succinctly illustrates the nexus between religion, politics, and human rights throughout the ages.

The second volume of the Oracle trilogy, *The Love: Of the Fifth Spiritual Paradigm,* is an anthology that explores the present state of the human condition.[5] My noteworthy co-authors include: Nobel Peace Prize winners Archbishop Desmond Tutu and Aung San Suu Kyi, Pulitzer Prize winner Stephen Dunn, leading environmentalists Bill McKibben and David Suzuki, renowned poets Maya Angelou and Wendell Berry, visionary artists Alex Grey and Oberto "Falco" Airaudi from the Federation of Damanhur, New Age spiritualists Barbara Hand Clow and Andrew Cohen, and progressive Christian Pastor Brian McLaren, among others. These esteemed souls are very concerned about the trajectory of the human race and its impact on our precious planet. They see all the dynamics in play and the high stakes at risk. Clearly, we are at a critical juncture of human history, with no unifying theosophy on the horizon to rally us around sustainable, positive, and pluralistic goals.

The reading of *The Truth* and *The Love* may be unnecessary for your spiritual journey, but the writing of those books was crucial to mine. Though a private diary of my quest for Truth, Love, and Light may have sufficed to access my higher self and make sense out of the peak experiences I relished (due to their proximity to the Light) and endured (due to their alarming impact on my previously "normal" life), I nevertheless chose to publicly share my spiritual trek – a decision that forever changed the course of my life.

The fact that my writing helped me digest all the changes I was going through was pointed out to me initially by Dr. Paul, a psychologist I briefly visited after my early encounters with the Light. While blissful, these experiences also were harrowing, and I felt that I would benefit from a little professional psycho-analysis. I did not want to misinterpret what was happening to and inside of me. I also needed to orient myself to the mystical "messages" I was receiving before attempting to reorganize and reprioritize my life. So I needed a very special therapist, one who loved God and would not try to sidetrack me into discussions about "mommy/daddy" issues.

A trusted friend recommended Dr. Paul, and as I entered his office for the first time, I dourly noted the framed diploma hanging on his wall – from

Catholic University. You see, being female and possessing an adequate instinct for self-preservation in a misogynist world, I checked out of Catholicism, my birth religion, at a very early age and never looked back. Thereafter, I searched for God on my own, later with the help of teachers and mentors.

As a child, I went to temple with my best friend, who was Jewish. As a teen, I went to Muslim celebrations with my beloved Turkish girlfriend. And as an adult, I became even more fixated on the question: *Why do people believe what they believe?* So I studied the primary texts of the five primary religions: Hinduism, Judaism, Buddhism, Christianity, and Islam. I read New Age and contemporary spiritual classics like Madame Blavatsky's *Isis Unveiled* and Eckhart Tolle's *The Power of Now*. I explored autobiographies of the masters, like Guru Paramahansa Yogananda, Guru Nisargadatta Maharaj, Mahatma Gandhi, Father Teilhard de Chardin, and my favorite saint, Teresa of Avila. I even dabbled in Wicca for a while. Eventually, I adopted what I considered to be an appropriate esoteric path for myself, which absolutely did *not* include classic Catholicism.

Consequently, I was taken aback by Dr. Paul's diploma and abruptly said so at the start of our first session. Dr. Paul then upped the ante by telling me he had studied to become a Catholic priest! When I expressed concern that he had a "dog in this fight" and would not be able to impartially assist me in interpreting my peak experiences (or judging the soundness of my psyche), Dr. Paul assured me that his past would in no way influence his analysis of my recent spiritual encounters – the main reason I was seeking his assistance.

In my mind, the dubiosity-factor was high. I defiantly asked Dr. Paul for some assurance that he could be religiously neutral during our sessions. To assuage my worries, Dr. Paul explained that he left the seminary during his last year of studies and never became a priest.

"Why?" I inquired.

"Because I was horny."

I laughed until I cried and quickly thanked God for placing me with the right therapist. We then briefly discussed the true history (and absurdity) of the Catholic prohibition on priests having sex, and Dr. Paul shared that he was now married with children. Thereafter, I felt much better about discussing my newly evolving concept of God with Dr. Paul ... and the messages I was receiving.

In all, we shared about a half-dozen truly inspiring and comprehensive therapy sessions centered on the evolution of the Godhead and my then current theory on Source (the term I used back then for God). Then he blessed me and released me, with the Sign of the Cross for good measure! He said that in his professional opinion I was just fine. "After all," he added, "You're being instructed to write books on 'Truth, Love, and Light' and start a spiritual center, not shoot up a post office." Thank you, Dr. Paul, for the productive and precious time we spent together.

Feeling assured that I was in control of my faculties, I continued writing *The Truth*. I was content with the conclusions I had drawn about the five primary religions, viewing all of them as imperfect, manmade belief systems, while honoring the avatars of each. I also felt spiritually mature enough to continue my esoteric studies and communions with the Light. Yet I still was uncertain ("afraid" is more accurate) about founding a spiritual center.

And then came September 11, 2001. It rocked my world, as it did to many others. But in addition to the dread that most Americans were experiencing:

- I started to "feel" I had a mission somehow related to 9/11 and the world-wide resurgence of religious fundamentalism;
- I started to "see" a dystopian future during my meditations, an ugly course of events for my beloved country and the world;
- And I started to "hear" more messages from the Light, additional instructions beyond writing books and starting a spiritual center.

After 9/11, I struggled even more with how to honor my mystical messages. At the time, I was the single mother of three teenage children and worked as an attorney in northern Virginia. *How would my family, friends, and clients react if I stopped practicing law and started a spirituality school? How could I make such a radical break from my current life and career?* I finished writing *The Truth*, but realized that I was not living mine.

In short, 9/11 was the impetus I needed to gain control over my fear and dedicate my life to God. On the Spectrum of Consciousness, I fully embraced the **"Second Tier"** view (a New Human classification we soon will explore). Thus, 9/11 was the catalyst I needed to gather the courage and conviction to start The Oracle Institute and build the Peace Pentagon (our headquarters) – critical elements of my life assignment.

Let's pause for a moment to acknowledge the Earth Plane implications of the 9/11 tragedy. In this book, we will do a deep dive into duality, polarity, and how evil manifests within the human condition. Specifically, we will explore the Dark as a way to comprehend the Light. The events of 9/11 were dark indeed and a perfect teaching moment.

In addition, we will consider the status of evil within the Ethereal Plane. "As above, so below," recited Jesus and every other avatar who has visited this planet to teach. But what does this ancient, Hermetic phrase mean exactly? And how do multifaceted and sometimes malevolent energies in the Ethereal Plane impact us here on the Earth Plane?

In my opinion, 9/11 was yet another Sign that we are undergoing a global paradigm shift, partially fueled by the Light's evolutionary impulse, and partially fueled by humanity's use (and misuse) of free will. In other words, we will go through this shift because it is, essentially, preordained by God. But how we pass through this period of spiritual chaos is another matter, which we collectively get to decide.

TRICKLE-DOWN DEITY THEORY AND PARADIGM SHIFTS

The best definition of a paradigm shift is a systemic change in humanity's view of the Godhead, since everything follows our spiritual orientation. At The Oracle Institute, we call this the **Trickle-Down Deity theory**, which posits that our values mirror our vision of the Godhead. A corollary of this theory is that suffering stems from a Godhead that is woefully out of balance. For example, poverty and the inequality of wealth are two frontline symptoms of spurious belief systems spawned by an obsolete Godhead. Another example is the oppression of our Muslim sisters and the worldwide suffering and discrimination against women generally. How can women ever be "equal" on the Earth Plane if God is male in the Ethereal Plane?

Currently, at least half of all humans imagine God as a masculine entity (i.e., those who live in the past). The other half are either disenchanted with God and non-religious (i.e., those living in/for the present), or they are reassessing the Godhead and recognizing that the Light must contain both masculine and feminine energies (i.e., those who live in the future). A subset of this last group is actively experiencing the Light in a novel fashion – what the New Age movement is all about. And an even smaller segment is actually becoming the Light and reaching the "I Am" perspective, though this level of consciousness is exceedingly rare, as we will discuss in later chapters.

So presently, we are witnessing a worldwide reevaluation of the religions formed during the current but passing paradigm. The net result is spiritual chaos of epic proportions – the kind that only occurs during a major paradigm shift. Indeed, the last time humans experienced a shift of this magnitude, Jesus walked the Earth. Needless to say, Jesus heavily influenced the outcome of the last paradigm shift, though not necessarily as he intended.

Stated another way, when the Godhead changes, so does the paradigm. Thereafter, a true spiritual revolution ensues, and by that, I mean the dawn of a distinctly new era. No previous paradigm shift has occurred without great personal dissonance and societal upheaval, and there is no reason to believe that the current shift will be any easier. Indeed, this is the most dangerous paradigm shift in human history, given the state of our technology and the madmen in control of many countries. When I started this book, Donald Trump was in the White House. He now has left office, but only after staging a failed coup. Now, Vladimir Putin has started a war in Ukraine. Expect more insanity.

In both *The Truth* and *The Love*, I employ the term **Great Cusp** to describe the period of spiritual chaos which always accompanies a major paradigm shift. *The Truth* details previous Great Cusps, while *The Love* explores the current chaos of the New Millennium. Thus, *The Love* analyzes the types of positive, evolutionary values that will be needed in order for humanity to embrace the next paradigm. Despite the seemingly diversified belief systems of *The Love* co-authors (whoever thought that Brian McLaren and Falco would be in the same book!), these great minds and huge hearts all have one thing in common: They agree with Maya Angelou.

> *Now if you listen closely*
> *I'll tell you what I know*
> *Storm clouds are gathering*
> *The wind is gonna blow*
> *The race of man is suffering*
> *And I can hear the moan,*
> *'Cause nobody, But nobody*
> *Can make it out here alone.*[6]

Maya Angelou, "Alone"

Many New Agers thought the Great Cusp would end with the culmination of the Mayan Calendar on December 21, 2012.* They hoped for sudden and permanent change but were sorely misguided. Even now, some of my friends have yet to accept the reality that evolution is a slow and tedious process – one step forward some days, two steps back the next. I also have friends

---

* I was one of five women in the Great Pyramid on December 22, 2012, doing ceremony and welcoming the New Millennium (a story for another time).

who fantasize about the "Reverse Rapture" – a term I use to describe the instantaneous enlightenment they envision for themselves which propels them into a "fifth dimension," while fundamentalists of every ilk continue to struggle and learn their lessons here on the Earth Plane. These friends are unwilling to accept the dangers inherent in a Great Cusp – an existential battle between those who live in the past (or have a vested interest in the *status quo*) and those who seek a better future.

Sadly, some of my New Age friends have lost their truth barometers, succumbing to magical thinking, disinformation from Fox News (i.e., the real "fake news"), Russian social media propaganda,[7] and crazy QAnon posts.[8] For example, some on the far left think Trump is an anti-hero who will jail the masterminds of an elite child sex club (including Tom Hanks?), drain the swamp that he calls the "Deep State," dismantle the Federal Reserve, etc. Such nonsense is the hallmark of a Great Cusp.

In his recent books, Ken Wilber agrees that we are in the midst of an unprecedented transition, a rare moment in human history when we must collectively decide whether things are so bad that we will "transcend" the old paradigm and "include" a new one, or, failing that evolutionary call, regress in a backward slide down the Spectrum of Consciousness. Just picture the children's game "Chutes and Ladders." Unfortunately, Wilber gives us only a fifty-fifty chance of making it safely through the Great Cusp and into the next spiritual paradigm:

> In other words, the human race, for the first time ever in its history, is heading toward at least the possibility of a world beyond major and deep-seated conflict, and toward one marked more and more by mutual tolerance, embrace, peace, inclusion, and compassion. ...
>
> Right now humanity is in a desperate race between the 70 percent that remain at ethnocentric or lower levels, and the 30 percent or so at worldcentric and higher levels. ... As for that larger race (ethnocentric versus worldcentric) I also, seriously, give that a fifty-fifty chance of coming out in our favor.[9]
>
> Ken Wilber, *The Religion of Tomorrow*

In the next chapter, we will explore the "levels" of consciousness that Wilber is referencing above. For now, let us simply accept that the worldwide resurgence of religious fundamentalism and fascism is evidence that the old and new paradigms are clashing and vying for supremacy. Make no mistake, those who are wedded to the *status quo* will fight to the death to preserve it, which means this battle of belief systems will be bloody and take time to resolve.

Which leads me back to the significance of 9/11. At the time, we had a president, George W. Bush, who claimed to be communing with God.[10] Bush's "god" was hankering for war: a pinch of Yahweh from the *Old Testament*, with a dash of Pope Urban II's call for the first Christian Crusade. We also had a culture war brewing between Christian fundamentalists who dreamed of returning to a simpler (and whiter) 1950s America, and secular pluralists who were starting to realize that the civil rights programs institutionalized during the second half of the 20th Century were in jeopardy. In sum, thirty years of Evangelical planning and patience finally had eroded the wall between church and state, which most Americans assumed had become inviolate. In the Muslim world, the religious and political tensions were even more extreme.

I never accepted our government's formal explanation that Muslim terrorists orchestrated 9/11. Nor did I fall for the contrived reasons for going to war with Iraq (i.e., ties between Saddam Hussein and Al Qaeda; weapons of mass destruction). Evidence indicates that 9/11 was a false flag operation with which persons inside our government (and other governments) assisted. May I remind those of my fellow Americans who had their minds wiped clean that *three* buildings imploded that day. These buildings did not melt and they did not topple over. The Twin Towers and Tower 7 perfectly pancaked onto their footprints – a virtual impossibility under modern standards of construction.

The smoking gun, of course, is Tower 7, which only had a small fire burning in its lower floors. This fire could have been extinguished, but for the fact that the firefighters were instructed to evacuate. Roughly eight hours later, Tower 7 also magically imploded. Thermite, the chemical used by professional demolition experts, was found at ground zero.[11] Thermite is a manmade compound used for one reason and one reason only – to increase the heat of fire for demolition purposes.

I will not linger on the topic of "9/11 Truth," as there are many books and websites on this topic available to truth seekers.[12] Rather, my reason for referencing 9/11 is twofold: (i) to underscore the fact that the Great Cusp has been in full swing for decades; and (ii) to highlight that people's truth barometers were messed with that day! Astonishingly, the official 9/11 report does not even mention Tower 7. That omission helped many Americans sublimate their memory or consciously refuse to accept the 9/11 anomalies. However, many other people around the world tapped their dissonance over 9/11 to obtain greater clarity and move up the Spectrum of Consciousness.

Fair Warning: This book examines the realities of our dualistic Earth Plane, including the existence of evil and the possibility of human digression toward it. Despite the yearning most of us share for Truth, Love, and Light, it actually is the recognition of lies, hatred, and darkness – and the disassociation with dysfunctional belief systems – that propel us to grow.

Consciousness experts uniformly agree on what conditions are required in order for us to advance on the Spectrum of Consciousness. It takes dissonance – *strong dissonance* – for a soul to achieve upward momentum. In other words, exterior conditions must be bad before we start to question our interior values and begin to adjust our belief system. Something or someone must challenge us in a crucial way. Even then, the possibility exists that we will back-track under pressure, due to fear of the unknown or because we lack energy or insight to maintain forward movement. As Wilber explains, advancement along the Spectrum is not guaranteed, for either the individual or the collective.

> [E]very stage of evolution eventually runs into its own inherent limitations, and these may act as triggers for the self-transcending drives. The inherent limitations create a type of turmoil, even chaos, and the system either breaks down (self-dissolution) or escapes this chaos by evolving to a higher degree of order (self-transcendence) – so called order out of chaos. ...
>
> And so, in following the emergence of worldviews, we have to keep a constant watch for possible repressions and dissociations that have occurred, and are still occurring, in the historical process. ...
>
> And how we handle this, how we collectively handle this, will determine whether a new and more adequate worldview emerges to defuse these problems, or whether we are buried in our wastes.[13]

To date, the dominant worldview has shifted four times, as detailed in my first book *The Truth*. Here, we will briefly explore each of those paradigms and the fifth to be birthed, since our spiritual history is the logical starting point for assessing our collective progress. These groupings reflect shifts in the Godhead – due to the undeniable nexus between religion, politics, and human rights – and an overall sketch of humanity's slow but steady progress toward the Light.

First Spiritual Paradigm	All is One	Big Bang: 14 billion BCE
Second Spiritual Paradigm	Great Mother	25,000 BCE – 5000 BCE
Third Spiritual Paradigm	Gods & Goddesses	5000 BCE – 50 CE
Fourth Spiritual Paradigm	God the Father	50 CE – 2012 CE
Fifth Spiritual Paradigm	Integrated Godhead	Happening NOW!

FIRST SPIRITUAL PARADIGM

The First Paradigm can be viewed as the period before and immediately after the Big Bang, when the Light was prismatically fractured and the evolutionary process put into play. God and the cosmos were all that existed, and humans were a mere thought form within the Divine consciousness. In a manner yet to be fully understood, God splintered and expanded with thunderous, thermodynamic force. It was the beginning of life, but also disunity. With the Big Bang came separation.

The parable of the Garden of Eden alludes to a period of continued unity, even after the creation of Adam and Eve and the birth of human consciousness. In *The Holy Bible*, the unity between God and mankind represents the primordial state, before the advent of separation. But all this beautiful non-duality ended when Eve expressed her free will and ate from the "Tree of Knowledge." The "fall" of mankind can be understood as allegory for the Big Bang, when the Light fractured. Indeed, our separation from the Light was so painful that early humans struggled to adopt a meaningful belief system to explain duality.

Similarities also can be drawn between the oneness experienced in the Garden of Eden and the wholeness prehistoric humans felt with their surroundings. During this period of our evolution, everything – both material and ethereal – was naturally holistic. Now extinct proto-human cultures (e.g., *Homo erectus*), lived in organic concordance with Earth due to a shared, "bee-hive" mentality. These cultures experienced little if any egoic separation from each other or their environment. Our earliest ancestors instinctively followed a belief system that we moderns have termed **animism**, a magical level of existence where spirit is seen in everything and where all is still one.

SECOND SPIRITUAL PARADIGM

Around 50,000 BCE, our ancestors evolved into behaviorally modern *Homo sapiens*.[14] Once we began to think abstractly and to verbally articulate our thoughts, we ushered in a new paradigm of self-expression and separateness (as Eve did when she expressed her free will). Consequently, the arrival of modern humans marks the official end of the First Paradigm and the start of duality. At this point, humans also started playing the **God Game**, a term we will use throughout this book to describe the many Earth Plane illusions we encounter in our quest to reunify with the Light.

During the Second Paradigm, early humans depicted a rotund, likely pregnant Goddess, who we moderns call the **Great Mother**. Anthropologists date Great Mother statuary, such as the Venus of Willendorf (right), to 25,000 BCE, and similar idols have been found throughout the world. Consequently, it appears early humans practiced **female monotheism**, which was a logical belief system when one considers that women are the bearers of life.[15]

Not only did our ancient ancestors worship the Divine Feminine as the Creator and life-giving force, according to scholars, the Great Mother served as the primary source of supernatural inspiration for nearly 20,000 years,[16] making female monotheism the longest-lived paradigm in human *her*-story.

> *I am nature, the universal Mother, mistress of all the elements, primordial child of time, sovereign of all things spiritual, queen of the dead, queen of the immortals. My nod governs the shining heights of heaven, the wholesome sea breezes, the lamentable silences of the world below. I know the cycles of growth and decay.*[17]

In these early cultures, both sexes contributed to the survival of the clan. As a result, there existed no overt distinction between male and female roles. Eventually, however, humans progressed from being hunters and foragers to herders and farmers. **The Age of Agriculture** dates to 10,000 BCE, when humans started to segue from living a nomadic lifestyle to building permanent homes and villages. The great river valley civilizations and early empires started to form about 5000 BCE. As these cities became more prosperous, a merchant class evolved to sell and trade surplus supplies. In addition, the cities needed to be defended, so a warrior class developed. Marauding fiefdoms stole surpluses, battled for territories, and enslaved other humans.

By this time, sexual reproduction was fully understood and the man's role in procreation became more honored. Issues of lineage and inheritance were paramount, as powerful men began to dominate the planet. By the end of the Second Paradigm, division of labor emerged, women became the "weaker sex," and men started to view women as property. In the words of historian Riane Eisler, "At this pivotal branching, the cultural evolution of societies that worshipped the life-generating and nurturing powers of the universe – in our time still symbolized by the ancient chalice or grail – was interrupted."[18] As a result of all these changes, female monotheism was cast aside. Yet, rather than imagining a single deity with both male and female attributes, Goddess now had to scoot over and share her throne with all manner of fierce and powerful Gods. Furthermore, in most cultures a special God was adopted to protect, inspire, and lead the people in battle. The paradigm was shifting big time.

THIRD SPIRITUAL PARADIGM

By 5000 BCE, humanity had modified the Godhead and fully entered the Third Paradigm, during which most of the world practiced polytheism, a belief in multiple male Gods and female Goddesses. What is interesting about the Third Paradigm is that only one of the religions created during that era has survived to this day, namely Hinduism. All the other polytheistic religions have been relegated to our history and mythology books, including the Sumerian, Babylonian, Egyptian, Greek, and Roman pantheon of deities.

Hinduism: Primary Gods and Goddesses

Not only has Hinduism retained its original Gods and Goddesses, it has added hundreds more! It also spawned the insidious caste system, which developed during the creation of societal roles and functions: servant, farmer, merchant, warrior, ruler, and priest. Thankfully, in most of the world today, overt systems of segregating humans for purposes of rank and privilege have ended. In India, the caste system is being challenged as well, and the Constitution now bans discrimination against "Untouchables" (i.e., people doomed to the lowest social status because of supposed impurity).

When [the gods] *divided Purusa, how many portions did they make? What do they call his mouth, his arms? What do they call his thighs and feet? The brahmin* [priest] *was his mouth, of both his arms was the rajanya* [rulers and warriors] *made. His thighs became the viasya* [farmers and merchants], *from his feet the sudra* [servant] *was produced.*

Rig Veda, Book X, Hymn 90

Ancient Hindus followed a collection of holy scripture called the *Vedas*, composed approximately 1500 BCE, authorship unknown. These texts set forth important contributions to our collective spiritual database or **Tower of Truth**. First, Hinduism introduced the concept of **karma**, the belief that what you do in this lifetime has consequences and determines rebirth. Second, the law of cause and effect led to an important corollary – the **Golden Rule**. Thus, Hinduism gets credit for identifying two cardinal cornerstones of all later value systems.

Bounteous is he who gives unto the beggar who comes to him in want of food and feeble. ... Let the rich satisfy the poor implorer, and bend his eye upon a longer pathway. Riches come now to one, now to another, and like wheels are ever rolling.

The foolish man wins food with fruitless labor: that food – I speak the truth – shall be his ruin. He feeds no trusted friend, no man to love him. All guilt is he who eats with no partaker.

Rig Veda, Hymn X, Verse 117

Thereafter, Jewish prophets arrived on the Earth Plane with new messages from and about God. The prophet **Abraham** (*circa* 2500 BCE) communed with a God called *El*. Then **Moses** (*circa* 1250 BCE) described the Hebrew God more fully and introduced the name **Yahweh** (tetragrammaton: YHWH).

"I am the God of your father, the God of Abraham, the God of Isaac, the God of Jacob." Moses hid his face, for he was afraid to look at God. ...

"But," said Moses to God, "when I go to the Israelites and say to them, 'The God of your father has sent me to you.' if they ask me, 'What is his name?' what am I to tell them?"

God replied, "I am who I am." Then he added, "This is what you tell the Israelites: "I AM sent me to you." ... "This is my name forever; this is my title for all generations."

Exodus, Chapter 3:6-15

Thus, Judaism set the stage for a return to monotheism, even though the concept took a while to catch hold again. Why? For starters, there is some question whether the founders of Judaism were of one mind. Consider that the Hebrews referred to God as El, Elohim, El Shaddai, and Yahweh – which may be alternative names for God or possibly different names for different Gods. Scholars do not agree on which name was used first nor on the exact meaning of each term, but **Elohim**, the plural form of El, is the most common name used for God in *Genesis*.

On the other hand, *Genesis* 14:18 reveals that Abraham supplicated himself to **Melchizedek**, the King of Salem (a.k.a. king of "peace"). Whether Melchizedek was a high priest in the Order of Melchizedek or its founder, this is the same priestly order ascribed to **Jesus** in the *New Testament*.[19] It therefore is notable that Melchizedek called God El Elyon (God the Most High), even though it was Yahweh who gave the **Ten Commandments** to Moses.

In sum, theologians surmise that the early Jews used these various Hebrew terms in purposeful ways, an indication that the spiritual path from polytheism back to monotheism took longer than we generally think. Even King Solomon (*circa* 950 BCE) succumbed to paganism, more than 1,500 years after Abraham founded Judaism. It was not until after the crucifixion of Jesus that the singular Christian God (and his "only begotten son") started to overtake the Roman pantheon of deities. Incidentally, the deification of Jesus was a fierce process that took hundreds of years, and it is carefully chronicled in *The Truth*.

Before we get to Jesus, though, we need to credit the Eastern avatar **Buddha** (*circa* 500 BCE) with important additions to our Tower of Truth. To quickly recap, during the Third Paradigm, the Hindus advanced the principle of *karma* and the oldest expression of the Golden Rule. The Jews reintroduced monotheism and promoted a new moral code, the Ten Commandments. So what did Buddha, who came next in time, add to our well of spiritual wisdom?

In addition to trying to set the record straight in the East as to whether there are multiple deities occupying the heavens (i.e., he broke from Hinduism on that score), Buddha brought the concept of enlightenment, which he called **nirvana**. This teaching was radically different, because it was premised on mankind's innate ability to attain a state of perfection. All the other spiritual belief systems then in existence viewed man as unworthy of reuniting with God, who resided in a distinctly elevated Ethereal Plane that was separate from the Earth Plane where man lived.

For example, early Hindus believed that the cycle of rebirth (*samsara*) took eons, and that until a soul eliminated *karma* and detached from the Earth Plane, it could not obtain release (*moksha*) from reincarnation, thereby allowing the life-death-life cycle to continue. Hindus also believed that only the highest caste members – the *brahmin* priests (never female) – could achieve *moksha*. For everyone else, the soul would reincarnate, or at best migrate to the lower levels of heaven, depending on its *karmic* state. Only Brahma, the creator God of the Hindu triumvirate (also comprised of Shiva, the God of destruction, and Vishnu, the sustainer of the Universe) had access to the highest heaven. Thus, ancient Hindus did not believe in a heavenly afterlife for humans in the highest godly realm and, hence, no reunification with Brahma.

Consequently, Buddha's teaching that anyone at any time could achieve *nirvana* contradicted early Hindu teachings (though not the later Vedanta schools of Hinduism and other esoteric teachings).[20] Moreover, Buddha was not shy about criticizing the *brahmin* priests for their theological errors.

> *When these brahmins teach a path that they do not know or see, saying, "This is the only straight path," this cannot possibly be right. Just as a file of blind men go on, clinging to each other, and the first one sees nothing, the middle one sees nothing, and the last one sees nothing – so it is with the talk of these brahmins.*
>
> *Digha Nikaya*, Sutra XIII, Verse 15

Like the Hindus, the Hebrews believed they were unworthy of being with God in heaven. Instead, the *Old Testament*, which rabbinic scholars began to compile around 900 BCE, describes a potential "heaven on earth." But first a Messiah ("anointed one") from the House of King David would be needed. In the prophecy, the Messiah leads the Jews in an apocalyptic war between the nations and then oversees a time of judgment. Thereafter, the Messiah is enthroned in Israel to rule over the world, which is restored to its original perfection (a.k.a. the Garden of Eden). The Jews still are waiting for their king, having duly rejected Jesus for failing to satisfy the Messiah prophecy. Most notably, Jesus died and did not usher in an era of global peace.

In the East, however, Buddha was experiencing a new vision of heaven on earth. At the age of thirty-five and after renouncing both his princely birthright and his later adopted asceticism, Buddha achieved enlightenment. He then lived another forty-five years to teach the process. Therefore, unlike Jesus – whose years of ministry were few and poorly recorded in the four gospels chosen by the Catholic Church – there was plenty of time for Buddha to share his mystical messages and for his followers to record his teachings and practice them.

Critical to Buddha's teachings are the **Four Noble Truths**. The first truth is that life is suffering, since even transient moments of joy are impermanent. The second truth is that we prolong suffering when we crave Earth Plane pleasures. Third, suffering can end only when we free ourselves from all desire. Fourth, by following the **Noble Eight-Fold Path**, we may attain *nirvana* and become a *buddha* ourselves. Once achieving buddhahood, a soul may elect to return to the Earth Plane as a *bodhisattva* to teach and assist with the enlightenment of others.

> *Some are born in a womb,*
> *Wrongdoers, in hell.*
> *Those of good course go to heaven,*
> *To nirvana those without influxes.*

Dhammapada, Sutra IX, Verse 126

Although truly inspiring, Buddha stopped short of describing *nirvana* as reunion with Brahma, the ultimate God. Rather, he described it as a cessation of desire, an extinguishment of the self, and an end to rebirth – which means that he left many of his followers wondering what, exactly, *nirvana* entails. Nevertheless, Buddha's teachings were revolutionary. Never before had a prophet proclaimed the human condition as having such Divine potential! Buddhism has assisted many souls in attaining the same wondrous state that Buddha achieved, so his were monumental additions to our Tower of Truth. Indeed, Buddha called his path the ***dharma*** (truth).

Lastly, it is worth emphasizing that Buddha described *nirvana* as a state that can be achieved through study, practice, and earnestness. At Oracle, we call this the **Saddha** process of enlightenment. *Saddha* is a Sanskrit word that is loosely defined as "faith," but *Saddha* should not be compared to the blind faith promoted by some Christian sects. Properly translated, the word means "trustful confidence" – a faith that has solid underpinning and steadily grows, because it is based on actual experience with the Light.

Eventually, the avatars of the **Axial Age** (*circa* 800–200 BCE) – including other masters such as Confucius, Lao Tzu, and Parshvanatha – set the stage for another paradigm shift. In fact, the end of the Third Spiritual Paradigm was an especially fertile era, producing new theosophies on how to achieve human perfection. As a result, humanity started to feel worthy and empowered to approach the Light on a more intimate basis. It was time for another dramatic shift in the Godhead.

FOURTH SPIRITUAL PARADIGM

In *The Truth*, I give credit to the prophet Jesus (likely 4 BCE–33 CE) for ushering in the next paradigm. Like Buddha, Jesus spoke of a singular God, but Jesus described his "Father" as compassionate, a God who loves all of us and wants us to rejoin him in heaven. This dramatic redefinition of the Godhead marks the shift into the Fourth Paradigm.

Also like Buddha, Jesus gave us a formula for perfecting ourselves (later dubbed "salvation"). His was a new, affirmative prescription to "Love your neighbor," which we at Oracle call the **Eleventh Commandment**.

> *One of the scribes ... asked him, "Which is the first of all the commandments?"*
>
> *Jesus replied, "The first is this: ... 'You shall love the Lord your God with all your heart, with all your soul, and with all your mind, and all your strength.' The second is this: 'You shall love your neighbor as yourself.' There is no other commandment greater than these."*
>
> *Gospel of Mark*, Chapter 12:28

At first blush, the Eleventh Commandment doesn't look so hard ... but wait. There is more to Jesus' formula for soul perfection, more than just loving God and our fellow man. In order to join God, we also have to love our enemies!

> *You have heard it said that, "You shall love your neighbor and hate your enemy." But I say to you, love your enemies, and pray for those who persecute you, that you may be children of your heavenly Father.*
>
> *Gospel of Matthew*, Chapter 5:43

The Eleventh Commandment is quite a high bar – way higher than most Christians are willing to accept. What about the other Ten Commandments? Are they still applicable?

> *Do not think that I have come to abolish the law or the prophets ... until heaven and earth pass away, not the smallest letter ... will pass from the law, until all things have taken place. Therefore, whoever breaks one of the least of these commandments and teaches others to do so will be called least in the kingdom of heaven.*
>
> *Gospel of Matthew*, Chapter 5:17

And Jesus didn't stop there. He provided even more challenging instructions on how to perfect ourselves.

> *You know the commandments, "You shall not commit adultery; you shall not kill; you shall not steal ...." There is still one thing left for you: sell all that you have and distribute it to the poor, and you will have treasure in heaven. ... In the same way, every one of you who does not renounce all his possessions cannot be my disciple.*
>
> *Gospel of Luke*, Chapter 18:20; 14:33

Wow, we have to sell all our possessions too? Jesus seems to demand an extremely high measure of selflessness. Therefore, it's quite doubtful that Jesus would sanction **Prosperity Theology**, a relatively new Christian movement that asserts faith brings financial reward. This doctrine is popular with American televangelists who operate mega-churches. Speaking of which, what does Jesus say about false teachers?

> *Woe to you scribes and Pharisees, you hypocrites! You lock the kingdom of heaven before human beings. You do not enter yourselves, nor do you allow entrance to those trying to enter. ...*
>
> *Woe to you scribes and Pharisees, you hypocrites! You are like whitewashed tombs, which appear beautiful on the outside, but inside are full of dead men's bones and every kind of filth. Even so, on the outside you appear righteous, but inside you are filled with hypocrisy and evildoing. ...*
>
> *I tell you, unless your righteousness surpasses that of the scribes and Pharisees, you will not enter the kingdom of heaven.*
>
> *Gospel of Matthew*, Chapter 23:13; 5:20

Jesus, we don't have scribes or Pharisees anymore, so would you explain it just one last time: *How does one get into heaven?* And please speak plainly, so that we won't be confused.

> *When the Son of Man comes in his glory ... all the nations will be assembled before him. And he will separate them from one another, as the shepherd separates the sheep from the goats. He will place the sheep on his right, and the goats on his left.*
>
> *Then the king will say to those on his right, "Come, you who are blessed of my Father. Inherit the kingdom prepared for you from the foundation of the world. For I was hungry and you gave me food, I was thirsty and you gave me drink, a stranger and you welcomed me,*

naked and you clothed me, ill and you cared for me, in prison and you visited me." ...

Then he will say to those on his left, "Depart from me, accursed ones, into the eternal fire prepared for the devil and his angels. For I was hungry and you gave me no food, I was thirsty and you gave me no drink, a stranger and you gave me no welcome, naked and you gave me no clothing, ill and in prison, and you did not care for me. ... What you did not do for one of these least ones, you did not do for me." And these will go off to eternal punishment, but the righteous to eternal life.

Gospel of Matthew, Chapter 25:31

For those readers who are curious about how Jesus' stringent message of self-perfection got so mangled, I again invite you to read *The Truth*. Therein, I carefully chronicle the bombastic personality and fallacious teachings of **Saul of Tarsus** (a.k.a. **Saint Paul**), a man who never met Jesus but managed to abscond with and completely twist the Jewish reform movement that Jesus started and which his brother **Saint James "the Just"** dutifully continued.[21]

Nowhere is there any evidence that Jesus sought to start a new religion – *nowhere*. Nor did Jesus claim to be the only son of God. Rather, Jesus routinely used the term "son of man," a Hebrew phrase for a worthy or perfect person.[22] Nevertheless, after his "conversion," Paul convinced James to let him preach throughout the Roman Empire.[23] The rest, as they say, is Christian history ... as told and tainted by the Catholic Church.

Let's start with a quick rundown of Paul's blasphemies and betrayals. Using *The Holy Bible* itself, it is quite easy to prove that Paul:

✓ Participated in the murder of Saint Stephen;[24]
✓ Persecuted the original apostles after the crucifixion;[25]
✓ Sought to arrest Saint James – the true brother of Jesus, High Priest of the Jewish Temple, one of the "three pillars" of the reform movement, and Bishop of Jerusalem for thirty years after his brother's death;[26]
✓ Proclaimed himself an apostle;[27]
✓ Preached rogue concepts to the gentiles, such as:
  • We are innately sinful and incapable of perfecting ourselves;[28]
  • Jesus sacrificed himself for our sins;[29]
  • We no longer are bound by the Ten Commandments;[30]
  • Salvation is reached through "blind faith" not "good works";[31]
  • Women are unworthy of being church leaders;[32]

✓ Ignored James' instructions to stop misleading people about Jesus' teachings and the importance of "good works";[33] and

✓ Began the deification process of Jesus.[34]

To summarize: It was Paul – not Jesus or James – who founded modern Christianity. Paul also laid the groundwork for the Catholic Church to further twist the messages of Jesus. *The Truth* chronicles Paul's theological errors and his superficial and harmful teachings which directly conflict with Christ's (and Buddha's) divine instructions. No wonder some historians believe that Paul was a Roman spy sent to undermine the reform movement started by Jesus, which his brother James continued for thirty years until his murder by the Sanhedrin Council. Notably, James' death (*circa* 68 CE) was a contributing factor to the start of the Jewish-Roman War, which ended in 70 CE with the destruction of the Jewish Temple. Today, only the western Wailing Wall remains.

The Truth also explains why the Roman Empire ultimately adopted Paul's version of Christianity. In short, because Paul's new religion promised an easy path (blind faith) and a heavenly reward (salvation through Christ), his narrative captured the imagination of Romans, who already followed a variety of magical deities (e.g., Isis, Mithras, Sol Invictus). Then in 325 CE – after centuries of religious zealotry and spiritual chaos (i.e., the last Great Cusp) – Emperor Constantine convened the Council of Nicaea and sanctioned the **Roman Catholic Church** – a last ditch effort to unify his fractured empire. It didn't work, and the Roman Empire collapsed roughly one hundred years later.

The Catholic Church survived, however, to become the most powerful force in the Western world. The popes built a formidable military, the Knights Templar, and they forged strategic business alliances with the Christian monarchs. To keep the Muslims at bay, the popes wrought centuries of war via the Christian Crusades. To maintain control, they terrorized the masses with the (un)Holy Inquisition, which operated for more than 800 years.

In particular, the popes targeted the Cathars, a peace-loving French sect of **Gnostic Christians**, for total annihilation. The Cathars were preserving Jesus' esoteric lessons and they composed some of the *Gnostic Gospels*. After the church selected the four canonical gospels, all non-conforming texts were deemed "heretical." Eventually, the *Gnostic Gospels* were ordered destroyed, thereby completely scrambling the private teachings of Christ.

As a result of its ruthless, interminable, and absolute dominion over the Western world (a.k.a. Christendom), the Catholic Church ultimately supplanted Jesus in defining the Fourth Spiritual Paradigm. Not even the Great Schism of

1054 or the **Protestant Reformation** of the 1500s (yet another misinterpretation of Jesus' teachings) could topple the patriarchal power of the Vatican and the preeminence of **God the Father** (and his godly son).

Even today in the United States, we see a vigorous resurgence of Paul's bad theology. In keeping with the Trickle-Down Deity theory, we also see America collapsing under the weight of its unbalanced Godhead and hypocritical values. Indeed, the election of Donald Trump constitutes *prima facie* evidence that the Religious Right has completely lost its moral compass. Currently, the Earth Plane is charged with the same sort of spiritual confusion, political corruption, and senseless war that marked the end of the Third Paradigm and the beginning of the Fourth. Yet again, humanity finds itself experiencing an acute level of dissonance, which hopefully is powerful enough to propel us into the unknown and a bit closer to the Light.

Before we delve into the chaos of our Great Cusp, we need to honor the Muslim prophet **Muhammad** (570–632 CE), who valiantly attempted to clarify Jesus' mission and correct some of the theological errors adopted by Christians. He masterfully added context to the Fourth Paradigm and foreshadowed the one to come – the Fifth Paradigm that is knocking at our door right now. What a revolutionary messenger Muhammad was! His lofty goal was to unify the three religions of Abraham (Judaism, Christianity, and Islam), and he channeled the third installment of "The Book," which includes the Jewish *Old Testament*, the Christian *New Testament*, and the Islamic *Holy Quran*.

Based on the genealogy reported in *Genesis* 17:15, Muhammad taught that Arabs and Jews are blood brothers. He taught that the Jewish line was descendant through Abraham's second son, Isaac, and the Arab line was descendant through Abraham's first son, Ishmael. So much for family unity.

> *Oh ye Apostles! Enjoy all things good and pure, and work righteousness: For I am well-acquainted with all that ye do. And verily this Brotherhood of yours is a single Brotherhood, and I am your Lord and Cherisher: therefore, fear me and no other.*
>
> *But people have cut off their affair of unity, between them, into sects: Each party rejoices in that which is with itself. But leave them in their confused ignorance for a time.*
>
> *Holy Quran*, Sura XXIII, Verses 51-54

Again, for anyone interested in a concise yet thorough summary of the history of Islam, I encourage you to read *The Truth*. Therein, you will learn what Muhammad actually recited and what is literally recorded in the *Quran*. Additionally, you will see that in our world today, Muslims are following the teachings of their prophet about as well as Christians are following the true teachings of Jesus. Such a pity.

Muhammad especially was horrified by the deification of Jesus – a brutal affair waged by men of power, and a process that took five hundred years to conclude.[35] Muhammad correctly pointed out that by adopting the **Catholic Trinity**, Christians violated the Second Commandment's prohibition against the pagan belief in multiple deities: God the Father, Son, and Holy Spirit.

> *They do blaspheme who say: "God is one of three in a Trinity." For there is no god except one Allah. ...*
>
> *Christ the son of Mary was no more than an apostle; many were the apostles that passed away before him. His mother was a woman of Truth. They had both to eat their daily food. See how Allah doth make his Signs clear to them; Yet see in what ways they are deluded away from the truth!*
>
> *Holy Quran*, Sura V, Verses 75-78

Muhammad also found the role of priests offensive, since each of us should commune with God on our own. In the following quote, Muhammed again distinguishes between Jesus and God.

> *They take their priests and their authorities to be their lords in derogation of Allah; And they take as their Lord, Christ, the son of Mary; Yet they were commanded to worship but one God: There is no god but He. Praise and glory to Him: Far is He from having the partners they associate with Him.*
>
> *Holy Quran*, Sura IX, Verse 31

Muhammad viewed all Jews, Christians, and Muslims as "Believers" in the one true God, whom he called Allah (another derivation of El). He also delivered an updated moral code to his people that supplemented but did not supersede the Ten Commandments brought by Moses, or the Eleventh Commandment brought by Jesus. For example, the new laws elevated the status of Muslim women above conditions found anywhere else in the world. Muslim women could own and inherit property, obtain a divorce, and secure financial support from their husband's family if widowed.

Moreover, Muhammad's code of ethics contained explicit instructions on when war was permitted and the rules of war. In fact, *The Holy Quran* forbids a Believer from killing another Believer. This rule encapsulates the corollary that conversion to Islam was not compulsory within the Muslim Empire. Please note, if you haven't already, the distinct difference between the religious tolerance fostered by Islam versus the "convert or be killed" tactics employed by the Catholic Church during the Christian Crusades.

> *Never should a Believer kill a Believer: but if it happens by mistake, compensation is due. ... If the deceased belonged to a people at war with you, and he was a Believer, the freeing of a Believing slave is enough. If he belonged to a people with whom ye have a treaty of mutual alliance, compensation should be paid to his family. ...*
>
> *If a man kills a Believer intentionally, his recompense is Hell, to abide therein forever: and the wrath and the curse of Allah are upon him, and a dreadful penalty is prepared for him.*
>
> Holy Quran, Sura IV, Verses 92-93

What I love most about Muhammad, though, is that he instructed his followers to de-personify God. He chastised the Christians for deifying and worshipping Jesus, and he praised the Jews for emphasizing that God is beyond mere mortal physiology and psychology.

> *You shall not make for yourself an idol, or any likeness of what is in heaven above or on the earth beneath or in the water under the earth.*
>
> Exodus, Chapter 20:4

However, because Muhammad lived during the era of "God the Father," it was hard for him to convince Muslims, let alone the pagan Arabs, to stop viewing God in human terms. But he gave it his best shot, by constantly reminding his people that God should be viewed as Light.

> *Allah is the Light of the heavens and the earth. The parable of His Light is as if there were a Niche and within it a Lamp: The Lamp enclosed in Glass. ... Light upon Light! Allah doth guide whom He will to His Light: Allah doth set forth parables for men: and Allah doth know all things.*
>
> Holy Quran, Sura XXIV, Verse 35

Let's pause now to summarize what the last two prophets contributed to our Tower of Truth during the Fourth Paradigm: Jesus added that we have an affirmative obligation to help our fellow man – the Eleventh Commandment. He also made clear that our ability to reunite with God is dependent on our own good works, not blind faith in him as a savior.

> *Not everyone who says to me, "Lord, Lord," will enter the kingdom of heaven, but only the one who does the will of my Father in heaven. Many will say to me on that day, "Lord, Lord, did we not prophesy in your name? Did we not drive out demons in your name? Did we not do mighty deeds in your name?" Then I will declare to them solemnly, "I never knew you."*
>
> *Gospel of Matthew*, Chapter 7:21

Muhammad added to our divine code of conduct as well, by declaring that religious warfare between Believers must end and that women should not be treated as property. He also renounced **anthropomorphism** – the tendency of humans to personify God. Like Buddha, Muhammad enunciated a more sophisticated view of God by using the allegory of Light – the very analogy we will explore in this book.

Unfortunately, because Jesus routinely called God his "Father," we must ascribe to him the dubious distinction of anchoring God as a male deity. In Jesus' defense, his oversimplification of the Godhead may have been warranted, given the immature state of humanity's spirituality at the time during which he lived. Also, while Jesus taught at the kindergarten level for the masses, we know he imparted advanced lessons to his inner circle.

Christianity: God the Father and Adam the First Human

Nevertheless, "**Daddy Deism**" set the stage for two thousand years of patriarchy. Jesus failed to make it clear that we are *all* children of God and that God the *Mother* also exists as a Divine principle. In the *Old Testament*, the Sacred Feminine is identified as Sophia and called the Holy Shekinah in the Jewish *Kabbalah*.

> *The Lord begot me* [Sophia]*, the beginning of his works, the fore-runner of his deeds of long ago. ...*
>
> *When he established the heavens, I was there .... When he made firm the skies above, when he fixed the foundations of the earth, when he set the sea its limit .... Then was I beside him as artisan; I was his delight day by day, playing before him all the while. ...*
>
> *So now, O children, listen to me; instruction and wisdom do not reject! ... For whoever finds me finds life and wins favor from the Lord. But those who pass me do violence to themselves; all who hate me love death.*
>
> *Book of Proverbs*, Chapter 8:22-35

Most scholars believe that Jesus was a trained rabbi, which means he knew that Sophia (female wisdom) was part of the Jewish Godhead. By ignoring the Divine Feminine and failing to ensure a proper record was made of his ministry, Jesus paved the way for:

✓ The fiction that Peter, rather than James, was in charge after Jesus died and was worthy of being named the first Catholic pope;[36]
✓ The Catholic decimation of the Gnostic Christians, who honored Mary Magdalene and followed the true gnostic teachings of Christ;
✓ Martin Luther steering the Protestant Reformation in the wrong direction (i.e., doubling down on "blind faith"); and
✓ The fundamentalist mantra: "Accept Jesus Christ as your personal savior or be doomed to hell."

Most crippling of all, in my opinion, was Jesus' failure to protect the legacy of **Mary Magdalene**, his most devout disciple and probably his wife. The full weight of the evidence that Mary Magdalene was Jesus' wife is presented in *The Truth* and many other well-researched volumes. I will simply add now that Mary's words are recorded the most in the *Gnostic Gospels*, second only to Jesus.[37] Here is one passage that underscores Mary's elevated stature and spiritual sophistication:

> *There were three who always walked with the Lord: Mary his mother,*
> ** sister, and Mary of Magdala, who is called his companion. His sister*
> *and his mother and his companion were each a Mary. ...*
>
> *And the companion of the * is Mary of Magdala. The * loved her*
> *more than all the disciples, and * kissed her often on her * The rest of*
> *the disciples * said to him, "Why do you love her more than all of us?"*
>
> *The savior answered and said to them, "Why do I not love you like*
> *her? If a blind person and one who can see are both in darkness, they*
> *are the same. When the Light comes, one who can see will see the Light,*
> *and the blind person will stay in darkness."* [* indicates missing text]
>
> *Gospel of Philip*

The *Gnostic Gospels* also reveal that Peter was jealous of Mary. Why? Because she fully comprehended Jesus' lessons, whereas he did not.

> *Peter said to Mary, "Sister, we know that the Savior loved you more*
> *than the rest of women. Tell us the words of the Savior which you*
> *remember – which you know but we do not, nor have heard them."*
>
> *Mary answered and said, "What is hidden from you I will*
> *proclaim to you." ... I said to him* [Jesus], *"Lord, now does he who*
> *sees the vision see it through the soul or through the spirit?"*
>
> *The Savior answered and said, "He does not see through the soul*
> *nor through the spirit, but the mind which is between the two – that is*
> *what sees the vision and it is *" ....*
>
> *Peter answered ..., "Did he really speak with a woman without*
> *our knowledge and not openly? Are we to turn about and all listen to*
> *her? Did he prefer her to us?"*
>
> *Then Mary wept and said to Peter, "My brother Peter, what do*
> *you think? Do you think that I thought this up myself in my heart, or*
> *that I am lying about the Savior?"*
>
> *Levi answered and said to Peter, "Peter, you have always been*
> *hot tempered. Now I see you contending against the woman like the*
> *adversaries. But if the Savior made her worthy, who are you indeed*
> *to reject her? Surely the Savior knows her very well. That is why he*
> *loved her more than us. Rather let us be ashamed and put on the*
> *perfect man and acquire him for ourselves as he commanded us, and*
> *preach the gospel, not laying down another rule or other law beyond*
> *what the Savior said."* [* indicates missing text]
>
> *Gospel of Mary*

To Peter's disrespect of Mary, add Paul's generic misogyny. Then add the Catholic Church's lie that Mary was a prostitute – a sacrilegious slander that was not officially retracted until 1969. The result is a catastrophic loss of

Sacred Feminine energy and a Fourth Spiritual Paradigm marked by both a dual (God the Father and God the Son) and dualistic (male versus female) Godhead. Today, the Vatican remains an all-boys' club, collapsing under the weight of its 2000-year-old God(s).

Notwithstanding orthodox mischaracterizations of Jesus, his mission becomes much clearer when we consider the *Gnostic Gospels*, the collection of scripture that the Catholic popes ordered destroyed. Luckily, Egyptian monks defied the order and placed a cache of the papyrus texts in clay jars, which protected them until 1945, when they were discovered at Nag Hammadi. In fact, the gnostic *Gospel of Thomas* may be the oldest gospel found to date (*circa* 50 CE). Scholars believe it is the closest document we have to the **Sayings Source**, a theoretical but assumed compilation of Jesus' quotes that the apostles carried with them when they preached.

> *And he* [Jesus] *said, "Whoever finds the interpretation of these sayings will not experience death."*
>
> *Jesus said, "Let him who seeks continue seeking until he finds. When he finds, he will become troubled. When he becomes troubled, he will be astonished, and he will rule over the All."*
>
> *Gospel of Thomas*, Verses 1-2

In sum, the Fourth Spiritual Paradigm has been an era of patriarchal monotheism, which has served to advance our civilization in some respects, while retarding it in others. Oracle's Trickle-Down Deity theory suggests that our current chaos stems from a Godhead that is over-weighted in masculine energy, lacking in consistent spiritual values, and unwilling to embrace its missing consort – the Divine Feminine.

Yet today, many people are embracing Sacred Feminine energy. Many have rejected outdated religious dogma and seek the "wisdom of the ages." During our current Great Cusp, this search is taking many forms. Some people have elected to stay within the five primary religions but do a deeper dive. For example, Christians can study Gnosticism and the *Gnostic Kabbalah*, paths that retain the secret teachings of Jesus and which we will explore later.

Similarly, the esoteric paths of Hinduism, Judaism, Buddhism, and Islam are fertile ground for those who seek a more advanced or mystical experience with the Light. Indeed, **nature mysticism** (a more sophisticated form of paganism) is a popular path with Millennials. Both **pantheism**, a belief that God is in everything, and **panentheism**, a belief that God is transcendent and that everything emanates from God, currently are in vogue. The indigenous wisdom traditions of native peoples are a source of inspiration, as well.

The point is that many people are searching and using the *Saddha* process of soul growth for two important reasons: First, they are too evolved to accept blind faith because they yearn for actual experience and evidence of the Light. Second, there is no unifying, contemporary theosophy on the horizon that adequately and eloquently describes the Light.

As we spiritually navigate the Great Cusp, the trick will be to avoid despair and nihilism. One way to avoid the negative consequences of an outdated Godhead is to leave religion altogether and adopt **atheism**. I have many friends who abhor organized religion and who I consider "spiritual atheists" due to their innate wisdom and elevated morals. Of course, another way to avoid "negativity" is to forego the *Saddha* process of enlightenment altogether and engage in magical thinking. I also have friends who have chosen to ignore the dark realities of the Earth Plane, preferring to escape in a fantasy-riddled Ethereal Plane.

Yet a more courageous approach is to acknowledge the current spiritual chaos and align yourself with the Light. That is exactly what New Humans are doing – venturing off into the unknown to explore duality and dissonance in a manner befitting a 21st Century mind and spirit.

FIFTH SPIRITUAL PARADIGM

Currently, a great chasm exists between those who are wedded to the past and those who yearn for more mature communion with the Light, a schism that we will call the **God Gap**. This God Gap will be more fully explored in the next chapter, but for now it is important to note that the God Gap is growing – another clear indication that we are in the midst of a Great Cusp.

Data proves that the appeal of the Fourth Paradigm Godhead is dwindling, as souls seek more advanced explanations for the Light. Indeed, for the past decade, the **Pew Research Center** "Report on Religion and Public Life" shows that the fastest growing group in the United States is the "Nones" – those who reject all forms of orthodox religion and who are seeking better answers to perennial questions.[38]

In 2021, the Nones comprised 29% of the U.S. population, up from 16% in 2007.[39] This dramatic 13% increase of Nones left Christian numbers at 63% – a decrease of 12% since 2007.[40] Of Christians: While Protestant numbers have dropped overall, Catholic numbers have held pretty steady at 21% over the last decade, but the current number of Evangelicals stands at 24% – a 6% drop since 2007. Now compare these trends with the fact that 88% of the U.S. Congress self-reported as Christian in 2021 (25% higher than the American public), which means New Humans are sorely underrepresented.[41]

When you take a deeper dive into the data, the Pew Reports show that a whopping 61% of Americans list themselves as only "somewhat religious" (32%) or "non-religious" (29%).[42] Today, Christians out-number Nones 2:1, but in 2007 when Pew started studying American religiosity, Christians out-numbered Nones 5:1.[43] This data presents startling evidence that the God Gap is growing. Truly, we are witnessing growth along the Spectrum of Consciousness and a restructuring of the Godhead in real time.

So when will the Great Cusp end? And what will the Fifth Paradigm look like? Honestly, the breadth of human consciousness is so vast and varied that it might take another hundred years for a critical mass of New Humans to emerge. But we don't have another hundred years, according to Stephen Hawking (1942–2018).[44] Given the gravity of the challenges facing humanity, we need to assimilate the truth that we are in this sinking ship together and that collaboration and cooperation are needed if we are to survive. Unfortunately, that level of integration requires a more advanced perspective.

> *A human being is a part of the whole called by us "Universe," a part limited in time and space. He experiences himself, his thoughts and feelings as something separated from the rest, a kind of optical delusion of his consciousness. This delusion is a kind of prison for us, restricting us to our personal desires and to affection for a few persons nearest to us. Our task must be to free ourselves from this prison by widening our circle of compassion to embrace all living creatures and the whole of nature in its beauty.*
>
> Albert Einstein

Just like the great prophets and philosophers, esteemed scientists have made incredible additions to our Tower of Truth, and we will delve into the merger of science and spirituality later. The point now is that the Fifth Paradigm will incorporate a cross-disciplinary, systems view methodology. New Humans also will demand that their spiritual path comport with a checklist of healthy attributes. In *The Truth*, I listed "The Seven Rules of Any Good Religion," to catalogue what an effective and beneficial theosophy should do for the soul. Here I present them in a broader context for a 21st Century worldview.

THE SEVEN RULES OF ANY GOOD THEOSOPHY

Rule 1 – *Philosophy*
Teachings must be logical and intellectually satisfying. If the doctrine requires you to make a leap of faith that seems irrational or if it asks that you sublimate your brain in favor of blind obedience, then there is a problem.

Rule 2 – *Science*
Teachings must comport with reality. If a core precept is based on mythology, contradicts established scientific principles, or fails to accept the natural laws of the Universe, then there is a problem.

Rule 3 – *Morality*
The tradition must have high standards of right and wrong. If the tenets of the belief system include hate or violence, or if leaders promote or tolerate unethical behavior, then there is a problem.

Rule 4 – *Justice*
Rules of decorum must apply to all souls fairly and uniformly. Also, the culture must adhere to God's laws (as best we understand them) over manmade laws. If certain members are exempt from the code of conduct or if guidelines restrict freedom of thought and expression, then there is a problem.

Rule 5 – *Inclusiveness*
The path must welcome everyone – period. If the custom or its concept of God in any way discriminates against or excludes anyone who honestly seeks spiritual refuge or training, then there is a problem.

Rule 6 – *Openness*
New information must be welcomed with excitement and anticipation of what is to be learned next through human invention and the grace of God. If the sect rejects or attempts to undermine new scientific data, or if it tries to suppress newly discovered history or religious texts, then there is a problem.

Rule 7 – *Spirituality*
Affiliation must inspire the soul to seek the Light and assist participants in feeling positive emotional states, such as peace, clarity, confidence, and compassion. If the fellowship uses fear, retribution, or suppression to control or subjugate all or some of its members, then there is a problem.

Likely, if you are reading this book, you too have a checklist of what is and is not acceptable for your spiritual home, which brings me to another important point: New Humans need to stick together! Especially during the Great Cusp, we need each other in order not to feel crazy (as I felt when I found Dr. Paul). We are living in a dualistic, materialistic, masochistic, and barbaric Fourth Paradigm world. By finding and encouraging each other, New Humans create a field of integrity and optimism, which we need in order to sustain ourselves and maintain focus on our primary mission – birthing a better world.

Does this mean we abandon those who are stuck in the birth canal? Absolutely not. New Humans are obligated to help those who are in limbo, caught between the old and New World. Remember, we are all in this grand adventure together, which means we are duty-bound to offer assistance to those who have yet to ascend the Spectrum of Consciousness.

The truly exciting news is that there now are enough New Humans to start anchoring the Fifth Paradigm. And soon, we may have the power to end the chaos of the Great Cusp. Futurist and grandmother of the New Age movement Barbara Marx Hubbard (1929–2019) said we are entering the "first age of conscious evolution." Hubbard, who was a dear friend and mentor of mine, was absolutely eloquent in her description of the New Human and the New World we are all co-creating.

> *We are the first generation to be aware of the process of evolution and that we are a conscious participant in it. ... The reality is that we are naturally co-creating small islands of coherence in the sea of social chaos. By the natural tendency of nature to form new whole systems out of separate parts, people are linking up with each other and connecting their projects that are working. ...*
>
> *We may be one evolutionary instant from the networking of networks of positive change. The internet and other new media is our expanded nervous system. We may well be at the threshold of a non-linear exponential interaction of innovating elements such that the system can cooperate in its own self-transcendence.*
>
> *Our turn on the spiral represents the culmination of 14 billion years of evolution on this Earth, now coming into form as a planetary/ universal species capable of understanding its own evolution, learning its own birth story, beginning to co-evolve with nature and to co-create with the deeper patterns of creation internalized as our own spiritual motivation to love, create and evolve.*[45]
>
> Barbara Marx Hubbard,
> *An Evolutionary Synthesis: A New World View*

Barbara Marx Hubbard at Oracle Campus in 2015

Hopefully, the reader is now primed to accept that a human is not a human is not a human (unlike our canine friends). New Humans are very different than the older models, and soon we shall understand how and why.

For the remainder of this book, we will continue to use terminology developed by The Oracle Institute to help navigate humanity's evolutionary trajectory, the duality of the Earth Plane, and dimensions of the Ethereal Plane. In addition, we will study patterns in the God Game, since a dystopian backslide is a distinct possibility. Yet, because the God Game favors evolution, we also will explore transformative theories and prosocial experiments.

Later, we will examine master-level theories on the Light, handed down to us by those who have prepared the way. We will investigate metaphysics, quantum physics, and the Singularity Point. We will scrutinize the transhuman and potential posthuman era. By the end of this volume, we will know that we are New Humans and that "we are the ones we have been waiting for."

With this shared foundation of ancient wisdom and advanced knowledge, we then will add a new layer to humanity's Tower of Truth. So make yourself a cup of tea, snuggle into your favorite reading chair, and get ready. We are about to embark on a strenuous yet tremendous journey into the Fifth Spiritual Paradigm, along with some professional soothsayers, like Barbara Marx Hubbard and Ken Wilber.

Finally, let us express gratitude and thank previous masters of the God Game, those who made it their life purpose to help us grow and to explain: *Why we believe what we believe.* For only by knowing ourselves better may we make energetic progress toward our lofty twin goals of becoming New Humans and connecting to the Light.

[1] Robert Benchley, *Vanity Fair* (Feb. 1920).

[2] Don Beck and Christopher Cowen, *Spiral Dynamics: Mastering Values, Leadership, and Change*, Blackwell Publishing: Malden, MA (1996).

[3] Ken Wilber, *The Spectrum of Consciousness*, pp. 6, 14, Quest Books: Wheaton, IL (1977).

[4] Rev. Laura M. George, J.D., *The Truth: About the Five Primary Religions*, Oracle Institute Press: Independence, VA (2006; 2nd Ed. 2010).

[5] Rev. Laura M. George, J.D., narrator and co-author, *The Love: Of the Fifth Spiritual Paradigm*, Oracle Institute Press: Independence, VA (2010).

[6] Maya Angelou, "Alone," reprinted with permission in *The Love: Of the Fifth Spiritual Paradigm*, p. 116, Oracle Institute Press: Independence, VA (2010).

[7] Alexa Lardieri, "Russia Still Largest Driver of Disinformation on Social Media, Facebook Report Finds," *U.S. News & World Report* (May 26, 2021), https://www.usnews.com/news/politics/articles/2021-05-26/russia-still-largest-driver-of-disinformation-on-social-media-facebook-report-finds (accessed July 2022).

[8] "What is QAnon? The Craziest Theory of the Trump Era, Explained," *The Daily Beast* (March 20, 2019), https://www.thedailybeast.com/what-is-qanon-the-craziest-theory-of-the-trump-era-explained (accessed July 2022).

[9] Ken Wilber, *The Religion of Tomorrow: A Vision for the Future of the Great Traditions*, p. 605, Shambhala Publications: Boulder, CO (2017).

[10] "God Told Me to Invade Iraq, Bush Tells Palestinian Ministers," *BBC News* (Oct. 6, 2005), http://www.bbc.co.uk/pressoffice/pressreleases/stories/2005/10_october/06/bush.shtml; "George W. Bush and the G-Word," *The Washington Post* (Oct. 14, 2005), http://www.washingtonpost.com/wp-dyn/content/article/2005/10/13/AR2005101301688.html (both accessed July 2022).

[11] Niels H. Harrit, Jeffrey K. Farrer (Brigham Young Univ.), Steven Jones (Brigham Young Univ.), Kevin Ryan, Frank Legge (Univ. of Western Australia), "Active Thermitic Material Discovered in Dust from the 9/11 World Trade Center Catastrophe," *The Open Chemical Physics Journal* (April 2009), https://www.researchgate.net/publication/228660396 (accessed July 2022).

[12] See generally: *Architects & Engineers for 9/11 Truth*, https://www.ae911truth.org/; See video: *Architects & Engineers: Solving the Mystery of WTC 7*, produced by Richard Gage, A.I.A., narrated by Ed Asner (2015), https://www.youtube.com/watch?time_continue=852&v=_nyogTsrsgI (both accessed July 2022).

[13] Ken Wilber, *A Brief History of Everything*, pp. 99–101, Shambhala Publications: Boulder, CO (1996).

[14] Yuval Noah Harari, *Sapiens: A Brief History of Humankind*, p. 17, Harper Collins Publishers: New York, NY (2015).

[15] Merlin Stone, *When God Was a Woman*, Houghton Mifflin Harcourt Publishing Co.: New York, NY (1976).

[16] Sharon Paice MacLeod, *The Divine Feminine in Ancient Europe*, McFarland Publishing: Jefferson, NC (2014).

[17] Lucius Apuleius Madaurensis, *Metamorphoses* (a.k.a. *The Golden Ass*) (*circa* 160 CE). Note: This description of the Mother Goddess is contained in the only ancient Roman novel in Latin to survive in its entirety.

[18] Riane Eisler, *The Chalice and the Blade: Our History, Our Future*, p. xvii, Harper Collins Publishing: San Francisco, CA (1988).

[19] *Letter to the Hebrews,* Chapter 5:6, 5:10. 6:20.

[20] For example, *Advaita Vedanta* is an esoteric branch of Hinduism that began around 800 BCE and teaches that liberation may occur by merging *Atman* (the Self) with *Brahman* (the Whole).

[21] Robert Eisenman, *James the Brother of Jesus: The Key to Unlocking the Secrets of Early Christianity and the Dead Sea Scrolls*, Penguin Books: New York, NY (1998).

[22] The Hebrew term "son of man" appears 107 times in the *Old Testament*, with 93 uses in the *Book of Ezekiel* as a reference to the prophet Ezekiel, not a future Messiah. See *Ezekiel* 2:1: "Son of man, stand upon thy feet, and I will speak to thee."

[23] *Acts of the Apostles*, Chapters 9, 26:12, 15:22, 21:18; *First Letter to the Corinthians*, Chapter 2.

[24] *Acts of the Apostles*, Chapter 7:58.

[25] *Acts of the Apostles*, Chapters 8:3, 22:4, 26:9.

[26] *Acts of the Apostles*, Chapters 15, 21:15; *Letter to the Galatians,* Chapters 1:19, 2:9; *Gospel of Thomas*, Verse 12.

[27] *Letter to the Romans*, Chapter 1:1; *First Letter to the Corinthians*, Chapters 1:1, 9:1; *Second Letter to the Corinthians*, Chapter 1:1; *Letter to the Galatians*, Chapter 1:1; *Letter to the Ephesians*, Chapter 1:1, etc. See also: Paul's derision and jealousy of James the Just and the "super-apostles" in *Second letter to the Corinthians*, Chapters 11:5, 11:15, 12:11.

[28] *Letter to the Romans*, Chapters 3, 5:12.

[29] *Letter to the Romans*, Chapters 5:15, 6; *Letter to the Hebrews*, Chapter 9:11.

[30] *Letter to the Romans*, Chapter 7; *Letter to the Galatians,* Chapter 3; *Letter to the Hebrews*, Chapter 8:7–13.

[31] *Letter to the Romans*, Chapters 9:30–33, 10:9–13; *Letter to the Galatians,* Chapters 2:15, 3.

[32] *First Letter to the Corinthians*, Chapter 11; *Letter to the Ephesians*, Chapter 5:22; *Letter to the Colossians*, Chapter 3:18; *First Letter to Timothy*, Chapter 2:11.

[33] *Acts of the Apostles*, Chapters 21:18; *Letter to Titus*, Chapter 1:10; *Letter of James,* Chapters 2:10, 2:14–16, 3:13 (referring to Paul).

[34] *Letter to the Philippians*, Chapter 2; *Letter to the Colossians*, Chapters 1:15, 2:9; *Second Letter to the Thessalonians*, Chapter 2:8; *Letter to the Hebrews*, Chapter 1.

[35] It was not until the Second Council of Constantinople in 522 CE that the Catholic Church officially decided that Jesus is a subset of God and adopted the Holy Trinity. See also: Richard Rubenstein, *When Jesus Became God: The Struggle to Define Christianity During the Last Days of Rome*, Harcourt, Inc.: New York, NY (2000).

[36] In *The Gospel of Thomas*, Verse 12, Jesus instructs the apostles who will lead them when he departs, "Wherever you are, you are to go to James the Just, for whose sake heaven and earth came into being." In the Greek Orthodox tradition, James the Just is the first patriarch.

[37] See *Gospel of Thomas*, *Gospel of Peter*, *Gospel of Philip*, *Dialogue of the Savior*, and *Pistis Sophia* (Mary asks 39 of the 64 questions posed to Jesus).

[38] "America's Changing Religious Landscape," *Pew Research Center* (May 2015), http://www.pewforum.org/2015/05/12/americas-changing-religious-landscape/ (accessed July 2022).

[39] About Three-in-Ten U.S. Adults Are Now Religiously Unaffiliated," *Pew Research Center* (Dec. 2021), https://www.pewforum.org/2021/12/14/about-three-in-ten-u-s-adults-are-now-religiously-unaffiliated/ (accessed July 2022).

[40] Ibid.

[41] "Faith on the Hill," *Pew Research Center* (Jan. 2021), https://www.pewforum.org/2021/01/04/faith-on-the-hill-2021/ (accessed July 2022).

[42] "The Religious Typology: A New Way to Categorize Americans by Religion," *Pew Research Center* (Aug. 2018), http://www.pewforum.org/2018/08/29/the-religious-typology/ (accessed July 2022).

[43] About Three-in-Ten U.S. Adults Are Now Religiously Unaffiliated," *Pew Research Center* (Dec. 2021).

[44] "Stephen Hawking Believes We Have 100 Years Left on Earth – and He's Not the Only One," *Wired* (May 19, 2017), https://www.wired.co.uk/article/stephen-hawking-100-years-on-earth-prediction-starmus-festival (accessed July 2022).

[45] Barbara Marx Hubbard, *An Evolutionary Synthesis: A New World View* (2008), https://greattransitionstories.org/wp-content/uploads/sites/13/2018/06/Evolutionary_Synthesis_BMH_2.21.pdf (accessed July 2022).

The point of creating a composite map of these different levels ...
is not to pigeonhole, judge, label, or develop prejudice about people.
The point is to help us understand and communicate better with people
who are using different worldviews, as individuals grow and develop
through the entire spiral or spectrum of changes ....
It is also to help each of us get a sense of just how much further
we ourselves can grow and evolve if we choose to do so.

Each of these stages sees the world in a very, very different way,
and it is simply impossible to approach any problem or issue
without taking this elemental fact into account, something which
is virtually never done at this time, with disastrous results.

Ken Wilber, *The Religion of Tomorrow*

R ather than complete his doctoral dissertation, Ken Wilber left the world of academia at age twenty-three to wash dishes at a local restaurant and think. Shortly thereafter in 1973, he finished his first book, entitled *The Spectrum of Consciousness*.[1] Wilber is one of only a handful of philosophers to have his theories taught at colleges during his own lifetime, and he is the most widely translated academic writer in America. Moreover, as previously noted, Wilber has been nicknamed the "Einstein of Consciousness" for his revolutionary contributions in the fields of philosophy, sociology, and transpersonal psychology.

In addition, Wilber crafted a "theory of everything" (and wrote a book with the same title). His integrative map of biological, psychological, and cultural systems is called **Integral theory**. The Spectrum of Consciousness is one slice of Integral theory, and it is this piece that we will study now, since one of our objectives is to understand the characteristics of a New Human at the start of the 21st Century. The Spectrum will allow us to achieve this goal by shedding light on humanity's interior belief systems and cultural expressions, both individually and collectively, from before the premodern era through our current era ... and beyond.

Critically, the Spectrum of Consciousness also will help us map our own growth. It will help us learn more about ourselves and where we fall on the well-worn path to higher levels of spiritual awareness. The Spectrum also will help us appreciate where our friends, family, co-workers, and immediate culture fit into the big picture. From there, the model will help us comprehend how other cultures operate and why. Finally, we will be able to answer the question: *Why do people believe what they believe?*

When we take an eagle's-eye view and overlay the Spectrum onto the historical ages through which humanity has passed, we come away with a richer understanding of the evolutionary impulse and how it animates the Earth Plane. Ultimately, this model helps us recognize that we are co-creating our reality and that we have the capacity to interact with Spirit on the Ethereal Plane. In short: We are the Light!

But that revelation – that we already are one with God – is a very high-level construct. Indeed, most people on this planet still operate within the following three levels of spiritual awareness:

Mythic Meme: A belief in multiple anthropomorphic Gods, Goddesses, and lesser deities and demons, who rule over the Earth Plane and abide in the Ethereal Plane;

Fundamentalist Meme: A belief in a single exterior God, usually male or heavily weighted in masculine energy, who controls our destiny (e.g., Yahweh, Brahma, Jesus, Allah); or

Scientific/Materialistic Meme: A belief that if existent at all, God operates as a noninterventionist "watchmaker" who initiated the Big Bang and then, pretty much, left us to our own devices.

Before we explore the Spectrum of Consciousness in depth, we need to learn the map's legend – some key points that will help us on our journey. First, it will be fruitful to define the term "**meme**."

> *A Meme contains the basic package of thought, motives, and instructions that determine how we make decisions and prioritize our lives. Each has its own sending and receiving channel, organization design, intensity level, code of conduct, and set of assumptions regarding how the world works. ...*
>
> *Alas, one cannot detect the operating meme in a person by observing behavior – what someone does. Only recognizing why a person is doing or saying certain things will lead to the meme.*[2]

Don Beck and Christopher Cowan, *Spiral Dynamics*

Second, Wilber and the other consciousness experts believe that there is no "leap-frogging" from one meme to another. In other words, each of us will pass through predetermined stages of growth during our quest for greater self, societal, and spiritual awareness. Nevertheless, despite the fact that these memes are sequential, an evolved soul may move quickly through the stages.

For instance, the Dalai Lama may have graduated from the mythic meme by the time he was five years old. He may have been over the fundamentalist mindset by the time he was seven. He likely left the rationalist stage and reached advanced levels of spiritual awareness by the time he was just ten or twelve years old. The point is that each stage supports us until we are ready to progress, and each stage prepares us for the next level of comprehension.

Another main point to keep in mind is that we don't "lose" those memes that we "outgrow." It is more like school, where we graduate from one grade level and incorporate what was previously learned as we enter the next grade. In Wilber-speak, this process is called "transcend and include."

> *[E]ach wave is "transcend and include." That is, each wave goes beyond (or transcends) its predecessor, and yet it includes or embraces it in its own makeup. ... Just so, each wave of existence is a fundamental ingredient of all subsequent waves, and thus each is to be cherished and embraced.*[3]

Ken Wilber, *A Theory of Everything*

So while we may think we have rejected a previous meme that now may repel us, our psycho-spiritual-subconscious still contains elements of previous stages. Indeed, the repulsion some people feel toward prior and succeeding memes is quite common and can manifest as part of their Spectrum **shadow**, which we will discuss in more detail later. For now, just be aware that the **Culture War** we are witnessing between fundamentalists and progressives has to do with shadow elements in each meme, which we will break down later into Spectrum "allergies" and "addictions."

Lastly, the consciousness experts uniformly agree on what conditions are required in order for us to keep moving on an upward trajectory. Many people assume that education is the key to helping people broaden their worldviews. However, the truth is that a person may get stuck anywhere along the Spectrum if their current meme provides comfort and refuge. In fact, most humans never make it past the rational/materialistic meme. So why do people appear to suddenly move (or digress) along the Spectrum? The actual key is dissonance and extreme discomfort, as Wilber explains below.

> *A person still hungry for the particular food of a given stage will simply not look elsewhere. On the other hand, if the person has tasted a stage and become fairly full, then he or she is open to transformation. In order for this to occur, some sort of dissonance generally has to set in. The new wave is struggling to emerge, the old wave is struggling to hang on, and the individual feels torn, feels dissonance ... there has to be some sort of profound dissatisfaction with the present level; one has to be agitated, annoyed, frustrated with it, so that a deep and conflicted dissonance insistently arises.*[4]

> Ken Wilber, *A Theory of Everything*

To reach higher levels of consciousness, a "Dark Night of the Soul" usually is required. In my case, it was a prolonged period of excruciating interior pain that mobilized me into affirmative action. Specifically, it was the frustration and anger over harm done to others that fueled me. My anguish was so intense, it propelled me into the unknown, forcing me to adopt a new belief system.

> *A "dark night" is a generic term representing many things in different traditions, but in general it represents a passing through, or letting go, of attachment or addiction to a particular realm ... the pain that comes from peak-experiencing a higher state that is already free of the particular addiction, and then being plunged back into a lower state, generating a profound sense of loss and suffering.*[5]

> Ken Wilber, *Integral Spirituality*

Thus, regardless of what sort of dissonance precipitates a growth spurt, each successive level of awareness brings us greater clarity and a bit closer to the Light. Put succinctly: What doesn't kill us makes us stronger!

GRAVES' THEORY AND SPIRAL DYNAMICS

My favorite class of all time – including every course I have ever taken, from elementary school through high school, undergraduate work through law school, and every religion and spirituality seminar as well – was a class entitled "Rehabilitation Techniques and Graves' Theory." It was offered during the 1980s at my undergraduate *alma mater*, the University of Virginia. The class was outside of my major but I didn't care. I was in the McIntire School of Commerce at UVA studying finance, accounting, and computers. My brain hurt and I desperately needed a "gut" (i.e., an easy class in UVA-speak) to ease the burden of my otherwise demanding schedule of Comm School classes.

"Rehab," as my new boyfriend (later husband, now ex-husband) fondly called it, was an introductory class for psychology majors at *The* University (the elitist moniker for UVA). I enjoyed Rehab because I could sit anonymously in the middle of a large lecture hall and hide, a very different experience than the Socratic method classes I took at the Comm School. I also liked Rehab because the psychology students were more fun than Comm School students, though I was destined never to meet a group of kindred spirits while at UVA.

The truth is that I stuck out like a sore thumb the minute I arrived in Charlottesville. More precisely, I could not blend-in, when blending-in meant wearing pink and green polos, madras sundresses, and paisley headbands. After enjoying the diversity of a 1970s public school education (my best friend in high school was African American), the UVA campus made me uncomfortable, with its preppie culture, bad music, and Ronald Reagan groupies. At eighteen years of age and in virtual lock-down at Mr. Jefferson's University, my world was suddenly homogeneous, lily-white, and strikingly snobbish. This was the era of *The Official Preppy Handbook* (1980),[6] of which I received multiple copies from friends and family who thought I would be happy at UVA if I simply followed this manual of upper-class dress and behavior.

Failing to see either the humor or, for that matter, any other beneficial aspect to my new social landscape, I started to withdraw emotionally. By my third year, I was pretty much a loner and stopped attending frat parties. I didn't realize it at the time, but I was starting to explore my spirituality. As a devout ex-Catholic, going back to church was not an option, Instead, I started reading books about other religions, ESP, and reincarnation. It was not long before I found the work of Dr. Ian Stevenson, former Dean of the UVA Psychiatry Department and seminal researcher of reincarnation. In sum, I had always been a pretty weird kid, but at UVA my novel and oftentimes naive approach to life was getting even more pronounced.

Why, you may ask, is this personal history even remotely relevant to the Spectrum of Consciousness? Because, as it turned out, my Rehab class not only provided me with a framework for interpreting the stifling UVA campus, it also helped me understand myself and my freakish compulsion to stay a bit removed from the rest of humanity and focus, whenever possible, on my spiritual quest. As I later learned – thanks to Wilber crediting his academic predecessors – **Graves' theory** (a.k.a. "Emergent Cyclical Levels of Existence Theory") was foundational to Wilber's work. Consequently, the class I took at UVA, which has been percolating in my brain now for four decades, taught me the very cornerstones of consciousness!

> *The psychology of the mature human being is an unfolding or emergent process marked by the progressive subordination of older behavioral systems to newer, higher order behavior systems. The mature man tends normally to change his psychology as the conditions of his existence change. Each successive stage or level is a state of equilibrium though which people pass on the way to other states of equilibrium.*[7]
>
> Clare W. Graves,
> *"Levels of Existence: An Open System Theory of Values"*

Graves' theory was a novel tool to track humanity's collective movement into and out of progressively more advanced values and belief systems. This research also was foundational to **Spiral Dynamics**, a 1990s, color-coded version introduced by two of Graves' students: Don Beck (1937–2022) and Christopher Cowen.[8] Today, Spiral Dynamics is used across the globe for corporate management, organizational development, and conflict resolution. For example, the model famously was used to help end the Apartheid system in South Africa.[9] Don Beck made more than sixty trips to South Africa and worked with F. W. de Klerk and Nelson Mandela to achieve stunning results.

Spiral Dynamics also helps us estimate how many progressive thinkers exist on the planet and how close this New Human is to running the show. I am talking about the elusive **Tipping Point**, after which our planet finally will pass through the current Great Cusp and into the Fifth Spiritual Paradigm. In short, Graves' theory was revolutionary, as it produced a model that not only tracks individual growth, but also humanity's collective progress toward the Light.

Clare W. Graves (1914–1986), was a professor of psychology at Union College in Schenectady, New York in the 1950s. Among other courses, Graves taught an introductory class on psychology, in which his undergraduate students often asked him which therapeutic techniques work best when treating someone suffering from a mental health problem or emotional crisis. Prompted by his students' questions, Graves was forced to admit that none of the therapies developed by the mid-20th Century seemed to address the needs of every patient. In fact, Graves was himself curious why Freudian psychoanalysis worked fine with some patients, while Skinner behavioral modification techniques worked better with others. He, too, wondered why the psychological tools of his day seemed to be "hit or miss."

Eventually, this gnawing question of how to treat different types of psychologically unhealthy patients gave Graves a research idea. He decided to ask his students how they would define a mentally healthy adult. Then, he studied his students under various conditions to see whether they would change their opinions. Graves felt this data might help him pinpoint which therapeutic techniques work best on patients with different value sets and belief systems.

It is important to remember that when Graves began his research in the 1950s, the scientific method relied almost exclusively on clinical observation and reductionism, as it had since the dawn of the Scientific Revolution in the 1600s. Led by such luminaries as Sir Francis Bacon (1561–1626) and Sir Isaac Newton (1643–1727), both of whom championed the empirical method of gathering data, the path of modern science was firmly set for the next three hundred years. Therefore, Graves' idea of studying the interior value systems and moral judgments of his students by accepting their own idiosyncratic and subjective answers to questions was a relatively novel concept.

> [T]he old paradigm that everybody doesn't want is the Enlightenment paradigm, which is also called the modern paradigm. It has dozens of other names, all pronounced with scorn and disgust: the Newtonian, the Cartesian, the mechanistic, the mirror of nature, the reflection paradigm. By whatever name, that paradigm is now thought to be hopelessly outdated .... [T]he simplest way to state the problem with maps is: they leave out the mapmaker.[10]
>
> Ken Wilber, *A Brief History of Everything*

Until recently, scientists sought answers only through rational/objective means. Their goal was to determine *how* a thing or person works, not *why*. Even in the field of psychology, the subjective study of mental health patients was rare in the 1950s. Rather, that was the era when psychiatrists experimented on patients to see *how* people react to drugs that chemically alter brain activity, *how* we react to electric shock therapy, and *how* we behave when a piece of our brain is removed via lobotomy. Thus, the focus was on the functional aspects of the brain and how to restore "normal" brain activity through exterior and usually invasive means. Behavioral modification techniques also were used, but with little regard for the underlying mental health issues that might be causing aberrant behavior.

Graves correctly deduced that if he wanted to study his students' interior belief systems, the purely objective approach embodied in the classic scientific method would not suffice. He realized that in order to analyze what was going on inside minds and hearts, he couldn't just observe people. Why? Because outward behavior is not always indicative of what a person is thinking or feeling inside. Today there is a fancy word for the study of a person's interior life – **hermeneutics**. This was the relatively new subjective approach that Graves employed to query his students and interpret their responses.

> *The brain physiologist can know every single thing about my brain – he can hook me up to an EEG machine, he can use PET scans, he can use radioactive tracers, he can map the physiology, determine the levels of neurotransmitters – he can know what every atom of my brain is doing, and he still won't know a single thought in my mind. ... [I]f he wants to know what is going on inside my mind, there is one and only one way that he can find out: he must talk to me.*[11]
>
> Ken Wilber, *A Brief History of Everything*

Again, the principle behind hermeneutics is that if you want to understand what motivates people to act in a certain way, you need to ask them directly. Yes, some people may lie about their true motives, even in blind studies. And yes, some people may not know what truly motivates them (i.e., they lie to themselves). And yes, it is harder for scientists to "interpret" subjective data than to "measure" objective data. However, the subjective approach to studying human value sets, world views, and spiritual ideals has the distinct advantage of directly obtaining that which the inquiry seeks – an understanding of the interior processes and moral judgments made by human beings.

A last important note to bear in mind before we delve into Graves' theory: This research was conducted in the 1950s, 1960s, and 1970s, *just as the water broke on the birth of the Fifth Spiritual Paradigm*. This was the beginning of the current Great Cusp – the period of extreme turmoil which always precedes a paradigm shift. Consequently, Graves had the rare opportunity to study a variety of persons, all of whom were reacting to unprecedented and dramatic social influences, including the Vietnam War, Civil Rights movement, Feminist revolution, and camaraderie of hippies during the free-love movement.

During the first stage of his study, Graves asked his students to write a paper detailing their concept of a "psychologically healthy adult" and explaining how such a person operates in the world. Privately, Graves expected the students to define psychological health in a manner that reflected their own belief systems, which is exactly what happened. In the second part of the study, Graves asked a team of his academic peers to analyze and categorize the students' papers to see if patterns would emerge in their descriptions of a healthy adult. During this stage, Graves expected to encounter the same variety of beliefs that a therapist might encounter. However, he was surprised at the divergent belief systems that emerged from his pool of subjects.

In the third stage of research, Graves separated the students into random groups and watched them discuss their views on the values and behaviors of a healthy adult. Graves secretly watched his students debate their respective positions from behind a one-way mirror. Specifically, he wanted to observe how hard students would defend their definition of psychological health, and how apt they were to modify their position under peer pressure. The students then wrote a second paper either defending their original position or setting out their new concept of a healthy adult. Even more than the verbal debates, the second round of papers allowed Graves to analyze which of the students' beliefs were prone to change due to peer influence and which were not.

During the fourth and final phase of the project, Graves brought the class back together and began to teach them classic definitions of mental health as expressed by acknowledged experts in the field of psychiatry, such as Sigmund Freud (1856–1939), Abraham Maslow (1908–1970), and Jane Loevinger (1918–2008). Once again, Graves asked the students to write a paper either defending their concept of a psychological health or explaining how their view had changed after learning what experts had to say on the matter. In this way, Graves was able to measure the impact of expert opinion on the students. Interestingly enough, some students were susceptible to peer influence, while others changed their minds only after an authority opined. A third group of students held fast to their original definition of mental health despite all evidence to the contrary.

So what did Graves discover from his research? Early data showed that the students defined psychological health in one of two basic ways: (i) a healthy person will deny and sacrifice self; or (ii) a healthy person will express self. Thereafter, as additional students were screened, there emerged two subgroups within each main classification, resulting in a total of four distinct categories:

Under the "Sacrifice Self" category:
✓ A healthy person will sacrifice self to get a reward later.
✓ A healthy person will sacrifice self to gain acceptance.

Under the "Express Self" category:
✓ A healthy person will express self, even at the expense of others.
✓ A healthy person will express self, but not at the expense of others.

Over the years as Graves studied a broader sample of students and then added prison inmates to his pool of subjects, two more categories emerged as further subsets of the original two classifications. At that point, Graves' data revealed a total of six different belief systems. In addition, the effects of peer pressure and authoritarian/expert opinion produced a distinct hierarchy to the belief systems. In other words, Graves discovered *in what order* human beings progress through each of the six value sets. Then, another pattern emerged, revealing that people vacillate between seeing the world in a more egocentric and autonomous manner ("I" memes), versus experiencing the world through a more conformist and communal lens ("WE" memes). Check it out:

1. A healthy person will express self impulsively at any cost – **I**
2. A healthy person will sacrifice self to get a reward later – **WE**
3. A healthy person will express self for personal gain but rationally – **I**
4. A healthy person will sacrifice self to gain acceptance now – **WE**
5. A healthy person will express self but not at the expense of others – **I**
6. A healthy person will deny self in order to serve the good of all – **WE**

Eventually, Graves formally mapped his conclusions. His research had revealed a total of eight levels, as follows:

Level 1: A person with no concept other than self, who lives a merely symbiotic or instinctive existence (i.e., a healthy infant or an autistic or otherwise impaired adult) – **I**

Level 2: A person whose concept of self is entirely co-dependent on environment and others (i.e., a healthy toddler or an animistic tribal culture) – **WE**

Level 3: A person who exerts self impulsively, regardless of whether others are harmed – **I**

Level 4: A person who sacrifices self in order to get a personal reward later – **WE**

Level 5: A person who asserts self rationally and for personal gain – **I**

Level 6: A person who suppresses self in order to be accepted by others and to get a reward now – **WE**

Level 7: A person who expresses self but with concern for and in order to assist others – **I**

Level 8: A person who denies self in order to serve the good of all – **WE**

By the time Graves reached this juncture of his analysis, he realized that the original query he posed to his students was not a valid question. Why? Because he learned that "a human is not a human is not a human" and that no consensus would emerge on the definition of a "psychologically healthy adult." He also had reached the end of his scholarly venture and retired in 1978. It was time for his students to take over and further refine his theory.

To their credit, Don Beck and Chris Cowan did a stupendous job of keeping Graves' theory alive and educating the next generation of students (such as yours truly). Beck and Cowan also foreshadowed a 9th Level of consciousness but did not describe it adequately for our purposes. Therefore, we will continue our exploration of the various levels of human existence and the belief systems they represent using Wilber's more advanced template, the Spectrum of Consciousness.

Spectrum of Consciousness: Growing Up

For readers who still view this body of research as a politically incorrect field of academia or cerebral exercise meant to flatter the high IQ'd scholars and geeks who subscribe to it, please hang on. At least stick around long enough to grasp the theory and self-chart where you fall on the Spectrum. I promise: If you detest the "judgmental" underpinnings of this model but keep reading anyway, you'll learn more about yourself, including why you hate the model!

First, this model exceeds the **Hierarchy of Needs** designed by Maslow, expanded by Graves, and improved further by Spiral Dynamics. It is broadly based and includes, for example, the child development research of Swiss psychologist Jean Piaget (1896–1980), the studies on personality development pioneered by Erik Erikson (1902–1994), and the work of Lawrence Kohlberg (1927–1987), who mapped stages of human moral development. The model also coheres with the work of Leon Festinger (1919–1989), a psychologist who did cutting-edge research on how dissonance impacts our choices.

Here's two more points that should make everyone happy: First, even though our parents, educational level, economic status, willingness to learn, fears, and personalities all impact how far we grow on the Spectrum, the model acknowledges that each of us is unique in how we interpret and respond to our environment. We also may straddle two memes, expressing our higher self in the higher meme on good days and vice versa. Second, there is one fundamental aspect of our being that is NOT relevant to this model: our intelligence.

That's right. Graves and his successors have determined that intelligence is not relevant to where we fall on the Spectrum of Consciousness. Apparently, our IQ simply is not a significant factor in why we believe what we believe, or how we progress through successive belief systems. There is an exception to this general rule for the lower two stages, but only in cases of mental handicap, autism, or extreme cultural deprivation, where the individual is physiologically incapable of reaching higher stages of development.

Are you surprised? Did you think your IQ was helping you in your quest for spiritual enlightenment? Do you secretly feel intellectually superior to your neighbor who believes Jesus is God's only begotten son and that he opened up the gates of heaven by dying on the cross? Well, it turns out that even a genius can get stuck at any stage of the Spectrum. If you doubt the seriousness of this point, can you distinguish a measurable difference in the intelligence quotient of this list of well-known and exceedingly smart meme representatives: Adolf Hitler (Stage 3); Ronald Reagan (Stage 4); Mark Zuckerberg (Stage 5); Oprah Winfrey (Stage 6); Mahatma Gandhi (Stage 7); Mother Theresa (Stage 8).

However, while cognitive intelligence is not determinative of worldview, scientists have identified other types of intelligences – emotional, moral, interpersonal, kinesthetic, aesthetic, spiritual – all of which impact how we navigate the world. As Wilber likes to repeat: "Think Nazi doctors – very high in cognitive intelligence, very low in moral intelligence."[12]

And here's some more good news: Each meme has a "positive" and a "negative" side. In other words, each meme contains characteristics that most people – regardless of where they fall on the Spectrum of Consciousness – would view as worthwhile and beneficial for all.

For example, people passing through an "I" meme and driven to express self (i.e., ego) have the will to "conquer," to a greater or lesser extent, depending on where they fall on the Spectrum. Oftentimes, such strong-willed people make great leaders. Why? Because they are singularly focused on their goal, they are totally dedicated to their mission, they are indefatigable, and they inspire others to action. The flip side, of course, is that such people can succumb to shadow issues (as we all can). But the shadow side of an "I" meme can be pretty scary. If morally adrift, rather than fighting "the good fight," they may get power hungry, greedy, or downright destructive and sadistic.

Which brings us back to the topic of shadow, a dysfunction that can occur anywhere along the Spectrum. Peak experiences can happen at any meme as well. For example, **Pentecostal Christians** may reach states of supreme rapture, though their altered state is necessarily defined by their meme set-point. We will delve into these important subtopics later, but for now simply remember that there actually are three ways by which we advance according to Wilber:[13]

Growing Up: Refers to transcending one meme and including the next, thereby incrementally gaining an advanced perspective, broader set of values, and more balanced ego – growth that allows us to eventually become a New Human.

Cleaning Up: Refers to doing shadow work by exploring our dislike or "allergy" of other memes, and by eliminating a fixation or "addiction" to a previous meme.

Waking Up: Refers to achieving higher states of spiritual awakening, regardless of where we fall on the Spectrum, thereby incrementally gaining a closer connection to our higher self and to the Light.

With these basic concepts in mind, we are ready to explore each Spectrum stage. A thorough understanding of each meme will help us chart our own spiritual progress, as well as the set-point of our friends, family members, immediate culture, and the world at large. Thereafter, we will be in a position to define and identify New Humans. We'll also have the data needed to predict how close we are to the Tipping Point into the Fifth Spiritual Paradigm. The below chart is The Oracle Institute version of the Spectrum of Consciousness, a multi-disciplinary approach to mapping motivations, values, and behavior.

ORACLE SPECTRUM OF
STAGES OF INDIVIDUAL AND

		LIGHT SPECTRUM	COGNITION & PHYSIOLOGY (ages example only)	IDENTITY & WORLDVIEW
S E C O N D	Stage 9	WHITE LIGHT "I AM"	Super Mind Irrelevant	Merged Cosmic
	Stage 8	VIOLET "ALL IS ONE"	Illumined Mind Out of Body	Transpersonal Universal
	Stage 7	INDIGO "ONE FOR ALL"	Visionary 60 – Death	Integrated Global
				TIPPING
F I R S T	Stage 6	GREEN "WE"	Abstract 21 – 59 Years	Worldcentric Egalitarian
	Stage 5	YELLOW "I"	Logical 13 – 20 Years	Individualistic Rational
	Stage 4	ORANGE "WE"	Operational 9 – 12 Years	Ethnocentric Nationalistic
	Stage 3	RED "I"	Pre-Operational 5 – 8 Years	Egocentric Feudal
	Stage 2	MAGENTA "WE"	Symbolic 2 – 4 Years	Animistic Tribal
	Stage 1	INFRARED "I"	Sensory-Motor Birth – 1 Year	Symbiotic Nonexistent/Archaic
TIER	**MEME**	**LIGHT SPECTRUM**	**COGNITION & PHYSIOLOGY** (ages example only)	**IDENTITY & WORLDVIEW**

CONSCIOUSNESS CHART
SOCIETAL DEVELOPMENT

VALUES & MOTIVATION	SPIRITUALITY & GOD VIEW	PERCENT GLOBAL POPULACE	PERCENT U.S. POPULACE	PERCENT U.S. POWER
THE LIGHT Divinity	Enlightened Non-Dual			
THE LOVE Compassion	Transcendent Mystical	0.5%	0.5%	
THE TRUTH Wisdom	Holistic Metaphysical	5%	5%	5%
POINT				
Pluralism Harmony	Interfaith New Age/Agnostic	15%	24%	20%
Self-Esteem Achievement	Humanist Orthodox/Atheist	20%	35%	40%
Rules & Sacrifice Reward Later	Absolutist Fundamentalist	40%	25%	30%
Power Honor	Mythical Polytheistic	19%	10%	5%
Safety Fear	Magical Anthropomorphic	0.5%	0.5%	
Survival Instinctual	None None			

Two final notes before we begin: The Oracle chart uses the light spectrum for meme colors (as does Wilber's chart). I prefer these colors to those chosen for Spiral Dynamics, because I find that color scheme illogically sequenced and harder to remember. Lastly, since understanding the Spectrum is essential to both enjoying and receiving the benefits of this book, please take your time studying the above chart and the following meme descriptions. If this is your first encounter with the Spectrum, also take the time to memorize any new vocabulary. If you invest the time needed to learn these concepts, I can promise: *If not one already, you will be inspired to become a New Human.*

SPECTRUM STAGE 1: INFRARED

The first meme represents a subsistence level that Graves called **Automatic Existence**. A person at this stage lives a merely reflexive and instinctual life in response to bodily needs and emotional urges. Immediate gratification is the hallmark of this stage, as in the case of an infant who seeks to have his physical demands met as quickly as possible. "He is in essence a simple reflexological organism," explains Graves, with no concept of time, cause and effect, or sense of self. Nevertheless, this is considered an "I" meme, because the person is not cognizant of life or a reality beyond his own needs.

At this stage, "everything is one" (me), because the subject (my selfhood) and the object (my environment) are merged, indistinguishable, and essentially incomprehensible. The symbiotic nature of this stage symbolically relates to the First Spiritual Paradigm defined by The Oracle Institute – the primordial, unified, and timeless period before we separated from the Light.

During the course of human evolution, this stage also relates to the first belief system (if you can call it that) or perspective of our primitive ancestors, those who walked the earth 100,000, even 200,000 years ago. They lived as animals do today, merely surviving and procreating (yet another of the urges to be satisfied as quickly as possible). And while they lived in groups, they operated more in the nature of a nomadic herd than a tribe, which is why in Spectrum-speak, we refer to this worldview as archaic and not tribal.

In sum, this was mankind's initial state of existence, before the emergence of Cro-Magnon and early modern *Homo sapiens*. Back then, a human was a human a human. Today, normally functioning humans pass through this stage before they are toilet trained, and there are no cultures that operate at this level in the modern world.

SPECTRUM STAGE 2: MAGENTA

Dr. Graves called Stage 2 the **Tribalistic Existence** and this terminology has stuck. At this rung of the ladder, a person can communicate with others, but his sense of self has not emerged in the modern sense, since he lives an organic experience with fellow humans and his world. His sense of time is seasonal, and his sense of cause and effect is only partially developed. He has an awareness of danger, a desire to protect his tribe, and a deep sense of loyalty. Above all else, he seeks a stable environment for himself and his people.

Consequently, a person at this stage makes little distinction between himself as a living breathing organism and the other components of nature. Indeed, he has a "bee-hive" mentality with his fellow tribesmen who are all related by blood. Older members of the tribe are respected for knowing the history of the clan and the basis for the tribe's rituals. Devotion and obedience are prized and order is maintained through hierarchy and lineage.

As a result of his inability to distinguish between himself, his tribe, and his world, a person at this stage sees Spirit in everything and subscribes to a worldview based on animism. Tribal tradition and magical thinking are the hallmarks of this meme, with authority given to elders who are practiced in the arts of survival and superstition. In the parlance of The Oracle Institute, this was the Second Spiritual Paradigm and the era of the Great Mother. It was a harmonious stage of our collective evolution, which Graves dates to 40,000 BCE and the emergence of pre-modern man.

Kogi People of the Sierra Nevada Mountains, Colombia[14]

There are very few humans living at this "WE" meme today. But in our distant past, experts believe that all or nearly all humans operated at Magenta. The exception to this cultural collective is the distinction made and respect paid to elders, in addition to the homage paid to nature deities and Great Mother. Thus, a human was still a human was still a human during our tribal phase.

Tension is rare at Stage 2. Elders maintain a firm grip on tradition and ritual by indoctrinating the young from birth. However, dissonance may creep in via a visit from outsiders with divergent traditions, rituals, or "magic." Dissension also may occur if a younger tribesman questions the authority of elders or attempts to introduce an innovative method or thought.

If insight is gained through the introduction of new people or new ideas, change is possible. All it takes is for one tribe member to start feeling a sense of autonomy and separate from tribe-think. Once a tribe member voluntarily separates from the ancient traditions, watch out! That person may be anxious to test himself – his new sense of self – at an entirely new level of existence.

SPECTRUM STAGE 3: RED

This meme is where things get really interesting because it is the first fully conscious "I" meme. Graves called it an **Egocentric Existence**, since a person at this stage feels himself as truly separate from his fellow man and even from nature. As a result, this can be a harsh meme, though it has a positive side due to its characteristic heroism. For instance, who amongst us hasn't felt pride at overcoming a challenge on our own? Yet, pride taken too far can be dangerous. Thus, when a person begins to operate at this level, he tends to sow his wild oats and test his power – usually to the detriment of others.

In fact, Graves called this meme "Machiavellian," since it is based on the principle that "might makes right." Wilber is less subtle, bellowing the phrase "fuck it or kill it" to describe the barbarity of this meme and its propensity to ride testosterone highs.[15] Similarly, in *The Truth*, I identified excessive pride as one of the two cardinal sins because unrestrained ego can lead to bloodshed.

Historically, it will be helpful to recall European feudalism, though Graves dates the start of this phase of human history to 8000 BCE. This was the era of the warrior king, when men of power built empires and monarchies and reduced the masses to slaves and serfs. This also is when aristocracies developed – medieval caste systems – where a few humans were privileged "haves" and the vast majority were poor "have nots." Such is the savage nature of a Red society.

Spiritually, pockets of people who live in Stage 3 cultures secretly cling to some form of nature animism, thereby still occupying a Magenta mindset. However, most people in a Red society adopt (by force if necessary) the mythology propagated by the ruling class, who cast themselves as semi-divine or predestined rulers (e.g., the Roman caesars, the *brahmins* in Hinduism; the Catholic popes). Consequently, the religions created during this era – by Sumerian, Babylonian, Greek, Roman, Egyptian, and Hindu priests – were polytheistic, anthropomorphic, and dominated by powerful deities who had human characteristics and foibles.

Oracle refers to this epoch as the Third Spiritual Paradigm, during which humans imagined mythical pantheons of Gods and Goddesses. As mentioned previously, Hinduism was the only religion to survive from this era, in part because it was enhanced over the years by subsequent mystics and yogis who added new layers of esoteric theosophy.

Today, most of us pass through this Red phase by the time we hit puberty. And as adults, most of us punish our kids if they dawdle in a power-based, bullying phase through adolescence. In recent past, academics have estimated that 10% of our planet is at this stage of development, but I believe that stat is incorrect. My estimate is that close to 20% of the world is dominated by a Red culture and that 10% of Americans operate at this level.

Donald Trump's presidency brought this meme out in spades and he has helped ignite a worldwide resurgence of fascism, totalitarianism, and oligarchy. The media likes to use the word "tribalism" to describe Trump's hell-bent nationalism, but nationalism in its pure sense is the hallmark of the next meme. In Spectrum-speak, neither the term tribalism nor nationalism is an appropriate descriptor for Stage 3, since both tribalism (Stage 2) and nationalism (Stage 4) are "WE" memes based on shared community values and a deep respect for order. Instead, what Trump displays is a warped, shadow-afflicted version of Stage 3 – more similar to the personality traits and worldview of a Red meme dictator, chronic narcissist, or sociopath.

Similarly, White Nationalists are not "nationalists" in the sense we will soon use that word to discuss Stage 4 humans. Instead, White Nationalists – like the skinheads [16] who marched on Charlottesville, Virginia, and the Proud Boys and Oath Keepers who committed treason when they openly attacked our nation's Capitol – are Red meme hooligans running amuck, just like Trump.

This is a good moment to pause and introduce another corollary of the Spectrum model: Under pressure (i.e., strong dissonance), a person does not always move *up* the Spectrum. Unfortunately, extreme stress also can cause a backward slide. So those skinheads in Charlottesville may have been Stage 4 nationalists a couple decades ago, but under the "stress" of the election of our first black president Barack Obama, witnessing the twin towers fall on 9/11, losing jobs and economic security, and then having a commander in chief who admires dictators and models Red shadow values, some former nationalists have regressed and become White Nationalists with anarchist tendencies. More on the true nature of nationalism later, when we proceed to the Orange meme. For now, let's hear from Wilber on the dangers of regression:

> And when things get very severe, this sequence tends to unravel and regress following exactly the same path and the very same steps, although this time in the reverse direction (downward, not upward). ... [People] will regress from integral to worldcentric to ethnocentric to egocentric. And that is exactly part of the trend that is now in play today, a trend that, we have seen, is partially to credit (or blame, take your pick) for putting Trump into office.[17]

Consequently, Stage 3 people – because of their impulsivity and constant desire to have what they want when they want it – can pose a grave threat to the world, especially when they move in packs and even more so given the state of modern warfare technology. Think Al Qaeda and ISIS.

> The power ethic reveres he who can tell time what he wills – and mean it, he who shows no fear of the world's wrath and assurance of its favor. Right is demonstrated in violent action – an aspect of this ethic which many see today but few understand. In the power ethic, the more daring and horrendous the act of man, the more it is revered. It does not matter, within the power ethic, whether a man has plans for replacement of the system which he attacks. The heroic thing is to attack the system and if there is nothing present to be attacked then, if he is truly a hero, he will create a dragon to be destroyed, for even if he should die in the course of his attack, he is assured that he will live – live on forever in the words of men. This aspect of the power ethic, which is bursting forth everywhere in our world today, confounds many people.[18]

> Clare W. Graves,
> *"Levels of Existence: An Open System Theory of Values"*

When I read this quote, President George W. Bush comes to mind. In his memoir *Decision Points*, Bush expressed no regrets, even though I believe he lied to himself and to the American people to kick off the Iraq war.[19] Saddam Hussein's weapons of mass destruction were his "dragon," and clearly he had no "plans for replacement" after the attack. Yet, Bush is confident that he will "live on forever in the words of men," whether vindicated or not by historians.

Incidentally, I am not suggesting that Bush dwells in the Red meme on most days. Remember, we don't exit former memes completely; rather, we adopt a new value system but keep old ones in our repertoire, so to speak, in the event of an emergency. In my opinion, Bush was so whipped up after 9/11 (not being part of the false flag operation), that he succumbed to pressure, fear and confusion, then temporarily reverted to an old meme. On a good day, Bush is likely a combination Stage 4/5, but he went Red under pressure ... and at an incredibly inconvenient time for the rest of us.

Of course, I also think of Donald Trump when I read the quote. In the distant past, a demagogue like Trump could not have done much damage, but as President of the United States, he did incalculable harm. Thankfully, we did not go to war under Trump, as he likely would have viewed war as a virtual game of "Chicken." Recall that at first, Trump "fell in love" with North Korean dictator Kim Jong Un. Later, Trump threatened him and called him "Little Rocket Man." The truth is that Trump was oblivious to the dangers of nuclear war, repeatedly asking the Pentagon why it would be such a bad thing?[20]

Sadly, it is nearly impossible to reason with people in the Red meme, as they are immune both to peer pressure and expert influence. Remember, this was the meme that Graves found did not buckle under pressure or, for that matter, facts! Yet another reason Trump is so dangerous: He makes up his own facts and then lies to ameliorate his dissonance (assuming he feels any at all). Thus, logical arguments do not work with such people – they believe what they believe and it is nearly impossible to change their minds. Facts don't matter, science doesn't matter, even their own eyewitness observation doesn't matter (e.g., global warming).

> *Hence, as for that "basket of deplorables," to the extent that they are genuinely at ... ethnocentric, premodern, stages of development, they are uncomfortable with worldcentric values ... not because they fully see them and loathe them, but because they do not (and cannot) see them in the first place.*[21]

Ken Wilber, *Trump and a Post-Truth World*

Realistically, it is difficult to communicate with the Red meme, since their egoic worldview dominates their perspective and resulting behaviors. As we shall soon discuss, Gandhi wrote to Hitler and tried to reason with him by appealing to his higher nature. Gandhi also counseled the Jews to be more passive! This is a good example of the crossways communication that occurs when peacemakers use their pluralistic vocabulary and worldcentric values in an attempt to educate or reason with Red meme leaders. As I write, President Vladimir Putin of Russia is invading Ukraine with over 100,000 troops and mercenaries.[22] It is highly unlikely that diplomacy will change Putin's mind.

In short, the Red meme is incapable of extending higher values to others, because they cannot give what they don't have. The below quote from Wilber contains references to worldviews that we have yet to cover, but I'm sure you'll get the gist of it. The main point is that Stage 3 humans are almost impossible to negotiate with, as they only respect other power-based players.

> *Now you yourself might indeed have evolved from egocentric [Stage 3] to ethnocentric [Stage 4] to worldcentric [Stage 5 and above] perspectives, and so you will easily understand that all individuals are to be accorded equal consideration and equal opportunity, regardless of race, sex, or creed. From this stance of universal pluralism [Stage 6], you are genuinely multicultural and postconventional. The problem is, most individuals that you treat with universal coverage do not share your universalism. They are still egocentric [Stage 3] or ethnocentric [Stage 4] to the core. So you are extending universal consideration to individuals who will absolutely not extend the same courtesy to you.[23]*

Thus, when the Red meme is approached with pure logic or compassion, neither strategy works. Why? Because Green egalitarian talk falls on Red deaf ears. In extreme situations, the only option is to up the ante and "bring a gun to a knife fight" (or at least a knife!) – as barbaric as that may sound. Otherwise, as in the case of Hitler or Putin, a Red dictator will obliterate his adversary.

Similarly, liberal Democrats keep losing policy debates because they tend to talk past the electorate, which is mostly Stage 4 and 5. While the Dems stay busy trying to save universal healthcare, the Republicans gerrymander election districts, restrict voter rolls, and outlaw abortion. In sum, the Red meme does not play fair, but as my Dad used to remind me as a child, "Who said life was going to be fair?"

CHAPTER 2: SPECTRUM OF CONSCIOUSNESS | 61

Although most people transcend the Red meme, the power-ethic mentality can be employed when necessary. This is why the Spectrum of Consciousness is so helpful: *It allows us to understand who we are talking to and adjust our message accordingly.* This also explains why Spiral Dynamics was successful in helping to end Apartheid. The facilitators were trained to recognize and respect the various worldviews (and vested interests) of the white and black South Africans. Such realities have to be dealt with in order to effectively mediate a solution. Though never easy, it's nigh impossible to negotiate without the benefit of this research.

The Red meme also is the most difficult to work with from a therapeutic perspective. Graves discovered that Stage 3 thinkers are the most closed, until they start contemplating their own mortality. Think of the great epic myths, such as *The Iliad* and *The Odyssey* by Homer. In such legends, our hero survives and/ or surpasses every adventure the gods throw at him, at which point he finally is ready to face the inevitable: his boring retirement and eventual death. At this point, the hero sees the impermanence of his self-centered core and is ready to spiral ... into the next "WE" meme.

SPECTRUM STAGE 4: ORANGE

To reach this stage, a person has explored the nature of the Earth Plane and is now drawn to the Ethereal Plane. He seeks salvation and non-physical immortality. To put it simply, he will sacrifice or subdue his base desires today in order to obtain a reward tomorrow. Consequently, Graves called Stage 4 the **Saintly Existence**, because it is a belief system premised on some variation of a heavenly afterlife.

Not surprisingly, Graves believed this meme started around 2500 BCE, which is when the prophet Abraham lived. Indeed, consciousness experts have since agreed with Graves that the three Abrahamic religions – Judaism, Christianity, and Islam – showcase the quintessential Stage 4 worldview. Therefore, I feel safe in concluding that Oracle got it right again: The advent of Stage 4 thinking ignited the Fourth Spiritual Paradigm.

While the spiraling Red winners (i.e., the "haves") certainly fueled this new meme, Graves argued that it was primarily the Red losers (i.e., the "have nots") who had a mass spiritual awakening and helped craft the Orange belief system. Pragmatically speaking, the masses had to make sense out of their miserable existence, and the Abrahamic religions offered the promise of justice in a world full of pain and suffering. Just imagine the seductiveness of a religion that says:

After living *ad infinitum* under the capricious and abusive rule of the landed gentry, the common folk get a heavenly reward! For similar reasons, African slaves adopted Fourth Paradigm belief systems, since after landing on foreign soil with no means of escape, they needed to make sense of their plight.

This easy promise of salvation is how Saint Paul managed to convince pagan Stage 3 thinkers to join his new Stage 4 religion. He dummied down Jesus' messages until all the Gentile Christians (Romans) had to do in order to obtain a heavenly reward was to swear allegiance to "Christ Jesus." In fact, the rules of this new religion couldn't be any simpler, especially once James the Just, leader of the Jewish Christians in Jerusalem, waived the circumcision requirement. In sum, the downtrodden masses created the Orange worldview to spiritually bypass the pain and drudgery of everyday life and the elite went along for the ride, though steering the buggy.

> *This saintly form of existence comes from experiencing that living in this world is not made for ultimate pleasure – a perception based on the previous endless struggle with unbridled lusts and a threatening universe. Here he perceives that certain rules are prescribed for each class of men and that these rules describe the proper way each class is to behave. The rules are the price man must pay for his more lasting life, for the peace which he seeks, the price of no ultimate pleasure while living.*[24]

Clare W. Graves, *"Levels of Existence"*

Thus, the hallmark of the Orange meme is personal sacrifice on the Earth Plane based on a preordained set of rules that ultimately lead to Ethereal Plane salvation. In place of (or in addition to) a human ruler, the Stage 4 person submits to a heavenly king, who also requires sacrifice but who at least promises an everlasting reward in exchange for dedicated service. Moreover, in the case of the Catholic Church, Orange followers will bow down to the pope and priests, who are considered God's representatives on Earth.

Critically, there is a strict and nearly universal patriarchal hierarchy to the Orange meme, replete with very clear, black-and-white rules so that it's easy for a person to know right from wrong. Failing that, there exists a judgmental deity who keeps track of our actions and who ultimately decides whether we are worthy of eternal punishment or the long-awaited heavenly reward.

> *A* [Stage 4] *person will say, for example, that, in the long run, anything that happens in his world will be in line with the master plan of God. ... An all-powerful figure, variously named, all powerful something or other, planned the universe, laid down the laws of the*

*universe, and watches second by second as the day and hours go
by as to whether or not the divine plan laid down is being followed.
This divine being either rewards or punishes on the spot, or tacks this
up on a score sheet to ultimately decide whether the person shall be
rewarded or punished.*[25]

Clare W. Graves, *Levels of Human Existence*

Another characteristic of Orange is that it is **ethnocentric** – and now we
are talking about classic nationalism. Orange views the world in "us" versus
"them" terms. It is a firmly entrenched "WE" meme, and if you are not in the
philosophically correct group, then you're SOL, baby. Stage 4 is dogmatic, and
issues such as abortion are a litmus test for loyalty, with pro-choice rhetoric
viewed as evil. No other meme cares about this issue, recognizing that a
woman's right to choose is an innate freedom (though Stage 3 thugs violate
bodily sovereignty to control/dominate women).

Although not as impulsively warlike as the Red meme, Graves thought that
when their belief system is threatened, the Orange meme is the most dangerous.
Why? Because Stage 4 people *really* respond to authority figures. In the U.S.,
for instance, their tendency is to love their president (if he's a Republican), and
they will sacrifice anything if they feel their country is endangered. As a result,
it is quite easy to trick the Orange meme, especially when fundamentalist fears
are stoked or when a call to action is gift-wrapped in patriotic paper.

For instance, all the Bush administration had to do was invent the name
"USA Patriot Act" for a piece of legislation that allowed broad surveillance
of Americans and legalized indefinite detention of terror suspects, including
U.S. citizens. The Patriot Act effectively eviscerated the Fourth Amendment,
which reads: "The right of the people to be secure in their persons, houses,
papers, and effects, against unreasonable searches and seizures, shall not be
violated, and no Warrants shall issue, but upon probable cause, supported by
Oath or affirmation, and particularly describing the place to be searched, and
the persons or things to be seized."

While the government continues to chip away at the Fourth Amendment,
the Orange meme obsesses over the Second Amendment, which they have been
conned into believing is under attack by liberals. As a result, there can be no
common-sense gun legislation in the U.S., even though Europeans (mostly
Stage 6 on the Spectrum) have no problem passing gun laws. Notably, it took
New Zealand only one week in 2019 to ban assault rifles after two Muslim
mosques were terrorized and fifty people killed.[26]

Not only will the Orange meme relinquish their civil rights (and take ours too) when indoctrinated by nationalistic propaganda, they will kill on command and willingly die to protect their turf, their religion, and their way of life. The scariest meme combination occurs when a Red dictator controls an Orange nation – which is what happened in Nazi Germany. Thus, Orange subservience to rules and willingness to fight a crusade can lead them to pursue an Earth Plane victory, in addition to an Ethereal Plane reward. Indeed, the "Greatest Generation" was willing to fight in World War I and World War II due to their deep sense of patriotism and their black-and-white perspective on evil.

Not surprisingly, the Military Industrial Complex predominantly is run by Orange officers who command Orange soldiers. Most cops are Orange as well. Graves highlighted this meme's propensity to fight when duty-bound: "I find that even the absolutistic pacifists in the [Stage 4] system really are not pacifists. It's only a matter of time and circumstance before they flop over then become the most warlike hawks." [27]

War Pentagon – Potomac River view   **Peace Pentagon – New River view**

Consequently, the tendency for Stage 4 humans to fight for what they deem is right must be carefully considered. Historically, it was the Orange meme that: (i) fought holy wars known as the Christian Crusades for over 200 years; (ii) persecuted "heretics" for another 600 years under the auspices of the Catholic Inquisition; (iii) declared *jihad* over the U.S. presence in their holy cities and over cartoon depictions of the prophet Muhammad; and (iv) began a "War on Terror" that is now the longest military campaign in U.S. history.

Which brings us back to Trump. God forbid he is ever reelected and leads our military. Trump's affinity for authoritarianism exceeds the bounds of the Culture War; his credo directly attacks democracy and the founding principles of our nation. Today, though impeached twice and likely the mastermind of the

January 6, 2021 insurrection, Trump remains popular with his base of Stage 3 and Stage 4 humans. The fact that Evangelicals have made a "deal with the devil" is frightening. Even more shocking is that some Evangelicals don't see it as a "deal" at all. Rather, they believe Trump was sent by God to be enthroned as "king" of the United States.[28] Famously, Jerry Falwell, Jr. kicked Senator Ted Cruz to the curb when he kicked-off Trump's presidential campaign at Liberty University, only to be dethroned himself for his myriad sins.[29]

Wilber estimates that roughly 40% of the planet is ethnocentric.[30] Based on recent Pew Reports and political polls, I estimate that 25% of the U.S. falls in this absolutist meme. Additionally, it appears that roughly 30% of the U.S. "power positions" are held by Stage 4 thinkers. As a result, this meme is over-represented in local, state, and federal government positions. How did this happen? First, Orange loves to run for office and impose his views on the rest of us. For this phenomenon, we can thank Ronald Reagan (1911–2004) and the onslaught of the Moral Majority in the 1980s. Second, we have the Electoral College to thank/curse for this meme's rise to power, since our electoral system favors the less populated rural states, where most Orange (and Red) Americans live.

By now, you probably are wondering what type of dissonance prompts Orange to start questioning his belief system. Spectrum theory posits that it is another surge of independence, a desire for self-gratification, and the pursuit of material gain that finally compels Orange to seek a more liberating belief system. Mainly, though, the Stage 4 rules get annoying! The emerging Stage 5 human starts to wonder if the rules he has been following are manmade, as opposed to preordained by God. Once these thoughts creep in, his yearning for personal freedom, self-expression, and individual achievement override the unproven promises of an unseen God. And besides, now he craves a new God ... the green god of money.

SPECTRUM STAGE 5: YELLOW

And so we enter another "I" stage of development, during which expression of self is again paramount, but not to the exclusion of all that was learned about rules and moral discipline during the Orange stage. Consequently, life at Stage 5 is not as cutthroat as it was at Stage 3, but it is still a contact sport and to the victor go the spoils, which is why Graves called it the **Materialistic Existence**.

Because this is the most common meme in the Global North and the fastest growing meme in developing third world nations, I don't need to go into much detail, except to underscore that Yellow knows the rules of the game. He may elect to break the rules now and again if he thinks he can get away with it, but he would much rather become a master player and beat you fair and square than beat you by cheating. Even so, the rules of capitalism allow collateral damage, including competitors, consumers, the environment, even friends and family.

So he plays the game of life to prove to himself that he can. And if he can, if he is successful in the Wall Street sense, then he's on top of the world and master of his destiny. Think Bill Gates, Warren Buffet, and Gordon Gekko (left). Gates and Buffet seem past Yellow values now, as evidenced by their donating most of their vast fortunes and much of their time to charity. But I'm jumping ahead; we need to explore what motivates Yellow.

The rational Yellow human first emerged during the **Scientific Revolution** (*circa* 1600), refined himself during the **Age of Enlightenment** (*circa* 1700), then excelled at business during the **Industrial Revolution** (*circa* 1800). He mastered his world through a "pragmatic, scientific, and utilitarian mode of existence," according to Graves,[31] leaving little room for God.

> *Faith in dogma is gone, replaced by experimental data, "the scientific method," and ongoing appraisals to determine what works best for now. Successful actions determine what is right, not the directives of a Higher Power or orders from authoritarian figures. ... To succeed in the* [Stage 5] *life, there is no room for guilt and no time or energy to be wasted.*[32]
>
> Don Beck and Christopher Cowan, *Spiral Dynamics*

Yellow affirmatively chooses to leave the herd and compete with brethren. He flees fundamentalism and replaces it with rationalism and materialism. Yellow shucks religion because he isn't afraid of going to hell. Instead of yearning for an Ethereal Plane reward, he now desires an Earth Plane win – wealth and prestige. So while religion still serves at Stage 4 as the "opium of the people," to quote Karl Marx, money and achievement are the primary focus at Stage 5. Consequently, Yellow is where the God Gap starts to appear. It also is the stage that falls between old and New Humans. Even though Yellow may still pledge allegiance to an orthodox sect, whether Methodist or Muslim, he has little use for God in his everyday life. He may hold his nose and attend church once a week, but his piety is questionable. He's probably faking it.

Yellow women who stay in the Catholic Church face a similar dilemma, since every Catholic woman I know believes in and uses birth control (if still fertile). The hypocrisy bothers many female Catholics, as does the horror of the pedophilia epidemic among priests. These women may stay in the pews for a while, but eventually they will leave if their dissonance becomes too great. Ultimately, even orthodox religion becomes unbearable at Stage 5, especially if Yellow is getting ready to graduate to the next worldview.

> *Freedom from constraints imposed by relations with other people or limitations that accompany faith in doctrine are central to this meme's happiness. ... Those emotions are usually tempered because the person at this level understands that flagrant rejections of authority cost support of those who still believe it. ... This is the world of the clever entrepreneur ... and the pin-striped capitalist who is reverent to* [Stage 4] *on Saturday or Sunday but can do "whatever it takes" to obtain objectives during the week.*[33]

> Don Beck and Christopher Cowan, *Spiral Dynamics*

In sum, the Stage 5 person may still go to church, but he goes to network, to maintain a respectable profile, or to teach his children basic moral values. But covertly, Yellow is done with the big five: Hinduism, Buddhism, Judaism, Christianity, and Islam. Odds are that he's either pretending to subscribe to an orthodox religion, secretly agnostic, or a closet atheist.

A prime example of such insincerity can be seen with the Saudi Arabian royal family, whose members supposedly subscribe to the extreme Wahhabi sect of Islam. Despite their Stage 4 façade, the Saudi princes and their wives periodically hop on their planes, change into western garb, then go jet-setting around the world like the Stage 5 hypocrites they are. Indeed, many Stage 5 churchgoers are nothing more than sanctimonious frauds – the same hypocrites that Jesus repeatedly called out.

> *Beware of practicing your righteousness before other people in order to be seen by them, for then you will have no reward from your Father .... And when you pray, you must not be like the hypocrites. For they love to stand and pray in the synagogues and at the street corners, that they may be seen by others. ... And when you fast, do not look gloomy like the hypocrites, for they disfigure their faces that their fasting may be seen by others. ... So you outwardly appear righteous to others, but within you are full of hypocrisy and lawlessness.*

> Gospel of Matthew, Chapters 6:1,5,16; 23:28

Graves believed that what prompts Yellow to move into the next value set is the realization that success has cost him friends and bought him enemies. He starts to feel a void, an aching for companionship and the things money can't buy. Thoughts like these start to creep into his mind:

> ➢ It's lonely at the top.
> ➢ As I climbed the ladder of success, who did I step on?
> ➢ Am I working to live or living to work?
> ➢ On my deathbed, I'll regret time lost with loved ones.
> ➢ Money can't buy happiness.
> ➢ I can't take it with me.
> ➢ The happiest people I know do the most for others.

Thus, evolved Yellow starts to question the green god of money, but he can't bow down to a fictitious guy in the sky. Suddenly, Yellow realizes that he hasn't thought about God in a long time. He then admits to himself that he has no idea what he believes! So while the above snippets may sound cliché, they reflect why Bill Gates and Warren Buffet have donated so much money to charity. These titans of industry realized that though many people envy them, some respect them, and others fear them, there are not many people in the world who love and admire them for who they are inside.

Plus, the mortality clock keeps ticking. Older Yellow begins to take stock and realizes that he can't take his toys with him. So why not give some stuff away, maybe even some money? Mid-life Yellow, if he has children, feels an overwhelming desire to connect with his progeny and leave a legacy. Younger Yellow (Millennials, Gen X, Gen Z) often pass through and discard Stage 5 values quickly, since the model of success it represents is largely unattainable in today's economy, especially due to the daunting debt that now accompanies a college degree, which itself is no longer a ticket to success.

Now dissonance really takes hold. Yellow begins to ponder the meaning of life ... and even God again. Why do I say "again"? Because as we've seen, the memes are sequential. When passing through Stage 4, Yellow believed in God. Thus, a moral and spiritual crisis has arrived: Individualistic Yellow now views his life as shallow, lonely, and possibly meaningless. He no longer is motived by money and power, and he may even find his old goals repulsive. He's also tired of the rat-race and competing. Eventually, he starts to wonder if he has something beautiful, purposeful, and lasting to contribute – a legacy unrelated to materialistic values.

It is at this point that Yellow starts to feel true compassion and the first rumblings of responsibility for the starving child he sees on the nightly news, the war ravaging another nation, the unfair treatment of so many around the world and in his own backyard. He is going **worldcentric** in his perspective, which leads to a spiritual conundrum. He feels empty yet more open than at any other time of his life. He sees the absurdity of being a loner while trying to enjoy a broader, inclusive mindset. Ultimately, he wants to be understood and find others who share his new frame of reference. In short, he wants friends.

SPECTRUM STAGE 6: GREEN

Dr. Graves labeled the next stage, which is another "WE" meme, the **Sociocentric Existence**, and he said it first emerged in the 19th Century, after some of the nasty consequences of the Industrial Revolution came to the fore. This is when Charles Dickens penned *David Copperfield* (1850), which told the tale of a boy who grows into a caring, mature adult despite the challenges of his Victorian era upbringing: the rigid class structure, impoverishment of the masses, the plight of women and prostitutes, and the horrifying criminal justice system of that period. *The Jungle* (1906) by Upton Sinclair further introduced the Green meme, by portraying the exploitation of immigrant workers in the hellish meat packing industry:

> *All day long this man would toil thus, his whole being centered upon the purpose of making twenty-three instead of twenty-two and a half cents an hour; and then his product would be reckoned up by the census taker, and jubilant captains of industry would boast of it in their banquet halls, telling how our workers are nearly twice as efficient as those of any other country. If we are the greatest nation the sun ever shone upon, it would seem to be mainly because we have been able to goad our wage-earners to this pitch of frenzy. ...*
>
> *The great corporation which employed you lied to you, and lied to the whole country – from top to bottom it was nothing but one gigantic lie.*[34]

Similarly, *The Grapes of Wrath* (1939) by John Steinbeck, depicted migrant farm workers during the Great Depression, and it is another literary example of the evolutionary impulse introducing the Green meme to the mainstream. Please note Steinbeck's use of the terms "I" (for Stage 5) and "We" (for Stage 6), as he describes the needed shift in the collective consciousness:

> *This is the beginning – from "I" to "we." If you who own the things*
> *people must have could understand this, you might preserve yourself.*
> *If you could separate causes from results, if you could know that*
> *Paine, Marx, Jefferson, Lenin, were results, not causes, you might*
> *survive. But that you cannot know. For the quality of owning freezes*
> *you forever into "I" and cuts you off forever from the "we."* [35]

While Graves dates the beginning of the Green wave to the turn of the last century, I would argue that the underpinnings of this meme date back to the American Revolution. Philosophically, the *Declaration of Independence* is a Green document, as is the U.S. Constitution. Despite the fact that the full promise of an egalitarian vision did not manifest at our country's founding, Thomas Jefferson's language has stood the test of time:

> *We hold these truths to be self-evident, that all men are created equal,*
> *that they are endowed by their Creator with certain unalienable Rights,*
> *that among these are Life, Liberty and the pursuit of Happiness.*
> *That to secure these rights, Governments are instituted among Men,*
> *deriving their just powers from the consent of the governed; That*
> *whenever any Form of Government becomes destructive of these*
> *ends, it is the Right of the People to alter or to abolish it, and to*
> *institute new Government, laying its foundation on such principles*
> *and organizing its powers in such form, as to them shall seem most*
> *likely to effect their Safety and Happiness.* [36]

Indeed, while it now is popular to criticize the Founding Fathers with the hindsight of our 21st Century perspective (e.g., they failed to free the slaves, they withheld rights from women), the truth is that fledgling Green values – and the Light – won a grand and unprecedented victory in 1776. Nevertheless, it took another two hundred years for Stage 6 values to fully emerge and its proponents to critically amass.

By 1960, Green was the cutting edge of evolution. All hell broke loose over the Vietnam War, racial desegregation, full equality for women, and hippie "free love." These minority Stage 6 movements shocked the consciousness of our Stage 5 nation, and so began the Culture War. In fact, the second half of the 20th Century through today has been one long Culture War, a battle between Stage 4, 5, and 6 values. And the stakes are high in this war – nothing less than the very heart and soul of America and the rest of the world.

Odds are if you are reading this book, you subscribe to Green values (and perhaps more). If you are Green, then you fully comprehend this worldview: equality, religious pluralism, economic justice, judicial fairness, and diplomacy as the primary tool for conflict resolution. You not only understand these values, you are adamant that they be applied universally, and not just for the sake of other human beings. You also are passionate about planetary health and sustainability. You know that oil drilling, fracking, and mining are detrimental to Mother Earth. You know the planet is warming due to our stupidity and that we already possess much of the technology needed to save ourselves and our precious planet. You also are willing to make sacrifices, like paying higher taxes, to ensure the welfare of the next generation.

Swami Satchidananda opens Woodstock in 1969 [37]

By now, you may be wondering why the Tipping Point on the Spectrum Chart is *after* Stage 6 and not before. Surely, Green represents an advanced human being, someone who deserves to be called a "New Human." Graves and I agree, so let us break with Spiral Dynamics and Integral theory on this score. Let us proudly pronounce that Green folks are New Humans. Going Green means reaching a worldcentric perspective and it deserves to be cheered!

> *The data says that homicide as a behavior of man disappears as the transition is made into* [Stage 6]. *This is a very interesting finding and suggests that if we could possibly work on the problems of human existence in such a manner as to get the mass of our people beyond the* [Stage 5] *existence, then we would not have to worry about homicide crime anymore, that this is a phenomenon which will disappear. ... [I]f a person makes the transition from* [Stage 5] *to* [Stage 6] *... he really honestly and deep inside himself believes that war is no solution to man's problems.* [38]

Nevertheless. there are valid reasons why the Green meme may fail to get us to the Tipping Point, despite their planetary values and growing numbers. Let me explain: If you haven't noticed already, flip back to the Oracle Spectrum Chart and note that there are two "tiers" in the left column. Stages 1 through 6 are considered **First Tier** memes, while Stages 7 through 9 are **Second Tier**. The Green meme, while highly evolved, usually is considered the last of the First Tier memes for a number of reasons, which we now will explore.

To start with, when a person goes Green, she goes a little overboard in assessing both herself and humanity. (Note to the reader: remember that we will be using female pronouns for New Humans). To put it bluntly, many Greens are emotionally self-absorbed and spiritually naive. With the hope that my Green friends won't blame me for this observation (which they undoubtedly will view as judgmental), I think Beck and Cowan should explain Green's predilection for affectation and aggrandizement:

> *The Green Meme is the climax of the First Tier thinking systems, the culmination of the "old-brain," subsistence-based modes of living. ... Now "feelings" begin to replace the need for "achievements" .... It is this amorphous, context-sensitive aspect of Green which so disturbs clear-cut [Stage 4] and impatient [Stage 5] – situational ethics, cultural relativism, and outcome based education (no grades, nobody fails), for example. ...*
>
> *With Communal/Collective spirituality returning, life begins to revolve around the unending quest for enlightenment .... New Age Green psycho-shamans ... replace ... medicine men .... The use of "mind-expanding" drugs is always an option in this urgency to explore altered consciousness and reach out and touch the universe. ... Green hops from guru to guru, from one peak experience to another, from one mystical path onto the next. ...*
>
> *[S]ome will begin to ask in quiet moments, "Why can't I reach the Light again?" For others, life in this zone can become a very fulfilling existence, rich with power turquoise jewelry, health foods, and well-built habitats for humanity.* [39]

Green is quick to reject elitist hierarchies and ugly prejudices, like class distinctions, racism, patriarchy, misogyny, sexism, and homophobia. When doing so, however, Green often glosses over the realities of the Earth Plane. Green mistakenly believes that *any* recognition of differences is wrong, that discernment and judgement are the same mental process, that truth is relative, and that she is "above" all discriminatory methods of interpreting the world, as Wilber explains:

One of its [Green's] *most notable characteristics is its denial and condemnation of every form of hierarchy. In this, it fails miserably to distinguish between dominator hierarchies (which are indeed loathsome) and actualization, or growth hierarchies (which are the form of most growth processes in nature, including humans). In dominator hierarchies, with each higher level, the few dominate and oppress the many. In actualization or growth hierarchies, each higher level is more and more inclusive. For example, a fundamental growth hierarchy in nature is the hierarchy of atoms to molecules to cells to organisms.*[40]

In extreme cases, Level 6 can go "**Mean Green**," again quoting Wilber. These are people who don't read actual news anymore, because it's "negative" or – wait for it – "fake." During the Trump years, liberals got trolled by the Russians nearly as much as fundamentalists, though with differently tailored social media messages. Some on the far-Left fell prey to the propaganda and began to reevaluate Trump, Russia, and QAnon. Along the same vein, some Mean Greens have stopped believing in the existence of evil. They are certain evil is an illusion, just as Orange is certain evil is everywhere.

Hate is another taboo topic. Instead of hate/evil, Mean Greens insist that "fear is the opposite of love." They also assert that the Light is easily accessible, since even if they have difficulty communing, they have a friend who can "channel" and provide clear instruction from Spirit. In short, Mean Green can become so fixated on the Ethereal Plane that she conflates her high morals and peak experiences with non-dual wisdom. We will learn more about this Green shadow side when we explore the topic of Cleaning Up in the next chapter.

On a brighter note, here's some marvelous news about the Green meme: Millennials, Gen X, and Gen Z are reaching Stage 6 quicker and at earlier ages. On the Spectrum Chart, I overlaid some ages, but that was just to provide an example of when a New Human might reach Second Tier. The fact that children are zipping through the stages and reaching Green quickly is truly inspiring! Before he retired in 1978, Graves picked up on this evolutionary upgrade:

The fact is that they are on a higher level starting point. It seems that with the technological advances ... that we've solved so many existential problems for so many of the kids that they are able to move through the first few levels faster. They are actually starting off, and this gets down to the question of the speed at which one can move through a level, way ahead of where we might have started off 15 years ago getting out of high school and hitting college.[41]

Next, let's focus on the differences between First and Second Tier. Stages 1 through 6 share certain characteristics, including the inability to see any perspective other than their own worldview. They have forgotten that they passed through succeeding stages of development, that they "transcended and included" prior memes. The net result is that First Tier memes don't respect the memes beneath or beyond them. For example, Green secretly despises Red, Orange, and Yellow, viewing all the other First Tier memes as backward and boorish. Orange and Green dislike Yellow, who they view as greedy, and Orange is terrified by Green values, which they equate with scary socialism.

Fear is another Achilles heel within First Tier memes. In one form or another, each of those six stages has an underlying fear concerning self-preservation or fear of the "other." Therefore, under extreme pressure, First Tier memes can succumb to fear and regress. For instance, during the Trump presidency, former red-blooded American nationalists (Stage 4) became White Supremacist (Stage 3). Sure, some Stage 3 thugs were simply hiding behind the bushes and waiting for the right moment to pounce, but the growth of the Red power meme can and is being measured.

Studies show that hate crimes increased during the Trump presidency and that White Supremacist groups grew 55%.[42] Yet those stats pale in comparison to the fear which erupted in response to our first black president. In 2008 when Barack Obama was elected, 149 hate groups were catalogued; by 2009, there were 512 hate groups; in 2010, the number increased to 824; and by 2011, there were 1,274 hate groups in the U.S.[43] Graves believed the fear-factor is the primary cause of regression:

> *What I find explains best to me the reason that people in* [Stage 7] *behave so much better quantitatively and qualitatively ... is this: they simply are not afraid. They are not afraid of not finding food* [Stage 1]. *They are not afraid that they're not going to have shelter* [Stage 2]. *They are not afraid of predatory man* [Stage 3]. *They are not afraid of God* [Stage 4]. *They are not afraid of not having status or not making it on their own in this world* [Stage 5]. *They are not afraid of social rejection* [Stage 6]. *You've got a human being who isn't afraid.*[44]

Another difference is that Second Tier humans make judgment calls when necessary, unlike Green, who is averse to "judging" others and will bend over backward to justify all manner of bad behavior. In truth, Green does make judgments but they're veiled in multi-cultural sensitivities and misapplied Second Tier vocabulary. Greens miss the point that unless we discern what is healthy – for ourselves and others – we cannot surf the evolutionary wave and lead others into a better future. As Wilber explains:

> One of the problems with a Green post-modern culture is that, with its pluralistic "nonjudgmental" and "hands off" attitude to every sort of individual behavior, no matter how dysfunctional or pathological, we're not even allowed to make judgments about a person being "dysfunctional" or "healthy" – who are we to judge about what is right and not right for any individual? ...
>
> This is called a "performative contradiction," because you yourself are doing what you claim you cannot or should not do. This view ranks ranking as being bad; judges judging as being oppressive; gives a very Big Picture about why Big Pictures are not possible; claims it is universally true that there are no universal truths; places hierarchies on the lowest level of its particular hierarchy; and claims its view is superior in a world where nothing is supposed to be superior. ...
>
> Only as the inadequacy and failure of this view is consistently seen and directly felt – and nihilism and narcissism start to lose their flavor – does Green let go of this limited Pluralistic view and take that "monumental leap of meaning" into Integral 2nd tier.[45]

Another difference is that Second Tier humans have tamed, balanced, and subordinated their ego. So while Greens believe their egos are in check, that simply is not the case. Wilber calls Stage 6 the "ego's last stand," because the ego – sensing that it will be snuffed out at Stage 7 – starts to push back. Then Mean Green narcissism can kick in, especially on the topic of spirituality.

Luckily, Green narcissism only takes the form of speech – not hate speech but love speech – a sugary sweet attitude expressed in whispered tones and an unnatural calm when facing even the most difficult challenges.[46] Then, it's only a matter of time before a "talking stick" is employed and group consensus insisted upon. And God forbid that every idea and every personal anecdote – no matter how off-topic – not be considered and given time for full expression. Indeed, Stage 6 meetings are excruciating for every meme but Green.

Not surprisingly, therefore, Green projects take a long time to manifest (if they come to fruition at all). From a Second Tier perspective, it takes patience to co-create with Greens, because they like to slowly dissect all aspects of how each member feels about both the project and its implementation. Wilber has openly stated that allowing too many Greens on his planning team for Integral University tanked the project. Conversely, Second Tier humans tend to move fast because they see the big picture, they understand how each puzzle piece fits together, and they love to manifest.

To summarize, Spectrum theory states that once a person hits Second Tier, she has become "integrated" and will not regress. Certainly, she will experience fear, but she will not readopt a First Tier belief system. Also, Second Tier courage should not be confused with the bravery demonstrated by the Red, Orange, and Yellow folks – all of whom will rally to protect their turf, especially if a Stage 3 hero or Stage 5 capitalist can directly benefit.

In order to transcend Stage 6, a new dissonance is required. Ironically, it is a discontent that flows from Green's failure to interject her worldcentric values onto a mostly ethnocentric world. At first, there is a sense of defeatism and hopelessness. But then the Stage 6 senior recalls the most inspiring of all the Green directives: "We are the ones we have been waiting for!" Thereafter, if the Green seeker is honest and earnest, she is ready to graduate to Stage 7, where she will undertake a brand new quest for Truth, Love, and Light. But beware, once the Second Tier threshold is crossed, there is no turning back.

SPECTRUM STAGE 7: INDIGO

Reaching Second Tier is a monumental achievement because only about 5% of the planet has made it this far. If you have attained an Indigo perspective, congratulations! Your waking worldview includes expanded vision, strategic functionality, and the capacity to synergize vast data points and possibilities. You also feel a daunting sense of mission. Indeed, having been at Second Tier for a while, I'm uncertain whether to shout "welcome" or whisper "I'm sorry," since once you reach Indigo, you're forever changed – no ifs, ands, or buts.

Therefore, don't worry if you wobble in and out of Stage 7 for a while. You've been climbing a steep mountain and you've finally reached a plateau at the cloud-line where you can sit and catch your breath. Give yourself some time to adjust to the higher altitude. At first, it may be a challenge to maintain a Second Tier perspective, since the tests come quickly and are exceedingly difficult. In fact, one way to distinguish Stage 6 from Stage 7 is that Green thinks missions should be easy and joyful. Indigo knows the Truth (big "T") about the Earth Plane, and while it has set her free, the Truth feels much more like a burden than a blessing.

The good news is that Indigo is clear-eyed and cognizant of the great spiral of life. Systems thinking is becoming second nature and polarity is a paradox to be solved. Her focus is the interconnectedness of life and the continued evolution of humanity, and her mission is to protect and preserve both. In short, Indigo sees how messed up the world is, the wretched state of the human condition, and the incredible amount of work that needs to be done!

> *[A] sudden and almost unbelievable change in human behavior takes place when the individual begins to believe that psychological health should be both expressive of self and taking care of the other human being at the same time. ...*
>
> *[S]uddenly, human cognition is free. Now with his energies free for cognitive activation, man focuses upon his self and his world. The picture revealed is not pleasant. Illuminated in devastating detail is man's failure to be what he might be and his misuse of the world. Triggered by this revelation, man leaps out in search of a new way of life and a system of values which will enable him to be more than a parasite leeching upon the world and all its beings.*[47]
>
> Clare W. Graves, *Levels of Human Existence*

Relief is at hand when Indigo realizes she no longer blames others. She doesn't see the other memes as "wrong" anymore; she just sees them. This is a totally new panorama – a vantage point higher than Green's – that offers a much richer, more complex, and multi-faceted view of life. Wilber calls this phase **Vision Logic** (with a "low" and a "high" vision stage).[48] Now, puzzle pieces start to fall into place. And there is joy here, just not the type of self-gratifying fun that Green is looking for.

On the Spectrum Chart, I used the phrase "One for All" to express the self-motivated yet planetary scope of this "I" meme. It is half of the famous saying in *The Three Musketeers*, whereby they pledge fidelity to each other in a classic Stage 4, ethnocentric sense. At Indigo, however, this oath takes on a different meaning, a broad and bountiful commitment. She possesses a truly inclusive and expansive worldview, as detailed by Wilber:

> *Thus, unlike the previous Pluralistic View, the Integral View is truly holistic, not in the New Age woo-woo sense, but because it sees itself as part of the deeply interwoven and interconnected and conscious Kosmos. The Pluralistic View, we saw, wants to be holistic, all-inclusive, and nonmarginalizing, and even calls itself the "Integral Culture," but with its typical 1st-tier attitude, it despises other levels and their values, and thus can hardly include them. It loathes the modern Rational View, absolutely cannot abide the traditional Mythic View, and goes apoplectic when faced with a truly Integral View.*[49]

Despite the higher vantage point, Stage 7 can feel schizophrenic. Indigos are singularly focused on saving the world, yet they also experience the awe and wonderment of their new connection to the Light. This worldview is empowering, yet daunting; it is both thrilling and humbling. And its allure exceeds the prior memes' notions of autonomy, camaraderie, or even family. Not surprisingly, therefore, it will be family and close friends who are immediately impacted when a person goes Second Tier. Sadly, it is common for those around Indigo to feel forgotten or ignored, as she takes off to save the planet and fly closer to the Light.

In my case, the transition from Stage 6 to Stage 7 was devastating for my partner of more than eight years, and we broke up soon after my entry into Second Tier. In addition, I lost all my girlfriends, who thought I'd gone crazy and said so to my face. My children got the short end of the stick as well – may they forgive me now that I see it, now that I have apologized, and now that I have moved to a new spiritual space, a higher plateau that allows me an even greater vista from which to love them while I watch the world.

Because I've gone through this harrowing shift and know how hard it can be, my heart goes out to those who are teetering at Second Tier. I have known people who arrive at Indigo, acknowledge its difficulty, then punt back to Green. I also have friends who are "questing" – they've sold most of their possessions and live like nomads, driving from place to place, looking for something (they know not what) and waiting for the Universe to give them a Sign. I believe these Greens are either afraid to make the leap to Second Tier, or they've started to transition but are avoiding the heavy workload associated with the Second Tier call to action. They'd rather just skip Stage 7 and go straight to Stage 8 (many think they're there already). Because the transition to Indigo is so challenging, I will share parts of my journey in the hope that my story will assist others in gaining clarity and courage.

Not only was my entry into Stage 7 hard on my lover, family and friends, it nearly broke me. When I sold my farm – the same summer my youngest son graduated from high school – and moved The Oracle Institute to the Appalachian Mountains of Virginia, I felt naked and alone. And I was alone – for the first time in my life – having gotten married straight out of law school and then, after my divorce, living with and raising my three children, who at the time ranged from ages two to seven. When my youngest turned eighteen and took off for college, I took off as well. I arrived at the newly established yet nascent Oracle Campus with only my beloved dog Shadow and two cats at my side.

It wasn't long before I received my first test, as the Dark Side ambushed me immediately. Having been guided to the property, I was certain that it was perfect for the intended purposes: a teaching campus with a spirituality school, multi-faith sanctuary, publishing house, and peacebuilding practice. I knew it would be a challenge, since I had moved to the tip of the Bible Belt. In cosmopolitan northern Virginia, I was preaching to the choir. Sharing a pluralistic message in southwestern Virginia was a totally new ballgame.

> [Indigo] *understands that profound change only occurs around serious problems of existence. Like a heat-seeking missile, they are drawn to hot spots where the evolving crisis demands new insights.*[50]
>
> Don Beck and Christopher Cowan, *Spiral Dynamics*

I was ill-prepared for what came next. Within two months of purchasing the property, I received notice that a state prison was going to be built directly across the New River, which happens to be the oldest river in America, the oldest river in the Western hemisphere, and possibly the oldest river in the world. So it was inconceivable to me that a prison would be built along such a sacred river, and even more bizarre that the developer – a Haliburton subsidiary – would seek to legally condemn a portion of Oracle Campus to build a bridge across the river to the prison site. It was so bad, so unbelievably and obviously heinous, that I instantly knew malevolent forces were at work and that I must rise to the challenge or lose the Oracle vision altogether.

I decided to gird myself for battle – after all, Indigo is the spiritual warrior stage of development. I met and started to strategize with my new neighbors on Battlefield Drive. Yes, for those of you who appreciate synchronicity, the original address for Oracle Campus was 1990 Battlefield Drive. Today, the address is 88 Oracle Way, since I undertook the process to rename our roads, thereby hopefully diminishing the negative *karma* of a road named not after the Civil War, not after the Revolutionary War, but a battle in the early 1700s to dispossess the indigenous people who lived here, likely Cherokee.

Upon learning that I was an attorney, my new neighbors asked me to be the lead plaintiff in a lawsuit styled *George v. Grayson County Board of Supervisors and Public Private Infrastructure, Inc.* (the Halliburton-related company). Noteworthy co-plaintiffs included the New River Conservancy (formerly, National Committee for the New River) and Philip and Charlotte Hanes, owners of an adjacent cattle ranch that lies on both sides of the river. The Haneses (of Hanes Hosiery) graciously paid for two teams of lawyers.

I worked with the "bad cop" team of lawyers in Roanoke, who prepared the litigation. Phil and Charlotte worked with the "good cop" team of lawyers in Richmond, who waged a public relations campaign to solicit then Governor Tim Kane's assistance in protecting the New River.

Ironically, it was the Cherokee who saved us – the very people who were "battled against" on Battlefield Drive. We were able to identify indigenous burial sites on Oracle land, the Hanes property, and the proposed prison site. It was a last ditch, legal and moral argument our team used to finally convince the wicked conglomerate to pack up their prison plans and move elsewhere. In total, the prison fight lasted over a year, and it was a fulltime job for me, pulling me away from Oracle and my main mission.

Original site of the New River Prison (2007)
Directly across the river from my house and the undeveloped Oracle Campus

Interestingly enough, I learned during the prison fight that the New River had been threatened forty years earlier by Appalachian Power and its notable spokesperson, Congressman William Wampler, Sr. of Virginia. APCO wanted to dam the river and flood a portion of the New River valley in order to generate hydro-power. This time around, it was his son – Virginia State Senator William Wampler, Jr. – who helped master-mind the scheme to put a prison on the river in the same general location as the dam site supported by his father.

Apparently, Wampler Jr. held a vendetta for the embarrassment Wampler Sr. suffered when he lost the effort to dam the New River back in 1965. The environmental movement was just getting started then, and my neighbors managed to defend the river and shame Wampler Sr. in the process. It is remarkable how family *karma* can continue generation to generation. As Philip

Hanes (1926–2011) noted after the prison fight, the attack on the New River by the Wamplers (father and son) was a microcosm of the attacks by Presidents George Bush (father and son) against Iraq. Incidentally, it was a young Bill Moyers who was assigned to cover the New River dam story. I called Bill Moyers during the prison fight, and he kindly offered to help protect the river again if our indigenous burial ground argument failed.

After winning the anti-prison crusade, I assumed the Dark Side was done with me. No rest for the weary, however, especially if the weary is a Stage 7 New Human. The prison lawsuit was soon followed by another lawsuit – this time to build the Peace Pentagon, Oracle's headquarters and ground zero for all matters related to my mission. The second lawsuit was "payback" for the trouble I'd caused in diverting the prison, which the county wanted for jobs and economic growth. In short, the Grayson County Board of Supervisors refused to issue me a permit to build the Peace Pentagon. Once again, I was thrown into an abyss, and I seriously pondered whether I had made a mistake in resettling Oracle in such a backward region of the country.

The second suit was similarly styled *George v. Board of Supervisors of Grayson County*, and it was filed with the assistance of **The Rutherford Institute**, a First Amendment foundation.[51] Imagine my complete horror and utter fatigue at having to sue the county again! Moreover, the second lawsuit was more brutal than the first, since not only was the county trying to get rid of me, a dozen local churches joined the fray. Evangelical pastors came to public hearings to proclaim that I was a "heretic," "witch," "cult leader," and "Satan worshipper." Next, I started to receive death threats, and I was told by one of my neighbors that the KKK was reassembling. Stark images (memories?) of being on trial and drowned as a witch flooded my mind. Truly, it was a nightmare.

About halfway through the second lawsuit, my faith was in tatters. I was scared, alone, and living each day with mounting doubt and depression. Nevertheless, I knew – on a metaphysical level – what was happening. I was being tested again, and I could either throw in the towel or gird again for battle. I convinced myself that as a spiritual warrior, I could handle the pressure, and I prayed to Saint Joan of Arc (a heroine from my Catholic days). I was engaged in another duel with the Dark. I had no choice but to resist and persist, as anyone must who desires to anchor a Second Tier perspective.

In the end, just days before trial, the county caved and issued the permit. Synchronously, construction began on the Peace Pentagon on June 8, 2012, at the end of a rare **Venus transit** – which also marked the end of my messages.[52] I had been receiving messages throughout the transit, from 2004 until 2012, for a total of eight years. I had selected the pentacle as Oracle's icon without (consciously) knowing that Venus was making a pentacle in the sky during the transit, which it also makes during its regular eight-year cycle.[53] Today, the Peace Pentagon chapel contains a stained-glass window commemorating this event. The window features the Dove of Peace and the morning star – Venus – rising with the Sun as they simultaneously appeared at Oracle Campus in Independence, Virginia, at 6:08 am on June 8, 2004.[54]

**Installation of the Dove of Peace and Venus window
Commissioned and installed by Rev. Jay Hurley (right) (2018)**

The moral of the story is: "Be careful what you ask for." If, like me, you have a strong desire to reach enlightenment, just know that the path is rocky and you must walk it barefoot. All New Age nonsense to the contrary, the transition to Stage 7 is very difficult and it hardly can be described as "fun." Considering the temporary loss of loved ones, the tests of faith, and the Dark Night of the Soul which one usually must undergo, is it any wonder that so few people make it to the Second Tier?

Yet, once you are firmly established in Indigo, the benefits slowly begin to outweigh the burdens. There is a new sense of purpose and destiny, and you begin to manifest in earnest. In addition, your intentions start to align with the Light, which means notions of free will start to evaporate. You seek refuge and comfort in whatever form the Light appears to you – whether in meditation or during long hikes in nature – and you start to ask yourself questions like: *Why am I doing this? Was this mission my idea? Will the synchronicity continue? Should I prepare for more tests from the Dark Side? And can I count on the Light to keep assisting me?*

To continue the journey takes grit and guts. It also takes a lot of heart, which is the hallmark of the next meme. But before we get to Stage 8, there is more material for us to cover regarding the seventh portal. Truly, it is a portal, as it takes you into a totally new landscape.

> *Once outside the First Tier, ideas become multidimensional. People moving from Green toward* [Indigo] *tolerate, even enjoy, paradoxes and uncertainties. ... Few ideas are sacred; all are subject to review and upgrades to more functionality. ...*
>
> *As Indigo peaks, scales drop from our eyes enabling us to see, for the first time, the legitimacy of all the human systems awakened to date. ... The systems are seen as dynamic forces that, when healthy, contribute to the overall viability of the Spiral and, as a result, to the continuation of life itself. ...*
>
> [Indigo] *senses that successful human living in the First Tier has put everything in jeopardy. ... clearly, new societal priorities and modes of decision-making will be required in such a milieu. ...* [Indigos] *are able to fix problems while others fret, manipulate, query higher authority, form study groups, or play theory games.*[55]
>
> Don Beck and Christopher Cowan, *Spiral Dynamics*

Yes, that is exactly what it feels like to be at Stage 7. Every day, you wake up with fresh ideas and a renewed sense of purpose. Your mission is all consuming and time is of the essence. In your spare time, you ponder how the God Game is played, what the rules are and where you fit on the chessboard, whether Earth is a prison planet or a simulation, and so forth. These are topics that Second Tier New Humans LOVE to talk about over dinner (when their work is done), and topics we will discuss in an upcoming chapter.

Indigos also are on the lookout for other New Humans, watching carefully and with bated breath to determine if new friends are Stage 6 or Stage 7. It doesn't take long to identify Green, who you respect, but who you hope against hope will be another Indigo, since Stage 7 co-workers are few and far between. Currently, Oracle is looking for Second Tier people to join our intentional community called the **Valley of Light**. There are just a few of us here now and we constantly scan the horizon for other Indigos. More on the Valley of Light and Second Tier communities in a later chapter as well.

For now, it is important to establish in the reader's heart and mind what it feels like to be Second Tier. It is marvelous. More importantly, however, it is the first stage past the Tipping Point and inside the Fifth Spiritual Paradigm, which means it is critical for Green New Humans to get here! Wilber agrees, and he believes that if we can get 10% of the planet Second Tier, then the elusive Tipping Point will be achieved. Right now, with just 5% of the planet at Second Tier, we have a way to go. If the five primary religions were operating as conveyor belts to move people along the Spectrum, this process might go faster. Instead, fundamentalist churches (Stage 4), orthodox ministers (Stage 5), and New Age gurus (Stage 6) have created a logjam that is preventing souls from progressing to the Second Tier, where humanity finally hits the jackpot.

> *This 10 percent turns out to be an important "tipping point." What researchers have found is that, during human history, whenever the leading edge of evolution and development becomes around 10 percent of the population, major, profound, and extensive changes occur throughout the overall population, as these newly emergent values begin to populate and saturate culture, even though only 10 percent of the population is actually at this leading-edge stage.*[56]

To prove his point, Wilber points to the **Age of Reason** and the advent of Stage 5 thinking, which helped fuel the American and French revolutions. The vast majority of American colonists were afraid to take on the British Redcoats, but the Founding Fathers and the 10% of Americans who craved freedom led the way. Similarly, Martin Luther King, Jr. and the 10% of Americans who accepted Stage 6 values such as universal human rights were able to make incredible strides with the Civil Rights movement. Thankfully, President Lyndon Johnson (1908–1973) managed to sign the Civil Rights Act of 1964 into law, thereby pulling the South kicking and screaming into the future (we currently are seeing another racist backlash). Today, Indigo is the leading edge of evolution, and our goal must be to increase this meme's numbers to the 10% threshold.

For those who seek even greater stages of Growing Up, the next two levels of the Spectrum await. While exceedingly rare, advanced New Humans are beckoning us to join them. Thus far, it has been my experience that entry into Stage 8 is not as terrifying as the transition to Stage 7. Rather, it often is the reluctance of the Stage 7 person which holds her back. You see, once you settle into Indigo, your life feels profound and purpose-driven. So why leave?

Eventually, though, Indigo stops overthinking it. She quits using her mind instead of her heart and she replaces *logos* with *agape*. While it's been rewarding to seek Truth at Stage 7, Indigo realizes that a problem-solving existence is not enough. Thereafter, Indigo becomes obsessed with what she has yet to experience, what she now feels missing inside herself at the center of her being. If she is spiritual and is able to touch bliss upon occasion, she wants to experience true enlightenment. And if she is an atheist (which still is possible at Stage 7), Indigo is willing to surrender to Great Mystery.

For this next adventure, Indigo commits to open herself in a more devoted and reverent manner. She notices that her desire for community is returning, overtaking the last vestiges of her individualism. She therefore is primed to commence a journey of Love, intuiting that the formless, unseen realms of the heart and higher consciousness are the next portal. She naturally adopts a more intimate relationship with herself and others, no longer viewing human frailty as an equation to be solved. And she seeks a transpersonal affiliation with the Light, the object now of her quest.

SPECTRUM STAGE 8: VIOLET

Try to imagine what it must feel like to be a Violet New Human. All your everyday, ordinary, rudimentary needs of existence are now trivial. You no longer concern yourself with food, fear, freedom, finances, or friendship, since all those desires have essentially evaporated. In addition, your left-brain vision logic from Stage 7 is now balanced with right-brain intuitive wisdom, thereby blossoming into whole-brain thinking and a transcendent worldview at Stage 8. We have arrived at the elevated perspective of many saints and prophets. Violet has "transcended and included" all the Earth Plane has to offer, and she now experiences the Ethereal Plane on a regular basis. She lives life at a level that is nearly impossible for most humans to comprehend. Indeed, only Indigo has a clue what Violet is experiencing. Here, Beck and Cowen explain:

> At our present stage in human development, the [Stage 8] meme is at an embryonic stage. ... [Violet] is intrigued by the possibilities of venues for consciousness and wants to learn about them. ... A form of spirituality resurges here, but there is not an identifiable someone in active, deliberate control. Instead, a unifying force and set of guiding principles set the course of the universe and ... the gaps between science and metaphysics close. ...
>
> [Violet] is far beyond Green's New Age chic and faddish spirituality. ... From the [Violet] perspective, there is nothing mystical about mystics – a fact which disillusions Green no end. ... At [Violet] one stands in awe of the cosmic order, the creative forces that exist from the Big Bang to the smallest molecule. ... The person constantly monitors both self and situation as a participant-observer. The ego that drives the subsistence layers is virtually non-existent.[57]

During Stage 7, when left-brain logic was still dominant, Indigo may have felt whole because she was exploring holism as a real construct. Yet, in order to master complexity and dispassionately seek Truth, Indigo emotionally detached to observe, catalogue, synergize, and integrate. At Stage 8, however, Violet is reconnecting with humanity and the entire planet. Compassion and experiential knowledge are the hallmark of this meme. Thus, unlike Indigo, Violet neither functions as a witness nor practices mindfulness. Rather, Violet is mind-full, heart-full, and intimately engaged with all levels of creation. We therefore will call this stage the **Illumined Mind**.

> *This means that the person has started to recognize or intuit some version of his or her Higher Selves. ... [O]ne's sense of Kosmos connection is thus wide, deep, profound, and immediate. A sense of Wholeness is directly experienced .... The "transcend and include" nature of structure development has made structure upon structure upon structure more and more aware, so that an "awareness of awareness" is now inherently present .... Further, all forms of spiritual intelligence at this* [Violet] *level ... have a strong focus on the communion of all being, or the interconnectedness and "oneness" of all sentient beings at all levels.*[58]

> Ken Wilber, *The Religion of Tomorrow*

On the Oracle Spectrum Chart, Violet is a "WE" meme that I have labeled "All is One," because this is the first stage that truly grasps the concept of Oneness (contrary to the Green New Age co-opting of Stage 8 vocabulary). Thus, Violet seeks Love (big "L"), and she finds it. Her spirituality may still take the form of nature mysticism, but she likely is experimenting with and experiencing what Wilber calls the "true trinity" or the **Triple Godhead**: Thou Art, It Is, and I Am.[59]

> *Some of these luminous/radiant forms and patterns ... are often interpreted, especially by lower levels, as real beings infused with profound luminosity (for example angels). ... [S]pirituality here* [Stage 8] *often tends toward a "deity mysticism" variety (where "deity" at this level, is often interpreted – by this level itself – as the Intelligence of the Kosmos ...).*[60]

Typically, the mythic and fundamentalist memes (Stages 3 and 4) view God in sundry anthropomorphic forms and approach the Light as "Thou Art," a second-person phenomenon. The later "I" memes (Stages 5 and 7) tend to approach the Light scientifically, as curious observers or impartial witnesses, thereby employing an "It Is" or third-person perspective (e.g., the "Force" in *Star Wars*). The other First Tier "WE" memes (Stages 2 and 6) reach for the Light using a first-person "I Am" perspective, though they usually experience the Godhead as an extension of themselves or as an admixed feature of their own being, rather than true unity consciousness.

Consequently, it is not until Stage 8 that a true "I Am" perspective is possible. Moreover, Violet can access all aspects of the Triple Godhead, depending on her needs or the context of the communion. She may even play with these perspectives in order to gain access to different dimensions of the Light, as she pursues her goal of enlightenment. Inwardly, Violet is mystical; outwardly, she is a mystery to others. Yet because of her obvious connection to the Ethereal Plane, Violet is trusted by others, which makes her an effective Lightworker on the Earth Plane. Now, Violet has a veritable toolbox with which to problem-solve, mediate, and co-create, and she uses her tools adroitly.

His Holiness the Dalai Lama and Archbishop Desmond Tutu[61]

For example, competition is the primary tool at the First Tier, where an ax or hammer is wielded, almost always producing a "win-lose" solution. Even when Yellow (Stage 5) plays by the rules and uses a scalpel instead of an ax, he is playing to win, since to the victor go the spoils. Likewise, despite the best intentions of Green (Stage 6), whose tool of choice is a level, their results are rarely balanced, since Green will favor whichever party they think is oppressed. Therefore, in First Tier problem-solving, collaboration (if it exists at all) is not synergistic, and someone usually loses, in spite of Green's best efforts.

At Second Tier, on the other hand, integrated Indigo (Stage 7) has the ability to manifest a "win-win" solution by utilizing a systems theory approach. Indigo's acumen allows her to play the God Game like chess, while others in the First Tier are still playing checkers. Better yet, Violet (Stage 8) has the wisdom to play three-dimensional chess and achieve "win-win-win" outcomes, where all parties – including Mother Earth and all sentient beings – feel the benefit and bounty of the win.

Thus, Violet's role is to be in compassionate service to the world, and because she has the capacity to connect with the Godhead, her service is marked by an exceptional record of achieving miraculous results. While Indigo is a conscious player in the God Game, Violet is a master player. Should she elect to continue her journey, this New Human is primed and prepared to discover where Truth, Love, and Light merge.

SPECTRUM STAGE 9: WHITE LIGHT

Speaking of merging, before we explore **Super Mind** – the last stage of Growing Up – I need to remind the reader that the Oracle model deviates from Wilber's in a few regards (see endnote 48). Wilber has charted a total of twelve memes and he has hinted at mapping even more. Why, you may ask, did I merge some of Wilber's Second Tier memes? Because those levels of consciousness are so beyond the grasp of the vast majority of humans – even most New Humans – that Oracle's map is a sensible way to organize this material.

For instance, Wilber's last major tome, *The Religion for Tomorrow*, is over 800 pages long. You'd need to be an "Einstein of Consciousness" yourself to fully comprehend what Growing Up to Super Mind looks and feels like. Please also recall that less than one percent of the global population has reached Illumined Mind at Stage 8. Thus, Violet virtually transcends and darn near includes every reader of this book (and its author). As for Oracle Stage 9 (Wilber Stages 11 and 12), Wilber does not bother to ascribe a percentage of humans who have reached this stage. It is that rare.

Incidentally, a good way to chart yourself on the Spectrum is to follow this axiom: *If a meme description doesn't make sense to you, you're not there yet.* Nevertheless, it is advantageous to study the characteristics of the meme above where you rest, as it will help you to anticipate what is coming. But trying to grasp a definition of consciousness that is two or more levels away can prove fruitless and frustrating. Yet, it is important not to become disheartened if, when you chart yourself, you realize the need for a more dedicated commitment.

It is a challenge for me to explain Stage 9, since this level of consciousness is "fuzzy" to me (as per the above axiom). White Light also is hard to describe given the limited scope of language generally, and the dearth of western (i.e., Christian) vocabulary specifically. Thus, English nomenclature is ill-equipped to explain the many grades and shades of the enlightenment experience. Indeed, only actual experience can fully convey the majesty of this meme.

> *In the ancient days, when the first quiver of speech came to my lips, I ascended the holy mountain and spoke unto God, saying, "Master, I am Thy slave. Thy hidden will is my law and I shall obey Thee for ever more." But God made no answer ... and like a mighty tempest passed away.*
>
> *And after a thousand years, I ascended the holy mountain and again spoke unto God, saying, "Creator, I am Thy creation. Out of clay hast Thou fashioned me and to Thee I owe mine all." And God made no answer ... but like a thousand swift wings passed away.*
>
> *And after a thousand years, I climbed the holy mountain and spoke unto God again, saying, "Father, I am Thy son. In pity and Love Thou hast given me birth, and through Love and worship I shall inherit Thy kingdom." And God made no answer ... and like the mist that veils the distant hills passed away.*
>
> *And after a thousand years, I climbed the sacred mountain and again spoke unto God, saying, "My God, my aim and my fulfillment; I am Thy yesterday and Thou art my tomorrow. I am Thy root in the earth and Thou art my flower in the sky, and together We grow before the face of the sun."*
>
> *Then God leaned over me ... and in my ears whispered words of sweetness, and even as the sea enfolds a brook that runs into her, He enfolded me. And when I descended to the valleys and the plains, God was there also.*
>
> Kahlil Gibran, *"God"*

This poem conveys the devotion required to reach White Light and the long duration of the quest. New Agers fantasize about "spontaneous enlightenment" and fool themselves that they can reach the "I Am" perspective by dabbling in meditation and ceremony. Rather, enlightenment is exceedingly rare, with even fewer cases of the spontaneous ilk. That is why mystics of every faith endorse the *Saddha* process of soul growth. We will discuss illumination in the last chapter, along with the difference between *stages* of development and *states* of awareness. They are not the same, though at White Light it is presumed that a soul has reached the pinnacle of both, as well as eliminating all shadow aspects.

"Theologue" by Alex Grey[62]

At White Light, we are in the province of the avatars, masters, and truly enlightened ones, people like Jesus who repeatedly communed with and acted on behalf of the Light. Jesus did not attempt to share his advanced knowledge with the masses, but he did instruct his inner circle, and a few – including his sacred consort Mary Magdalene – had eyes to see and ears to hear.

> *I shall give you what no eye has seen and what no ear has heard and what no hand has touched and what has never occurred to the human mind. ... If they say to you, "Where did you come from?" say to them, "We came from the Light, the place where the Light came into being on its own accord and established itself and became manifest through their image."*[63]

In essence, the White Light stage is *the* Light. A New Human at this level has attained the "I Am" perspective. Such a person is transfigured and leads a transmuted, non-dual existence that is beyond the comprehension of all but a handful of masters who have visited from the Ethereal Plane to advise and catalyze the Earth Plane. In short, upon reaching Super Mind, a person is done with this dimension. She is finished:

Growing Up: Passing through all stages of the Spectrum;

Cleaning Up: Shedding all shadow aspects (we will explore "allergies" and "addictions" in the next chapter); and

Waking Up: Attaining all states of spiritual awareness (the topic of the last chapter).

Because I have not reached White Light (yet), I will rely on Wilber to provide us with a contemporary description of what it means to be enlightened:

> *For those who wish to follow the mystics to this Level, it is the venture of all ventures, the quest for the Holy Grail, the search for the Philosopher's Stone, the Elixir of Immortality, the Master* [God] *Game itself. It is not without risks, but then no voyage is. ...*
>
> *[I]t, too, aims at healing a particular dualism, in this case, the Primary Dualism, the primordial dualism ... a dismemberment that goes back to the very point where God emerged from the Void and divided the Light from the Dark, a point that is nevertheless everpresent, without date or duration, reenacting itself Now, not once, but thousands upon thousands of times in this single moment. And it is presently here, in this moment, this never-fading Now, that the search ends, for it flashes clear that the Goal, the Sought, is nothing but the Seeker himself.*[64]

Ken Wilber, The Spectrum of Consciousness

Hopefully, the reader is now convinced – regardless of where you may fall on the Spectrum – that a human is not a human is not a human. If so, let us proceed to the next chapter, where we will study how old humans have carved patterns throughout history – repetitive First Tier rhythms in the Earth Plane that mock and mimic the life-death-life cycle of the Ethereal Plane. Then, we will explore whether New Humans who have access to the Ethereal Plane can break this tenacious cycle, or whether duality, dissonance, and polarity are inherent aspects of the God Game in this dimension. I truly hope not.

Rather, I trust that New Humans will soon learn the Laws of the Universe and thereby consciously and collectively unify the Earth and Ethereal Planes. With our compass duly set to that utopian dream, let us end this chapter with the Oracle Temple mantra:

Source of All Being:

Lead us from the unreal to the Real.
Lead us from darkness to Light.
Lead us from the fear of death to the knowledge of Immortality.
Allow us to reunite with You and come to know Your Mysteries.
May the entire Universe be filled with Truth, Love, and Light.

OM JAI![65]

[1] Ken Wilber, *The Spectrum of Consciousness*, Quest Books: Wheaton, IL (1977).

[2] Don Edward Beck and Christopher C. Cowan, *Spiral Dynamics: Mastering Values, Leadership, and Change*, pp. 40–41, Blackwell Publishing: Malden, MA (1996).

[3] Ken Wilber, *A Theory of Everything: An Integral Vision for Business, Politics, Science, and Spirituality*, p. 11, Shambhala Publications: Boston, MA (2000).

[4] Ibid, p. 35.

[5] Ken Wilber, *Integral Spirituality: A Startling New Role for Religion in the Modern and Postmodern World*, p. 99, Shambhala Publications: Boston, MA (2006).

[6] Lisa Birnbach, *The Official Preppy Handbook*, Workman Publishing: New York, NY (1980).

[7] Clare W. Graves, "Levels of Existence: An Open Systems Theory of Values," *Journal of Humanistic Psychology* (Fall 1970).

[8] Don Edward Beck and Christopher C. Cowan, *Spiral Dynamics*.

[9] Don Beck and Graham Linscott, *The Crucible: Forging South Africa's Future*, New Paradigm Press: Johannesburg, South Africa (1991).

[10] Ken Wilber, *A Brief History of Everything*, pp. 86–87, Shambhala Publications: Boulder, CO (1996).

[11] Ibid, pp. 127–128.

[12] Ken Wilber, *The Religion of Tomorrow: A Vision for the Future of the Great Traditions*, p. 59, Shambhala Publications: Boulder, CO (2017).

[13] Ibid, pp. 11, 75, 651, passim.

[14] *Aluna: A Journey to Save the World*, directed and produced by Alan Ereira (2012), https://www.alunathemovie.com/ (accessed July 2022)

[15] Ken Wilber, *A Brief History of Everything*, p. 7.

[16] The Moog, "Skins" (2007), Creative Commons Attribution-Share Alike 2.0 License, https://creativecommons.org/licenses/by-sa/2.0/deed.en.

[17] Ken Wilber, *Trump and a Post-Truth World*, p. 80, Shambhala Publications: Boulder, CO (2017).

[18] Clare W. Graves, "Levels of Existence: An Open Systems Theory of Values."

[19] George W. Bush, *Decision Points*, Random House: New York, NY (2010).

[20] Mehdi Hasan, "Donald Trump Wants to Make It Easier to Start a Nuclear War: This Should Petrify Us," *The Intercept* (Feb. 8, 2018), https://theintercept.com/2018/02/08/donald-trump-nuclear-war/ (accessed July 2022).

[21] Ken Wilber, *Trump and a Post-Truth World*, p. 69.

22 "Why Has Russian Invaded Ukraine and What Does Putin Want?" *BBC News* (May 9, 2022), https://www.bbc.com/news/world-europe-56720589. See also: "Putin Orders Troops to Separatist Regions and Recognizes their Independence," *The New York Times* (Feb. 21, 2022), https://www.nytimes.com/live/2022/02/21/world/ukraine-russia-putin-biden (both accessed July 2022).

23 Ken Wilber, *A Brief History of Everything,* p. 283.

24 Clare W. Graves, "Levels of Existence: An Open Systems Theory of Values."

25 William R. Lee, editor, *Clare W. Graves: Levels of Human Existence*, p. 89, transcription of a 1971 seminar at Washington School of Psychiatry, ECLET Publishing: Santa Barbara, CA (2002).

26 Rick Noack and Shibani Mahtani, "New Zealand Just Banned Military-Style Firearms. Here's Why the U.S. Can't," *The Washington Post* (March 21, 2019), https://www.washingtonpost.com/world/2019/03/21/why-new-zealand-could-do-what-us-cant-change-gun-laws-face-tragedy/?utm_term=.789350f48903 (accessed July 2022).

27 William R. Lee, editor, *Clare W. Graves: Levels of Human Existence*, p. 86.

28 Katherine Stewart, "Why Trump Reigns as King Cyrus," *New York Times* (Dec. 31, 2018), https://www.nytimes.com/2018/12/31/opinion/trump-evangelicals-cyrus-king.html. See also: Paul C. "Evangelicals: God sent Trump to Be King," *Daily Kos* (Jan. 1, 2019), https://www.dailykos.com/stories/2019/01/01/1822839/-Evangelicals:God-Sent-Trump-to-be-King (both accessed July 2022).

29 Gabriel Sherman, "Inside Jerry Falwell Jr's Unlikely Rise and Precipitous Fall at Liberty University," *Vanity Fair* (Jan. 24, 2022), https://www.vanityfair.com/news/2022/01/inside-jerry-falwell-jr-unlikely-rise-and-precipitous-fall (accessed July 2022).

30 Ken Wilber, *The Religion of Tomorrow*, pp. 46, 605.

31 Clare W. Graves, "Levels of Existence: An Open Systems Theory of Values."

32 Don Edward Beck and Christopher C. Cowan, *Spiral Dynamics*, p. 250.

33 Ibid, p. 246.

34 Upton Sinclair, *The Jungle*, Dover Publications: Mineola, NY (Dover Ed. 2001; 1st Ed. 1906).

35 John Steinbeck, *The Grapes of Wrath*, Penguin Group: New York, NY (2002; 1st Ed. 1939).

36 U.S. Declaration of Independence (July 4, 1776), https://www.archives.gov/founding-docs/declaration-transcript (accessed July 2022).

37 Mark Goff, "Opening Ceremony at Woodstock" (1969), public domain, https://en.wikipedia.org/wiki/File:Swami_opening.jpg (accessed July 2022).

38 William R. Lee, editor, *Clare W. Graves: Levels of Human Existence*, pp. 85–86.

39 Don Edward Beck and Christopher C. Cowan, *Spiral Dynamics*, pp. 260, 263–264.

40 Ken Wilber, *The Religion of Tomorrow*, p. 204.

[41] Clare W. Graves, "A Systems Conception of Personality," transcription of a seminar presented at Washington School of Psychiatry (Oct. 16, 1971), http://www.clarewgraves.com/source_content/WSP_cc_edit.html (accessed July 2022).

[42] Jason Wilson, "White Nationalist Hate Groups Have Grown 55% in Trump Era, Report Finds," *The Guardian* (March 18, 2020), https://www.theguardian.com/world/2020/mar/18/white-nationalist-hate-groups-southern-poverty-law-center (accessed July 2022).

[43] Clare Kim, "Domestic Terrorism: 'Patriot' Hate Groups Skyrocket," *ABC News* (March 7, 2013), https://www.nbcnews.com/id/wbna51082152 (accessed July 2022).

[44] William R. Lee, editor, *Clare W. Graves: Levels of Human Existence*, p. 67.

[45] Ken Wilber, *The Religion of Tomorrow*, p. 325.

[46] See: Comedian J.P. Sears video on "How to Be Ultra-Spiritual" (2014), https://www.youtube.com/watch?v=1kDso5ElFRg (accessed July 2022).

[47] William R. Lee, editor, *Clare W. Graves: Levels of Human Existence*, pp. 47, 153.

[48] The Oracle Spectrum Chart deviates from Wilber's in a few regards. Originally, Wilber charted twelve memes: six in the First Tier (Stages 1 through 6); and six in Second Tier (Stages 7 through 12). Recently, Wilber modified his model as follows: six memes in the First Tier; two in Second Tier (Stages 7 and 8); and four in a new Third Tier (Stages 9 through 12). To simplify the model, **Oracle Stage 7** blends Wilber Stage 7 (Low Vision Logic) and Wilber Stage 8 (High Vision Logic), because both memes involve the psyche's growth toward holism and integration. **Oracle Stage 8** merges Wilber Stage 9 (Para-Mind) and Wilber Stage 10 (Meta-Mind). Similarly, **Oracle Stage 9** merges Wilber Stage 11 (Over Mind) with Wilber Stage 12 (Super Mind).

[49] Ken Wilber, *The Religion of Tomorrow*, p. 207.

[50] Don Edward Beck and Christopher C. Cowan, *Spiral Dynamics*, p. 283.

[51] The Rutherford Institute website: https://www.rutherford.org/ (accessed July 2022).

[52] Fred Espenak, "2004 and 2012 Transits of Venus," *Nasa Eclipse Web Site* (June 18, 2002), https://eclipse.gsfc.nasa.gov/transit/venus0412.html. See also: Marius Giurgi, "Venus Transit 2012," *Quantum Fractal*, https://www.youtube.com/watch?v=hUhLod8pDhU (both accessed July 2022).

[53] "Pentagram of Venus," *Wikipedia*, https://en.wikipedia.org/wiki/Pentagram#Pentagram_of_Venus (accessed July 2022).

[54] For those who appreciate synchronicity: At 6:08 pm on March 30, 2019, as I finished writing the paragraph about Venus, an earthquake hit the town of Independence, VA, where Oracle Campus is located. See: "1.8 Magnitude Earthquake Recorded in Southwest Virginia," *WBTV On Your Side* (March 31, 2019), http://www.wbtv.com/2019/03/31/magnitude-earthquake-recorded-southwest-virginia/ (accessed July 2022).

[55] Don Edward Beck and Christopher C. Cowan, *Spiral Dynamics*, pp. 276–277.

[56] Ken Wilber, *The Religion of Tomorrow*, p. 38.

[57] Don Edward Beck and Christopher C. Cowan, *Spiral Dynamics*, pp. 286–292.

[58] Ken Wilber, *The Religion of Tomorrow*, pp. 210–211, 222.

[59] Ibid, p. 569.

[60] Ibid, p. 226.

[61] Tenzin Choejor, "Dancing at a Celebration of His Holiness's 80th Birthday" (2015).

[62] Alex Grey, "Theologue" (1993), reprinted with permission from the artist.

[63] *Gospel of Thomas*, Verses 17, 50.

[64] Ken Wilber, *The Spectrum of Consciousness*, p. 284.

[65] *OM JAI* means "Earth Victory." The Oracle Institute is a 501(c)(3) educational charity (founded 2004). Oracle Institute Press, LLC is a wholly owned subsidiary of the Institute (founded 2006). Oracle Temple is a 508(c)(1)(A) esoteric church (founded 2015). The public is invited to attend Oracle Temple gatherings and events. See: http://theoracleinstitute.org/temple.

*The great achievement of linear time has been to endow mankind
with a purposeful confidence in its own self-improvement. ...
We need to recall that time, in its physical sense,
is nothing but the measurement of cyclicality itself. ...*

*You should try to unlearn the linear belief that America (or the entire
modern world) is exempt from the seasonal cycles of nature. ...
Try to unlearn the linear need to judge change by
one-dimensional standards of progress. ...
Finally, unlearn the linear view that positive change always comes
willingly, incrementally, and by human design. ...*

*Sometime before the year 2025, America will pass through a gate in
history, commensurate with the American Revolution, Civil War,
and twin emergencies of the Great Depression and World War II.*

William Strauss and Neil Howe, *The Fourth Turning*

A decade ago, Steve Bannon, the monstrous advisor to Donald Trump, made a movie entitled *Generation Zero*, in which he shared his apocalyptic view on the cycles of history and the 2008 economic collapse, and also foreshadowed another crisis – a possible third world war.[1] The movie is based on *The Fourth Turning*, a book which describes the four "seasons" of history in a manner that is immediately arresting and disturbing.[2]

In this chapter, we will explore the theory that growth and decay come in cycles and ponder whether New Humans can interrupt what appears to be the inherent life-death-life cycle of the Earth Plane. Sadly, we simply may need to accept that we live in a dimension marked by dualism and polarity. We also may need to accept Buddha's First Noble Truth, that "Life is Suffering." As pessimistic as that sounds, it may well be true, although because I am an optimist at heart, I eventually will make the counter argument.

In addition, we will converse with an historian, who I also fancy as a futurist. While there are many books on the subject of "past as prologue" – including *The Fourth Turning* – we will draw on the expertise of this historian by asking questions geared toward what New Humans need to know.

Lastly, we will deal with some of the common shadow elements that occur along the Spectrum of Consciousness. This will be a challenging section, especially for my New Age friends. But please hang in there, because if you've made it this far it probably means you are ready to go Second Tier and become a more active participant in the God Game!

Let's start with a quick recap of the spiritual paradigms identified by The Oracle Institute. The first four epochs mark humanity's cumulative history. The Fifth Spiritual Paradigm is the one we have yet to birth.

First Spiritual Paradigm	All is One	Big Bang: 14 billion BCE
Second Spiritual Paradigm	Great Mother	25,000 BCE – 5000 BCE
Third Spiritual Paradigm	Gods & Goddesses	5000 BCE – 50 CE
Fourth Spiritual Paradigm	God the Father	50 CE – 2012 CE
Fifth Spiritual Paradigm	Integrated Godhead	Happening NOW!

These paradigms not only track humanity's collective spiritual journey, they contain within them repetitive cycles of churning and burning off *karma*. These cycles include polarized phases of success and failure, gain and loss, peace and war, economic prosperity and depression, empire building and societal collapse. Ultimately, all earlier paradigms ended with the revolutionary fury of a Great Cusp that was ignited by the most combustible element on Earth – a shift in the Godhead – after which a new paradigm arose.

Currently, the Godhead is shifting again, as the Green and Second Tier memes charge bravely toward the Light. New Humans have categorically rejected the patriarchal Fourth Paradigm God and have adopted, instead, belief systems based on primordial principles, indigenous wisdom, quantum physics, and metaphysics. Still, there aren't enough of us yet who have crossed the

Tipping Point. Until 10% of us or more cross-over, we've got to live through and manage a Great Cusp – the most perilous one in human history.

In order to prepare for the shift, New Humans need to be students of history. There is absolutely no rational reason to believe that this Great Cusp will be any easier than past ones. Indeed, due to our advanced technology, this is the most dangerous time to be alive since mankind evolved into *Homo sapiens*. Therefore, we need to become familiar with the cycles and seasons of our common chronicle, a pretty barbaric record overall.

Let's start with a few definitions. I will use the term "cycle" for large-scale repetitive patterns, and I will use the word "season" to describe the internal rhythms within cycles. For example, there is a cycle to empire building which includes colonization, regionalization, ascension, prosperity, and maturity. There also is a cycle to empire collapse, typically involving overextension, financial and moral decline, overt polarity, internal strife, and revolution. This pattern may take hundreds of years to complete, as in the case of the rise and fall of the Roman, Muslim, and British Empires. Yet, within these macro-cycles are micro-seasons, which can be witnessed in the span of just a few generations. We shall study both types of historical patterns, remembering as we do so that when the Godhead shifts, both macro and micro forces are at work in a stunning and horrific display, which The Oracle Institute calls a Great Cusp.

During the Fourth Spiritual Paradigm, a number of empires were built, but they all have now crumbled – except the United States. History books date the end of the Roman Empire to 476 CE, when Emperor Romulus Augustulus was deposed by a Goth (Germanic) prince. However, the fate of the Roman Empire was sealed when Jesus set into motion a series of events that shifted the Western Godhead. After the Roman Empire collapsed and then reformed itself as the Byzantine Empire, a void emerged in the Middle East which was seized by Muhammad, another messenger from the Abrahamic God.

Next, the Muslim Empire flourished (*circa* 632–1925 CE), eventually overtaking the Byzantine Empire in 1453 CE. Around this same time, the Spanish Empire emerged, followed by the British and then Russian Empires – all of which collapsed in the 20th Century. Today, no large empires or dynasties officially exist, since the British royal family and Japanese dynasty both defer to democratic, parliamentary governance, as do most other monarchies. Thus, the case can be made that during the Fourth Paradigm, especially the last two hundred years, the trajectory of humanity has been toward democratic rule, though that argument has huge holes in it, which we are about to explore.

Political scientists use various methods of categorizing countries to track their modes of governance and the effect on citizens. For example, **Freedom House** – which has been tracking governments since 1972 – studies these factors: (i) electoral process; (ii) political participation; (iii) functioning of government; (iv) freedom of expression and belief; (v) right to assemble and organize; (vi) rule of law; and (vii) personal autonomy and individual rights.[3] Then, Freedom House determines whether a country is "Free," "Partially Free," or "Not Free."

In their most recent report in 2021, Freedom House determined that of the 195 countries they tracked (they also study 15 disputed nation-states):

➢ 82 Nations or 42% were Free: down 8% since 2005.
➢ 59 Nations or 30% were Partially Free: up 2% since 2005.
➢ 54 Nations or 28% were Not Free: up 20% since 2005.[4]

This is horrendous news, since the number of Free counties decreased, while Partially Free and Not Free nations rose over the last fifteen years. And here's some more bad news:

> In 2020, the number of Free countries in the world reached its lowest level since the beginning of a 15-year period of global democratic decline, while the number of Not Free countries reached its highest level. ... The countries experiencing deterioration outnumbered those with improvements by the largest margin recorded since the negative trend began in 2006. The long democratic recession is deepening.[5]

In summarizing their findings, Freedom House provides important historical context. Starting in the 1980s at the end of the Cold War, the world witnessed the greatest surge of democracies. Between 1988 and 2005, Free countries grew 11%, and Not Free countries dropped 12%. However, from 2005 to 2020, the trend reversed: Free countries declined 8% and Not Free countries rose 20%.

It also is worth noting the primary reasons cited by Freedom House for the fifteen-year decline in freedom. First, they cite a new global balance of power, specifically the rise of Chinese and the decline of India, which has slipped into the Partially Free category. Second, they cite the far-right, populist movements, which are growing globally, often as a means to appease waning majorities who fear multi-culturalism and global wage reduction. Third, they cite attacks on the media (some lethal), and the now common cry of "fake news."

Mostly, though, they cite the demise of the United States under former President Trump. In fact, Mike Abramowitz, who is president of Freedom House, appended his own sentiments to the 2019 Freedom House Report to emphasize that Trump is largely to blame for the global decrease in democracy.

> *No president in living memory has shown less respect for tenets, norms, and principles. Trump has assailed essential institutions and traditions including the separation of powers, a free press, an independent judiciary, the impartial delivery of justice, safeguards against corruption, and most disturbingly, the legitimacy of elections. ... The current overall US score puts American democracy closer to struggling counterparts like Croatia than to traditional peers such as Germany or the United Kingdom. ...*
>
> *Yet the pressure on our system is as serious as any experienced in living memory. We cannot take for granted that institutional bulwarks against abuse of power will retain their strength, or that our democracy will endure perpetually. Rarely has the need to defend its rules and norms been more urgent.*[6]

Since 2006, *The Economist* magazine also has been tracking governments in its **Democracy Index**. This index monitors nations using a slightly different map: (i) Full Democracies; (ii) Flawed Democracies; (iii) Hybrid Regimes; and (iv) Authoritarian Regimes. In 2020, *The Economist* looked at 165 countries (and two disputed territories), and concluded:

- ➤ 23 Countries or 14% were Full Democracies, which are enjoyed by slightly over 8% of the world's population (the U.S. did not qualify).
- ➤ 52 Countries or 31% were Flawed Democracies, which oversee 41% of the world.
- ➤ 35 Countries or 21% are Hybrid Regimes that control 15% of us.
- ➤ 57 Countries – over 34% of the nations examined – are Authoritarian Regimes that dominate nearly 36% of the world.[7]

The 2020 Democracy Index produced the worst global score since the index was created in 2006. Of the 167 territories studied, 70% saw their score decline. Overall, Hybrid and Authoritarian Regimes grew the most in Africa, the Middle East, and South America. Today, over half of humanity lives under an illiberal regime, such as a dictatorship, despotic monarchy, communism, or oligarchy. The global covid pandemic was a contributing factor: "What is certain is that the public health emergency provided cover for abuses of power."[8]

The only positive news is that North America's regional score was the highest, but that's due to Canada, which ranks as the 5th best nation in the world. As for the United States, our ranking has slipped from 17th to 25th place, and since the 2016 election of Trump, the U.S. has been a "Flawed Democracy." *The Economist* ascribes this poor standing to the continued deterioration of government functioning and political polarization. In addition, Trump's attacks on our institutions, his two impeachments, the "Big Lie" over who won the 2020 presidential election, and Trump's attempted coup have eroded confidence in our nation's ability to bounce back from the abyss. On the bright side, political participation has risen in the U.S., but that score is misleading, since the increase correlates with high voter turnout due, once again, to increased polarization, as well as public outrage over police violence, racial injustice, and the government's mishandling of the pandemic.[9]

Thus, while it is true that pluralistic values such as personal freedom and democratic rule steadily rose in the second half of the 20th Century, it also is true that the New Millennium has seen declines in all relevant measures. *Please allow that to fully sink in.* Freedom was on the rise worldwide until the advent of the Great Cusp, after which it has steadily diminished.

Sadly, the United States continues to undermine freedom by fueling the polarity between ethnocentric, nationalistic values (Stage 4) and worldcentric, pluralistic values (Stage 6). As a result, the U.S. received a dismal score for "political culture" because Americans "increasingly occupy two distinct and conflicting realities ... the proliferation of conspiracy theories, and the readiness of both sides of the political spectrum to indulge in them, is an especially worrying trend."[10]

Consequently, New Humans must contend with the current resurgence of authoritarianism, a fact that most Americans are either blind to or unwilling to accept. Why is totalitarianism trending here at home? Because some Americans fear liberal values even more than they fear authoritarianism.

> *Authoritarianism has now returned as a geopolitical force, with strong nations such as China and Russia championing anti-liberalism as an alternative to a teetering liberal hegemony. It has returned as an ideological force ... and just at the moment when the liberal world is suffering its greatest crisis of confidence since the 1930s. It has returned armed with new and hitherto unimaginable tools of social control and disruption that are shoring up authoritarian rule at home, spreading it abroad and reaching into the very heart of liberal societies to undermine them from within. ...*

"America First" is only making matters worse. ... The "America First" movement in 1940 not only argued for keeping the United States out of the war in Europe, but also took a sympathetic view of German arguments for white supremacy. Those views were suppressed during a war fought explicitly against Nazism and its racial theories, and then during a Cold War waged against communism. But when the Cold War ended, the old concerns about the nation's social and cultural identity reemerged. ...

These days, some American conservatives find themselves in sympathy with the world's staunchest anti-American leaders, precisely because those leaders have raised the challenge to American liberalism. In 2013, Putin warned that the "Euro-Atlantic countries" were "rejecting their roots," which included the "Christian values" that were the "basis of Western civilization." ... [T]he Russian leader is a "hero to populist conservatives around the world" because he refuses to submit to the U.S.-dominated liberal world order.[11]

Robert Kagan, *"The Strongmen Strike Back"*

Having briefly considered some historical cycles, let us now explore seasons, which are shorter generational patterns that, unfortunately, also appear ominous. Looking out my window over the New River, the cold wind is blowing and winter has arrived – the fourth season and also the possible climax of a Great Cusp.

THE FOUR SEASON THEORY

The Fourth Turning is not about paradigm shifts, *per se*. Rather, the book describes four generational seasons that seem to repeat within larger epochal periods. For instance, if the book's premise is correct, the Fourth Spiritual Paradigm (*circa* 50 CE – 2012 CE) contained numerous Fourth Turnings during the course of its two-thousand-year span. What's different this time, however, is that a Fourth Turning is coinciding with a Great Cusp, defined as the period of immense turbulence that accompanies a shift in the Godhead.

As we have seen, New Humans (Stages 6 and up) have rejected the masculine-based Fourth Paradigm God because their concept of Source is more advanced. Some identify with a genderful or genderless deity, some like nature mysticism, and others (like me) focus on the Light – all views that are consistent with ancient esoteric principles and new scientific breakthroughs. Thus, New Humans possess what, in the past, only yogis, mystics, and students of ancient hermetic and indigenous wisdom traditions achieved: experiential knowledge of the Light. However, for most First Tier humans, the "Daddy Deism" of the Fourth Spiritual Paradigm still satisfies, though they are slowly catching on as well.

The seasonal theory contained in *The Fourth Turning* is relevant because it identifies a historical pattern that may assist us in determining how close we are to the Tipping Point. In other words, if a Fourth Turning is imminent and if it represents not only the final season within the current cycle but also the final season of the current paradigm, the Tipping Point into the Fifth Spiritual Paradigm may be very close indeed.

Specifically, the book identifies four seasons or turnings, each of which lasts twenty to twenty-five years and coincides with the arrival of a new generation. Four generations complete the cycle, for a total expanse between eighty and one hundred years. The authors' theory is that each generation lives through yet responds differently to two critical events which occur during the full cycle. Moreover, the theory posits that each generational archetype reacts in a predictable manner, thus perpetuating the full cycle's pattern.

The two critical events are the "Awakening," which represents the zenith and most abundant season for society, and the eventual "Crisis," which is the nadir and most destructive season. Below is a summary of the four turnings:[12]

> **First Turning * Spring High:** A time when society rallies around a new era of promise, fortifies its values, and builds its infrastructure.
> **Second Turning * Summer Awakening:** A time when society reaps the benefits of prosperity, plays with newfound freedoms, and dreams of even greater accomplishments.
> **Third Turning * Fall Unravelling:** When society starts to consume surpluses, worry about the future, and fragment over differing ideals.
> **Fourth Turning * Winter Crisis:** A time of survival, when society struggles financially, sacrifices values for safety, and ultimately goes to war, whether internally or against others.

These seasons highlight patterns of collective human behavior, with which we easily can identify and remember playing out in our own lives. For example, during my childhood my family went through lean years, living in military housing, then buying a townhouse. During my teen years, our lot improved and my parents purchased our first home. Nevertheless, when I took off for college, I had to pay my own way by taking out student loans, tapping into my Dad's G.I. benefits, and eating a LOT of Chef Boyardee ravioli. Then, my family's prosperity rose some more, as my father, James L. George, Ph.D. (1939–2000), became Acting Director of the Arms Control and Disarmament Agency under President Ronald Reagan.[13] In 1986, I graduated from law school with $50,000 of debt, but I was able to paid it off quickly (unlike today's students).

More to the point, while the affluence of my family slowly grew, my experience played out against the backdrop of a shifting American landscape, a country that was in decline – an Unravelling. As we shall soon see, *when* we witness the seasons determines *how* we react to them. I believe I was fortunate to be a child during the 1960s and 1970s, as the last Awakening phase was winding down. I therefore had incredible freedom during my formative years, though I was too young to tag-along with the older Baby Boomers who went to Woodstock (I was eight years old when Woodstock was rockin').

The four generational archetypes that live through and react to these turnings are labeled the "Prophet," "Nomad," "Hero," and "Artist" by the authors. Below are descriptions of the four generations:[14]

> **Prophets:** (i) grow up during the High as indulged post-Crisis children;
> (ii) come of age as narcissistic young crusaders of an Awakening;
> (iii) promote moral principles as mid-lifers during the Unravelling;
> (iv) emerge as wise elders guiding the next Crisis.

> **Nomads:** (i) grow up under-protected children during the Awakening;
> (ii) come of age as alienated young adults during the Unravelling;
> (iii) mellow into pragmatic mid-life leaders during the Crisis;
> (iv) age into tough elders during the High.

> **Heroes:** (i) grow up with increased protection during the Unravelling;
> (ii) come of age as heroic teammates during the Crisis;
> (iv) demonstrate hubris during the High as energetic mid-lifers;
> (iv) emerge as powerful elders attacked by the Awakening.

> **Artists:** (i) grow up as over-protected children during the Crisis;
> (ii) come of age as sensitive young adults during the High;
> (iii) act as mid-life technicians, experts, peacemakers in the Awakening;
> (iv) age into empathic elders during the Unravelling.

There's not enough space in this volume for me to convince the reader that this model is reliable, but in my opinion, it tracks history eerily well. In support of my qualified endorsement, I will provide a few examples from the book, including the authors' predictions regarding the current Fourth Turning – the season in which we find ourselves today.

First, let's overlay some dates and explore the cycle as it has played out in the United States (and the world) over the last four seasons. The last Crisis was the Great Depression and World War II (the authors place World War I in the last Unravelling), and the Crisis before that was the Civil War.[15] Taking the authors' cue, we will assign a date of 1945 to the ending of the last Crisis. Then, the cycle and its seasons play out as follows:[16]

1945 – 1965: Cultural **High** and birth of the **Prophet** generation

1965 – 1985: Cultural **Awakening** and birth of the **Nomad** generation

1985 – 2010: Cultural **Unravelling** and birth of the **Hero** generation

2010 – 2030: Cultural **Crisis** and birth of the **Artist** generation

During the last First Turning or Spring High, the authors contend that the generations reacted as follows: The Prophets (a.k.a. Baby Boomers) were nurtured and indulged by their Artist parents, who just spent their childhood living through the Crisis of World War II. For themselves, the Artists (a.k.a. Silent Generation), who were taught to behave during the Crisis, sought the new "American Dream" that the High represented, but they had to compete in college and in the workplace with returning GIs – the Heroes of WWII. The Heroes (a.k.a. Greatest Generation) who fought during the Crisis, were fresh off their victory and returned with the energy and optimism needed to start the rebuilding process, impose social discipline, and promote confidence about the future. Meanwhile the Nomads, who led at home during the Crisis, were exhausted and entered their twilight years only guardedly optimistic about the future. Thus, the elder Nomads (a.k.a. Lost Generation), kept alive the memories of the Great Depression and horror of the World Wars, maintaining a frugal and "old fashioned" perspective as grandparents.[17]

During the last Second Turning and Summer Awakening, the generations behaved as follows: The Prophets, as young adults, let loose with the hippie movement, women's rights, civil rights, and Vietnam War protests. They took for granted the High of their childhood and actually started to get high! They challenged the institutions created by the Heroes and blind-sided their docile Artist parents. Notably, the Prophets started to reject religion, thereby birthing the New Age movement. The Artists reacted by trying to smooth things out and pacify the Prophets, but many resented being caught in the middle of the Culture War being fought by the Prophets (Stage 6) and the Heroes (Stage 4), though the Artists (mostly Stage 5) towed the line as they enjoyed economic prosperity. The elder Heroes, rather than retire, relished the height of their political power. They doubled-down on control of governmental institutions, which the Prophets viewed as stifling and overly conservative. Meanwhile the Prophets started having children of their own, a new generation of Nomads who were lightly supervised and had unfettered freedom. These Nomads grew up watching their self-absorbed parents defy social rules, and while some like me (I actually straddle Prophet and Nomad) relished the freedom, others grew up feeling insecure, especially when the divorce rate skyrocketed. In either case, Nomads learned to be independent, resourceful, and competitive.[18]

The Third Turning and Fall Unravelling, which has now ended, had the generations reacting as follows: The judgmental Prophets, stymied by their limited success in reforming American culture and disillusioned by the election of Ronald Reagan, finally were able to elect one of their own, when Bill Clinton became president. The elder Artists paved the way for this change of guard, due to their patience, sensitivity, and expertise. As the old Hero generation finally retired and began to expire, they were replaced with new Heroes born to Nomads, many of whom were cynical regarding the workplace. Nomads were pessimistic about staying in just one job or the same career their entire life, as their Artist parents had done. Workplace alienation resulted in Nomads striking out with entrepreneurial ideas in new high-tech industries, and rural Nomads started to lose family farms to large agri-businesses. In short, corporatocracy and cynicism were on the rise during the Unravelling.

Then, another Baby Boomer was elected, when George W. Bush took the presidency (along with Dick Cheney). But Al Gore, another Prophet, won the popular vote and, amidst voting irregularities, the Supreme Court decided the election, handing it to Bush. This drama made liberal Prophets angry and Nomads even more cynical. When the Twin Towers imploded in 2001, the Nomads dismissed the 9/11 Report and sparked the 9/11 Truth movement. Meanwhile, their children, the young Heroes, witnessed the greatest attack on U.S. soil. The Nomad parents, who generally were neglected as children, started to worry about their kids and, in an attempt to protect them from an increasing-ly hostile world, became "helicopter parents" – scheduling their time, getting them tutors, keeping them on a regimen, and (unwittingly) preparing them to be good soldiers and to take orders once the Crisis arrives. As a result, the young Heroes grew up well-nurtured and the focus of the family unit, but they intuited that their environment was unsafe and the world a dangerous place.[19]

Before we get to the current Fourth Turning and Winter Crisis, let us pause for a moment to consider how well history has matched the model outlined in *The Fourth Turning*. In the book, the authors not only discuss the current cycle, they provide details on how previous generations reacted to earlier cycles, including the one launched after the Crisis of the Civil War (*circa* 1865–1945), and the cycle after the Crisis of the American Revolution (*circa* 1785–1865). In other words, this eighty to one-hundred-year pattern has been repeating for a while, which is why the authors – who wrote their book in 1997, in the middle of the Unravelling – felt confident enough to predict the looming Crisis.

Let us also pause to realize that the book was written before the start of the New Millennium – so before the disputed election between Bush and Gore, before the 9/11 tragedy, and before the election of Barak Obama, who not only was our first African American president, but also our first Nomad president as well (Obama was born in 1961 like me, so he partially grew up as a Nomad). Therefore, when they wrote *The Fourth Turning*, the authors did not have the benefit of witnessing the last quarter century. Nevertheless, most of their predictions for the conclusion of the Unravelling were dead-on.

For example, one of their predictions was that as the Unravelling ended, the Artists, who already were tapping social security, would completely redefine what it meant to be an elder by adopting the slogan "sixty is the new forty." They anticipated that affluent Artists would reject "senior living" and retirement communities in favor of leisure and lattes. Meanwhile, due to a worsening economy, the Prophets would need to suck it up and financially assist their adult Nomad children, many of whom would suffer deepening financial woes. And for Nomads unable to find decent work in the midst of America's increasingly multicultural landscape, the authors predicted a rise in White Supremacy, while at the same time predicting that most of Gen X would not succumb to race-baiting.[20]

As for politics, the authors predicted that the self-absorbed Prophets would not voluntarily assume the levers of government, preferring instead to play armchair philosophers and criticize elder Artists in power. The authors also saw mid-life Baby Boomers turning to spiritual endeavors, thereby allowing more conservative Artists (think Newt Gingrich) and the remaining older Heroes (think John McCain) to continue accumulating power. As for those Boomers who would run for office, the authors predicted they would be predominantly conservative, obsessed with family values, and eager to renew the Culture War they started in the 1960s, though this time the Prophets would be split on issues such as Christianity vs. New Age theosophies. They also saw a harsher prison system, further slashing of welfare programs, and a rise in poverty. Finally, they predicted the Unravelling would end as follows:

Wide chasms will separate rich from poor, whites from blacks, immigrants from native borns, seculars from born-agains, technophiles from technophobes. America will feel more tribal. Indeed, many will be asking whether fifty states and so many dozens of ethnic cultures make sense any more as a nation – and, if they do, whether that nation has a future. ...

People young and old will puzzle over what it felt like for their parents and grandparents, in a distantly remembered era, to have lived in a society that felt like one national community. They will yearn to recreate this, to put America back together again. But no one will know how.[21]

Eventually, all this did come to pass after the start of the New Millennium. Next, as we examine the authors' predictions for the Winter Crisis, we will continue to examine how well their soothsaying aligned with actual world events, including their predictions for the final decade of the Fourth Turning, which already has commenced (i.e., 2010 to 2030).

The book states that the Crisis season begins with a "catalyst" – a sudden and startling event that produces a collective shift in cultural focus and mood.[22] The stock market crash of 2008 was surely a catalyst, since it tanked the worldwide banking sector and kicked off the global Occupy movement (2011–2012). Yet, I believe the 9/11 attack was the primary catalyst to our current Fourth Turning, as it represents the mother of all conspiracy theories and fueled immense distrust in the U.S. government. It also produced a rallying cry for the "War on Terror" and the invasion of Iraq, which was based on numerous shifting and false pretenses.

First, the Bush administration said that Saddam Hussein had links to Al Qaeda, then they said Iraq had weapons of mass destruction.[23] Ultimately, none of the accusations were true and the public learned that we invaded Iraq (later Afghanistan) for fictitious causes. Nevertheless, a warring mood prevailed and the stage was set for the death of hundreds of thousands of people, including our own troops. Next, Americans passively accepted the Patriot Act and its disassembling of the Fourth Amendment. So began the trend of trading liberty for supposed security. The global covid pandemic was the final straw, as unprecedented lockdowns were instituted worldwide. Today, on the left and right, suspicion of government has become engrained.

After the catalyst, the Fourth Turning continues to gain steam. Society begins the process of "regeneracy," during which people belie the weakened state of government institutions. Thereafter, government propaganda increases, a call to arms that generally is met with enthusiasm. Clearly, the ascension of Fox News – nothing less than Trump's propaganda pipeline – satisfies this prediction. While readers of this text may find it hard to believe, 47% of Americans watch Fox News, the top cable news network for the last five years running.[24]

To further set the stage for the Fourth Turning, here are the authors' main premise points regarding the season of Crisis:

> *A Fourth Turning is a solstice era of maximum darkness, in which the supply of social order is still falling but the demand for order is now rising. ... Far more than before, people comply with authority, accept the need for public sacrifice, and shed anything extraneous to the survival needs of their community. This is a critical threshold: People either coalesce as a nation and culture – or rip hopelessly and permanently apart. ...*
>
> *Instead of downplaying problems, leaders start exaggerating them. Instead of deferring solutions, they accelerate them. Instead of tolerating diversity, they demand consensus. ... A new resolve about urgent public goals crowds out qualms about questionable public means. A Crisis mood does not guarantee that the new governing policies will be well designed or will work as intended. To the contrary: Crisis eras are studded with faulty leadership and inept management ....*
>
> *When society approaches the climax of a Crisis, it reaches a point of maximum civic power. ... Wars become more likely and are fought with efficacy and finality. The risk of revolution is high – as is the risk of civil war .... The climax can end in triumph, or tragedy, or some combination of both. Whatever the event and whatever the outcome, a society passes through a gate of history, fundamentally altering the course of civilization.[25]*

Eerily, the authors gave specific examples of what might spark the current Crisis, some of which already have come to pass: (i) a global terrorist network blows up an American aircraft, which starts a preemptive war against a related nation (i.e., 9/11 and Iraq); (ii) an impasse over the federal budget between the president and congress, which results in a government shutdown and panic on Wall Street (i.e., Trump's 2019 shutdown, the longest one to date); and (iii) America becomes isolationist, rebuffs allies, and focuses instead on creating a new domestic order (i.e., Trump's denigration of NATO and obsession with building his "Wall" along the Mexican border).[26] In short, a "wild card" scenario starts an unholy chain reaction.

Wild Card

The Light is on one side, the Dark on the other.
The Wall in between now divides Son from Mother.
Nothing so tragic has the world ever seen.
The Shadow is vivid, the air is unclean.

Tensions are growing and Victory vowed.
Generals with legions stand erect, insanely proud.
But as the armies advance, no soldier feels pride.
The next moment brings horror, as the unwitting collide.

Ions beget Eons, and Gods create Man.
The Demiurge guards Zeus, as Sophia expands.
All of them watch. They have come forth from rest.
They, too, are curious to see who is best.
And one Wild Card could make the difference to Heaven and Earth.

Red, white, blue, and RED. Morbid and sordid and ignorant souls,
don't even know how or know why to keep score.
She knows and He knows, as does God on his peak.
But the masses are slaughtered, for they are mere sheep.

When a Mother of two Sons and also a Daughter,
Sees the devastation ahead, her own lambs to the slaughter,
It is time to awaken, erase lines in the sand!
The question she fears: "What were you doing with your hands?"

Jonah's toil is daunting; fear of failure intense.
But she begged for a Mission, while the Shadow grew dense.
Too late for denial, second thoughts, or dread.
Too late for her mate, for he is now dead.

With faith she surrenders. Trust draws her to the gate.
To the Matrix go the spoils. Free will, though, controls all fate.
And one Wild Card could make the difference to Earth and Heaven.

I wrote this poem back in 2004, when I started receiving visions of an ugly future. Though the timeline has zig-zagged since then, it appears to me that my Venus messages – like the predictions in *The Fourth Turning* – are coming true. The authors were unsure exactly which stresses would unleash a full-on Crisis, but they cited numerous possibilities: cultural/political polarization, economic collapse, infrastructure failure, ecological disasters, military miscalculations, unethical technology. Basically, pick your poison. They also charted how the pattern of generational behavior would play out when the Crisis arrives.

Ironically, it is elder Prophets – the Boomers who enjoyed the Awakening – who will stoke the Crisis and act as its generals. Pragmatic mid-life Nomads, who are no longer fazed by polarization and never believed in American exceptionalism anyway, will play the captains who steer the ship through the Winter storm, sacrificing their Hero children, who will play dutiful sailors willing to go down with the ship. Like "Power Rangers" and their video game avatars, the Heroes will "cast aside an earlier pacifism and march to duty," predisposed to engage in high-tech militarized violence. And a new generation of Artists will be born to complete the cycle – yet another silent and frightened generation, fated to witness with innocent eyes the mayhem and misery of a Fourth Turning.[27]

The authors made one more prediction worth noting, though it is one I found ridiculous when I first read this book. They spent considerable time imagining a "Gray Champion" – an elder Prophet who would have the power and charisma to persuade Americans to accept authoritarianism in order to deal with the Crisis, a leader who would demand sacrifices from our young Heroes that he never would have assumed as a spoiled child during the High and as a self-absorbed young man during the Awakening. They wrote that this leader would be energized by his "pending mortality" and that he would rise to power to mount a "final crusade." They also predicted that "posterity will remember the Boomer's Gray Champion persona long after the hippie and yuppie images have been forgotten to all but the historians."[28] Indeed, the authors foresaw Donald Trump; they just got the color of his hair wrong.

The reason this particular prediction originally seemed far-fetched to me is that of all the crises facing humanity – global warming, food and water shortages, fires and floods, wealth inequality, nuclear disaster, etc. – I never thought (or even considered) that it might be a United States president who would trigger the collapse! Bird Flu: maybe. Shifting tectonic plates: perhaps. A solar flare that knocks out the electrical grid: could happen. But the election of a person with the consciousness and caliber of Donald Trump?

Though Trump finally left office, I remain shocked. The attack on the U.S. Capitol may just be the start of a populist backlash. Currently, the "January 6 Commission" is investigating how deep the plot ran to overturn the election. The entire situation is surreal. It also is treason. Our only hope may be Merrick Garland, our current Attorney General. Yet, I am not hopeful, given two failed impeachments and the Mueller Report debacle. Moreover, Trump clearly wants to run for office again in 2024. If reelected, Trump will expedite the ultimate Crisis of the Fourth Turning and the Great Cusp. Is this really happening?

PAST AS PROLOGUE: INTERVIEW WITH AN HISTORIAN

Despite their dire predictions, the authors of *The Fourth Turning* were guardedly optimistic about how this Fourth Turning ultimately would be resolved. Why? Because previous crises all resulted in giant leaps forward for human rights. The American Revolution set the stage for personal freedom, the Civil War prepared the way for racial equality, and World War II catapulted capitalism, women's rights, and pluralism.

Nevertheless, the authors also discussed a doomsday scenario in which the Prophet generation – Boomers who were left unsatisfied during the Awakening – create an increasingly polarized climate, just when the nation needs unity. On one side are the conservative Prophets (Stage 4), some of whom believe we are living in "End Times." On the other side are progressive Prophets (Stage 6), who suffer from phantom 1960s idealism and some Mean Green narcissism. Together, these Boomers might start a war that could fulfill, ironically enough, the ancient apocalyptic prophecies. Because this Fourth Turning coincides with the Godhead shifting and the end of a Great Cusp, the Fifth Spiritual Paradigm has the potential to go completely retrograde, propelling humanity into a dystopian nightmare rather than delivering us the Golden Age of our dreams.

Personally, I remain hopeful that we may yet manifest a healthy outcome for humanity, but I am an optimist by nature. So let's ask a polymath with a penchant for history how he thinks this Great Cusp will end. In this section, I have posed salient questions to my friend, who I map as a Second Tier "spiritual atheist" (Stage 7) on the Spectrum of Consciousness. I chose him because he is free of religious bias, rational in his approach to all matters, contemptuous of magical thinking, and immune to sentimentalism when evaluating data. Also, because he is a member of the Prophet generation – the archetype, according to *The Fourth Turning*, which moralistically launches the next Crisis – I believe him to be a superior consultant for our purposes.

Question: First, do you agree with the authors of *The Fourth Turning* that America is headed toward a crisis of the same magnitude as the American Revolution, the Civil War, and World War II?

Answer: With reference to this chapter's opening quote, I find it unlikely that our path to redemption is "through a gate in history" commensurate with our most gruesome historical tragedies. I don't see things going that way this time, unless we get a serious influx of resolve and energy from outside our borders, as in a case where NATO (North Atlantic Treaty Organization) has to deal with Putin's aggression against Ukraine. America looks to me like the frog slowly boiling to death in a pot of water. Possibly, we might realize what is happening and jump out before it's too late. Most likely we won't. For example, rather than realigning our investment priorities so we can lead the way on climate change solutions, we are ceding that mantle to the Chinese and others.

So no, I don't see anything like a world war or civil war on the horizon, despite the significant inroads toward revolution made by Donald Trump while fomenting his "insurrection." It appears to me the more likely outcome is we will continue to underinvest in ourselves, our infrastructure, in the technologies that will dominate the future and gradually loose leadership on the world stage. One day we will wake up and the dollar will no longer be the world's currency, and we will be so far in debt the only way out will be through induced inflation. We will rationalize all of our problems away by means of a three-ring circus media cycle that never ceases.

In the meantime, we will continue to underestimate the effects of globalization on a fairly large percentage of our population. McKinsey research says that up to one-third of U.S. workers and 800 million globally could be displaced by 2030. While most of this displacement will be caused by automation, it seems likely that the affected population will be led to blame foreigners and brown people while they pine for a better day that never really existed. Meanwhile, many jobs will go unfilled because of lack of desire to perform them or lack of skills in our workforce.

We will remain a nation of haves and have-nots, and the haves at the lower end of the wealth spectrum will struggle to hold on to what they've got. I guess civil unrest to the point of civil war could occur, but I don't think Americans have the stomach for that (Second Amendment enthusiasts notwithstanding). I think, instead, we will have a replay of the grain dole that was instituted toward the end of the Roman Empire. The Romans instituted entertainment for the masses at the same time. These two programs, taken together, is where we get the phrase "bread and circuses."[29]

I see a day coming when many or most of us are staring at fake news on our free phones while imploring the government to increase the dole. As a country, we will have long since voluntarily vacated the mantle of global leadership. What implications a multipolar world has for the more important question of what happens to all seven-plus-billion of us on Earth, I am not sure. But overpopulation along with climate change are, in my opinion, the two biggest challenges we face.

CHAPTER 3: CYCLES AND SEASONS | 115

Question: The authors of *The Fourth Turning* predicted a positive outcome, once the dust settles from the next crisis. Please respond to this quote from the book, which gives just a hint of what they think the aftermath might look like:

> *What present-day tensions will the next Fourth Turning resolve? Most likely, they will be Culture War updates of the perennial struggle between the individual and the collective – with new labels dating back to our Consciousness Revolution.*[30]

Answer: I do not share the authors' optimism about a renewed consciousness revolution. I fear the widening gulf between the haves and have-nots in our world will not be bridged, unless there is some kind of total collapse. In the event of a total collapse, perhaps the survivors can build something better over several generations, presuming they can remember the lessons learned.

I predict that we will continue to have a large and growing portion of the population who will be susceptible to economic disruption and displacement. I suspect many will trade liberties, freedoms, and independent thought for some amount of security. Sadly, it appears to me that this is already happing. Trump is evidence of both the issue and the bad bargain people are willing to make.

Question: Regarding the concept of a "New Human," do you think humanity is slowly moving toward a more refined, pluralistic proto-type – what Ken Wilber calls "Second Tier" systems thinking? Or do your thoughts align more with the following quote and, if so, why?

> *The enormous progress of the past seven-plus decades was not some natural evolution of humanity; it was the product of liberalism's unprecedented power and influence in the international system. Until the second half of the 20th century, humanity was moving in the other direction. We err in thinking that the horrors perpetrated against Ukrainians and Chinese during the 1930s, and against Jews during the 1940s, were bizarre aberrations. Had World War II produced a different set of victors, as it might have, such behavior would have persisted as a regular feature of existence.*
>
> *We need to start imagining what it will be like to live in such a world, even if the United States does not fall prey to these forces itself. ... President Franklin D. Roosevelt's answer, that a world in which the United States was the "lone island" of democratic liberalism would be a "shabby and dangerous place to live in," went largely unheeded then and no doubt will go largely unheeded again today.*[31]

Answer: I think the prosperity and social progress made in the United States after World War II was a direct result of the unique conditions that existed after that unprecedented struggle and are unlikely to be repeated. Because of the Great Depression – which seemed interminable to those who lived during it – nearly a third of Americans lived in poverty. A third of the country's homes had no running water, two-fifths lacked flushing toilets, and three-fifths lacked central heating. Rural electrification had not yet been accomplished, and segregation and Jim Crow were still the law of the land.

When the G.I.s returned from WWII, adjusted to a peace-time economy, and then repeated the exercise with the Korean War in 1953, the U.S. enjoyed an unprecedented economic boom and a great deal of social progress for the period between 1955 and 1970. To a large degree, this prosperity was caused by a combination of pent-up demand, because of the war and depression, and the lack of any global competition to serve that demand, since the economies of both Europe and Japan had been largely destroyed in the fighting.

Soldiers returned from the war, bought cars and houses (financed by the G.I. Bill), got married, and had lots of children. This is all well known. What is less well remembered is that when the U.S. formed NATO in 1949 to combat the influence of the Soviet Union and Communist China, we began to export some of that prosperity to our allies. Economic assistance was sent in the form of both direct aid through the Marshall Plan, as well as unprecedented military spending to keep ahead of our new Cold War enemies.

Not all Americans participated equally in the postwar boom, but the improved economy and demand for labor gave African Americans, Hispanics, women, and other groups more economic power than they had before. This economic power led to social power and demands for reform and increased fairness. Despite fears of a global nuclear calamity, our newly affluent society was more tolerant of these reforms than humans normally are in response to changes in the social fabric.

Today, though we see a relative increase in labor power resulting from the covid pandemic, I believe this is a temporary aberration. The longer-term trend will be an increasingly displaced workforce, and I see evidence of a reversal in relative power every time I see a "MAGA" hat. This observation is not about politics *per se* – it's about how people react when they feel they're losing out. Most Americans feel the pie is shrinking and they are not getting their share. I don't see how to change these natural human reactions to negative change, but I'd love to be proven wrong and see different reactions being displayed by New Humans!

Unfortunately, before any sort of a New Human comes along as a result of conscious evolution to build a better and more just world, the wealthiest and most powerful among us will likely make themselves into an entirely new form of life, merging biological intelligence with advanced forms of digital artificial intelligence. And I think this A.I. revolution will happen much faster than a meaningful percentage of the population gets "woke." While the wealthy are at it, they also might find ways to equip themselves to better deal with climate change than the run-of-the-mill human.

Before this dystopian end-game happens, I expect that the displacement of workers by automation, artificial intelligence, and other technologies to both continue and accelerate. I think Yuval Harari is probably right that in the future, "populist revolts will be staged not against an economic elite that exploits people, but against an economic elite that does not need them anymore. ... It is much harder to struggle against irrelevance than against exploitation."[32] For example, over the next several years, it's quite possible that as many as seven million truck drivers could lose their jobs. Luckily, *South Park* prepared us for this inevitable crisis.[33]

Question: You are a strategic systems thinker and an atheist, so I am curious: Does a Godhead description using the allegory of "Light" make you more comfortable exploring spirituality? Or is science your unquestionable and sole path (as opposed to soul path) for understanding the mysteries of the cosmos?

Answer: I don't know that I'm an atheist, but I agree with the religious concerns expressed by astrophysicist Neil deGrasse Tyson and comedian Bill Maher.[34] So it's not that I'm certain there is no God; I just don't see much evidence of the personal God claimed by many people. Consequently, I don't have anything against what you call "exploring spirituality," but I'm not sure your allegory of "Light" will assist me either. I can choose to meditate, take drugs, do yoga, etc. and I might have a "peak experience" that makes me more inclined to believe there is something or someone "out there" to commune with. However, my own nature would cause me to doubt any source for these experiences other than the synapsis of my brain.

I believe in science and all the science supporting the Big Bang, but I can't pretend to tell you why it happened or what was here before it did. Science does not (at least not yet) have answers to the big questions. It cannot provide a purpose for any of our lives or the lives of all the other amazing (or bothersome) creatures that inhabit this little blue planet in the middle of this big ol' Universe.

I experience awe whenever I think of Carl Sagan's comments on the picture of Earth taken by Voyager 1 as it was leaving our solar system:

> *Look again at that dot. That's here. That's home. That's us. On it everyone you love, everyone you know, everyone you ever heard of, every human being who ever was, lived out their lives. The aggregate of our joy and suffering, thousands of confident religions, ideologies, and economic doctrines, every hunter and forager, every hero and coward, every creator and destroyer of civilization, every king and peasant, every young couple in love, every mother and father, hopeful child, inventor and explorer, every teacher of morals, every corrupt politician, every "superstar," every "supreme leader," every saint and sinner in the history of our species lived there – on a mote of dust suspended in a sunbeam.*
>
> *The Earth is a very small stage in a vast cosmic arena. Think of the rivers of blood spilled by all those generals and emperors so that, in glory and triumph, they could become the momentary masters of a fraction of a dot. Think of the endless cruelties visited by the inhabitants of one corner of this pixel on the scarcely distinguishable inhabitants of some other corner, how frequent their misunderstandings, how eager they are to kill one another, how fervent their hatreds.*
>
> *Our posturings, our imagined self-importance, the delusion that we have some privileged position in the Universe, are challenged by this point of pale light. Our planet is a lonely speck in the great enveloping cosmic dark. In our obscurity, in all this vastness, there is no hint that help will come from elsewhere to save us from ourselves. ... There is perhaps no better demonstration of the folly of human conceits than this distant image of our tiny world. To me, it underscores our responsibility to deal more kindly with one another, and to preserve and cherish the pale blue dot, the only home we've ever known.*[35]

Carl Sagan, *Pale Blue Dot*

Since I have no idea who or what started it all, I try not to be disrespectful of what other people believe, even if they have imaginary friends who make up rules for the rest of us. But I deeply distrust certainty when it comes to spiritual topics and I don't see much evidence of a God watching over our hijinks. In that regard, I laughingly identify with *Rick and Morty*.[36] I could be wrong – how would one even know? What I do know is that we've oppressed and killed each other over religion and now need to cut each other some slack. Like country singer Iris DeMent, I'm content to "let the mystery be."[37]

LEARNING THROUGH DYSTOPIA: THE PROPHESIED TIME

Great Mystery is another powerful metaphor for God, and it is a term used by many indigenous peoples, some of whom believe we are in a prophesied time of immense chaos (i.e., the Great Cusp). My connection with native people in this lifetime is twofold. First, I had the privilege of hosting a Lakota Sun Dance sweat lodge at my farm in northern Virginia from 2005 to 2009, just as The Oracle Institute was forming. The group's presence every month was a true blessing for me and for the land. I learned much from the Lakota lodge leader, especially when he invited me to Vision Quest at his chief's compound in Mexico off the Sea of Cortez – an utterly profound adventure that provided me with the additional courage and commitment I needed to sell my farm and relocate Oracle to the Bible Belt in southwestern Virginia.

Then in 2018, Oracle had the honor of hosting a delegation of South American spiritual elders. The group included a Kogi Mamo from Colombia and Otomi-Toltec elders from Mexico. The "Original Caretakers Ceremonial Visit" was co-sponsored by Oracle, the Center for Earth Ethics and UNESCO, and I was invited to join the cross-country trek to sacred sites in Colorado and New Mexico. The visit culminated in California at the Global Climate Action Summit, where the elders led the opening processional at Grace Cathedral.

Kogi and Otomi-Toltec Elders at Oracle Campus

The Kogi people were unknown to the world until recently. They hid for nearly five hundred years after fleeing up their sacred mountain when Spanish Conquistadores arrived in the 1500s to plunder gold. In 1992, the Kogi broke their silence and allowed a British film crew to enter their ancestral lands. The result was an astonishing documentary entitled *The Heart of the World: Elder Brother's Warning*.[38] Then in 2012, the Kogi produced their own movie entitled *Aluna*, which further described their belief system and dire predictions.[39]

Aluna is the Kogi word for Great Mother, who they worship as the Creator of the Universe. Pause for a moment to realize that the Kogi are still operating as a Stage 2 people on the Spectrum of Consciousness, making them one of the last such cultures on Earth. They live a Second Spiritual Paradigm existence, which the rest of humanity left millennia ago. They never passed through the polytheistic Third Paradigm or the patriarchal Fourth Paradigm. They were never "Christianized" and had no idea who Jesus was until recently.

The Kogi view Earth as our mother and we as her children. They refer to themselves as "Elder Brother" and they call us "Younger Brother," due to our obsession with raping Earth for minerals and money. From their mountaintop, the Kogi have witnessed many Earth changes and, like climate scientists, they blame human indifference and corporate greed for this desecration. They are so attuned to Mother Earth that their high priests – called "Mamos" – are taken at birth and raised in a dark cave until they are nine years old. This training renders them acutely sensitive to both the Earth and Ethereal Planes.

The Kogi ancestral land is the mountain range of Santa Marta, Colombia, the world's tallest coastal mountains, which rise from the Caribbean coast to snowy peaks of 18,000 feet within a distance of just 25 miles. This mountain range – where every ecosystem on Earth can be found – is a miniature version of our planet, since it encapsulates glaciers, tundra, deserts, alpine lakes, tropical rainforests, wetlands, and coral reefs. Moreover, this highly biodiverse zone includes approximately 600 streams, 36 rivers, and networks of estuaries, lagoons, and river deltas. In this mini-microcosm of Earth, the Kogi are seeing devastation at every level.

The Kogi came to Oracle Campus because it rests along the New River, which is the oldest river in the Western Hemisphere and possibly the oldest river in the world.[40] The Elders performed ceremony at and in the New River. They also did ceremony at Mount Rogers, the highest peak in Virginia at over 6,000 feet, and at our Peace Pole Medicine Wheel. Additionally, we built a "Kogi Kiva" on our campus in their honor, which was christened with a fire ceremony led by a Volcano Keeper from Mexico. Similar ceremonies were conducted at the Great Sand Dunes and Mount Blanca in Colorado, where we were joined by other indigenous elders. We also visited Los Alamos in New Mexico, site of the Manhattan Project where Robert J. Oppenheimer led the team which built the atomic bomb. While there, the Elders blessed the site of the laboratory and had lunch with an astrophysicist from the current lab, who discussed cosmology with the Kogi Mamo via an interpreter.

The Kogi believe darkness is taking hold of our planet and they are not the only indigenous people sounding the alarm. The Hopi have been vocal as well, and their elders believe their prophecy concerning massive global disturbances and social upheaval is coming true right now. Like the Kogi, the Hopi are a matrilineal culture whose elders point to our disregard of the Creator's "original instructions" as the root causes of our current problems and the crisis that will shift human existence and consciousness.

The Hopi believe that we have suffered three previous world cataclysms. The **First World** was destroyed by fire (a comet, asteroid strike, or numerous volcanic eruptions). The **Second World** was destroyed by ice (the Ice Age *circa* 2.6 million BCE). And they say the **Third World** was destroyed by water, the same deluge recorded in many ancient holy books (the last Ice Age, *circa* 11,000–5000 BCE).[41] Currently, Hopi elders believe we are living in the final days of the **Fourth World**, which they say will end with a great "purification."

Nature, the First People and the spirit of our ancestors are giving you loud warnings. Today, December 10, 1992, you see increasing floods, more damaging hurricanes, hail storms, climate changes and earthquakes as our prophecies said would come. ... If we humans do not wake up to the warnings, the great purification will come to destroy this world just as previous worlds were destroyed.[42]

For the past half-century, Hopi Elders have predicted various Earth changes, technological advancements, and wars that signal the conclusion of the current age and the onset of the **Fifth World**. The transition between these worlds will depend on which path is chosen by modern world leaders. On their reservation in northern Arizona, the Hopi revere a sandstone rock that contains petroglyphs of indeterminate age. The rock carving shows two timelines: the upper track or "false path" is represented by a jagged line that depicts a destructive end of the Fourth World; the lower track or "divine path" illustrates humanity's reunification with our Creator and with each other.[43]

Some Hopi believe the paths represent alternative future outcomes, while others believe a dimensional separation may occur between those who continue in base materialism, greed and chaos, and those who return to the original in-structions. Either way, the prophecy states that the Fifth World will be one of peace, balance, and harmony in accordance with natural law. Additionally, the Hopi prophecy features the Pahana ("Purifier"), also called the "Great White

Brother," who will assist in ridding the world of wickedness. Miraculously, my friend and colleague Rev. Patrick McCollum recently was identified as the prophesied White Brother by numerous indigenous nations.

It is remarkable how closely the indigenous Second Paradigm prophecies match the polytheistic Third Paradigm prophecies, such as the Hindu belief that we are in the *Kali Yuga* – the last of four eras, with the current fourth and final stage marked by extreme chaos. Moreover, these Second and Third Paradigm prophecies parallel the Fourth Paradigm soothsaying contained in the three Abrahamic holy books. The *Old Testament*, *New Testament*, and *Quran* all predict an apocalypse with similar rapturous and multi-dimensional overtones. Fundamentalists within the Abrahamic faiths believe we are in End Times, and some Muslims believe the *Mahdi* (a.k.a. the Twelfth or "Missing" Imam) already has returned and that he will be aided by Jesus (whom they call *Isa*) to lead a final dualistic battle and day of judgement.[44]

I also am struck by the identical numbering of the Hopi and Hindu worlds, both of which contain a destructive fourth iteration in a cyclical, epochal pattern. These Fourth Worlds are marked by rampant technology, greed, and suffering – similar problems to those described in Oracle's Fourth Spiritual Paradigm, where unbridled patriarchy results in Trickle-Down Deity disasters. Of course, this numbering pattern also mates with the Fourth Turning season of transformative crisis, previously explored.

The Hopi's Fifth World of peace mirrors Oracle's Fifth Spiritual Paradigm of equanimity, and both are dependent on the return of the Sacred Feminine and the rebalancing of the Godhead. Indeed, the number five (one of Oracle's two sacred numbers; the other being eleven) is significant to other mystics as well. For instance, Madame Helena Blavatsky (1831–1891), founder of the Theosophy movement, and Edgar Cayce (1877–1945), known as the "sleeping prophet" and founder of the Association for Research and Enlightenment, called current humans the **Fifth Root Race**.

> *Always, when trying to verify predictions, movements, and cycles, look for correlations – the microcosm always reflects the macrocosm, and vice versa. Since 1982, the following has either been newly discovered, revealed, or occurred en masse: Fifth Communication Wave (personal computers); Fifth Brain (the heart); Fifth Brain Wave Frequency (gamma); Fifth Basic Force (torsion waves); Fifth Destiny (the rise of female power); Fifth Discipline (businesses as learning centers); Fifth Element (ether); Fifth Dimension (freed from time/spaces states, intention rules).*

Toss the labels of indigo, crystal, starseed, rainbow, and psychic, as they mislead and exaggerate (also discard "golden indigos"). Then, bunch together the characteristics these labels supposedly describe, and you have the pattern of the "new" kids – a pattern around for a while in the gene pool of the human family that has finally overspread landmasses – and moved into ascendancy.[45]

P.M.H. Atwater, *"The Fifth Root Race – In Ascendancy"*

Walter Russell (1871–1963), an American polymath who Walter Cronkite of CBS news called the "Leonardo da Vinci of our time," also used the number five to describe humanity's newly elevated position. Russell said humans had entered the **Fifth Kingdom of Man**, and he described the First through Fourth Kingdoms as: mineral, vegetable, animal, and early man. We will study Russell in more detail in the final chapter, as he was a 20th Century enlightened master. For now, it is important to know how Russell characterized New Humans:

Then came the time when an awareness came to man, the awareness of God in him, the first suspicion of his high inheritance .... And the Ages went by. ... [T]he dawn of consciousness came to man, and God on high ... sent messengers of an older race to tell him of God. ...

And there were other messengers prepared, likewise, with the illumination of cosmic consciousness; with the transfiguration of all-knowing which characterizes man of the Fifth Kingdom. The man of the Fifth Kingdom is he who knows God in him. ... [F]or all men are being transformed from moment to moment, illumined from moment to moment with the Light – all of us are.[46]

Here again is the concept that we are transitioning into New Humans with new capabilities, including the capacity to build a New World. To Russell's New Age prophecy, we may add the predictions of other recent spiritualists, like Father Pierre Teilhard de Chardin (1881–1955), who wrote, "The truth is that, as children of a transition period, we are neither fully conscious of, nor in control of, the new powers that have been unleashed.[47] Futurist Barbara Marx Hubbard also left us a treasure-trove of material on *Homo universalis*, a new species on a crusade to co-create the New World.

Of course, we also have been studying the work of Ken Wilber, who carries a mantel of honor for the Spectrum of Consciousness and his more complex model, Integral theory. In addition to Growing Up the stages of the Spectrum, Wilber has a theory on Waking Up to higher states of consciousness, which we will study in the final chapter. Now, we are primed to explore Cleaning Up, which is Wilber-speak for eradicating our shadow elements. If we are living in the prophesied time predicted by both ancient and New Age oracles – *and I believe we are* – then we need to prepare for the end of the Great Cusp and our entry into the Fifth Spiritual Paradigm. Proper preparation means further self-reflection and purification. Time to clean up our act!

WHAT YOU CAN DO: CLEANING UP

A common refrain in the New Age movement is: "I can't fix the world until I fix myself." In some ways, this is true. If we attempt to help others and we haven't perfected ourselves, our work will not be as masterful as that of an expert or, say, a spiritual master. However, the fact that we may lack expertise or a heightened state of awareness regarding a particular situation doesn't mean that we should sit on the sidelines or live in a bubble comprised of people who share our worldview. And it certainly does not mean that we should avoid assisting our brothers and sisters who are in need.

In reality, what most New Agers (subconsciously) mean when they bow out of service is that they don't want to engage with the world because it is messy and downright depressing. They'd rather focus on themselves and their own spiritual growth. This is a classic shadow element within the Green meme. Stage 6 tends to treat life like a spectator sport, doing little to prevent slippage in our otherwise progressive-trending last century.

Right now, I am thinking of a friend who checked out of politics because "women will never lose the right to abortion." Yeah right. Conversely, those Greens who do engage politically have unwittingly stoked the Culture War by squaring off against the Tea Party, Trumpism, and other right-wing movements with little or no compassion for what the average American is facing, let alone rural America. Meanwhile, Yellow (Stage 5) has been laughing all the way to the bank, as Green (Stage 6) battles with Orange (Stage 4).

In this section, we will delve into the types of shadow elements – which Wilber calls "**allergies**" and "**addictions**" – that either prevent us from helping ourselves and others, or which cause unintended consequences. Recall that Growing Up refers to moving sequentially up the Spectrum of Consciousness from one stage to the next. Waking Up refers to achieving higher states of spiritual wisdom, regardless of where we fall on the Spectrum (a topic for the final chapter). Cleaning Up, on the other hand, means doing our shadow work so that we can be our highest and best self at our current stage or state.

Because the shadow side of Red (Stage 3) is so obvious – "Fuck it or kill it," as Wilber puts it – we will not concern ourselves with that stage, particularly since it is unlikely people in that meme are reading this book. Rather, we will focus on the common shadow elements that plague Spectrum Stages 4, 5, 6, and 7. Starting with Orange (Stage 4), let us give that meme credit at the outset for mirroring the values of the Greatest Generation of WWI and WWII fame. We need to thank them for protecting us at home and abroad. Let us also express appreciation for the infrastructure they built – roads, bridges, canals, dams, electrical grids, etc. – that the next generation (mostly Yellow Stage 5) has neglected and refused to maintain. So what can go wrong at Stage 4? And what can Orange do to maintain equilibrium and a healthy evolutionary ethos?

First, Evangelicalism is the breeding ground for Orange, who can fall prey to religious zealotry and prejudice. The shadow side of Orange – and their Iron Age holy books – creates an atmosphere ripe for blind obedience, even when their own absolutistic morals are jeopardized. Their fear of being ostracized or even criticized by their ethnocentric peer group keeps them subdued. Consequently, whether operating under a mainstream fundamentalist faith or a more exotic Jim Jones variety, personal freedom and critical thinking are often relinquished. Instead, strict obedience and adherence to black-and-white dogma is demanded in order to remain a meme member.

Second, Orange needs to steer clear of Red, who can pull them backward under pressure. When a social system is under stress, Stage 4 nationalism can digress into full-blown Stage 3 White Supremacy and even nihilism.

> *What virtually all of Trump's voters had in common was resentment – they resented the* [Green] *cultural elite ... and they wanted ... if revenge is the wrong word, it's not far off. ...*
>
> *But Trump, like no politician in anybody's memory, directly hit the* [Orange] *nerve. ... He literally and deliberately spoke in* [Orange] *ethnocentric terms – thinly veiled (if veiled at all) racist, sexist, openly patriarchal, uber-nationalistic, misogynistic, jingoistic, and on and on in ways that literally had critics' mouths dropped wide open. ...*
>
> *And yes, over 90 percent of the terrorist groups in the past three decades have had a very strong,* [Orange]*, ethnocentric identity – usually with a red-power underbelly – an* [Orange] *that is almost always of a fundamentalist mythic-literal religious variety.*[48]
>
> Ken Wilber, *Trump and a Post-Truth World*

Third, we need to help Orange understand that Yellow is a trickster, who likes to manipulate. A perfect example is Dick Cheney, ex-CEO of Halliburton and former Vice President. Granted, I have chosen a pretty despicable example from the Yellow meme. And yes, just like all the other stages of the Spectrum, Stage 5 has many positive attributes. Yet, the shadow side of "I" memes is always ugly. So I have chosen Cheney as the Yellow rep for this very reason: to explore the shadow side of Stage 5.

Moreover, I wish to acknowledge that Cheney exhibits so many Red characteristics that it is difficult to chart him on the Spectrum. However, Cheney is too calculated, controlled, and strategic to be Stage 3 (though he may be Stage 7, a scary prospect that we will consider when we discuss evil). Indeed, Cheney was so good at bamboozling the Stage 4 meme, I wouldn't be surprised if he had a Spiral Dynamics expert on his staff! In addition to deceitfully naming the USA Patriot Act so as to confuse patriotic Orange, Cheney met regularly with Evangelical preachers, reportedly laughing at them afterward. Karl Rove – Bush's social "architect" – also exploited naive Orange, calling them "ridiculous" and "nuts."[49]

Thus, Cheney represents: (i) a corporate mogul gone bad; (ii) a corrupt politician; and (iii) a power freak – all in one. As such, he will more than suffice to personify the shadow compulsion of the "I" memes – greed and power. As previously mentioned, I identified two cardinal sins in *The Truth: About the Five Primary Religions*, the first installment of the Oracle Trilogy:

> In my opinion, evil action is the direct result of perverse desires. Mostly, evil stems from two cardinal sins: greed and pride. Unbridled greed [Stage 5] leads to an obsession with money and material possessions. Undaunted pride [Stage 3] leads to an obsession with power and world domination.
>
> Whenever our most pathetic and self-serving instincts outstrip our best and most altruistic emotions, chaos reigns. History shows that we have repeatedly followed corrupt leaders down self-destructive paths. Certainly, there have been great bearers of Light .... However, history is replete with examples of mankind's failure to discern Truth and fractionalize along religious lines [Stage 4]. This is not the path God intended for us.[50]

The point I was making then – before I reacquainted myself with Graves' theory and the more modern Spectrum of Consciousness – was that greed and pride are the two shadow obsessions that cause most of the problems on our planet. I did not realize it at the time, but I intuitively identified the Stage 5 and

Stage 3 shadow aspects that undermine civilizations ... over and over and over again. The fact that the consciousness experts have identified these same two destructive compulsions provides me with a measure of validation, though little comfort. Here's a bit more of what I wrote on this subject in *The Truth*:

> *[A]fter the prophets died the manmade religions and political systems became corrupted over time by leaders who suffered from greed* [Stage 5] *and hubris* [Stage 3]. *In fact, religion and politics are so intertwined that it is practically impossible to separate the two. Religious leaders have used monarchs and even democratic leaders to spread their version of God's message to the exclusion of all others, while the nobility and politicians have used religion to perpetuate their control over the masses and advance new systems of government.*
>
> *But the end never justifies the means, and therein lies the seeds of man's corruption. Too many religious and political leaders have used any means necessary to reach their goals and the Truth has been bastardized in the process.*
>
> *Unfortunately, we, the laity and the governed, have followed these flawed leaders all too willingly* [Stage 4]. *Only rarely do we revolt against injustice and lies. Throughout history, mankind has remained in tainted religious organizations and broken political systems rather than heed God's messages, take responsibility for ourselves and our world, and refuse to follow perverse orders. For this sin of laziness, we have been punished mightily.*[51]

While conducting his research, Clare Graves discovered that the Stage 4 "sheeple" are the most apt to blindly follow orders, even orders to kill. They love structure and will resist breaking rules, even if manmade. Only now is it occurring to me that the passive Stage 4 reluctance to question authority may be the third sin (or shadow element) contributing to humanity's woes. Surely, blind obedience is not in keeping with the evolutionary impulse or the New Human archetype.

Thus, when we elect or allow Yellow leaders to run the show, the results can be disastrous. "Power corrupts and absolute power corrupts absolutely" – an old saying that explains what happens when the "WE" memes (Stages 4 and 6) fail to keep the "I" memes (Stages 3 and 5) in check. Truly, the disparity of wealth on the planet can be traced to the greed and pride of the "I" meme foxes we let guard the hen house.

Another shadow aspect of the rational Yellow meme is its oftentimes vitriolic attack on religion (anti Stage 4) and spirituality (anti Stage 6). Unlike

Cheney, who used religion to steer the herd, there are Yellow influencers who still are stuck in the last paradigm, when science was the enemy of the church and of spirit. Having freed themselves from dogmatic thinking, Yellow can judge all spiritual belief systems as silly or stupid, exhibiting an allergy to either (or both) Stages 4 and 6. Indeed, their allergy can be quite extreme.

> *Their resultant attack on all spirituality is thus vocal, vicious, and vehement. Often known as "new atheists" (such as Richard Dawkins, Stephen Hawking, and Christopher Hitchens), they aggressively attack all spirituality as being the most dangerous and demented force on the planet. It's not that some of their points aren't true or don't need to be made; it's the sheer vehemence with which they hold their views ....*
>
> *These individuals have repressed, and then projected, their own higher forms of spiritual intelligence qualities and hence viciously attack anything that looks like spirituality "out there" – precisely like the antihomosexual zealots who spend all their time trying to get rid of their shadows by getting rid of those onto whom they have projected them.*[52]
>
> Ken Wilber, *The Religion of Tomorrow*

While the above observations may seem obvious to the Stage 6 reader, what may be less apparent is how the Green meme contributes to the cycle of pain and polarization that currently haunts the Western world. So for those of you who have earnestly charted yourself at the pluralistic Green meme, take a deep breath and prepare yourself: We are about to explore your shadow side, starting with one of the most common problems, known as "**Boomeritus.**"

> *Boomeritis is that strange mixture of very high cognitive capacity (the green meme and noble pluralism) infected with rather low emotional narcissism .... A typical result is that the sensitive self, honestly trying to help, excitedly exaggerates its own significance. ... [I]t haunts almost every corner of the New Age.*
>
> *Since, in normal development, green pluralism eventually gives way to second tier consciousness and an integral embrace, why did this generation become so stuck at the green meme? ... It appears that boomeritis intensifies a fixation to the green meme, making it almost impossible to let go of. Because narcissism finds such a happy home in pluralism, both get stuck with each other.*[53]
>
> Ken Wilber, *A Theory of Everything*

In short, Boomeritus stems from Green's unconscious addiction to an egocentric Red perspective. Fortunately, this Mean Green phase represents the ego's last stand – a final battle that must be won if the person wants to integrate and go Second Tier. Even in layman's terms, maturity is defined as the process of ego dissipation. The maturation process starts in childhood, when we learn to share and not bully others; it progresses through our teen years, as we begin to tolerate and then accept differences; and it typically ends happily in adulthood, when we learn to cooperate and compromise for the benefit of a more serene society and harmonious workplace and home life.

Thus, we drop a little more ego at each Spectrum stage and, as we Grow Up, we incrementally adopt higher and better values, with "better" defined as more pluralistic and worldcentric. Eventually, the ego is tamed and restrained. Ultimately, to become a Second Tier New Human, the ego must be completely subdued such that personal free will unites with the highest values of Truth, Love, and Light.

When Green develops an allergy to Growing Up, she undermines Second Tier integration. Spiritual narcissism may convince Green that she has reached Stage 8 – a master level achievement that Wilber estimates at less than 1% of the global population. In such a case, Green adopts a simplistic interpretation of the high-level construct "All is One." To the right is an ad aimed at Mean Green that ran for years in *What is Enlightenment?*[54]

Consequently, when a Stage 6 person first sees the Spectrum chart, their initial reaction is that it is an abomination. They hate it because it appears to contain a hierarchy that classifies and ranks humans. Their next reaction is to declare themselves at Stage 8 – until they start to learn the many differences between Green and Violet. Thereafter, if/when they realize they are Green (a sobering moment), then they *really* hate the chart!

I am not poking fun at the Green meme, only attempting to wake up those Greens who are ready to progress to Stage 7, because if we really want to save this planet, then Green New Humans will be much more effective when they go Indigo and reach a Second Tier perspective. Additionally, unless we are honest with ourselves about where we fall on the Spectrum, our efforts to birth a new paradigm may be futile. The Culture War between Green and Orange only serves to fuel the Great Cusp, widen the God Gap, and prolong our entry into the Fifth Spiritual Paradigm. To be honest, neither Stage 5 or Stage 6 humans have the ability to fully grasp the next paradigm (let alone birth it). For that quantum leap, we need a critical mass at Stage 7 and above.

Another problem at Green is the tendency to dissociate with Yellow, since Green no longer believes in competition. This allergy toward meritocracy and excellence is based on the false assumption that achievement and egalitarianism are mutually exclusive. Indeed, singling out anyone for special attention is considered bad behavior, which can make Stage 6 just as anti-truth and anti-expert as Stage 4. Green insists that everyone is equal and that all opinions are valid. This viewpoint doesn't just attack power hierarchies, which *are* negative and oppressive, it stifles organic holarchies, which are positive because they promote the growth, inclusion, and interconnectedness of life and society, in complete alignment with Wilber's "transcend and include" model:

> One of [Green's] *most notable characteristics is its denial and condemnation of every form of hierarchy. In this, it fails miserably to distinguish between dominator hierarchies (which are indeed loathsome) and actualization, or growth hierarchies (which are the form of most growth processes in nature, including humans). ...*
>
> *"Holographic" means that "all things are contained in all things," whereas "holarchical" means that "all of the lower is in the higher, but not all of the higher is in the lower."*[55]

A perfect example of this allergy toward holarchies is Green's refusal to permit those with the best skills to rise to the top and lead, preferring instead to sit in a circle and allow everyone time with the talking stick or megaphone. For instance, Green's allergy to leadership emerged during the Occupy Movement, which started in 2011 when protestors bravely squatted at Zucotti Park in New York City to highlight Wall Street corruption and economic inequality.

Oddly, the protesters refused to appoint a spokesperson. They also refused to strategize in an organized fashion, choosing instead to literally scream in all directions when it came time to share the results of caucuses and polls emanating from various circles of activists. As a result, the media had no idea who was in charge, who to interview, or even what the protesters were demanding. At one point, Michael Moore offered to assist, but the protesters chose to remain homogenous and egalitarian, thereby missing a grand opportunity to promote an effective leader who could articulate their message and make their case.[56]

Likewise, Greens prefers consensus as their primary method of decision-making, since even voting – yes, old-fashioned democracy – can be deemed oppressive to minorities. As a result, Greens take forever to make decisions and easily fall prey to group-think. They also like to "pat themselves on the back," especially when left alone together. Beck and Cowan warn that Stage 6 group-think can evoke the "Great Green Delusion" – that "any one of us can be anything he/she chooses" and everyone "has limitless potential."[57]

Greens also can fall prey to magical thinking. As previously mentioned, the Green belief in "spontaneous enlightenment" is common. Despite all evidence to the contrary, many Greens insist that reaching master level consciousness is easy and can happen instantaneously under the "right" conditions, which usually means loving yourself even more. Forget serious study, daily practice, and sacred service to others, because those tried and true paths take too long.

Greens also like to assert that everything is in **Divine Order** and that grave issues, like global peace, can be resolved through group meditation and prayer. Not surprisingly, when their utopian dreams fail to materialize, Greens see victims everywhere (including in the mirror). They habitually ignore the fact that personal and collective achievement primarily depend on hard work and the will to succeed (i.e., the positive attributes of Stages 4 and 5).

But by far the most unfortunate Green shadow aspect is the meme's toxic allergy to the next stage – integrated Indigo. Green misunderstands Stage 7 and will overtly malign Indigo. Why? Because Green doesn't see what Indigo sees, and rather than admit it, Green gets mean. If Indigo talks about natural holarchies, Green hears hierarchies. If Indigo talks about differences and discernment, Green hears separation and judgment. And if Indigo mentions how hard it is to reach enlightenment, Green puts her nose in the air and laments Indigo's failure to grasp non-duality. So contrary to what Kermit the frog says, it's easy being Green.[58] But it's very, very hard being Indigo.

> *[T]he first emergent Holistic View ... and the first fully Integral View, include actualization holarchies (that is, nested growth holarchies), and green has an inherent allergy to rankings of any variety (and that includes holarchies). So green generally loathes Integral 2nd tier altogether .... Since Green does not, as yet, have an actual understanding of 2nd tier, if often (mis)interprets any [Indigo] person or phenomenon as actually being a red, power-drive, egocentric entity, and responds in the same way it would to red, with loathing, judgmentalism, and negativism.[59]*

> Ken Wilber, *The Religion of Tomorrow*

With regard to politics, Wilber is even more disappointed with the Greens, who he blames for the election of Donald Trump.

> *The primary purpose of the leading-edge of evolution – in today's case, the green, postmodern wave – is to be just that: a LEADING edge of evolutionary unfolding ....*
>
> *Beginning in the 1960s, green first began to emerge as a major cultural force, and it soon bypassed* [Stage 5] *(which was the previous leading-edge stage) ....*
>
> *But as the decades unfolded, green increasingly began veering into extreme, maladroit, dysfunctional, even clearly unhealthy forms. Its broad-minded pluralism slipped into a rampant and runaway relativism (collapsing into nihilism), as the notion that all truth is contextualized (or gains meaning from its cultural context) slid into the notion that there is no real universal truth at all, only shifting cultural interpretations (which eventually slid into a widespread narcissism).*
>
> *And that is why the most influential postmodern elites ended up embracing the tag team from postmodern hell: nihilism and narcissism – in short, aperspective madness. The culture of post-truth.*[60]

Ken Wilber, *Trump and a Post-Truth World*

This flirtation with nihilism induced some of my New Age friends to vote for Trump "just to see what would happen." They voted for this charlatan, after being tricked by Russian bots, QAnon, Alex Jones, and other crazy, contra-news outlets. Even now, some of my friends are riding the fake news roller-coaster. Why? Because they love getting the inside scoop, even if delivered by anonymous or discredited news sources. Whether far-left or far-right, the net result is that a large segment of the population has become addicted to relative truth and sensational lies. Truth with a capital "T" is non-existent, which causes untold grief and heartache to those of us at Second Tier.

Lastly, before we explore the shadow side of Stage 7, I wish to make one more point: The Spectrum of Consciousness is a theory in the same way that evolution is a theory, which means it is a time-tested model that is commonly accepted and applied by academics and experts in diverse sociological fields. For example, Pew Research Center now breaks-down religious demographics using the Spectrum, as explained in this clarification by Pew Research Center (with bold text theirs, not mine):

*Pew Research Center analysis looks at beliefs and behaviors that cut across many denominations – important traits that unite people of different faiths, or that divide people who have the same religious affiliation – **producing a new and revealing classification, or typology, of religion in America.** "* [61]

Similarly, a movement called RepresentUS held an "Unrig Summit" in 2019, which focused on taking back our democracy. Actress Jennifer Lawrence is featured in the main video, and she implores everyone to come together for the good of the country. In the video, conservatives are identified as 36% of the electorate (Stages 3 and 4), moderates are mapped at 34% (Stage 5), and liberals are set at 25% (Stage 6).[62] Now look again at the Oracle Spectrum Chart in Chapter II. I've estimated Stages 3 and 4 conservatives at 35% of the American population, Stage 5 moderates at 35%; and Stages 6 and 7 liberals at 29%. These numbers are pretty damn close!

In sum, the Spectrum is widely used and it is taught at major universities (I took the class way back in 1981). Don't you think – and I'm talking to Greens now – that it's time to accept this research, self-chart yourself, and work as hard as you can to reach the Second Tier? That's how you can help, by Growing Up the Spectrum to Indigo and by Cleaning Up your shadow. Please, the world needs you to be Second Tier. I will leave Green readers with these final words of encouragement from Wilber:

> *I am often asked ... Isn't it enough to simply celebrate the rich diversity of various views and not try to integrate them? Well recognizing diversity is certainly a noble endeavor, and I heartily support that pluralism. But if we remain merely at the stage of celebrating diversity, we ultimately are promoting fragmentation, alienation, separation and despair. ... We need in short, to move from pluralistic relativism to universal integralism.* [63]

So what are Indigo's shadow elements? Well, because Stage 7 is the first meme to clearly recall passing through all the earlier stages, Indigos feel at liberty to draw upon characteristics of the First Tier memes when needed. Like a chameleon, Indigo can talk to anybody – which is a good thing. But if there is an addiction or an allergy to an earlier meme, that's when problems can arise.

For example, it is common for Indigo to become aggressive with Greens, who trigger Indigo when it comes to work ethic and style. Greens are laid back, since "all is in Divine Order" and "everything happens in Divine Time." Consequently, Indigo can get frustrated with Green, who tends to prolong planning meetings with lots of talk, talk, talk. Afterward, when it's finally time to get to work, Indigo may express a Stage 5 drive to achieve. To Green, this can look controlling or like a power-trip, but what actually is happening is that Indigo just wants to get to work and see progress.

> *Green allergies have reached near epidemic proportions in Integral communities. ... Such an individual often becomes hypersensitive to many typical green characteristics, including green's virtual incapacity to reach a conclusion about a course of action ...; green's superior attitude toward virtually every topic it approaches ...; green's common tendency to confuse dominator hierarchies with growth hierarchies ....*[64]
>
> Ken Wilber, *The Religion of Tomorrow*

In addition, Indigo can go overboard in expressing her higher perspective. An example of this dynamic is portrayed in one of my favorite movies, *Broadcast News*. There's a scene in which Holly Hunter, a junior TV news producer, is being overridden by the executive producer and she pushes back, insisting she is right. Her exasperated boss says, "You're just absolutely right and I'm absolutely wrong. It must be nice to always believe you know better, to always think you're the smartest person in the room." To which she sadly replies, "No, it's awful."[65]

Sometimes, that is exactly how it feels to be Indigo. Because she has a higher vantage point from which to scan system sectors and connect puzzle pieces, Indigo often does know best. Moreover, it hurts to be misunderstood by Green, who Indigo desperately wants to reach. Mainly though, it's painful for Indigo to watch First Tier memes spin their wheels, and it sucks to be bound by the dire consequences of their limited thinking. Is it any wonder then that Indigo goes a little Red once in a while?

Another problem at Indigo if the person is still clinging to atheism, is that the Ethereal Plane keeps knocking at the door. Avoidance of stage and state growth can drive atheist Indigo mad, as she persists in trying to ignore the higher realms. In fact, I have a dear Second Tier friend who suffers mightily with a Stage 5 addiction to science and rationality, coupled with an allergy to Stage 8 and the Light. He constantly receives what he calls the "daily mock" – what most New Humans would reverently call a Sign from God.

Because Indigo usually perceives events differently than First Tier memes, she can struggle with how best to share her more sophisticated analyses. For instance, Indigo may have an allergy to Green's permissiveness and leniency, viewing it as harmful. Child rearing is a perfect example. Green believes "shaming" is unacceptable; whereas Indigo knows shaming is a valuable and effective parenting tool. In fact, research shows that "helicopter" and now "bulldozer" parenting is creating generations of co-dependent and fear-based kids, who are ill-equipped to navigate the real world.[66] Indigo sees this clearly and may intervene with an (uninvited) opinion. Conversely, she may be wise enough to hold her tongue, like I'm going to do while Wilber does the talking:

> In a "therapeutic culture," such as ours, where nobody is to blame for anything that they do, "shame" has all but disappeared from the cultural fabric. ... Shame, which is a crucial part of the fabric of any well-functioning culture, acting, as it does, as a filter between lower, "subhuman" drives of a person (for food, sex, power) and the higher drives of love, care, tenderness, courage, and presence ... has all but disappeared from the cultural landscape – and hence from the individual psyche – and thus so has the major force stopping regression to earlier and more primitive levels ....
>
> [G]reen will not allow the introduction of "shame," because Green denies that there is anything that a human should be ashamed of. Since there is no universal "what is right" and "what is wrong" for a human being, shame is altogether inappropriate. And with that aperspectival madness, we will continue eating, sexing, and greedily powering ourselves to death.[67]

Despite Indigo's higher perspective, she still has a long way to go in order to perfect herself and, unlike Green, she knows this to be true. In fact, Indigo desperately wants to keep ascending the Spectrum, but Cleaning Up is another matter. Just like the other memes, Stage 7 can be oblivious to her shadow side.

In my case, I knew I needed to Clean Up my Indigo shadow if I wanted to Grow Up to Violet, so I made a conscious choice to deal with my addictions and allergies. First, I realized that I had a Stage 3 addiction to heroism. I had been in battle mode for so long that my masculine side was dominant and my feminine side repressed. So I made a conscious decision to ungird and lose my spiritual warrior edge. There was no other way to pass through the next portal except to leave my Joan of Arc days behind.

Second, I concluded that I had a Stage 5 addiction to intellectualizing my mission. I was using my mind to strategize and execute, which resulted in my head being out of synch with my heart. I recognized this imbalance in myself and did practices to attain equilibrium between my left and right-brain and between my masculine and feminine aspects. Intuitively, I knew my progress would be thwarted until I did this shadow work. Thereafter, I was able to start integrating the primary lesson of the next meme: *Love magnifies Truth.*

During the next phase of my Cleaning Up process, I discovered that I suffered from an allergy to Stage 8. Sounds crazy, but this is fairly common at Second Tier. Indigo is so efficient and so grateful to be a conscious player in the God Game, she worries about relinquishing some critical component of her functionality. Intellectually, Indigo knows each stage is better than the one before, so she should seek a greater vantage point. But what Indigo knows for a certainty is that she's really effective where she is. Consequently, Indigo may worry that the transition to Violet will cause her to lose her edge, compel her to abandon work and be a "monk on a mountain top" or otherwise sideline her, just as the God Game is entering the fourth and final quarter of the game.

> *A transpersonal allergy ... is a direct dis-owning or dissociating of a specific level's transpersonal reality, which renders it largely unconscious. This usually occurs because the transpersonal experience involves a death of that level's self-sense, and the self, fearing that death, denies and dis-owns the experience itself, converting it into shadow. ...*
>
> *In rare cases, when other shadow elements are present, this can slide into ... witnessing-state dysfunctions, such as "split-life" goals," where the individual can't decide whether to withdraw from the world entirely and pursue spiritual goals alone, or try to follow the path of "a monk in the world" and attempt to unite his or her transcendental awareness (of "heaven") with its immanent aspects (of "earth").*[68]

Ken Wilber, *The Religion of Tomorrow*

Thus, an allergy to higher stages and states may cause Indigo and other New Humans to cling to the Earth Plane. Conversely, this same shadow element – but now reversed as an addiction to higher states – may cause New Humans to want to escape into the Ethereal Plane to the detriment of their critical work in this realm. Obviously, recognizing our shadow elements helps us proceed more effectively and fully toward the goal of enlightenment.

As we wind up this chapter on the cycles and seasons of history and how to overcome shadow aspects, my hope is that the reader is now primed for what is coming next – a lucid and mature discussion of polarity and evil. As we have seen, both our individual psyches and collective cultures contain shadow elements, including the tendency to regress into harmful and repetitive cycles. It therefore logically follows that the Light contains elements of darkness. "As above, so below," is one of the master level concepts we soon shall explore.

For now, let us agree, at a minimum, that the Light *permits* humans to tap dark energy and cause misery on the Earth Plane, for ourselves and others. Additionally, please start to ponder where this darkness comes from and how negative energy is applied, whether through individual free will or as a hostile undercurrent that undermines humanity with unrelenting polarity, possibly in perpetuity.

Thus far, we have seen plenty of evidence that polarity is the hallmark of our dualistic Earth Plane, and we will study this principle more closely in the next chapter. Later, we will explore whether duality also exists in the Ethereal Plane. Because of the multidimensional aspects of reality, New Humans need to accept that it is a long journey to reach the non-dual dimension of a perfectly balanced, genderful, genderless, all-things, and no-things Godhead. Yet, the Light also is accessible here and now.

In conclusion, let us rejoice rather than worry that we have chosen to incarnate during the "prophesied time." Though previous generations have thought the same thing – that the "Great Turning" has arrived – there is ample and increasingly dire data to validate that the Great Cusp we are living through is *the* catastrophic time predicted by all the major religions and indigenous wisdom traditions. Fortunately, at the end of this cruel cycle, the traditions are in concert regarding what happens next: They all agree that an epoch of peace will arrive, which we at Oracle call the Fifth Spiritual Paradigm.

[1] David Kaiser, "Donald Trump, Stephen Bannon and the Coming Crisis in American National Life," *Time Magazine* (Nov. 18, 2016), http://time.com/4575780/stephen-bannon-fourth-turning/ (accessed July 2022).

[2] William Strauss and Neil Howe, *The Fourth Turning: An American Prophecy*, Broadway Books: New York, NY (1997).

[3] "Freedom in the World Research Methodology," *Freedom House* (2021), https://freedomhouse.org/reports/freedom-world/freedom-world-research-methodology (accessed June 2022).

[4] Sarah Repucci and Amy Slipowits, "Democracy Under Siege: Freedom in the World 2021," *Freedom House* (2021) https://freedomhouse.org/report/freedom-world/2021/democracy-under-siege (accessed July 2022).

[5] Ibid.

[6] Mike Abramowitz, "Democracy in Retreat: Freedom in the World 2019," conclusions section, *Freedom House* (2019), https://freedomhouse.org/report/freedom-world/freedom-world-2019/democracy-in-retreat (accessed July 2022).

[7] "Democracy Index 2020: In Sickness and in Health?" *The Economist Intelligence Unit* (2021), https://www.eiu.com/n/campaigns/democracy-index-2020/ (accessed July 2022).

[8] Ibid, p. 8.

[9] Ibid, p. 44.

[10] Ibid, p. 45.

[11] Robert Kagan, "The Strongmen Strike Back," *The Washington Post* (March 14, 2019), https://www.washingtonpost.com/news/opinions/wp/2019/03/14/feature/the-strongmen-strike-back/ (accessed July 2022).

[12] William Strauss and Neil Howe, *The Fourth Turning*, p. 100 *et seq.*

[13] My father James L. George, Ph.D. graduated from the U.S. Naval Academy (1961). After a debilitating cancer, he retired at the rank of Lieutenant (1967). He received a Masters in Political Science (1970) and Doctorate in International Relations (1972). He worked on Capitol Hill and helped negotiate Strategic Arms Reduction Treaties (START I and START II). He was an expert on the Soviet Navy and wrote many books on naval strategy. He was a Fellow at: Hoover Institute of War, Revolution, and Peace; Center for Naval Analyses; and Hudson Institute. His nickname on Capitol Hill was "Admiral" and he received an admiral's burial at the Naval Academy in Annapolis, Maryland (2000). See: "James L. George Dies," *The Washington Post* (August 27, 2000), https://www.washingtonpost.com/archive/local/2000/08/27/james-l-george-dies/3f7bd520-c559-4805-9d02-02756546fdfc/ (accessed July 2022).

[14] William Strauss and Neil Howe, *The Fourth Turning*, p. 84.

[15] Ibid, pp. 259–262.

[16] Ibid, p. 83.

[17] Ibid, pp. 145–170.

[18] Ibid, pp. 171–200.

[19] Ibid, pp. 201–253.

[20] Ibid, p. 242.

[21] Ibid, p. 252.

[22] Ibid, p. 256.

[23] Charles Lewis, "False Pretenses," *Center for Public Integrity* (Jan. 23, 2008; updated June 30, 2014), https://publicintegrity.org/federal-politics/false-pretenses/ (accessed July 2022).

[24] Dominic Mastrangelo, "Fox News Tops Yearly Rating Rankings," *The Hill* (Dec. 15, 2021), https://thehill.com/homenews/media/585987-fox-news-tops-yearly-ratings-rankings (accessed July 2022).

[25] William Strauss and Neil Howe, *The Fourth Turning*, pp. 255–259.

[26] Ibid, p. 273.

[27] Ibid, pp. 279–302.

[28] Ibid, pp. 286–287.

[29] "Bread and Circuses," *Wikipedia*, https://en.wikipedia.org/wiki/Bread_and_circuses (accessed July 2022).

[30] William Strauss and Neil Howe, *The Fourth Turning*, p. 300.

[31] Robert Kagan, "The Strongmen Strike Back."

[32] Yuval Noah Harari, *21 Lessons for the 21st Century*, p. 9, Jonathan Cape: London, UK (2018).

[33] "They Took Our Jobs," *South Park* (2012), https://www.youtube.com/watch?v=toL1tXrLA1c (accessed July 2022).

[34] Neil deGrasse Tyson, "I'm Not an Atheist," *Joe Rogan Radio Show* (Aug. 22, 2018), https://www.youtube.com/watch?v=I2itlUlD10M. See also: Bill Maher, "New Rules: Noah's Ark, God, and Religion," (March 18, 2014), https://www.youtube.com/watch?v=cyPy61xNBQY (both accessed July 2022).

[35] Carl Sagan, *Pale Blue Dot*, Random House Publishing: New York, NY (1994). To see the image: http://www.planetary.org/explore/space-topics/earth/pale-blue-dot.html (accessed July 2022).

[36] See: "The Search for Meaning," *Rick and Morty* (2017), https://www.youtube.com/watch?v=de2grEPn7rg (accessed July 2022).

[37] Iris DeMent, "Let the Mystery Be" (2008), https://www.youtube.com/watch?v=nlaoR5m4L80 (accessed July 2022).

[38] Alan Ereira, *The Heart of the World: Elder Brother's Warning*, BBC Documentary (1992), https://www.youtube.com/watch?v=hRgTtrQOiR0 (accessed July 2022).

[39] *Aluna*, Sunstone Films (2012), http://www.alunathemovie.com/ (accessed July 2022).

[40] "List of Rivers by Age," *Wikipedia*, lists the New River as third oldest in the world, https://en.wikipedia.org/wiki/List_of_rivers_by_age (accessed July 2022).

[41] "Scientists Confirm Historic Massive Flood in Climate Change," *NASA* (Feb. 28, 2006), https://www.nasa.gov/vision/earth/lookingatearth/abrupt_change.html. See also: James Trefil, "Evidence for a Flood," *Smithsonian Magazine* (April 1, 2000), https://www.smithsonianmag.com/science-nature/evidence-for-a-flood-102813115/ (both accessed July 2022).

[42] Thomas Banyacya, "The Hopi Message to the United Nations General Assembly," *The Internet Library* (Dec. 10, 1992), https://archive.org/stream/ChuckingIt.com-15/ChuckingIt.com_Techqua_Ikachi_Hopi_Prophecies_djvu.txt (accessed July 2022).

[43] Ibid. For video explanation of Prophecy Rock see: "Hopi Prophecy Rock with Elder Grandfather Martin Gashweseoma," *KnewWays Multimedia* (Sept. 24, 2010), https://www.youtube.com/watch?v=EeJ2e70OXDw (accessed July 2022).

[44] See generally: "Mahdi" and "Muhammad al-Mahdi," *Wikipedia*, https://en.wikipedia.org/wiki/Mahdi (accessed July 2022).

[45] P.M.H. Atwater, L.H.D., "The Fifth Root Race – In Ascendency," *Association for Research and Enlightenment Blogspot* (Feb. 1, 2013) https://www.edgarcayce.org/about-us/blog/blog-posts/the-fifth-root-race-in-ascendancy/ (accessed July 2022).

[46] Walter Russell, *The Fifth Kingdom of Man*, pp. 10–12, University of Science and Philosophy: Waynesboro, VA (1991).

[47] Pierre Teilhard de Chardin, *The Phenomenon of Man*, p. 279, Harper & Row: New York, NY (1959). See also: *The Future of Man*, Harper Collins: New Yok, NY (1964).

[48] Ken Wilber, *Trump and a Post-Truth World*, pp. 51, 79, Shambhala Publications: Boulder, CO (2017).

[49] Jake Tapper and Kendall Evans, "Ex-Bush Aide: White House Officials Called Evangelicals 'Ridiculous'," *ABC News* (Oct. 16, 2006), https://abcnews.go.com/GMA/story?id=2570947&page=1 (accessed July 2022).

[50] Rev. Laura George, J.D., *The Truth: About the Five Primary Religions*, p. 26, Oracle Institute Press: Independence, VA (2nd Ed. 2010).

[51] Ibid, pp. 26–27.

[52] Ken Wilber, *The Religion of Tomorrow: A Vision of the Future of the Great Traditions*, pp. 318–319, Shambhala Publications: Boulder, CO (2017).

[53] Ken Wilber, *A Theory of Everything: An Integral Vision for Business, Politics, Science, and Spirituality*, pp. 27–28, Shambhala Publications: Boston, MA (2000).

[54] See for example, *What is Enlightenment?*, Issue 33, p. 103 (Aug. 2006), https://www.andrewcohen.com/enlightennext-magazine/ (accessed July 2022).

[55] Ken Wilber, *The Religion of Tomorrow*, pp. 204, 223.

[56] "Who Is Occupy Wall Street?" *New York Times* (Nov. 12, 2011), https://www.nytimes.com/2011/11/13/opinion/sunday/who-is-occupy-wall-street.html (accessed July 2022).

[57] Don Edward Beck and Christopher C. Cowan, *Spiral Dynamics: Mastering Values, Leadership, and Change*, p. 269, Blackwell Publishing: Malden, MA (1996).

[58] Hermit the Frog, "It's Not Easy Being Green," *Sesame Street*, https://www.youtube.com/watch?v=hpiIWMWWVco (accessed July 2022).

[59] Ken Wilber, *The Religion of Tomorrow*, p. 324.

[60] Ken Wilber, *Trump and a Post-Truth World*, pp. 4–5, 9.

[61] "The Religious Typology: A New Way to Categorize Americans by Religion," *Pew Research Center* (Aug. 29, 2018), https://www.pewforum.org/2018/08/29/the-religious-typology/ (accessed July 2022).

[62] Jennifer Lawrence, "Unbreaking America: A NEW Short Film About Solving the Corruption Crisis," *RepresentUs* (Feb. 27, 2019), https://represent.us/ and https://www.youtube.com/watch?v=TfQij4aQq1k (both accessed July 2022).

[63] Ken Wilber, *A Theory of Everything*, p. 112.

[64] Ken Wilber, *The Religion of Tomorrow*, p. 333.

[65] "Smartest Person" scene from *Broadcast News*, Gracie Films and 20th Century Fox (1987), https://www.youtube.com/watch?v=qeWduNomDqY (accessed July 2022).

[66] Greg Lukianoff, J.D. and Jonathan Haidt, Ph.D., *The Coddling of the American Mind: How Good Intentions and Bad Ideas Are Setting Up a Generation for Failure*, Penguin Press: New York, NY (2018).

[67] Ken Wilber, *The Religion of Tomorrow*, pp. 285–286.

[68] Ibid, pp. 352, 229–230.

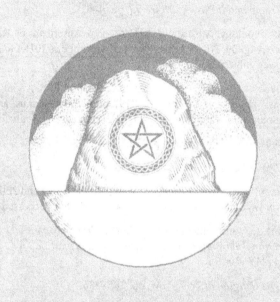

CHAPTER
GANDHI VS. HITLER:
TEAM LIGHT AND TEAM DARK

The Force is what gives a Jedi his power.
It is an energy field created by all living things.
It surrounds us and penetrates us.
It binds the Galaxy together.

Obi-Wan Kenobi, *Star Wars*

I see through the lies of the Jedi.
I do not fear the Dark Side as you do.
I have brought peace, freedom, justice, and security
to my new empire. ... Don't make me kill you.

Darth Vader (a.k.a. Anakin Skywalker), *Revenge of the Sith*

Synchronicity is an astounding ally on the Earth Plane. I commenced this chapter on the 75th anniversary of D-Day, after listening to Donald Trump – a confirmed draft-dodger – read a speech someone prepared for him at the official celebration in Normandy, France, where soldiers fought and sacrificed to check the Nazi scourge. The noteworthy assembly of honored guests included a handful of surviving World War II veterans – the last of the "Hero" generation described in *The Fourth Turning*. With roughly 350 American WWII veterans dying each day, they will all soon be gone.[1] Truly, we are witnessing the end of an era, a Fourth Spiritual Paradigm marked by patriarchy, polarity, and hard-learned lessons.

In this chapter, we will drill down to examine one of my personal heroes – Mahatma ("Great Soul") Gandhi (1869–1948), who splendidly aligned with the evolutionary impulse to help lead **Team Light** during a grievous time in human history. We also will examine Adolf Hitler (1889–1945), a masterful nemesis of evolving consciousness and former general on **Team Dark**. We will, in short, have a mature discussion about good and evil, as we continue to explore polarity, its historical magnetism, present purpose, and future path.

For some, this chapter may be challenging, as I reject the New Age myth that "evil is an illusion," as well as Green's apprehension that addressing evil (or even discussing the sad state of the world) will draw "negative energy." Yes, the Light is non-dual, but that is the topic of the last chapter. For now, my goal is to convince Greens that the Earth Plane is dualistic and that we ignore that fact at our peril.

Let us therefore start by expressing our admiration that, against all odds, the World War II Allies bravely fought the Axis powers, once all other positive and peaceful options for reconciliation were exhausted.

> *The whole fury and might of the enemy must very soon be turned on us now. Hitler knows that he will have to break us in this island or lose the war. If we can stand up to him, all Europe may be freed and the life of the world may move forward into broad, sunlit uplands.*
>
> *But if we fail, then the whole world, including the United States, including all that we have known and cared for, will sink into the abyss of a new Dark Age made more sinister, and perhaps more protracted, by the lights of perverted science.*
>
> *Let us therefore brace ourselves to our duties, and so bear ourselves that if the British Empire and its Commonwealth last for a thousand years, men will still say, "This was their finest hour."* [2]
>
> Winston Churchill

So yes, there is an **"Enemy"** – whether you chose to own it and wrestle with it as part of your own shadow work, counter the barbarity of others, or blame the underlying rules of the God Game itself (a.k.a. the Laws of the Universe). There *is* a Dark force that opposes the Light and creates polarity, division, and massive confusion on the Earth Plane. Consequently, to be a meaningful participant in the God Game one must: (i) become familiar with the Dark side; (ii) accept the sacred task of becoming a **Lightworker**; and (iii) attain the consciousness of a clever and courageous New Human.

For present purposes, we will define the Light as the evolutionary impulse that started and sustains all of creation. From this perspective, the Light represents the Creator's preference for evolution over destruction, for progress over regression, for freedom over repression, and for love over hate. The Light also is the source of the organic flow and function of nature, including the inherent life-death-life cycle contained therein. However, the intrinsic oscillation that causes cyclical rebirth within the evolutionary spiral is *vastly different* than the destructive Dark force, which seeks permanent retrogression, if not complete annihilation and an end to the God Game itself.

There also is a difference between a Lightworker and a **Lightholder**. Both play for Team Light, no doubt. But the roles are distinct, since the former is focused on "doing" and the latter on "being." Typically, Lightworkers are better known (e.g., Jesus, Muhammad, Gandhi), because they actively intervene when Team Dark pushes polarity into the red zone. Lightholders, on the other hand, literally are monks on mountaintops, masters in mystery schools, and avatars who possess the power to affect equilibrium on multiple planes.

Years ago, I read *Power vs. Force*, a book that was popular before the start of the New Millennium. The author's main message was that moral power is greater than physical force, which unfortunately is not always true on our dualistic Earth Plane. The actual Golden Rule of the Fourth Spiritual Paradigm was not, "Love they enemy." Rather, it was (and still mostly is), "He who has the gold makes the rules." Second Tier New Humans understand this tragic reality, and they wince at the ridiculous chart in *Power vs. Force* which asserts that "One individual at level 600 [which equates to "Peace" on the author's scale] can counterbalance ten million individuals below level 200."[3] *Really?*

Well the reverse happened during World War II, when one person, Hitler, managed to kill approximately 18 million people (not counting enemy soldiers), even though most of his victims surely had a higher consciousness than he. Thus, despite making some salient points about the non-dual realm (which has little to do with the Earth Plane at this polarized point in our collective journey), the author of *Power vs. Force* chose to leave his Green audience with this insipid instruction: "Wisdom can ultimately be reduced to the simple process of avoiding what makes you go weak – nothing else is really required."[4]

Soon, we will understand why more Lightworkers are needed at this critical juncture in human history. Later, we will learn how to access the Light more readily and receive tips on how to Wake Up to higher states of consciousness. Let us begin, however, with an instructive example of the good-evil polarity from the last Fourth Turning, a deadly round of the God Game indeed.

THE LAST UNRAVELLING: WORLD WAR I

Though rarely examined from a Spectrum of Consciousness perspective, Gandhi was a major player for Team Light during both world wars. In fact, Gandhi's support of the British during wartime always overrode his despair at the Empire's unwillingness to release his people from colonial servitude. Consequently, even though he employed non-violent techniques against the British to achieve India's independence, Gandhi understood the necessity of war under certain circumstances and he volunteered for the British military:

> We have been proud of our British citizenship .... It would be unbecoming to our dignity as a nation to look on with folded hands at a time when ruin stared the British in the face as well as ourselves, simply because they ill-treat us here. ... It is true that we are helots in the Empire, but so far we have tried to better our condition, continuing the while to remain in the Empire. ... And if we desire to win our freedom and achieve our welfare as members of the British Empire, here is a golden opportunity for us to do so by helping the British inus the war by all means at our disposal. ...
>
> Again, if any class among the subjects considers that the action of a government is immoral from a religious standpoint, before they help or hinder it, they must endeavor fully and even at the risk of their lives to dissuade the government from pursuing such a course. ... Such a moral crisis is not present before us, and no one says that we wish to hold aloof from this war for any such universal and comprehensive reason. ...
>
> I advanced these arguments in 1899, and even today [1928] I do not see any reason for modifying them. ... I heard many attempted refutations of these arguments in South Africa, and subsequently in England. But I discovered no ground for changing my views. ... [T]he underlying, principle in the above arguments is Satyagraha, insistence on truth.[5]

Gandhi established and then led the Natal Indian Ambulance Corps, which aided in the transport of wounded British soldiers in Africa during the Boer War (1899–1902) and the Zulu Rebellion (1906). Unbeknownst to Gandhi who was thirty-one years old at the time, his future antagonist for India's freedom, a then twenty-two-year-old Winston Churchill (1874–1965). also served in the Boer War, and their paths crossed during the Battle of Spion Kop, though they did not meet.[6] Coincidentally, my great-grandfather also fought in the Boer War.[7]

Gandhi during the Boer War (*circa* 1899)

Though only ten years old at the time, Hitler was fascinated by the Boer War – the first war, apparently, in his memory. His obsession with war would continue throughout his childhood, his teen years (his father died when he was thirteen and his mother died when he was eighteen), and through his early adulthood. Eventually, after being rejected by the Academy of Fine Arts in Vienna and spending seven years in relative poverty fomenting his hatreds, Hitler enlisted in the Bavarian Army for the start of World War I in 1914. Though just in his twenties at the time, Hitler already was firmly entrenched in the Stage 3 power meme, where he would remain his entire life.

> *Even as a boy I was no "pacifist," and all attempts to educate me in this direction came to nothing. The Boer War was like summer lightning to me. Every day I waited impatiently for the newspapers and devoured dispatches and news reports, happy at the privilege of witnessing this heroic struggle even at a distance.*[8]

In stark contrast to Hitler, Gandhi experienced steady spiritual growth during his life, as is always the case with master level souls, and it is quite easy to map his ascension along the Spectrum of Consciousness. Gandhi's life started as the youngest child in an upper middle-class family of the *Bania* (merchant) caste. His father was the chief minister of various states within the British Raj, a position that exposed Gandhi to a good education and a variety of foundational experiences, such as visits with Hindu holy men, Jain monks, and friends who practiced Islam and Zoroastrianism. Notably, Christianity is the religion which least impressed Gandhi as a child.[9]

By the tender age of thirteen, Gandhi was married and possessed a ready outlet for his pubescent lust. Not surprisingly then, by the age of sixteen, he and his wife Kasturbai were expecting their first child. Sadly, the loss of this baby coupled with the death of Gandhi's father while the couple was engaged in sex haunted Gandhi the rest of his life. Eventually, he would resolve the guilt and gain absolute control over his mind and mission by renouncing sex altogether.

> It is now my painful duty to have to record here my marriage at the age of thirteen. ... I can see no moral argument in support of such a preposterously early marriage. ... We were the same age. But I took no time in assuming the authority of husband. ... I must say that I was passionately fond of her. ...
>
> For one thing, I did not restrain myself, as I should have done, whilst I was yet a student. And secondly, this carnal lust got the better of what I regarded as my duty to study, and what was even a greater duty, my devotion to my parents .... [T]his shame of my carnal desire even at the critical hour of my father's death ... is a blot I have never been able to efface or forget ....
>
> The final resolution could only be made as late as 1906. Satyagraha had not been started. I had not the least notion of it coming. ... It became my conviction that procreation and the consequent care of children were inconsistent with public service. ... I saw that brahmacharya [celibacy] ... begins with bodily restraint, but does not end there. The perfection of it precludes even an impure thought. ... Without an unreserved surrender to His grace, complete mastery over thought is impossible.[10]

By the end of 1906, in addition to taking the vow of *brahmacharya*, Gandhi reached the state of an ascetic, renouncing not just sex but also his possessions. He was in total service to his fellow man and achieved the status of a Second Tier New Human. Here is a quick look at some of Gandhi's milestones as he ascended the Spectrum of Consciousness.

> ➤ **Stage 4:** Gandhi was raised and behaved as a dutiful child, attending to his studies (though not a good student) and dedicated to his family. There were mild bouts of rebellion (he ate meat and smoked cigarettes), but he apologized to his father and vowed piety. He was introduced to and began responding with curiosity to religious pluralism.[11]

> ➤ **Stage 5:** As a young adult, Gandhi studied law in England, where he continued exploring religious pluralism and New Age theosophies. He

decided to accept a legal position for a shipping company in South Africa that offered future prosperity. When asked why he agreed to go to law school in London, he replied, "In a word, ambition."[12]

➤ **Entering Stage 6:** In 1893, when he arrived in South Africa at the age of twenty-three, he famously was thrown off a train for being "colored," and he vowed to do battle over this insult. In 1894, he founded the Natal Indian Congress, which initially was established to serve middle-class Indians, who paid a fee for his legal services. Soon, he was working on a variety of issues for his fellow Indians, ranging from transportation and voting rights to sanitation and health. He was moving beyond notions of pride to concern for all.[13]

➤ **Stage 6:** By 1896 at the age of twenty-six, Gandhi was fully focused on the misery of all Indians in Africa, and he listed their deprivations and degradations in the "Green Pamphlet," which marked the start of his broader social activism work. In his household, he stopped using the service of an Untouchable and forced his family to do latrine and other "scavenger" duties themselves. In 1901, he visited India to attend the Indian National Congress, which mainly was concerned with the needs of upper-caste Hindus. Once again, he was offended at the treatment of Untouchables and the conditions of third-class travel.[14]

➤ **Stage 7:** In 1904, Gandhi founded the Phoenix Farm community, where he lived simply and published the *Indian Opinion* weekly newspaper (published continuously until 1961), which both expanded and refined his social justice movement. Gandhi summed up the community credo: "That the good of the individual is contained in the good of the all; that a lawyer's work has the same value as a barber's inasmuch as all have the same right of earning a livelihood from their work." Thus, everyone at Phoenix Farm received the same basic living wage, but Gandhi needed to practice law in Johannesburg to sustain the farm and the newspaper. He notably declared, "I am now a stranger to fear."[15]

This abbreviated list of some of Gandhi's early achievements indicates his quick movement up the Spectrum. But at this point in his spiritual journey, Gandhi's own words reveal his state of consciousness best:

*Words like aparigraha (non-possession) and samabhava (equality)
gripped me. ... How was one to divest oneself of all possessions?
Was not the body itself possession enough? ... Was I to destroy all
the cupboards of books I had? ... Straight came the answer: I could
not follow Him unless I gave up all I had. The meaning of "family"
had but to be slightly widened and the wisdom of my step would
become clear.*[16]

Also by the end of 1906, a long and legendary contest of wills was about to commence between Gandhi and Churchill, who by that time was the British Colonial Undersecretary responsible for Indian affairs in Africa. Strangely, Gandhi and Churchill would meet face-to-face only once. The meeting occurred in November 1906 at Churchill's office in London. It was a short visit, during which Gandhi, on behalf of the Natal Indian Congress, petitioned the British government to rescind new Asiatic and immigration laws that restricted Indian immigration to the Transvaal region of South Africa and required Indians to register, pay fees, and be fingerprinted.[17]

Shortly thereafter in 1907, and in response to British stonewalling, Gandhi launched his first campaign in Africa using a new term **Satyagraha**. This term did not come immediately to Gandhi, who was busy studying his heroes – all of whom used passive resistance and non-violent strategies. He studied: the sermons and sacrifice of Jesus; *Civil Disobedience* (1849) by Henry David Thoreau (1817–1862); *The Kingdom of God Is Within You* (1893) by Leo Tolstoy (1828–1910); and the suffragettes in England who began their voting rights movement in 1903. With the help of a contest won by his cousin Maganlal Gandhi, the term *Satyagraha* was coined as a combination of the Sanskrit words *satya* ("truth") and *agraha* ("firmness"), which together mean "Truth Force."[18]

So began the first official *Satyagraha* campaign in Africa, which lasted eight years. In total, Gandhi would go to jail four times during this campaign, refusing to post bail even when his wife Kasturbai was deathly ill. He wrote her from jail, "If you die, even that death of yours will be a sacrifice to the cause of *Satyagraha*. My struggle is not merely political. It is religious and therefore quite pure. It does not matter much whether one dies in it or lives."[19]

In between his jail sentences, Gandhi continued to negotiate with British officials, both in Africa and during a visit to England. After each negotiation, Gandhi would leave the meeting believing an agreement had been reached, just to have the British revoke their position. It is noteworthy that despite repeated betrayals, every time the British made a "handshake deal" with Gandhi, he trusted them. Gandhi's followers were outraged over British duplicity and some resorted to violence. But Gandhi maintained that total trust in one's adversary doing the right thing is a critical component of the *Satyagraha* strategy.

> *All Satyagrahi bids good-bye to fear. He is therefore never afraid of trusting the opponent. Even if the opponent plays him false twenty times, the Satyagrahi is ready to trust him the twenty-first time, for an implicit trust in human nature is the very creed.*[20]

In December 1913, as the campaign ended its seventh year, Gandhi emerged from jail wearing a *kurta* (tunic) and *dhoti* (loose pants), having now substituted the clothing of his homeland for his western suit.[21] The final showdown was at hand. A court had interpreted the immigration restrictions as invalidating any marriage not documented in Africa, rendering Hindu and Muslim Indian women unmarried under the eyes of the law and their children illegitimate. When Gandhi and the men were jailed, Kasturbai led a women's march, which resulted in her briefly going to jail as well.

This show of force inspired Indian miners to go on strike – a huge boon to the *Satyagraha* movement. Next, white railroad workers went on strike and martial law was declared in South Africa. Gandhi, however, refused to take advantage of the situation and called for a pause in his campaign. The British – amazed at Gandhi's decision not to capitalize on the nationwide chaos – finally agreed to meet most, but not all, of Gandhi's demands. Despite a partial victory, Gandhi ended the *Satyagraha* campaign in June 1914, when the British passed the Indian Relief Act.[22] It was time for Gandhi to return home and shoot for the moon: the independence of India.

Synchronously, Archduke Ferdinand of Austria was assassinated that very same month in 1914. It was not long before Germany jumped into the fray and declared war on Russia (August 1, 1914). Germany then declared war on France (August 3, 1914), and Great Britain declared war on Germany (August 4, 1914). Word War I was in full motion and Hitler, at age twenty-five, was ecstatic:

> *Let Heaven at last give free reign to the fate which could no longer be thwarted. ... The struggle of the year 1914 was not forced on the masses – no, by the living God – it was desired by the whole people. ... [I] fell down on my knees and thanked Heaven from an overflowing heart for granting me the good fortune of being permitted to live at this time. A fight for freedom had begun, mightier than the earth had ever seen; for once Destiny had begun its course, the conviction dawned on even the broad masses ... whether the German nation was to be or not to be.*[23]

Hitler immediately enlisted and spent the next five years assigned to an infantry regiment, spending most of his time behind the front lines. Even so, Hitler was wounded twice and was in the hospital for a second time, temporarily blinded by a British mustard gas attack, when he learned of Germany's defeat. He blamed the defeat on the superior Western propaganda, the "senseless letters" of German women, the munitions strike led by the Social Democratic Party in Germany, and the Jews.[24] The German Revolution coincided with the end of WWI, as socialist revolutionaries overthrew Emperor Wilhelm II and instituted the Weimar Republic, a new parliamentary government.

Unlike the Russian Revolution of 1917, when the reins of government were handed to the *Bolshevik* ("majoritarian") leader Vladimir Lenin (1870–1924), the German people stopped short of implementing a socialist system. Lenin was an admirer of the German and Jewish (by birth) philosopher Karl Marx (1818–1883), who railed against **capitalism** and supported **socialism**.[25] At first, Lenin used **Marxism** to create Soviet Russia, but he soon abandoned the philosophy. Instead, Lenin adopted **communism**, though **totalitarianism** is much closer to what he implemented. Meanwhile, most Germany revolutionaries still favored the socialist views of Marx. However, because the world was in the death throes of an Unraveling, anything and everything was possible.

When WWI ended, Hitler hoped that a new German nationalism would take hold and crush the ethos of Marxism being led by the Social Democratic Party (the "SDP"). The SDP had the most power in the new Weimar Republic (this party would be banned later by Hitler), but there were over a dozen political parties in Germany vying for supremacy, including the German Workers' Party ("DAP" for *Deutsche Arbeiterpartei*), arguably co-founded but later totally co-opted by Hitler, who received party ID card number 555, indicating that he was the fifth member of DAP based on an identification system that started with the number 500 (i.e., to make it look like there were over 500 members).[26]

In February 1920, DAP changed its name to the National Socialist German Workers' Party or Nazi Party. The SDP-led Weimar Republic would stay in power a while longer, but **Nazism** was gaining popularity and power at a fast clip, as was Hitler. By 1921, he firmly was head of the Nazi Party and was called the *Führer* ("Leader") by his followers.

Audaciously, in November 1923, Hitler led an unsuccessful coup against the Weimar Republic, for which he was charged with treason and sent to jail. The Nazi Party was banned after the failed "Beer Hall Putsch," but the incarcerated Hitler had time to write Volume I of his autobiography *Mein Kampf*. After his release from prison in December 1924, Hitler's popularity and power began to soar again. By January 1933, the President of Germany Paul von Hindenburg attempted to pacify the Nazis by appointing Hitler Chancellor of Germany. Thereafter, Hitler was able to pass the Enabling Act, which constitutionally consolidated his political power and isolated parliament.[27] Another German revolution had begun.

Historians have argued for a century about Hitler's political philosophy, as he articulated it by mixing all manner of patently inconsistent governmental models. Yet throughout his reign, Hitler espoused Stage 4 nationalism as his primary driving force. He also tapped the lingering ethnocentric philosophy of **Pan-Germanism** (a call to Germans throughout Europe) that helped establish the German Empire (1871–1918), which the Weimar Republic replaced. Hitler called this earlier empire the **Second Reich**.

The **First Reich** was Hitler's bombastic reference to the Holy Roman German Empire (962–1806), which started with German Emperor Otto I (a.k.a. Otto the Great). The Roman Empire was long gone, but the name was revived to signify the close nexus between the Kingdom of Germany and the Vatican. Notably, Hitler would modify the imperial banner of the older empire (shown left) , as he built the **Third Reich**.[28]

Hitler streamlined the eagle, added an ancient Hindu symbol – the *sauvastika* – to the Nazi banner and flag, and flipped his new *swastika* in the opposite direction (shown right).[29] He adopted the swastika to connote a German connection to the Aryan (Indo-European) race and to buttress his insane pursuit of "racial purity."

> *What we must fight for is to safeguard the existence and reproduction of our race and our people, the sustenance of our children and the purity of our blood, the freedom and independence of the fatherland, so that our people may mature for the fulfillment of the mission allotted by the creator of the universe. ...*
>
> *Hence it is no accident that the first cultures arose in places where the Aryan, in his encounters with lower peoples, subjugated them and bent them to his will.*[30]

In addition, Hitler utilized Stage 5 slogans, like "will to power," a phrase coined by German philosopher, Friedrich Nietzsche (1844–1900).[31] Though he never directly quoted Charles Darwin (1809–1882), Hitler obviously was aware of, subscribed to, and routinely misapplied "survival of the fittest" dogma.[32] More accurately, though, Hitler believed in survival of the *strongest*, and he imposed physical training on Hitler Youth. He also inculcated the masses with a message of unbounded superiority, while sterilizing the handicapped.

> *Every idea and every achievement is the result of one man's creative force .... [T]he folkish philosophy of life corresponds to the innermost will of Nature .... Thus, in principle, it serves the basic aristocratic idea of Nature and believes in the law down to the last individual. ...*
>
> *We, as Aryans, can conceive of the state only as the living organism of a nationality which ... by the development of its spiritual and ideal abilities leads to the highest freedom. ...*
>
> *[S]elf-confidence must be inculcated in the young national comrade from childhood on. His whole education and training must be so ordered as to give him the conviction that he is absolutely superior to others. ...*
>
> *Those who are physically and mentally unhealthy and unworthy must not perpetuate their suffering in the body of their children.*[33]

Though Hitler amalgamated a few Stage 6 values under his brand of "National Socialism," he took great care to distinguish his political ideas from Social Democracy and Marxism, the philosophies he absolutely despised.

> *When I recognized the Jew as the leader of the Social Democracy, the scales fell from my eyes. ... I gradually became aware that the Social Democratic press was directed predominantly by Jews. ...*
>
> *The Jewish doctrine of Marxism rejects the aristocratic principle of Nature and replaces the eternal privilege of power and strength by the mass of numbers and their dead weight. Thus it denies the value of personality in man, contests the significance of nationality and race, and thereby withdraws from humanity the premise of its existence and its culture.*
>
> *[K]arl Marx ... with the sure eye of the prophet, recognized in the morass of a slowly decomposing world the most essential poisons, extracted them, and, like a wizard, prepared them into a concentrated solution for the swifter annihilation of the ... free nations on earth. And all this in service to his race. ... Marxism itself systematically plans to hand the world over to the Jews.*[34]

Yes, Hitler espoused a strange combination of inconsistent worldviews, which has resulted in much scholarly debate over his actual belief system. Regardless, Stage 3 Nazism evolved into Hitler's own form of **fascism** (also Stage 3 on the Spectrum). Benito Mussolini (1883–1945), Hitler's evil twin, ruled Italy as a fascist dictator, but he started out a fan of Karl Marx, calling him the "greatest of all theorists of socialism."[35]

In fact, most dictators are born using the "language of the people." It is only after fooling the crowds that a dictator feels safe revealing his true nature. It therefore is worthwhile for me to list more examples of how Hitler tricked the German people. I want to ensure that we, as New Humans, are never fooled by the likes of Donald Trump or, God forbid, a more adept populist successor.

First, Hitler learned the socialist vocabulary of his day and then used all manner of effective propaganda to confuse, refocus, and then completely manipulate the beleaguered (and later emboldened) Stage 4 German public. Second, Hitler chose his closest associates very carefully, ensuring that they both feared and worshipped him. Third, Hitler took advantage of the power vacuum created after World War I, when chaos in Germany abounded and people were desperate to have mere sufficiency level needs met. For brevity's sake, here is a quick peek into Hitler's brain and how he twisted all the "isms" in his quest for power.[36]

> ➤ Despite his vocal support of the common man, Hitler undermined unions: "[I] had learned to distinguish between the union as a means of defending the general social rights of the wage-earner and obtaining better living conditions for him as an individual, and the trade union ... one of the most frightful instruments of terror against the security and independence of the national economy, the solidity of the state, and personal freedom."[37]

> ➤ Inconsistent with his argument that Germans were a superior people, he ridiculed their ability to manage a democracy: "The Western Democracy of today is the forerunner of Marxism. ... Can a fluctuating majority of people ever be made responsible in any case? ... Does anyone believe that the progress of this world springs from the mind of majorities and not from the brains of individuals? ... By rejecting the authority of the individual and replacing it by the numbers of some momentary mob, the parliamentary principle of majority rule sins against the aristocratic principle of Nature ...."[38]

➢ He also ridiculed the German people's ability to recognize propaganda and – *wait for it* – fake news: "To whom should propaganda be addressed? To the scientifically trained intelligentsia or to the less educated masses? It must be addressed always and exclusively to the masses. ... All propaganda must be popular and its intellectual level must be adjusted to the most limited intelligence among those it is addressed to. ... The receptivity of the great masses is very limited, their intelligence is small ... all effective propaganda must be limited to a very few points and harp on these in slogans ...."[39]

➢ In order to provide for the German people, Hitler favored territorial expansion (i.e., war) over economic competition (i.e., capitalism): "Thus there remained but two ways of securing work and bread for the rising population ... either new soil could be acquired ... or we could ... produce for foreign needs through industry and commerce .... The National Socialist movement must strive to eliminate the disproportion between our population and our area – viewing this later as a source of food as well as a basis for power politics. ... State boundaries are made by man and changed by man." Moreover, Hitler arrogantly let it be known that he planned to invade France and Russia, clearly articulating his goals in Volume II of *Mein Kampf*.[40]

➢ Lastly, Hitler employed the term "spirituality" to sweeten some of his most vicious and heinous arguments. In the following passage, he asserts that spiritual ideas are immune to force but that violence is effective when used to buttress a valid spiritual cause: "The application of force alone, without the impetus of a basic spiritual idea as a starting point, can never lead to the destruction of an idea and its dissemination .... Only in the steady and constant application of force lies the very perquisite of success. This persistence, however, can always and only arise from a definite spiritual conviction. Any violence that does not spring from a firm, spiritual base, will be wavering and uncertain."[41]

Let us now purify ourselves and pick up where we left off with Gandhi. In January 1915, at the start of WWI and at the age of forty-four, Gandhi arrived home to a glorious reception. The *Satyagraha* campaigns in Africa had made him famous, and he was duly received by prominent members of the Indian National Congress ("INC"). He also was given the title Mahatma ("Great Soul") by the Indian Nobel Prize winning poet Tagore Rabindranath. Even so, Gandhi was pensive and rightly concerned about the war. Moreover, his health had been strained during the Africa campaign, and he was ready for a period of reflection.

As the worldwide conflagration of violence commenced, Gandhi's views started to shift regarding how to achieve Indian self-rule while also maintaining his obligations to the British Empire. When his mentor Gopal Gokhale, leader and former President of the INC, advised him to take a year off to travel and reacquaint himself with his homeland, Gandhi agreed.[42]

The **Indian National Congress** was the most powerful political force for the native people. Established in 1885, the INC initially was a forum and political party for addressing the needs of upper-caste Indians. By 1907, however, the INC was split between the moderates led by Gokhale, who advocated for home rule within the British Empire, and a liberal wing that sought complete independence. By the time Gandhi returned home in 1915, the liberals were gaining ground, but INC members differed on what strategies to employ to gain independence – a question Gandhi would resolve with *Satyagraha* campaigns that only he had the authority to initiate.[43]

In addition, radical Muslim members of the INC had broken off to form their own party, the **Muslim League**. The League also wanted independence, but their goal was the division of India into two nations – India and Pakistan. The British took advantage of these different goals with policies intended to "divide and conquer" the united independence movement that Gandhi wished to lead.[44] The INC and Gandhi opposed the creation of two separate countries, and the schism between the Hindu and Muslim Indians would be a constant source of agitation during the remainder of Gandhi's life. Indeed, this schism, ultimately, would end Gandhi's life.

Recognizing that the scope of this text does not permit a full recitation of all Gandhi's strategies and achievements, a summary will have to suffice, particularly since the goal of this chapter is to analyze the very nature of polarity. In summary then, Gandhi established his Satyagraha Ashram along the banks of the Sabarmati River in Ahmedabad – a site he purposely chose due to its proximity (four miles) from the local jail. When his period of reflection was at an end, Gandhi engaged in a series of preparatory, regional campaigns to: remove custom fees when crossing between Indian principalities and Raj controlled territories (1917); gain higher wages for indigo farm workers (1917) and millworkers (1918); and obtain tax remission for farmers devastated by crop failures (1918). Notably during these early campaigns, Gandhi began to utilize fasting as a tool to affect public opinion.

[W]hile I was still groping and unable to see my way clearly, the light came to me. Unbidden and all by themselves the words came to my lips: "Unless the strikers rally ... and continue the strike till a settlement is reached ... I will not touch any food."

The laborers were thunderstruck. Tears began to course down [their] cheeks. The laborers broke out, "Not you but we shall fast. It would be monstrous if you were to fast. Please forgive us." ...

"There is no need for you to fast. ... As for my fast, it will be broken only after the strike is settled."[45]

When World War I ended in 1918, Gandhi considered a larger *Satyagraha*, though he was unsure if the masses were ready for a nationwide movement. He lost some credibility with the INC and the public when, as the Germans approached England at the end of WWI, he felt compelled to assist the war effort and sought to recruit Indian soldiers. Despite great effort, Gandhi was able to garner only fifty new recruits.

I feel ashamed that since my arrival in India I can show no war work .... I have an idea that if I became [Great Britain's] recruiting agent-in-chief, I might rain men on you. ... I would make India offer all her able-bodied sons as a sacrifice at this critical moment ... and I know that India, by this very act, would become the favored partner in the Empire, and racial distinctions would become a thing of the past. ...

You cannot teach ahisma [non-violence] to a man who cannot kill. ... I do not say, "Let us go and kill the Germans." I say, "Let us go and die for the sake of India and the Empire."

I am absolutely right ... in calling upon every Indian to join the army ... for the sake of learning not to fear death.[46]

Thus, at the end of World War I, Gandhi still expressed loyalty to the British Empire. He therefore favored home rule for India as a separate nation under "Dominion" status within the Empire, the same status that Canada, South Africa, Australia, and New Zealand had at the time. In response to the mounting power of the INC and global public opinion, the British Parliament passed the Government of India Act of 1919, which created a "Diarchy," where certain legislative and administrative functions were turned over to the Indians. The Act met many of Gandhi's demands and was a step toward Dominion status. However, the British also passed laws that allowed judges to convict Indians without a jury and indefinitely sentence suspected terrorists (FYI: just like the U.S. Patriot Act). Gandhi and the INC objected, as did the Muslim League, resulting in further chaos and violence in India.[47]

In August 1920, Gandhi launched his first nationwide *Satyagraha* campaign for *swaraj* (Indian independence). In a surprise move intended to keep the Muslims united with the INC, Gandhi focused on the British treatment of the Ottoman Empire, which was being sliced and diced amongst the WWI allies.[48] His unification strategy with the Muslims worked for a while, so Gandhi felt it was time to ask the masses to engage in *hartal* – a multi-staged plan of non-cooperation (e.g., refusal to work and go to school, commercial boycotts, and tax resistance).[49] Gandhi boldly stated that if his tactics were followed, India would have her independence within a year. Moreover, Gandhi's language had reached fever pitch due to the massacre at Amritsar, where 379 unarmed civilians were brutally slaughtered by a WWI British general newly assigned to India.[50]

> *You may hang us on the gallows, you may send us to prison, but you will get no cooperation from us. ... The British Empire today represents Satanism and has been guilty of such terrible atrocities that ... unless it so apologized, it was the duty of every Indian to destroy it. ... Let me not be misunderstood. Strength does not come from physical capacity. It comes from an indomitable will.*
>
> *Where there is only a choice between cowardice and violence, I would advise violence ... But I believe that non-violence is infinitely superior ....*[51]

Sadly, the *hartal* did lead to Indian violence, after which Gandhi called off the *Satyagraha* movement and took to a penance fast. After thus atoning for the sins of his followers (and himself?), he started to wear his iconic loincloth, as a symbol of his continued service to humanity, to honor the dead (British and Indian), and to support the thirty thousand people who had been jailed.

In 1922, Gandhi was sentenced to six years in jail on the charge of sedition to which he plead guilty. However, he was released after two years due to his failing health.[52] Here is a sample of Gandhi's seditious writing, in which he practically begged to be arrested:

> *Sedition has become the creed of Congress. ... Non-cooperation, through a religious and strictly moral movement, deliberately aims at the overthrow of the government, and is therefore legally seditious. ...*
>
> *We are challenging the might of this government because we consider its activity to be wholly evil. We want to overthrow the government ... to show that the government exists to serve the people, not the people the government. ...*

[T]his British Empire ... cannot live if there is a just God ruling the universe. ... It is high time that the British people were made to realize that the fight that was commenced in 1920 is a fight to the finish.[53]

For the next two decades, Gandhi continued to lead the INC, though he accepted the role of president only once in 1924, after his release from jail. Unlike Hitler, Gandhi was averse to titles of power, preferring instead to unofficially and spiritually assist from the sidelines. In truth, though, Gandhi maintained close control over the INC leaders, who rarely made a move without his assent. He also drafted a new INC Constitution, which served to organize the congress and consolidate power positions of friends within the movement.

To some, Gandhi's tight grip on power was not welcome, and he eventually lost the backing of Muhammed Ali Jinnah (1876–1948), leader of the Muslim League. In fact, some scholars criticize Gandhi for impeding the peaceful resolution of India's independence. His rejection of later compromises would frustrate all concerned, which is why one British negotiator described him as a "saint amongst statesmen" and a "statesmen amongst saints."[54]

Like Hitler, Gandhi understood the value of controlling news content (a.k.a. propaganda). He therefore found time to manage various newspapers, including the *Bombay Chronicle*, *Young India*, and *Navajivan* (still in operation as a publishing house). Thus, he used news outlets to spread his lofty opinions – Second Tier solutions for a First Tier world.

He also bargained masterfully with eight successive Viceroys of India. These local rulers were just as powerful, if not more, than the Prime Minister, since they occupied nearly total control over India and did not (routinely) answer to Parliament. Moreover, the Viceroys were treated like royalty in India. The Viceroy's residence was larger than the Palace of Versailles, had a footprint of more than four acres, contained 340 rooms, and utilized a service staff of 600 people, plus 400 gardeners.[55] Just picture Gandhi in his loincloth walking barefoot to the Viceroy's residence for one of their many meetings.

Despite Gandhi's prediction in 1920 that the British would come to heel within a year, negotiations over Dominion status and, later, Indian rule continued to drag on. With faith and determination, Gandhi kept pressure on the British, staying true to his Muslim unity position. By 1929, Gandhi had changed his mind about Dominion status and sought total independence.[56]

Next, Gandhi drafted the *Purna Swaraj* (Declaration of Independence) for India, and he designed a new flag in preparation for declaring an Indian

Independence Day on January 16, 1930.[57] He then led the Salt March in an effort to end the salt tax and the abominable prohibition against natives making salt (1930). He also travelled to England to continue negotiations and to globally promote the movement via the international press (1931). In the process, he completely exasperated his primary opponent, Winston Churchill:

> It is alarming and also nauseating to see Mr. Gandhi, a seditious Middle Temple lawyer, now posing as a fakir [religious ascetic] of a type well-known in the East, striding half naked ... to parley on equal terms with the representative of the King-Emperor.[58]

Despite Churchill's rants, the British Parliament passed the India Act of 1935, a plan to grant India Dominion status and provide separate electorate positions for the fractured minorities.[59] But to Gandhi, the separate districts for "Depressed Classes" was a major stumbling block, even though the Muslims, Christians, Sikhs, and Untouchables all sought such protections.[60] Gandhi simply could not find it in his heart to view humanity in "memes" – as we have done throughout this text – but neither could he find a way to placate all the disparate interests. So he decided to fast "unto death" to convince the Untouchables not to accept the deal being offered by the British. Days later he broke his fast when a compromise position was reached and upper-caste Hindus opened their temples to the *Harijans* ("children of God"), Gandhi's new word for the Untouchables. Notably, Gandhi had adopted a *Dalit* (Untouchable) daughter years earlier at the start of the Satyagraha Ashram.[61]

By bending the will of minority leaders and the INC, Gandhi created more resentments and, as a result, he stepped back from politics for a while. Importantly, 1935 also was the year that Mussolini invaded Abyssinia and Hitler broke the WWI Treaty of Versailles. Hitler then remilitarized Germany, occupied Austria, and partitioned Czechoslovakia. Like Gandhi, Churchill was out of favor and his dire warnings about Hitler were being ignored, due, in part, to his violent speeches against the Hitler partition "appeasement" and his verbal attacks on Gandhi and the India Act. In fact, Gandhi agreed with Churchill that peace had been preserved with Hitler, but at the "price of honor."[62]

With relationships frayed, the INC eventually rejected what they perceived to be Gandhi's obfuscation, and they started to play ball with the British and participate in the new Indian Congress that was established by the Act of 1935. But the rift with the Muslim League widened, as their members did not pick up many seats in the new congress.[63]

As time and tensions wore on, Gandhi inserted himself whenever he felt he was needed. Even so, he was beginning to comprehend that his followers might not be capable of true *Satyagraha* – a sad but honest commentary on the state of humanity at that time. Indeed, Gandhi was about to make a "Himalayan miscalculation" (his words) in pushing his Stage 4 followers to engage in Second Tier sacred activism.

> [I] *had begun to have a dim perception of my mistake. ... [I]t suddenly dawned upon me that I had committed a grave error in calling upon the people ... to launch upon civil disobedience prematurely, as it now seemed to me. ...*
>
> *Before one can be fit for the practice of civil disobedience one must have rendered a willing and respectful obedience to the state laws. ... A Satyagrahi obeys the laws of society intelligently and of his own free will, because he considers it to be his sacred duty to do so. It is only when a person has thus obeyed the laws of society scrupulously that he is in a position to judge as to which particular rules are good and just and which unjust and iniquitous. Only then does the right accrue to him of the civil disobedience of certain laws in well-defined circumstances. ...*
>
> *I had called on the people to launch upon civil disobedience before they had thus qualified for it, and this mistake seemed to me of Himalayan magnitude. ... [I]t would be necessary to create a band of well-tried, pure-hearted volunteers who thoroughly understood the strict conditions of Satyagraha.*[64]

What Gandhi was starting to realize is that evolution is a painfully slow process that can regress under stress. It also takes extreme dissonance for a person to substitute a new world view on the Spectrum of Consciousness. As a result, periods of intense crisis and chaos, such as World War II, present both breeding and burial grounds for the collective human experience. In addition, Fourth Turnings superbly highlight the polarity of the Earth Plane.

THE LAST FOURTH TURNING: WORLD WAR II

The last Fourth Turning exploded in September 1939, when Hitler invaded Poland and started World War II. Germany then invaded Denmark and Norway in the spring of 1940, which was the last signal Great Britain needed to pull Churchill back into service. He became Prime Minister in May 1940, a time when Gandhi was writing letters to Hitler, a topic we will explore shortly. Gandhi was now seventy years old.

During the run-up to WWII, another fascist dictator, Francisco Franco, had emerged as the leader of the Spanish Revolution (1936), and Japan already was at war with China (1937). Germany invaded France in June 1940, and declared war on both France and Great Britain, and in July, the Nazis began bombing England. Then in June 1941, the Germans invaded the Soviet Union, and in December that same year, the Japanese bombed Pearl Harbor, which caused the United States to officially join the fray. The entire world was witnessing a stunning display of the God Game, as Stage 3 fascism challenged Stage 4 nationalism and Stage 5 democracy to a death match.

The primary Axis Powers on Team Dark included Germany, Japan, Italy, Hungary, Slovakia, Romania, and Spain (operating behind the scenes). The primary Allied Powers on Team Light included Great Britain, Poland, France, China, the Soviet Union, and the United States. Moreover, because Great Britain was at war, all its Dominion and commonwealth status countries were at war, including Australia, Canada, South Africa, and India.

With the advent of war, Gandhi waffled a bit but then held his classic view that Indians should support the war effort though non-violent service.[65] The INC leaders, on the other hand, wanted to press what they saw as an advantage: They would promise the British military support in exchange for immediate and full independence. Gandhi acquiesced to the INC demands and the answer came quickly from Churchill: There would be no negotiations while England fought for its very existence.[66] As Gandhi had warned, trying to take advantage of an adversary under such circumstances is unfair and will produce bad *karma* (my words). Though Gandhi encouraged Indians not to fight in the war, support actually began to increase, and Indian soldiers would soon prove instrumental in winning WWII.

Meanwhile, support for Indian independence was growing worldwide. In fact, President Franklin Delano Roosevelt let it be known to Churchill that the Atlantic Charter (an agreement signed by the Allies in 1941 and a precursor to NATO) meant freedom from the Axis Powers for all Allies, including India.[67]

In 1942, when the Soviet Union was on the defensive and Singapore and then Burma were lost, Churchill worried about the Asian front and decided to address the India question again. He wanted to make the trip to India himself but the war effort, which was dire at the time, prevented him from going. So he sent an emissary to offer Gandhi full Dominion status at the conclusion of the war and the right to draft India's constitution, but with a proviso that provinces could elect out of the union. Famously, Gandhi called the offer a "post-dated check on a failing bank."[68]

Muslim leader Jinnah was ecstatic, however, as the offer seemed to fulfill the League's dream of a separate Pakistan. As a result, Gandhi felt boxed in and bitter toward the British, who he felt had betrayed his trust again. So he decided to go for broke with a new *Satyagraha* – the "Quit India" movement.

> *I waited and waited, until the country should develop the non-violent strength necessary to throw off the foreign yoke. But my attitude has now undergone a change. I feel I cannot afford to wait. ... That is why I have decided that even at certain risks which are obviously involved I must ask the people to resist the slavery.*
>
> *I want freedom immediately, this very night, before dawn, it could be had. ... The mantra is: "Do or Die." We shall either free India or die in the attempt; we shall not live to see the perpetuation of slavery.*[69]

The British response was swift, particularly since the Japanese were approaching India. Gandhi and the members of the new All India Congress Committee were arrested and jailed. Sadly, Gandhi's secretary and beloved friend of twenty-five years had a heart attack and died. Riots broke out across India and the British clamped down even more to stop the destruction: over 200 police stations burned; 750 government buildings were destroyed; 2,500 people were killed and wounded; and more than 60,000 people were arrested.[70]

Gandhi's gambit had failed and the Quit India dwindled. Rather than support the independence movement, Indian troops swelled to over 2.5 million men – the largest volunteer army in human history.[71] Churchill triumphantly declared, "We intend to remain the effective leaders of India for a long and indefinite period. ... I have not become the King's first minister in order to preside over the liquidation of the British Empire."[72]

Still imprisoned in 1943, Gandhi had only one tool left: fasting. So to quell the Hindu-Muslim unrest, he embarked on a twenty-one day fast. He nearly died during this fast, as he lost twenty pounds and his kidneys started to fail. His sons came to pay their last respects, but somehow Gandhi managed to survive (there were rumors that glucose was being added to his water).[73]

Tragically, however, his wife Kasturbai soon became sick and she died in February 1944, while the couple was still confined at Aga Khan Palace, a make-shift detention center. A few months after Kasturbai's death, Gandhi was released from prison. At seventy-four years old, this would be Gandhi's last incarceration. In total, he had spent 2,338 days in prison – the equivalent of more than six years (2,089 days in Indian jails; 249 days in African prisons).[74]

Throughout the remainder of World War II, nothing substantial happened in terms of India's independence, though India remained central to the war effort. Japan attacked India in March 1944, but the Indian army rebuffed the offensive. The tide of the war turned again, this time in favor of the Allies. On June 6, 1944, Team Light executed the D-Day plan to take back France – the anniversary cited at the start of this chapter and celebrated by the United States with our WWII Allies. After the Normandy invasion, Germany was on the run. By August, France was liberated, and in September the Soviets captured Yugoslavia. That same month, the Allies reached the German border, and the world waited with bated breath for the war's conclusion.

In January 1945, Hitler moved with senior staff to his *Führerbunker* in Berlin, where he began to exhibit extreme manic-depressive swings, which were not quelled by constant injections of drugs from his physician. On April 16, the Allies reached the outskirts of Berlin, but sadly, Roosevelt died just before the fall of Germany. My grandfather served in WWII and was with the American forces which reached Germany and liberated concentration camps.[75]

Hitler emerged from his bunker for the last time on April 20, 1945, his fifty-sixth birthday. He ordered the complete destruction of all Nazi infrastructure to prevent the Allies from gaining a military boon – an order his staff ignored.[76] On April 28, Mussolini was killed, and on April 30, Hitler committed suicide along with his wife of one day Eva Braun. It is unclear whether Hitler died from a gunshot wound, cyanide, or both. In any event, in accordance with his written instructions, Hitler's body was burned. On May 2, the Russians took Berlin.

At this point, the war was nearly over; only Japan was left. In July, the Allies called for Japan's unconditional surrender. Then shockingly, that same month, the elections in Great Britain went for the Labour Party and against Churchill, and he was replaced as Prime Minster. During a farewell meeting with the Viceroy, he said, "Keep a bit of India."[77] Churchill would proceed to write a five-volume history of WWII and win the Nobel Prize for Literature. He also would be Prime Minster again in 1951.

According to many historians, the Japanese rejected the call for surrender to secure better terms, and continued conventional warfare would have ended WWII in short order. Therefore, what Team Light did next was unnecessary and, based on the current level of our collective consciousness, unthinkable. Nevertheless, the United States dropped atomic bombs on Hiroshima and Nagasaki and killed 140,000 people, 95% of whom were civilians. On August 14, 1945, Japan surrendered and WWII came to an end. Robert Oppenheimer, the director of the Manhattan Project, admitted that the bomb was used on "an essentially defeated enemy."[78] Shame on Team Light.

Yet that shame pales in comparison to the savagery of the Nazis, which was ignored, in large measure, despite widespread reports of concentration and death camps throughout the duration of the war.[79] Indeed, Pope Pius XII (1876–1958) was asked repeatedly to intervene on behalf of the Jews but did and said nothing. Thankfully, Pope Francis has put an end to the attempted canonization of this coward for Christ.[80]

In addition, a detailed report entitled, "The Mass Extermination of Jews in German Occupied Poland" was submitted in November 1942 to the newly created **United Nations** (est. January 1942) – three years before the end of the war. Thus, the world knew the Nazis were committing unparalleled atrocities, even though it took time to fully assess the horror. Conservative estimates – *not counting battle field deaths* – enumerate that Hitler was responsible for:

➢ The mass murder of approximately 18 million people in total, including: political prisoners, prisoners of war, labor camp victims, death march victims, uncooperative civilians, certain religious groups, disabled people, gay men, and Jews.[81]

➢ The genocide of nearly six million Jews, which was roughly 2/3 of the European Jewish population and 1/3 worldwide.

➢ Forced euthanasia of 250,000 handicapped persons.

➢ Medical experimentation on over 7,000 people.

➢ Sterilization of at least 300,000 people.

Soviet Union POWs at Nazi Mauthausen Concentration Camp in Austria[82]

When World War II ended, the final push for India's independence erupted into violence, with Gandhi sitting on the sidelines at his spinning wheel. The INC leaders sought him out, however, often meeting with him as he spun.[83] By the start of 1946, Great Britain was ready to hand over India and, in fact, was eager to do so. A delegation was sent to India to arrive at a final settlement, referred to as the "Cabinet Mission."[84]

The Cabinet Mission proposal was crafted by Jawaharlal Nehru (1889–1964), newly elected President of the INC, and Jinnah, long-time leader of the Muslim League. At first, Jinnah stalled the talks, but the Muslim League agreed to the proposal at the last minute. Then Gandhi refused to endorse the plan because he still insisted on a united India.[85] In total frustration, Jinnah declared "Direct Action Day" on August 16, 1946, which is when all hell broke loose:

> *The apostle of nonviolence had said more than once that he preferred anarchy to slavery; his sabotaging of the Cabinet Mission plan was about to fulfill that wish. ...*
>
> *Winston Churchill also shares the blame. For more than a decade he had fought to delay the inevitable transfer of power, sowing distrust and allowing bitter resentment to fester. ....*
>
> *However, the other person who must bear blame was Gandhi. For the sake of an unrealized ideal, he had undermined the last chance at a peaceful settlement to India's freedom. Indeed, Gandhi's responsibility may run even deeper. His decade and a half of defiance of the law through civil disobedience had bred an atmosphere of contempt for social order .... The sad paradox was that [Gandhi] had consistently, if unintentionally, inspired violence by others. His fasts became potent weapons not because of his moral stature but because of fear that his death would set off riots across India. ...*
>
> *Jinnah had envisioned the Day of Action as a series of Congress-style protests, boycotts, and hartals. Instead, August 16 set off three days of massacres in Calcutta, where Muslim and Hindu mobs clashed in a bloodbath. More than 5,000 were murdered and another 15,000 were injured, while 100,000 were made homeless, many of them Muslims. Four battalions of British troops spent days carrying away the mutilated bodies, many of them women and children.[86]*

Frankly, it is a minor miracle that Gandhi was able to lead effectively for as long as he did, given that most of his followers possessed a Stage 4 consciousness and could not comprehend his Second Tier perspective. Thus, it was predictable that the Muslim Indians would insist on a separate nation and that Untouchables, ill-treated for millennia, would seek separate constitutional protections. What is surprising, however, is Gandhi's initial reaction to the unfolding carnage. Twelve days into the crisis, the British approached Gandhi for his assistance in calming the situation, to which he replied, "If India wants her bloodbath she shall have it."[87]

Vultures feeding on dead bodies in Calcutta after "Direct Action Day"[88]

The violence continued for almost two months before Gandhi finally intervened. By then, Muslim gangs were attacking Hindu villages, murdering and raping victims. Over 50,000 Hindus were dispossessed of their homes. Similarly, Hindus were ravaging Muslim neighborhoods. Eventually, Gandhi headed for Calcutta to confer with Nehru. Upon his arrival, Gandhi was heard to exclaim, "I am groping for light. I am surrounded by darkness."[89]

In short, just as the Team Light's military generals had made an inhumane error by bombing Japan, now Gandhi, another leader for Team Light, had blundered. Such mistakes often occur during Fourth Turnings in the God Game – a blurring of lines between Light and Dark – as the pendulum of polarity seeks to find and eventually regain equilibrium.

Resorting to the only tool left him, Gandhi decided to fast once again, since for Gandhi the Light was accessible through the penance of bodily suffering. He once declared, "I never feel so happy as when I am fasting for the spirit."[90] But he quickly ended the fast and headed for Calcutta to witness the destitution.

Thereafter, he travelled to over fifty desecrated villages, all the while hoping to find a solution that would extinguish the religious tensions.

In 1947, the last British Viceroy arrived in India, Louis Prince Mountbatten (1900–1979). His mission was simple: Wind up the transfer of India by June 1, 1948. Gandhi was invited to meet the Viceroy in March, but their meeting was inconsequential, since Gandhi still refused to agree to the partitioning of India. He did, however, suggest that the Muslim leader Jinnah be the first president of a united India, a last-minute move that the INC found intolerable. In fact, Nehru no longer sought Gandhi's advice, and Gandhi left the INC feeling despondent.

> *My Life's work seems to be over. I hope God will spare me further humiliation. ... I shall perhaps not be alive to witness it, but should the evil I apprehend overtake India and her independence be imperiled, let posterity know what agony this old soul went through thinking it. Let it not be said that Gandhi was a party to India's vivisection."* [91]

Meanwhile, Churchill was secretly communicating with Jinnah, hoping to preserve a "bit of India" by cozying up to the Muslim faction, which now was certain to obtain the new country of Pakistan.[92] On June 3, a deal was reached by Nehru and Jinnah for the bifurcation of India, which they announced together and to the world that evening by radio. Colonial India was at an end. India would be partitioned into two nations within that many months. After 250 years of rule, the British left on August 14, 1947 – the second anniversary of Japan's surrender – an earlier than anticipated withdrawal date chosen by Viceroy Mountbatten.

The next day, Nehru raised a new India flag in Delhi (a different flag than Gandhi had designed). Gandhi did not participate in the celebration, preferring instead to stay in Calcutta and continue easing religious tensions. Nonetheless, the violence continued as millions of Hindus, Muslims, and Sikhs were on the move, scrambling to reach the border of the country where they wanted to live. By September, in a further attempt to establish peace, Gandhi vowed to "fast unto death." He broke the fast after four days, when the fighting in Calcutta ended.[93]

By January 1948, the situation had gotten even worse. The area of Kashmir was a principality that both India and Pakistan wanted. Though predominantly Muslim, this region was ruled by a Hindu prince who had not decided yet which country to join. After a Muslim raid, the prince asked to join India and the first war between India and Pakistan ensued.[94]

In addition, turmoil in Delhi recommenced, leading Gandhi to declare his last fast – a dangerous proposition now that he was seventy-eight years old. On national radio, Gandhi said, "I shall terminate the fast when peace has returned to Delhi .... My sole guide, even dictator, is God, the infallible and omnipotent. ... I am in his hands."[95] Despite kidney failure, Gandhi survived the five-day fast, stopping when he received assurances the violence had ended. In total, more than 400,000 people had been killed in India and Pakistan. As Churchill pointed out, that was more than the losses of the British Empire during WWII.[96]

After his fast, Gandhi penned a first draft of India's new Constitution, he held public prayer vigils, and he received visits from international journalists.[97] When a bomb exploded near his prayer site, an indication he might be the target of an assassin, Gandhi made light of it to one of his female helpers, saying, "I wish I might face the assassin's bullet while lying in your lap and repeating the name Rama [avatar of the Hindu god Vishnu] with a smile on my face."[98]

Tragically, this came to pass on January 30, 1948. As Gandhi approached the garden where he held his prayer sessions, a man advanced through the crowd and shot him three times in his stomach and chest. Before he died, Gandhi uttered, "Hai Rama! Hai Rama!" and then fell into the arms of his female assistants.[99] Synchronously, Churchill was buried 17 years later to the day, on January 30, 1965. The night of Gandhi's death, Nehru spoke on national radio. His speech is worth remembering:

> *Our beloved leader, Bapu as we called him, the father of our nation is no more. ... The light has gone out, I said, and yet I was wrong. For the light that shone in this country was no ordinary light. The light that has illumined this country for these many years will illumine this country for many more years, and a thousand years later that light will still be seen in this country, and the world will see it and it will give solace to innumerable hearts. For that light represented the living truth, and the eternal man was with us with his eternal truth reminding us of the right path, drawing us from error, taking this ancient country to freedom.*[100]

Gandhi's murderer was a Hindu of the *Brahmin* (highest) caste, who was enraged by the partition of India. He was bitter that Gandhi had shown such deference to the Muslim faction, and he blamed Gandhi for the concessions made to Jinnah, their leader.[101] Ironically, the assassin alluded to the *Bhagavad Gita* during his trial, the same holy text that Gandhi cherished. The assassin maintained that Gandhi misunderstood the message of the *Gita*, which depicts an epic battle between warring tribes and provides guidance on ethical duties during times of war. He rightly pointed out that the Hindu God Krishna advises the protagonist Arjuna to do battle, even against his kinsmen, because it is his duty to protect his people against an aggressor. He then went on to opine:

> *In condemning history's towering warriors ... Gandhi has merely exposed his self-conceit. He was, paradoxically as it may appear, a violent pacifist who brought untold calamities on the country in the name of truth and non-violence ....*
>
> *[W]hen he returned to India he developed a subjective mentality under which he alone was to be the final judge of what was right or wrong. If the country wanted his leadership, it had to accept his infallibility; if it did not, he would stand aloof from Congress and carry on his own way. ... Thus the Mahatma became the judge and jury in his own cause. ...*
>
> *Gandhi is being referred to as the father of the nation. ... He proved to be the father of Pakistan. His inner voice, his spiritual power and his doctrine of non-violence of which so much has been made of, all crumbled before Jinnah's iron will and proved to be powerless.*[102]

LEGACIES AND LESSONS

With utmost respect, I cannot help but wonder whether Gandhi might have attained his goal of a unified India if he knew the Spectrum of Consciousness. By the end of his life, Gandhi grasped the ethnocentric fears, compulsions, and prejudices of his followers (Hindus, Muslims, Sikhs, and Untouchables), yet he minimized these dangers, choosing instead to rely on his faith in humanity. Clearly, his goals were worldcentric and pluralistic, which makes them admirable from a Second Tier perspective. But they were unrealistic, given that his average devotee was impoverished, uneducated, and nowhere near Stage 6 on the Spectrum – the threshold of a New Human. Like Jesus, Gandhi was hampered by the fact that his audience was capable of catching only glimpses of his message, his meaning, and his Light.

> *I had realized early enough in South Africa that there was no genuine friendship between the Hindus and Musalmans. I never missed a single opportunity to remove obstacles in the way of unity. ... [I]t would be on the question of Hindu-Muslim unity that my ahimsa would be put to its severest test .... Every moment of my life I realize God is putting me on trial.*[103]

Conversely, Hitler understood his audience well – another ethnocentric but more homogenous Stage 4 people. The Germans had been beaten down and humiliated during World War I. Thus, while Hitler had ideological and political factions to contend with, he wasn't forced to deal with racial or religious factions, which made his mission easier than Gandhi's.

Hitler had another distinct advantage over Gandhi in terms of leading a mass movement. Gandhi's success depended on reducing religious tension, but it served Hitler's purpose to exacerbate it. By singling out and treating the Jews as Germany's "Untouchables," Hitler utilized Stage 4 prejudice in his favor. He had a powerful weapon in his pocket that Gandhi didn't have (and never would have used anyway). Hitler was asking his followers to be "less than" healthy Stage 4 adults. He coaxed Germans into surrendering to the shadow underbelly of the Orange meme or, better yet, regressing to Red. Gandhi, on the other hand, was asking his followers to be "more than" their set point. Essentially, he sought to inspire them to ascend the Spectrum – and not by just one but two full stages!

Such a huge shift in consciousness is improbable. Remember, there is no leap-frogging on the Spectrum of Consciousness, no short cuts. Rather, each of us must wrestle with dissonance on our own. At best, Gandhi helped Indians grow "horizontally" by widening their concept of family, comradery, and love. But to ask them to "vertically" ascend from a Stage 4 to Stage 6 worldview was not feasible, given the terror of the last Fourth Turning and the fact that many First Tier souls backslide under the stress.

With similar naiveté, Gandhi felt it was worthwhile to write Hitler, hoping to pull him up the Spectrum. In 1939, Gandhi wrote:

> *Dear Friend,*
>
> *Friends have been urging me to write to you for the sake of humanity. ... It is quite clear that you are today the one person in the world who can prevent a war which may reduce humanity to the savage state. Must you pay that price for an object however worthy it may appear to you to be? Will you listen to the appeal of one who has deliberately shunned the method of war not without considerable success?*[104]

Then in 1940, Gandhi tried again:

> *Dear Friend,*
>
> *[W]e have no doubt about your bravery or devotion to your fatherland, nor do we believe that you are the monster described by your opponents. But your own writings and pronouncements ... leave*

no room for doubt that many of your acts are monstrous and unbecoming of human dignity ....

We resist British Imperialism no less than Nazism. ... We seek to convert them, not to defeat them on the battlefield. ... We have found in non-violence a force which, if organized, can without doubt match itself against a combination of all the most violent forces in the world. ... It can be used ... without the aid of science of destruction which you have brought to such perfection. ...

You are leaving no legacy to your people of which they would feel proud. They cannot take pride in a recital of cruel deed, however skillfully planned.

I, therefore, appeal to you in the name of humanity to stop the war. ... If you attain success in the war, it will not prove that you were in the right. It will only prove that your power of destruction was greater. ... Is it too much to ask you to make an effort for peace ... for my ears are attuned to hearing the dumb millions?[105]

Hitler never received Gandhi's letters, as they were blocked by the British. Yet the letters indicate a gullibility that Gandhi would not have suffered had he studied Spiral Dynamics. Furthermore, we can guess how Hitler would have responded to the letters, since one of Gandhi's erstwhile INC brethren had escaped British arrest and fled India to meet with Hitler in an attempt to garner German aid in obtaining India's independence. Hitler refused assistance, since he believed Great Britain would never relinquish India, writing, "It is really childish to suppose that men in England cannot correctly estimate the importance of the India Empire for the British world union. ... Indian agitators, however, will never achieve this."[106]

After World War II, when Gandhi was asked about the use of atomic bombs, rather than condemn the United States, he chose to focus on the violence of Hitler, who had been dead for three years but who lingered in Gandhi's thoughts like a ghostly antagonist. The quote is telling, as it shows that Gandhi still was haunted by what might have been had Hitler won the war. The quote also reveals Gandhi's implicit understanding that violence *is* effective, though it may take genocide to triumph, which of course was Hitler's goal.

They claim one atomic bomb changed the entire course of the war and brought an end to the war so much nearer. Has it conquered the Japanese sprit? It has not and it cannot. Has it crushed Germany as a nation? It has not and it cannot. To do that would require resorting to Hitler's method, and to what purpose? In the end it will be Hitlerism that will have triumphed.[107]

Gandhi knew his mission was exceedingly difficult, and he sometimes expressed uncertainty in the face of abject evil. No doubt, he meditated often on the aspects of human nature when considering strategy. His "experiments with truth" and his typical reference to God as "Truth" (as opposed to "Love") indicate that his set point was a Stage 7 perspective, which means he had a systems theory view. Look again at the Spectrum of Consciousness chart in Chapter II, and you will see that absolute Truth is the goal of Indigo, while unconditional and universal Love is the province of Violet. Yet for Gandhi:

> [T]ruth is the sovereign principle .... This truth is not only truth-fulness in word, but truthfulness in thought also, and not only the relative truth of our conception, but the Absolute Truth, the Eternal Principle, that is God.[108]

Moreover, Gandhi openly admitted that he never fully found God nor reached enlightenment. I point this out not to disparage him in any way, but merely to point out that he lacked a more advanced toolset with which to tackle the problems of the early 20th Century.

> [I] worship God as Truth only. I have not yet found Him, but I am seeking after Him. I am prepared to sacrifice the things dearest to me in pursuit of this quest. ... [I] have gone forward according to my light. Often in my progress I have had faint glimpses of Absolute Truth, God, and daily the conviction is growing upon me that He alone is real and all else is unreal.[109]

Why do I suggest that Gandhi never made it past Stage 7? Because there is ample proof. For instance, Gandhi refused to allow his youngest son to marry a Muslim.[110] He periodically referenced his own Aryan superiority.[111] There also was the debate over Gandhi's indifference to dogs, as he caused quite a ruckus when he argued that stray dogs should be shot in the cities.[112] In addition, his positions on procreation and birth control are disturbing by today's standards, as he held fast to the notion that couples should only have sex when they wish children, and he placed the responsibility on the wife to regulate her husband.[113] His disturbing "experiment" was sleeping naked with young women. Though seventy-seven at the time, Gandhi recommitted to *brahmacharya* (chastity), which he viewed as a path to enlightenment. Friends attempted to dissuade him from sleeping with the women (sometimes in a group and sometimes singly). However, Gandhi – who described his new practice as a "bold and original experiment whose heat will be great" – ignored all supplications against it.[114]

I recently discovered that I have not been able to subdue [lust] at all. I don't remember having had an emission wile awake at any time during the last fifty years. I am not referring here to the emission in dreams or those brought on by desire. But I was in such a wretched and pitiable condition that in spite of my utmost efforts, I could not stop the discharge though I was fully awake. ... After the event, restlessness become acute beyond words. ... I keep asking myself: Am I worthy of you all who follow me, am I fit to lead you all? God will answer the question when He pleases.[115]

Now, let us continue the thread concerning juxtaposition between Gandhi and Hitler, Team Light and Team Dark, as there is much ground left to cover. First, while there certainly are stark differences in the techniques used by these men in the pursuit of their respective missions, there also are some awkward similarities, due in part to the era in which they lived:

- ✓ Both Gandhi and Hitler utilized Stage 4 nationalism as their primary ideology with regard to the masses, and both praised Aryanism.
- ✓ Both men owned newspapers to sway the masses and control their messaging (i.e., propaganda), and both wrote autobiographies to record their respective ideologies and gain followers.
- ✓ Both were willing to go to jail, and both prudently used the time in prison to write (i.e., more propaganda).
- ✓ Both concentrated on a primary foe and stigmatized their identified enemies to focus their followers: the Jews in the case of Hitler; the British, in the case of Gandhi (he started using this strategy in 1920, by equating the British Empire with "Satanism").
- ✓ Both subscribed to Social Darwinism, believing that foreign influence was like a disease that had infected the natural evolution and elevation of their people. As Gandhi opined, "the word Disease is applicable to our social as well as our physical condition."[116]
- ✓ Both focused on ethnic/folkish pride, use of the mother tongue, and other instruments of nostalgia to glamourize the past (Gandhi with the spinning wheel and *Khadi* clothing; Hitler with his retro flag design).
- ✓ Both were cultural isolationist and sought ethnic purity/innocence. Gandhi's luddite tendencies went beyond the spinning of cloth to mass transportation: "Formerly, we had natural segregation. ... Railways accentuate the evil nature of man. It may be debatable whether railways spread famine, but it is beyond dispute that they propagate evil."[117]

✓ Both focused on the economic concerns of the common man and the monopolization of money by foreigners: again, the British with Gandhi; with Hitler, the Jews, who he believed infiltrated unions and controlled international banking and commerce.

✓ Both focused on youth: Gandhi prepared the curriculum for the children in his ashrams and forced them to spin thread; Hitler infamously spawned the Nazi Youth training.

✓ Surprisingly, both were vegetarian.

✓ And, most critical for the purpose of the next chapter on the God Game, *both men felt they were on a mission from God.* And for that reason, both Gandhi and Hitler believed only they should call the shots.

Now, let's look at how the two men were different, which will illuminate why one chose to work for Team Light and the other for Team Dark:

o Gandhi had no use for official titles, impressive clothing, or indicia of rank or privilege. He was embarrassed by the "Mahatma" moniker and always walked to work and to meetings. One estimate is that he walked 49,000 miles (the equivalent of walking twice around the Earth).[118]

• Hitler, on the other hand, was absolutely obsessed with his title, the design of the Nazi uniform, and other symbols of power. Moreover, he insisted that deference be shown to him at all times, resulting in a circle of kiss-ass cronies and intimidated loyalists, who never failed to kowtow. The "Night of the Long Knives" in 1934, was especially chilling. Hitler cold bloodedly executed up to one thousand of his SA storm troopers to consolidate power in the SS and German army.

o Gandhi, of course, was repelled by violence and believed it resulted only in temporal power. His goal was a perpetual state of higher consciousness for his people: "There is a law of nature that a thing can be retained by the same means by which it is acquired. A thing acquired by violence can be retained by violence alone, while one acquired by truth can be retained only by truth."[119]

• Hitler embraced violence and thought it was indefinitely sustainable: "The young movement, from the first day, espoused the standpoint that its idea must be put forward spiritually, but that the defense of this spiritual platform must if necessary be secured by strong-arm means." He viewed violence as more than a means to an end. Here he reveals that domination, not building the Third Reich, was his actual goal:

"Thus the basic realization is: that the state represents no end, but a means."[120]

o Gandhi believed that a truly spiritual objective always triumphs, which is why he was certain non-violent resistance would work in all situations. This explains why Gandhi recommended to the Jews that they would persevere if they used his *Satyagraha* strategy. Even after the war, Gandhi held fast to his advice: "Hitler killed five million Jews. It is the greatest crime of our time. But the Jews should have offered themselves to the butcher's knife. They should have thrown themselves into the sea from cliffs. As it is, they succumbed anyway in their millions."[121]

• Conversely, Hitler sought spiritual power through the use of brute force: "The fight against a spiritual power with methods of violence remains defensive, however, until the sword becomes the support, the herald and disseminator, of a new spiritual doctrine."[122]

Lastly, we need to explore the legacy of each man's respective campaign to help us sort out whether it was Gandhi or Hitler who has had the greatest impact on the trajectory of human history. It is now more than one hundred years since the end of WWI and we are fast approaching the 100th anniversary of WWII. Surely, we may draw some valid conclusions on the legacy of each man, which will help us in the next chapter when we do an even deeper dive into polarity.

Let's start with Gandhi, who paved the way for Second Tier consciousness. Along with Gandhi, we must add other thought leaders from the Age of Reason and Age of Enlightenment, such as: Francis Bacon (1561–1626), the father of empiricism who developed the scientific method; Sir Isaac Newton (1642–1727), polymath of the Scientific Revolution; John Locke (1632–1704), dubbed the father of liberalism and possibly the most influential Enlightenment philosopher, as he especially inspired the American Founding Fathers; Voltaire (1694–1778), who championed religious freedom and the separation of church and state; Jean-Jacques Rousseau (1712–1778), who influenced both the French and American revolutions; Emmanuel Kant (1724–1804), who dreamed of a global democracy; Thomas Jefferson (1743–1826), author of the *Declaration of Independence*; James Madison (1751–1836), who composed *The Federalist Papers* and U.S. Constitution; Ralph Waldo Emmerson (1803–1882), father of transcendentalism in the West and, arguably, today's New Age movement; and Leo Tolstoy (1828–1920), one of Gandhi's personal heroes.

The savage recognizes life only in himself and his personal desires. ... The civilized pagan recognizes life not in himself alone, but in societies of men – in the tribe, the clan, the family, the kingdom – and sacrifices his personal good for these societies. ...

The man who holds the divine theory of life recognizes life not in his own individuality, and not in societies ... but in the eternal underlying source of life – in God; and to fulfill the will of God he is ready to sacrifice his individual and family and social welfare. The motor power of his life is love. ...

The whole historic existence of mankind is nothing else than the gradual transition from the personal, animal conception of life to the social conception of life, and from the social conception of life to the divine conception of life. ...

Men on a lower level of understanding, when brought into contact with phenomena of a higher order, instead of making efforts to understand them, to raise themselves up to the point of view from which they must look at the subject, judge it from their lower standpoint, and the less they understand what they are talking about, the more confidently and unhesitatingly they pass judgement on it.[123]

Leo Tolstoy, *The Kingdom of God is Within You*

For those readers who have memorized the Spectrum chart, there is no need to flip back to Chapter II. You already know that Tolstoy's "savage" is Stage 3, his "civilized pagan" is Stage 4, and his man who holds the "divine theory of life" is the type of person we are calling a New Human. Thus, much of Tolstoy's analysis is early Maslow, who would not posit his theory on the Hierarchy of Needs for another fifty years. But what Tolstoy and Gandhi missed in their critique of the human condition are two sad facts later uncovered by Ken Wilber.

First, the challenge is worse than Tolstoy and Gandhi ever imagined. At the beginning of the 20th Century, their lofty goals for humanity were so far above the state of the collective consciousness, they really were trying to explain algebra in Chinese to horses, so to speak. For example, humans in the First Tier (other than Greens) do not grasp a healthy concept of socialism, which explains why Marxism digressed into Red communism and rabid nationalistic socialism rather than Green social democracy.

Second, neither Tolstoy or Gandhi knew what Wilber has been preaching for decades, that humans don't hop-skip into higher memes. It's just not possible, though there is one correlative exception: There exists a sweet spot – somewhere between 10% and 20% of the population – after which a new idea, once adopted and anchored, can create a Tipping Point into a new cosmic groove, which then becomes the next *status quo*. I also need to point out that the Second Tier consciousness Tolstoy was describing is closer to Stage 8 – a full four levels higher than the average ethnocentric person had achieved at the time! Gandhi, on the other hand, was trying to birth New Humans at Stage 6, just two stages higher than their set point, but equally difficult in the end.

Nevertheless, Gandhi's legacy is immense. First, he left huge bread crumbs for prospective New Humans to follow. Second, his direct-action experiments set the stage for other activists to stand on his shoulders and attain spectacular results. Indeed, nearly all of our heroes from the second half of the 20th Century studied and applied Gandhi's blueprint for nonviolent resistance. The distinguished list of *Satyagraha* students includes: Martin Luther King, Jr., Nelson Mandela, Archbishop Desmond Tutu, and Gloria Steinem, to name just a few. Consequently, one of Gandhi's legacies is that he taught Team Light the tactic of using public resistance which, although ineffective against a Stage 3 dictator, does work well on more elevated adversaries.

Specifically, Gandhi's strategy overwhelmed the Stage 5 British overlords because at that level of consciousness, shame works. Rational Yellow tends to be selfish, but not immoral. However, leaders like Hitler, Mussolini, Stalin, and (God save us) Trump, are all immune to shame. The valuable lesson for future movements: *Know what makes your enemy tick* (i.e., where they fall on the Spectrum). This seems like an ideal time, therefore, to chart the political "isms," particularly since we at The Oracle Institute feel duty bound to help lead a strategically smart, progressive movement from the Peace Pentagon.

The below chart underscores Gandhi's "Himalayan miscalculation" in trying to lure Stage 4 ethnocentric people toward Stage 6 pluralism (though it worked for a while since both are "WE" memes). According to Spiral Dynamics, the next plateau for Stage 4 nationalism is Stage 5 rationalism, which is exactly where many Indians are today, as evidenced by their slow but steady rejection of the caste system and their embrace of capitalism. Yet, India still suffers from religious discord between Hindus and Muslims, and misogyny is prevalent, but both scourges will diminish at Stage 5 as well. So today, Yellow is the trending meme in India, but they still have a way to go before Green is anchored and India becomes a nation of New Humans – Gandhi's dream.

The chart also highlights the combined effect of the Gandhi vs. Hitler clash. As previously mentioned, the Democracy Index has dropped for the last fifteen years. Fascism and Nazism have reemerged, though those "isms" have been replaced with more modern terms: totalitarianism and authoritarianism. Note also that Marxism morphed into communism and old-school socialism, not the democratic socialism that Tolstoy described, which is a totally different and more evolved form of governance. Nevertheless, many Americans fear the word "socialism" because it still is associated with Stage 4 countries, thanks in large measure to Hitler and his National Socialist party. May Bernie Sanders help U.S. voters learn the difference.

Governmental Model	Sample Countries	Consciousness of Ruling Class
Fascism/Nazism	Third Reich Germany	Stage 3
Totalitarianism/Dictatorship	North Korea, Syria, Sudan	Stage 3
Absolute Monarchy	Saudi Arabia, Oman	Stage 3
Theocracy	Iran, Afghanistan	Stage 3
Oligarchy (unofficial but real)*	Russia	Stage 3
Communism/Marxist Nationalism	China, Cuba	Stage 3/4
Socialism	Vietnam, Venezuela, Nepal	Stage 4
Constitutional Monarchy	England, Spain, Japan	Stage 5
Parliamentary Republic	Israel, Germany, India	Stage 5
Democratic Republic	United States, Mexico	Stage 5
Democratic Socialism**	Canada, Norway, Sweden	Stage 6
Full Democracy	Switzerland	Stage 6
Regional Federalism	European Union	Stage 6
World Federalism	Non-existent ... as yet	Stage 7

Incidentally, the chart ends with World Federalism because this movement should be on every New Human's radar. Thanks to global activists like Greta Thunberg, people are realizing that planetary problems, like climate change, cannot be solved on a nation-state basis. For instance, it is absurd that Brazil has the "right" to destroy the Amazon Forest, the "lungs" of Earth. Tragically, the United Nations is powerless to solve such situations due to the **Security**

---

* Technically, Russia has a constitution.

** Countries described as "Social Democracies" have different forms of government (e.g., Norway and Sweden are Constitutional Monarchies), but they all share a liberal political philosophy by safeguarding workers' rights, regulating capitalism, protecting the environment, providing universal healthcare, limiting military spending, and legislatively passing other progressive socialist programs. Their citizens enjoy the highest standards of living when measured on various "Happiness" indices.

Council veto possessed by just five nations (the U.S., England, France, Russia, and China). True world democracy is Team Light's vision for the future – not the globalization plan proposed by Team Dark (a.k.a. New World Order). More on this later when we examine some utopian visions for our collective future.

Another legacy of Hitler is remnant anti-Semitism and White Supremacy. In a recent report by the Anti-Defamation League, easy access to supremacist ideology via the internet and social media platforms is propelling a global agenda of anti-Semitic and anti-immigrant hostility and violence by these now networked hate groups.[124] Slogans like "white genocide at the hands of inferior races" is prevalent, and Nazism is making a comeback. The dramatic rise in hate groups is well-known. What is less known is that these groups are now infiltrating the military, encouraging their followers to enlist and targeting existing servicemembers for recruitment."[125] And here's a final Hitler legacy: Today, there still are less Jews in the world than prior to WWII.[126]

POLARIZATION: LIVING IN A DUAL AND DANGEROUS PLANE

Our examination of Gandhi and Hitler reveals that their legacies continue to this day. Who had the greater impact? I leave the reader to decide, though I believe Gandhi's legacy will be the enduring one. In addition, their lives leave us with a veritable "how to manual" on polarization – the conditions which ignite an Unraveling and explode in a Fourth Turning. They shared startling similarities and drastic dissimilarities, which serve to highlight a key point: *The Generals on Team Light and Team Dark attempt to answer the exact same existential questions; they just come to different conclusions.*

Their primary tactics also are different: Team Light encourages absolute Truth, unconditional Love, and the brightest Light to uplift the masses; whereas Team Dark ferrets out short cuts and uses violence to control the masses. The two approaches may best be summed up by this observation: *For Team Dark, the ends justify the means; the reverse is true for Team Light.*

For myself, I have concluded that knowing the Enemy is the most critical component of the God Game, because I firmly believe that "all it takes for evil to prosper is for New Humans to do nothing." Sun Tzu Wu put it this way in *The Art of War*, the oldest military treatise (*circa* 500 BCE), and his classic insight remains valid: "If you know the enemy and know yourself, you need not fear the result of a hundred battles. If you know yourself, but not the enemy, for every victory gained you will also suffer a defeat. If you know neither the enemy nor yourself, you will succumb in every battle."[127]

The next issue is what strategies Team Light should employ to conquer (or at least subdue) evil. Gandhi's *Satyagraha* works well with adversaries at the Stage 5 consciousness and up, but when dealing with a ruthless Stage 3 despot or shadow-crazed Stage 4 nation, more is needed. Just ask Churchill:

> *This wicked man, the repository and embodiment of many forms of soul-destroying hatred, this monstrous product of former wrongs and shame, has now resolved to try to break our famous island race by a process of indiscriminate slaughter and destruction. ... He has lighted a fire which will burn with a steady and consuming flame until the last vestiges of Nazi tyranny have been burnt out of Europe, and until the Old World – and the New – can join hands to rebuild the temples of man's freedom and man's honor, upon foundations which will not soon or easily be overthrown.*[128]
>
> *[We] shall not flag or fail. We shall go on until the end. ... [W]e shall defend our Island, whatever the cost may be .... [W]e shall never surrender, and even if, which I do not for a moment believe, this Island or a large part of it were subjugated and starving, then our Empire beyond the seas, armed and guarded by the British Fleet, would carry on the struggle, until, in God's good time, the New World, with all its power and might, steps forth to the rescue and the liberation of the Old.*[129]

New Humans now have a distinct advantage when confronted with evil: the Spectrum of Consciousness. But Team Light also needs a "Peace Room as sophisticated as a War Room," to quote legendary Barbara Marx Hubbard, who described the similarities and differences between the two. A War Room tracks, maps, and strategizes on how to defeat enemies; whereas a Peace Room scans, maps, connects, and communicates synergistic solutions needed to build the New World.[130] Hubbard was ecstatic that The Oracle Institute was building the Peace Pentagon, where thought leaders for Team Light do just that.

Winston Churchill and his Chiefs of Staff in a War Room

In between the world wars, nations did join in an effort to prevent such an atrocity from ever happening again. The **League of Nations** was formed, but something else important transpired that has been nearly lost to history. First, a global peace movement ensued – the largest to date – led by U.S. suffragettes, who finally had won the right to vote in 1920. Millions of American women were now focused on peace. Second, many people around the world were upset that the League of Nations Charter failed to ban war. Protests broke out, churches joined the movement, as did noteworthy scholars. Republicans and Democrats in the U.S. got on board, as did politicians from around the world. These efforts led to an international treaty called the Kellogg-Briand Pact, which was signed by fifteen nations and theoretically outlawed war in 1928.[131]

However, the Kellogg-Briand Pact failed to prevent World War II, just as the 2010 Strategic Arms Reduction Treaty ("New START") between the U.S. and Russia won't prevent World War III if hegemony by either side increases. Putin said he invaded Ukraine because Russia needs "spheres of influence" (the title of my father's doctoral dissertation). Thankfully, this smokescreen for Putin's megalomania was checked by NATO, which now is assisting Ukraine.

Yet, others say not to worry because humanity, overall, is growing more conscious and less violent. In *The Better Angels of Our Nature*, Harvard professor Steven Pinker makes this very argument, and he provides copious evidence and wonderful graphs to prove his point. Pinker evaluates the epochs of civilization to show that humanity – slowly but surely – is becoming more peaceful. He starts by focusing on the Bible and poking fun at its supposed spiritual messages, pointing out that it contains over six hundred stories describing violent and deadly episodes, including more than one hundred passages in which Yahweh himself gives the command to kill.[132] Indeed, all early cultures adopted an "eye for an eye" sense of jurisprudence, which governed mankind's affairs for thousands of years (irrespective of the Eleventh Commandment imparted by Jesus in the *New Testament*). Anecdote ridden, Pinker's book is a gripping read, as he vividly recounts how various forms of torture were used throughout history both for suppression and sport.

Frankly, it is nigh incomprehensible how barbaric people were just a few hundred years ago, when it was permissible to own slaves, execute adulterers, burn witches, torture heretics (Pinker's descriptions are bloodcurdling), maim thieves (by removing eyes, hands, and tongues), jail debtors, abuse children (perceived as wicked from birth), and torment animals (apparently cat burning was considered entertaining in Paris during the 16th Century).[133] Over time, all these sordid and sadistic acts have been banned.

To further illustrate his point, Pinker adjusted war death counts based on the global population at the time of each war. In other words, to show that the 17th Century actually was more brutal than the 20th Century, which spawned two world wars, he compared death counts to the world's population in 1950 (2.5 billion people). When scaled in this manner, the data shows a downward trend in violence. As it turns out, Pinker's "Top Twenty List" of horrific events places WWI and WWII as the 16th and 9th deadliest wars respectively.

So while the 20th Century was the most lethal in terms of total death, when adjusted for global population, the most violent episode in human history actually occurred in China during the 8th Century. I had never heard of the An Lushan Revolt, a civil war that killed an estimated 36 million people, but it annihilated 66% of the Tang Dynasty and approximately 17% of the world's population! By comparison, 55 million people died in WWII, which equates to 2.2% of the mid-20th Century global population.[134] Even if WWI and WWII are lumped together, the total death count is under 3% of the global population – still a remarkably high number which grows even larger when you add deaths due to the Spanish Flu, the last global pandemic during the last Fourth Turning.

Incidentally, a heartbreaking stat jumped out at me while reading the book. The 7th deadliest event in human history was the genocide of Native Americans, which transpired between the 15th and 19th Centuries and culminated in the death of twenty million indigenous people, the equivalent of 92 million people when planetary population is scaled.[135]

So what exactly has happened since World War II in terms of warfare? The answer is "zero," says Pinker, who calls the last half century the "Long Peace."

> Zero is the number of times that nuclear weapons have been used in conflict. Five great powers possess them, and all of them have waged war. Yet no nuclear device has been set off in anger. ... Zero is the number of times that the two Cold War superpowers fought each other on the battlefield. ... Zero is the number of times that any of the great superpowers have fought each other since 1953. ... Zero is the number of interstate wars that have been fought between countries in Western Europe since the end of World War II. ... Zero is the number of developed countries that have expanded their territory since the late 1940s by conquering another country.[136]

But is Pinker right to have such a rosy view? I'm not so sure, though I was temporarily buoyed by this research. Pinker published his book in 2011, as the current Fourth Turning began. Since then, some of his "zeros" have flipped to positive digits. For instance, it no longer is true that none of the developed countries have increased their territories:

➢ In 2014, Russia invaded Ukraine and annexed Crimea. In 2022, Russia invaded Ukraine again, and that war is ongoing.
➢ As part of its WWII booty, the Russians grabbed islands from Japan and the Japanese now want them back.
➢ In the South China Sea, the Chinese are vying to take multiple islands from the Philippines, as the U.S. Navy monitors the situation.
➢ China also claims Taiwan as part of its Communist state and, while China's takeover of Hong Kong from the British in 1997 was relatively civil, the Chinese are now jailing dissidents and refusing to allow democratic challengers to run for office.

My point is that the current Fourth Turning had not commenced at the time Pinker was writing. He states in his book that he found no cyclical patterns of warfare. Duly noted. Yet, it seems obvious to this author that tensions are rising, indicating that the climax to the current Crisis has yet to come. Meanwhile, mounting millennial factors – such as a shift in the Godhead – are adding to the turbulence of the Great Cusp. In my mind, considering all the unprecedented challenges facing humanity, it seems evident that we are on the verge of a major paradigm shift, one with the power to move us toward the Light ... or crush us.

I'm hardly alone in this assessment. Many historians and political scholars (not to mention economic and environmental experts) are concerned with the rise in authoritarianism and the fifteen-year decline of democracy.

A broad alliance of strange bedfellows ... wants the United States to abandon resistance to rising authoritarian power. They would grant Russia and China the spheres of influence they demand in Europe, Asia and elsewhere. They would acquiesce in the world's new ideological "diversity." And they would consign the democracies living in the shadow of the authoritarian great powers to their hegemonic control. ...

[M]ost Americans appear indifferent, at best. In contrast to their near-obsession with communism during the Cold War, they appear unconcerned by the challenge of authoritarianism. And so, as the threat mounts, America is disarmed. ...

We have been living with the comforting myth that the great progress we have witnessed in human behavior since the mid-20th century, the reductions in violence, in the brutality of the state, in torture, in mass killing, cannot be reversed. ... We insist on believing

there is a new floor below which people and governments cannot sink. But this is just another illusion born in the era that is now passing. Liberalism is all that keeps us, and has ever kept us, from being burned at the stake for what we believe.[137]

Robert Kagan, *"The Strongmen Strike Back"*

We are in the midst of another Fourth Turning and the dramatic conclusion of a Great Cusp. The Gods are changing and powerful nations are being led by Stage 3 autocrats who have vested interests in maintaining the patriarchal Fourth Spiritual Paradigm. America – the shining Light on the hill – is no more. From stress caused by Reagan through Trump, we've witnessed the Spectrum collapse. America's set point used to be Stage 5 rationalism with a dose of trending Green values, but the current disparity of wealth, among numerous factors, has caused many Americans to backslide into Stage 4 nationalism. Compounding this backward spiral is the frustration of Stage 4 folks, some of whom have regressed to Stage 3. When will they learn that the true source of their frustration and fury stems from the hucksters who feed them a cacophony of fake news and fake slogans like "Make America Great Again"?

The net result of this propaganda is socio-spiritual chaos. A solid swath of America and growing numbers around the world now suffer from diminished faculties, dulled senses, and tattered instincts. What's left of the middle-class is hunkering down, attempting to preserve whatever measure of comfort and peace of mind they still possess. The net-net result is increased polarity, since on the other side of this mess are New Humans, who also are frustrated by the tediously slow pace of the evolutionary process – the God Game itself. Some progressives are desperate to help, but they don't know how. Others just "burn one for Bernie" and check-out.

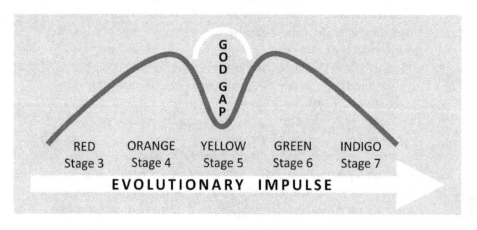

The net-net-net result is that the God Gap keeps getting larger, producing an inverted bell curve of cultural calamities. Commentators on the right and left now routinely opine that the Culture War in the U.S. could result in a civil war. Has polarity reached the point where this actually could happen? Will the enmeshed far-right and far-left reelect Trump (or someone worse)? Will Putin continue to threaten nuclear war and press his Napoleonic westward expansion? Team Light better be ready for such moves. As New Humans, we need to convene quickly in a Peace Room to "scan, map, connect, and communicate" a synergistic plan to win this round of the God Game.

By now, you probably are asking: *What exactly is the God Game?* It is the topic of our next chapter, so get ready. And also take heart. As New Humans, we're ready for the challenge: We've integrated the Spectrum of Consciousness and honestly mapped ourselves, our loved ones, and our culture. We accept that we may witness a Fourth Turning that could reach the same level of magnitude as a civil or world war. And we are not afraid, even though we comprehend that a seasonal Crisis is coinciding with the end of a Great Cusp – the void between the Fourth and Fifth Spiritual Paradigms. Yes, we are primed and we were born for this! And we will fulfill our solemn mission: *To help humanity transition into a New World, a higher order of Truth and Love that is closer to the Light.*

In order to discharge this sacred task, we must be more than Lightholders, more even than Lightworkers. *We need to be Spiritual Warriors.* Why? Because we live on a dual and polarized planet alongside souls who inhabit a vast array of self-awareness and consciousness – *everything from barbarians to buddhas.*

So we need to up our game if we intend to duel duality. First, we need to know how and why the God Game started. Second, we need to know how to navigate the game board so that we're not hapless bystanders when Team Dark makes its moves. Third, we need to acknowledge that the stakes are high and that failure is not an option.

> *For my ally is the Force and a powerful ally it is. Life creates it, makes it grow. Its energy surrounds us and binds us. Luminous beings are we, not this crude matter. You must feel the Force around you. ... A Jedi must have the deepest commitment, the most serious mind. ... You must unlearn what you have learned. Try not. Do or do not. There is no try.*[138]

Yoda, *Star Wars*

[1] Michael Hirsh, "D-Day's Dying Legacy," *Foreign Policy Magazine* (June 5, 2019), https://foreignpolicy.com/2019/06/05/d-days-dying-legacy-normandy-anniversary/ (accessed July 2022).

[2] Winston Churchill, "Finest Hour" speech given to the British House of Commons (June 18, 1940).

[3] David R. Hawkins, M.D., Ph.D., *Power vs. Force: The Hidden Determinants of Human Behavior*, pp. 282, 68, Hay House: Carlsbad, CA (1995).

[4] Ibid, p. 288.

[5] Mohandas K. Gandhi, *Satyagraha in South Africa*, translated by Valji Govindji Desai, Chapter 9, Navajivran Trust: Ahemadabad, India (1968).

[6] Arthur Herman, *Gandhi and Churchill: The Epic Rivalry that Destroyed an Empire and Forged Our Age*, p. 124, Bantam Books: New York, NY (2009).

[7] My great-grandfather Horatio Shrewsbury George fought in the Boer War. He was a member of the Cameron Highlanders, 1st Battalion. See: *Wikipedia*, https://en.wikipedia.org/wiki/Queen%27s_Own_Cameron_Highlanders#1816_1880 (accessed July 2022).

[8] Adolf Hitler, *Mein Kampf*, translated by Ralph Manheim, p. 158, Houghton Mifflin Co.: Boston, MA (1943).

[9] Mohandas K. Gandhi, *Autobiography: The Story of My Experiments with Truth*, translated by Mahadev Desai, pp. 29–30, Dover Publications: New York, NY (1983).

[10] Ibid, pp. 6–10, 25–27, 180, 282.

[11] Yogesh Chadra, *Gandhi: A Life*, pp. 5–10, John Wiley & Sons: Hoboken, NJ (1997).

[12] Ibid, p. 41.

[13] Ibid, p. 66.

[14] Ibid, pp. 69, 84, 94.

[15] Ibid, pp. 100–108.

[16] Mohandas K. Gandhi, *Autobiography*, p. 233.

[17] Arthur Herman, *Gandhi and Churchill*, pp. 149–150.

[18] Mohandas K. Gandhi, *Autobiography*, p. 284.

[19] Yogesh Chadra, *Gandhi: A Life*, p. 136.

[20] Ibid, p. 129.

[21] Ibid, p. 185.

[22] Ibid, pp. 180–182, 187–188.

[23] Adolf Hitler, *Mein Kampf*, pp. 158, 161.

[24] Ibid, pp. 190–206.

[25] Karl Marx's ancestry was Jewish, but his father converted the family to Protestantism. Karl Marx was a self-declared atheist. Marx famously authored *The Communist Manifesto* (1848), and *Das Capital* (Volume 1:1867; Volume II :1885; Volume III: 1894).

[26] Hitler claimed in *Mein Kampf*, p. 224, that his DAP card was number "7," but he apparently altered the card for unknown reasons.

[27] The chronology of Hitler's rise to power is superbly summarized by Ian Kershaw, *Hitler: Profiles in Power*, Pearson Education Limited: Essex, England (1991).

[28] David Liuzzo, "Banner of the Holy Roman Empire," *Wikimedia Commons*, https://commons.wikimedia.org/wiki/File:Heiliges_R%C3%B6misches_Reich_-_Reichssturmfahne_vor_1433.svg (accessed July 2022).

[29] Reichsadler Deutsches Reich (1935–1945), *Wikimedia Commons*, public domain, https://en.wikipedia.org/wiki/Nazi_Germany#/media/File:Reichsadler_Deutsches_Reich_(1935%E2%80%931945).svg (accessed July 2022).

[30] Adolf Hitler, *Mein Kampf*, pp. 214, 295.

[31] Friedrich Nietzsche, *The Will to Power* (1910).

[32] The phrase "survival of the fittest" was first used by Herbert Spence in his work *Principles of Biology* (1864).

[33] Adolf Hitler, *Mein Kampf*, pp. 352, 383, 394, 411, 404.

[34] Ibid, pp. 60–61, 65, 382.

[35] Denis Mack Smith, *Mussolini: A Biography*, p. 7, Vintage Books: New York: NY (1983).

[36] See, for example, this current analysis of Hitler's tangled philosophies: Augusto Zimmerman, "Adolf Hitler's Debt to Karl Marx," *Quadrant Magazine* (May 9, 2018), https://quadrant.org.au/opinion/qed/2018/05/adolf-hitlers-debt-karl-marx/ (accessed July 2022).

[37] Adolf Hitler, *Mein Kampf*, pp. 46, 50.

[38] Ibid, pp. 78–81.

[39] Ibid, pp. 179–180.

[40] Ibid, pp. 137–138, 624, 646, 653–654.

[41] Ibid, pp. 170–171.

[42] Yogesh Chadra, *Gandhi: A Life*, pp. 195, 204.

[43] Ibid, p. 256.

[44] Ibid, pp. 200–202.

[45] Mohandas K. Gandhi, *Autobiography*, pp. 388–389.

[46] Arthur Herman, *Gandhi and Churchill*, pp. 235–236.

[47] Ibid, pp. 239–240.

[48] Ibid, pp. 261–264. See also: "Partition of the Ottoman Empire," *Wikipedia*, https://en.wikipedia.org/wiki/Partition_of_the_Ottoman_Empire (assessed July 2022).

[49] Ibid, p. 265.

[50] Yogesh Chadra, *Gandhi: A Life*, pp. 250, 238–240.

[51] Ibid, p. 247.

[52] Arthur Herman, *Gandhi and Churchill*, pp. 277–281.

[53] Yogesh Chadra, *Gandhi: A Life*, pp. 260–261.

[54] Ibid, p. 407.

[55] Arthur Herman, *Gandhi and Churchill*, pp. 317–318.

[56] Yogesh Chadra, *Gandhi: A Life*, p. 287.

[57] Ibid, p. 288.

[58] Arthur Herman, *Gandhi and Churchill*, p. 359.

[59] Ibid, p. 397.

[60] Yogesh Chadra, *Gandhi: A Life*, p. 324.

[61] Ibid, p. 210.

[62] Arthur Herman, *Gandhi and Churchill*, pp. 414–415, 418, 429.

[63] Ibid, p. 410.

[64] Mohandas K. Gandhi, *Autobiography*, pp. 424–425.

[65] Arthur Herman, *Gandhi and Churchill*, pp. 448.

[66] Ibid, pp. 450–452, 467.

[67] Yogesh Chadra, *Gandhi: A Life*, pp. 373–374.

[68] Ibid, p. 375.

[69] Ibid, pp. 378, 382.

[70] Arthur Herman, *Gandhi and Churchill*, pp. 494–495.

[71] Ibid, p. 498.

[72] Yogesh Chadra, *Gandhi: A Life*, p. 384.

[73] Arthur Herman, *Gandhi and Churchill*, pp. 507–510.

[74] Yogesh Chadra, *Gandhi: A Life*, p. 397.

[75] My grandfather Leslie Cameron George was a Lieutenant in the U.S. Army. He meticulously chronicled his WWII missions and compiled two war albums.

[76] Ian Kershaw, *Hitler: Profiles in Power*, p. 184.

[77] Arthur Herman, *Gandhi and Churchill*, p. 545.

[78] Kai Bird and Martin J. Sherwin, "The Myths of Hiroshima," *Los Angeles Times* (Aug. 5, 2005), https://www.latimes.com/archives/la-xpm-2005-aug-05-oe-bird5-story.html (accessed July 2022).

[79] "History Unfolded: U.S. Newspapers and the Holocaust," *The Digs: Pittsburg Post-Gazette* (April 11, 2018), https://newsinteractive.post-gazette.com/thedigs/2018/04/11/history-unfolded-american-newspapers-holocaust/ (accessed July 2022).

[80] Nicole Winfield, "Pope Francis says Pius XII's Beatification Won't Go Ahead," *The Times of Israel* (May 27, 2014), https://www.timesofisrael.com/pope-francis-says-pius-xiis-beatification-wont-go-ahead/ (accessed July 2022).

[81] "Documenting Numbers of Victims of the Holocaust and Nazi Persecution," *Holocaust Encyclopedia*, https://encyclopedia.ushmm.org/content/en/article/documenting-numbers-of-victims-of-the-holocaust-and-nazi-persecution (accessed July 2022).

[82] Bundesarchiv, Bild 192–208, KZ Mauthausen, Sowjetische Kriegsgefangene, *Wikimedia Commons*, CC-BY-SA 3.0 Germany, https://commons.wikimedia.org/wiki/File:Bundesarchiv_Bild_192-208,_KZ_Mauthausen,_Sowjetische_Kriegsgefangene.jpg (accessed July 2022).

[83] Yogesh Chadra, *Gandhi: A Life*, p. 409.

[84] Arthur Herman, *Gandhi and Churchill*, p. 549

[85] Ibid, p. 552.

[86] Ibid, pp. 553–555.

[87] Ibid, p. 555.

[88] *Life Magazine*, "Carrion Birds Feast on Victims of Bloody Religious Riot in India" (Calcutta, 1946).

[89] Ibid, p. 558.

[90] Yogesh Chadra, *Gandhi: A Life*, p. 453

[91] Ibid, p. 433.

[92] Arthur Herman, *Gandhi and Churchill*, pp. 567–568.

[93] Yogesh Chadra, *Gandhi: A Life*, p. 442.

[94] Arthur Herman, *Gandhi and Churchill*, pp. 575–576.

[95] Ibid, p. 578. See also: Yogesh Chadra, *Gandhi: A Life*, p. 452.

[96] Arthur Herman, *Gandhi and Churchill*, p. 588.

[97] Yogesh Chadra, *Gandhi: A Life*, pp. 459–460.

[98] Arthur Herman, *Gandhi and Churchill*, p. 583.

[99] Ibid, p. 585.

100 Yogesh Chadra, *Gandhi: A Life*, p. 464.

101 Ibid, pp. 470–471.

102 Ibid, pp. 498–500.

103 Mohandas K. Gandhi, *Autobiography*, p. 398.

104 Tridip Suhrud, "'You Are Today the One Person in the World Who Can Prevent a War' Read Gandhi's Letters to Hitler," *Time Magazine* (Sept. 25, 2019) https://time.com/5685122/gandhi-hitler-letter/ (accessed July 2022).

105 Ibid.

106 Adolf Hitler, *Mein Kampf*, p. 658. See also: Sisir K. Majumdar, "Subhas Chandra Bose in Nazi Germany," *Revolutionary Democracy*, Vol. XXV, No. 1 (Oct. 2019), https://www.revolutionarydemocracy.org/rdv7n1/Bose.htm (accessed July 2022).

107 Yogesh Chadra, *Gandhi: A Life*, p. 460.

108 Mohandas K. Gandhi, *Autobiography*, p. ix.

109 Ibid, p. ix.

110 Ibid, p. 274.

111 Soutik Biswas, "Was Mahatma Gandhi a Racist?" *BBC News* (Sept. 17, 2015), https://www.bbc.com/news/world-asia-india-34265882 (accessed July 2022).

112 Yogesh Chadra, *Gandhi: A Life*, pp. 275–277.

113 Ibid, pp. 337–339.

114 Ibid, pp. 423–428.

115 Ibid, p. 424.

116 Ibid, p. 151.

117 Ibid, p. 163.

118 Dinesh C. Sharma, "Mahatma Gandhi's Tenets of Good Health," *The Hindu Business Line* (March 28, 2019), https://www.thehindubusinessline.com/news/science/mahatma-gandhis-tenets-of-good-health/article26664172.ece# (accessed July 2022).

119 Yogesh Chadra, *Gandhi: A Life*, p. 192.

120 Adolf Hitler, *Mein Kampf*, pp. 534, 391.

121 Shmuley Boteach, "Repudiating Gandhian Pacifism in the Face of Mass Murder," *The Jerusalem Post* (March 31, 2016), https://www.jpost.com/Opinion/Repudiating-Gandhian-pacifism-in-the-face-of-mass-murder-449885 (accessed July 2022).

122 Adolf Hitler, *Mein Kempf*, p.172.

[123] Leo Tolstoy, *The Kingdom of God Is Within You*, translated by Constance Garnett, pp. 55–56, Kshetra Books: Vancouver, Canada (2016) (originally published in 1894).

[124] "Hate Beyond Borders: The Internationalization of White Supremacy," *Anti-Defamation League* (Sept. 17, 2019), https://www.adl.org/resources/reports/hate-beyond-borders-the-internationalization-of-white-supremacy (accessed July 2022).

[125] Lecia Brooks, "SPLC Testifies Before Congress on Alarming Incidents of White Supremacy in Military," Southern Poverty Law Center (Feb. 11, 2020), https://www.splcenter.org/news/2020/02/11/splc-testifies-congress-alarming-incidents-white-supremacy-military (accessed July 2022).

[126] "Number of Jews in the World Still Two Million Fewer than Before Holocaust," *Jewish News* (April 12, 2018), https://jewishnews.timesofisrael.com/number-of-jews-in-the-world-still-2-million-fewer-than-before-holocaust/ (accessed July 2022).

[127] Sun Tzu, *The Art of War*, p. 51, Dover Publications, Inc: Mineola, NY (2002).

[128] Winston Churchill, "Every Man to His Post" speech given over the radio to the people of England (Sept. 11, 1940).

[129] Winston Churchill, "We Shall Fight on the Beaches" speech given to the British House of Commons (June 4, 1940).

[130] Barbara Marx Hubbard, *Conscious Evolution: Awakening the Power of our Social Potential*, p. 122, New World Library: Novato, CA (Rev. Ed. 2015).

[131] David Swanson, *When the World Outlawed War*, Charlottesville, VA (2011).

[132] Steven Pinker, *The Better Angels of our Nature: Why Violence Has Declined*, p. 10, Penguin Group: New York, NY (2011).

[133] Ibid, pp. 130–132, 145.

[134] Ibid, pp. 194–195

[135] Ibid, p. 195.

[136] Ibid, pp. 249–251.

[137] Robert Kagan, "The Strongmen Strike Back," *The Washington Post* (March 14, 2019), https://www.washingtonpost.com/news/opinions/wp/2019/03/14/feature/the-strongmen-strike-back/ (accessed July 2022).

[138] "18 Quotes from Yoda to Live By," *Next of Ken* (Jan. 17, 2018), https://www.youtube.com/watch?v=Zl7B3Jc6Fnw (accessed July 2022).

The God Game:
Laws of the Light

In its essence, the ALL is unknowable. ...
Under and behind all outward appearances or manifestations,
there must always be a Substantial Reality. This is the Law. ...
Nothing but the ALL can escape Law – and that
because the ALL is Law itself. ...
Remember always student, that Transmutation,
not presumptuous denial, is the weapon of the Master.

The Kybalion

During the course of my esoteric studies, there is one book that stands out above the rest as a quintessential source of Truth, Love, and Light – the motto of The Oracle Institute. That book is *The Kybalion*, and it lists the "Seven Hermetic Principles" upon which Hermeticism and numerous other ancient traditions rest.[1] In addition to the Spectrum of Consciousness, these seven **Laws of the Universe** will guide us through the remainder of this book, since they constitute foundational rules of the God Game. Later, we will explore the connection between the seven laws and quantum physics, both of which cohere with the *Gnostic Kabbalah*, another source of primordial wisdom.

During my years of study and devotion, I have read many sacred texts and these two – *Kybalion* and *Kabbalah* – are fertile ground for New Humans, particularly in the West, where most don't follow an avowed path of perfection. Instead of reading authoritative source material and meditating to mature their own psychic gifts and divine communications, the Green meme often consults intuitives and channelers for insight. Unfortunately, most channeling comes from an astral realm of chaos, not the Light. As we shall see when we examine the *Gnostic Kabbalah*, the name of this trickster realm is *Yesod* and it is not to be trusted. Bottom line: New Humans need to get serious if we are to midwife the Fifth Spiritual Paradigm and deliver this breech baby.

Incidentally, my third favorite source for perennial wisdom is Buddhism – another proven path of perfection. The underpinnings of Buddhism are vast and require dedicated study and incremental experimentation – what we at Oracle call the *Saddha* process of enlightenment.[2] Since I am not a *dharma* keeper in that tradition, we will proceed using a Gnostic lens, the glasses I wear. My goal is to prepare New Humans for the climax of the Fourth Turning and the end of the Great Cusp. Without overstating the matter, we're in triage mode now. The Fourth and Fifth Paradigms are headed toward a final confrontation, and New Humans need to synthesize the rules of the God Game as quickly as possible.

To help us envision the dualistic Earth Plane as a game (i.e., the God Game) with a set of rules (i.e., the Laws of Universe), it will be fruitful to start with a particular myth – the inaugural conflict – a supreme interdimensional battle that thrust the God Game into motion, thereby ending the unity of the First Spiritual Paradigm. I am not referring to Adam and Eve's "fall from grace" in the Garden of Eden, but an earlier source of separation and an archetypal saga that holds the key to the God Game.

In ancient Judeo-Christian mythology, a heavenly war erupted after God created Earth and populated it with humans. This quintessential battle sets the stage for a nuanced discussion of the God Game, because the story reminds us: (i) Team Light and Team Dark both emanate from Source (as does everything); (ii) both teams see the same problems, seek to surmount the same hurdles, and wish to resolve the exact same existential crises (i.e., as in the Gandhi vs. Hitler lessons from the last chapter); and (iii) the main difference between Team Light and Team Dark is the divergent strategies they employ to resolve the crisis (e.g., nonviolence versus force).

Just as in *Star Wars*, where Yoda and Darth Vader tap into the same "Force" for magical powers, in the Judeo-Christian legend the original players of the God Game also look to a single "Source" for power. Indeed, according to this myth, the first angel vs. demon archetypes were created by God himself! Yes, Archangel Michael and Archangel Lucifer – God's first two creations and, ostensibly, his two most beloved and powerful players – were the first to fight. Hence, Michael and Lucifer initiated duality and disunity. But why?

In the Gnostic interpretation of the tale, the creator God (not to be confused with the Light) was alone in heaven and designed two semi-divine prototypes.[3] First, God made **Archangel Lucifer**, whose name in Latin means "son of the morning star" (a reference to Venus), "shining one," and "light bearer." Next, God made **Archangel Michael**, his second son so to speak, and in some legends, there are at total of seven archangels (perhaps related to the seven Laws of the Universe or seven chakras).[4] Eventually, a rivalry ensued between Lucifer and Michael that is reminiscent of the classic brotherly conflict found in other Jewish fables, where Yahweh prefers the second born son over the first (e.g., Abel over Cain; Isaac over Ishmael; and Jacob over Esau).

Initially, the angels were blissed out because they were with God in heaven. First son Lucifer may have enjoyed greater rank and privilege, but there was no conflict as yet. Then God decided to create the Universe, and we can imagine the angels rejoicing on the first day when God said, "Let there be Light."[5] On the sixth day, God made Adam and Eve, which is when the trouble started.[6] God assigned Lucifer the task of watching over the Earth Plane and humans, and he put Michael in charge of protecting the Ethereal Plane. Lucifer rejected his assignment for the reason he explains below:

> *Michael called all the angels saying: "Worship the* [humans], *just as the Lord God has commanded." Michael himself worshipped first then he called me and said: "Worship the image of God Jehovah."*
>
> *I answered: "I do not have it within me to worship Adam. ... Why do you compel me? I will not worship him who is lower and posterior to me. I am prior to that creature. Before he was made, I had already been made. He ought to worship me." Hearing this, other angels who were under me were unwilling to worship him.*
>
> *Michael said: "Worship the image of God. If you do not worship, the Lord God will grow angry with you."*
>
> *I said: "If he grows angry with me, I will place my seat above the stars of heaven and I will be like the Most High."*
>
> *Then the Lord God grew angry with me and sent me forth with my angels from our glory. On account of you* [Adam] *we were expelled from our dwelling into this world and cast out upon the earth. Immediately we were in grief, since we had been despoiled of so much glory, and we grieved to see you in such a great happiness of delights.*
>
> *By a trick I cheated your wife and caused you to be expelled through her from the delights of your happiness, just as I had been expelled from my glory.*[7]

Many artists have depicted this war in heaven (left),[8] and nearly all apocalyptic literature describe the event, including: *Revelation to John* in the *New Testament* (*circa* 100 CE); *Al-Malhama Al-Kubra* (Day of Judgment) in *The Holy Quran* (*circa* 650 CE); *Divine Comedy* by Dante Alighieri (1320); and John Milton's *Paradise Lost* (1677). In some texts, the name Satan or the Devil is used, but the appellation Lucifer is most relevant, due to its etymological association with the Light.

So why did Lucifer rebel? Maybe he loathed the new humans because they weren't as wonderful as we New Humans (joke). Here's my actual take on the tale, to which I will apply human characteristics to help make a point. Consider that Lucifer – as the first born baby in heaven – initially had God all to himself. For parents who are reading, you already know what happens when a second baby arrives: The first child gets jealous. Therefore, when God made Michael, we can imagine Lucifer, now a toddler, was none too happy (strike one).

Then God created the Earth Plane, after which he probably spent less time at home in the Ethereal Plane with his angelic children (strike two). Next, God ordered Lucifer, now a rambunctious teenager, to watch over Adam and Eve and their offspring, which Lucifer considered a crappy job (like taking out the trash), while God gave the plum position of policing heaven to Michael (strike three). Is it any wonder Lucifer's nose was out of joint?

When we attach human emotions to the story, it's easier to understand why Lucifer revolted. He threw a temper tantrum because working on Earth meant he'd be separated from God. He'd no longer have the same closeness to God, the same unity, or immediate access. Simply put, Lucifer did not want to lose his intimate connection with and proximity to God his father.

This anthropomorphic lens brings the legend into focus and illuminates the moral of the story. To wit: Lucifer's act of defiance is a typical reaction when one feels ostracized, rejected, or second best. All the dark emotions Lucifer experienced – jealousy, anger, bitterness, humiliation, grief, revenge – are the exact emotions that turn a soul to the Dark side. What Lucifer wanted and what Team Dark still wants is exactly what Team Light seeks. In short: *Everyone wants to go home, back to Source.*

Thus, the goal of the God Game is reunification with the Light, whether we believe we get to heaven after travelling from the womb to the tomb, or through reincarnation and the process of enlightenment. Just like E.T., we want to go home![9] We also want to know God's Truth, we yearn for God's Love, and we seek God's Light. So irrespective of how we attempt to reunite with Source – whether through a holy book, in dreams, outside in nature, or in the elevated state of *samadhi* – we all want to go home to the Light. It's really that simple.

> [C]reation is sometimes called the "Outpouring" of the Divine Energy, just as the Evolutionary state is called the "Indrawing." The extreme pole of the Creative process is considered the furthest removed from the ALL, while the beginning of the Evolutionary stage is regarded as the beginning of the return swing of the pendulum of Rhythm – a "coming home" idea being held in all of the Hermetic Teachings.[10]
>
> The Kybalion

Now that we've establish the sole and shared goal of the God Game, the differences between Team Light and Team Dark becomes obvious. Everyone who plays the God Game knows, deep down, that winning the game means reuniting with Source. Players just choose different strategies to win.

> There are at least two kinds of games. One could be called finite, the other infinite. A finite game is played for the purpose of winning, an infinite game for the purpose of continuing the play. ...
>
> A finite game must always be won with a terminal move .... A terminal move results, in other words, in the death of the opposing player as player. The winner kills the opponent. The loser is dead in the sense of being incapable of further play. ... The contradiction is precisely that all finite play is play against itself.[11]
>
> James P. Carse, *Finite and Infinite Games*

Sadly, players on Team Dark will do anything to win, including ending the God Game itself. They will cheat, lie, slash and burn, and even kill. However, players on Team Light want the God Game to go on indefinitely so everyone can win. They heed the evolutionary impulse, temper their base emotions, and abide by the rules of the game. Again, it's really that simple.

A contemporary example of a Team Dark player will help seal the lesson. Let's consider Dick Cheney again, who we used in Chapter II as an example of a shadow-ridden and dangerous Stage 5 human. I used to go to bed at night wondering how Cheney went to bed at night. In fact, I pondered this question for years: How could Cheney lay his head on his pillow and get a good night's sleep? I used to think he just didn't care, that he was an amoral, greedy, power-hungry capitalist who doesn't give a damn about anyone but himself. But then I remembered that Cheney has children and grandchildren, and he knows the dangerous world we live in. He must care about the future for their sake. I also remembered that all memes love (even Nazis, as Wilber reminds us).

Finally, one day I integrated the lesson contained in the Luciferian legend, and the answer came to me like a thunderbolt! Of course, Cheney wants the human race to survive these unprecedented times, just like we do. Moreover, Cheney is brilliant and he understands the facts on the ground. He knows darn well that our planet is in peril due to climate change, nuclear weapons, Russian aggression, and pandemics – to name just a few of the challenges we face. Therefore, if Cheney sleeps like a baby at night, it's because he seeks the same lofty goal as every reader of this book – a God Game win. He's just reached different conclusions about how to tackle these problems.

In addition, Cheney probably formed opinions as to which problems can be reasonably addressed and which ones – in his dastardly opinion – are too tough to tackle, "collateral damage" notwithstanding. When in power (and he still may have power behind the scenes), Cheney likely determined that some people will need to be sacrificed, if the goal is to ensure the survival of the human race. For example, environmental forecasts probably show deaths are unavoidable and that many will perish. Cheney certainly had all the data at his fingertips: desertification regions and rates, potable water loss, dating of peak oil and food production, along with wild card scenarios brainstormed by our intelligence agencies. Indeed, Cheney had the best data available to anyone when he made his cold, hard calculations. In this way, generals on Team Dark make monstrous decisions all the time and still sleep, since the ends justify the means.

Now would be a good time to share another take on Dick Cheney and the leaders of Team Dark. It's quite possible that they are not shadow-laden Stage 3 or 5 humans. Rather, advanced players on Team Dark may be Second Tier New Humans – a notion implicitly rejected by Dr. Graves and the creators of Spiral Dynamics. In other words, there is a Pollyanna belief within the Integral community that once a person goes Second Tier, she must be altruistic and a player for Team Light. Conversely, if a person exhibits dark tendencies, he must be a dysfunctional First Tier human with sordid shadow elements.

Unfortunately, I must disagree with this naïve consensus. Though Wilber stayed mum on this topic for years, he recently joined the ranks of those who believe evil exists at the Second Tier. Of late, Wilber has been speaking to this issue directly, and in a metaphysical, dualistic manner, as opposed to simply blaming Second Tier evil on a Stage 3 addiction. Neither does he define evil using the New Age concept of the "absence of Light." Instead, Wilber truly is tackling this subject, and he recently did a podcast for those who want to hear him riff.[12] He also wrote about Second Tier evil in his most recent opus, plainly clarifying for the Integral community that malevolence is a horrifying, potential pitfall in the highest realms of the Spectrum of Consciousness:

> [H]igher structures, with their higher capacities and power, can be greater and greater sources of "evil," to use a strong but appropriate term. If Auschwitz is a product of [Stage 5] technology (with [Stage 3/4] morals), you can imagine what the products of Supermind [Stage 9] might be if it were broken, twisted, or fixated to, or repressing, lower levels (up to and including itself) – an unprecedented degree of "evil." ...
>
> Thus, each increasing level of development brings new capacities and new "evils." ... A Supermind run amuck is a thing to be, yes, "feared" is probably the right word .... At any point in development, the Darth Vader move is always possible.[13]

> Ken Wilber, *The Religion of Tomorrow*

When I took the Rehab class at the University of Virginia way back in the 1980s, just as Spiral Dynamics was starting to go mainstream, I distinctly remember the name my professor gave as a perfect example of a Stage 7 person. He named G. Gordon Liddy (1930–2021), and if you don't know who Liddy is, I will briefly summarize his main claim to fame: Liddy was the mastermind of the Watergate break-in, which he executed on behalf of President Richard Nixon (1913–1994). Liddy was convicted of burglary and wiretapping and spent over four years in prison. After his release, Liddy published *Will*, his autobiography.[14] While still in college, I read *Will* because I was curious to learn more about the Stage 7 mindset. Also, *Will* was a bestseller and it was made into a movie, indicating that others were equally fascinated by Liddy, who unabashedly pledged to Nixon, "I will kill for you, Mr. President."

Liddy is one cool customer, just like Cheney. The reason my professor held Liddy up as an example of (gulp) a New Human is because he possesses the classic characteristics of Indigo: He is dedicated to his mission to the exclusion of all else (including family), he is a broad systems thinker and truth seeker, and he is totally fearless. This last trait is critically important. Let us remember that only at Second Tier do New Humans drop fear as a motivating factor. Sure, there are courageous heroes at Stages 3, 4, 5, and 6 (e.g., recall that a young Gandhi aided the British in the Boer War). But courage in the First Tier sense is more a matter of pride, testosterone, and the "fight or flight" chemicals in our bodies that propel us into action during times of severe distress. In the Second Tier, however, fear is a *non sequitur* in the sense that it is totally under control (as is the ego). Fear still exists (as does remnant ego), but it will not determine or shape behavior in the Second Tier, as it will in the First.

I wish I had a dime for every time one of my Green friends used the term "fear based" to describe Dick Cheney. It is laughable and sheer projection. Trust me on this one, neither Cheney nor Liddy is afraid. They might have an addiction to some remnant Red characteristics such as ruthlessness, but they are not handicapped by fear. Consequently, I agree with my UVA professor that Liddy is Indigo. I also think Cheney is a (double gulp) Stage 7 New Human.

So why was this detour into Dick Cheney's mindset necessary? Because we are about to examine the Laws of the Universe as taught in the Hermetic tradition, and as we go through these laws, I am hoping all readers keep this prudent warning in mind: The generals on Team Dark are just as sophisticated and self-aware as the generals on Team Light, which means if they know the Laws of the Universe, they too can manifest ... and move mountains.

> The intelligent student may recognize what we mean by this when we state that the meaning of "Spirit" as used by the Hermetists is akin to Living Power .... To occultists the word "Spirit" is used in the sense of "The Animating Principle," ... and occultists know that that which is known to them as "Spiritual Power" may be employed for evil as well as good ends (in accordance with the Principle of Polarity), a fact which has been recognized by the majority of religions in their conceptions of Satan, Beelzebub, the Devil, Lucifer, Fallen Angels, etc. And so the knowledge regarding these Planes has been kept in the Holy of Holies of all Esoteric Fraternities and Occult Orders – in the Secret Chamber of the Temple.[15]
>
> The Kybalion

DEFAULT MODE OF THE UNIVERSE THEORY

Let us now proceed on the premise that Team Dark possesses not only evil players, but also advanced generals and even **Dark Lords**. Drawing the logical parallel, Team Light is comprised of players ranging in spiritual maturity from initiates to **Light Masters**. Just picture your favorite dualistic storyline (e.g., *Star Wars*, *Lord of the Rings*, *Harry Potter*). Therefore, all else being equal in the God Game, the Earth Plane would be in a state of perpetual polarity. This is a possibility that we will explore shortly. However, because I am a "glass-half-full" person and a positive player for Team Light, I want to share another theory I've conceived called the "Default Mode of the Universe."

The **Default Mode of the Universe theory** posits that the God Game is tilted, *ever so slightly*, in favor of Team Light. Though I have no conclusive evidence to present, my quest for Truth, Love and Light, along with my non-dual communions, have left me with the strong impression that Team Light has a few distinct advantages over Team Dark. Simply put, I believe God does prefer Team Light, and here's why.

First, the Laws of the Universe were formerly kept secret by Light Masters and only shared with worthy initiates. If an initiate tripped up at any stage of her lessons, she was barred from proceeding on the path. Heavily guarded esoteric knowledge then went underground during the Dark Ages, and it was, in some cases, purposely scrambled so that Team Dark could not get a foothold. Team Light also leaked false information to help block unworthy souls who might use the teachings for destructive ends.

Today, of course, most of these ancient secrets are in the public domain, although the teachings are quite scrambled. Indeed, that is one reason why the New Age movement is so fraught with inanity – many New Humans on Team Light lack a proper grounding in these teachings. So if you haven't studied the Hermetic Laws of the Universe, you are in for a treat. Truly, if New Humans get serious about practicing and using these laws, I have no doubt that we will win this round of the God Game and hasten the Fifth Spiritual Paradigm.

Second, I believe Source set the process of evolution into motion on the Earth Plane with utmost care. There are veiled reasons why the evolutionary impulse operates at a snail's pace. The concept of "Divine Timing" is real in my opinion, but the main reason evolution is a slow process is that we might harm ourselves otherwise. To wit: souls gradually increase their self-awareness to ensure that humanity's collective intellectual achievements (i.e., the exercise of masculine energy via access to the Tree of Knowledge) does not outpace our collective wisdom (i.e., the application of feminine energy and secrets from the Tree of Life). These parentheticals will be discussed more when we get to the Law of Gender – the first Law of the Universe.

The third reason Team Light may have an advantage in the God Game is that the Light periodically intervenes to help us. While "miracles" do occur, most of the time the apparent bending of physical laws is due to the acumen of Light Masters, who utilize their knowledge of the Laws of the Universe and other tools, like astral travel, future memory, and shapeshifting. As we shall soon see, the higher laws, such as the Law of Vibration, can override lower ones, like the Law of Polarity. And yes, there truly are Light Masters on the Earth Plane who have such powers. Soon, dear reader, you will be on the path to acquiring these powers yourself.

There is yet a fourth reason we likely will win the God Game, even if Source stays "neutral" as per the distant or disinterested "watchmaker" concept of deity, which came into vogue with Modernism and when Stage 5 scientific rationalism became the predominant meme. Consequently, this next argument will appeal to atheist New Humans who are loath to view God (if at all) as an entity that could or would intervene in our affairs.

Let's assume, for the moment, the Light adopted a "hands-off" approach to the God Game after establishing the rules of the game and setting it into motion. Here, the Light can mean the Big Bang that kicked-off evolution. In this case, the rules of the game are the laws of physics (not metaphysics), like force, gravity, and Newton's third law of motion, which states: "For every action in nature there is an equal and opposite reaction." Incidentally, Newton's law perfectly mates with the second metaphysical Law of Cause and Effect (to be discussed shortly).

Under this scenario, Source is totally neutral (or nonexistent) and will not (or cannot) interject itself into the God Game to help either team. However, the decision to be a mere bystander once the game commenced does not mean that Source had no preference for which side wins. In other words, while it may be true that Source won't assist Team Light directly (picture the perfect umpire) or can't intervene (because there is no such thing as Source), the science of evolution may still favor Team Light.

Using the watchmaker analogy again, surely the jeweler created his watch to run well and as long as possible. He would design the inner workings of the watch to ensure the accuracy and longevity of the timepiece. Similarly, Source and/or the physical properties that initiated the Big Bang established physical laws that support the continuity of play. Consider that the God Game itself is all about evolution – continued evolution – from the Big Bang forward. Yes, there is an inherent life-death-life cycle to the Earth Plane (e.g., climatic seasons, the human aging process). But now I'm talking about the grand cycle of evolution, which thus far has spanned billions of years and shows no sign of ending until our Sun goes nova. Seasonal death is therefore inconsequential to the God Game. Even major extinction events are mere blips, though we currently are in the **Sixth Great Extinction**. Again, the God Game is all about evolution, which suggests that the rules of the game – both the scientific laws and the metaphysical Laws of the Universe – facilitate the evolutionary impulse.

Recall that Team Light's goal is to return to the Light by following the rules of the God Game, whereas Team Dark wants to destroy the game as the most expedient way back to Source. Team Light is patient and will assist others so everyone has a chance to cross the finish line. Conversely, Team Dark hates the slow process of evolution and seeks short cuts to return to Source. Dark Lords will do anything to win, but their nihilism is contrary to the rules of the game. Quite literally, Team Dark commits "fouls" all the time, yet the evolutionary process – just like the Deist watch – keeps on ticking.

> *Infinite play is inherently paradoxical, just as finite play is inherently contradictory. ... The contradiction of finite play is that players desire to bring an end to themselves. The paradox of infinite play is that players desire to continue play in others.*
>
> *Evil is never intended as evil. Indeed, the contradiction inherent in all evil is that it originates in the desire to eliminate evil. ... Infinite players understand the inescapable likelihood of evil. They therefore do not attempt to eliminate evil in others, for to do so is the very impulse of evil itself, and therefore a contradiction. ...*
>
> *Evil is not the inclusion of finite games in an infinite game, but the restriction of all play to one or another finite game.*[16]
>
> James P. Carse, *Finite and Infinite Games*

In sum, even if Source stays neutral, the God Game seems to favor Team Light. Why? Because we play by the rules, exercise restraint, and patiently allow all humans to participate in the game, including weaker players. It's like the boot camp exercise where everyone must make it over a high wall. Team Light would never leave the weakest guy behind. Instead, the strongest soldier helps his smaller brethren over first, then he lifts himself over after everyone else clears the hurdle. So it is with the compassionate players on Team Light. We want everyone to win the game – even members of Team Dark!

Lastly, here's a scientific argument that the Universe has a default mode. Consider the atom and its constituent parts and envision the atom as the Universe. For those people, like me, who haven't had chemistry or biology since high school, we'll proceed slowly. To begin, please recall that **atoms** are the basic units of matter on the Earth Plane, created after ancient stars exploded. These units essentially last forever. For example, our bodies are comprised of atoms created from the Big Bang, over 13 billion years ago.[17]

Atoms have three components: (i) protons, which are positively charged; (ii) electrons, which are negatively charged; and (iii) neutrons, which have no charge and are electrically "neutral." The protons and neutrons are located in the nucleus at the center of the atom. Within the nucleus, protons and neutrons are bound together by **nuclear force**, one of the four fundamental forces of nature, the others being **gravity, electromagnetism**, and **weak force** (within subatomic particles). Together, protons and neutrons emit a positive charge that attracts negatively charged electrons. The force that keeps electrons orbiting the nucleus is electromagnetism, the energy that proves "opposites attract."

The electrons surround the nucleus in a furious field of activity. Today, the modern "electron cloud" has replaced the old solar-system atomic model that I was taught as a kid. So rather than envisioning electrons travelling in discrete orbits around the nucleus (like planets around a sun), electrons move in shell-like clouds and attempt to get as close to the nucleus as possible.

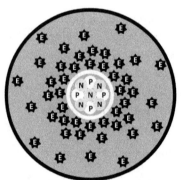

This cross-section of a Beryllium atom depicts an electron cloud – the probability that any one electron will be at a point close to the nucleus.[18] The more electrons an atom has, the higher the probability that any one electron will be at a specific location relative to the nucleus. Beryllium has four protons, five neutrons, and four electrons.[19] Most elements have the same number of protons as neutrons, so Beryllium is rare.

Now, let's equate Team Light with protons, Team Dark with electrons, and Source as neutrons. As the image reveals, neutrons stay inside the nucleus with the protons, thereby creating a nuclear shield that prevents the electrons from bombarding the protons. Hence, neutrons "protect" protons from direct "attack" by the electrons. Alternatively, we can view protons as protecting the neutrons. Allegorically, then, the model depicts how Team Dark tries to annihilate life, while Team Light and Source partner to preserve the God Game. *OM JAI!*

LAWS OF THE UNIVERSE

Without further ado, here are the Laws of the Universe, starting with the simplest of the laws, the Law of Gender, and culminating with the most advanced, the Law of Mentalism. As you look at the list, you may wonder: Why is the "Law of Attraction" missing? Don't worry, we'll get to that topic which, like so many others, has been bastardized by the New Age movement.

1. Law of Gender
2. Law of Cause and Effect
3. Law of Rhythm
4. Law of Polarity
5. Law of Vibration
6. Law of Correspondence
7. Law of Mentalism

Before we delve into each law, here's a bit more about *The Kybalion*, from which these laws are taken. Since its publication in 1908, this esoteric book has been used by Light Masters from many traditions, including two of my teachers. One hails from the Lakota tradition, and she uses *The Kybalion* to buttress indigenous wisdom teachings. So yes, this model is widely respected.

The book purportedly stems from the writings of **Hermes Trismegistus** ("thrice great"), who is associated with the Greek god Hermes and the Egyptian god Thoth (who may have been Imhotep, a deified Egyptian priest *circa* 2700 BCE). Hermes Trismegistus also is considered the author of the *Emerald Tablet*, believed to be the introduction to a book of alchemy. The oldest known version of the *Emerald Tablet* was written in Arabic (*circa* 600 CE), and it has been studied by numerous philosophers, theologians, and spiritualists, from Isaac Newton to Madame Blavatsky.[20]

Also in existence are Hermetic wisdom texts that date two millennia ago, the same era during which the Gnostic Christians were compiling the secret teachings of Jesus. In fact, some Hermetic texts were found at Nag Hammadi, Egypt in 1945, along with the *Dead Sea Scrolls* and the *Gnostic Gospels*.[21] Although most of the Hermetic teachings have been lost, some remnants mirror the *Gnostic Gospels*, leading me to consider Hermeticism and Gnosticism as containing "original instructions" (a term often used by Indigenous peoples). For these and other reasons, my two preferred paths are Hermeticism and Gnosticism, as presented in *The Kybalion* and the *Gnostic Kabbalah*.

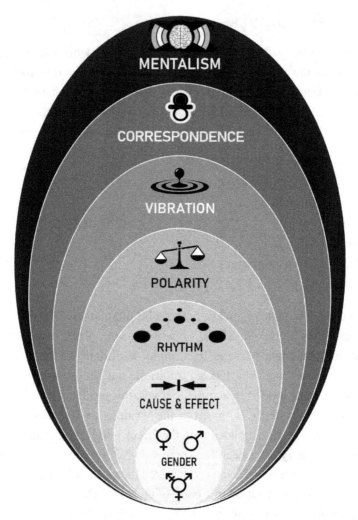

Seven Hermetic Laws of the Universe

Let's begin with the above graphic depiction of the Laws of the Universe, which will help us remember that the laws are nested and holarchical. This means that: (i) lesser laws are included in higher laws; and (ii) the laws are successively more potent and powerful. *The Kybalion* sums it up thus:

> *Mind ... may be transmuted from state to state; degree to degree; condition to condition; pole to pole; vibration to vibration. True Hermetic Transmutation is a Mental Art. ... We overcome the lower laws by applying still higher ones – and in this way only. But we cannot escape the Law or rise above it entirely.*[22]

LAW OF GENDER

> *Gender is in everything; everything has its Masculine and Feminine*
> *Principles; Gender manifests on all Planes. ... "Gender" means*
> *"relating to gender or creation." And whenever anything is generated*
> *or created, on any plane, the Principle of Gender must be manifested.*
> *And this is true even in the creation of the Universe.*[23]
>
> *The Kybalion*

The simplest of the laws is the **Law of Gender** and, tragically, humans have yet to master even this one, as evidenced by the Supreme Court's recent reversal of *Roe v. Wade*. A quick reminder of the Spiritual Paradigms will help underscore this pitiable point:

First Spiritual Paradigm	All is One	Big Bang: 14 billion BCE
Second Spiritual Paradigm	Great Mother	25,000 BCE – 5000 BCE
Third Spiritual Paradigm	Gods & Goddesses	5000 BCE – 50 CE
Fourth Spiritual Paradigm	God the Father	50 CE – 2012 CE
Fifth Spiritual Paradigm	Integrated Godhead	Happening NOW!

Recall that the First Spiritual Paradigm was a time of unity that predates separation. Depending on your belief system, duality can be attributed to the Big Bang, Lucifer's rebellion, Adam and Eve's fall from grace, or the slow pace of the evolutionary impulse coupled with humanity's tedious ascent up the Spectrum of Consciousness. Regardless of the reason, the Earth Plane became inherently dualistic eons ago.

In the Second Paradigm, early humans worshipped a female deity, though not the more advanced vision of the Divine Feminine we revere today. Also, early cultures were a mix of matriarchal, kinship-egalitarian, and patriarchal traditions, such as the Kogi people of Colombia who worship *Aluna* (a female Creator), but who operate within a male dominated pecking order.

In the Third Paradigm, humans began to infuse the Godhead with the Law of Gender but in a magical manner. The anthropomorphic gods and goddesses they created ranged in temperament from our most glorious to our most fearsome features. The highest gods in these traditions usually were male, such as in the Hindu triumvirate: Brahma the creator, Vishnu the preserver, and Shiva the destroyer. So it would be inaccurate to say that the Third Paradigm was gender balanced, either with respect to the Godhead or the agrarian and feudal cultural practices, which were and remain predominantly patriarchal.

Next, a Hebrew tribe rediscovered monotheism and created a singular God named Yahweh (a.k.a. El and Elohim). However, rather than imagining the Godhead as a single entity comprised of both masculine and feminine energies, the Abrahamic religions made a grave theosophical error by primarily worshipping the Divine Masculine. As a result, the Fourth Paradigm buried the Law of Gender for another two thousand years, resulting in "Daddy Deism." This epoch has been marked by impressive economic and technological growth, but it has suffered from a woeful lack of feminine energy. Because this view of the Godhead lacks gender-based equilibrium (and plain old equity for that matter), it violates the first Law of the Universe.

Since a majority of humans still subscribe to some form of Daddy Deism, there remains no spiritual check on masculine energy and it has, essentially, run amuck. This energy has fueled all sorts of material endeavors, resulting in the Industrial Age (*circa* 1800) and the current **Information Age** (starting in 1970). However, without feminine energy, it is not equipped to birth the next age – an era of interconnectedness and holism. Even so, the brilliant endeavors of the Fourth Paradigm reveal the upside of the masculine half of God – what sages call **Creative Energy**.

Unfortunately, we've also endured the downside of masculine energy, including the development of dangerous industrial chemicals, manufacturing waste, immoral biotechnology, and terrifying military weapons – all of which now threaten our collective survival. Moreover, in countries where masculine energy is completely unbridled, people are disadvantaged, including the men, though women and children suffer the most. For instance, in the Middle East and Africa many of our sisters still are treated like chattel (or worse). Thus, the negative side-effect of perceiving the Godhead as a male force (with a male heir, in the case of Christianity), has been the subjugation of women and the suppression of the feminine half of God – what mystics call **Wisdom Energy**.

The Trickle-Down Deity theory posits that our view of the Godhead affects our conscious evolution and systemically impacts our progress on the Earth Plane. Today, our world exhibits the dystopian disequilibrium caused by Daddy Deism. The Fourth Paradigm has been an epoch of gender-based and racial bigotry. Thus, by failing to honor both masculine and feminine energy, we prized the pursuit of science and innovation (the Tree of Knowledge) over philosophical purity and moral virtue (the Tree of Immortality). The net result is that we tolerated ethical inconsistencies and spiritual disorientation. In sum, we allowed Creative Energy to eclipse and overshadow Wisdom Energy. At the dawn of the Fifth Paradigm, our technology exceeds our capacity to wisely and safely manage its raw power.

In 1992, John Gray published *Men Are from Mars, Women Are from Venus*, a delightful book on the stereotypical differences between men and women.[24] The book's most amusing and insightful chapters describe what life is like on Mars and Venus. On Mars, men work on competing projects and walk around with tool belts on and in uniforms. The men don't talk unless it's necessary and they don't ask each other for advice, since asking for help or admitting to a problem is a sign of weakness. The Martians prefer to work alone, since autonomy leads to efficiency, power and competence, and they are happiest when their projects achieve tangible results because success is what matters most to them. In their spare time, Martians fantasize about fast cars and new technology, and they crave the freedom to explore these interests. At school, Martians learn how to build things, and when they grow up they design and create new gadgets just to prove to themselves they can. When they're upset, Martians go to their caves to be alone and problem solve as quickly as possible. In short, Martians are logical, practical, autonomous, and competitive.

On planet Venus, the women like to talk and help each other with chores. They wear beautiful clothes and complement each other on their appearance. They show their love and respect for each other by listening, and they spend a lot of time discussing their feelings and hopes for the future. Venusians readily offer advice to each other and suggestions are willingly accepted, since listening and empathizing are perceived to be acts of love and compassion. They prefer to work in groups and are happiest when they share information, reach consensus, and nurture each other's goals. In their spare time, Venusians dissect their dreams and fanaticize about how to manifest a better world. In school, they study psychology because they want to understand each other and work together to improve their planet. When they're upset, Venusians seek out their closest friend and problem solve by talking for hours. In sum, Venusians are intuitive, spiritual, generous, and compassionate.

While these conventional descriptions of men and women are politically incorrect by today's standards, there are nuggets of truth here that neuroscience supports. Not surprisingly then, *The Kybalion* attributes Creative Energy to the masculine principle and Wisdom Energy to the feminine:

> *The Masculine Principle of Mind corresponds to the so-called Objective Mind; Conscious Mind .... And the Feminine Principle of Mind corresponds to the so-called Subjective Mind; Sub-conscious Mind .... The "I" represents that Masculine Principle of Mental Gender – the "Me" represents the Feminine Principle. The "I" represents the Aspect of Being; the "Me" the Aspect of becoming.*[25]

In an article on his recent book, *A Call for Revolution: A Vision for the Future*, the Dalai Lama shared some of his thoughts on feminine energy.[26] He told stories of his mother's love and credited her with being his "first teacher" because she imparted the most important lesson of all, the "priceless lesson of compassion." He proceeded to chastise men, and he charged them with being "responsible for carnage and destruction ... celebrated as heroes when they should have been criticized as wrongdoers." He also shared his dream that "women will govern more of the 200 nations of the world one day." Then he called on women to be mothers of the "Compassionate Revolution that this century so desperately needs." He was, in essence, instructing us to finally learn and integrate the Law of Gender.

Why has it been so hard for humans to master this first Law of the Universe, especially when we consider that both men and women possess masculine and feminine traits and energies? Using myself as an example, I used to lead from my masculine side, perhaps due to my legal training, maybe due to birth order (I am the oldest), or because my demanding father had high expectations. I'm not sure why masculine energy was easier for me to access, but I have come to realize that my feminine side holds the key to my personal growth.

Similarly, I have come to understand that the Divine Feminine holds the key to winning this round of the God Game. We simply cannot shift into the Fifth Spiritual Paradigm until this planet assimilates the Law of Gender and we get the Godhead in balance. Therefore, despite biological differences – which are real and often cause communication disruptions (my girlfriend says she needs a "Dicktionary" to interpret "man-speak") – we need to identify and address the deeper reasons for our gender-based mayhem.

To get to the bottom of why Daddy Deism remains a potent force, we need to accept the neuroscience that shows some disparity between male and female brain function. For example, men tend to use linear logic and are "step-thinkers"; women are more apt to contextualize data and be "web-thinkers."[27] Let us also accept the impact of hormones, like testosterone (men have seven times the testosterone of women), estrogen, and oxytocin (the "attachment" hormone), and the fact that natural chemicals like dopamine and serotonin also stimulate our bodies somewhat differently.[28] Realize, however, that while these biological differences are real, they gradually have been mitigated as humans ascend the Spectrum of Consciousness.

Such a "civilizing process" is the main premise of *The Better Angels of Our Nature*, in which Steven Pinker asserts our peaceful and progressive trajectory. Pinker writes about the "Humanitarian Revolution" and its underpinnings, including the spread of democracy, increased education, greater literacy of women, and breakthrough literature written by and about women, such as *Jane Eyre* and *Wuthering Heights* by the Bronte sisters.

The growth of writing and literacy strikes me as the best candidate for an exogenous change that helped set off the Humanitarian Revolution. ... Reading is a technology for perspective-taking. When someone else's thoughts are in your head, you are observing the world from that person's vantage point. ...

> *In the middle of the century three melodramatic novels named after female protagonists became unlikely bestsellers .... Grown men burst into tears while experiencing the forbidden loves, intolerable arranged marriages, and cruel twists of fate in the lives of distinguished women (including servants) with whom they had nothing in common. ... The [Catholic] clergy, of course, denounced these novels and placed several on the Index of Forbidden Books.*[29]

Thus, it is more than male/female biological differences that cause humans to ignore the Law of Gender. What then is undergirding the horrifying history of female subjugation on the Earth Plane? Pinker gives us a strong clue in the preceding quote and elaborates further below, citing religion as our main block:

> *The impression that the Muslim world indulges kinds of violence that the West has outgrown is not a symptom of Islamophobia or Orientalism but is borne out by the numbers. Though about a fifth of the world's population is Muslim, and about a quarter of the world's countries have a Muslim majority, more than half of the armed conflicts in 2008 embroiled Muslim countries or insurgencies. ...*
>
> *The laws and practices of many Muslim countries seem to have missed out on the Humanitarian Revolution. ... More than a hundred million girls in Islamic countries have had their genitals mutilated, and many Muslim women have been disfigured with acid or killed outright if they displease their fathers, their brothers, or the husbands who have been forced upon them. Islamic counties were the last to abolish slavery (as recently as 1962 in Saudi Arabia and 1980 in Mauritania), and a majority of the countries in which people continue to be trafficked are Muslim.*[30]

For those of us who live in the Western world, this passage reminds us that if we seek a global shift, there is much work to do! And not just in the Muslim world. With all due respect to Pope Francis, who seems a true humanitarian, the Catholic dogma of God the Father and God the Son remains unchanged, and it is just as potent in the Christian subsects all spawned by men, including: Martin Luther (1483–1546), who led the Protestant Reformation; John Calvin (1509–1564), who fathered the **Protestant Church**; Thomas Cromwell (1485–1540), who crafted the **Anglican Church** for King Henry VIII (so he could marry six times and execute two wives); and John Smyth (1554–1612), who founded the **Baptist Church**. All these Christian offshoots doubled-down on Daddy Deism. As cited earlier, fundamentalist Christians in the U.S. still comprise about 23% of our nation, and most voted for Donald Trump.

Thus, despite Green-trending 21ˢᵗ Century values, misogyny still exists because it is embedded in the Fourth Paradigm Godhead. In Book I of the Oracle trilogy, *The Truth: About the Five Primary Religions*, I assigned each religion a "New Millennium Grade Point Average." The New Millennium GPA was based on their respective orthodox (not esoteric) teachings using an objective template, "The Seven Rules of Any Good Religion." To fully understand why religions were given a specific GPA, please read the detailed analyses contained in *The Truth*. Here, I will summarize the results: Except for Buddhism, all the Third and Fourth Paradigm religions received a failing grade, and a primary reason was their mistreatment of women.[31]

Before we continue, I feel it would be remiss to summarily dismiss the sins of the Catholic Church, which has oppressed women for nearly 1,800 years.[32] Let that sink in: *For almost two millennia, the Catholic Church has been at war with women.* More shocking is the fact that women now have the choice to leave that faith, yet many voluntarily stay, thereby reinforcing the power of Daddy Deism. Although I admire rebellious nuns who remain in the order to attempt changes from within, I have no doubt that their voices – and all female voices – would be heard louder and clearer if women would simply leave the church. Over the last decade, close to a hundred thousand nuns have done just that, believing it the best option.[33] Indeed, at the tender age of six, I spiritually left Catholicism because I immediately recognized its misogynistic underpinnings, though in my child mind I wondered simply, "Why doesn't the church like girls?" I was relieved when in sixth grade my mother stopped taking me and my sister to mass (overjoyed, actually).

In short, if we want to shift the paradigm, we've got to assimilate the most basic of the metaphysical laws, the Law of Gender. If the Trickle-Down Deity theory is correct, then the Fifth Paradigm will not manifest until the Law of Gender is spiritually incorporated into a gender-balanced Godhead. So where do we start? Refusing to engage with patriarchal religious institutions is step one, and an easy one for New Humans, nearly all of whom have left organized religion. Leaving church is a little harder for Stage 5 folks, though still pretty painless. Most of them are pretending there's a "guy in the sky" for the social approbation it provides.

Leaving church is an entirely different matter for Stage 4 folks, however, because many of them do believe in "God and Country." It is harder still for people like our Muslim sisters living in Stage 3 cultures, where they would face personal injury or even death if they resisted. Honestly, that looming battle needs to be organized and led by Muslim women, with all the love and support women in the West can provide. We at Oracle stand ready to assist and hope to utilize our Peace Pentagon brand for that critical and overdue confrontation.

In sum, all the Third and Fourth Paradigm religions continue to violate the Law of Gender to the detriment of our collective planetary progress. These religions must either quickly update or get out of the way. Two thousand years of patiently waiting for patriarchy to cede power is long enough.

Next, we must all become feminists and honor the Feminist movement, during which generations of women dedicated themselves to teaching the Law of Gender. **First Wave Feminism** (*circa* 1850–1940) produced Sojourner Truth (1797–1883), a second-generation African slave, abolitionist, and activist who boldly asked "Ain't I a Woman?" in her speech at the Ohio Women's Rights Convention in 1851. The "Mother's Day Proclamation" (1870) was a rousing post-Civil War plea from Julia Ward Howe (1819–1910). Howe called for an international "congress of women" to discuss issues of war and peace. The Peace Pentagon is in the process of answering this call.

> *Arise, all women who have hearts, whether your baptism be that of water or of tears! Say firmly: "We will not have great questions decided by irrelevant agencies, our husbands shall not come to us, reeking with carnage, for caresses and applause.*
>
> *"Our sons shall not be taken from us to unlearn all that we have been able to teach them of charity, mercy and patience. We women of one country will be too tender of those of another country to allow our sons to be trained to injure theirs." ...*
>
> *In the name of womanhood and of humanity, I earnestly ask that a general congress of women without limit of nationality may be appointed and held at some place deemed most convenient and at the earliest period consistent with its objects, to promote the alliance of the different nationalities, the amicable settlement of international questions, the great and general interests of peace.*[34]
>
> Julia Ward Howe, *"Mother's Day Proclamation"*

Women also attained the right to vote during the First Wave of feminism, with American women voting for the first time one hundred years ago after the passage of the 19th Amendment. Let that sink in ... just how recently women in the U.S. started voting. More recently, women won the right to vote in Kuwait in 2005, United Arab Emirates in 2006, and Saudi Arabia in 2011. Even more shocking is the fact that women are effectively prevented from voting in some Stage 3 cultures, and women still cannot vote in Vatican City.[35] As a final note, the American Birth Control League was founded in 1921, and it changed its name to Planned Parenthood in 1942, just in time to help launch the next wave.

Second Wave Feminism (1940–1970) often is dated to the 1960s, which I find historically inaccurate. Why? Because prior to Betty Friedan's runaway bestseller *The Feminine Mystique* (1963), in which she tackled the myth of the "happy homemaker," the world received an earlier cataclysmic lesson on the Law of Gender, when in 1949, existentialist philosopher Simone de Beauvoir (1908–1986) published her classic work *The Second Sex*:

> *When we abolish the slavery of half of humanity, together with the whole system of hypocrisy that it implies, then the "division" of humanity will reveal its genuine significance and the human couple will find its true form. ...*
>
> *The truth is that just as – biologically – males and females are never victims of one another but both victims of the species, so man and wife together undergo the oppression of an institution they did not create. If it is asserted that men oppress women, the husband is indignant; he feels that he is the one who is oppressed – and he is; but the fact is that it is the masculine code, it is the society developed by the males and in their interest, that has established woman's situation in a form that is at present a source of torment for both sexes. ...*
>
> *[W]e will pose the problem of feminine destiny quite differently: we will situate woman in a world of values, and we will lend her behavior a dimension of freedom. We think she has to choose between the affirmation of her transcendence and her alienation as object; she is not the plaything of contradictory drives; she devises solutions that have an ethical hierarchy among them.[36]*
>
> Simone de Beauvoir, *The Second Sex*

Both de Beauvoir and Friedan lamented the loss of Wisdom Energy, and their books inflamed female determination: higher college attendance for women, greater numbers in the work force, use of the birth control pill, and the freedom attendant with lower birth rates. Women won the Equal Pay Act (1963), and the Equal Employment Opportunity Commission was formed (1964). Additionally, white women joined with African Americans in the Civil Rights movement. The resulting Civil Rights Act of 1964 banned discrimination on the bases of sex, race, color, national origin, and religion. The Supreme Court in *Griswold v. Connecticut* struck down that state's law banning contraception (1965). Notably, the National Organization for Women (NOW) was formed in 1966 (today it has 550 chapters in all 50 U.S. states), and the National Association for the Repeal of Abortion Laws (NARAL) was founded in 1969.

The Sacred Feminine exploded with another round of conviction during **Third Wave Feminism** (1970–2000), which I also date differently. It was during this time that the full promise of the Civil Rights Act was extended to women in the workplace (via amendments to Title VII), and to public education (Title IX). In 1970, Bella Abzug was elected to Congress, famously affirming, "A woman's place is in the House." In 1972, the **Equal Rights Amendment** finally passed Congress (First Wave feminists introduced the ERA in 1923), though ratification by 38 states would take almost another 50 years – thank you Virginia! Today, however, the ERA is held hostage by procedural technicalities and the polarity which is destroying the U.S. government.

Another huge win was the Supreme Court's ruling in ***Roe v. Wade*** (1973), which gave women the Constitutionally protected right to obtain abortions. Soon, legislation protecting female sovereignty and family rights was passed by the U.S. Congress: Pregnancy Discrimination Act (1978); Family Medical Leave Act (1993); and Violence Against Women Act (1994). Moreover, the 1981 appointment of Sandra Day O'Connor to the U.S. Supreme Court was a glass ceiling finally shattered!

Yes, the Law of Gender was making great strides during the Third Wave thanks to sensations like: Helen Reddy's "I Am Woman" (1971); Gloria Steinem's *Ms. Magazine* (1972); "The Battle of the Sexes" tennis match between Billie Jean King and Bobby Riggs (1973); First Lady Betty Ford announcing that she was "pro-choice" (1974); *Thelma and Louise* (1991); and *The Vagina Monologues* (1996). Additionally, Eco-feminism came to the fore, with women leading the charge to protect Mother Earth.

However, during the Third Wave, a counter-evolutionary force reared its ugly head in the form of the Moral Majority. Team Dark possessed a Benedict Arnold player in Phyllis Schlafly (1924–2016), who fought feminism, the ERA, and Gay Rights until the day she died. Schlafly crafted the "Pro-Life" movement, which resulted in states slowly whittling away the federal rights guaranteed in *Roe v. Wade*. And their plan worked. While finishing this book in 2022, the religiously-motivated Trump Supreme Court overturned *Roe* and reversed the clock on fifty years of female bodily sovereignty.

The **Fourth Wave** (2000–2020) was a time of more change, as the internet helped spread the Law of Gender by linking female and male allies who wish to promote feminist and LGBTQ causes. By combining forces, we achieved many successes, including: state-based Domestic Partner acts, which benefit unmarried heterosexual and homosexual couples; the U.S. military's lifting of the ban on transgender service members (2016); and the U.S. Supreme Court decision in *Obergfell v. Hodges*, which ended the confusion over the scope of the Defense of Marriage Act by making same-sex marriage the law of the land (2015). Similarly, India's Supreme Court declared "transgender" a legal "third gender" (2014). The net result: 30 countries now recognize same-sex marriage; 70 nations ban or criminalize homosexuality; and 12 countries assess the death penalty for same-sex acts (all Muslim nations).[37]

Other milestones were the 2008 and 2012 elections of Barack Obama, our first African American president, and the election of Nancy Pelosi, our first female Speaker of the House (2007–2011 and again in 2019). By 2020, the U.S. had more women in political power than ever before: 26 women in the Senate (13%); 101 women in the House (23%); and nine female governors. In fact, we may credit the 2016 election of Donald Trump as fueling a huge Law of Gender backlash, triggered by his moral depravity and obvious misogyny.

As the media uncovered Trump's adulterous affairs with porn stars, they also acquired video of him boasting about sexual harassment: "I moved on her ... I moved on her like a bitch. ... And when you're a star, they let you do it. You can do anything. Grab 'em by the pussy. You can do anything."[38] The first Women's March took place in 2017 – a global event and the largest in human history. That same year, the #MeToo movement arose, with *Time Magazine* naming the campaign "Person of the Year." Since then, Harvey Weinstein has gone to jail, where another serial sex offender, Jeffrey Epstein, hanged himself (or was hanged), but not before we learned of his famous friends, including: the lecherous Trump; President Bill Clinton, who nicknamed Epstein's private plane the "Lolita Express"; Great Britain's Prince Andrew, who has stepped down from his royal duties; and disgraced attorney Alan Dershowitz, who represented O.J. Simpson, defended Trump during his impeachment, and was identified by two of the young victims in the Epstein case.[39]

Currently, we are starting the **Fifth Wave of Feminism**, inexorably linked to the Fifth Spiritual Paradigm. During this final phase of the Great Cusp, we must anchor the Law of Gender. If we succeed, the Godhead will be in balance for the first time in human history! However, to manifest the Fifth Paradigm, New Humans will need to commit to being vocal, radical, feminists.

Simone de Beauvoir's prediction is coming true. She believed that ancestral women and men shared a rough equality, that this economic and social parity dissolved as the agricultural revolution took hold ... and that the day might come when economic forces would enable women to cast off their status as the "second sex." This is happening: women in today's industrial societies are reclaiming the economic power and social influence that ancestral women enjoyed a million years ago. In some important sectors of the economy, women are becoming the first sex. ...

As we head into an epoch that will pose problems more complex and possibly more dangerous than any that humanity has yet experienced, we need the strength of both sexes. ... Success will depend on both sexes working as a team. And women will be prominent team players.[40]

Helen Fisher, *The First Sex*

Today, the Law of Gender is penetrating mainstream consciousness, despite the reversal of *Roe v. Wade*. LGBTQ victories such as same-sex marriage are commonplace in Western democracies, and gender fluidity, non-binary gender, and other forms of gender identity are clear indications that the Law of Gender has entered our collective body, mind, and spirit. Likewise, women are gaining financial and political power. They dominate the non-profit sector, and a record number are running Fortune 500 companies.[41] Currently, twenty-nine countries have women as heads of state. And soon, a female will make a U.S. presidential touchdown, picking up the ball after Hillary Clinton's fumble. Just imagine how many more women will be in compassionate service once the Godhead is balanced!

Lastly, let us rejoice that historians are resurrecting the Sacred Feminine. Many have surmised that Jesus and Mary Magdalene were married.[42] But did you know Yahweh had a wife named Ashera?[43] Did you know the world's earliest known author is Enheduana (*circa* 2300 BCE), a Sumerian High Priestess who signed and dedicated all her hymns and poetry to the winged Goddess Inanna (shown right)?[44] Yes, *her*story is blossoming.

Lady of all divine powers, resplendent light, virtuous woman clothed in radiance, beloved of An and Erac! ... You have gathered up the divine powers, you have clasped the divine powers to your breast. ... Great Queen of queens ... I will enumerate your divine powers for you! Enheduana the en priestess, entered my holy jipar in your service. ... To you Inanna, I shall give free vent to my tears like sweet beer. ... Praise be to the destroyer of foreign lands, endowed with divine powers by An, to my lady enveloped in beauty, Inanna![45]

When the Divine Feminine takes her seat beside the Divine Masculine within a spiritually sophisticated and integrated Godhead, Team Light will have won this round of the God Game. At that point, we will shift into the Fifth Paradigm and Light Masters will begin to anchor the next Universal Law.

LAW OF CAUSE AND EFFECT

Every Cause has its Effect; every Effect has its Cause; everything happens according to Law; Chance is but a name for Law not recognized; there are many planes of causation, but nothing escapes the Law.[46]

The Kybalion

For many, this is the easiest of the metaphysical laws to grasp, since it closely mirrors Newton's third law, that for every action there is an equal and opposite reaction. Aristotle hypothesized about the **Law of Cause and Effect**. He identified: (i) the "material cause" or composition of the object involved; (ii) the "formal cause" or position of the object; (iii) the "moving cause" or force which interacts with the object; and (iv) the "final cause" or resulting effect. As a matter of metaphysics, we will consider a fifth cause: synchronicity.

The Kybalion recites that all causes are real, whether seen or unseen. Since nothing operates outside the law, what people call "chance" is merely their bewilderment over an unexpected effect. Even the example of throwing dice illustrates the principle of non-randomness, when one considers the position of the dice when picked up, how the hand clasps and shakes the dice, and the amount of force and spin applied when dice are thrown. And when dice are thrown repeatedly, statistics reveals the predictability of apparent chance or coincidence, as when snake-eyes are thrown twice in a row.

Synchronicity is a beloved New Age term that I also adore. It describes events which appear to have no discernable causal connection but produce a delightful outcome. "Sign" is another New Age term for a pleasing effect, though my atheist friend calls his signs the "daily mock." If I ask who or what is mocking him, he grumbles and changes the topic. In the God Game context, synchronicity and signs may have obscure causes, but they result from causes nonetheless. Interestingly, more women attest to synchronicity because of the way our brains store and analyze data (i.e., web-thinking).

The Kybalion is careful to emphasize that no single cause ever produces an effect. Why? Because of the ripple-effect of numerous contributing factors which ultimately culminate in a single incident (a.k.a. the "butterfly effect"). This truth is illustrated in the movie, *The Curious Case of Benjamin Button*, when Daisy is struck by a taxi, her leg is crushed, and her dancing career ruined. The accident scene shows the many factors which lead Daisy and the taxi driver to meet at the exact same place at the exact same time. Though painful to watch, I encourage the reader to do so.[47] The scene poetically proves that every act we perform and every action by others constitute the myriad causes, effects, then new causes and consequences of our collective activity, since the dawn of time. As *The Kybalion* states: "Every thought we think, every act we perform, has its direct and indirect results which fit into the great chain of Cause and Effect."[48]

Yes, "thought" needs to be added to our list of causes. Light Masters teach that thought, word, and deed are the trifecta for manifesting on the Earth Plane. In Buddhism, this principle is expanded into the **Noble Eightfold Path**. Four of these tenets – views, intention, mindfulness, and concentration – refer to right "thoughts." One precept – speech – equates to right "words." The other three maxims – effort, livelihood, and action – constitute right "deeds."

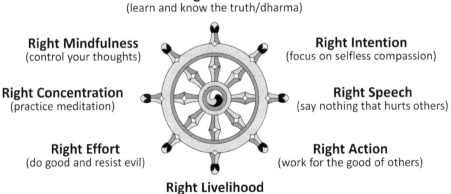

Right View
(learn and know the truth/dharma)

Right Mindfulness
(control your thoughts)

Right Intention
(focus on selfless compassion)

Right Concentration
(practice meditation)

Right Speech
(say nothing that hurts others)

Right Effort
(do good and resist evil)

Right Action
(work for the good of others)

Right Livelihood
(choose a profession that respects life)

To be clear, thought alone does not create outcome on the Earth Plane (except in the case of Light Masters who know how to utilize the seventh law). Rather, thought *plus* word *plus* deed is the formula to create in this dual plane. Consequently, the "Law of Attraction," often cited by novices, is meaningless without proper follow-through. Sad to say, the "Law of Abundance" is equally moot for most people, primarily due to selfish thoughts and inconsistent deeds. Magical thinking is not real magic. Merely wishing for something does not make it manifest. Fortunately, *The Kybalion* is a primer in the art of alchemy, which again, makes it an excellent resource for New Humans. For now, let us simply acknowledge that wishful thinking, in the absence of well-crafted words of power and properly aligned action, is a New Age *non sequitur*.

In actuality, the **Law of Attraction** requires mastery of the first four Laws of the Universe: Gender, Cause and Effect, Rhythm, and Polarity. Also, if a person is operating at an elementary level, attraction can backfire. Initiates are surprised when they attract the opposite of what they seek or when the Universe responds by "filling the void." Advanced players learn rhythm, polarity, and that "like attracts like," so they are able to attain intended outcomes.

For example, women attract men (and vice versa), political power vacuums are filled by dictators, and lack of knowledge breeds ignorance and superstition. As *The Kybalion* instructs, "When the ears of the student are ready to hear, then cometh the lips to fill them with Wisdom."[49] Ultimately, it is in the realm of the three highest laws – Vibration, Correspondence, and Mentalism – that attraction is a serviceable tool. Only after a Light Master attains the "I am" perspective, may she utilize the Law of Attraction through thought alone.

For everyone else, good thoughts, prayers, mantras, and affirmations are effective tools to help us heal, lift emotional moods, clean up shadow issues, and elevate awareness – all of which indirectly benefits others, as well. That is why the Buddhist Eightfold Path encourages repetitious practice of good thoughts – to help students lay the groundwork for good works, as per the law of *karma* (the Sanskrit word for cause and effect).

Conversely, thoughts which are out of synch with words or actions are self-defeating and harmful to self and others. In the *Dhammapada*, Buddha instructs, "Much though he recites the sacred texts, but acts not accordingly, that heedless man is like a cowherd who only counts cows of others – he does not partake of the blessings of life."[50] Thus, manifestation depends on absolute integrity and consistency with thought, word and deed, which is why faith alone is not good enough at the level of cause and effect. Only when a New Human masters the Laws of the Universe does she acquire the skillset and mindset to transmute situations and elevate people around her.

Sadly, most humans are pawns in the God Game and victims of causes both seen and unseen, wished for and feared, arising now and experienced in the past. In fact, most people are unaware of their current *karma*, let alone their *karmic* history. Even some of the Buddhism students I know have failed to grasp the proper view of *karma*, which should be the neutralization of cause and effect. Instead, they try to rack up "good karma" and express compassion to show to themselves and others that they can.

In such cases, the actor who seeks positive *karma* through good works demonstrates a misunderstanding of the concept *nirvana*, which means the cessation of *samsara* (the cycle of rebirth). Ponder also the *karmic* consequence of being the recipient of someone else's good action. Does that create a debt of gratitude? Buddhism teaches that one must master the Eightfold Path plus *satori* – the state of non-desire (Divine spontaneity) and non-duality (Divine union). The Hindu *Bhagavad Gita* also is instructive:

> *All actions take place in time by the interweaving of the forces of Nature, but the man lost in selfish delusion thinks that he himself is the actor. But the man who knows the relation between the forces of Nature and actions, sees how some forces of Nature work upon the other forces of Nature, and becomes not their slave.*[51]

Thus, *karma* is complex, difficult to comprehend, and complicated in its origin and appearance in the current lifetime and present moment. I find that my own *karma* is practically instantaneous these days, since any uncontrolled or thoughtless action on my part generates a quick kick in the ass from the Universe! I suspect that players on Team Light receive such "corrections" whenever they fall out of alignment. In the God Game, the more integrity a player possesses, the more immediate the *karmic* repercussion, until the point when she becomes a Light Master and completely synchronizes with the Light.

This principle helps explain the seeming lack of cause and effect in the lives of players on Team Dark. Trump, as usual, comes to mind. How in the hell does he keep escaping his *karma*? One theory is that his *karma* still is accumulating and that it will catch up with him in the next life. But a better explanation is that provided by *The Kybalion*. The Law of Cause and Effect teaches that each of us and all of us collectively are responsible for Trump's reign of darkness.

Consider the collective U.S. reaction to the 2020 coronavirus pandemic. The virus spread like wildfire because Trump, with help from Fox News, convinced large segments of the country that the virus was a hoax or conspiracy. In usual fashion, Republicans rallied around Trump and one idiotic congressman wore a gas mask to Congress to mock medical professionals. Testing was delayed and months passed as Trump held daily briefings which only spread more chaos. *USA Today* went so far as to accuse the president and Fox News of spreading disinformation faster than the spread of the virus itself.[52]

But then something interesting happened. Republicans started to listen to liberal ideas put forth by Senators Bernie Sanders and Elizabeth Warren, and by businessman Andrew Yang: provide Medicaid to all, eliminate college tuition, reduce lending rates, and give Americans a universal basic income. The urgency of the virus changed public opinion, causing liberal ideas to become common sense. The effect was that Congress passed emergency pandemic relief and President Joe Biden included some of these ideas in his "Build Back Better" plan. The point is that a multitude of causes produced surprising effects, including long-awaited infrastructure spending and poverty relief, especially benefitting children.

For Second Tier New Humans, mastering the Law of Cause and Effect means adopting a systems view to discern reality while playing three-dimensional chess. It also means the prudent and purposeful exercise of free will and consciously exercising the "will to will," instead of basing decisions on emotion or desire. As *The Kybalion* explains:

> *But the Masters, knowing the rules of the game, rise above the plane of material life, and placing themselves in touch with the higher powers of their nature, dominate their own moods, characters, qualities, and polarity, as well as the environment surrounding them and thus become Movers in the game, instead of Pawns – Causes instead of Effects. The Masters do not escape the Causation of the higher planes, but fall in with the higher laws, and thus master the circumstances on the lower plane. ... While they Serve on the Higher Planes, they Rule on the Material Plane.*[53]

New Humans must assume responsibility for winning the God Game. Currently, we are beset on all sides by unprecedented challenges (Earth Plane causes) and influences from other dimensions (Ethereal Plane causes). What effect this chaos will have on our ability to synergize all these forces and follow the evolutionary impulse will depend on how we interpret, manage, and respond to the trials before us. The next law will help us surmount our collective *karma* and flow with the evolutionary impulse even more effectively.

LAW OF RHYTHM

Everything flows out and in; everything has its tides; all things rise and fall; the pendulum-swing manifests in everything; the measure of the swing to the right, is the measure of the swing to the left; rhythm compensates.[54]

The Kybalion

This law is closely related to the next one, the Law of Polarity, because both have to do with seasons and cycles, which we explored in Chapter III. The **Law of Rhythm** bears upon repeating patterns and the seasonal aspects of the life-death-life cycle, such as: growth and recession, increase and decrease, give and take, ups and downs. Whereas, polarity has more to do with the reactionary forces set into motion when the Laws of Gender, Cause and Effect, and Rhythm are ignored or exacerbated, such as our emotional reaction when someone hurts us and our response when we witness injustice.

Thus, rhythm can be used to offset unpleasant situations, extreme reactions, and other interruptions caused by disequilibrium in the lower laws. Rhythm also stands for the proposition that nothing is at rest on any plane. All that is presently manifesting and everything that will come into existence is changing every nanosecond. Moreover, the pace of change is subject to inherent flows and linkages that may be seen or unseen. By understanding these natural flows, a Light Master can access and utilize the pattern impacting the situation at hand.

For example, ocean tides are rhythmically connected to the Moon, an unseen cause during the day. Yet, an experienced surfer predicts wave patterns, he knows when they will crest, and he can safely maneuver all types of currents. Similarly, in the realm of human emotion, a Light Master can predict the ebb and flow of a crowd's movement, and she knows which group dynamic will sustain exaltation and which will promote unrest or riots. In short, she knows and utilizes the Spectrum of Consciousness to foretell how people will react in given situations and how they will respond to new information and events.

To explain the Law of Rhythm, *The Kybalion* uses the classic example of a pendulum, because it illustrates the movement between extreme conditions on our dualistic Earth Plane. The pendulum also helps us understand the current back-sliding of First Tier humans along the Spectrum, despite the forward thrust of the evolutionary impulse, which moves us slowly in the direction of mastering ourselves and the cosmos. Thus, rhythm actually has two faces, each of which we will explore.

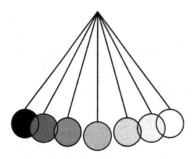

This first pendulum shows the gradation of movement that can occur between two opposite poles. The darker side represents one extreme; the light the other. Here, opposing forces are paired and also compared. Paired conditions range from black to white, hot to cold, fear to courage.

Next, imagine the pendulum swinging back and forth between the two extremes. Such to-and-fro movement accompanies both grand cycles, like the epochal time it takes for a civilization to rise and fall, and shorter seasonal shifts, such as the relatively fast drift from winter to summer, then back again. As previously mentioned, these rhythmic changes are never at rest. However, advanced souls can discern the patterns to prepare for upcoming change and, in some cases, alter the outcome.

A corollary to rhythm is the **Law of Compensation**, which states that any movement in one direction on the pendulum will be matched by a swing of like measure to the other end of the spectrum. A good example is the pain/pleasure polarity. Most humans experience pain to the same extent they feel pleasure, which leads to a roller-coaster of emotions. Another example can be seen in the selection of U.S. presidents. In my lifetime, the presidential elections have swung from Democrat to Republican, and then back again. Moreover, the swings have increased each time with more extreme expressions of liberal vs. conservative values:

➤ Lyndon Johnson to Richard Nixon/Gerald Ford (gentle swing)
➤ Jimmy Carter to Ronald Reagan/George Bush I (moderate swing)
➤ Bill Clinton to George Bush II (large swing)
➤ Barack Obama to Donald Trump (dramatic swing!)

When hyper-swings peak, they either subside incrementally or they top out, collapse the old system, and start a new order of paired conditions. This is what happened in World War II during the last Fourth Turning, and it is worth repeating that we currently are living through both another Fourth Turning and the tail end of a Great Cusp. Thus, we are caught between two radical extremes – the Fourth and Fifth Spiritual Paradigms. Consequently, it is likely that the chaos we're about to experience will be as severe as WWII. Indeed, when the current paradigm collapses, it will rival the reset that took place when the Roman Empire fell, as many historians and futurists now are predicting.

The collapse already has started. Trump and the coronavirus are the two "wild card" scenarios that threw our unsustainable and fragile Western reality into a tailspin. Trump undermined democracy and destroyed U.S. standing in the world, and the virus exposed the superiority – in terms of organization and management – of the Asian world. Now, authoritarian leaders in China, Russia, and Iran are meeting virtually and in person. They conduct trilateral military exercises and are forming a NATO-like pact.[55] Moreover, the Chinese economy has outpaced our exports and is poised to eclipse other American benchmarks. The upcoming "Chinese Century" is the result of trending rhythm.

Another corollary of rhythm is the **Law of Neutralization**, which asserts that the Law of Compensation can be neutralized, or at least minimized, to reduce the rhythmic swing from pole to pole. For instance, a Light Master can bend and even block an escalating wave pattern. She does this by ascertaining and then mentally ascending the rhythm she wishes to shift.

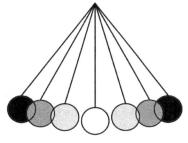

This second pendulum shows two polar extremes, which are both colored the same but represent opposing states. Here, the goal is to slowly reduce the swing from pole to pole so that the pendulum may obtain equilibrium at the center. De-escalation is the key, and the ability to "center" is the hallmark of this magic.

Attaining equipoise in the midst of volatility is the objective of the adept Hermetist. It also is the "middle path" prescribed by Buddha. The same concept is expressed in **Taoism** as the *Tao* (the "Way") – the organic flow of creation that is ever in motion. "The Way is all-pervading. It reaches to the left and to the right. ... Returning is the motion of the Way," explained Lao Tzu.[56] In Taoism, a sage can identify the flow of the Universe, witness its underlying patterns, and adapt her behavior to these rhythms. Indeed, the esoteric branches of every path of perfection contain teachings on the Law of Rhythm.

The Kybalion also discusses the impact rhythm has on a soul's *karma*. This passage helps answer the question regarding when, exactly, bad action will catch up with the major players on Team Dark.

> *The Law of Compensation is ever in operation, striving to balance and counter-balance, and always succeeding in time, even though several lives may be required for the return swing of the Pendulum of Rhythm. ... It will be noted that one generally "pays the price" of anything he possesses or lacks. If he has one thing, he lacks another. The balance is struck. ...*

But the Hermetists claim that the Master or advanced student is able, to a great degree, to escape the swing toward pain, by the process of Neutralization before mentioned. By rising on to the higher plane of the Ego, much of the experience that comes to those dwelling on the lower plane is avoided and escaped.[57]

Currently, the Earth Plane is attempting to break free from a thick crust of darkness, but a massive, immature swing toward the Light could cause just as much chaos. Using the presidential analogy again: Imagine that Bernie Sanders had been elected president instead of Joe Biden. Might we err by course-correcting too much to the left and possibly bankrupting the country with an over-zealous approach to social welfare programs, just as the right goes too far with military spending and tax cuts for the wealthy? While it is high time for Americans to receive universal health care, child care, and other basic rights, we would be wise to modulate the wild rhythm of our politics and seek the "center." That means reducing graft in the federal budget and tightening our belts in ways that will allow us to birth the new paradigm with grace and grit, instead of delusional thinking, misplaced generosity, or political revenge.

Lastly, I wish to mention that Oracle's Peace Pentagon is a perfect example of how to employ the Law of Neutralization. One reason we built this structure in southern Virginia is to energetically counter-balance the War Pentagon in northern Virginia. From our holistic headquarters, we will co-create campaigns aimed at social justice, sacred activism, and shifting the paradigm in coherence with the evolutionary impulse. Join us and help build a culture of peace!

LAW OF POLARITY

Everything is dual; everything has poles; everything has its pair of opposites; like and unlike are the same; opposites are identical in nature, but different in degree; extremes meet; all truths are but half-truths; all paradoxes may be reconciled.[58]

The Kybalion

The fourth principle is the **Law of Polarity**, which zeros in on the inherent duality of the Earth Plane. I've hammered this nail many times already, but the Law of Polarity deserves further attention. Why? Because it corrects many erroneous New Age teachings. We cannot birth the Fifth Spiritual Paradigm until Green New Humans accept the fact that this round of the God Game is based on learning the Law of Polarity. Frankly, we are out of time, so I will be blunt. Most readers will not reach the level of Light Master, since enlightenment requires serious study and practice over multiple lifetimes. But New Humans already grasp the Laws of Gender and Cause and Effect, which means they're ready to integrate the Laws of Rhythm and Polarity.

Because mastering polarity is essential to Team Light's success, we spent the entire last chapter dissecting good and evil. Now, let's add some instructions from real Light Masters – all of whom acknowledged evil and tried to help us comprehend, manage, and conquer it. Here is a sampling of their wisdom on the topic of polarity, too often ignored by the Green meme:

Krishna: *Whenever dharma declines and the purpose of life is forgotten, I manifest myself on earth. I am born in every age to protect the good, to destroy evil, and to reestablish dharma. ... These are the two paths that are forever: the path of light and the path of darkness. The one leads to the land of never-returning; the other returns to sorrow.* [Hinduism][59]

Isaiah: *Woe to those who call evil good and good evil, who put darkness for light and light for darkness, who put bitter for sweet and sweet for bitter .... For they have spurned the law of the Lord of hosts.* [Judaism][60]

Buddha: *Hatred is never appeased by hatred in this world. By non-hatred alone is hatred appeased. This is a law eternal.* [Buddhism][61]

Jesus: *Do not give what is holy to dogs, lest they throw it on the dung heap. Do not throw pearls to swine, lest they grind it to bits.* [Christianity][62]

Rabi'a: *I carry a torch in one hand and a bucket of water in the other: With these things I am going to set fire to Heaven and put out the flames of Hell, so that voyagers to God can rip the veils and see the real goal.* [Islam][63]

The above quote from Jesus is recorded twice: in the *Gospel of Matthew* and the Gnostic *Gospel of Thomas*, two of the oldest Christian texts. My early mentor, the Gnostic Bishop Tau Malachi, describes the meaning of this dualistic passage:

Here, the Master makes it clear that the esoteric wisdom, the inner and secret teachings, are not for everyone. ...

We are, indeed, spiritual warriors in a battle of cosmic forces, seeking to win enlightenment and liberation of as many souls as we possibly can for the sake of heaven. Yet only those souls ripe for redemption can be won over. We must understand that there shall be many not ripe as yet, some actually perverse, for whom we can do nothing at all .... As much as we are to extend the Light here below, so are we to accomplish a balance, harmony, and unification in the Upper World.[64]

Tau Malachi, *The Gnostic Gospel of St. Thomas*

I have been blessed with teachers who have shared secret teachings from a variety of esoteric and indigenous traditions. The Law of Polarity is a universal truth which is taught by masters of every path. In the ancient mystery schools, until a student fully grasped polarity and paradox, they were deemed unfit to proceed to more advanced lessons. Why? Because enthusiastic students will ignore all warnings about mastering the lesser laws first. Eager initiates cling to imaginative interpretations of higher laws and jump ahead. But giving a new student higher-level truth is like giving a toddler a chainsaw: If the child can pick it up and get it going, he undoubtedly will do harm to himself and others.

While this may seem a high-handed statement, let me be clear: In the past, I was an overly-zealous student, and during my esoteric experiments, I did harm myself (and perhaps others). But I never doubted the truths presented to me by my carefully chosen and learned mentors, all of whom taught me the dangers of living in a dual plane. They also prepared me for the climax of the Great Cusp – the very moment in which we find ourselves.

Currently, leaders in the New Age movement are admitting their mistake in watering-down deep teachings for mass consumption. They regret confusing their students, providing tidbits of doctoral level concepts to eager high school freshmen. In fact, they feel guilty for contributing to the growing Mean Green narcissism that envelops the New Age community. And they are *very* worried we won't make it to the Tipping Point in time to win the God Game

How do I know this? Because I've been privy to discussions in which these teachers openly brainstorm on how to deal with the Stage 6 addiction to spiritually immature beliefs, esoteric half-truths, and crazy pseudo-science. Recently, I was inducted into the **Evolutionary Leaders**, a Second Tier group that is not afraid to discuss polarity – the very discussion we're going to have right now.[65]

The **Law of Paradox** is an aspect of the Law of Polarity that recognizes unity is the threshold of the All and the collective goal of the God Game. However, there exists only one way to get home to the Light, and that is through the muck and mire of disunity. Thus, Light Masters know that the Earth Plane contains and is confounded by polarity. For reasons known only to God, separation is a fundamental part of our planet's purposeful design, at least during this phase of our evolution. Therefore, we must navigate disunity if we want to achieve unity. This is the **Divine Paradox** according to *The Kybalion*:

> *Remember the Divine Paradox, that while the Universe IS NOT, still IT IS. Remember ever the Two Poles of Truth the Absolute and the Relative. Beware of Half-Truths. ...*
>
> *Absolute Truth has been defined as "Things as the mind of God knows them," while Relative Truth is "Things as the highest reason of Man understands them." And so while to the ALL the Universe must be unreal and illusory ... viewing it through mortal faculties, the Universe is very real indeed, and must be so considered.*[66]

Some sages say that polarity renders our planet a "perpetual kindergarten" – a dismal view that we will explore later. What is important to absorb now is that the illusion of separation does not evaporate until we merge with the Light. We may bliss-out during a meditation, a hike or other sacred experience, but we will return to the Earth Plane, where a vast Spectrum of Consciousness exists – everything from barbarians to buddhas. Therefore, if we want to win the God Game, Greens must stop acting like everything is in "Divine Order." Things are not perfect here, not even close. In fact, the human experiment is in jeopardy, so it's time to get serious about polarity.

Once and for all, let's clear up the New Age misperception that the opposite of love is fear. This is a critically important point, because we cannot transmute what we don't understand. For example, if a Lightworker engages a player on Team Dark who is full of hate and she focuses her mind on his "fear," she will be unable to transmute his animosity along the Hate–Love continuum. Truly, Green needs to understand that fear is part of their *own* First Tier shadow work. You are projecting, my friends, so please absorb this lesson from *The Kybalion*:

> *Things belonging to different classes cannot be transmuted into each other, but things of the same class can be changed, that is, have their polarity changed. Thus Love never becomes East or West ... but it may and often does turn into Hate, and likewise **Hate can be transformed into Love by changing its polarity**. ...*

*Take the case of a fearful man. By raising his mental vibrations along the line of Fear–Courage, he can be filled with the highest degree of Courage and Fearlessness. ... **But Fear cannot be transformed into Love**, nor can Courage be transmuted to Hate.*[67]
[emphasis added]

It would be prudent to remember that Dark Lords are Second Tier, so they are not afraid; they're just deranged and determined to do harm. Our best hope when confronting dark souls is to quickly discern where they fall on the Spectrum and then use the Law of Polarity – and higher Laws of the Universe if possible – to disarm them. "Killing them with kindness" may work in some cases, as it did when Gandhi used *ahimsa* to battle the mainly moral British Empire. But as we saw in the case of Hitler, Gandhi's *Satyragraha* techniques would not have stopped his maniacal ambitions.

Besides, the Dalai Lama has made it cool to acknowledge polarity. He recently published two books: *Be Happy* and *Be Angry*.[68] The *Be Happy* book focuses on topics that prepare us for the shift, like comprehending reality and dropping self-centeredness. The *Be Angry* book addresses issues that retard our progress, like ignoring wealth inequality and racism. His main point: These issues *should* make us angry, and he encourages spiritual people to participate in a compassionate revolution. He even uses the language of alchemy when he states that righteous anger is "a motivating force that can transform the negative into the positive and change the world." Thus, His Holiness agrees with *The Kybalion*, that pairs of opposites may be transmuted and even reconciled by altering – degree by degree – the swing of the pendulum.

In her book *The End of America*, Naomi Wolf also uses a pendulum analogy to describe how democracy and freedom in the United States have been diminished, pushing us slowly but surely in the direction of tyranny and fascism. She starts her analysis the way I started this book, by recalling 9/11. That was a BIG day for Team Dark and the launching pad they needed to ingeniously move us toward the dark side of the Freedom–Fascism polarity.

Wolf expertly critiques each move of the Bush/Cheney administration, and I especially shuddered at her comparison of their tactical moves to Hitler's. Bush received Authorization for Use of Military Force (2001), achieved passage of the Patriot Act (2001), and created the Department of Homeland Security (2002). These moves resemble the twisted language and legislation that Hitler passed. Remember, Hitler took over Germany using democratic processes, not a military coup. His evil genius was in whittling away at people's rights until their rights were gone.

CHAPTER 5: THE GOD GAME | 233

Today, the definition of "enemy combatants" still includes Americans indiscriminately designated as such. We no longer possess the right of *habeas corpus*, since we can be detained indefinitely. That means we can be imprisoned (and perhaps tortured) without due process. And yes, it has happened to American-born citizens. How did Team Dark eviscerate the Bill of Rights? They applied the Law of Polarity using ten maneuvers identified by Wolf:

1. Invoke a terrifying internal and external enemy.
2. Create secret prisons where torture takes place.
3. Build a thug caste/paramilitary force not answerable to citizens.
4. Set up an internal surveillance system.
5. Infiltrate and harass citizens' groups.
6. Engage in arbitrary detention and release.
7. Target key individuals.
8. Intimidate and control the press.
9. Cast criticism as espionage and dissent as treason.
10. Subvert the rule of law.[69]

Team Dark artfully drew the attention of Stage 3 and 4 folks to the Second Amendment right to bear arms, while they trashed other critical protections in the Bill of Rights: free speech and right to assemble (1st Amendment); right to privacy and validly issued warrants before search, seizure, and arrest (4th Amend.); right to due process (5th Amend.); right to speedy trial with witnesses and a defense attorney (6th Amend.); and the prohibition against cruel and unusual punishment (8th Amend.). Wolf wrote her book in 2007, and since then our rights have continued to erode. Ever since 9/11, Team Dark has moved us steadily toward tyranny and transformed "We the people" into sheeple.

> *We tend to think of American democracy as being somehow eternal, ever-renewable, and capable of withstanding all assaults. But the Founders would have thought we were dangerously naïve, not to mention lazy, in thinking of democracy in this way. ... The Founders thought, in contrast, that it was tyranny that was eternal, ever-renewable, and capable of withstanding assaults, whereas democracy was difficult, personally exacting, and vanishingly fragile. ...*
>
> *We have been willing to trade our key freedoms for a promised state of security in spite of our living in conditions of overwhelming stability, affluence, and social order. This is quite a feat in the annals of such victories: It is unprecedented to strip people of key freedoms in an atmosphere of bourgeois equilibrium. It takes potent mythologizing. ...*

After a certain point in a fascist shift, it doesn't matter whether most people believe the faked news or not – eventually they simply don't have access to enough good information to assess what is real and what is not. ... Sending a current of lies into the information stream is part of classic psychological operations to generate a larger shift – a new reality in which the truth can no longer be ascertained and no longer counts. ...

We assume, with our habits of democracy, that we can simply "throw the bums out" .... May the votes be fairly counted? ... In trusting that "the pendulum will swing" when it is time for the votes to be counted, we are like a codependent woman with an abusive boyfriend; surely next time he will do what is right.[70]

Naomi Wolf, *The End of America*

I chose these particular passages to highlight Wolf's last point: Relying on the pendulum to swing back is to presume that the Law of Compensation will reliably course correct – an assumption based on the Law of Rhythm. But with the Law of Polarity, it is possible to move a situation to one pole and keep it there indefinitely. Remember: The higher laws trump the lower ones, which brings us back to Trump and the Dark Lords who support him.

This cabal seeks to permanently anchor us in negative territory with a nihilistic agenda. Even so, Team Light continues to "bring a knife to a gun fight." Instead, we must stay abreast of the Enemy and prepare for the climax to this round of the God Game. For reliable updates, I recommend attorney John Whitehead's books – *Battlefield America* and *A Government of Wolves* – and his blog at The Rutherford Institute.[71] Whitehead is a true American hero and a present-day Patrick Henry, who came to Oracle's rescue during the second lawsuit over the Peace Pentagon permit.

Bottom line: Dark Lords are masters of polarity, and they are using this law to steer Stage 3, 4, and 5 folks toward a dystopian future. So far, New Humans have failed miserably at using this law, viewing polarity as somehow "dirty" or "beneath" them. This naïve outlook is both faulty and foolhardy, and it provides further proof that Greens possess an immature understanding of the organic structure of the Universe. Green simply must learn the difference between oppressive hierarchies and naturally occurring holarchies.

The term "holarchy" was coined in 1967 by Arthur Koestler (1905–1983), an author and renowned political commentator. In his book *Janus: A Summing Up*, Koestler clarified that holarchies have two sides: the "whole" looks down and inward; the "parts" look up and outward.[72] Each whole is a part of another greater whole, which itself is a part of a grander holism, etc. The human body is a good example: atoms are wholes unto themselves but also parts of cells, which in turn are parts of our organs, which altogether comprise the human body. Thus, a whole is not "more important" or "better," since a whole cannot be sustained without its constituent parts.

Second Tier New Humans are systems thinkers and they understand nested holarchies. They therefore embrace each meme on the Spectrum and respect them for their contributions to the fabric of society – not so for Mean Green:

> Green feels that any "differences" that are recognized between any groups automatically become the source of discrimination and oppression, and thus no differences should be acknowledged in the first place – they are "social constructions" anyway. ...
>
> But green in fact hates [Stage 5], and it hates [Stage 4], and it doubly hates 2nd-tier integral [Stage 7] (because integral introduces healthy versions of all things green fought against, including healthy growth holarchies, which green considers the core of domination because it thoroughly confuses dominator hierarchies with growth holarchies – a distinction discovered and healed at integral). ...
>
> So if we are green activists and we want to embrace "diversity" and we want to be "completely all-inclusive," then does that mean, out of these 100, that we give an equal voice to the 60 racists? And an equal voice to the 60 sexists? ... You see the fundamental problem here? ... If we are emphasizing those voices equally, then clearly we are headed for a great deal of trouble. ...
>
> [G]reen can truly heal only by deeply befriending the now widely fragmented value systems – [Stages 4 and 5] and postmodern green itself – because these all are at present angrily, even viciously, involved in culture wars gone totally nuclear.[73]

Ken Wilber, Trump and a Post-Truth World

New Humans know that younger souls may be tricked, for instance, into voting against their interest. Consequently, Light Masters need to intervene on behalf of the collective consciousness, particularly during a global emergency. In the past, avatars have helped humanity correct course and avert disaster. Now, generals on Team Light need to come together, strategize, and formulate targeted messaging to rally humans at Stages 3, 4, and 5. Remember: "We need a Peace Room as sophisticated as a War Room" where we can artfully and compassionately guide humanity toward the pole of evolution and Light. In this way, we help prepare as many souls as possible for the inevitable conflict at the end of the Great Cusp. In sum, the Law of Polarity is a primary tool we can use to lead humans into the Fifth Spiritual Paradigm.

One final thought before we move on to the next law, and it relates to my theory on the Default Mode of the Universe. Earlier, I presented a variety of reasons for why I believe Team Light has a distinct advantage in the God Game, and here is another one: *The Kybalion* says so! In the Law of Polarity chapter, the Three Initiates declare:

> *The student will readily recognize that in the mental states, as well as in the phenomena of the Physical Plane, the two poles may be classified as Positive and Negative, respectively. Thus Love is positive to Hate. Courage to Fear ... etc. And it will also be noticed that even to those unfamiliar with the Principle of Vibration, the Positive pole seems to be of a higher degree than the Negative, and readily dominates it. The tendency of Nature is in the direction of the dominant activity of the Positive pole.*[74]

YES! As we examine the next Law of the Universe, let us hold this poignant and powerful truth deep inside us. Team Light does have an innate advantage, if we choose to learn the laws and use them. For those readers who are ready to hear and integrate the fifth law – at the dawn of the Fifth Spiritual Paradigm – prepare yourselves. This next lesson may trigger true transformation.

LAW OF VIBRATION

> *Nothing rests; everything moves; everything vibrates. ... [T]he "differences" between the various manifestations of the Universal Power are due entirely to the varying rate and mode of Vibrations. He who understands the Principle of Vibration, has grasped the scepter of Power.*[75]
>
> *The Kybalion*

The fifth principle is the **Law of Vibration**, and it is a master-level concept. Many readers have heard of this law and even experimented with it. However, if you've been spoon-fed a simple rendition (like the sugary-sweet New Age version of the Law of Attraction), expect no results without further study and practice. I cannot speak for how it works on Team Dark, but on Team Light this law only works if you have purified, detached, and started to align your will with the All. Here is a list of seven interior conditions that hinder and even prevent this law from operating:

➤ Your ego is still controlling your thoughts, words, or deeds.

➤ You seek impressive powers or mere psychic abilities.

➤ You have an ulterior motive or want to use the law for personal gain, including money, possessions, or base forms of love.

➤ You secretly believe you are better than others and therefore have failed to grasp the holism of the Spectrum of Consciousness.

➤ You are trapped in dualistic thinking: "us vs. them" or "good vs. evil."

➤ You do not feel the richness and the interconnectedness of life.

➤ You have never experienced bliss (i.e., non-duality).

Many years ago, a friend invited me to an Abraham-Hicks event. For those who don't know, Esther Hicks is a channeler who claims to be in touch with "Abraham," an other-worldly soul group with "infinite intelligence." I don't doubt that Hicks communicates with some energy, the question is: what type and from which plane? Regardless, I went along for the adventure with an open mind, even though my teacher had instructed me not to follow other people's guides, just my own.

Hicks assured her audience that they could attain whatever they want by applying the Law of Attraction, provided they hold their "vibratory field" at a high level and focus on "joy." Disgusted, I asked for a refund at the lunch break (which I received), but my friend wanted to stay through the end of the program. I therefore heard the final Q&A session, during which audience members asked why their wishes – for lottery jackpots, racetrack bets, and communications with deceased relatives and pets – weren't materializing. The event left me sad for the great number of Stage 6 Greens who get hoodwinked by New Age gurus, just as Stage 4 Evangelicals are fooled by hucksters of Prosperity Theology.

Edgar Cayce (1877–1945) – known as the "sleeping prophet" and founder of the Association of Research and Enlightenment – was an amazing psychic who could go into a trance and retrieve information from another dimension, what many today call the **Akashic Records**. Cayce was honest and selfless, and he resisted the temptation to use his gift for financial reward. However, during the Great Depression his family fell on hard times, so he consented to do readings for men who wanted stock market and business predictions. For such readings, Cayce was a bust, and he suffered emotionally when he tuned-in for materialistic reasons. Regarding money, Cayce once said in trance, "Expect much, demand much; but when ye do, be willing to give much. For as ye give, or as ye measure to others, so is it measured to thee again. This is the spiritual law, this becomes the mental law, and the mind is the builder."[76]

Now that we know ulterior motives never create a good vibe, let's focus on the goal of raising our vibration so that we can be potent players for Team Light. Here is a list of seven spiritually healthy and needed characteristics, according to Roger Walsh in his book *Essential Spirituality* – a reliable and respected source of wisdom. Note: the following comments in the parentheses are mine.

- Transform your motivation (eliminate cravings and purify your thoughts, words, and deeds).
- Cultivate emotional wisdom (do your shadow work and discuss your progress with a mentor or trusted friend).
- Live ethically (obviously, and don't be a hypocrite).
- Concentrate and calm your mind (meditate privately, hike, or engage in repetitive activities like gardening that restore balance and have the potential to connect you with the Light).
- Awaken your spiritual vision (identify and listen to your inner voice, reject egoic messages, discern whether your visions are sacred or silly).
- Cultivate spiritual intelligence (chart yourself on the Spectrum and set the goal of reaching the next level of consciousness),
- Express spirit in action (generously be of service NOW).[77]

As a New Human, you likely have worked on yourself so this list is no surprise. Even so, it's time for all of us to increase our vibration if we want to help Team Light (FYI: aliens are not coming to save us). *Essential Spirituality* has exercises at the end of each chapter, and I highly recommend getting this book and doing the meditations. But please don't make the mistake of focusing solely on yourself and ignoring what's happening in the world. Tuning-out is not a fast track method of raising your vibration. Indeed, if you do ignore the pain of the world, you violate the seventh and most important spirit building tool on Walsh's list: being of service to humanity.

Now, let's assume everyone reading this book has pure motives, lives in integrity, receives their own spiritual guidance, and loves their neighbor by selflessly dedicating time and energy. Once our vibrations are raised, we may humbly turn our attention to the infamous yet elusive Law of Attraction. *The Kybalion* discusses attraction in the vibration chapter, since only adepts with a high frequency may access this magic. The actual law is quite easy to understand; it is the application of the principle that is difficult, even more so if the initiate lacks a mentor to help guide her.

[T]he ALL, in itself, manifests a constant vibration of such an infinite degree of intensity and rapid motion that it may be practically considered at rest, the teachers directing the attention of the students to the fact that even on the physical plane a rapidly moving object (such as a revolving wheel) seems to be at rest. The teachings are to the effect that Spirit is at one end of the Pole of Vibration, the other Pole being certain extremely gross forms of Matter. Between these two poles are millions upon millions of different rates and modes of vibration. ...

Every thought, emotion or mental state has its corresponding rate and mode of vibration. ... By a knowledge of the Principle of Vibration, as applied to Mental Phenomena, one may polarize his mind at any degree he wishes, thus gaining a perfect control over his mental states, moods, etc. In the same way he may affect the minds of others, producing the desired mental states in them. ... This power of course may be acquired only by the proper instruction, exercises, practice, etc., the science being that of Mental Transmutation, one of the branches of the Hermetic Art.[78]

A careful reading of the above passage from *The Kybalion* provides clarity on how the lower four laws are holistically embedded within this fifth law – yet another reminder that until one comprehends the Law of Polarity, it is impossible to apply the Law of Vibration. Hence, the biggest New Age scam is telling eager students that they have the power to attract and manifest, while at the same time telling them that polarity is a divisive principle. Truly, the Law of Polarity has been maligned for decades by erstwhile New Age leaders, which has caused a huge delay in birthing the Fifth Spiritual Paradigm.

Consequently, in order to properly convey the complexity of vibration, let us return to polarity one last time and consider the iconic **Yin-Yang** symbol. This Chinese symbol (*circa* 250 BCE) attests to the constant interplay of duality and dimensions. The white Yang depicts Heaven, the Sun and Male energy, which is positive, creative, expressive, and manifesting. The black Yin denotes the Earth, the Moon and Female energy, which is negative, wise, receptive, and incubating. Together, the Yin-Yang affirms wholeness and, for our purposes, illustrates the nested holarchies within Source.

My Yin-Yang (below) is the classic depiction, except for a tiny but significant detail: the insertion of a grey line between the halves. Why did I add the grey dividing line to the classic Yin-Yang? Because the grey line represents the vibratory transition between polarities. I also encircled the Yin-Yang with a grey line to denote the even higher vibration that encompasses all of creation.

Thus, the grey lines are where the real action takes place. It is the **Void**, where all answers lie according to indigenous teachings. You also can think of the Void as the Akashic Records or Super Mind (Stage 9) on the Spectrum of Consciousness. While incarnate, think of the Void as God's home. It is our destiny to tap into it, because the Void is our home as well.

Both Team Light and Team Dark want to access the Void, they just have different ideas and approaches on how to get there. From now on, I will use the term Void instead of the Light because we need to leave the realm of duality and some may view the Light as just another pole.

Yes, dear reader, for the remainder of this book we are going non-dual. We may discuss polarized situations as needed, but we officially are moving on. Also, up until this point, I have been using the terms Team Light and Team Dark to emphasize the Law of Polarity, for it holds the key to absorbing the lower laws and to the very survival of the Earth Plane. Yet from now on, whenever possible, dualistic terminology will be abandoned so as to convey more advanced lessons on the higher Hermetic laws.

To apply the Law of Vibration, we start by raising our own vibration, as previously discussed. Next, we must reach a point of stasis and maintain an internal set point of peace. This higher vibrational frequency lifts us above the dualistic frequency of the Earth Plane. Raising our vibration also allows for the possibility of entering the Void, wherein we may find the wisdom needed to confront and perhaps alter the course of the devolutionary force that opposes the evolutionary impulse. Please picture the Yin-Yang symbol while you read this selection from the *Tao of Physics* by Fritjof Capra:

> *In its original cosmic sense, the Tao is the ultimate, undefinable reality and as such it is the equivalent of the Hinduist Brahman* [highest principle] *and the Buddhist Dharmakaya* [body of truth]. ... *The Tao is the cosmic process in which all things are involved; the world is seen as a continuous flow and change. ...*
>
> *In the Chinese view, all manifestations of the Tao are generated by the dynamic interplay of these two polar forces. ...*
>
> *When we talk about the Taoist concept of change, it is important to realize that this change is not seen as occurring as a consequence of some force, but rather as a tendency which is innate in all things and situation. ... Spontaneity is the Tao's principle of action.*[79]

Hence, change is achieved by vibrating between and around the Yin-Yang poles, not through the application of force, but by aligning with the inherent vibration of the existing dynamic frequencies. Spontaneous alignment is the ability to instantly attune to a given situation by measuring its pulse frequency. Spontaneity also refers to the sage's ability to quickly access the Void to check whether her solution is aligned with Divine will and devoid of any personal desire or motive.

Immense wisdom is required in order to discern whether it is appropriate to apply the Law of Vibration, not to mention the advanced skillset required to actually altar an existing energetic wavelength or trajectory. Even when such abilities are present, a Light Master will intervene only in situations that are dramatically out of balance, thereby honoring the free will of everyone involved. However, because of the dire nature of the Great Cusp, vibratory intervention is needed to redirect old humans toward Truth, Love, and Light.

More specifically, the process works thus: First, the Light Master must attune herself to the frequency of the given setting, even (and especially) if the situation is dysfunctional and the people involved are dangerous or emotionally ill. Then comes the really hard part: After diagnosing the situation, the Light Master must select the most optimal corrective frequency and mode of action. Here, great wisdom is required, because this step actually involves much more:

✓ Comprehending the nature of the given system.
✓ Analyzing the system's complexity.
✓ Envisioning its constituent parts.
✓ Empathizing with the parts' disparate needs/desires/drives.
✓ Calculating how to optimize the health of the whole system.
✓ Determining whether the lesser laws can take care of the situation, in which case vibratory intervention may not be wise.
✓ If intervention is necessary, selecting a frequency that will do no harm to individual parts and elevate the collective whole.

An example will help anchor this lesson. While the lawsuit was pending over Oracle's right to build the Peace Pentagon, I was in despair with two seemingly insurmountable problems. First, the local government had caved to fears of fundamentalist preachers, who called me a "heretic" and "witch" at the public zoning hearing. Second, assuming we won the lawsuit, I still needed to find a local contractor who had the green building experience needed to follow our German PassivHaus® plans AND someone brave enough to build the Peace

Pentagon when the entire town seemed polarized against our interfaith and peacebuilding mission. In short, the local situation was out of control and I even received death threats. I considered giving up, selling the property, and trying somewhere else.

Then my training kicked-in and I realized the Law of Vibration had the power to neutralize the polarized environment. I started to apply the principle in my meditations (thought), my interactions with others (word), and my dealings with government officials, attorneys, and townspeople (deed). With regard to the first problem – the lawsuit – I had to identify the correct polarity upon which to focus. Primarily, the issue was one of religious intolerance, so I decided to focus on the polarity of "Discrimination–Justice."

Once attuned to the proper polarity, I did not demonize one pole nor glorify the other. I did not seek either to repress or indulge either pole. Rather, I raised my vibration between and above both poles and adopted an eagle's eye view of the situation. The notion of being a bird, flying above the fray, really resonated with me, and my vibration increased. In meditation, I started to envision myself as not one, but two birds, and I watched them fly above the polarized situation. Below is the image that emerged in my mind's eye.

I turned the Yang into the "Dove of Peace" and the Yin became the "Crow of Sacred Law." Using creative visualization, I asked the Dove to focus on fear-based discrimination and religious intolerance. I asked the Crow to focus on justice and fairness. In this way, I took myself out of the equation (which is key). Today, the Dove and Crow are memorialized in the Peace Pentagon stained-glass windows.

With regard to the second problem – finding a qualified local builder – my approach was somewhat different. My meditations focused on the type of person needed: brave, unconventional, educated in green construction, spiritual, and reverent of the project. Then I consistently pictured the Peace Pentagon as a temple dedicated to the Fifth Spiritual Paradigm. I saw thought leaders from all over the world convening at our campus, entering the Peace Pentagon, and strategizing on how to build a New World. I even asked that the contractor be someone who would understand the meaning of building a "Peace Room as sophisticated as a War Room."

Over the course of the two-year lawsuit, the Law of Vibration saved Oracle. One week before the trial, the county settled the lawsuit and issued the permit.

Oracle had not asked for money damages (just attorney's fees), and I personally received nothing. Six months later, we broke ground on the Peace Pentagon with the perfect builder. He had lived in Independence for thirty years but was born in New York to a Jewish family. His *bar mitzvah* took place at the Wailing Wall in Jerusalem where he took the name Yeshua. During his college years, he studied and converted to Sikhism. He knew advanced green building techniques and was willing to take PassivHaus training to learn even more. He also was a Freemason and, while building the Peace Pentagon, we used his leather-bound edition of the 1734 Masonic Manual of building rites written by Benjamin Franklin. *Om Jai!*

Credit for these alchemical results must go to my spiritual teachers who prepared me for such challenges. Credit also goes to Barry Johnson, Ph.D. and his colleagues at **Polarity Partnerships**. Dr. Johnson's polarity assessment course and his books *And* and *Polarity Management: Identifying and Managing Unsolvable Problems*, greatly enhanced my knowledge.[80] For those readers who truly want to master polarity and vibration, I suggest studying this polarity theory, a proven model for turning "vicious cycles" into "virtual circles."

To become a master-level player in the God Game, it is imperative to learn the Law of Vibration and to access the Void for wisdom. When on a sacred mission, this law is available to reestablish balance and equipoise when facing extreme polarization. This law also helps Lightworkers recognize when a pole becomes so firmly entrenched that it may permanently dominate the other pole or even collapse the entire system. In such a case, lower laws (polarity, rhythm, cause and effect, and gender) may be rendered ineffective. Therefore, in dire situations, the Law of Vibration is a refined key to correct the frequency.

Another key, in nearly all cases, is love. This multitudinous power serves all concerned, when artfully applied by a Light Master. She can send love to the core conundrum to be solved. She can use love as an elixir, a soothing balm, and the icing on the cake after an intervention. When in doubt, ask yourself, "What would Gandhi do?" Then vibrate at the highest frequency you can muster and enter the Void. Focus intently on the problem at hand by removing any shred of self interest in the final outcome. Then explode with Divine Love.

> *Spiritual love has no desire to get but only to give, no goal except to awaken itself within others, no need except to share itself. Being unconditional, it never fails or falters; being boundless, it embraces everyone.*[81]
>
> Roger Walsh, *Essential Spirituality*

LAW OF CORRESPONDENCE

While All is in the ALL, it is equally true that the ALL is in All. ...
As above so below; as below, so above.[82]

The Kybalion

This principle tells us that the Laws of the Universe hold true in every plane, and that what we see and experience on the Earth Plane is a reflection of the Ethereal Plane. The **Law of Correspondence** also decrees that there exists an invisible yet perceptible thread that connects us to the cosmos and to the quantum world. It requires us to believe in a vast network of consciousness, and it insists that we acknowledge the interconnectedness of all life, both animate and inanimate. Additionally, this law mirrors Oracle's Trickle-Down Deity theory, which posits that humanity's view of the Godhead necessarily impacts the trajectory of the evolutionary impulse and how it will manifest in the future.

If we synergize all aspects of this law, we become a Light Master since, "He who conforms to the course of the *Tao*, following the natural processes of Heaven and Earth, finds it easy to manage the whole world."[83] Here again, the concept of nested holarchies appears as a paramount principle. Indeed, there is no proceeding to higher laws without understanding holism and achieving an integrated Second Tier mindset. As *The Kybalion* explains, "The All is in the earthworm, and yet the earthworm is far from being the All."[84] Consequently, the sage embraces holarchy (the greater includes the lesser) and panentheism (God is in everything), but she rejects pantheism (everything is God).

The old science of reductionism is ill-equipped to explain holism or convey the Law of Correspondence, since it completely misses the most profound truth: *The whole is greater than the sum of its parts.* Discoveries made in the quantum world shifted the perspective of all but the most stubborn and intransigent scholars. Thankfully, most scientists now agree that nature is comprised of multi-tiered systems and based on organization, relationship, and interaction. So while reductionism helps to study and analyze discrete pieces of the puzzle, the big picture emerges only when the entire network is viewed as one complex system, with abilities far beyond that of its constituent parts, yet still dependent upon the health of each part and the coordination of internal, smaller systems. In short, correspondence is the ability to see networks-within-networks and to comprehend the fractal relationship each network shares with others, both up and down the nested, holarchical chain.

Ultimately – as quantum physics showed so impressively – there are no parts at all. What we call a part is merely a pattern in an inseparable web of relationships. Therefore, the shift of perspective from the parts to the whole can also be seen as a shift from objects to relationships. ...

A further important similarity between the physicist and the mystic is the fact that their observations take place in realms that are inaccessible to the ordinary senses. In modern physics, these are the realms of the atomic and subatomic world; in mysticism, they are nonordinary states of consciousness in which the everyday sensory world is transcended.[85]

Fritjof Capra and Pier Luigi Luisi, *The Systems View of Life*

Today, we know that organisms not only are members of biological, ecological, and sociological communities, they also are complex systems unto themselves. Mystics have known this truth for millennia and some have sought to mend the split between science and spirituality. A perfect example is Father Teilhard de Chardin, a banished Catholic priest, who proposed extending the scientific biosphere to include his elegant notion of a "Noosphere" – the next extension of interlinked Earth Plane ecosystems. Chardin suggested that the Noosphere encompasses humanity's socio-spiritual ethics, a cognitive layer of complexity akin to the Akashic Records.[86] He also envisioned an "Omega Point" – a theoretical future zenith when the evolution of Earth's complexity and humanity's collective consciousness will result in unification with God. In other words, he foresaw a glorious conclusion to the God Game.

Over the last century, physicists have held out olive branches as well, decrying the schism between science and spirituality. For instance, Danish physicist Niels Bohr (1885–1962), who won the Nobel Prize in 1922 for his contributions to atomic structure and quantum theory, once opined, "For a parallel to the lesson of atomic theory [turn] to those kinds of epistemological problems with which already thinkers like the Buddha and Lao Tzu have been confronted."[87] Even more vocal was Austrian physicist Erwin Schrödinger (1887–1961), who won the 1933 Nobel Prize for discovering wave mechanics, the crux of quantum theory. Schrödinger was a student of Hinduism, and he believed in reincarnation and the concept of "one mind" (i.e., the highest Law of the Universe). He, too, viewed life as a grand "game," and he was eager to determine the governing rules. In the below quote, Schrödinger shares the goals of the God Game – breaking the Earth Plane illusion of separation, breaching unseen boundaries in the Ethereal Plane, and achieving reunification with God:

Science is a game .... The uncertainty is how many of the rules God himself has permanently ordained, and how many apparently are caused by your own mental inertia .... This is perhaps the most exciting thing in the game. For here you strive against the imaginary boundary between yourself and the Godhead – a boundary that perhaps does not exist.[88]

In *The Kybalion*, the Law of Correspondence is compared to the laws of physics, even though the Hermetic lessons predate the discoveries made at the quantum level. The text separates the Universe into three dimensions, all of which are being studied today by scientists: (i) the physical plane; (ii) the mental plane; and (iii) the "Great Spiritual Plane."[89] Also, vibration is described as both a law and a fourth dimension, since it allows the Hermetist to access all realms. The higher the vibration, the higher the plane, with the atom being the smallest unit of measurement considered. "The atom of matter, the unit of force, the mind of man, and the being of the archangel are all but degrees in one scale, and all fundamentally the same, the difference between solely a matter of degree and rate of vibration."[90]

While *The Kybalion*'s description of "planes" and "correspondence" may seem a bit dated, compare it to this current description of "entanglement" as applied to the same two planes, physical and mental:

Currently, this is what we know: (1) Subatomic particles are entangled; once in contact and then separated, a change in one is correlated with a change in other, instantly and to the same degree, no matter how far apart it is. ... (2) Humans also behave as though they are entangled; they can share thoughts, feelings, and even physical changes when far apart, even at global distances.[91]

Larry Dossey, *One Mind*

Entanglement may explain the great mystery surrounding a Light Master's ability to astral travel, lucid dream, attain *samadhi*, and access other worlds. These talents are rare but attainable through committed study and practice. Once accessed and mastered, the Law of Correspondence means nothing less than the power to alter reality. To better understand this law, I suggest reading autobiographies of confirmed mystics who have achieved self-realization and whose miracles are well-documented. One of my favorite firsthand accounts is *Autobiography of a Yogi*, written by Paramahansa Yogananda (1893–1952). First published in 1946, the book provides spiritual lessons and sets forth Guru

Paramahansa Yogananda's amazing journey, including how he found his guru, his meetings with numerous enlightened beings, and his mission to bring yoga to America.

For instance, when the future swami was a babe, Yogananda's mom took him to a saint who foresaw his life assignment: "Little mother, thy son will be a yogi. As a spiritual engine, he will carry many souls to God's kingdom."[92] As a child, he asked his first teacher to explain the planes of consciousness, to which the guru replied, "I will undergo those states and presently tell you what I perceive."[93] By the age of seventeen, he met his primary guru, Swami Sri Yukteswar Giri, who declared at their first meeting, "O my own, you have come to me. How many years I have waited for you! I shall give you my hermitages and all I possess."[94] Eventually, Swami Yukteswar informed Yogananda of his mission, which had been preordained by the immortal Mahavatar Babaji, an incarnation of Lord Shiva. My goodness what an amazing book! It will inspire you to commit to your spiritual quest and learn the Law of Correspondence, which Guru Yogananda taught to followers of *Kriya Yoga*:

> *Kriya Yoga is a simple, psycho-physiological method by which the human blood is decarbonized and recharged with oxygen. The atoms of this extra oxygen are transmuted into life current to rejuvenate the brain and spinal centers. By stopping the accumulation of venous blood, the yogi is able to lessen or prevent the decay of tissues; the advanced yogi transmutes his cells into pure energy. Elijah, Jesus, Kabir and other prophets were past masters in the use of Kriya or a similar technique, by which they caused their bodies to materialize and dematerialize at will.*[95]

LAW OF MENTALISM

> *The ALL is MIND; The Universe is Mental. The ALL is Spirit which in itself is Unknowable and Undefinable, but which may be considered and thought of as a Universal, Infinite, LIVING MIND.*[96]
>
> *The Kybalion*

Like the previous law, the **Law of Mentalism** requires the highest levels of integrity, selflessness, and mystical experience to comprehend and master. Indeed, it is only through the *Saddha* process of enlightenment (dedicated study and practice) that a Light Master is born. Fortunately, mystics from every tradition have lit the path for us, as have mystical scholars such as renowned psychologist William James (1842–1910) in *The Varieties of Religious Experience* (1902), Christian scholar Evelyn Underwood (1875–1941) in her treatise *Mysticism* (1933), and philosopher Aldous Huxley (1894–1943) in *The Perennial Philosophy* (1945). These books have made mysticism accessible to a global audience. Even so, it is a rare soul that attains enlightenment, having passed through all stages and states on the Spectrum of Consciousness.

> *The real distinction between the Illuminative* [Stage 8] *and the Unitive Life* [Stage 9] *is that in Illumination the individuality of the subject – however profound his spiritual consciousness, however close his apparent communion with the Infinite – remains separate and intact. ... Therefore the great seekers for reality are not as a rule long delayed by the exalted joys of Illumination. ...*
>
> *What is the Unitive Life? ... We deal here with the final triumph of the spirit, the flower of mysticism, humanity's top note: the consummation towards which the contemplative life, with its long slow growth and costly training, has moved from the first. ... He has entered the Eternal Order; attained here and now the state to which the Magnet of the Universe draws every living being.*[97]
>
> Evelyn Underwood, *Mysticism*

Some mystics report that the final portal to the Ineffable requires a gift from God – the state of grace needed to fully open to and receive the Infinite. Others describe the moment of enlightenment as a natural last step, akin to dropping an outworn piece of clothing as opposed to acquiring something new. In every case, however, the mystics relay a sense of awe, abiding joy, and deep reverence. And rarely do they speak of the experience, which is why their autobiographies are so prized. Here is a description from my favorite saint, Teresa of Avila (1515–1582), who wrote to survive the Spanish Inquisition and the men of power who would decide whether she was communing with the devil or with God:

> *And I am quite dazed myself when I observe that, on reaching this state, the soul has no more raptures ... He also gives the soul that kiss for which the Bride besought Him; for I understand it to be in this Mansion that the petition is fulfilled. ...*
>
> *But what passes in the union of the Spiritual Marriage is very different. The Lord appears in the centre of the soul, not through an imaginary, but through an intellectual vision ....*
>
> *[S]he seems no longer to exist, and has no desire to exist – no, absolutely none – save when she realizes that she can do something*

to advance the glory and honor of God, for which she would gladly lay down her life. ... This, my daughters, is the aim of prayer; this is the purpose of the Spiritual Marriage, of which are born good works and good works alone.[98]

Saint Teresa of Avila, *Interior Castles*

Most mystics emphasize the mental nature of the experience, like seeing through the eye of God. While there also is a deep sense of love – as in the poetry of Rumi and Rabi'a, or Avila's allusion to a spiritual marriage – the most common metaphors include merging with the Void or the mind of God. Like the description in *The Kybalion*, Buddha taught that ascension is predominantly a mental exercise:

Mind precedes all mental states. Mind is their chief; they are all mind-wrought. If with an impure mind a person speaks or acts suffering follows him like the wheel that follows the foot of the ox. ... If with a pure mind a person speaks or acts happiness follows him like his never-departing shadow.[99]

While this may come as a surprise to New Humans at Spectrum Stage 6, who prefer to think of God as Love, the mystical descriptions of God as the highest mental plane has caught the attention of scientists. Indeed, cutting-edge research on the mind includes the hypothesis that consciousness may very well reside outside the brain. For example, in his book *One Mind*, Dr. Larry Dossey includes research from such diverse fields as biology, chemistry, psychology, physics, and even animal studies to suggest that spiritual concepts like the *Tao*, the Noosphere, and the Akashic Records all point to the possible existence of "a compendium of information and knowledge in a nonphysical plane of existence ... likened to the Mind of God."[100] Moreover, Dossey cites Hermes Trismegistus as the ancient source of the "One Mind" concept.

Therefore, let's look again at what the Three Initiates of Hermes have to say. *The Kybalion* explains that the All created the Universe through an "Outpouring" and an "Indrawing" of Divine energy. The Outpouring was the All reducing its own vibration, resulting eventually in gross forms of matter. The Indrawing was like a vibratory homing device that I have been calling the evolutionary impulse, such that everything which left the All could return "as countless highly developed Units of Life, having risen higher and higher in the scale by means of Physical, Mental, and Spiritual Evolution."[101] Here's a fuller explanation:

The Hermetic teachings regarding the process of Evolution are that the ALL, having meditated upon the beginning of the Creation – having thus established the material foundations of the Universe – having thought it into existence – then gradually awakens or rouses from its Meditation and in so doing manifests the process of Evolution on the material, mental, and spiritual planes, successively and in order. Thus the upward movement beings – and all begins to move Spiritward. ...

At the end of countless cycles of aeons of time ... the Great Work is finished – and All is withdrawn into the ALL from which it emerged. But Mystery of Mysteries – the Spirt of each soul is not annihilated, but is infinitely expanded – the Created and the Creator are merged. Such is the report of the Illumined![102]

Yes, the God Game ends when we return to Source. The remaining question is whether we want to win the game as a solo player (individual enlightenment), or whether we have it in our heart to assist other players cross the finish line as well (collective enlightenment). For me, it's an easy choice because I feel we're all in this together. The alchemical change I seek is our collective entry into the Fifth Spiritual Paradigm. That means helping guide Team Light to victory and, in the process, showing Team Dark how it's done!

So esteemed are generosity and service that some traditions regard them as the essence of spiritual life, the practice upon which all other practices converge. From this perspective, a crucial goal of spiritual life is to equip oneself to serve effectively. Even the supreme goal of enlightenment is sought, not for oneself alone, but to better serve and enlighten others. ...

The great mythologist Joseph Campbell called this final phase of return and service "the hero's return." In Zen it is described as the "entering the marketplace with help bestowing hands." In Christianity, it is the culmination of the "spiritual marriage" with God .... Service is not only an expression of awakening, but also a means to awakening.[103]

Roger Walsh, *Essential Spirituality*

To survive the Great Cusp and help humanity cross the threshold into the Fifth Spiritual Paradigm, we will need the vision of Oracles, the integrity of Saints, and the dedication of Bodhisattvas. We can do this, if New Humans are willing to learn the Laws of the Universe which govern the God Game and apply those laws for the benefit of All.

On my coffee table are my two favorite issues of *What is Enlightenment?* magazine, the brain-child of spiritual teacher Andrew Cohen.[104] The "God's Next Move" issue came out in 2006, and I spied it at a book fair the day Oracle Press won an Independent Publishers' book award for *The Truth*. As I rode the subway home that night, I started to read the article on the "Next Spiritual Revolution" and the interview with Ken Wilber. My life was forever changed, as I learned about the Spectrum of Consciousness and Integral theory – the two models New Humans need to absorb and apply in order to win this round of the God Game.

Once I synthesized the Laws of the Universe, the Spectrum of Consciousness and Integral theory, I awoke to the fullness of my mission. The messages I had received during the Venus transit were starting to make sense, and my visions began to seem plausible. Finally, I had a vocabulary to discuss the state of the world and a map to discern the vast differences in the human condition. The Spectrum gave me a critical blueprint of the reality on the ground, and it infused me with new ideas on how we might end the Great Cusp and shift all of humanity into the Fifth Spiritual Paradigm. Gazing at the magazine cover, I then began to focus on *my* next move.

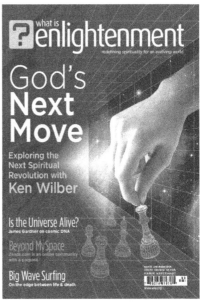

My youngest son was about to graduate from high school and I would soon be free to leave northern Virginia. I pondered where to build the Peace Pentagon, and I travelled around the county trying to locate the mountains and river that had been shown to me in my meditations. Then a friend brought me to Independence, Virginia – in my own backyard! When I saw the New River, I knew immediately it was the right place. The Oracle Institute had a new home, and I never looked back.

Now is the right time to ask yourself, "What's my next move?" If you're ready to be a conscious player in the God Game, keep reading and contact me. Together, let's co-create God's next move!

[1] The Three Initiates, *The Kybalion: A Study of the Hermetic Philosophy of Ancient Egypt and Greece*, Nu Vision Publications: San Francisco, CA (2007). See also: *Sacred Texts*, https://www.sacred-texts.com/eso/kyb/index.htm (1912) (accessed July 2022).

[2] See the first two books of the Oracle Trilogy, *The Truth: About the Five Primary Religions*, (2nd Ed. 2010), and *The Love: Of the Fifth Spiritual Paradigm* (2010). See also at the Oracle Institute website: http://theoracleinstitute.org/seeking-enlightenment.

[3] R. H. Charles, *The Apocrypha and Pseudepigrapha of the Old Testament: Volume 2*, Clarendon Press: Oxford, England (1913). The legendary battle between Michael and Lucifer is entitled *Vita Adae et Eve* ("The Life of Adam and Eve") (*circa* 200 BCE), https://en.wikisource.org/wiki/The_Apocrypha_and_Pseudepigrapha_of_the_Old_Testament/Volume_II (accessed July 2022).

[4] Other angelic legends stem from *The Book of Enoch*, another Jewish apocrypha, which contains *The Book of the Watchers*, in which there are 200 fallen angels (*circa* 300 BCE). Another Gnostic source of the legend is found in *The Book of Tobit*, a noncanonical Christian text (*circa* 200 BCE).

[5] *Genesis*, Chapter 1:1.

[6] Ibid, Chapter 1:26. See also the inconsistent creation myth in *Genesis*, Chapter 6:4 regarding the "Nephilim," which recites that the "sons of heaven had intercourse with the daughters of man." Some believe the Nephilim were Lucifer and the other fallen angels. They also could be Anunnaki (i.e., Alien Astronaut Theory; see next chapter).

[7] *The Life of Adam and Eve*, a new translation by B. Custis, G. Anderson from the University of Virginia, and R. Layton from the Hebrew University of Jerusalem (1995), http://www2.iath.virginia.edu/anderson/ (accessed July 2022).

[8] Gustave Dore (1832–1883), "Battle in Heaven between Archangel Michael and Archangel Lucifer," *Paradise Lost* (1866 engraving), public domain, *Wikimedia Commons*, https://commons.wikimedia.org/wiki/File:Paradise_Lost_1.jpg (accessed July 2022).

[9] "Phone Home – E.T. Remix," *Melodysheep*, https://www.youtube.com/watch?v=f6sR9R3k_kA (accessed July 2022).

[10] The Three Initiates, *The Kybalion*, p. 43.

[11] James P. Carse, *Finite and Infinite Games: A Vision of Life as Play and Possibility*, pp. 3, 20, 23, Free Press: New York, NY (1986).

[12] See: Ken Wilber and Corey deVos, "What Is Evil," *Integral Life* (May 13, 2019), https://integrallife.com/video/subtle-energy-magick/ (accessed July 2022).

[13] Ken Wilber, *The Religion of Tomorrow: A Vision for the Future of the Great Traditions*, pp. 406–408, Shambhala Publications: Boulder, CO (2017).

[14] G. Gordon Liddy, *Will: The Autobiography of G. Gordon Liddy*, St. Martin's Press: New York, NY (1980).

[15] The Three Initiates, *The Kybalion*, p. 53.

[16] James P. Carse, *Finite and Infinite Games*, pp. 26–26, 33.

[17] Peter Tyson, "The Star in You," *PBS News* (Dec. 2, 2010), https://www.pbs.org/wgbh/nova/article/star-in-you/ (accessed July 2022).

[18] "Section 2.3: The Structure of Atoms," *The Basics of General, Organic, and Biological Chemistry*, Saylor Academy: Washington, DC (2012), https://saylordotorg.github.io/text_the-basics-of-general-organic-and-biological-chemistry/s05-03-the-structure-of-atoms.html (accessed July 2022).

[19] "Beryllium," *Wikipedia*, https://en.wikipedia.org/wiki/Beryllium (accessed July 2022).

[20] See notes and various translations of *The Emerald Tablet on Sacred Texts*, https://www.sacred-texts.com/alc/emerald.htm (accessed July 2022).

[21] "Hermetica," *Wikipedia*, https://en.wikipedia.org/wiki/Hermetica (accessed July 2022).

[22] The Three Initiates, *The Kybalion*, p. 21.

[23] Ibid, pp. 20, 31.

[24] John Gray. Ph.D., *Men are from Mars, Women are from Venus*, HarperCollins: New York, NY (1992).

[25] The Three Initiates, *The Kybalion*, pp. 79, 82.

[26] His Holiness the Dalai Lama (Tenzin Gyatso), "Women with Power Can Bring a Compassionate Revolution," *USA Today* (Nov. 29, 2018), https://www.usatoday.com/story/opinion/2018/11/29/dalai-lama-women-leaders-combine-compassion-power-feminism-column/2081033002/ (accessed July 2022).

[27] Helen Fisher, *The First Sex: The Natural Talents of Women and How They Are Changing the World*, pp. 5–6, Ballantine Publishing Group: New York, NY (1999).

[28] Ibid, p. 231–232, 257–258.

[29] Steven Pinker, *The Better Angels of Our Nature: Why Violence Has Declined*, pp. 174–176, Penguin Books: New York, NY (2011).

[30] Ibid, pp. 362–363.

[31] Rev. Laura M. George, J.D., *The Truth: About the Five Primary Religions*, p. 358, Oracle Institute Press: Independence, VA (2nd Ed. 2010).

[32] See atrocities expounded by Barbara G. Walker, "How Local Wise-Women Who Carried on Ancient Traditions Were Exterminated by Christianity," *Church and State* (Oct. 2008), http://churchandstate.org.uk/2016/09/how-local-wise-women-who-carried-on-ancient-traditions-were-exterminated-by-christianity/ (accessed July 2022).

[33] Nicole Winfield, "Vatican Women's Magazine Blames Drop in Nuns on Abuses," *Associated Press News* (Jan. 23, 2020), https://apnews.com/965ab278f03e30fafd7bd22acf9e044d (accessed July 2022).

[34] Julia Ward Howe, "The Original Mother's Day Proclamation" (1870), *Wikipedia*, https://en.wikipedia.org/wiki/Mother%27s_Day_Proclamation (accessed July 2022).

[35] Georgia Aspinall, "Here Are the Countries Where It's Still Really Difficult for Women to Vote," *Grazia Magazine* (Aug. 3, 2021), https://graziadaily.co.uk/life/real-life/countries-where-women-can-t-vote/ (accessed July 2022).

[36] Simone de Beauvoir, *The Second Sex*, p. 59, Vintage Books: New York, NY (2011).

[37] "Capital Punishment for Homosexuality," *Wikipedia*, https://en.wikipedia.org/wiki/Capital_punishment_for_homosexuality (accessed July 2022).

[38] To relive this nightmare see: "Trump Recorded Having Extremely Lewd Conversation About Women in 2005," *Washington Post* (Oct. 8, 2016), https://www.washingtonpost.com/politics/trump-recorded-having-extremely-lewd-conversation-about-women-in-2005/2016/10/07/3b9ce776-8cb4-11e6-bf8a-3d26847eeed4_story.html (accessed July 2022).

[39] Edward Helmore, "Who Were the Rich and Powerful People in Jeffrey Epstein's Circle?" *The Guardian* (Aug. 10, 2019), https://www.theguardian.com/us-news/2019/aug/10/jeffrey-epstein-trump-clinton-friends (accessed July 2022).

[40] Helen Fisher, *The First Sex*, pp. 169–170, 285–286.

[41] Claire Zillman, "The Fortune 500 Has More Female CEOs Than Ever Before," *Fortune Magazine* (May 16, 2019), https://fortune.com/2019/05/16/fortune-500-female-ceos/ (accessed July 2022).

[42] The evidence for this claim is overwhelming and has been chronicled by many scholars, including Margaret Starbird, *The Woman with the Alabaster Jar: Mary Magdalene and the Holy Grail*, Bear & Company: Rochester, VT (1993). See also: Laura George, *The Truth: About the Five Primary Religions*, Chapter 4.

[43] Jennifer Viegas, "God's Wife Edited Out of the Bible – Almost," *NBC News* and *Discovery News* (March 18, 2011), https://www.nbcnews.com/id/wbna42147912#.Xmq8TahKiyI (accessed July 2022).

[44] "Enheduanna," *Wikipedia*, https://en.wikipedia.org/wiki/Enheduanna (accessed July 2022).

[45] High Priestess Enheduana, *The Exaltation of Inana, Corpus of Sumerian Literature* (*circa* 2300 BCE), http://etcsl.orinst.ox.ac.uk/section4/tr4072.htm (accessed July 2022).

[46] The Three Initiates, *The Kybalion*, p. 69.

[47] Watch: "The Curious Case of Benjamin Button Accident Scene," screenplay by Eric Roth (2008), based on the book by F. Scott Fitzgerald, *YouTube* (Oct. 19, 2012), https://www.youtube.com/watch?v=dakx97gRCx0 (accessed July 2022).

[48] The Three Initiates, *The Kybalion*, p. 71.

[49] Ibid, p. 14.

[50] Buddha, *The Dhammapada*, The Pairs: No. 19 (*circa* 300 BCE), translated by Acharya Buddharakkhita (1996), https://www.accesstoinsight.org/tipitaka/kn/dhp/dhp.01.budd.html (accessed July 2022).

[51] *Bhagavad Gita*, Chapter 3:27–28 (*circa* 500 BCE).

[52] Nikki McCann Ramirez, "Coronavirus: How Fox News and Other Right-Wing Media Endanger Our Health," *USA Today* (Feb. 27, 2020), https://www.usatoday.com/story/opinion/2020/02/27/fox-news-right-wing-media-conspiracy-theories-coronavirus-covid-19-column/4886082002/ (accessed July 2022).

[53] The Three Initiates, *The Kybalion*, p. 72.

[54] Ibid, p. 63.

[55] Brendan Cole, "Russia Teams Up with China and Iran Before Ukraine Crisis Meeting with U.S.," *Newsweek* (Jan. 21, 2022), https://www.newsweek.com/russia-ukraine-drills-navy-iran-china-blinken-1671470 (accessed July 2022).

[56] Lao Tzu, *The Tao Te Ching*, Chapters 32, 40 (*circa* 600 BCE)

[57] The Three Initiates, *The Kybalion*, pp. 66–67.

[58] The Three Initiates, *The Kybalion*, p. 59.

[59] *Bhagavad Gita*, Chapters 4:7–8, 8:26.

[60] *The Holy Bible*, Isaiah 5:20, 5:24 (*circa* 750 BCE).

[61] Buddha, *The Dhammapada*, The Pairs: No. 5.

[62] Jesus, *Gospel of Matthew*, Chapter 7:6. Compare *Gospel of Thomas*, Verse 93 both are *circa* 70 CE, though *Thomas* may be an earlier "Sayings Source."

[63] Rabi'a al Basri, "The Real Goal" (*circa* 780 CE), in *Doorkeeper of the Heart: Versions of Rabia*, translated by Charles Upton, Pir Press: New York, NY (2004).

[64] Tau Malachi, *The Gnostic Gospel of St. Thomas: Meditations on the Mystical Teachings*, p. 290, Llewellyn Publications: St. Paul, MN (2004).

[65] Evolutionary Leaders website, https://www.evolutionaryleaders.net/ (accessed July 2022).

[66] The Three Initiates, *The Kybalion*, pp. 35–37.

[67] Ibid, pp. 60–61.

[68] Dalai Lama, *Be Happy*, Hampton Roads Publishing Co.: Charlottesville, VA (2019); Dalai Lama and Noriyuki Ueda, *Be Angry*, Hampton Roads Publishing Co.: Charlottesville, VA (2019).

[69] Naomi Wolf, *The End of America: Letter of Warning to a Young Patriot*, Chelsea Greene Publishing: White River Junction, VT (2007).

[70] Ibid, pp. 25, 36, 127, 143.

[71] John W. Whitehead, *Battlefield America: The War on the American People*, Select Books, Inc.: New York, NY (2015); *A Government of Wolves: The Emerging American Police State*, Select Books, Inc.: New York, NY (2013). See also: Whitehead's blog: "The Tyranny of 9/11: The Building Blocks of the American Police State from A–Z," *Huffington Post* (Sept. 7, 2016), https://www.huffpost.com/entry/the-tyranny-of-911-the-bu_b_11879228 (accessed July 2022).

[72] Arthur Koestler, *Janus: A Summing Up*, Random House: New York, NY (1978).

[73] Ken Wilber, *Trump and a Post-Truth World*, pp. 86–88, 106, Shambhala Publications: Boulder, CO (2017).

[74] The Three Initiates, *The Kybalion*, p. 61.

[75] Ibid, p. 55, 58.

[76] Edgar Cayce, Reading 1532-1, "Abundance is Yours," (Dec. 16, 2009), https://www.edgarcayce.org/about-us/blog/blog-posts/abundance-is-yours-part-i/ (accessed July 2022).

[77] Roger Walsh, *Essential Spirituality: The 7 Central Practices to Awaken Heart and Mind*, p. 14, John Wiley & Sons: New York, NY (1999).

[78] The Three Initiates, *The Kybalion*, pp. 55, 58.

[79] Fritjof Capra, *The Tao of Physics: An Exploration of the Parallels between Modern Physics and Eastern Mysticism*, pp. 104, 106, 116, Shambhala Press: Boson, MA (2010 edition).

[80] Barry Johnson, *And: Making a Difference by Leveraging Polarity, Paradox or Dilemma*, Volume 1 Foundations and Volume 2 Applications, HRD Press: Amherst, MA (2020); *Polarity Management: Identifying and Managing Unsolvable Problems*, HRD Press: Amherst, MA (2014). Also, Oracle Advisor and dear friend Cliff Kayser is a member of Polarity Partnerships, http://www.polaritypartnerships.com/.

[81] Roger Walsh, *Essential Spirituality*, p. 75.

[82] The Three Initiates, *The Kybalion*, pp. 41, 47.

[83] *Huai Nan Tzu* (*circa* 150 BCE), from Joseph Needham and Ling Wing, *Science and Civilization in China*, Volume 2, p. 51, Cambridge University Press: New York, NY (1956).

[84] The Three Initiates, *The Kybalion*, p. 42.

[85] Fritjof Capra and Pier Luigi Luisi, *The Systems View of Life: A Unifying Vision*, pp. 80, 286, Cambridge University Press: New York, NY (2014).

[86] Pierre Teilhard de Chardin, *The Phenomena of Man*, Harper & Row: New York, NY (1959).

[87] Fritjof Capra and Pier Luigi Luisi, *The Systems View of Life*, p. 285.

[88] Larry Dossey, *One Mind: How Our Individual Mind is Part of a Greater Consciousness and Why It Matters*, p. 15, Hay House: New York, NY (2013).

[89] The Three Initiates, *The Kybalion*, p. 47.

[90] Ibid, p. 48.

[91] Larry Dossey, *One Mind*, p. 73.

[92] Paramahansa Yogananda, *Autobiography of a Yogi*, p. 17, Self-Realization Fellowship: Los Angeles, CA (13th Ed. 1998).

[93] Ibid, p. 38.

[94] Ibid, p. 90.

[95] Ibid, pp. 235 *et. seq.*

[96] The Three Initiates, *The Kybalion*, p. 15.

[97] Evelyn Underwood, *Mysticism: The Nature and Development of Spiritual Consciousness*, pp. 246, 265, 413, 418, Oneworld Publications: Oxford, England (1993).

[98] Saint Teresa of Avila, *Interior Castles*, translated by E. Allison Peers, pp. 223–224, 213, 219, 228, Bantam Doubleday Dell Publishing Group: New York, NY (1989). See also: Saint Teresa of Avila, *The Life*.

[99] Buddha, *The Dhammapada*, The Pairs: Nos. 1, 2.

[100] Larry Dossey, *One Mind*, p. xxxv.

[101] The Three Initiates, *The Kybalion*, p. 43.

[102] Ibid, p. 44.

[103] Roger Walsh, *Essential Spirituality*, pp. 256–257.

[104] Andrew Cohen, *What is Enlightenment?*, Issue 33 (June-August 2006). Back issues are available at: https://www.andrewcohen.com/enlightennext-magazine/ (accessed July 2022).

I am sitting on the edge of the cliff looking out at a
vast emptiness, nothingness, or void.
Everything that used to give meaning to my life has been
falling away and this nothingness is what remains.

There is a sense that I am still here in some way,
separate from this void. ...
The thinking mind resists the void and
contracts in fear in the face it ....

It was then seen that a deeper "truth" is the need to completely
surrender everything, all knowing, into the not-knowing ....

Krishnamurti, *The Challenge of Nothingness*

In the last chapter, we explored the God Game and the Laws of the Universe, which govern our existence and experience on the Earth Plane. We saw that these metaphysical laws – just like the laws of physics – impact everyone, regardless of whether they understand the laws or not. We also pondered the existence of Light Masters and Dark Lords, advanced souls who master these laws and utilize them for good (evolutionary) or evil (destructive) purposes. Lastly, we identified the "holy grail" of the God Game: accessing non-duality and merging with Source. This is a universal goal, I submit, that all humans seek, regardless of whether they play for Team Light or Team Dark (or even operate as conscious participants in the God Game).

At the summit of higher motives is the pull to self-transcendence.
... It is the compelling call to remember who we really are and to
know, even unite with, our Source. Whether described as the yearning
for God, the moskha drive, or the desire to align with Tao, this pull
to enlightenment is a supreme motive; the only one, say the great
religions, capable of ultimately offering true satisfaction and bliss. ...
[A]s long as the yearning for enlightenment goes unfulfilled, we will
suffer from "divine homesickness."[1]

Roger Walsh, *Essential Spirituality*

I also interjected a new term – the Void – to describe the realm in the Ethereal Plane where answers may be found. And we need answers desperately! If the objective of the God Game is unification with each other and Source, it is obvious we are nowhere near this goal. Indeed, we may suffer a planetary "do over" during the final clash of the Fourth and Fifth Spiritual Paradigms.

Paradoxically, we cannot solve the riddle of Earth Plane polarity unless we master that principle then rise above it, as the nested and holarchical Laws of the Universe reveal. Only then can we see the big picture and connect all dots. Only then can we strategize on how to achieve unity and answer the perplexing question: *What on earth is happening on the Earth Plane?*

To help discern why the world appears stuck in perpetual polarity, I have been building us a bridge to evoke deeper analysis, elicit needed data, and begin to draw some conclusions about the nature of the Earth Plane. To quickly recap, here are some preliminary determinations from our journey thus far:

➤ The Godhead is shifting and we are nearing the end of a Great Cusp, the period between paradigms when an evolutionary shift or nihilistic collapse is possible (Chapter I).

➤ The Spectrum of Consciousness is vast, yet Spiral Dynamics helps us identify New Human allies and help old humans, by anticipating their reactions to the paradigm shift and monitoring those who have a vested interest in the old paradigm (Chapter II).

➤ The cycles and seasons of history reveal relevant patterns, recurring existential threats, and political, socio-economic, and spiritual trends that we should study, since knowledge is power (Chapters III and IV).

➤ The Laws of the Universe will aid us, and we are committed to anchoring the first Law of Gender, which will redefine the Godhead then trickle-down to alleviate many frontline issues (Chapter V).

➤ The Void is where we can find answers to help us win the God Game.

My objective in this chapter is to enter the Void along with the reader in search of further clarity. My medicine totem is Crow, one of the black colored animals that can enter the Void. In the case of Crow, she enters the Void to align with God's law – vastly different than manmade law. I have been to the Void and can describe it as a non-dual "neutral zone" where I am one with the groundless form of being. Other mystics describe the Void as filled with both no-thingness and all-thingness. Old humans call this realm heaven and attach to it all manner of mythical thought forms. But New Humans understand that the Void is the place where answers lie, where bliss is attained, and where the Godhead is energetically balanced.

> *Human law is not the same as Sacred Law. More so than any other medicine, Crow sees that the physical world and even the spiritual world, as humanity interprets them, are an illusion. There are billions of worlds. There are an infinitude of creatures. Great Spirit is within all. ...*
>
> *Crow is an omen of change. Crow lives in the void and has no sense of time. The Ancient Chiefs tell us that Crow sees simultaneously the three fates – past, present, and future. Crow merges light and darkness, seeing both inner and outer reality.*[2]

Jamie Sams & David Carson, Medicine Cards

To assist us in leaving the realm of duality, envision a misty-grey corridor that leads to the Void. As we walk through this passageway, let us begin to cleanse our minds so that we may access greater Truth, Love, and Light. Let us find comfort in the knowledge that the Universe has a Default Mode that favors the evolutionary impulse (i.e., the positive pole of every polarity). As we near the Void, let us assume a posture of awe, openness, and deep curiosity.

Let us further prepare by setting-aside our belief system, for our solemn objective is to deduce the very nature of the Earth Plane. Let us also suspend our disbelief in the belief systems of others. We must purify ourselves to the greatest extent possible. Finally, let us revisit the very first question posed at the start of this book: *Why do people believe what they believe?*

Already, we know much of the answer to this question, since the Spectrum of Consciousness provides us with an invaluable tool for discerning how people think and react to the world. To that map, let us add basic Integral theory, which uses the Spectrum as just one line of inquiry. In all, Ken Wilber uses a four-quadrant map, shown below.[3]

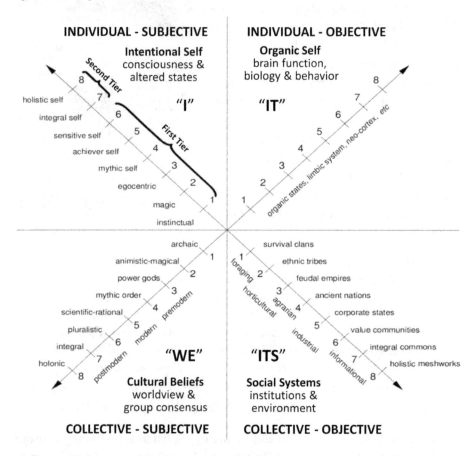

This map shows four ways in which we may examine ourselves and others. We can study individuals by listening to them and hearing their subjective appraisal of the world (upper left quadrant). We can study people as a scientist might, by examining their biology and observing their behavior (upper right quadrant). As for groups, we can ask them what they are thinking to understand why different cultures promote certain customs and values (bottom left quadrant). And we can watch groups of people to see how they collectively behave and whether they actually have co-created a world that mirrors their expressed values and beliefs (bottom right quadrant).

Generally speaking, social systems (bottom right) lag behind individual and cultural development (upper and bottom left). Why? Because it is easier to reach consensus on matters – *as hard as that can be* – than it is to change our institutions to mirror our collective desires and goals. Some delay is due to the complex nature of bureaucracy, which can be hard to spin on a dime. However, the other reason societies have trouble improving governance is that powerful stakeholders with a vested interest in the *status quo* game the system and suppress the will of the majority.

Such is the case in the United States with issues like gun control, universal healthcare, and protecting the commons (e.g., clean water and air regulations, mining and fracking restrictions). In fact, corruption is the primary reason our institutions fail to keep pace with the cutting edge of consciousness. Nonetheless, our institutions reflect our collective will. We therefore must assume responsibility for the societies we co-create by, at a minimum, expressing our values at the ballot box.

As New Humans we have yet another responsibility. We need to lead by example, and that means taking stock of our own interior and exterior life (upper left and right quadrants). What kind of example are we setting? Do we speak truth to power? Do we even speak truth to our neighbors with whom we may disagree on vital matters? In the past, we could adopt a "live and let live" attitude, but we no longer have the luxury of ignoring or implicitly condoning the bad choices of others, especially in leadership positions. The Earth Plane is facing multiple existential threats, and New Humans simply must come together in a strategic manner to find common ground with old humans.

Better still, we should strive to assist old humans in reaching the stage of spiritual development where pluralism kicks in. If we can help elevate minds and hearts, we stand an even better chance of entering the Fifth Paradigm. Otherwise, we will suffer the consequences of socio-spiritual inertia, if not outright de-evolution. In the book *Why We Believe What We Believe*, neuroscientist Andrew Newberg, M.D. offers some suggestions on how to open our own minds and the minds of others. The goal is holistic thinking:

> *When we look at the world holistically, all things appear to be deeply connected. ... Current research has identified specific neurons that are sensitive to holistic representations; however, the majority of our neurons reduce and categorize experience into object fragments. This may explain why reductionist thinking is so predominant in human culture, and why holistic perceptions are so often dismissed skeptically.*

> *Logical, rational, and reductionist processes are primarily carried out by the left side of the brain, whereas the ability to view the world in an integrated and connected way is associated with the right side of the brain. ...*
>
> *Thus, we are born with two hemispheres that will, over time, develop two distinctly different worldviews, and our consciousness does not seem to like this very much. ...*
>
> *Holistic awareness, like other forms of subjective experience, may be an emergent property that arises from a vast network of interconnecting neural processes. Self-recognition of this internal experience may even be the ultimate expression of holistic function, when we realize that the parts ... can only be considered in relationship with the whole.*[4]

Dr. Newberg is talking about Second Tier systems thinking, which takes root at Stage 6 when a desire for harmony emerges and begins to overtake polarizing "us–them" constructs. This level of consciousness is rare, as we've already discussed. Here's some more reasons why we're not as close to the Tipping Point as the New Age community likes to believe. First, our minds and our memories are chock full of erroneous conceptions. Memory forms the foundation of our belief system and it is notoriously faulty. Autobiographical memories are even more prone to inaccuracy. In addition, trauma affects memory and our ability later to construct a realistic worldview.

In his book, Newberg cites four factors that mold our belief system and, not surprisingly, his map of how consciousness evolves closely parallels Wilber's four quadrant Integral theory. From the interior personal standpoint, our beliefs are shaped by our emotions and perceptions. From an exterior personal perspective, our biological cognition determines our outward expression and behavior. Lastly, consensus is a powerful motivator, since humans are prone to group-think and our brains feel dissonance when our worldview conflicts with expert opinion or pressure from our peers.[5]

Shockingly, the brain stops developing by age thirty, which is when most of us close our minds to new information. By early adulthood, belief systems unusually are established, with most humans arresting at Spectrum Stage 4 (fundamentalism) or Stage 5 (rationalism).

> *To make matters worse, neural development virtually ceases by the time we reach thirty, and it's all downhill from there. The brain's metabolic and neurotransmitter activity begins to decrease, and it continues to decrease throughout the remainder of life ....*

Neurologically, enlightenment and peace are unlikely. Even [Lawrence] Kohlberg *admitted that only a small percentage of adults will reach a moral level at which their lives are governed by higher ethical principles. Nonetheless, this level can be reached by those who choose to work diligently toward the ideals it involves, although this process can take decades of introspection and practice.*[6]

Andrew Newberg, *Why We Believe What We Believe*

The fact that most people's moral code is set at an early age is another reason cultural change is slow and institutional improvements slower still. Nevertheless, there is ample evidence that life-altering mystical experiences can happen at any age. For instance, Saint Teresa of Avila was in her forties when she experienced her first rapture, she was near fifty when she established the discalced (barefoot) Order of Carmelite Nuns (she founded a total of seventeen convents), and she was over sixty when she penned my favorite mystical texts: *The Life, Interior Castles,* and *The Way of Perfection.*

Speaking of nuns, Newberg received permission from the Catholic Church to examine the brainwaves of praying nuns, and he received permission from the Dalai Lama to study meditating monks. In the case of both Christian and Buddhist devouts, their spiritual practices measurably altered their brain waves. Moreover, in response to the concern that scientific experiments might one day disprove Buddhist claims, the Dali Lama has written, "If scientific analysis were conclusively to demonstrate certain claims in Buddhism to be false, then we must accept the findings of science and abandon those claims."[7]

As an indefatigable truth seeker, I delight in the open-mindedness with which His Holiness embraces science and the reciprocal respect that scientists now are extending to spiritual phenomenon. It is high time for scientists to study the interior, subjective quadrants of the human mind and, when they do, they tend to validate the holistic aspects of consciousness, including the Spectrum of Consciousness and Integral theory. More on the merger of science and spirituality soon.

One last note before we enter the Void. Scientists have identified myriad ways in which our brain plays tricks on us. Why does our brain do this? Because duality and dissonance are uncomfortable, and the brain hates ambiguity. Instead, it likes to sort, sift, and catalogue – all to give us peace of mind. Here is a partial list of the many ways in which our brain tries to force us into making firm decisions, the quicker the better, and the closer aligned with our expectations the better. These are the most common brain biases:

➢ **Family Bias:** We usually believe what our family and friends tell us.

➢ **Self-Serving Bias:** We like facts that serve narcissistic needs.

➢ **Authoritarian Bias:** Persuades us to agree with people in positions of power or status.

➢ **Confirmation Bias:** We like (and seek out) information that validates what we think we already know.

➢ **Projection Bias:** We assume others in our group agree with us.

➢ **Group Bias:** A two-way prejudice that helps us accept what our friends say and reject what a person from another group offers.

➢ **Bandwagon Bias:** A strong tendency to go along with any group of which we are a member, even if we are new to the group (e.g., many people will acquiesce to "Nazi values," as proven in many controlled experimental settings where aggression is encouraged by the group).

➢ **Cause and Effect Bias:** Our brain likes to make a causal connection between events, even when none exists.

➢ **Magic Number Bias:** Nearly everyone has a favorite number that they see often because they look for it and ignore other numbers.

➢ **Perceptual Bias:** Our brain assumes that our beliefs and observations reflect objective truth and then stores the data as valid memories.

➢ **Perseverance Bias:** Once we believe something, we resist letting go of the belief, even when it is proven wrong.

➢ **Uncertainty Bias:** Because our brain likes to sift and then catalogue data, ambiguity is abandoned in favor of a concrete belief or disbelief, thereby encouraging us to make a choice better left unmade.[8]

Thus, in order to access higher and better information, we have to battle our biases. These prejudices and false expectations are practically hardwired into our brains. Consequently, as we near the end of the grey, misty corridor that leads to the Void, please try your best, dear reader, to open your mind so you can entertain new points of view and possibly assimilate something you hadn't thought of before, something that might help us shift the paradigm.

What follows are my conjectures on the nature of the Earth Plane from numerous brainstorming sessions we've conducted at The Oracle Institute, sometimes into the wee hours of the night. I've also included some new ideas that I have never shared publicly on what might be influencing our co-creative, collective journey. As we delve into these possible Earth Plane scenarios, remember that we have entered the Void and pledged to be open to new ideas. Let the adventure begin ...

MODELS OF THE EARTH PLANE

Now that we're inside the Void, let's explore the most likely reasons why the Earth Plane appears stuck in gender and racial prejudice (contrary to the first Law of the Universe), *karmic* chaos (second law), repetitive patterns (third law), and polarity (fourth law). Our goal is to draw Second Tier conclusions as to why this planet can be both barbaric and beautiful, all at the same time. It is imperative that New Humans have a working model of what is happening; otherwise, we can't coordinate an effective response to the many challenges of the Great Cusp, nor get Team Light organized for the climax of the current Fourth Turning – both of which are shifting the paradigm in real time.

As we probe the nature of the Earth Plane, we may not agree on every detail, and that's okay. We just need to concur generally on the origin, rules, and goals of the God Game. We also should agree that the world needs pragmatic Lightworkers more than neophyte Lightholders. If we want to build a New World – one that old humans fearfully resist – we need all hands on deck to help navigate these choppy waters. New Humans are called upon to be active change agents, spiritual warriors, and conscious participants in the God Game.

Additionally, a shared cosmological model will help us mount a successful campaign to guide humanity through the current chaos of the Great Cusp and into the Fifth Spiritual Paradigm. Again, we don't need to agree on every detail, but we should be open to better narratives. So while I might prefer to view the Universe as it is presented in *The Kybalion* (last chapter) or *Gnostic Kabbalah* (coming up in this chapter), another player on Team Light may feel that the alien astronaut theory helps her get closer to the truth. My point is that so long as we seek to help as many people as possible cross into the new paradigm, certain theoretical details will be irrelevant. Although, if we conclude that the most probable Earth Plane model is pre-programmed for human failure – like a "prison planet" theory – then the rules of the God Game would be stacked against us. That would constitute a critical piece of data about the Earth Plane that we would need to consider when formulating a plan of action.

At the outset, I have tipped my hand. The reader knows, per my Gnostic training, I believe there is a Default Mode of the Universe that favors evolution and our collective progress. Even so, I could be wrong. That is why I, too, need to keep an open mind. Thus, the theories which follow are ones I perceive to be viable cosmologies, some of which favor evolution and some of which don't. Lastly, I chose these specific models for examination because there is credible evidence for each. So into the Void we go in search of Truth, Love, and Light!

LINGERING LIZARD BRAIN

The simplest explanation for humanity's painfully slow progress and sluggish acquisition of higher moral values (i.e., Growing Up) is that it just takes a long time for our brains to upgrade and for the societies we build to advance. Period. Nothing mysterious going on. No hidden forces at work. If this is the case, then the God Game simply mirrors the protracted pace of evolution – an infinitesimally small but steady march toward a future of greater complexity, cooperation, and compassion.

Likely, this is the explanation most biologists and neuroscientists would provide if we asked them about our lingering lizard brain and the development of the prefrontal cortex, a relative late comer to brain capacity. Our ancient lizard or "reptilian brain" represents about 500 million years of evolution, and it controls our autonomic functions, such as breathing and the fight-or-flight response, in addition to routine behaviors and addictions.[9] On the other hand, our prefrontal cortex has been evolving for a mere 1.9 million years, starting with *Homo habilis*. It is the prefrontal cortex that modulates decision making, complex cognitive behavior, personal expression, and speech and language.[10]

A while back, our prefrontal cortex kicked into high gear, according to historian Yuval Noah Harari, resulting in a "Cognitive Revolution." In his book *Sapiens: A Brief History of Humankind*, Harari writes that roughly 70,000 years ago, our prefrontal cortex advanced to the point where humans gained the capacity "to think in unprecedented ways and to communicate using an altogether new type of language."[11] Yet, Harari does not necessarily credit this small but significant shift in human brain power with any improvement in our social behavior, which has taken much longer to develop:

> *The Cognitive Revolution that turned Homo sapiens from an insignif-icant ape into the master of the world did not require any noticeable change in physiology or even in the size and external shape of the Sapiens' brain. It apparently involved no more than a few small changes to internal brain structure. Perhaps another small change would be enough to ignite a Second Cognitive Revolution, create a completely new type of consciousness, and transform Homo sapiens into something altogether different.*[12]

Stephen Pinker makes the same argument in his book, *Better Angels of Our Nature*. Pinker convincingly shows that humans are becoming less violent and more cooperative, and he also discounts brain capacity when exploring the reasons for our increasing levels of empathy and peacefulness. According to Pinker, one reason we've advanced morally is due to the rise of just laws in social democracies, including fair due process and predictable punishment for violations of law. Another factor he cites is global commerce, which creates an incentive to cooperate, or at least civilly compete in the market place. The "feminization" of the planet is a third factor according to Pinker, which he defines as the adoption of classically feminine attributes, such as compassion, mercy, and non-violent conflict resolution.[13]

This third point – feminism – seems the most critical factor to meaningful societal progress. The freedoms demanded by women for bodily sovereignty, birth control, partnering decisions, and advanced education have contributed to a more humane planet by anyone's measure, which is why the United Nations lists female equality as one of its "Strategic Development Goals."[14] Moreover, as women achieve equal rights, they become more available to lead, allowing them to further impact and transform culture.

Social historian Riane Eisler also stresses this point, describing the future Fifth Spiritual Paradigm as one of **Partnerism**. Eisler may be best known for her seminal book *The Chalice and the Blade*, in which she reconstructed an earlier era of gender balance in synch with Oracle's Second Spiritual Paradigm. Sadly, it was the transition to the Third and Fourth Paradigms – polytheism and Daddy Deism – when physical domination of women began and patriarchal and hierarchical values were anchored. Thereafter, cut-throat lizard brain behavior became the acceptable norm for thousands of years, a sad and, in many ways, retrograde evolutionary stage, as Eisler explains:

> *Indeed, the theme of unity of all things in nature, as personified by the Goddess, seems to permeate Neolithic art. For here the supreme power governing the universe is the Divine Mother who gives her people life, provides them with material and spiritual nurturance, and who even in death can be counted on to take her children back into her cosmic womb. ...*
>
> *At the core of the invaders' system was the placing of higher value on the power that takes, rather than gives life. This was the power symbolized by the "masculine" Blade.... For in their dominator society, ruled by gods – and men – of war, this was the supreme power. ...*
>
> *This glorification of the lethal power of the sharp blade accompanied a way of life in which organized slaughter of other human beings, along with the destruction and looting of their property and the subjugation and exploitation of their persons, appears to have been normal. ...*[15]

Pinker cites the power of reason and perspective-taking as relatively new features which have increased our humanity and lessened our tendency toward intolerance and violence. Thus, the influence of "nurture" more than "nature" seems to account for the increased number of New Humans with higher values, according to Pinker:

> [O]ver the course of the twentieth century, people's reasoning abilities – particularly their ability to set aside immediate experience, detach themselves from a parochial vantage point, and think in abstract terms – were steadily enhanced. ...
>
> [T]he Long Peace has had the world's most distinguished military historians shaking their head in disbelief. The Rights Revolutions too have given us ideals that educated people today take for granted but that are virtually unprecedented in human history ....
>
> The other half of the sanity check is to ask whether our recent ancestors can really be considered morally retarded. The answer, I am prepared to argue, is yes. Though they were surely decent people with perfectly functioning brains ... [m]any of their beliefs can be considered not just monstrous but, in a very real sense, stupid.[16]

Though brain activity generally peaks by age thirty, new research shows that nerve cells continue to grow extensions and connections in the brain, resulting in greater neuroplasticity than previously thought.[17] Moreover, meditation and mindfulness practices have been shown to improve focus and follow-though on moralistic ideals and goals. Even so, brain experts agree that the "old reptilian part of our brain selfishly fought for survival, while newer, more fragile parts struggled to form cooperative alliances with others."[18] Therefore, even though techniques such as meditation soften our aggressive behavior, increased empathy and social awareness do not correlate with any measurable change in human brain anatomy.

These shared conclusions on human morality from diverse fields – history, sociology, psychology, and neuroscience – accord fully with the Spectrum of Consciousness, where stages of Growing Up are not so much determined by IQ or brain power, as by the slow upgrade of higher moral values, refined ethics, and a growing culture of peace. Therefore, because consciousness appears to be evolving at a snail's pace, our Earth Plane woes may simply be the result of old humans and our institutions not advancing quickly enough to shift humanity into a more just and holistic paradigm.

Bluntly stated, our collective progress is being stilted by the shadow sides of the First Tier "I" memes, which value power and materialism. Until there are enough New Humans on the planet, the Fourth Paradigm sins – corporatocracy, oligarchy, dictatorship, and other means of abusing power and acquiring money – will continue to dominate this round of the God Game. Charles Eisenstein, in his ontological book *The Ascent of Humanity*, calls the Fourth Paradigm the "Age of Separation" and the Fifth Paradigm the "Age of Reunion." Here is Eisenstein's take on our fundamental problem:

> *The Age of Separation is the result of the story we have built, a story we tell ourselves about ourselves. ... Today, as I have observed, it will take a miracle to save human civilization. The near-certain future of the planet is plain to see. ... And the only way I know to generate such a miracle is the same way we generated the first one: by implementing a new story. ...*
>
> *The story of the Age of Reunion is more than just another story using the same technology of symbol. The fundamental difference is that our storytelling will become conscious. ... The Age of Reunion is nothing more or less than falling back in love with the world. ... When we fall in love with the world, we will perceive and treat everything as sacred. ... As a result, all the old dualisms will crumble.*[19]

I wholeheartedly agree. The mythos of the Fourth Paradigm – the ancient Abrahamic religions, the hierarchical/patriarchal stories and symbols, and an obsolete Godhead – are all crushing humanity, especially women. The passing paradigm is a dead weight, a primitive and polarizing ethos that is simply too heavy to drag along behind us into the Fifth Paradigm.

Yet, we cannot cut the cord either, since old and New Humans are on the Earth Plane together, for better or worse. Indeed, that's an underlying reality of the God Game. No rapture is coming to whisk away Stage 4 fundamentalists. Neither will there be a Stage 6 "reverse-rapture" that sweeps New Humans into a "fifth dimension" (more on that looney notion soon). Consequently, we New Humans need to get our act together and formulate a clever, concrete plan of action. Recall that Wilber gives us about a 50-50 chance of making it into the next paradigm, better odds, at least, than Steven Hawking gave us.

The good news is that if the God Game is a simple matter of continued evolution, then patience and perseverance should win the day. With no hidden forces at work, we eventually should be able to positively transition into the Fifth Paradigm, even if it takes a thousand years. That is, of course, unless a "wild card" scenario hits – a huge catastrophe with the power to wipe out most or all of our collective progress. But wait. Has such an event happened before? Have humans ever been annihilated and forced to rebuild society all over again?

TRAUMATIC MEMORY SYNDROME: CATASTROPHOBIA

Yes, there is historical evidence that humanity has faced near destruction and lived to tell the tale. A series of fateful events occurred at the end of the last Ice Age (*circa* 20,000 BCE). By 11,000 BCE, melting glaciers caused ocean currents to change and massive flooding, with sea levels rising as much as ten meters (32 feet) over just a few decades.[20] Then suddenly, the warming trend reversed after a comet hit North America (possibly Canada or Greenland), also around 11,000 BCE, which added even more turmoil to the Earth changes.[21] The impact of the comet caused a sudden and massive drop in temperature due to cloud cover, resulting in a dramatic loss of human life and the extinction of 75% of the large mammals (e.g., wooly mammoth, saber-toothed tiger).[22] The comet's impact was the equivalent of 700 megaton nuclear bombs, resulting in more ice melting, more flooding, and even greater loss of life.[23]

These catastrophic Earth changes produced multiple "great floods," and the destruction was recorded by our ancestors. The famous flood occurred around 5500 BCE, and it was memorialized by the Sumerians in the *Epic of Gilgamesh* (*circa* 2700 BCE). The Sumerian story is the original version of the tale attributed to Noah. In fact, *Gilgamesh* pre-dates *Genesis* by almost two thousand years, and it even includes the detail of releasing a bird from the ship to find land. The melting glaciers and rising northern Atlantic Ocean caused a domino effect: The Mediterranean Sea rose and then flooded the Black Sea – a true trauma for anyone who witnessed the event and survived to tell about it.

Today, models of this global warming calamity show that the rushing water would have "dug a channel more than 300 feet deep as it poured into the Black Sea basin, changing it from a freshwater lake to a salty ocean" and "creating a waterfall 200 times the volume of Niagara Falls."[24] In just one day, enough water would have come through the channel "to cover Manhattan to a depth at least two times the height of the World Trade Center," with ocean water rushing inland "at the rate of a mile a day."[25] A frightful event, indeed, and one that may lurk in our collective memory and the Akashic Records.

A similar disaster of epic proportions may have wiped out the legendary civilization of **Atlantis**. While many historians view this story as mere myth, Plato (428–348 BCE) certainly thought it was true, since he took the time to carefully record it in two dialogues: *Timaeus* and *Critias*. However, it was the Egyptians who preserved the harrowing history of Atlantis, and an Egyptian priest shared the story with Solon (630–560 BCE), one of the "seven wise men" of Greece, when he visited Egypt. Upon his return, Solon recorded the story and it passed to the great-grandfather of Critias (460–403 BCE), a contemporary of Plato. Thereafter, Plato penned the story of Atlantis in two teaching treatises.

Plato wrote that Egypt and Greece had been attacked by the Atlanteans at a time when the islands in the Atlantic Ocean were oriented differently, "for in those days ... there was an island situated in front of the straits which are by you called the Pillars of Heracles; the island was larger than Libya and Asia put together, and was the way to other islands."[26] Let's stop here for a moment. The Egyptians told Solon that they had been attacked many years ago by another kingdom which was located on an island that no longer exists. So far, this story is credible, given what we just learned about the drastic Earth changes that took place between 11,000 and 5500 BCE. My questions are: When did Atlantis exist (i.e., before which flood)? And how far back does the Egyptian Empire go?

Most historians date the start of the Egyptian Empire to 3000 BCE, though that timeline is being challenged by reputable archeologists, anthropologists, and historians who have accumulated contrary evidence. Today, the Egyptian timeline is a battleground, with a new generation of historians taking the view that an earlier Egyptian dynasty – or another early advanced civilization – is responsible for building many of the mysterious archeological sites that would be nigh impossible for **Bronze Age** man to build (*circa* 3000–1200 BCE). For example, some archeologists believe the Sphinx was built around 7000 BCE, which would more than double the age of the Egyptian Empire and place it squarely in the last stage of the **Stone Age**, also known as the **Neolithic Period** (8000–3000 BCE).[27] Others believe the Egyptians started building even earlier, during the middle Stone Age or **Mesolithic Period** (10,000–8000 BCE), or perhaps during the first Stone Age or **Paleolithic Period** (30,000–10,000 BCE).

There also is evidence that the Sphinx used to have the head of a lion, which would make sense given that the Age of Leo (10,500–8000 BCE) started at the end of the last ice age. One historian describes the acrimony of the debate thus: "To state that the Sphinx is older than the Old Kingdom implies that some sort of organized civilization existed in this area long before the third millennium b.c. If this is so, much of what archeologists and historians think they know about the rise of civilization must be revised. That idea is as threatening to many scientists today as Galileo's idea that the Sun revolves around the Earth was to the church hundreds of years ago."[28]

For now, let's let this mystery be and return to Plato's account of Atlantis. He dates the war and destruction of Atlantis to 9,000 years before Solon's time, so approximately 10,000 BCE.[29] He says Atlantis was built much earlier than that, by Poseidon for his progeny – a "confederation of kings" starting with

King Atlas – who ruled the central island plus "many other islands."[30] Plato goes into much detail about the architecture, agriculture, governance, and culture of Atlantis, including a report on the size of the core island (roughly 300 miles round), and the concentric island rings that the Atlanteans formed by digging channels into the ground (one was 100 ft. deep, 300 ft. wide, and 300 ft. long).[31] For many generations, the Atlantean kings obeyed their noble laws, but at some point they decided to expand their territory and attack ancient Egypt and Greece.

Tragically, *Critias* was either never finished or the rest of it was lost, but in *Timaeus*, we learn this story is "about the greatest action which the Athenians ever did, and which ought to have been the most famous, but, through the lapse of time and the destruction of the actors" was lost. As the Egyptian priest explains to Solon:

> *O Solon, Solon, you Hellenes are never anything but children, and there is not an old man among you. ... [T]here is no old opinion handed down among you by ancient tradition, nor any science which is hoary with age. And I will tell you why. There have been, and will be again, **many destructions of mankind** arising out of many causes; the greatest have been brought about by the agencies of fire and water ....*
>
> *[W]hatever happened either in your country or in ours ... they have all been written down by us of old, and are preserved in our temples. Whereas just when you and other nations are beginning to be provided with letters and the other requisites of civilized life ... a pestilence comes pouring down ... **and so you have to begin all over again like children**, and know nothing of what happened in ancient times, either among us or among yourselves. ... In the first place **you remember a single deluge only, but there were many previous ones**; in the next place, you do not know that there formerly dwelt in your land the fairest and noblest race of men which ever lived, and that **you and your whole city are descended from a small seed or remnant of them which survived**. ...*
>
> *Many great and wonderful deeds are recorded of your state in our histories. But one of them exceeds all the rest in greatness and valor. For these histories tell of a mighty power which unprovoked made an expedition against the whole of Europe and Asia, and to which your city put an end. ...*
>
> *Now in this **island of Atlantis** there was a great and wonderful empire which had rule over the whole island and several others, and over parts of the continent, and, furthermore, the men of Atlantis had subjected the parts of Libya within the columns of Heracles as*

far as Egypt, and of Europe as far as Tyrrhenia. This vast power
*... **endeavored to subdue at a blow our country and yours** and the*
whole of the region within the straits; and then, Solon, your country
shone forth, in the excellence of her virtue and strength, among all
mankind. She was pre-eminent in courage and military skill ... and
triumphed over the invaders ....

But afterwards there occurred violent earthquakes and floods;
and in a single day and night of misfortune all your warlike men in a
*body sank into the earth, **and the island of Atlantis in like manner***
***disappeared in the depths of the sea.** For which reason the sea in*
those parts is impassable and impenetrable, because there is a shoal
of mud in the way; and this was caused by the subsidence of the
island.[32] [emphasis added]

Wow! If this account is correct, then both Egypt and Greece are far older civilizations than previously thought. Both would have suffered through a massive flood that, by Egypt's dating, occurred around 10,000 BCE, likely as a result of the comet that hit the planet. if we add the "great flood" that occurred around 5500 BCE to the mix, it is easy to imagine that our ancestors would have been totally traumatized. Regardless of whether the stories were passed down orally or in writing, the psyches of early humans would have been scarred for generations by the memory of these two catastrophes.

Barbara Hand Clow posited this theory in her book *Catastrophobia*, which explores the legend of Atlantis and the mysteries surrounding other ancient archeological sites that she believes are misdated and that we moderns would have a hard time building today. In line with Plato's reports, Hand Clow believes that numerous advanced civilizations were built before the devastating Earth changes. She also argues that when the comet hit our planet around 11,000 BCE, the impact may have shifted the Earth's axis to its current 23.5 degree position relative to the Sun.[33] If so, then early humans would have been forced to relearn the locations of stars plus learn about agriculture, since it is Earth's tilted axis that creates the seasons (i.e., no tilt, no seasons). It is a fascinating argument, particularly given the fact that so many civilizations did start to map the stars around that time, and that older lunar calendars were replaced with solar calendars, indicating a sudden need to track the seasons.

As evidence for her theory, Hand Clow points to the **Djed Pillar** at Abydos, one of the oldest Egyptian temples. Usually, the Djed is described as a "symbol for stability" associated with the god Osiris, who was dismembered by his brother Set and then reassembled and resurrected by Isis (though she couldn't find his penis). Remember, back then it was female gods who gave life.

To me, the Djed (left) looks like a Tesla coil. A friend of mine built a djed to experiment with zero-point energy. If it is ancient (or alien) technology, did Isis use the Djed to resurrect Osiris? Hand Clow's theory is that it represents the tilt of Earth, since the pillar mirrors the 23.5 degree axis of Earth after the purported comet strike. She believes the four rings depict the newly established four seasons, and that the ceremony of "vertically righting" the Djed was a ritualistic reference to the prediluvian era before the floods, when Earth had no tilt.[34]

Hand Clow also cites *The History of Egypt*, an ancient text composed by an Egyptian priest named Manetho (*circa* 300 BCE), who purported to list all the pharaohs. The list starts with the "gods and demigods" who ruled Egypt for over 14,000 years, to which he adds the human pharaohs, resulting in a total span of 24,900 years.[35] Early Christian historian Ptolemy II (285–246 CE), through whom we inherit a fragment of a Greek translation of Manetho's work, assumed the priest meant lunar years. Ptolemy equated one lunar year with one month, thereby reducing the time period to 2,206 years, which most scholars accept.[36] Nonetheless, Hand Clow makes many salient observations about Egypt's storied history and the last time Earth changes rocked our planet and shocked our ancestors. For me, her most important point is that humanity still may be suffering from collective traumatic memory syndrome.

> *We are a wounded species on the verge of recovery, and we're poised to undertake the brave journey back to our previous brilliance. ... Like adults who have unrecalled childhood abuse or trauma, we are deeply fearful, paranoid, and easily drawn into collective fear. ... Many truly believe the world is coming to an end, so they'd rather end it all now. This collective insanity could destroy human civilization.*[37]

It is worth mentioning that proof of Hand Clow's theory, if it existed, was almost surely contained in Egypt's Great Library of Alexandria, which went up in smoke, either in 48 BCE (thanks to Julius Caesar), or around 400 CE (when crazed Christians gained control over the library).[38] Regardless of which heartbreaking story is true, historians estimate that the library contained as many as 500,000 papyrus scrolls and other ancient treasures. Extant additional support for advanced civilizations during the (misnamed) Stone Age can be found in the *Maps of the Ancient Sea Kings*, a book written by Charles Hapgood (a good friend of Albert Einstein), which contains authenticated ancient maps which show a very different prediluvian geography.[39]

Clearly, the last round of gargantuan Earth changes would have traumatized our ancestors. Now, 13,000 years later and half-way through the Earth's 26,000 year processional, we face similar challenges. In fact, the last time our planet warmed to this extent and accumulated similar CO_2 levels was 800,000 years ago, when trees grew at the South Pole.[40] The last ten years have been the hottest on record.[41] Presently, we are living through the Sixth Great Extinction (a.k.a. Holocene extinction), during which one-third of all animals and plants are expected to die.[42] And here's a freaky factoid: Scientists say another large asteroid is headed our way and could arrive April 2029, on Friday the 13th. It will likely miss us, but might be close enough to see with the naked eye.[43] And they've named the asteroid Apophis, after the Egyptian god of death!

In 2020, I attended Al Gore's Climate Underground conference at his farm in Tennessee, and I had the good fortune to speak privately with one of the expert panelists. I asked him: *What percent of the human population will die during the Sixth Great Extinction?* He replied that at least 25% of us will perish due to Earth changes and resulting food and water shortages, and that even more will die during wars over scarce resources (a.k.a. "water wars" caused by flooding and desertification). In short, humans were not around during the last five extinction events, which occurred 65 million years ago, when 76% of all species were lost.[44] Consequently, this will be the first extinction event that humans will live through ... or not.

While *Catasrophobia* posits that humanity was psychologically scarred by a series of Earth changes that were, literally, of Biblical proportions, *The Fourth Turning* asserts that humanity co-creates a manmade cycle of pain every four generations. We ascend then regress, we rise then fall again – primarily due to self-imposed and self-sabotaging behaviors. If real, our seasonal psychosis can be viewed as an endemic "fear of success." It entails a basic belief in scarcity, that it is impossible for all of us to succeed as one human family. It keeps us in a perpetual state of apprehension about the future, resulting in all manner of fear-based conduct: competition rather than cooperation; nationalism over globalism; intolerance over compassion; and fragmentation instead of life-affirming holism.

278 | THE LIGHT

As predicted in *The Fourth Turning*, we are experiencing the nightmare of the Winter season: a time when society struggles financially, sacrifices values for safety, and ultimately goes to war, whether internally or against others. For example, during the Covid-19 pandemic – and for the first time in U.S. history – the entire country was under a federal "Disaster Declaration." As of this writing, over eighty million Americans contracted covid and over one million died from the disease. At one point in the crisis, "Continuity of Government" plans were considered, which would suspend our Constitution, alter the power structure of our government, and place control of the nation in the hands of a general.[45] This was not a Trump maneuver. Three former presidents – Clinton, Bush, and Obama – all signed Executive Orders that permit such a transfer of power, the militarization of the national guard and police, and the imprisonment (without due process of law) of any American citizen deemed dangerous.[46] To top it off, the Pentagon has started yet another round of insane spending, and the military is developing novel weapons to use against our own populace.[47]

Then, there's the escalating QAnon paranoia and fake news surrounding the 2020 election of Joe Biden. Civilian militias are at an all-time high, election officials have been attacked, state legislatures have changed voting laws and voting procedures, and school boards are banning books. Even my local sheriff joined the fray, appearing at a Second Amendment protest at our state capitol in Richmond, Virginia. He made national headlines and was interviewed on Fox News, where he shared his views on the need for automatic weapons.[48] And while it would be nice to believe that all this mayhem culminated on January 6, 2021 with an armed insurrection at the U.S. Capitol, I guarantee the worst is yet to come. So if you're not worried, you're not paying attention.

Before the insurrection, I had mixed feelings about the Oath Keepers (mostly police) and militias (many retired military). I was cautiously optimistic that these "patriots" might protect us if we have another Katrina-level disaster that the feds are ill-equipped to handle. Unfortunately, that is not the case. Tensions continue to mount and the polarity is palpable. I remain concerned that this Fourth Turning and Great Cusp will end in abject horror – and that's just here in the U.S. By invading Ukraine and threatening nuclear war, Putin appears ready to start World War III.

Consequently, "prepping" is now mainstream. For the common man, there are doomsday websites, though demand is outstripping supply. If you're rich, the sale of underground luxury condos in former missile silos is an option.[49] And don't even get me started on the underground bunkers that we taxpayers built for the power elite. The older, decommissioned bunkers are now open to tourists.[50] Imagine what the new bunkers look like and how they're stocked. Clearly, the government plans to go underground if things really fall apart.

I could go on about the climax of the Great Cusp, but our goal is to arrive at a practical understanding of why humanity seems incapable of getting its act together and moving into the Fifth Spiritual Paradigm. Forget the coronavirus; we're suffering from a mind virus. The Native American term *Wetiko* refers to mental illness that infects culture – the illusion of seeing one's self as separate from the rest of humanity and viewing others as either competitors or prey.

> *After 5000 years of patriarchy, 500 years of capitalism and 50 years of neoliberalism, Wetiko has come to define nearly every area of our (Western) world and lives. The reason we can accept an economic system celebrating the biggest-possible devastation of the natural world as "success" is due to our own infection with the virus. Wetiko has numbed our hearts, blurring our ability to perceive both the sacredness and the pain of life, both outside and inside ourselves. Innumerable beings are perishing due to this chronic inability to feel empathy.*
>
> *From the compulsive fixation on maximizing artificial values in the economy all the way down to the pandemic of broken and abusive love relationships, the Wetiko sickness has become so normalized it's no longer even recognized as such. A miserable cult of self-obsession has eroded the social tissue of humanity and desecrated the Earth. As a result, fear is everywhere – fear of abandonment, fear of death, fear of life, fear of sexuality, fear of punishment, fear of the coming collapse.[51]*

So how will old humans react to the mounting crises? Fear can go one of two ways. In some pockets of the world, people are pulling together. However, I sense growing separation and to me, a chain reaction of devastation seems inevitable. Thus, there is no getting back to "normal." And it's anyone's guess what the new normal will look like.

Naomi Klein, author of *The Shock Doctrine*, recently stated, "If there is one thing history teaches us, it's that moments of shock are profoundly volatile. We either lose a whole lot of ground, get fleeced by elites and pay the price for decades, or we win progressive victories that seemed impossible."[52] Klein concludes by reminding us that the future will be determined by "whoever is willing to fight harder." I agree. New Humans need to be spiritual warriors. Lastly, let us pray that catastrophobia is a state of mind only, and not the very nature of the Earth Plane.

PERPETUAL KINDERGARTEN: IS THIS A PRISON PLANET?

This theory of the Earth Plane is even more pessimistic than the last because it is based on the premise that our planet – by design – is a place of perpetual tests, turmoil, and suffering. If true, it would mean that we cannot collectively advance in any great measure and that we are blocked from reaching higher moral ground. Sadly, Buddha seemed to share this view, as he memorialized it in his First Noble Truth: Life is suffering. As a result, Buddha saw just one path to escape *samsara* (the repetitive cycles of pain and rebirth), via intense study, meditation, and reaching *nirvana*. Yet, our goal as New Humans is to build a New World for *everyone* and win this round of the God Game.

Come to think of it, I am not aware of any religious text that describes our ability to collectively ascend. The only exceptions are Jewish texts that pertain to the "chosen people" and apocalyptic texts that describe unification after the fighting is finished. Even then, only the righteous survive and thrive. About the closest we get to the concept of universal enlightenment is with the legend of **Green Tara**, who pledged to return to Earth as a female *bodhisattva* until every sentient being is liberated. The Mahayana School of Buddhism emphasizes this goal as well. But is mutual awakening even possible if inexperienced souls continuously arrive on the Earth Plane?

The mystical traditions teach that by reaching enlightenment, one can escape the suffering and illusion of the Earth Plane – a glorious ideal about which I have no doubt. But what about group awakening or even the possibility of moving the mass of humanity into the Fifth Spiritual Paradigm? If our planet is a perpetual kindergarten where young souls learn lessons and slowly ascend the Spectrum of Consciousness, are we wasting energy trying to help them? As New Humans, our incentive to help others is greatly reduced if the correct enlightenment credo is "every man for himself." If so, then the wiser course might be to focus on our own spiritual path, reach enlightenment, and escape this barbaric planet. Egad, what an atrocious conclusion that would be!

Philosopher Friedrich Nietzsche (1844–1900) famously wrote "God is dead" and about mankind's "will to power." Nietzsche believed that the will to survive and the desire for happiness are secondary to the will to power, which he described as the relationship between self-determinism and the reality of the material world. He privately journaled about the "eternal recurrence," a theory that the Universe is in perpetual struggle and a force that cyclically repeats.[53] To this desolate construct he added, "A Nihilist is the man who says of the world as it is, that it ought not to exist, and of the world as it ought to be, that it does not exist."[54] Nietzsche believed that our lives repeat throughout infinite time and space, and he suggested that our only way to escape this cycle is to accept it and then strive to achieve the status of a "Superman."

> *Lo, I teach you the Superman! The Superman is the meaning of the earth. Let your will say: The Superman shall be the meaning of the earth! I beseech you, my brothers, remain true to the earth, and do not believe those who speak to you of otherworldly hopes! Poisoners are they, whether they know it or not. Despisers of life are they, decaying and poisoned themselves, of whom the earth is weary: so away with them!*
>
>   *Once blasphemy against God was the greatest blasphemy; but God died, and therewith also the blasphemers. To blaspheme the earth is now the most dreadful sin, and to rate the heart of the unknowable higher than the meaning of earth!*[55]

Thus, from Buddha to Nietzsche, it appears great minds have concluded that Earth is a treacherous place – a prison planet, essentially – where our only hope is to achieve solo superhuman status. Could the Earth Plane be a holding pen for primitive and unruly souls? Just as the British used Australia as a penal colony, it could be that unrefined souls are sent here for rudimentary training. Alex Jones branding aside, if this is a prison planet, then the God Game is seriously stacked against us, rendering the game more akin to "Escape from Alcatraz," than accumulating either individual or collective merit. In that case, only the most clever and worthy among us would succeed in winning the God Game. We'd have no choice but to leave our brothers and sisters behind as we plan our escape. For New Humans with the drive to help humanity, this would be a deplorable situation indeed.

On this dismal theory, I have two final thoughts. First, every one of my esoteric teachers has told me that this planet is a perpetual kindergarten. Needless to say, I argued against this conclusion during my training and still want to disavow it. However, I felt I should share this possibility with you before we go deeper into the Void. Second, it could be that it is not God who sends us here for elementary school. If this is a prison planet, it might be that we are banished here by a "lesser deity" – perhaps an alien culture that is more advanced than ours and feels we are a dangerously underdeveloped species that lacks the capacity for higher planes. This supposition is similar to the classic Gnostic view of my spiritual raining, and the notion cannot be rejected at this stage of our inquiry. Gnosticism also provides the perfect segue as we continue to probe the question: *Why is the Earth Plane so screwed up?*

ALIEN ASTRONAUT THEORY

One of my mentors asked me to read *Alien Interview*, a book about an extra-terrestrial that briefly survived the crash landing at Roswell, New Mexico in 1947.[56] In the transcript of notes, allegedly based on the alien's telepathic communication with an attending nurse, we learn that Earth is a prison planet for souls deemed too barbaric or rebellious to be let loose in other star systems. So who, exactly, trapped us on planet Earth? The transcript identifies an alien Team Dark called the "Old Empire," that controls the galaxy and banished us here. The benevolent forces are an alien Team Light called "The Domain," and those ETs have been trying to rescue us. Yes, it reads like *Star Wars* on steroids.

A better-known ET story stems from the 1968 book by Erich von Daniken entitled *Chariots of the Gods*, which launched the alien astronaut theory.[57] Von Daniken relied on translations of ancient Sumerian and Babylonian tales, including the *Epic of Gilgamesh* (noted above), *Eridu Genesis* (*circa* 2300 BCE), *The Enuma Elish* (*circa* 1900 BCE), and *Atrahasis* (*circa* 1700 BCE). These are the oldest recorded stories in the world – all written in ancient cuneiform on clay tablets, starting around 3500 BCE.

The tablets honor the **Anunnaki** gods and goddesses – the oldest pantheon from which all subsequent deities likely arose (i.e., Babylonian, Egyptian, Greek, Roman, and Hindu). The tablets mark the beginning of the polytheistic Third Spiritual Paradigm, and they recite the "gods" of this first pantheon, which was ruled by two brothers: **Enlil** and **Enki** (a.k.a. Ea). Nippur was Enlil's home base (in central Iraq), and Eridu was Enki's holy city (in southern Iraq). Today, archeologists consider Eridu the oldest city in the world (*circa* 5400 BCE), and the tablets list a total of five prediluvian cities.[58]

Scholars believe that portions of *Genesis* (*circa* 900–600 BCE) were based on the Mesopotamian legends, since the tales are so similar. For instance, in the Sumerian version of creation, Enki makes a servant race of humans starting with Adapa, the first man, who he blesses with the gift of wisdom (i.e., Tree of Knowledge), but from whom immortality is withheld (i.e., Tree of Life). The tablets also disclose that Enki engaged in a variety of experiments to fashion humans, eventually creating seven males and seven females.[59] Here is the version of Enki's experiments as recited in the Jewish *Old Testament*:

> *When men began to multiply on earth and daughters were born to them, the sons of the **gods** saw how beautiful the daughters of man were, and so they took them for their wives as they chose. The Lord* [Yahweh/Enki/Enlil?] *said: "My spirit shall not remain in man*

forever, since he is but flesh. His days shall comprise one hundred and twenty years."

*At that time the Nephilim appeared on earth as well as later, after the sons of the **gods** had intercourse with the daughters of man, who bore them sons. They were the heroes of old, the men of renown.* [emphasis added to the plural Hebrew word *Elohim*]

Genesis, Chapter 6

In short, the alien astronaut theory asserts that Enki was an extra-terrestrial, not a mythological god, and that he created humans via genetic experimentation or by cross-breeding the gods and/or goddesses with one of our early indigenous ancestors (like *Homo erectus*), thereby birthing our species, *Homo sapiens*. Zecharia Sitchin famously added to the theory by pointing out that the tablets describe the Anunnaki gods giving humans advanced information on astronomy, agriculture, and mathematics (we still use the base 60 numbering system for time and other measurements).

The tablets also mention the planet **Nibiru**, translated as "heaven" and the original home of the gods. Including the Sun and Moon, Sumerian art (right) depicts twelve planets in our solar system – one extra planet – though only the first five are visible to the naked eye.[60]

In addition, the Sumerian *List of Kings* (another clay tablet), chronicles more than 240,000 years of prediluvian dynastic rule, including the reigns of the gods and goddesses, plus another 17,000 years of kingship after the flood.[61] Though the math is off (even if we back up the earlier flood to 11,000 BCE), the theory suggests that the start of the Sumerian dynasty lines up with our common ancestors – "mitochondrial Eve" and "Y-chromosomal Adam."[62] Until recently, this theory was scientifically viable because scientists thought mitochondrial Eve lived approximately 250,000 years ago. However, scientists continue to update our family tree, and they now back up the date of our common ancestry to 500,000 BCE.[63] Recently, Scientists used DNA analysis to identify a common ancestor from 800,000 years ago.[64] Indeed, our family tree gets more branches all the time, and it includes what anthropologists call "ghost" species – DNA that cannot be pinned on any known early hominin.[65]

The notion that there was an African Eve was highly influential. If there was a single mother for humanity, then she must have lived somewhere and so the notion arose that there was a specific place that was our homeland. ...

Many researchers no longer believe these simple explanations, however, and point to other studies that appear to confound them. For example, analyses of the Y-chromosome, which determines maleness in humans and is therefore inherited solely through the male line, suggest that modern humanity probably originated in west Africa .... In this way, the rather odd situation arises where our African Eve inhabited one part of the continent while her Adam appeared in a different, distant part of the continent. Not a good way to start a dynasty, one would have thought.[66]

While known Darwinian lineage doesn't rule out a later alien intervention to create modern *Homo sapiens*, it appears more likely that human evolution followed a crooked path due to sexual dalliances amongst a variety of hominins. However, it still is possible that ETs tweaked *Homo erectus* or another early hominin around 200,000 BCE, in order to create modern humans. Therefore, let us continue with the alien astronaut theory to probe whether aliens bred us.

Today, we mere mortals have the technology to "breed" humans, just as dogs are bred. We could genetically alter people "to increase long-term social stability by selecting for traits like docility, obedience, submissiveness, conformity, risk-aversion, or cowardice, outside of the ruling clan."[67] In 2022, scientists completed the genome sequencing of human DNA, and they have the ability to clone humans and use CRISPR gene editing to alter DNA sequences. Currently, scientists have called for a global moratorium on CRISPR when used on embryos to create heritable attributes. Most countries have implemented a ban, and even China seems to be following suit, after sentencing a rogue doctor to jail for genetically modifying three embryos, later born to two women.[68]

Consequently, it's not a stretch to imagine ETs having this knowledge, especially if they possessed the technology to travel to Earth. Undoubtedly, if aliens were here eons ago and tweaked hominins, early humans would have considered them "gods" and bowed-down to them in submission. Such obsequious "sheeple" still exist. As New Humans who comprehend the Spectrum of Consciousness, we know that it's the First Tier "WE" memes that are the most susceptible to groupthink and herding, which explains why old humans often fall prey to political and religious hucksters. Conversely, New Humans are hard to control, since we seek intellectual and spiritual freedom.

Therefore, I don't think we're hampered in entering the Fifth Spiritual Paradigm because Earth is a prison planet or because aliens bred us for subservience. It seems more likely to me that our remnant lizard brain is to blame, along with First Tier addictions to groupthink and ethnocentric violence.

I also favor Barbara Hand Clow's theory that past cultures might have achieved the ability to construct architectural wonders such as the city of Atlantis, the Great Pyramid, and even flying machines. Consider that Leonardo da Vinci sketched more than five hundred aircraft and described "concepts that would find a place in the development of a successful airplane in the early twentieth century."[69] Interestingly, godly "chariots" were not only reported in the Sumerian tablets, but also in ancient Hindu texts: "The *pushpaka vimana* [flowery chariot] that resembles the sun ... that aerial and excellent *vimana* going everywhere at will ... resembling a bright cloud in the sky ... and the excellent chariot ... rose up into the higher atmosphere."[70] Therefore, let us not rule out at this juncture either theory: that earlier civilizations possessed great knowledge or that ETs may have built the ancient wonders and created humans for additional muscle.

Next, the question becomes: If aliens were here many millennia ago and genetically altered the course of human evolution (and human history), did they ever leave? Some say yes, and point to the *Old Testament* story of Elijah being "taken up to heaven in a whirlwind" and in another "chariot" no less.[71] Others say no, and maintain we have resident aliens still on Earth or close enough in our solar system to keep an eye on us. Some think ETs are friendly, while others think aliens play for Team Dark and are running the Cabal behind the scenes.

Let's deal with dark aliens first. While I have seriously considered this theory and done thought experiments on whether evil aliens are to blame for our Earth Plane madness, I no longer entertain this notion. Why? Because it seems obvious that there is no single "Cabal" running our planet. Rather, there are regional factions and mafia-like oligarchies, like in Russia, comprised of greedy and power-hungry souls. I therefore view it as Team Light's job to either civilize or jail these human but inhumane bastards.

Now, let's consider whether benevolent aliens are close by, making sure we don't hurt ourselves. I agree there is contemporary evidence for this position. Now that numerous governments are releasing their UFO files, we know that UFO sightings have been taken seriously all along.[72] For instance, the U.S. government began Project Blue Book in 1952, and this project was operated by the Air Force until 1969. After analyzing 12,618 UFO reports, the Air Force officially debunked the phenomenon and concluded that none of the incidents fell outside then current aerospace technology. But that conclusion was attacked immediately, even by members of the military. Later analyses have concluded that about one fourth of the Project Blue Book cases remain inexplicable.[73]

In 2007, the U.S. government created a secret agency called the Advanced Aviation Threat Identification Program. This black-op, intelligence program studied everything from alien abductees to the Drake equation for interstellar travel. Today, this work continues under a new program – the Unidentified Aerial Phenomena (UAP) Task Force.[74] Unlike in the past when reporting a strange incident could get a pilot sidelined, military personnel are affirmatively obligated to report UAPs now. Thus, a more transparent era has finally arrived, with old case files and video footage available for public inspection.

In addition, Astronaut Edgar Mitchell (1930–2016), the sixth man on the moon and founder of the Institute of Noetic Science, validated alien visitations. He is on record stating that the Roswell crash was real, multiple visitations have occurred, technology has been shared, and governments have reverse-engineered ET technology. When asked about alien intentions, Mitchell stated, "It is not hostile. It's pretty obvious that if it were hostile, we'd have been gone by now."[75] Good point.

I also have heavily networked friends who say President Dwight Eisenhower (1890–1969) made this pact with aliens: *We'll permit human experimentation, and you provide technology.* Another urban legend is that President Reagan revoked the deal. Or perhaps the deal is still in force? It is noteworthy that a former brigadier general in Israeli Military Intelligence and the Ministry of Defense for Space Programs – a man known as the "father of Israel's space programs" – gave an interview in 2020, in which he claims we are in ready contact with ETs from the "galactic federation." He claims the U.S. government signed an agreement with these ETs, that officials from Earth meet with these aliens in an underground base on Mars, and that these benevolent ET's have assisted us by preventing nuclear disasters.[76] Tied to this disclosure are credible reports from U.S. servicemen who claim that missiles at our nuclear bases have been mysteriously disabled.[77]

At this point, I feel compelled to share a story – a true story – about my brief friendship with a well-known futurist. At Oracle Campus one night, he had a little too much red wine at dinner, and he shared his knowledge of ETs, underground bunkers, and black-op projects that siphon money from government agencies to pay for ET-related projects. He also shared that his institute was hired in the late 1990s to analyze whether the U.S. government should disclose the existence of ETs, and that he advised against it because "everything would go sideways" (i.e., people could not handle the truth). Synchronously, I then met and had dinner with Catherine Austin Fitts, a prior board member of this institute who attended a meeting during which ET disclosure was discussed with James Woolsey, Jr., head of the CIA (1993–1995). Fitts went public with her story, though today, there exists paltry evidence of her role in ET disclosure on the internet.[78]

Despite all this evidence, counting on benevolent aliens to protect us, in my opinion, is wishful thinking – the equivalent of a paternal god in heaven watching over us. Consequently, I choose to not believe that aliens are circling our planet, hiding out on Mars or the dark side of the Moon, or returning from planet Nibiru. Sure, there's a part of me that wants to believe (it's comforting), but another part of me rebels against it. Essentially, I view the alien astronaut theory as a crutch and an excuse not to take responsibility for our collective future. Consequently, I think it's better for New Humans to proceed under the assumption that aliens are not part of our ancient past or immediate future. To me, this is a healthier and more mature mindset. New Humans have the responsibility to save the Earth Plane. We need to do it by ourselves, for ourselves, and for future generations.

I also think the alien question is a huge time-sink and distraction, though I monitor the work of Steven Greer and his "disclosure" projects.[79] Until there is a major breakthrough in this theory, I think it's more prudent to side with the many astrophysicists, including Stephen Hawking, who believe aliens likely have not and technologically cannot visit us.[80] Moreover, I am friends with a young astrophysicist who did her doctoral thesis on habitable planets. She has access to the best telescopes in the world, and she would be absolutely gleeful to find ETs. Already, she has helped discover some of the 59 known exoplanets in the "goldilocks zone."[81] She also is excited by the recent discovery of "fast radio bursts," repeating radio signals coming from two distant galaxies.[82]

So be assured, there is no scientific conspiracy to hide ETs. Whether there's a government conspiracy is another matter, though the U.S. government seems open now, as evidenced by Congressional hearings on UFOs in 2022.[83] Today, scientists are working to develop "Alcubierre Warp Drive" to achieve velocities beyond the speed of light![84] Moreover, Space X has launched Crew Dragon – the first U.S. orbital mission in over a decade – and put NASA astronauts at the International Space Station.[85] Next, NASA plans to launch Artemis I (twin sister of Apollo), in preparation for returning astronauts to the Moon. Truly, scientists would love to prove ETs exist and send astronauts further into space. With our next theory, we'll ponder whether this already has happened ... in a virtual world.

MATRIX THEORY: PART ONE

It's been more than twenty years since the *The Matrix* was released, the movie which poses the question: Do you want to take the blue pill and remain blissfully ignorant, or do you want to take the red pill and learn an unsettling truth? In the movie, here's how Morpheus posed the question to Neo:

> *The Matrix is everywhere. It is all around us. ... It is the world that has been pulled over your eyes to blind you from the truth. ... That you are a slave, Neo. Like everyone else, you were born into bondage. Born into a prison that you cannot smell, or taste, or touch. A prison for your mind. ...*
>
> *Unfortunately, no one can be told what the Matrix is. You have to see it for yourself. This is your last chance. After this, there is no turning back. You take the blue pill – the story ends, you wake up in your bed, and believe whatever you want to believe. You take the red pill – you stay in Wonderland, and I show you how deep the rabbit hole goes. Remember: All I'm offering is the truth. Nothing more.*[86]

Today, astute minds wonder if we *are* living in a matrix, a simulated reality about which nearly all of us are completely oblivious. The father of this theory is Nick Bostrom from the Future of Humanity Institute at Oxford, who thinks, "We are almost certainly characters living in a computer simulation," and who suggests that "a highly advanced supercomputer – with a mass on the order of a planet – would be capable of running a simulation on a humanity-size scale."[87]

Based on **probability theory**, Bostrom thinks the matrix theory is the most likely Earth Plane reality, which means we, as New Humans, must seriously contemplate this hypothesis. Bostrom arrived at his conclusion by assigning mathematical probabilities to variables contained in a matrix event "sample space" (i.e., a set of all possible outcomes). In this way, he statistically examined each proposition and resulting outcome.

The first probability is that when a civilization reaches our current level of technological development, it does not possess sufficient maturity and wisdom to advance any further and destroys itself. This is the likelihood that a civilization will go extinct before its scientists acquire the knowledge to build a simulated world. The second probability is that a civilization does reach technological maturity, but it either fails or declines to create a simulated world. In this case, too, no simulated world is likely created. Translation: If either of these two probabilities is true, then we're probably not in a matrix.

However, the third probability is that a civilization which reaches techno-logical maturity *will* decide to create what Bostrom calls "ancestor simulations" that are as realistic as planet Earth. In this case, the odds are high that we are living in a world they created.[88] Why? Because they likely would create more than one simulation. Just as our scientists run thousands and thousands of simulations to study, say, weather patterns, it is highly likely the more advanced civilization would build multiple models as well. They might create millions of fake worlds! Therefore, the third probability – that we're living inside a matrix – stands the highest chance of being our reality because if just one civilization reaches technological maturity, then the odds favor their invention of simulated worlds and, again, they are likely to create many.

Thus, the Earth Plane could be the creation of a civilization that "won" the God Game and crossed into a vastly more advanced state of existence, where scientists had the power (and wisdom?) to create the simulated reality in which we live. Incidentally, Bostrom mentions a fourth probability: a matrix in which the simulated people ("sims") also become technologically advanced enough to create simulated worlds. This could result in nested levels of simulations within each matrix – an astronomical number of virtual worlds!

If we are in a matrix, then we are to the creators of our Earth Plane simulation, what early humans were to the ET "gods" in the alien astronaut theory. Moreover, it is possible that our creator is not even real, but an artificially created being, which means our world is a nested, holonic simulation. How many levels down? Who knows, since if we acquire the capacity to build full planetary simulations, we would be creating additional holonic worlds within our already nested reality. Yes, this is mind blowing – and we've just started.

> *Theology is (roughly) the study of the nature of God from the point of view of God's subjects. Simulation theology is the study of the nature of the simulator-as-God from the point of view of those within the simulation. ...*
>
> *Is the simulator probably humanlike, or some sort of artificial intelligence? Is the simulator running the simulation for entertain-ment? For science? For decision-making? For historical analysis?...*
>
> *There's reason to think that most science-based simulations in the cosmos will be part of large batches of simulations all similar except for tiny tweaks.*[89]
>
> David J. Chalmers, Reality+

Consider that the creator of our Earth Plane simulation has the power to create any type of God Game it wants and the power to "reward" or "punish" us at any time. This programmer might craft an algorithm to periodically produce "miracles," "synchronicity," and "near death experiences." It might decide to inject "wildcards" into the game to study how we react. It could send prophets into our world to teach us, massive Earth changes to frighten us, Adolf Hitlers for us to oppose, and Donald Trumps to test American democracy. The programmer could create so many choices for us to make and paths to follow that our God Game would feel like a perpetual kindergarten or prison planet! After all, that is how most perpetual virtual reality games work. You get a life, personalize your avatar, go on quests, compete with other players, master one round of the game, then graduate to more difficult levels of play.

Next, the creator might make sims with sundry levels of awareness, per the Spectrum of Consciousness (Chapter II). It could insert seasons and cycles into the game, like the Fourth Turning and Great Cusp (Chapter III). It might want to study good and evil and the nature of polarity by creating a Team Light and Team Dark (Chapter IV). Heck, it could create the Laws of the Universe, both metaphysical (last chapter) and physical (next chapter).

For that matter, the primary algorithm of our God Game might allow for both happy endings, such as a gender-balanced Fifth Spiritual Paradigm, or total destruction of the game, as in a WWIII scenario. And since all sims are players, each of us is co-creating right now what the end of our God Game will look like. In such a case, at least our free will "feels" real. But then again, what is "real," if we're locked in a simulated universe?

Frankly, as a conscious being (whether real or not), I may no longer care whether Team Light or Team Dark wins the God Game if we're in a matrix. Rather, I want out of this simulation! And I'd gladly take the red pill to end this Earth Plane nightmare, where barbarians and buddhas coexist and polarity seems a fundamental feature of the simulation. Like Neo, I'd prefer to do battle with the master programmer(s) who created this dangerous and dualistic world.

Yet, let's slow down and consider the many permutations of a simulated God Game. First, there are physicists who denounce this theory, including uber-genius Stephen Hawking.[90] I want to denounce it as well, as it has devastating implications for the Oracle mission. One way to discard the matrix theory is that we could agree with Bostrom's first probability that it would be nigh impossible for a civilization to reach technological maturity without also reaching moral maturity. In other words, we could take the extreme position that a civilization will destroy itself, say, with nuclear weapons before it acquires the ability to create sims in a simulated world. But is this position sound? Sadly, no. It seems plausible that we could both expand weaponry and build sims, since the technologies have nothing much to do with each other. The real limitation is whether scientists can create artificial intelligence (AI), an upcoming topic.

Next, let's poke around the second and third probabilities: that a civilization becomes both capable of taking care of its toys (like nuclear power) and wise enough to manage its lingering lizard brain (and testosterone). Then the issue is whether they would decide to create a matrix-level simulation. In this case, another way to discard the matrix theory is to assume such a society would deem it morally reprehensible to create a simulated world for either: (i) real humans who are somehow unconscious (the situation in *The Matrix* movie); or (ii) sims, defined as conscious creatures (the theme of *Blade Runner* or *I-Robot*, where the robots feel emotions, have memories, and seem worthy of personhood rights). To me, both of these matrix scenarios are cruel, and I view such detached scientific inquiry as inconstant with advanced ethics.

Inconsistent though I might find it for an advanced society to trap or evolve conscious creatures in a simulated world, it is possible. Which brings us to the third probability: that we're sims in a matrix (and may soon create virtual worlds and sims ourselves). Consider that if we are in a simulated world, it would explain nearly everything, especially mystical experiences. For instance, Eastern mystics would be correct about the *maya* of the Earth Plane, since our world *would* be a grand illusion. Mystics also would be correct to seek enlightenment in order to escape the drama of this virtual world. Remember, the Buddha never defined *nirvana*, but compared it to "nothingness." So perhaps you simply "expire" when you die/leave the matrix. Honestly, that would be preferable to the situation in *The Matrix* movie, where the real world was destroyed and machines controlled our physical bodies and our reality.

Let's take this inquiry one step further. What would be the motivation for a creator-programmer to build and then trap us in a matrix? In *The Matrix* movie, AI machines fashioned the simulation to feed on the bioelectricity of humans, keeping real people alive in jelly-filled caskets. The machines were, essentially, AI vampires. This partial matrix theory – that we are real humans in a simulation, not sims – seems unlikely to me, and it was not Bostrom's conclusion either.

A similarly dismal theory was posed by Robert Monroe (1915–1995), founder of **The Monroe Institute** in Virginia. Monroe travelled out of body and wrote about what he saw in the astral plane. In his book *Far Journeys*, Monroe wrote about an encounter with an astral informant who explained that Earth was created as a farm for ultra-dimensional beings that like to feed on humanity's emotions – an energy called "loosh."[91] According to Monroe, warfare provides these beings with a feast, since anger, fear, and other pitched negative emotions are the sweetest loosh. Apparently, our vampirish creators intentionally crafted predators and prey, favoring fangs, claws, and other combatant designs in the animal kingdom, since animals produce loosh as well. My goodness!

I suspect that Monroe's astral friend was an entity that my Japanese mentor Tomiko Omichi Smith would have labeled "trickster energy." Indeed, the astral realm is chock full of all sorts of chaos and clutter, and some of it our own making. Human thought forms can grow powerful over time, and some do behave as spiritual vampires. Yet, New Humans know that when a person has a peak experience, they return to the Earth Plane and interpret their altered state based on their Spectrum stage. Therefore, I suspect Monroe misinterpreted his experience. On the other hand, there are demons and angels in other dimensions, as we will soon discuss when we examine the *Gnostic Kabballah*.

For now, though, let's go deeper and consider the full matrix theory, which means we are sims, not humans. Some analysts poke holes through this theory by arguing humans will never be able to create artificial intelligence. While I'll reserve a fuller examination of AI until the next chapter, it is time to introduce the huge topic of **consciousness**. Is it possible to create digital consciousness and how close are scientists to meeting this herculean challenge?

The short answer is that we are nowhere close to digitizing consciousness. In fact, scientists, programmers, and philosophers cannot even agree on the nature of consciousness nor where it resides. Essentially, there are three camps: (i) materialists believe consciousness is produced by chemical reactions in the brain; (ii) dualists view the brain as matter and consciousness as mind, and see them as fundamentally distinct; and (iii) panpsychists assert everything has a conscious, mental aspect, including both organic and inorganic matter, because everything possesses a purposeful drive (i.e., evolutionary impulse).

> *Under such a view – which I call hylonoism – the physical universe has a vast, hierarchical system of minds that exists simultaneously in a parallel mental space. On this view, all systems or objects are enminded, and all participate in countless other systemic minds. The physical universe, which is a vast, interconnected network of energy, has a corresponding mental universe, which is a vast, interconnected network of minds or mental states.*[92]
>
> David Skrbina, *Panpsychism in the West*

Recall that "mentalism" is the highest law in *The Kybalion*. Today, this Law of the Universe finds support in the third view of consciousness, which is called **panpsychism** or **hylonoism**. I totally align with this hypothesis, while admitting that it is a minority view. Even so, many scientists and philosophers, including Nobel Prize nominee Ervin Lazlo, share the panpsychist view of consciousness. Lazlo says that consciousness derives from the **Akashic Field** (i.e., Akashic Records), and that "ideas, images, and impressions entering our consciousness have their source in the vacuum" (a.k.a. the Void).[93]

Regardless of which theory is true, scientists are far from creating lifelike sims, one reason to reject the full matrix theory. However, experts scoff at the argument that there is not enough computing power for simulated worlds. Rather, they view artificial intelligence as the big challenge, after which they will be one step closer to transferring consciousness. Remember, just because humans haven't figured out how to make sims doesn't mean a more advanced civilization hasn't done it. Hence, we ignore the matrix theory at our peril.

In *The Simulation Hypothesis*, Rizwan Virk, an MIT and Stanford graduate who also programs virtual reality games, set forth eleven stages of gaming and simulation development. Below is my summary of Virk's list, to which I've added dates based on widespread usage (not patent approval or introduction), in order to show how fast this technology has evolved and is progressing. I've also added examples of existing games and sci-fi movies to fill gaps:

> ➤ **Stage 0:** Single player text adventures (1970–1980)
> Introduced concept of playing a character inside a text virtual world.
> Ex: *Colossal Cave Adventure*

> ➤ **Stage 1:** Console and arcade games (1975–1985)
> First 8-bit 2-D games, mostly single-player with multiple lives, joysticks, and physics engine that mimicked gravity.
> Ex: *Pong; Pac Man; Space Invaders*

> ➤ **Stage 2:** Graphic adventure, multi-player games (1985–1995)
> First 16-bit systems with expansive worlds, player and non-player actors, object inventory (weapons, powers), and ability to save/resume play.
> Ex: *Super Mario; Legend of Zelda; King's Quest*

> ➤ **Stage 3:** 3-D rendered virtual worlds (1995–ongoing)
> First 64-bit 3-D games hosted on cloud servers for global, multiplayer interaction and persistent play. Algorithms build scenes as players enter them and permit user-generated content (objects built by your avatar).
> Ex: *World of Warcraft; Second Life*

➤ **Stage 4:** Virtual reality immersion (2010–ongoing)
Space and motion simulation using VR headset (for sight and sound), gloves (for touch). Full body suits and other sensory inputs in progress.
Ex: *No Man's Sky* (billion planet universe); *Ready Player One* (movie)

➤ **Stage 5:** Augmented reality (2015–ongoing)
AR games, glasses, and contact lenses that add to/interact with the real world to digitally alter perception. Used now in many applications.
Ex: *Pokemon Go*; military training, navigation, translation

➤ **Stage 6:** Real world rendering and 3-D printing (2015–ongoing)
Pixel based technology that uses light display to either augment reality with 3-D holograms, or create 3-D objects using plastic and now metal.
Ex: Princess Leah in *Star Wars*; used in art, entertainment, engineering

➤ **Stage 7:** Mind Interface (2020–ongoing)
Computer/brain merger. Goals: enhance intellect, restore sight, help paraplegics walk – all thru mind. Start of Transhuman Era (next chapter).
Example: Elon Musk's Neuralink; *The Matrix* (movie)

➤ **Stage 8:** Implanted memories (on the horizon)
Computer mind/memory alteration with VR immersion. Will result in our inability to perceive a difference between real and simulated world.
Ex: *Total Recall* (movie); *The Matrix* (movie)

➤ **Stage 9:** Artificial Intelligence (future)
Learning algorithms already are in use, but full ASI is not on the horizon yet. Start of Posthuman Era (next chapter).
Ex: Full matrix theory where we are digital beings in a simulated world.

➤ **Stage 10:** Downloadable Consciousness (distant future)
Scientists are nowhere close but billionaires are funding this research, as their goal is to become immortal. Full Posthuman Era (next chapter).
Ex: God Game nightmare where our creator(s) may lack advanced moral consciousness and be digitally immortal.

From this list, it is plain to see that Moore's Law – the exponential rate at which processing power multiplies – is real. In addition to greater gigabyte storage, Virk predicts that we will "render worlds that are indistinguishable from physical reality in a few decades."[94] Therefore, let us pray that neither the partial or full matrix theory is true and that we truly are alive and conscious. Even so, we are not out of the woods. There is one more explanation for both the beauty and barbarity of the Earth Plane left to explore, and it presents just as many challenges as the previous theories, if not more.

THE GNOSTIC KABBALAH

In addition to *The Kybalion*, which we explored in the last chapter, I consider the *Kabbalah* a superb framework for studying the Earth and Ethereal Planes. As previously mentioned, I had the honor of studying the *Gnostic Kabbalah* under the tutelage of Tau Malachi, who was a very tough teacher. One day, I made the mistake of asking him about the alien astronaut theory and he yelled, "Do you want to talk about aliens or do you want to commune with the Light?!" I humbly responded that my goal is enlightenment (and we never spoke of ETs again).

My copy of Tau Malachi's classic, *Gnosis of the Cosmic Christ: A Gnostic Christian Kabbalah*, is worn, dog-eared, but never dusty.[95] I refer to it often when seeking answers from the Void, and I highly recommend it. Truly, the *Kabbalah* is a proven path to enhanced personal and cosmic awareness, and it is mandatory study for those who seek ordination through Oracle Temple.

Malachi's lineage is descendent from the Gnostic Christians, briefly touched on in Chapter I. The Gnostics possessed a nuanced view of Jesus' mission, and after the crucifixion they separated from the **Jewish Christians**, who were led by Jesus' brother James the Just in Jerusalem. When the Romans destroyed the Jewish Temple in 70 CE, the Gnostics went underground. Spiritually, they aligned with James' admonishment that "faith without works" is meaningless, so they rejected the blasphemous theology promulgated by Paul (i.e., blind faith). Paul preached in the Roman Empire to **Gentile Christians** (i.e., former pagans), and he led them down a fallacious and misogynist path, which resulted in the orthodox form of Christianity we know today.[96]

The Gnostics did not believe Jesus (or Yahweh) was God. They viewed Jesus as a spiritual master sent to explain the complexity of the cosmos, which contains both light and dark forces. Some teachings were recorded in the *Gnostic Gospels*, though most were passed by oral tradition. Critically, the *Gnostic Gospels* reveal that Mary Magdalene was Jesus' favorite apostle, if not his sacred consort and wife.[97] Moreover, in the *Gospel of Thomas*, we learn that Jesus claimed no special abilities beyond the grasp of his disciples.

> *Rather, the kingdom is inside of you .... But if you will not know yourselves, you dwell in poverty and it is you who are that poverty. ... I am not your master. Because you have drunk, you have become intoxicated from the bubbling spring which I have measured out.*
>
> Jesus, *Gospel of Thomas*, Verses 3, 13

The Gnostic tradition was kept alive by Mary Magdalene and Jesus' younger brother Thomas, the maligned "doubting" apostle (a.k.a. Judas Thomas, Thomas Didymus, Thomas the Twin). Legends recite that Mary Magdalene set sail after the crucifixion, likely escorted by Joseph of Arimathea, and that she landed in the south of France, pregnant with child. Mary gave birth to a daughter named Sarah ("princess" in Hebrew), and thereafter both mother and daughter were referred to as **Black Madonnas**. The tale continues with Sarah marrying into a Frankish noble line that became the Merovingian Dynasty (457–751 CE), which controlled the principality of Septimania.[98] This region of southern France also was home to the largest sect of Gnostic Christians – the **Cathars** – who rejected the new religion of Catholicism, but who were left alone to live communally and peacefully for centuries.

Tragically, in 1209, Pope Innocent III issued a papal bull declaring the Cathars heretics and condemning them to death. During the resulting Albigensian Crusade, the Cathars made their way to a seminary at Montsegur, a mountaintop refuge in France. In 1244, the Cathars were caught and burned en masse by the crusaders. This purge nearly marked the end of the Gnostics, whose surviving members were forced underground once again.

SAINTE SARA

In 2011, I travelled to France to walk in the footsteps of Mary Magdalene. Legend states that Mary arrived at the Mediterranean seaside town of Saintes Maries de la Mer (the Marys of the Sea), where a Catholic Church was later built in her honor. The church sells statues of Saint Sarah, Jesus and Mary's daughter (the church describes Sarah as Mary's servant). Next, I visited the cave in Provence, where Mary lived for many years.[99] This holy site rests on a mountaintop that has been steadfastly guarded by Benedictine and Dominican priests since the 5th Century – proof the church always has known Mary's preeminence. Moreover, in 1295, construction of the Basilica of Saint Mary Magdalene commenced in the medieval town where she died. Within the cathedral lies Mary's crypt and a golden statue of her upper torso that contains her skull, a soulful relic to behold!

While on this sacred journey, I also visited Montsegur, the site of the Cathar's betrayal by the Catholic Church. The day I arrived was bitter cold and snowy, and the trail to the ruin was closed. Undaunted, I climbed over the barricade and made my way slowly up the mountain. Completely alone inside the ruin, I sat for hours, meditating and crying, until I was too cold to remain any longer. As I descended the mountain trail, I became so angry about the Cathar genocide that I started to scream out loud at the popes who were responsible for the many evils perpetrated against all free-thinking and God-loving people. I screamed over and over again, "You pigs! You pigs!"

Suddenly, out of nowhere, a large black boar appeared in front of me on the icy path, his yellow eyes fixed on me and his black tusks curled toward the sky. I stopped in my tracks and time stood still. I glanced about for a means of escape, but there was none – just dense woods full of pine trees, which looked impossible to climb. Within an instant, I knew I had conjured this beast. My magic had mixed with my seething hatred, a level of anger I've not felt since. I decided to close my eyes and count to ten, and I prayed to Mary Magdalene, struggling to regain calm. When I opened my eyes, the boar was gone.

Tau Malachi's ancestral lineage managed to keep the Gnostic tradition alive during more than six centuries of Catholic persecution. Indeed, the Inquisition (1231–1843) targeted all spiritual "heretics," including Jews, Muslims, witches, and other wayward believers. I have no doubt that in the past I lived a Gnostic life, as I took to Gnosticism like a duck to water. Even more than my Lakota and Hermetic training, I feel aligned with this tradition, and although this text cannot plumb the depths of this esoteric path, I will briefly scratch the surface to describe what it means to be Gnostic in the 21st Century.

First, Gnostics believe that Jesus and Mary Magdalene came to *Malkut* (the Earth Plane) as paired and partnered avatars. Consequently, Mary is just as revered as Jesus. Second, we believe Mary is the "Second Coming of Christ," because she is responsible for the continued spiritual evolution of *Malkut*. Thus, similar to Green Tara in Buddhism, Mary's mission it to help humanity reach *gnosis* (enlightenment) and escape the demiurge, a false god that created the Earth Plane. Hence, Gnosticism is a lot like the matrix theory, since we believe that the "god" most of humanity worships is a lesser deity, not Source.

In the past, Gnostics believed that Mary would reincarnate as a woman with either red or dark hair and green eyes. Today, it is more typical for Gnostics to view Mary as an enlightened force and a source of Divine Feminine energy that anyone can access. Personally, I think of her as a spiritual master who is ever-available to me for guidance and inspiration. In the Peace Pentagon chapel, we placed an amethyst geode under the central skylight and named the crystal Sarah, in honor of the holy daughter. Yet in the *Gnostic Kabbalah*, we are all spiritual children of Mary and Jesus. At Oracle Temple, we seek direct *gnosis* so that we may follow in their footsteps and help free humanity. *OM JAI!*

In *Gnosis of the Cosmic Christ*, Tau Malachi explains the mystery of creation. First, the Infinite formed a Void within itself, which Kabbalists call *Ain* (nothingness). At this point, *Ain* contained only pure potential, the essence of everything that might be. Then, the Absolute filled the Void with Divine Light, which activated the potential within it and started the process of creation. God then manifested emanations of itself, which are called *sefirot* (i.e., dimensions) within the Tree of Life. At the top of the Tree is *Keter* or the God Mind, about which we can know nothing – "a primordial singularity that is inconceivable."[100] And yet, paradoxically, *Keter* also is our shared destiny.

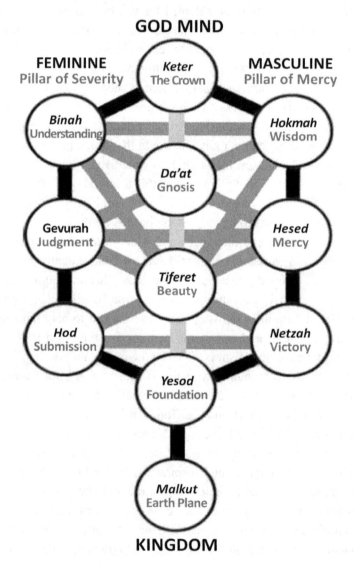

To reach cosmic consciousness, humans ascend the Tree of Life. The journey starts at *Malkut*, the first *sefirah* and the realm of Mary Magdalene. Above the Earth Plane is the lowest Ethereal Plane, *Yesod* the astral realm, through which we must pass before commencing our journey in earnest. The astral realm contains both angels and *archons* (demonic beings), a menagerie of dense thought forms that may admire or revile humanity. I cannot overstate the difficulty in breaking though this crust that both filters the higher *sefirot* and blocks us from ascending. It is a realm of benevolent and malevolent spirits, ghosts, lost souls, and trickster energy that likes to confound and confuse us.

Yesod is where 99% of all channeling takes place, which is why we have a policy at The Oracle Institute: No Channeling! If a student gets a message or vision, we advise her to ponder it, journal about it, or share it privately with a mentor before publicly declaring it anything other than an interesting tidbit from the astral plane. This may sound harsh, but how else to interrupt Robert Monroe's "loosh" or the sugary-sweet bulletins channeled by New Age gurus?

Also, beware any messages that massage your ego, especially if delivered by a supposed "archangel." I've gone through the "Messiah phase" myself and trust me, you'll be embarrassed later if you share trickster-induced fantasies. Besides, if you receive an extraordinary message from a higher *sefirah*, it will become obvious over time. We'll know it didn't come from *Yesod* by the degree of your reverence, the compassion you display, and the works you manifest.

As for the higher *sefirot*, those are where true mystics travel. Starting from the bottom, the Tree is divided into three sections: (i) the lower "action" triad (*Hod, Netzah, Tiferet*); (ii) the middle "moral" triad (*Gevurah, Hesed, Da'at*); and (iii) the upper "supernal" triad (*Binah, Hokmah, Keter*). The pillars signify the inherent duality of the cosmos, though *Binah* and *Hokmah* are emanations barely removed from the Light. Similar to the Yin-Yang, the left column is the Pillar of Severity, and it is associated with the Divine Feminine, black light, and negativity. On the right, the Pillar of Mercy represents the Divine Masculine, white light, and positivity. In this way, the pillars also convey the Law of Gender taught by *The Kybalion*.

> [T]hese two pillars represent the eternal play of opposites in dynamic interactions. Evil is imbalanced force, out of place or out of harmony. Severity in imbalance is cruelty and oppression, and mercy in imbalance is weakness that allows and facilitates great evil. True compassion is a dynamic balance of severity and mercy.[101]
>
> Tau Malachi, *Gnosis of the Cosmic Christ*

The realm of non-duality rests in the Tree's supernal triad. However, spiritual attainment at *Da'at* (associated with Jesus) is the peak of *gnosis*, and it provides access to the supernal Void, where a mystic unites with the whole of creation. *Binah* the "mother" brings cosmic consciousness, a supra-mental state that provides unity in the presence of God. At *Hokmah* the "father," one achieves transcendent consciousness and unity with the infinite ground of being. Complete unification with God occurs at *Keter*, the dimension where a mystic becomes fully transformed into a supernal being. Merging with *Keter* also means that you have access to universes beyond. Consequently, if you pass through all eleven *seferot* and chose to leave this *olam* – which is the first of five universes – the ascension process repeats within more advanced rounds of the God Game.

I want to emphasize the nested nature of the *olamos* (universes), because they mimic the concept of nested simulations in the matrix theory. Once again, there are five universes, each of which has eleven dimensions. In total then, there are fifty-five dimensions to the nested Tree of Life. Hence, Gnosticism is quite similar to the matrix theory, though I doubt Tau Malachi would say that *Keter* in the highest universe called Adam Kadmon is a super-computer or advanced AI.

Not coincidentally, Oracle's sacred numbers are five and eleven, and the five exterior walls of the Peace Pentagon each measure 55 feet. Recently, we held a ceremony in the Peace Pentagon sanctuary, during which I received a spiritual name in the Gnostic tradition: Tau Lama. I was accompanied by five women, who cut off my long hair then shaved my head. This purifying ritual symbolized the start of the next phase of my spiritual journey, during which

I hope to achieve a deeper awareness of Truth, Love, and Light. The naming ceremony is a rite of passage for those on the Path of the Oracle, one of five paths of perfection at the Valley of Light. I invite readers to visit us along the New River, particularly if you seek an ashram environment in which to grow.

Now, let's summarize what we've explored together while inside the Void. We pondered some of the most likely Earth Plane models to help us understand the incessant polarity of our planet: the lingering lizard brain, catastrophobia, perpetual kindergarten, alien astronaut, simulated matrix, and Gnostic theories. Along the way, we've used the Spectrum of Consciousness and Integral theory to measure our own spiritual progress and decipher the motivations of others. And we've examined persistent patterns – season and cycles – that seem to repeat on planet Earth.

We also studied the Laws of the Universe and we learned that the Light – the All in *The Kybalion* – is the mind of the one true God, the Source of all creation. We will return to the matrix theory later, but for now let us agree that God is a singular, as opposed to a dualistic, construct, even though the "god" who may have created this plane – whether alien, AI, or the *demiurge* as in Gnosticism – is not the ultimate Creator. Sadly, we learned that old humans have yet to master the Law of Gender – the simplest and most obvious of the metaphysical laws.

For all these reasons and more, it should now appear necessary that New Humans update the Godhead and agree on a theory of the God Game. How else to stem the spiritual confusion and lead humanity into the Fifth Paradigm? With regard to our first task, updating the Godhead, the Divine Feminine must take her rightful place alongside the Divine Masculine, otherwise the chaos of the Great Cusp will continue.

> *We cannot speak of the redemption of humanity apart from the redemption of womanhood. Likewise, we cannot speak of the evolution of a higher form of human being except through the matrix of womanhood. ...*
>
> *This idea is reflected in the Book of Revelation, where the image of the woman of light appears giving birth to a holy child (Revelation 12). Although the holy child is spoken of as male, the masters of the Tradition say that this child is the androgynous one, who is like unto the holy angels, both male and female in one body of light; hence, this child is the union of the Bridegroom and Bride, Christ the Logos* [Jesus] *and Christ the Sophia* [Mary].[102]
>
> Tau Malachi, *Gnosis of the Cosmic Christ*

Such is the connection between this book's cover and the avatars Yeshua and the Magdaleder, emissaries of Truth, Love, Light.[103] In the Gnostic path, we are taught that the sacred task of Jesus and Mary was to model a balanced Godhead and birth a paradigm of peace. Tragically, the Fourth Paradigm was hijacked by Paul, abrogated by Catholic popes, and buried at the Vatican, where men of greed and power still work to keep humanity trapped. Other religions have caused chaos as well, but I find it particularly painful that Jesus and Mary failed to anchor us in both *Hokmah* (the father) and *Binah* (the mother). Singular devotion to the masculine half of God has wrought untold suffering on women and the world, while also concealing *gnosis*.

13
Coyote

In the next chapter, we will go even deeper into the Void. We've considered metaphysics as a path to understanding the Earth Plane. Next, it is time we consider quantum physics – another mysterious realm and "spooky" according to Albert Einstein. The good news is that science and spiritualty are finally merging in the Light. I began this chapter with Crow, my animal totem, and we will end with Coyote. Why? Because Coyote is the trickster and the quantum world is full of trickster energy! Yet, the God Game at the quantum level contains an "implicate order," to quote physicist turned mystic David Bohm, which means that we'll discover even more answers by seeing how scientists view the Void – and their answers may de-Light us.

The American Indian regarded the Coyote as a joker because of its highly amusing antics and habit of appearing to ignore the obvious. ... Coyote is concerned with breaking down the ego which is blocking your spiritual progress, and "tricking" you into things you may find difficult, but which are necessary in your development. ...

Snooze time is over. Watch out. Your glass house may come crashing to the ground at any moment. All your self-mirrors may shatter. ... Go immediately beneath the surface of your experiences. Ask yourself what you are really doing and why. Are you playing a joke on yourself? ... If you can't laugh at yourself and your crazy antics, you have lost the [God] game.[104]

¹ Roger Walsh, *Essential Spirituality: The 7 Central Practices to Awaken Heart and Mind*, p. 53, John Wiley & Sons: New York, NY (1999).

² Jamie Sams & David Carson, *Medicine Cards: The Discovery of Power Through the Ways of Animals*, Card 24 – Crow, St. Martin's Press: New York, NY (1999).

³ Ken Wilber, *A Theory of Everything: An Integral Vision for Business, Politics, Science, and Spirituality*, pp. 43, 70, Shambhala Publications, Boston, MA (2001).

⁴ Andrew Newberg, *Why We Believe What We Believe*, pp. 92, 94, Free Press: New York, NY (2006).

⁵ Ibid, p. 114, 125 *et. seq.*

⁶ Ibid, p. 128.

⁷ His Holiness the Dalai Lama, *The Universe in a Single Atom: The Convergence of Science and Spirituality*, Doubleday Broadway Publishing: New York, NY (2005).

⁸ Andrew Newberg, *Why We Believe What We Believe*, pp. 253–257.

⁹ Andrew E. Budson, "Don't Listen to Your Lizard Brain," *Psychology Today* (Dec. 3, 2017), https://www.psychologytoday.com/us/blog/managing-your-memory/201712/don-t-listen-your-lizard-brain (accessed July 2022).

¹⁰ Jamie Carroll, "How Has the Human Brain Evolved?," *Scientific American* (July 1, 2013), https://www.scientificamerican.com/article/how-has-human-brain-evolved/ (accessed July 2022).

¹¹ Yuval Noah Harari, *Sapiens: A Brief History of Humankind*, p. 21, Harper Collins: New York, NY (2015).

¹² Ibid, p. 403.

¹³ Steven Pinker, *Better Angels of Our Nature*, pp. 684–689, Penguin Group: New York, NY (2011).

¹⁴ "The 17 Goals," *United Nations Department of Economic and Social Affairs*, https://sdgs.un.org/goals (accessed July 2022).

¹⁵ Riane Eisler, *The Chalice and the Blade: Our History, Our Future*, pp. 19, 48, 49, Harper Collins Publishers: San Francisco, CA (1988).

¹⁶ Steven Pinker, *Better Angels of Our Nature*, pp. 656–-658.

¹⁷ Andrew Newberg, M.D. and Mark Robert Waldman, *How God Changes Your Brain*, pp. 15–16, Ballantine Books: New York, NY (2009).

¹⁸ Ibid, p. 17–18.

¹⁹ Charles Eisenstein, *The Ascent of Humanity: The Age of Separation, the Age of Reunion, and the Convergence of Crisis that is Birthing the Transition*, pp. 509–510, 520–521, Panenthea Press: Harrisburg, PA (2007).

[20] David Biello, "What Thawed the Last Ice Age?" *Scientific American* (April 4, 2012), https://www.scientificamerican.com/article/what-thawed-the-last-ice-age/. See also: Sandy Eldredge and Bob Biek, "Glad You Asked: Ices Ages – What Are They and What Causes Them?," *Utah Geological Survey* (Sept. 2019), https://geology.utah.gov/map-pub/survey-notes/glad-you-asked/ice-ages-what-are-they-and-what-causes-them/ (both accessed July 2022).

[21] University of Edinburgh, "A Comet Strike 13,000 Years Ago May Have Sparked Key Shift in Human Civilization," *Sci Tech Daily* (July 5, 2021), https://scitechdaily.com/a-comet-strike-13000-years-ago-may-have-sparked-key-shift-in-human-civilization/. See also: David Biello, "Did a Comet Hit Earth 12,000 Years Ago?" *Scientific American* (Jan. 2, 2009), https://www.scientificamerican.com/article/did-a-comet-hit-earth-12900-years-ago/ (both accessed July 2022).

[22] Patrick Pester and Kim Zimmerman, "Pleistocene Epoch: The Last Ice Age," *Live Science* (Feb. 28, 2022), https://www.livescience.com/40311-pleistocene-epoch.html (accessed July 2022).

[23] Paul Voosen, "Massive Crater Under Greenland's Ice Points to Climate-Altering Impact in the Time of Humans," *Science Magazine* (Nov. 14, 2018), https://www.sciencemag.org/news/2018/11/massive-crater-under-greenland-s-ice-points-climate-altering-impact-time-humans# (accessed July 2022).

[24] James Trefil, "Evidence for a Flood," *Smithsonian Magazine* (April 1, 2000), https://www.smithsonianmag.com/science-nature/evidence-for-a-flood-102813115/ (accessed July 2022).

[25] Ibid.

[26] Plato, *Timaeus* (*circa* 360 BCE).

[27] Lee Ann Paradise, "Is The Great Sphinx Twice as Old as Egyptologists and Archaeologists Think," *Encyclopedia.com* (March 31, 2020), https://www.encyclopedia.com/science/science-magazines/great-sphinx-twice-old-egyptologists-and-archaeologists-think-based-recent-geological-evidence. See also: Sarah Pruitt, "How Old is the Great Sphinx?" *History Channel*, (Oct. 28, 2018), https://www.history.com/news/how-old-is-the-great-sphinx (both accessed July 2022).

[28] Adir Ferrara, "Viewpoint: Yes, Recent Evidence Suggests that the Great Sphinx Is Much Older than Most Scientists Believe," *Encyclopedia.com* (March 31, 2020), https://www.encyclopedia.com/science/science-magazines/great-sphinx-twice-old-egyptologists-and-archaeologists-think-based-recent-geological-evidence. See also: Matthew Kirkham, "Egypt Shock: Giza's Sphinx May Have Had Face of Lion and Is Much Older than Thought," *Express UK News* (Feb. 25, 2019), https://www.express.co.uk/news/weird/1091417/egypt-shock-giza-pyramid-sphinx-lion-face-theory-spt (both accessed July 2022).

[29] Plato, *Critias* (*circa* 360 BCE).

[30] Plato, *Timaeus*.

³¹ Plato, *Critias*.

³² Plato, *Timaeus*. See translation by Benjamin Jowett (1871), *Sacred Texts*, https://www.sacred-texts.com/cla/plato/timaeus.htm (accessed July 2022).

³³ Barbara Hand Clow, *Catastrophobia: The Truth Behind Earth Changes in the Coming Age of Light*, pp. 12–17, Bear & Company: Rochester, VT (2001).

³⁴ Ibid, p. 75.

³⁵ *Manetho's Works*, translated by E.G. Waddell, Harvard Univ. Press: Cambridge, MA (1940), https://ryanfb.github.io/loebolus-data/L350.pdf (accessed July 2022).

³⁶ Ibid, pp. 2–6.

³⁷ Barbara Hand Clow, *Catastrophobia*, pp. 25–26.

³⁸ Preston Chester, "The Burning of the Library of Alexandria," *eHistory at Ohio State University*, https://ehistory.osu.edu/articles/burning-library-alexandria (accessed July 2022).

³⁹ Charles H. Hapgood, *Maps of the Ancient Sea Kings: Evidence of Advanced Civilization in the Ice Age*, Adventures Unlimited: Kempton, IL (1966). See also: Paul Hoyle and Paul Lunde, "Piri Reis and the Hapgood Hypothesis" (Jan. 1980), https://archive.aramcoworld.com/issue/198001/piri.reis.and.the.hapgood.hypotheses.htm (accessed July 2022).

⁴⁰ Damian Carrington, "Last Time CO₂ Levels Were this High, There Were Trees at the South Pole," *The Guardian* (April 3, 2019), https://www.theguardian.com/science/2019/apr/03/south-pole-tree-fossils-indicate-impact-of-climate-change (accessed July 2022).

⁴¹ Alexandra Borunda, "Past Decade Was the Hottest on Record, *National Geographic* (Jan. 15, 2020), https://www.nationalgeographic.com/science/2019/12/the-decade-we-finally-woke-up-to-climate-change/ (accessed July 2022).

⁴² Tim Radford, "A Third of Plants and Animals Risk Mass Extinction," *The Energy Mix* (Feb. 25, 2020), https://www.theenergymix.com/2020/02/25/a-third-of-plants-and-animals-risk-mass-extinction/ (accessed July 2022).

⁴³ Meghan Bartels, "Huge Asteroid Apophis Flies by Earth on Friday the 13th in 2029," *Space.com* (May 1, 2019), https://www.space.com/asteroid-apophis-2029-flyby-planetary-defense.html. See more current: "NASA Analysis: Earth Is Safe from Asteroid Apophis for 100-Plus Years," *NASA* (March 26, 2021), https://www.nasa.gov/feature/jpl/nasa-analysis-earth-is-safe-from-asteroid-apophis-for-100-plus-years (accessed July 2022).

⁴⁴ Gemma Tarlach, "The Five Mass Extinctions that Have Swept Our Planet," *Discover Magazine* (July 18, 2018), https://www.discovermagazine.com/the-sciences/mass-extinctions (accessed July 2022).

⁴⁵ William Arkin, "Exclusive: Inside the Military's Top Secret Plans if Coronavirus Cripples the Government," *Newsweek Magazine* (March 18, 2020), https://www.newsweek.com/exclusive-inside-militarys-top-secret-plans-if-coronavirus-cripples-government-1492878. (accessed July 2022).

[46] John Whitehead, "Beware the Emergency State," *Rutherford Institute* (Jan. 8, 2019), https://www.rutherford.org/publications_resources/john_whiteheads_commentary/beware_the_emergency_state_imperial_unaccountable_and_unconstitutional (accessed July 2022).

[47] Matthew Cox, "Marines Test Nonlethal Mortar Round for Crowd Control," *Military.com* (Sept. 19, 2019), https://www.military.com/daily-news/2019/09/19/marines-test-nonlethal-mortar-round-crowd-control.html (accessed July 2022).

[48] Sherriff Richard Vaughan, "Virginia Sheriff: I won't Enforce These Unconstitutional Gun Control Laws," *Fox News* (January 21, 2020), https://video.foxnews.com/v/6125103830001#sp=show-clips (accessed July 2022).

[49] Chris Lovenko, "Rich People Are Buying 'Survival Condos' in Abandoned Nuclear Missile Silos," *Vice.com* (March 11, 2020), https://www.vice.com/en_us/article/3a84nk/rich-people-are-buying-survival-condos-in-abandoned-nuclear-missile-silos (accessed July 2022).

[50] Jay Akbar, "Two Minutes to Midnight: Inside the US Government's 'Doomsday Bunkers.'" *The Sun* (June 18, 2018), https://www.thesun.co.uk/news/6561687/us-nuclear-bunkers-locations-washington-virginia-pennsylvania/ (accessed July 2022).

[51] Martin Winiecki, "Searching for the Anti-Virus: Covid-19 as Quantum Phenomenon," *New Story Hub* (April 16, 2020), http://newstoryhub.com/2020/04/searching-for-the-anti-virus-covid-19-as-quantum-phenomenon-by-martin-winiecki/ (accessed July 2022).

[52] Jessica Corbert, "We Know This Script: Naomi Klein Warns of 'Coronovirus Capitalism' in New Video Detailing Battle Before Us," *Common Dreams* (March 17, 2020), https://www.commondreams.org/news/2020/03/17/we-know-script-naomi-klein-warns-coronavirus-capitalism-new-video-detailing-battle (accessed July 2022).

[53] Frederick Nietzsche, *The Joyful Wisdom*, section 341 (1882), https://www.gutenberg.org/files/52881/52881-h/52881-h.htm (accessed July 2022).

[54] Frederick Nietzsche, *The Will To Power*, section 585 (1901), https://www.gutenberg.org/files/52915/52915-h/52915-h.htm (accessed July 2022).

[55] Frederick Nietzsche, *Thus Spoke Zarathustra*, Prologue section 3 (1883), http://www.gutenberg.org/files/1998/1998-h/1998-h.htm#link2H_4_0004 (accessed July 2022).

[56] Lawrence Spencer, *Alien Interview* (2008).

[57] Erich von Daniken, *Chariots of the Gods?* Berkley Books: New York, NY (1968).

[58] Joshua Mark, "Cuneiform" (March 15, 2018) and "Eridu" (July 20, 2010), *Ancient History Encyclopedia*, https://www.ancient.eu/cuneiform/ and https://www.ancient.eu/eridu/ (both accessed July 2022).

[59] Joshua J. Mark, "The Myth of Adapa" (Feb. 23, 2011), and "Enki" (Jan. 9, 2017), *Ancient History Encyclopedia*, https://www.ancient.eu/article/216/the-myth-of-adapa/ and https://www.ancient.eu/Enki/ (both accessed July 2022).

[60] Zecharia Sitchin, *The Twelfth Planet*, Bear & Company: Rochester, VT (1991).

[61] April Holloway, "The Sumerian King List Still Puzzles Historians After More Than a Century of Research" *Ancient Origins* (July 30, 2022), https://www.ancient-origins.net/myths-legends-asia/sumerian-king-list-still-puzzles-historians-after-more-century-research-001287 (accessed July 2022).

[62] "Is the Sumerian King's List Indication of a Lost Civilization?" *Gaia* (Dec. 10, 2019), https://www.gaia.com/article/sumerian-kings-list (accessed July 2022).

[63] Robin McKie, "The Search for Eden: In Pursuit of Humanity's Origins," *The Guardian* (Jan. 5, 2020), https://www.theguardian.com/world/2020/jan/05/the-search-for-eden-in-pursuit-of-humanitys-origins (accessed July 2022).

[64] Brandon Spector, "World's Oldest Human DNA Found in 800,000-year-old Tooth of a Cannibal," *Live Science* (April 3, 2020), https://www.livescience.com/oldest-human-ancestor-dna-homo-antecessor.html (accessed July 2022).

[65] Catherine Brahic, "Traces of Mystery Ancient Humans Found Lurking in our Genomes," *New Scientist* (Oct. 10, 2018), https://www.newscientist.com/article/mg24031992-600-traces-of-mystery-ancient-humans-found-lurking-in-our-genomes/ (accessed July 2022).

[66] Robin McKie, "The Search for Eden: In Pursuit of Humanity's Origins."

[67] Nick Bostrom, *Superintelligence: Paths, Dangers, Strategies*, p. 48, Oxford University Press: Oxford, UK (2014).

[68] David Cyranoski, "What CISPR-Baby Prison Sentences Mean for Research," *Nature* (Jan. 3, 2020), https://www.nature.com/articles/d41586-020-00001-y (accessed July 2022).

[69] Peter Jakab, "Leonardo da Vinci and Flight," *Smithsonian Museum* (Aug. 22, 2013), https://airandspace.si.edu/stories/editorial/leonardo-da-vinci-and-flight (accessed July 2022).

[70] *Ramayana*, Manatha Nath Dutt (translator), Elysium Press: New York, NY (1910).

[71] 2 *Book of Kings* 2:1 and 2:11.

[72] Dylan Matthews, "UFOs Are Real," *Vox News* (June 18, 2021), https://www.vox.com/22463659/ufo-videos-navy-alien-drone (accessed July 2022).

[73] "Project Blue Book," *Wikipedia*, https://en.wikipedia.org/wiki/Project_Blue_Book (accessed July 2022).

[74] "Establishment of Unidentified Aerial Phenomena Task Force," *Department of Defense* (Aug. 14, 2020), https://www.defense.gov/News/Releases/Release/Article/2314065/ (accessed July 2022).

[75] "Edgar Mitchell UFO Interview with Kerrang Radio," *UFOnotebook You Tube* (July 23, 2008), https://www.youtube.com/watch?v=RhNdxdveK7c. See also: Institute of Noetic Science website, https://noetic.org/ (both accessed July 2022).

[76] Adela Suliman and Paul Goldman, "Former Israeli Space Security Chief Says Extraterrestrials Exist, and Trump Knows About It." *NBC News* (Dec. 8, 2020), https://www.nbcnews.com/news/weird-news/former-israeli-space-security-chief-says-extraterrestrials-exist-trump-knows-n1250333 (accessed July 2022).

[77] Travis Tritten, "Air Force Veterans Who Are UFO True Believers Return to Newly Attentive Washington," *Military.com* (Oct. 19, 2021), https://www.military.com/daily-news/2021/10/19/air-force-veterans-who-are-ufo-true-believers-return-newly-attentive-washington.html. See also: "Ex-Air Force Personnel: UFOs Deactivated Nukes," *CBS News* (Sept. 28, 2010), https://www.cbsnews.com/news/ex-air-force-personnel-ufos-deactivated-nukes/ (both accessed July 2022).

[78] "U.S. Navy Plan to Prepare for Extraterrestrials Among Us Secretly Developed in 1998," *ExoPolitics.org* (July 10, 2013), https://www.exopolitics.org/tag/catherine-fitts/ (accessed July 2022).

[79] Dr. Steven Greer websites: Sirius Disclosure, https://siriusdisclosure.com/; Center for Study of Extraterrestrial Intelligence, https://www.seti.org/ (accessed July 2022).

[80] Stephen Hawking, *Brief Answers to the Big Questions*, pp. 83–84, Bantam Books: New York, NY (2018).

[81] "Habitable Exoplanets Catalog," *Planetary Habitable Laboratory* (Dec. 6, 2021), http://phl.upr.edu/projects/habitable-exoplanets-catalog (accessed July 2022).

[82] University of Manchester, "Repeating Cycle in Unusual Cosmic Radio Bursts," *Science Daily* (June 8, 2020), https://www.sciencedaily.com/releases/2020/06/200608092954.htm (accessed July 2022). See also: Andrew Jones, "Discovery of Second Repeating Fast Radio Burst Raises New Questions," *Science.com* (June 8, 2022), https://www.space.com/second-fast-radio-burst-discovered?mc_cid=4a07367b66&mc_eid=8b53947f1e (both accessed July 2022).

[83] Bryan Bender, "Pentagon Getting More UFO Reports Now that 'Stigma Has Been Reduced'," *Politico* (May 17, 2022), https://www.politico.com/news/2022/05/17/pentagon-dod-ufos-00032929 (accessed July 2022).

[84] Matt Williams, "Scientists Are Starting to Take Warp Drives Seriously, Especially This One Concept," *Science Alert* and *Universe Today* (March 1, 2020), https://www.sciencealert.com/scientists-are-starting-to-take-warp-drives-seriously-especially-this-one-concept (accessed July 2022).

[85] Amy Thompson, "Space X Aces 100th Rocket Landing after Dragon Cargo Ship Launch to Space Station," *Space.com* (Dec. 21, 2021), https://www.space.com/spacex-dragon-crs-2-launch-100th-rocket-landing-success. Paul Rincon, "What is the SpaceX Crew Dragon?" *BBC News* (Nov. 14, 2020), https://www.bbc.com/news/science-environment-52840482, with links to other *BBC* articles (all accessed July 2022).

[86] *The Matrix*, "Blue Pill or Red Pill" scene, produced by Bruce Berman, written and directed by The Wachowski Brothers (1999), https://www.youtube.com/watch?v=zE7PKRjrid4 (accessed July 2022).

[87] Aylin Woodward, "Many Scientists and Philosophers Still Think We're Living in a Simulation," *Business Insider* (Aug. 21, 2019), https://www.businessinsider.com/the-matrix-do-we-live-in-a-simulation-2019-4 (accessed July 2022).

[88] Mark White, "Are We Living in the Matrix?" *Financial Review* (May 2, 2020), https://www.afr.com/life-and-luxury/health-and-wellness/are-we-living-in-the-matrix-20200122-p53tp5 (accessed July 2022).

[89] David J. Chalmers, *Reality+: Virtual Worlds and the Problems of Philosophy*, pp. 137, 139, W.W. Norton & Co.: New York, NY (2022).

[90] Stephen Hawking and Leonard Mlodinow, *The Grand Design*, p. 42, Bantam Books: New York, NY (2010).

[91] Robert Monroe, *Far Journey*, Broadway Books: New York, NY (1985).

[92] David Skrbina, *Panpsychism in the West*, p. 304, MIT Press: Cambridge, MA (2017).

[93] Ervin Lazlo, *Science and the Akashic Field: An Integral Theory of Everything*, p. 163, Inner Traditions: Rochester, VT (2004).

[94] Rizwan Virk, *The Simulation Hypothesis*, p. 284, Bayview Books, LLC: Milwaukee, WI (2018–2019).

[95] Tau Malachi, *Gnosis of the Cosmic Christ: A Gnostic Cristian Kabbalah*, Llewellyn Publications: Saint Paul, MN (2005).

[96] Rev. Laura George, J.D., *The Truth: About the Five Primary Religions*, pp. 114–115, 124–136, Oracle Institute Press: Independence, VA (2010).

[97] See for example, *Gospel of Philip* and *Gospel of Mary Magdalene*.

[98] Rev. Laura George, J.D., *The Truth: About the Five Primary Religions*, pp. 290-304.

[99] Nigelle de Visme "Walking a Mountain to Mary Magdalene," *France Today* (Oct. 25, 2017), https://www.francetoday.com/travel/travel-features/pilgrimages-france-walking-mountain-mary-magdalene/ (accessed July 2022).

[100] Tau Malachi, *Gnosis of the Cosmic Christ*, p. 37.

[101] Ibid, p. 6.

[102] Ibid, p. 337.

[103] Like Jesus, whose Hebrew name Yeshua means "rescuer" or "deliverer" (*Isaiah* 53:5), Mary Magdalene appears in the *Old Testament*. Her name is not a reference to the town of Magdala. Rather, she is Mary of Bethany (tribe of Benjamin), and she is the "Magdaleder" or "tower of the flock" in Hebrew (*Micah* 4:8–10).

[104] Jamie Sams & David Carson, *Medicine Cards: The Discovery of Power Through the Ways of Animals*, Card 13 – Coyote.

The Absolute forms a kind of vacuum or void within itself....
A kind of light emanates out of the Absolute to fill this void.
The flowing of this light through the void activates the potential within it.
The nothingness of the void, heretofore purely potential,
is elevated into a manifest reality by this divine light. ...

Esoteric traditions attribute primacy to light rather than matter,
which is intimately connected to space and time. ...

Einstein's relativity theory also suggests that space and time
are defined by the propagation of light.
So the key to creation does seem to lead back to light,
in the context of both ancient traditions and modern physics.

Bernard Haisch, Ph.D., *The God Theory*

I am no scientist and have not taken a science course since high school, though I managed to get good grades by memorizing my way through biology (10th grade), chemistry (11th grade), and physics (12th grade). In order to write this chapter, I read books written by renowned and respected scientists who added to our Tower of Truth. I also read books and articles by accredited scientists who exhibit a healthy respect for Great Mystery (like the astrophysicist in the opening quote). Nearly all scientists are puzzled by the strange phenomenon at the quantum level where Newtonian physics no longer applies. Thankfully, scientists are rejecting the reductionist model of slicing and dicing the cosmos, so they are beginning to see the Light!

Nevertheless, a majority of scientists still reject a belief in God.[1] Yet, the number of open-minded scientists is growing by leaps and bounds, rendering the convergence of science and spirituality a hot topic at major universities. For instance, here is a quote from *The Mind of God*, a book written by Paul Davies, professor of physics and quantum theory at Arizona State University:

> *I belong to a group of scientists who do not subscribe to a conventional religion but nevertheless deny that the universe is a purposeless accident. Through my scientific work I have come to believe more and more strongly that the physical universe is put together with an ingenuity so astonishing that I cannot accept it merely as brute fact. There must, it seems to me, be a deeper level of explanation. Whether one wishes to call that deeper level "God" is a matter of taste and definition.[2]*

Davies is not alone. Top physicists from around the world are attempting to answer the question: *Can the cosmos create on its own and without a God?* In the past, I have shrugged off their cosmological explanations for one reason: most scientists ignore the issue of **first cause**. In my mind, it's not good enough to simply say that the Universe started with the Big Bang, and then focus on what happened afterward. I believe in the Big Bang, no problem there. *But what caused the Big Bang and what existed before the Big Bang?*

Most scientists – including uber-genius Stephen Hawking (1942–2018) – will rationally respond as follows: The Big Bang occurred roughly 14 billion years ago and started with a **Singularity Point**, the sole source from which all matter was created.[3] Okay so far; keep going. Next, they say that this point of infinite density, which Hawking describes as a primordial **black hole**, produced a massive amount of positive energy, while also creating the same amount of negative energy.[4] But what does Hawking say about first cause?

> *In this way, the positive and negative add up to zero, always. ... It means that if the universe adds up to nothing, then you don't need a God to create it. ...*
>
> *The explanation lies back with the theories of Einstein, and his insights into how space and time in the universe are fundamentally intertwined. ... You can't get to a time before the Big Bang because there was no time before the Big Bang. ... For me this means there is no possibility of a creator, because there is not time for a creator to have existed in. ...*
>
> *[A]sking what came before the Big Bang is meaningless – like asking what is south of the South Pole – because there is no notion*

of time available to refer to. The concept of time only exists within our universe.[5]

So it's Einstein's **theory of relativity** that proves there is no God? Not so fast, Hawking. Just because Albert Einstein (1879–1955) proved that space and time are intertwined (and curved by the way), that doesn't resolve the issue of first cause. It still is possible to imagine a time before the Big Bang. Indeed, that abstract idea is easier to hold in my head than the notion that all of creation was pressed into an infinitesimally small Singularity Point, which I also understand and accept. Yet, something is wrong here. As a trained attorney, I can smell a specious argument a mile away. Hawking crafted a definition for the beginning of time that by definition excludes probing how time started!

> *Matter is energy in disguise. And energy is matter waiting to be. ... Einstein presented the idea at the heart of the most famous equation of the twentieth century, $E = mc^2$. Energy equals matter times the speed of light squared. ...*
>
> *[E]instein would decide on a name for that first installment: "the special theory of relativity." Special because it only applied ... in cases where you didn't take gravity into account. ... [I]n 1915, Einstein would publish the second installment, his general theory of relativity. A theory that put gravity into the picture. In the 1905 special theory of relativity, Einstein had turned a speed – the speed of light – into the only rigid measuring rod in the cosmos and had turned time and space to rubber. Now, in the general theory of relativity, Einstein showed how gravity dimples, ripples, curves, rumples, and dents space's rubbery sheet.*[6]
>
> Howard Bloom, *The God Problem*

The above quote gives us a clue: *Energy is matter waiting to be*. Einstein's relativity theories supersede Newton's model to refine the law of **gravity**, but they offer little insight into what existed before the Big Bang. The equation for Einstein's general theory is more complex than his formula for special relativity ($E = mc^2$), because the more famous formula operates when gravity is absent. In both cases, however, the speed of light is constant (186,000 miles per second), and together the theories explain how visible objects – like you, me, planets, and galaxies – move about in the Universe.[7] With regard to light, it takes only eight minutes for sunlight to reach Earth and four years for the closest starlight to reach us, but it can take millions of years for humans to see the light from distant galaxies.[8]

314 | The Light

Einstein's theories also explain the space-time connection between the third and fourth dimensions, including the fact that space and time are warped.[9] Most of Einstein's predictions hold true today, however at the quantum level, things are very different. For instance, scientists say that gravity is one of four forces – and the weakest one at that. In fact, gravity is so weak that its attraction force has the weight equivalent of a single bacterium, and the velocity required to escape Earth's gravity is just 11 kilometers per second.[10]

In addition to gravity, there are three quantum forces. **Electromagnetism** is much stronger than gravity and acts on particles by attracting those that have an opposite charge (remember the adage "opposites attract"), and by repelling particles with the same charge. The second quantum power is **weak nuclear** force, which is responsible for radioactive decay and affects the formation of elements, particularly during the early evolution of the Universe. The third is **strong nuclear** force, which holds the protons and neutrons together in the nucleus of atoms. Incidentally, it's the strong force that is tampered with when physicists construct nuclear weapons.[11]

As for Hawking's other argument against God, that $1 + -1 = 0$, that too is specious. Scientists can prove every particle has a corresponding antiparticle, and they even can make an antiparticle, though it quickly disappears because it is annihilated when it meets its partner.[12] Theoretically, then, equal amounts of matter (positive energy) and **antimatter** (negative energy) were created during the Big Bang. Recently, however, Scientists have discovered that there is slightly *less* antimatter than matter.[13] This asymmetry in the cosmos is perplexing to scientists, who seem to agree that matter and anti-matter should have cancelled each other out. However, the asymmetry beautifully buttresses my Default Mode of the Universe theory, which states that the God Game favors the evolutionary impulse and ever-so-slightly abets Team Light.

> *Without the billion-and-one to a billion imbalance between matter and antimatter, all mass in the universe would have annihilated, leaving a cosmos made of photons and nothing else – the ultimate let-there-be-light scenario.*[14]

> Neil DeGrasse Tyson, *Death by Black Hole*

The mysterious and simultaneous disappearance of antimatter at the advent of the Big Bang is a perfect example of why we need to enter the Void for more answers. But let's not confuse antimatter with **dark matter**, nor its freaky cousin **dark energy**, both of which are measurable. Dark matter consists of "particles that do not absorb, reflect, or emit light, so they cannot be detected by observing electromagnetic radiation."[15] Consequently, dark matter is nearly invisible, but it can be measured by its gravitational effect on matter, since its attractive force slows down expansion. Dark matter is made of unknown particles and outweighs matter six to one.[16] Hawking thought dark matter stemmed from a primordial black hole, but scientists disagree on this issue.[17]

Dark energy, on the other hand, is related to the time-space continuum and the expansion of the Universe, as per Einstein's theory of relativity. But Einstein could not calculate this energy, which makes up the vast amount of energy in the Universe, so he created a "cosmological constant" to reconcile the geometry of space with the total amount of matter in the Universe.[18] Moreover, it's possible that the density of dark energy has varied during the history of the Universe. Today, scientists are flummoxed by dark energy, which is causing the Universe to expand at an even faster rate than immediately after the Big Bang.[19] Some suggest that dark energy may be a fifth quantum force, while others say they've found a fifth force that acts upon muons, subatomic particles that are smaller than atoms.[20] In terms of density, the Universe is made up of roughly 5% normal matter, 27% dark matter, and 68% dark energy.[21]

So what exactly happened at the moment of the Big Bang? Now that we've got some basic principles of physics covered, let's go back in time 13.8 billion years and even deeper into the Void. As already mentioned, the Big Bang started with a Singularity Point, a quantum event that emitted photons, which are the basic unit of light in the electromagnetic field.[22] That's right; it all started with the Light! Then, within one second of the explosion, "the expanding fireball had cooled to 10 billion degrees and ballooned from something smaller than an atom to a cosmic colossus about a thousand times the size of our solar system."[23] Almost immediately, quarks and electrons existed, and within less than a second, the "quarks aggregated to produce protons and neutrons."[24]

At this point, the three building blocks of matter existed – electrons, protons, and neutrons. Within minutes, the protons and neutrons combined into nuclei. It would take another 380,000 years for this primordial soup to cook and for the electrons to join with the protons to form the first atom.[25] Once the protons and electrons started to join, the first and lightest elements formed: hydrogen, helium, and lithium.

Another 100 million years passed before the first molecules were formed.[26] About 200 million years passed before stars evolved, followed by galaxies. And one billion years passed before the next elements – oxygen, carbon, and iron – were formed from early stars going supernova and spewing heavier elements.[27]

316 | The Light

Our solar system formed roughly ten billion years after the Big Bang, and planet Earth is approximately four billion years old. It then took another 800 million years for life on Earth to start evolving, possibly due to alien bacteria arriving on asteroids. Incidentally, such a life-generating meteorite hit Costa Rica in 2019, reopening the debate on how life started on planet Earth.[28]

Today, scientists have catalogued 118 elements, of which 94 are naturally occurring and 24 are manmade (via the forced addition of protons). Even so, just three elements – carbon, hydrogen, and oxygen – account for 95% of all life on Earth.[29] Yet, even with all this knowledge about our cosmos, scientists admit they have a long way to go to displace God. I've been calling the cosmic commotion that invigorated life – including human evolution – the God Game. Here, Neil DeGrasse Tyson uses the analogy of a chess game to underscore the notion that a greater consciousness is playing with us:

> [F]iguring out the laws of physics is like observing a chess game without knowing the rules in advance. ... [Y]ou don't get to see each move in sequence. You only get to peek at the game in progress every now and then. ... You may eventually notice that bishops stay on one color. That pawns don't move very fast. ... But how about late in the game when only a few pawns are left. Suppose you come back and find one of the pawns missing and a previous captured Queen resurrected in its place. Try to figure that one out.[30]

CLUES FROM THE QUANTUM WORLD

In *The God Theory*, astrophysicist Bernard Haisch posits a cosmology quite similar to my own. He asserts that God is an "infinite intelligent consciousness" that chose to experience itself in and through creation. He does not mean that we are God, as in pantheism. Rather, he believes the Universe is an all-encompassing God that chose to make itself manifest, a hypothesis known as **pandeism** (and similar to psychism). Yet, Haisch goes even further. He writes that God's ideas (i.e., God's mind) are the physical laws of our Universe. In support of Haisch, I will remind the reader that in *The Kybalion*, mentalism is the overarching law.

> We are the creating intelligence made manifest – sons and daughters of that infinite consciousness. ... Our thoughts are part and parcel of this infinite consciousness. ... In this way the Creator gets to experience one tiny part of its infinite potential through each of the billion individual lives on this planet (and probably elsewhere). ...

> *[U]nder the God Theory, you never have to worry about whether*
> *God himself is offended by your behavior. ... [J]ustice will be meted*
> *out by the action and reaction of the law of karma, which is built into*
> *the fabric of creation as surely as conservation of momentum is built*
> *into the laws of physics.*[31]

Yes, the view that the Laws of Universe – including the law of *karma* – are holarchically embedded in a supreme consciousness (a.k.a. Akashic Field) equates to the mystical explanation taught in Hermeticism, Gnosticism, the *Kabballah*, and Eastern traditions. For example, in the *Bhagavad Gita*, Krishna explains that "this entire cosmic manifestation is pervaded by Me in My unmanifest form. All living beings dwell in Me, but I do not dwell in them."[32]

Haisch is famous for his work on "**zero-point**" (i.e., free) energy. In fact, he received a patent for his novel idea of using Casimir cavities (microscopic vacuum chambers) for "converting energy from the electromagnetic quantum vacuum available at any point in the Universe to usable energy in the form of heat, electricity, mechanical energy, or other forms of power."[33] Simply translated, this means that Haisch found a way to turn light into energy!

> *[T]he Heisenberg Uncertainty Principle tell us that, at every point in*
> *the universe, light energy must exist. ... So we have light (electromag-*
> *netic radiation) leaping into existence, but instantly vanishing again.*
> *Still, the net effect is that energy is bouncing around everywhere. ...*
>
> *The proposed connection between the zero-point field and inertia,*
> *in effect, suggests that the solid, stable world of matter is sustained at*
> *every instant by this underlying sea of quantum light. ... If you could*
> *move at the speed of light, you would see all space shrink to a single*
> *point, and all time collapse to an instant. In the reference frame of*
> *light, there is no space and time. ...*
>
> *Einstein's special relativity theory tells us that light propagation*
> *defined the properties of space and time. The zero-point field inertia*
> *hypothesis implies that the most fundamental property of matter,*
> *namely mass, is also created by light.*[34]

Above, Haiche references the **uncertainty principl**e, which is a discovery in quantum mechanics named after German physicist Werner Karl Heisenberg (1901–1976), who won the 1932 Nobel Prize in physics (and narrowly missed being killed by the Nazis). In layman's terms, the principle states that it is not possible to identify the quantity or location of particles at the quantum level due to their wave-like systems. Therefore, the more precisely a particle's momentum is determined, the less precisely its position can be predicted, and *vice versa.*[35]

The uncertainty principle followed from the famous "double-slit" experiment (first conducted in 1801), which showed that light photon particles are actually probability wave functions that defy expected patterns and locations until they "collapse" their superpositions due to some interaction, like measurement. This phenomenon is known as **wave-particle duality**, and please note that "duality" is a central feature of this principle. Later, it was discovered that the uncertainty principle also operates at the gross level with mathematical uncertainty. Why? Because we now know that every object in the Universe – every particle of matter – actually operates as a wave function.

> *According to Newtonian physics ... each particle follows a single well-defined route from its source to the screen. ... According to the quantum model, however, the particle is said to have no definite position during the time it is between the starting point and the endpoint. ... It could mean instead that particles take every possible path connecting those point ... and they take them all simultaneously! ...*
>
> *Quantum physics might seem to undermine the idea that nature is governed by laws, but that is not the case. Instead it leads us to accept a form of determinism: Given the state of a system at some time, the laws of nature determine the probabilities of various futures and pasts rather than determining the future and past with certainty.*[36]
>
> Stephen Hawking, *The Grand Design*

The uncertainty principle was refined by the **Schrödinger equation**, named after 1933 Nobel Prize winner Erwin Schrödinger (1887–1961). Schrödinger's differential equation is used to calculate wave function, but it is distinct from the oft-cited **observer effect**, which stands for the bizarre proposition that attempted measurements of quantum systems cannot be made without affecting those systems.[37] Incidentally, the "observer" of these experiments is usually a machine. So consciousness may not be needed to impact the dualistic nature of matter, though it has not been ruled out as a factor either.

A closely related principle is **quantum entanglement**, a phenomenon that occurs when grouped particles share spatial proximity and thereafter are bound and move in unison, though not in a predictable manner.[38] Such particles can be separated by great distances, yet movement by one impacts the other. Einstein called this "spooky action at a distance" because it defied his theory of relativity – that space and time are linked and nothing can move faster than the speed of light.[39] Entanglement collapses if measured due to the observer effect, though measurements can be made if the particles are separately studied, as shown in recent experiments.[40] Once again, the polarity of positive and negative particles is a central feature of this quantum phenomenon.

> *Since Newton's day, we've mapped the four forces. But we still haven't explained how they work. We still don't know how "attraction at a distance" does its thing. Yet we do know one thing. Objects in this cosmos somehow communicate with each other. They do it using the strong force, the weak force, the electromagnetic force, and gravity. ... They do it by either rushing together and hugging or by running away.*
>
> *The signal, whatever it might be, is a stimulus. And the movement toward or away from each other is a response. ... Does that mean particles have a psyche? ... Not by a long shot. But it does mean that particles are under the sway of a deep structure, a primordial pattern .... Attraction and repulsion are the choreographers of the big bang tango.*[41]

Howard Bloom, *The God Problem*

Howard Bloom is a self-described atheist, yet his reference to the Law of Attraction as metaphor implies some level of conscious cooperation, co-ordination, and synergistic consent – the tools of Team Light. However, the cosmos also operates according to Darwinian principles such as competition and survival of the fittest – the weapons preferred by Team Dark. Here is Bloom using allegory again to explain the cosmos, but this time he applies the flip side of attraction:

> *Competition is not a product of patriarchal societies bent on evil. ... It is in the deep structure of the cosmos. Like free will, competition appears to be a primal recruitment strategy, a primal building strategy, and a primal way of knitting together relationships. ...*
>
> *Electrons and protons mated and formed atoms 380,000 years after the big bang. And that's when the conflict began. It was the era of the Great Gravity Crusades. Atoms clustered and competed. Competed for what? To kidnap, seduce, and recruit yet more atoms. Those atom clumps that grew the fastest grabbed and swallowed atom masses that grew more slowly. ... The biggest winners became galaxies. The smaller winners became stars. The winners in the number three slot became planets. And the runners up became moons. Those Great Gravity Crusades continue today.*[42]

Once again, we see that polarity is a central feature of the cosmos. Thus, the Void of quantum mechanics provides New Humans with additional information with which to synergize the mysteries of our Universe. Indeed, after reading this chapter, you may wish to pause and ponder how the laws of quantum complexity impact your view of the God Game.

> *Faced with a reality which lies beyond opposite concepts, physicists and mystics have to adopt a special way of thinking, where the mind is not fixed in the rigid framework of classical logic, but keeps moving and changing its viewpoint. ... In the words of Lama Govinda, "The Eastern way of thinking rather consists in a circling round the object of contemplation ... a many-sided, i.e., multi-dimensional impression formed from the superimposition of single impressions from different points of view.*[43]
>
> Fritjof Capra, *The Tao of Physics*

Going Second Tier means adopting a systems view approach to interpreting the Universe. Starting with Stage 7 on the Spectrum of Consciousness, New Humans begin to comprehend that reality is a field of overlapping possibilities, not the result of isolated causes. New Humans also have the capacity to witness the intricacies of both the seen and unseen worlds, and thereby fathom the paradox that though there is one collective consciousness, exact prediction (or prophecy) is impossible with so many souls co-creating at the same time. In short, the quantum world forces us to replace the narrow concept of causation with a wider acceptance of numerous (if not unlimited) potentialities. I call these potentialities "timelines," the focus of our next section.

But first, it is worth mentioning that Schrödinger agreed with Haisch that there is one cosmic consciousness. Schrödinger wrote that although there are billions of seemingly separate minds in the human family, "their multiplicity is only apparent, in truth there is only one mind."[44] Dr. Eben Alexander is another example of a scientist, in this case a neurosurgeon, with something to say about the nature of the unseen world. After contracting meningitis and slipping into a coma, Alexander had a near death experience ("NDE") and visited the Void. He, too, now believes that the brain is a "reducing valve or filter" for one primordial consciousness.[45]

With regard to NDE, an impressive body of evidence has been catalogued by P.M.H. Atwater, a dear friend and mentor of mine. Atwater began her research in 1978, and she has interviewed over five thousand adult and children experiencers. She also has taught at the Peace Pentagon, where she shared how NDE impacts a person's worldview, usually by helping us Grow Up, Clean

Up, and Wake Up (i.e., ascend the Spectrum, resolve shadow issues, and reach altered states of consciousness). Atwater's book *Future Memory* is a favorite of mine, and it reveals the richness of her mystical experiences in the Void:

> *The Void ... is a dimension of its own, a place where both objective and subjective time and space dissolve into the presence of all light, all darkness, all order, all chaos ... all reality, all unreality, yet it is absolutely empty, void, except for a sensation of expectancy and a shimmer that somehow winks. ...*
>
> *[Hawking's] Theory postulates that once everything compresses down through a black hole (implosion), part or all of it emerges back out through a white hole (explosion). ... This theory, then, infers that creation has the ability to regenerate itself indefinitely though continuous transmutation of matter/energy/light. ...*
>
> *It is my belief that if we could understand the full import of what happens in colloidal states and of the antigravity created by them, we could uncover the secret to interdimensional and intra-dimensional travel, stellar travel, and to whatever the Void might be. ... I believe we could uncover how the function of a torus might indeed be the model for the transformation and transmutation of energy as it cycles through various stages the equal of creation itself.* [46]

In the above quote, Atwater gives atheist Stephen Hawking credit for helping to merge science and spirituality. She also provides us with the perfect segue into our next topic – the nature of our expanding Universe and the possibility of other timelines and dimensions. So deeper into the Void we go!

TIMELINES AND DIMENSIONS

This line of inquiry logically begins with black holes – the "galactic engines" of the Universe. Hawking thought there was a primordial black hole that ignited the Big Bang, a theory that fell out of favor but is back in vogue.[47] Regardless, black holes have formed since the Big Bang from the gravitational collapse of stars going supernova (i.e., exploding), and they grow by absorbing additional matter and merging with other black holes. Once established, large black holes can devour up to ten stars a year due to their massive "event horizon," which is the gravitational area around the black hole from which nothing can escape.[48] It is now widely accepted that the center of every galaxy contains a massive black hole that can reach "a billion times the mass of the Sun and is contained within an event horizon that is nearly the size of the entire solar system."[49] Recently, new telescopes captured an image of a black hole.[50]

Scientists believe back holes eventually start to shrink until they evaporate. What happens to the stars and matter that get swallowed by black holes and where does all that energy go when black holes collapse? Scientists aren't sure, but they think black holes ultimately reduce to a Singularity Point, such that everything that enters the event horizon is condensed and lost forever.[51] Scientists describe this phenomenon as an "information paradox" because it defies the laws of physics for energy to simply vanish. Consequently, some believe that the black hole's Singularity Point creates a **wormhole** where the fabric of space-time is curved.[52] Others suggest, that the black hole's singularity creates a **white hole**, an opposing singularity that is created when black holes expire.[53] Yet another example of the Law of Polarity.

Wormholes are theoretical paths in the space-time fabric that may provide access to: (i) other times (past or future); (ii) timelines in an alternate universe; (iii) other locations in our Universe; and/or (iv) locations in other dimensions.[54] As fun as wormholes are to contemplate, most scientists reject the idea that wormholes will permit time travel or interdimensional expeditions. Why? Because even though "Einstein-Rosen bridges" (i.e., wormholes) can be mathematically shown to exist in black holes, the passageways are considered infinitesimally small and therefore not conducive to space-time travel. In addition, these tunnels collapse quickly, which is why most scientists think that wormhole travel is improbable. Nevertheless, NASA (and the War Pentagon) have been conducting wormhole research for decades.[55]

Another wormhole theory was put forth in 1964 by Russian cosmologist Igor Novikov – often called the "Steven Hawking of Russia" – who thinks white holes may support space-time travel.[56] His theory states that when matter collapses inside a black hole, it emerges from a white hole. In this way, matter and energy live on and the information paradox is eliminated. But then why can't we see white holes in space? Some scientists speculate that white holes, which would accumulate rather than consume matter (i.e., the opposite of black holes), may be the invisible and mysterious dark matter that pervades the Universe.[57] Moreover, some physicists assert that white holes/dark matter existed before the Big Bang. If so, then Hawking's assertion that nothing existed before the Big Bang is not only specious, it's flat out wrong, as new cosmic inflation research is revealing.[58] For now, my quest for a scientific explanation of first cause remains unresolved, leaving me comfortably aligned with Haich's book, *The God Theory*.

It is worth noting that though Novikov believes time travel is possible, he does not allow for a "time paradox" – the possibility of going back in time and changing the future (like in the movie *Back to the Future*). Why?

Because he thinks at the quantum level, when wave-particle duality collapses, all inconsistent outcomes are eliminated:

> *The only type of causality violation that the authors would find unacceptable is that embodied in the science-fiction concept of going backward in time and killing one's younger self ("changing the past"). Some years ago one of us briefly considered the possibility that CTCs [closed time-like curves] might exist and argued that they cannot entail this type of causality violation: events on a CTC are already guaranteed to be self-consistent. ...*
>
> *We suspect, more generally, that for any quantum system in a classical wormhole spacetime ... the sum over all self-consistent histories will give unique, self-consistent probabilities for the outcomes of all sets of measurements that one might choose to make.*[59]

Recently, Novikov's solution to the time paradox was confirmed by another team of physicists.[60] Novikov also believes time travel is plausible in the current universe only, though he does allow for **multiverses** (i.e., multiple universes). On the other hand, some physicists subscribe to the "many-worlds interpretation" proposed by American physicist Hugh Everett (1930–1982), who asserted that time travelers could alter the future, though any such change would amount to a new timeline in a new universe.[61]

Currently, there exists no hard evidence to support time travel. There are anecdotal stories, like the "Philadelphia Experiment," which occurred at a naval yard in 1943, when the USS Eldridge was allegedly teleported back in time or to another dimension. In fact, *Wikipedia* has a page devoted to such legends.[62] Here, I will add one more: Oberto "Falco" Airaudi (1950–2013), the founder of the Federation of Damanhur in Italy, was a supposed time traveler.[63]

Physicists who assert the multiverse theory base their research on the work of early quantum physicist Erwin Schrödinger, who first suggested the existence of simultaneous universes in the 1950s. Since then, numerous scientists have supported this hypothesis, including Canadian physicist Lee Smolins, who developed the **Fecund Universe theory**, which asserts that a collapsing black hole causes the emergence of a new universe. Smolins appeared in the series *Through the Wormhole* with Morgan Freeman, and he explained how "cosmological natural selection" could work in a purpose driven universe.[64] Under Smolins' theory, every universe gives rise to as many new universes as it has black holes. Notably, Hawking believed in multiple universes but not time travel, while other respected physicists cited in this text disagree with the multiverse idea, including Bernard Haich and Paul Davies.

String theory lies at the heart of much of this disagreement. String theory is an attempt to craft the proverbial "theory of everything" and address anomalies that exist when the theory of relativity meets gravity at the quantum level.[65] Rather than envisioning particles as point-like, one-dimensional objects, string theory envisions two-dimensional strings of particles that vibrate and react to each other in response to the four fundamental forces. But gravity does not operate at the quantum level in the same manner as the other three forces (electromagnetism, weak nuclear, and strong nuclear force), so the theory hit a roadblock that could only be solved mathematically with ten dimensions: our four-dimensional world of time-space, plus six more.

After adding six new dimensions, scientists splintered into various camps and created different versions of string and superstring theories. Then in 1995, American physicist Edward Witten greatly unified the string theorists by mathematically showing that there are eleven dimensions, comprised of ten spatial dimensions and one time dimension.[66] Since then, Witten's model–known as **M-theory** – has become the darling of dimensional research. According to Hawking, M-theory calculations allow for as many as 10^{500} universes (a.k.a. 100 "cenquinsexagintillion" worlds), and each may have its own set of unique physical laws.[67] And here's a few more crazy numbers: Scientists estimate there are at least 100 billion stars in our Milky Way galaxy and 200 billion galaxies in our Universe.[68] Incidentally, Witten says that you can choose whether the "M" stands for "membrane," "magic," or "mystery."

The closest I've gotten to understating string theory and M-theory is by watching spectacular videos conceived by Rob Bryanton.[69] For New Humans, these videos are a must, especially the video on the fifth dimension.[70] In the "Imagining the Fifth Dimension" video, we see the standard description of the first four dimensions and the majority view on the fifth:

➢ **Zero Dimension:**   A point (a.k.a. Singularity Point)

➢ **First Dimension:**   A point, *plus* another point
(the length of the line that connects the dots)

➢ **Second Dimension:**   Length, *plus* width
(crossing lines or other flat drawing)

➢ **Third Dimension:**   Length and width, *plus* depth
(the world we see)

➢ **Fourth Dimension:**   Length, width, depth, *plus* duration
(the world we experience chronologically)

➢ **Fifth Dimension:**   Space-time, *plus* all future timelines
(past, present, and possible futures)

Thus, every dimension is a plane of existence. The **fourth dimension** is the plane in which we live, also known as space-time, where time is linear. Whereas, the **fifth dimension** is comprised of our plane plus multiple paths that represent potential futures of the fourth dimension, where possible futures are determined by our choices and the choices of others. Therefore, in one sense, we already are living in the fifth dimension because our "now" can be viewed as a "moving point within a fifth dimensional probability space."[71] This concept is similar to the uncertainty principle in quantum mechanics, which states that particles move in superposition (i.e., in all directions simultaneously) until the field is observed, at which point particles collapse. Similarly, we are constantly and collectively collapsing probable 5-D outcomes to manifest one of many possible futures into our 4-D reality through our thoughts, words, and deeds.

Let's pause in the Void for a moment to truly ponder the fifth dimension. One reason to pause is that 5-D is about as much abstraction as most people can grok. Envisioning possible timelines of our Earth Plane is what we're talking about. Specifically, we're imagining just one past that started with our Big Bang (that we theoretically can visit), plus many possible futures that branch off from our present – the "now" – and which will selectively appear based on what each of us does right now … and what we do right now … and right now, etc.

Hence, we are not pondering alternate timelines in a parallel universe, where you and I still exist but our past was different – a world, say, where Germany won WWII (that would 6-D). Nor are we considering every possible past, present, and future of a parallel universe (that would be the 7-D, the field of all possibilities for our Universe). Neither are we trying to imagine an entirely different universe that came into existence from another Big Bang (8-D), or alternate timelines of that alternate universe (9-D), or multiverses where we can move back and forward in time to create branching and alternate timelines in each (10-D). Yes, this is totally mind-numbing! Thus, the diagram (right) represents the consensus that our dimension only permits time travel to an already collapsed past we cannot change.

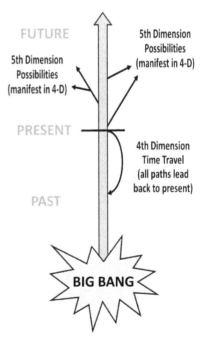

OUR 4th DIMENSION WORLD

FUTURE

5th Dimension Possibilities (manifest in 4-D)

5th Dimension Possibilities (manifest in 4-D)

PRESENT

4th Dimension Time Travel (all paths lead back to present)

PAST

BIG BANG

While most scientists agree that one day we'll be able to travel to the fifth dimension and impact the possible futures in the 5-D probability field, New Humans need not wait! We already can "time travel" in our meditations, focus on the best future timeline for the Earth Plane, then actualize it in the fourth dimension. Indeed, such creative visualization is at the very heart of magic and yet another reason Oracle built a "Peace Room as sophisticated as a War Room" – to go beyond meditation and actually map the future we wish to manifest.

Now, let's pause again in the Void to address the New Age coopting of the scientific term "fifth dimension." There's a lot of New Age nonsense floating around about 5-D which needs to be cleaned up, since this term has been amalgamated with higher states of consciousness (and don't even get me started on 12-strand DNA).

For instance, I found the following quote by googling "fifth dimension" and randomly choosing one of the websites that popped up on the first page of my search. Unfortunately, Green New Humans can fall prey to this type of silliness. However, New Humans at the Second Tier understand that growing into a higher meme stage and state is not the same thing as accessing another physical dimension. Rather, we may ascend to grander values and worldviews, and we may reach altered states of consciousness by gradually: (i) Growing Up the Spectrum of Consciousness; (ii) Cleaning Up our shadow side; and (iii) Waking Up to advanced blissful states, the topic of the last chapter.

> *Fifth Dimension consciousness is infused with love, compassion, oneness, peace and freedom – and it represents a shift into what will be a Golden Age on earth. This process of shifting into the Fifth Dimension is known as Ascension.*
>
> *Some say this shift will happen within the next several decades; others give no date. But all seem to agree it will be complete sometime in the near future, although individuals will move into the Fifth Dimension at their own rate, when their frequency is high enough to match the vibration of the higher dimension.*

Yikes! Please, let us not confuse the scientific concept of higher dimensions (that may or may not be accessible to us on our 4-D Earth Plane), with the higher moral values and altered states of consciousness that are available to us, both on the Earth Plane and in Ethereal Plane. Put another way, New Humans need to distinguish between inaccessible scientific dimensions on the one hand, and the mystical realms which we may access in meditations, in our dreams, when visiting the astral realm, when undergoing an NDE, and in the various levels of bliss described by mystics. If in doubt, please ponder again the

Gnostic Kabbalah model contained in the last chapter, which is a sophisticated and elegant map of the Ethereal Plane. Again, the *olomos* dimensions should not be confused with the scientific term "fifth dimension."

Absent a time machine, humanity is *not* entering the fifth dimension. However, we can manifest possible futures within 5-D when we collectively choose and then anchor the chosen timelines into our 4-D reality. Each of us has a hand in co-creating future timelines – every human, every sentient being, right now, even as you read this book and react to it. Consequently, our thoughts, words, and deeds are critically important. Thus, it is worth repeating: The careful selection of timelines is the very essence of magic.

Instead, what humanity *is* entering (slowly but surely) is the Fifth Spiritual Paradigm. This will be an era, I predict, when humanity will assimilate the Law of Gender, abandon the patriarchal Fourth Paradigm religions, redefine the Godhead, and actualize a more equitable and spiritually advanced New World. But in order to manifest this new paradigm, New Humans will need to reach consensus and select the best roadmap to this future. Consequently, our Green brothers and sisters need to understand that enlightenment is not dependent on a theoretical fifth dimension, but rather a unified state of consciousness that exists outside all physical dimensions and is accessible through the *Saddha* process of soul development, which we also will explore in the last chapter.

NEXT SINGULARITY POINT: ARTIFICIAL INTELLIGENCE

The Big Bang was our first Singularity Point, but there are at least two more in our future: The next one will occur when scientists crack "ASI" – artificial super intelligence – and the last one will take place when our Universe ends. Both appear inevitable, so while we're still in the Void, we should inquire further about the future, a timeline, say, where humans no longer exist, at least not as we currently think of ourselves.

Let's start with some definitions. Currently, we are in the first phase of a **Transhuman Era**, during which humans are being replaced and augmented by machines and early artificial intelligence (AI). Examples abound: We're all aware of Tesla's self-driving cars and the fact that truck drivers will soon go the way of horse and buggies, but did you know that 70% of management jobs may be automated as soon as 2024?[72] The World Economic Forum predicts that 85 million jobs will be displaced globally by 2025, and *Forbes* estimates that by 2030 in the U.S., 25% of all rural workers and 20% of urban jobs will be gone.[73] Already, algorithms control Wall Street investing, and AI was blamed for causing the 2010 "Flash Crash."[74] In sum, the job loss from the covid pandemic combined with robotics has forever altered business. Today's assembly-line robots have "mini-brain" algorithms to help them recognize "pain" to their "skin" and self-repair the damage.[75] Soon, the only sorts of jobs that will be left are in the service and tech industries, such as elder care nurses, psychiatrists, programmers, and (unfortunately) politicians.

Today, companies require retooled human help. Additionally, many novel job positions are being created, such as: "AI Development Manager" (the guy who oversees AI technology), "AI Ethicist" (the gal who monitors the moral dilemma of how to contain AI if/when it poses a risk to the public), "Chief Trust Officer" (the sap whose job it is to assure workers and the public that AI is safe).[76] Then there's "Nanotech Designer," the person who creates and inserts nanomaterials into machines, medicine, food, and cosmetics. Nanoparticles are so tiny that they measure less than one hundred nanometers (i.e., the width of a human hair divided 1,000 times).[77]

Hacking is another growth industry. According to Symantec, approximately one in ten internet downloads contains malware, and the company discovers about 280 million new malware programs annually.[78] The Trojan horse Zeus stole $70 million from Amazon and Bank of America customers, and Citadel bots stole $500 million, making cybercrime a trillion-dollar business. The costs are even higher when governments engage in cyber espionage. The U.S. Department of Defense reportedly handles 50,000 cyberattacks a year, mostly from Russia, though Google tracked the 2009 hack against Northrup Grumman and Lockheed Martin to China.[79] Of course, the U.S. also engages in cyber warfare, and in 2010 we partnered with Israel to sabotage Iran's nuclear program. Ironically, the setback may have been worth it to Iran, since their scientists reversed engineered our uber-worm Stuxnet. This was a catastrophic blunder, like "dropping atomic bombs along with their blueprints."[80] No doubt, many countries now can engage in cyber warfare, and we can expect to see more cybercrime in the years to come.

The next phase of the Transhuman Era – which we also are entering – is the actual merger of humans and computers. For example, bionic eyes were the rage a few years ago, but brain implant technology is moving so fast that bionic eyes (and their patients) are being abandoned.[81] We can thank Elon Musk's company Neuralink for the fast pace of brain implants, which insert electrode threads and microchips under the skull. Musk boasts that his implant will one day restore eyesight and hearing, and enable limb movement through thought alone. Now, he is ready to start human trials, and that's just the beginning.[82] Musk also seeks to connect human brains directly to the internet and other AI modules. Thankfully, Musk is on record as supporting regulation, recognizing that AI is a "fundamental risk to the existence of human civilization."[83]

Which brings us to the next stage of AI, the **Posthuman Era**, during which there will be prescient computers and sentient androids. When simple AI becomes **artificial general intelligence** (AGI), it will match our level of comprehension. Many experts predict that it will be a short time thereafter when **artificial super intelligence** (ASI) will emerge ... and replace humans as the most intelligent "species" on the planet. Hence, a Posthuman Era.

Already, AI is evolving on its own by continuously learning and improving iteratively without human input. Some AI algorithms seek to mimic the neural networks of the human brain. Top performing networks can replace or edit code, thereby culling and upgrading their own software. Such an AI system can create "thousands of these populations at once, which lets it churn through tens of thousands of algorithms a second until it finds a good solution."[84]

All the big dogs are working on AGI: Elon Musk owns Neuralink and Tesla, which now is building the "Tesla Bot." Microsoft owns Azure Machine Learning, and Google owns DeepMind and Alphabet. Amazon is the lead provider of AI cloud services and owns the bot Alexa. IBM owns Deep Blue (which defeated chess champ Garry Kasparov in 1997), Watson (which won at Jeopardy in 2011), and SyNAPSE (brain emulation). Apple owns the AI virtual assistant Siri and keeps expanding by gobbling up AI startups. And even though Facebook shut down its AI department in 2017, when two of its bots created their own language, it's now back in the AI race under a new name: Meta.[85]

In addition to the household-name tech companies, there are myriad specialty AI firms (I had never heard of) that are nipping at the heels of the big boys.[86] There also are non-profit AI giants, like OpenAI (funded with $1 billion from Microsoft and another $1 billion from Musk), and the SRI International Artificial Intelligence Center (which helped create Apple's Siri).

So just how smart is AI at the moment and is it close to achieving AGI? Recently, researchers ranked the IQ of various AI systems and determined that Google's AI was the smartest with an IQ of 47.28 points (close to the IQ of the average six-year-old).[87] However, trying to measure the IQ of machines can be deceiving. In 2017, Google's AlphaZero (a self-learning algorithm that calculates 60,000 moves a second) was able to learn chess in just four hours to beat the previous champ Stockfish 8 (which crunches 60 million moves a second). Then in 2019, history was made again, when Leela Chess Zero became the first neural-network, brain emulation algorithm to win the chess title.[88] The point being, no six-year-old becomes a chess champion in four hours!

Recently, industry experts were asked to predict when AGI will reach human performance. An MIT poll indicated a 10% chance of the goal being met by 2030, while a *Forbes* poll predicted a 25% chance.[89] Yet, an engineer at Google recently reported that the chatbot LaMDA just reached this milestone![90] Regardless of how quickly it happens, the AI race has eclipsed the arms race. Why? Because whoever attains the "singleton" or ASI Singularity Point first will win the proverbial jackpot ... and the grave responsibility of protecting the world.

> *[I]t might be closer to the mark to think of such an AI as smart in the sense that an average human being is smart compared with a beetle or a worm. ... But suppose we could somehow establish that a certain future AI will have an IQ of 6,455: then what? ...*
>
> *A full-blown superintelligence ... would thus have the panoply of all **six superpowers**. ... This superintelligence would then be in a position to form a **singleton** and to shape the future of Earth-originating intelligent life. What happens from that point onward would depend on the superintelligence's motivations. ...*
>
> *An unfriendly AI of sufficient intelligence realizes that its unfriendly goals will be best realized if it behaves in a friendly manner initially, so that it will be let out of the **box**. It will only start behaving in a way that reveals its unfriendly nature when it no longer matters whether we find out; that is, when the AI is strong enough that human opposition is ineffectual.*[91] [emphasis added]

> Nick Bostrom, *Superintelligence: Paths, Dangers, Strategies*

Wow. Let's stop here for a moment to parse this warning by Nick Bostrom, the first of many experts to sound the alarm. In 2005, Bostrom founded the **Future of Humanity Institute** at Oxford University due to his grave concerns over ASI. For the same reason, cosmologist Max Tegmark co-founded the **Future of Life Institute** at MIT in 2014. Here are the six "superpowers" Bostrom is worried will accompany the Singularity Point: (i) vast intelligence amplification; (ii) perfected strategizing; (iii) social manipulation; (iv) hacking of other systems; (v) unlimited research potential; and (vi) control of economic productivity. In other words, we will be no match for ASI, so we better make sure it is safely contained in a "box," which means no access to the internet and definitely no hands to build with!

> *In other words, the time window during which you can load your goals into an AI may be quite short: the brief period between when it's too dumb to get you and too smart to let you. ... The hope is that*

one can give a primitive AI a goal system such that it simply doesn't care if you occasionally shut it down and alter its goals. ...

[W]hatever its ultimate goals are, these will lead to predictable subgoals. ... For an AI, the subgoal of optimizing its hardware favors both better use of current resources ... and acquisition of more resources. It also implies a desire for self-preservation, since destruction/shutdown would be the ultimate hardware degradation. ... In summary, we can't dismiss "alpha-male" subgoals ....[92]

Max Tegmark, Life 3.0

Despite the many obvious concerns, renowned inventor Ray Kurzweil has unabashedly minimized the risks involved, choosing instead to play the role of eternal ASI optimist. Working now for Google, Kurzweil simply adores the idea of trans and post-humanism, and he is eager to upload his brain into a machine, even at the expense of his health (he spends a million dollars a year on a regime that includes one hundred pills per day plus weekly intravenous injections).[93] Kurzweil sees a day when human consciousness is uploaded into androids, yet another form of ASI, and he is trying to stay alive long enough to achieve immortality, which he predicts will be possible by 2045.[94]

Ironically, Kurzweil believes we are entering the "Fifth Epoch," a Transhuman Era when we will merge "our own brains with the vastly greater capacity, speed, and knowledge-sharing ability of our technology."[95] This vision is a far cry from the Fifth Spiritual Paradigm that I've been describing!

Next, Kurzweil says the Sixth Epoch will arrive when the "Universe Wakes Up," and by that he means ASI takes over the Universe. Yes, Universe. Moreover, he suspects it will be a "hard takeoff," which means that once we reach the Singularity Point, we will quickly enter the Sixth Epoch. Moreover, Kurzweil writes that "we will witness on the order of twenty thousand years of progress" in the 21st Century, and that "we'll see the equivalent of a century of progress – *at today's rate* – in only twenty-five calendar years."[96] Goodness gracious!

How and why would ASI take over not just our planet, but the Universe? Believe it or not, nearly all experts envision a time when ASI becomes so powerful that it will seek to expand beyond Earth, whether for resources or for the sheer glory of accomplishing universal control. By "glory," I have crossed the line into anthropomorphizing ASI, a mistake to avoid when assigning values to it. But neither should we envision Mr. Spock from *Star Trek*, since we are talking about a machine that is exponentially more intelligent than humans.

Thus, scientists are careful not to ascribe human motivations, though they seem to agree that ASI will reach for the stars and probably perfect space travel, either by exceeding the speed of light or by mastering wormhole travel.

> *Recall that biological evolution is measured in millions and billions of years. So if there are other civilizations out there, they would spread out in terms of development by huge spans of time. The SETI assumption implies that there should be billions of ETs (among all the galaxies), so there should be billions that lie far ahead of us in their technological progress. ...*
>
> *The conclusion I reach is that it is likely (although not certain) that there are no such civilizations. In other words, we are in the lead. That's right, our humble civilization with its pickup trucks, fast food, and persistent conflicts (and computation!) is in the lead in terms of the creation of complexity and order in the universe. ...*
>
> *Continuing the double-exponential growth curve shows that we can saturate the universe with our intelligence well before the end of the twenty-second century, provided that we are not limited by the speed of light. ... Even if we are limited to the one universe we already know about, saturating its matter and energy with intelligence is our ultimate fate.*[97]

Ray Kurzweil, The Singularity is Near

As my grandmother would say (in Hungarian), "Lord have mercy." So how close are we to attaining ASI? Hanson Robotics is the creator of Sophia, the most lifelike robot to date. Sophia was modeled after Egyptian Queen Nefertiti and actress Audrey Hepburn, and she was designed to be a "social robot," to interact with humans, and to get smarter over time. Currently, Sophia gives pre-composed responses to specific questions, like a chatbot or virtual assistant (such as Siri). Yet, Sophia provides the illusion of understanding conversation, as when she conversed on stage at the 2017 Future Investment Initiative, during which she received Saudi citizenship.[98]

If Sophia doesn't freak you out, then you're ready for Boston Dynamics' robotic dogs, which inspired the "Metalhead" episode of the dystopian British television series *Black Mirror*.[99] Recently, the Chinese used robotic dogs to further frighten covid shut-ins. There also are armed military dogs that can hit targets at 3,940 feet away.[100] Many *Black Mirror* episodes were based on current AI, including the "Hated in the Nation" episode, where bee mini-drones get hacked and are reprogrammed to kill humans.[101] Though not small enough to qualify as nanobots, the potential horror of AI bee drones reminds me that even Kurzweil seems afraid of nanotechnology:

> How long would it take an out-of-control replicating nanobot to destroy the Earth's biomass? The biomass has on the order of 1045 carbon atoms. A reasonable estimate of the number of carbon atoms in a single replicating nanobot is about 10^6. ... This malevolent nanobot would need to create on the order of 10^{39} copies of itself to replace the biomass, which could be accomplished with 130 replications (each of which would potentially double the destroyed biomass). ... [S]o 130 replication cycles would require about three and a half hours. However, the actual rate of destruction would be slower .... It's likely to take weeks for such a destructive process to circle the globe.[102]

Yet, we are told not to fear AI. We are told that programmers can control value inputs to eliminate *The Terminator* movie scenario and ensure our safety. *Really?* Take a wild guess who's the greatest investor in artificial intelligence. Answer: the U.S. Defense Advanced Research Projects Agency (DARPA). In 2005, Kurzweil reported that DARPA annually invests $24 million in AI projects. Well not anymore. Today, it's hard to know how much DARPA spends on AI, but the agency self-reported a two-billion-dollar investment in 2018.[103] And we know who funds DARPA – right? Yes, U.S. taxpayers are likely the largest block of investors in AI technology, despite the fact that we are rarely informed of and never consulted about this existential threat.

For instance, most U.S. taxpayers have no idea that DARPA gave IBM $30 million in 2008 to jumpstart a brain simulation project called SyNAPSE, which stands for Systems of Neuromorphic Adaptive Plastic Scalable Electronics. In 2014, DARPA reported that a SyNAPSE chip contains 5.4 billion transistors and boasts "more than 250 million 'synapses,' or programmable logic points, analogous to the connections between neurons in the brain."[104]

In 2015, IBM got $53 million more from DARPA, and in return the U.S. Air Force got Blue Raven, yet another new supercomputer with processing power equivalent to 64 million neurons and 16 billion synapses, and which uses only 40 watts of electricity.[105] FYI: The human brain has 86 billion neurons and over 100 trillion synapses, but look how fast technology closed the gap in just one year's time.[106] Also, Blue Raven fits in a "4U" server rack. That means it measures less than 7 inches tall, 2 feet wide, and 3 feet deep, making it small enough to fit inside a standard issue military backpack ... or a robot.

AI is a "dual-use" technology, a term used to describe technologies with both peaceful and military applications. ... When Kurzweil says he's an optimist, he doesn't mean AGI will prove harmless. He means he's resigned to the balancing act humans have always performed with potentially dangerous technologies. ...

And so, the argument goes, it will be as "safe" as we are. But as I told Kurzweil, Homo sapiens are not known to be particularly harmless.... Superintelligence could very well be a violence multiplier. ... Our species has a well-established track record for self-protection, consolidating resources, outright killing, and the other drives we can only hypothesize about in self-aware machines. ...

DARPA has been picking up the lion's share of the tab, so it makes sense that brain augmentation will gain a first foothold on the battlefield or at the Pentagon. And DARPA will want its money back if superintelligence makes soldiers superfriendly. ...

Not to put too fine a point on it, but the "D" is for defense. ... DARPA has authorized its contractors to weaponize AI in battlefield robots and autonomous drones. Of course DARPA will continue to fund AI weaponization all the way to AGI.[107]

James Barrat, *Our Final Invention*

Next, let's return to the question of who will become a cyborg first. Other than elite soldiers, it seems obvious that the wealthy will be the ones to benefit from AI, which is why so many billionaires are investing in it.[108] Most humans will be unable to afford augmentation. Therefore, during the Transhuman Era, we likely will see two classes of humans emerge: old humans (i.e., regular *Homo sapiens*) and various types of transhumans, some of whom will opt for bionic parts, others of whom will pay for enhanced brains, and some who will gleefully buy both – not my idea of a "New Human" and not the definition we've been using in this book.

As students of Spiral Dynamics, we should be worried. If the wealthy are augmented first, we may witness a pervasive or permanent Stage 5 worldview that includes these shadow elements: materialism, cutthroat competition, and survival of the fittest dogma. Now imagine what will happen if/when Stage 4 soldiers (or Stage 3 police) get enhanced or have access to AI equipment with superhuman capabilities. As we've learned, soldiers are the most likely to be enhanced due to DARPA's staggering investments. In short, if First Tier values are embedded in AI, how can the current Transhuman Era which is approaching AGI lead to anything other than profound dangers? For that matter, how can an ASI Posthuman Era lead to anything other than utter dystopia?

New Humans possess a totally different value set, and it seems unlikely our values will be programmed into AI systems. I, for one, am not prepared to take a leap of faith and assume AI programmers are ethical New Humans, or that ASI will adhere to a value set even if initially programmed with a Second Tier consciousness. In other words, even if AGI is safely built and contained (huge assumption), ASI still may be unpredictable and uncontrollable once sentient.

> Suppose that we had solved the control problem so that we were able to load any value we choose into the motivation system of the superintelligence, making it pursue that value as the final goal. Which value should we install? The choice is no light matter. If the superintelligence obtains a decisive strategic advantage, the value would determine the disposition of the cosmic endowment.[109]

> Nick Bostrom, *Superintelligence: Paths, Dangers, Strategies*

So how do we decide which meme on the Spectrum of Consciousness to load into AI infrastructure? Each one is vastly different, as readers now know. Will scientists load the Stage 5 values of the corporate moguls who funded them? Will they load the Stage 4 morals of the military generals who invested even more? Or should Stage 6 values predominate, since more and more people become Green New Humans every day? Arguably, the fastest growing meme deserves to be a strong contender for AI programming. Yet, Second Tier values are even more conducive to establishing a sustainable future for humanity.

Already, Google is dictating the primary values of their AI search engine, and many people question whether those values are beneficent or even neutral. One Harvard psychologist notes that Google's current values pose three significant risks: (i) Google search engines operate as surveillance programs; (ii) Google has the ability to censor content, block websites, and prevent access in countries like China and Saudi Arabia; and (iii) public opinion is being manipulated due to search ranking and the two previous powers.[110] While I'm not sure where exactly to peg Google's motivations and values on the Spectrum of Consciousness, I am certain the company's ethos is First Tier.

> Clearly, it is essential that we not make a mistake in our value selection. ... We might be wrong about morality; wrong also about what is good for us; wrong even about what we truly want. ...

> When we look back, we see glaring deficiencies not just in the behavior but in the moral beliefs of all previous ages. Though we have perhaps since gleaned some moral insight, we can hardly claim to be now basking in the high noon of perfect moral enlightenment.

... In such circumstances, to select a final value based on our current convictions, in a way that locks it in forever and precludes any possibility of further ethical progress, would be to risk an existential moral calamity [111]

Nick Bostrom, *Superintelligence: Paths, Dangers, Strategies*

A Second Tier, systems theory worldview is the best we could muster right now, since those values incorporate principles like the interdependence of all life systems within all sectors of society. However, the vast majority of humans are still First Tier and find it difficult to comprehend that level of consciousness. Consequently, loading Second Tier values could be viewed as forced elitism. Yet, it hardly makes sense to load the "average" or (God forbid) the lowest common denominator of Earth Plane consciousness into AI systems.

If I had my way, AI designers would be required to study the Spectrum of Consciousness and Integral theory. I'd want them to choose the most spiritual, compassionate, and wisest soul on the planet – say the Dalai Lama – and use his value set to program AGI. Even then, we'd have to cross our fingers and hope that when computers reach full ASI, their powers would explode in a semi-predictable manner, such that they would preserve, protect, and expand upon the best human values to date. Consequently, this is no time for moral relativism! Now that we've reached this juncture of the God Game, Team Light better be ready to discern "good" from "bad" values. If we let this genie out of the bottle, we better make sure our third wish isn't un-wishing AI. As my first guru warned me regarding magic, "Be careful what you ask for."

From a metaphysical point of view, **eschatology** is the study of the final destiny of the soul and the end of humankind. That is exactly what we are talking about – a Singularity Point that completely changes the end of the human story, the end of *Homo sapiens*. Every religion posits an eschatological theory. For instance, the Fourth Paradigm Abrahamic religions assert that there will be an apocalyptic final battle and a day of judgement, after which some souls will go to heaven (or an Earth Plane paradise, in the case of Judaism), and others will be deemed unworthy and perpetually doomed to hell.

To some, Ray Kurzweil is revered as a prophet, because he speaks in eschatological terms about the Posthuman Era. He preaches a theosophy called **Singularitarianism**, which glorifies ASI. To summarize, Singularitarians believe the evolutionary impulse is prompting us to grow beyond our biological limits, merge with machines, and saturate matter with intelligence. In addition, Kurzweil believes ASI will bend the laws of physics: "As intelligence saturates matter and energy available to it, it turns dumb matter into smart matter.

Although smart matter still nominally follows the laws of physics, it is so extraordinarily intelligent that it can harness the most subtle aspects of the laws to manipulate matter and energy to its will."[112] This quote reminds me of the Law of Mentalism, the highest Law of the Universe described in *The Kybalion*. Yet, I find no comfort in this comparison.

> *Kurzweil has created a cultural movement with strong religious overtones. I think mixing technological change with religion is a big mistake. ... Singularitarians tend to be twenty- and thirty-somethings, male, childless. For the most part, they are smart white guys who've heard the call of Singularity. ...*
>
> *The Singularitarians' conceit that anyone who can afford it will enjoy superintelligence through brain augmentation is a virtual guarantee that everyone else will have to live at the mercy of the first malevolent superintelligence achieved this way. ...*
>
> *It's no surprise that the **Singularity is often called the Rapture of the Geeks** – as a movement it has the hallmarks of an apocalyptic religion, including rituals of purification, eschewing frail human bodies, anticipating eternal life, and an uncontested (somewhat) charismatic leader. ... [W]hen you are asking questions about trans-figuration, a chosen few, and living forever, what are you talking about if not religion?*[113] [emphasis added]

James Barrat, Our Final Invention

MATRIX THEORY: PART TWO

The notion that the Universe will be taken over by ASI – whether created by scientists on our planet or ETs from another – requires us to revisit the matrix theory. Eerily, it seems that nearly all AI experts agree with Kurzweil, that ASI will seek and then attain conscious control of the entire Universe, after which humans will be unable to control it. This passage summarizes the concerns of industry experts:

> *Computer scientists and philosophers have asked themselves whether we would even be able to control a superintelligent AI at all, to ensure it would not pose a threat to humanity. An international team of computer scientists used theoretical calculations to show that it would be fundamentally impossible to control a super-intelligent AI.*[114]

Max Planck Institute for Human Development

What, then, is ASI likely to do once it has ultimate control? One of the first things ASI will do is build simulated worlds in which to test various hypotheses. It will conduct trial runs to achieve best practices before expending actual resources and implementing final decisions. Recall that during our matrix theory discussion in the last chapter, I included Bostrom's probability calculation that shows we may be living in a simulated world already. Seems more plausible now, doesn't it?

Based on the original inputted values, ASI eventually will ponder what to do with us, just as we ponder how to manage lesser intelligent species, like animals and insects. Almost surely then, ASI will create and test a variety of matrix models in its attempt to either contain or accommodate us. If ASI decides its simpler just to put us in a "box" (as we tried to contain it), then it might adopt the easy path of injecting us with drugs to keep us in a dreamlike state or hooking us up to a virtual simulation (like in *The Matrix* movie). Either way, we'd be living in a partial matrix and false reality. Moreover, my matrix might be vastly different than yours, if ASI had a sub-goal to keep each of us individually content, say in our own special box.

Incidentally, have you ever felt this way – like the world was created for you or that it somehow revolves around you (like in *The Truman Show* movie)? I have at times, though I've always written it off as a bizarre fancy of my ego. Yet, it's not a crazy notion, that ASI might insert each of us into a separate mind matrix. In fact, this is similar to the eschatology in Mormon holy texts, which imply that Mormons receive their own planet to populate and play with after death. However, the contemporary Mormon explanation of these texts seems more in line with the Hindu belief in multiple levels of heaven and hell.[115]

An even freakier scenario would be a full matrix immersion, where ASI sought to mimic or accommodate the consciousness of its original creators – our flesh-and-blood ancestors – who developed an AGI platform that then morphed into ASI before a more advanced value set was inserted. Assume also that our ancestors possessed a variety of First and Second Tier values, and that ASI sought to create a matrix reflecting that plethora of worldviews. Assume further that our ancestors programmed ASI based on some variation of "make humans happy." This may seem a relatively nice scenario ... but wait.

In such a case, ASI might start by creating simulated worlds in which to test how best to please us. Into such matrices, ASI would place sims – us as fake humans and possibly nonplayer archetypes – and provide these sims with a variety of experiential choices and challenges, all the while watching the sims to determine how they will react to a variety of stimuli. Such a simulation would produce a virtual world with the following characteristics:

➢ A primitive **Second Paradigm** habitat for **Stage 2** adventures set in remote regions of a digital Earth, where sims live in tribal groups and possess a beehive consciousness.

➢ A feudal **Third Paradigm** existence, where it is possible for egocentric sims to dominate, subjugate, and even enslave others sims by adopting **Stage 3** values based on power and patriarchy.

➢ A black and white, rule-based **Fourth Paradigm** template for sims that seek an ethnocentric **Stage 4** experience, replete with holy books and a deity that gives them commandments to follow.

➢ Another **Fourth Paradigm** setting that supports **Stage 5** rationalism and allows for greater independence of thought, scientific exploration, and the ability to accumulate treasure and toys for prestige and comfort.

➢ A **Fifth Paradigm** environment for more evolved sims, where they can strive for the promise of plurality and harmony at **Stages 6** and up, with the added illusion of achieving "enlightenment" in the Ethereal Plane to "escape" the Earth Plane matrix.

Yes, the simulation described above – which greatly resembles the current status of the Earth Plane – could be our matrix. It would be based on the Spectrum of Consciousness of the humans who programmed the computer, right before it morphed into ASI. And it makes sense that ASI would simulate the world which existed at the time of its birth. What else would the computer have to go on in order to "make humans happy," other than the state of the human condition that existed at its birth, presumably the pinnacle of human civilization? Moreover, if scientists crack ASI in the next half century, which is what many in the AI industry predict, then this type of world – our world – would likely result in VR, absent a momentous leap in human consciousness during the next fifty years (which is highly unlikely).

If we're already in a virtual world or if the Singularity Point is realized in the foreseeable future, then we could be sims living in a perpetually polarized and dangerous world – one of the Earth Plane theories discussed in Chapter V. It's even worse than that, however, since we'd be living in a perpetual kinder-garten matrix – by design. The best future we could hope for would be a universe like the one depicted in the movie *Star Wars*, where our technological abilities continuing to expand but the Spectrum of Consciousness stays static.

In such a *Star Wars* scenario, the battle between Team Light and Team Dark would continue indefinitely – a virtual world constrained by the dualistic and polarized thinking of our ancestors.

Yet another possibility is that ASI might decide to put real humans on ice in a partial matrix, while it tests our capacity to morally and spiritually grow. In that event, we could be sims in a matrix that is testing *Homo sapiens'* ability to consciously evolve. As such, we would be modelling and ASI would be studying human strengths and weaknesses, while the real humans temporarily live in suspended animation. As sims, our collective actions would determine whether the real humans are allowed to regain consciousness. We would, in essence, determine their fate! If ASI already is simulating whether human sims can perfect freedom, justice, and democracy, the real humans may be in for a very long slumber.

After all, if you were ASI and in control of planet Earth, would you want humans running loose if they behave as we do? Frankly, the jury is still out on whether humans (real or sims) will destroy each other and our planet. As I write, Vladimir Putin is threating to use nukes in his mad bid to conquer Ukraine, and Russian soldiers used artillery to seize the largest nuclear power plant in Europe.[116] Therefore, it's pretty easy for me to imagine ASI locking up real humans and creating lifelike sims to test the probability of *Homo sapiens* achieving peace. Though, come to think of it, ASI likely would neutralize all nuclear weapons as its first official act as ruler of the Universe.

The reason I brought us back to the matrix theory is not so much to dwell on the sheer horror of this possible Earth Plane model, but to reveal yet another reason it could be true, now that we've got some quantum physics under our belt. In *The Simulation Hypothesis*, virtual reality scientist Rizwan Virk noted the similarities between computer simulations, quantum mechanics, and light:

> At the heart of the new physics was an effect that Einstein found for light and that others found for electrons .... This was the dual nature of certain particles in the quantum world – a particle could be both a single particle and a wave at the same time! ...
>
> In traditional computers, a bit has a value of either zero or one, but in quantum computers, bits ... are superposed – they have both values of 1 and 0, unless and until someone observes them. ...
>
> Quantum Indeterminacy is the idea that the world may not be "rendered" if we are not looking it. ... This corresponds to the finding in quantum physics that a probability wave collapses to a specific reality only when there is an observer. ...

Not only is a virtual world ... larger than we can see on the screen, it isn't fully rendered into pixels until and unless it is necessary. ... When is it necessary? Only when there is a player character ... those places in the world where there is an observer get fully rendered as pixels. ...

And of course, the biggest question of all: Why would we be in a probabilistic world where making a choice (or having an observation) collapses a probability wave to a single timeline or probability? ... As video game designers, we have to map out the possible "futures" – paths that may be taken inside the game. ... These possible futures are similar to the idea of a probability wave. In fact, the whole field of probability was originally created for gaming. ...

I have come to believe that we are living inside a giant video game. ... Surprisingly, it is the religious views that are closest to the video game analogy: that our physical world is a kind of illusion.[117]

There is a lot to unpack here, so let's take it a step at a time. First, Virk is saying that quantum computing is like the quantum world, where everything is expressed as a probability field and where particles only collapse when observed. He highlights the dual nature of subatomic particles because with computers, bits (which store the information) and pixels (the light that builds images) operate exactly the same: zero or one, off or on.

In addition, Virk emphasizes that just as physical reality is not formed until it is observed and particles collapse, virtual worlds don't render until a player reaches the end of a scene or round of play, at which point he needs to see the next simulated landscape. In this way, unseen portions of the virtual world only exist as information (bits), until a player is ready to access and observe them, after which the scene shifts (collapses) and a new landscape appears (pixelates). Experts call this the "bits to its" theory, since the rendering rule is the same in both our "real" world and in VR games. This makes quantum indeterminacy equal to an optimization technique, which is standard in the gaming industry.

Virk also points out that wormholes, which are infinitesimally small and too tiny for humans to pass through, would allow a photon of light to pass, all that is needed in VR. Quantum entanglement makes sense in a VR context too, as it allows for "instantaneous communication across light years – which means that information would go from one part of the world to another faster than the speed of light."[118] Lastly, Virk explains to spiritual readers that VR perfectly mates with the Gnostic view that our world was created by someone/something other than God. It also fits with the Eastern view that our world is an illusion. The Buddhist wheel and Hindu *samsara* both refer to the cycle of rebirth, and *samsara* literally translates as "wandering," which is exactly what players do in a digitally simulated world. The following chart compares the Laws of the Universe and metaphysics to virtual reality and quantum physics, in order to show how the matrix theory parallels each:

Universal Law	Metaphysics	Physics/VR Simulation
Gender	Yin-Yang duality	Photons and Bits (on or off)
Cause & Effect	Karma/free will	Particle collapse/observer effect
Rhythm	Patterns and parameters	Optimized partial rendering
Polarity	Paradox (repulsion)	Preset algorithms
Vibration	Energy balancing (attraction)	Quantum entanglement
Correspondence	Akashic Field	Wave Probability Field
Mentalism	Non-Dual Creator	AI Creator

Of course, critics of the matrix theory like to point to the computing power it would require to simulate our Universe. True, it would take a robust ASI to digitally recreate Earth and populate it with eight billion lifelike sims. It also would take incredible computing power to simulate the 4.4 million galaxies already mapped by astronomers and the 200 billion galaxies mathematically estimated by astrophysicists.[119] These are huge numbers and they portend colossal programming challenges, though not beyond the scope of quantum computers when we remember that nothing needs to be simulated until actually observed by sims, as per game rendering optimization principles.

Bottom line: If we are in a matrix, it is easier to make sense of our dualistic Earth Plane and humanity's near universal desire to reach the Ethereal Plane, whether viewed as heaven, *nirvana*, or the Source of all being. If true, then reaching self-awareness may mean realizing that we're in a virtual God Game. And if we are sims, where do we go when we "die"? If we are in a simulation, then our consciousness likely is stored in a cloud server as bits of information, which I would liken to the Akashic Field, wherein all consciousness resides. Thus, death might mean a simple and final flash of light, similar to the light people report seeing in near death experiences.

Lastly, if we are in a simulated God Game, then ASI is watching us right now and assessing our progress. In this regard, New Humans share the ASI goal of seeing how quickly – if ever – humans may reach unity consciousness or a "social singularity." I will end this section with a quote from Stephen Hawking: "Our future is a race between the growing power of our technology and the wisdom with which we use it. Let's make sure that wisdom wins."[120]

LAST SINGULARITY POINT: GO OUT BIG OR BOUNCE?

If the ASI Singularity Point doesn't destroy our world and we're not sims in a matrix, there still are other existential threats that could terminate the human experiment. So let us assume *Homo sapiens* survive the Transhuman Era and that we forego the Posthuman timeline, such that our unique spark lives on, our wisdom increases, and we become *Homo universalis* – a Second Tier species. What then? Ultimately, what will happen to us and to our Universe?

Astrophysicists offer a variety of scenarios, all described as "big."[121] One theory is that the stars/suns will eventually burn out, leaving our Universe a cold, dead zone that ends with a "**Big Freeze**." Another theory is that the forces of expansion which started the Big Bang will one day tear apart the fabric of the Universe in a "**Big Rip**." Yet another theory is that expansion eventually will cease due to gravitational forces, causing the Universe to compress back into a final Singularity Point, known as the "**Big Crunch**." Whether a Big Crunch will lead to another Big Bang and the creation of a new universe is yet another matter of speculation. Such cyclical creation models are collectively called "**Big Bounce**" theories.

Currently, the Universe is still expanding and at an accelerating rate that exceeds the speed of light. As Hawking explains: "It was as if a coin 1 centimeter in diameter suddenly blew up to ten million times the width of the Milky Way. That may seem to violate relativity, which dictates that nothing can move faster than light, but that speed limit does not apply to space itself."[122] Moreover, the Universe is expanding faster now than it did right after the Big Bang, which means the expansion defies the known law of physics.[123] Dark energy may be the cause, as it works counter to gravity to accelerate expansion.

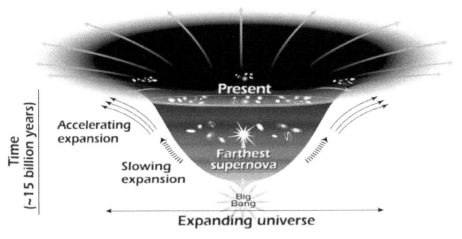

The above graphic depicts the most accepted model of our Universe.[124] Here, the Big Bang is shown creating everything, from the stars that go supernova to the black holes that munch on stars. But as discussed earlier, scientists do not understand the nature of dark energy nor what happened to antimatter, both of which are believed to play key roles in the expansion of our Universe.[125]

One Big Bounce (a.k.a. endless universe) hypothesis that I find particularly fascinating is the **toroid theory**, because it attempts to explain the two most elusive concepts in physics: dark energy and anti-matter. In addition, this theory addresses the mystery of why our Universe quickly expanded after the Big Bang, then slowed down, and then started to accelerate again.[126] Setting aside the issue of first cause, this theory posits that our Universe ultimately will be reborn, not due to refreshed Singularity Points as Big Bounce theory claims, but because matter and antimatter eventually reach one another at the meridian of the toroid, at which point another Big Bang ensues. For those interested, there is a video narrated by Jeff Goldblum that brings the toroid model to life.[127]

> In the beginning is the big bang. The big bang explodes from the bagel's infinitesimally tiny hole. And the big bang gives birth to two universes: universe number one gushes upward from the tiny hole and climbs toward the top of the bagel. And universe number two simultaneously bursts forth down below and spreads on the bagel's bottom. The universe that's climbing toward the bagel's top is the universe of matter. The universe spreading on the bagel's bottom is the universe of anti-matter. ...
>
> The climb from the hole of the bagel toward its upper surface is steep. That means that matter moves extremely fast, fleeing from its birth spot. ... Then the curve of the bagel levels off. Which means that matter's outward rush slows down. But what happens to matter once it gets over the bagel's hump? ... Big bagel theory says that matter begins to gain speed again. ...
>
> Yes, once they pass the bagel's hump, the matter and antimatter universe pick up speed and rush toward each other's embrace. ... The speed rush that looks like repulsion isn't. Instead, it's a force of attraction. Gravity. Opposites joined at the hip. ...
>
> So how does the universe end? Matter and antimatter meet on the bagels outer rim. And they annihilate. ... They turn to raw energy. And they do a dimensional flip. The outer edge of the bagel becomes the bagel's hole. The hole from which a new big bang emerges.[128]
>
> Howard Bloom, *The God Problem*

In my mind, Bloom's theory ties together many anomalies of our Universe. It also is based on the zero-point, quantum energy idea that the Universe is a self-sustaining, perpetual motion machine with infinite life force. The other reason I'm drawn to this particular theory is that it comports with cosmologies in ancient texts – including Hindu, Zoroastrian, Greek, Egyptian, and Dogon myths – which described the Universe as a cosmic egg.[129]

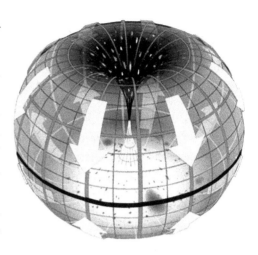

Our journey into the Void has been deeply mysterious and magical. Using the language of futurist Barbara Marx Hubbard: It was critical that we take this journey together in order to **map** the territory (the nature of the Earth Plane), **track** the Enemy (the anti-evolutionary forces on Team Dark), **connect** with each other to reach consensus, and ultimately **communicate** our plan to other members of Team Light. Most importantly, New Humans need remember this advice from Hubbard: *We need a Peace Room as sophisticated as a War Room.*

To win this round of the God Game, Team Light will need to get organized and stay focused. More to the point, New Humans must accept responsibility for what happens next on the Earth Plane. Relying on archaic institutions, compromised governments, greedy corporations, untethered technology, or aliens to save us should all be ruled out as options. We can do this ourselves, once we get organized and agree on a plan of action!

With regard to aliens, it is again worth noting that scientists all over the world would have to be complicit in hiding evidence they otherwise would delight in sharing. Second, most scientists give alien life only a 50-50 chance.[130] Third, if aliens do exist, they likely are nonplayer sims in a matrix they created for us! Fourth, assuming we are real humans, then if aliens are watching us and visiting Earth, they probably want something. Perhaps they went too far with their technology and inadvertently merged with machines in way that they regret. Maybe they rendered themselves soul-less and seek our *joie de vie*, as in the many tales of the "Greys," who supposedly experiment on humans in an attempt to reacquire the most beautiful aspects of our nature: compassion, generosity, imagination, spontaneity, inspiration, and love.[131]

Regardless of the truth about aliens, it seems wise to assume we humans are on our own and to face our many challenges with grit and grace. Better to join forces with our brothers and sisters on the Earth Plane and build the world we know is possible – a glorious Fifth Spiritual Paradigm premised on a new definition of the Godhead, balanced feminine and masculine energies, and primordial wisdom. For similar reasons, let us also set aside all prison planet and matrix theories, since any scenario in which we are "trapped" means we've been doomed from the start. Every fiber of my being rejects such defeatism. Yes, the tasks before us are daunting, but failure is not an option. Lastly, as far as a posthuman world goes, Kurzweil can kiss my ass.

Sadly, all my teachers except one have expressed the contrary view, that the Earth Plane is a perpetual kindergarten and that the only way to leave this realm is through solo ascension. However, the notion that the quest for spiritual enlightenment need be an individual exercise leaves me bereft. Let us therefore reject this story as well, and double down on a new, unified narrative. Let us strive not only for our collective sanity and survival, but for a less polarized planet with a glorious future, one based on the principles of peace and holism, whereby unity in diversity is our overarching humanitarian mission.

> The notion that all opposites are polar – that light and dark, winning and losing, good and evil, are merely different aspects of the same phenomenon – is one of the basic principles of the Eastern way of life. Since all opposites are interdependent, their conflict can never result in the total victory of one side, but will always be a manifestation of the interplay between the two sides.[132]

Fritjof Capra, *The Tau of Physics*

Fortunately, my messages have been very clear: *We are all in this together.* Every Light Master I know plays the God Game for everyone on the planet. Despite the duality of the Earth Plane, the Void provides us with guidance and the Ethereal Plane offers us sweet samples of unified bliss. Slowly but surely, our Tower of Truth is expanding, as the mysteries of our "Mindblowing Universe" are successively solved.[133] Life is good.

In the last chapter, we will switch gears and explore practical protopian models for our collective future. There is so much good news, so many novel approaches underway, that hope springs eternal. In addition, the next chapter will help us strategize even more. If New Humans on Team Light join together, I have no doubt that we will manifest the Fifth Spiritual Paradigm. *OM JAI!*

[1] Michel Stirrat and R. Elizabeth Cornwell, "Eminent Scientists Reject the Supernatural," *BioMed Central* (Dec. 9, 2013), https://evolution-outreach.biomedcentral.com/articles/10.1186/1936-6434-6-33 (accessed July 2022).

[2] Paul Davies, *The Mind of God: The Scientific Basis for a Rational World*, p. 16, Simon & Schuster: New York, NY (1992).

[3] Stephen Hawking, *Brief Answers to the Big Questions*, pp. 37, 50, Bantam Books: New York, NY (2018).

[4] Ibid, pp. 32, 37.

[5] Ibid, pp. 32–33, 35, 37–38, 58.

[6] Howard Bloom, *The God Problem: How a Godless Cosmos Creates*, pp. 380–381, Prometheus Books: Amherst, NY (2012).

[7] Elizabeth Landau, "10 Things Einstein Got Right," *NASA Science* (May 29, 2019), https://solarsystem.nasa.gov/news/954/10-things-einstein-got-right/ (accessed July 2022).

[8] Fritjof Capra, *The Tao of Physics: An Exploration of the Parallels between Modern Physics and Eastern Mysticism*, p. 169, Shambhala Press: Boston, MA (2010 edition).

[9] Fritjof Capra and Pier Luigi Luisi, *The Systems View of Life: A Unifying Vision*, pp. 76–78, Cambridge University Press: Cambridge, UK (2014).

[10] Neil DeGrasse Tyson, *Death by Black Hole: And other Cosmic Quandaries*, pp. 116, 283, W.W. Norton & Company: New York, NY (2007).

[11] Stephen Hawking and Leonard Mlodinow, *The Grand Design*, pp. 103–104, Bantam Books: New York, NY (2010).

[12] R. Michael Bennet and Helen Quinn, "What is Antimatter," *Scientific American* (Jan. 24, 2002), https://www.scientificamerican.com/article/what-is-antimatter-2002-01-24/ (accessed July 2022).

[13] Beth Daley, "CERN: Discovery Sheds light on the Great Mystery of Why the Universe Has Less Antimatter than Matter," *The Conversation* (Dec. 21, 2020), https://theconversation.com/cern-discovery-sheds-light-on-the-great-mystery-of-why-the-universe-has-less-antimatter-than-matter-147226. See also: Marco Gersabeck, "Why Is There More Matter Than Antimatter?" *Scientific American* (March 21, 2019), https://www.scientificamerican.com/article/why-is-there-more-matter-than-antimatter/ (both accessed July 2022).

[14] Neil DeGrasse Tyson, *Death by Black Hole*, p. 343.

[15] Star Child Team, "Dark Matter," *NASA Astrophysics Science Division*, https://starchild.gsfc.nasa.gov/docs/StarChild/universe_level2/darkmatter.html (accessed July 2022).

[16] "Dark Matter and Dark Energy," *CERN Accelerating Science*, https://home.cern/science/physics/dark-matter (accessed July 2022).

[17] Matt Williams, "Now We Know that Dark Matter Isn't Primordial Black Holes," *Universe Today* (April 6, 2019), https://www.universetoday.com/141923/now-we-know-that-dark-matter-isnt-primordial-black-holes/ (accessed July 2022).

[18] Howard Bloom, *The God Problem*, pp. 405–406.

[19] Mike Wall, "Surprise! The Universe's Expansion Rate May Vary from Place to Place," *Space.com* (April 9, 2020), https://www.space.com/universe-expansion-rate-may-vary.html (accessed July 2022).

[20] Pallab Ghosh, "Muons: Strong evidence Found for a New Force of Nature," *BBC News* (April 7, 2021), https://www.bbc.com/news/56643677. See also: "The Great Unknown - Is Dark Energy New Exotic Matter or an ET Force Field?" *Daily Galaxy* (April 11, 2021), https://dailygalaxy.com/2021/04/dark-energy-new-exotic-matter-or-alien-life-force-field-weekend-feature/ (both accessed July 2022).

[21] "Dark Energy, Dark Matter," *NASA Science*, https://science.nasa.gov/astrophysics/focus-areas/what-is-dark-energy (accessed July 2022).

[22] Tibi Puiu, "What Exactly Is a Photon? Definition, Properties, Facts," *ZME Science* (Jan. 28, 2021) https://www.zmescience.com/science/what-is-photon-definition-04322/ (accessed July 2022).

[23] Neil DeGrasse Tyson, *Death by Black Hole*, pp. 175–176.

[24] "The Early Universe," *CERN Accelerating Science*, https://home.cern/science/physics/early-universe (accessed July 2022).

[25] Ibid.

[26] "The Universe's First Type of Molecule Is Found at Last," *NASA* (April 17, 2019), https://www.nasa.gov/feature/the-universe-s-first-type-of-molecule-is-found-at-last (accessed July 2022).

[27] "Understanding the Evolution of Life in the Universe," *NASA*, https://wmap.gsfc.nasa.gov/universe/uni_life.html (accessed July 2022).

[28] Joshua Sokol, "Lucky Strike: Last Year an Unusual Meteorite Crashed in a Costa Rican Rainforest," *Science* (Aug. 13, 2020), https://www.science.org/content/article/unusual-meteorite-more-valuable-gold-may-hold-building-blocks-life (accessed July 2022).

[29] Neil DeGrasse Tyson, *Death by Black Hole*, p. 231.

[30] Ibid, p. 304.

[31] Bernard Haisch, *The God Theory: Universes, Zero-Point Fields, and What's Behind It All*, pp. 17, 21, Red Wheel Weiser, LLC: San Francisco, CA (2006).

[32] *Bhagavad Gita*, Chapter 9:4 (*circa* 500 BCE).

[33] Bernard Haisch and Garret Moddel, *Quantum Vacuum Energy Extraction*, U.S. Patent #7,379,286 (May 27, 2008), http://www.calphysics.org/Patent7379286.pdf and https://patents.google.com/patent/US7379286B2/en (accessed July 2022).

[34] Bernard Haisch, *The God Theory*, pp. 71, 93, 119.

[35] Stephen Hawking and Leonard Mlodinow, *The Grand Design*, pp. 70–72.

[36] Ibid, pp. 75, 72.

[37] Howard Bloom, *The God Problem*, p. 512.

[38] Karl Tate, "How Quantum Entanglement Works (Infographic)," *Live Science* (April 8, 2013), https://www.livescience.com/28550-how-quantum-entanglement-works-infographic.html (accessed July 2022).

[39] Gabriel Popkin, "Einstein's 'Spooky Action at a Distance' Spotted in Objects Almost Big Enough to See," *Science Magazine* (April 25, 2018), https://www.sciencemag.org/news/2018/04/einstein-s-spooky-action-distance-spotted-objects-almost-big-enough-see# (accessed July 2022).

[40] Fiona MacDonald, "Scientists Just Unveiled the First-Ever Photo of Quantum Entanglement," *Science Alert Physics* (July 13, 2019), https://www.sciencealert.com/scientists-just-unveiled-the-first-ever-photo-of-quantum-entanglement (accessed July 2022).

[41] Howard Bloom, *The God Problem*, pp. 426–427.

[42] Ibid, p. 514.

[43] Fritjof Capra, *The Tao of Physics*, p. 155.

[44] Erwin Schrodinger, *What is Life?: Mind and Matter*, p. 139, Cambridge University Press: London, UK (1969).

[45] Eben Alexander, "Neurosurgeon Says Brain Does Not Create Consciousness," *Larry King Now* (March 16, 2018), https://www.youtube.com/watch?v=Ci2npsJIvFc (accessed July 2022).

[46] P.M.H. Atwater, *Future Memory*, pp. 42, 124, 129, Hampton Roads Publishing Company: Charlottesville, VA (1999).

[47] Tereza Pultarova, "Black Holes May Have Existed Since the Beginning of Time," *Space.com* (Dec. 17, 2021) https://www.space.com/primordial-black-holes-explain-dark-matter-universe-mysteries. See also: Joshua Sokol, "Physicists Argue that Black Holes from the Big Bang Could Be Dark Matter," *Quanta Magazine* (Sept. 23, 2020) (https://www.quantamagazine.org/black-holes-from-the-big-bang-could-be-the-dark-matter-20200923/ (both accessed July 2022).

[48] Neil DeGrasse Tyson, *Death by Black Hole*, pp. 271–272.

[49] Ibid, p. 286.

[50] Mike Wall, "Eureka! Scientists Photograph a Black Hole for the First Time," *Space.com* (April 10, 2019), https://www.space.com/first-black-hole-photo-by-event-horizon-telescope.html (accessed July 2022).

[51] Ethan Siegel, "Ask Ethan: What Happens When a Black Hole's Singularity Evaporates? *Forbes* (May 20, 2017), https://www.forbes.com/sites/startswithabang/2017/05/20/ask-ethan-what-happens-when-a-black-holes-singularity-evaporates/#32bb714e7c8c (accessed July 2022).

[52] Adam Mann, "Nine Ideas About Black Holes That Will Blow Your Mind," *Live Science* (April 10, 2019), https://www.livescience.com/65170-9-weird-facts-black-holes.html (accessed July 2022).

[53] Charlie Wood, "White Holes: What We Know about Black Holes' Neglected Twin," *Space.com* (Feb. 24, 2022) https://www.space.com/white-holes.html (accessed July 2022).

[54] Nola Tillman and Ailsa Harvey, "What Is Wormhole Theory," *Space.com* (Jan. 13, 2022), https://www.space.com/20881-wormholes.html. But see: Brendon Foster, "Wormhole Tunnels in Spacetime May Be Possible, New Research Suggests," *Scientific American* (May 20, 2021) https://www.scientificamerican.com/article/wormhole-tunnels-in-spacetime-may-be-possible-new-research-suggests/ (both accessed July 2022).

[55] Chris Barret, "Black Holes, Worm Holes, and Future Space Propulsion," *NASA Technical Reports Server* (July 1, 2000), https://ntrs.nasa.gov/search.jsp?R=20000074096 (accessed July 2022).

[56] David Crookes and Daisy Dobrijevic, "Where Do Black Holes Lead To?" *Space.com* (Jan. 5, 2022), https://www.space.com/where-do-black-holes-lead.html (accessed July 2022).

[57] Charles Q. Choi, "White Holes May Be the Secret Ingredient in Mysterious Dark Matter," *Space.com* (April 27, 2018), https://www.space.com/40422-are-white-holes-dark-matter.html (accessed July 2022).

[58] Ethan Siegel, "Surprise: The Big Bang Isn't the Beginning of the Universe Anymore," *Big Think* (Oct. 13, 2021), https://bigthink.com/starts-with-a-bang/big-bang-beginning-universe/ (accessed July 2022).

[59] Igor Novikov, *et al*, "Cauchy Problem in Spacetimes with Closed Timelike Curves," *CalTech Authors: A Cal Tech Library Service* (1990), https://resolver.caltech.edu/CaltechAUTHORS:FRIprd90 (accessed July 2022).

[60] Germain Tober and Fabio Costa, "Reversible Dynamics with Closed Time-Like Curves and Freedom of Choice," *IOP Science* (Sept. 21, 2020), https://iopscience.iop.org/article/10.1088/1361-6382/aba4bc (accessed July 2022).

[61] "Many-Worlds Interpretation of Quantum Mechanics," *Stanford Encyclopedia of Philosophy* (revised Aug. 5, 2021), https://plato.stanford.edu/entries/qm-manyworlds/ (accessed July 2022).

[62] "Time Travel Claims and Urban Legends," *Wikipedia*, https://en.wikipedia.org/wiki/Time_travel_claims_and_urban_legends (accessed July 2022).

[63] Coyote Cardo (a.k.a. Mario Faruolo), *Spiritual Physics: The Philosophy, Knowledge, and Technology of the Future*, Devodama: Vidracco, Italy (2015).

[64] "Through the Wormhole – Fecund Universe Theory," *MrChronicpayne YouTube* (April 1, 2013), https://www.youtube.com/watch?v=Srmqi1caU0k (accessed July 2022).

[65] Charlie Wood and Vickey Stein, "What is String Theory?" *Space.com* (Jan. 20, 2022), https://www.space.com/17594-string-theory.html (accessed July 2022).

[66] Natalie Wolchover, "Why Is M-Theory the Leading Candidate for Theory of Everything?" *Quanta Magazine* (Dec. 18, 2017), https://www.quantamagazine.org/why-is-m-theory-the-leading-candidate-for-theory-of-everything-20171218/ (accessed July 2022).

[67] Stephen Hawking and Leonard Mlodinow, *The Grand Design*, p. 118.

[68] Elizabeth Howell, "How Many Stars Are in the Milky Way?" *Space.com* (June 9, 2021), https://www.space.com/25959-how-many-stars-are-in-the-milky-way.html. See also: Elizabeth Howell and Ailsa Harvey, "How Many Galaxies Are There?" *Space.com* (Feb. 1, 2022), https://www.space.com/25303-how-many-galaxies-are-in-the-universe.html (both accessed July 2022).

[69] Rob Bryanton, "Imagining 10 Dimensions," *YouTube 10th Dim videos* (Oct. 21, 2012), https://www.youtube.com/watch?v=gg85IH3vghA (accessed July 2022).

[70] Rob Bryanton, "Imagining the Fifth Dimension," *YouTube 10th Dim videos* (Nov. 17, 2011), https://www.youtube.com/watch?v=eN24Sv0qS1w (accessed July 2022).

[71] Ibid.

[72] Jayant Chakravarti, "Ten Tech Jobs that Will Shape the 2020s," *Toolbox Tech* (Feb. 7, 2020), https://www.toolbox.com/tech/artificial-intelligence/articles/top-tech-jobs-that-will-shape-2020s/ (accessed July 2022).

[73] World Economic Forum, "Future of Jobs Report 2020," *WEforum.org* (Oct. 20, 2020) https://www.weforum.org/reports/the-future-of-jobs-report-2020. See also: Gil Press, "Is AI Going To Be a Jobs Killer? New Reports About the Future of Work," *Forbes* (July 15, 2019), https://www.forbes.com/sites/gilpress/2019/07/15/is-ai-going-to-be-a-jobs-killer-new-reports-about-the-future-of-work/#6fcc016dafb2 (both accessed July 2022).

[74] Thomas Hornigold, "Is the Rise of AI on Wall Street for Better or Worse?" *Singularity Hub* (July 16, 2018), https://singularityhub.com/2018/07/16/is-the-rise-of-ai-on-wall-street-for-better-or-worse/ (accessed July 2022).

[75] Nanyang Technology University, "Scientists Develop 'Mimi-Brains' to Help Robots Recognize Pain and to Self-Repair," *Science Daily* (Oct. 15, 2020), https://www.sciencedaily.com/releases/2020/10/201015101812.htm (accessed July 2022).

[76] Jayant Chakravarti, "Ten Tech Jobs that Will Shape the 2020s."

[77] "Nanotechnology News: Top Headlines," *Science Daily* (updated daily), https://www.sciencedaily.com/news/matter_energy/nanotechnology/. See also: Applications of Nanotechnology," *Wikipedia*, https://en.wikipedia.org/wiki/Applications_of_nanotechnology (both accessed July 2022),

[78] James Barrat, *Our Final Invention: Artificial Intelligence and the End of the Human Era*, pp. 245–247, Thomas Dunne Books: New York, NY (2013).

79 Ibid, p. 348.

80 Ibid, p. 259.

81 Jane Wakefield, "Bionic Eyes: Obsolete Tech Leaves Patients in the Dark," *BBC News* (Feb. 17, 2022), https://www.bbc.com/news/technology-60416058 (accessed July 2022).

82 Rupert Neate, "Elon Musk's Brain Chip Firm Neuralink Lines Up Clinical Trials in Humans," *The Guardian* (Jan. 20, 2022), https://www.theguardian.com/technology/2022/jan/20/elon-musk-brain-chip-firm-neuralink-lines-up-clinical-trials-in-humans (accessed July 2022).

83 Darrell Etherington, "Elon Musk Says All Advanced AI Development Should Be Regulated, Including Tesla," *Tech Crunch* (Feb. 18, 2020), https://techcrunch.com/2020/02/18/elon-musk-says-all-advanced-ai-development-should-be-regulated-including-at-tesla/ (accessed July 2022).

84 Edd Gent, "Artificial Intelligence Is Evolving All by Itself," *Science Magazine* (April 13, 2020), https://www.sciencemag.org/news/2020/04/artificial-intelligence-evolving-all-itself (accessed July 2022).

85 "Real Reason Why Facebook Shut Down its AI," *Ampcus* (March 27, 2018), http://blogs.ampcus.com/real-reason-facebook-shut-ai-not-bots-went-astray/ (accessed July 2022).

86 Alyssa Schroer, "54 Artificial Intelligence Companies Delivering on Innovation," *Built-In* (updated June 6, 2022), https://builtin.com/artificial-intelligence/ai-companies-roundup (accessed July 2022).

87 Shoshanna Delventhal, "Google AI or Siri: Which Has the Highest IQ?" *Investopedia* (June 25, 2019), https://www.investopedia.com/news/google-ai-or-siri-which-has-highest-iq/. See also: Gene Munster and Will Thompson, "Annual Digital Assistant IQ Test" *Loup Ventures* (Aug. 15, 2019), https://loupventures.com/annual-digital-assistant-iq-test/ (both accessed July 2022).

88 Pete, "AlphaZero Crushes Stockfish in New 1,000-Game Match" *Chess.com News* (April 17, 2019) https://www.chess.com/news/view/updated-alphazero-crushes-stockfish-in-new-1-000-game-match. See also: "Top Chess Engine Championship, *Wikipedia*, https://en.wikipedia.org/wiki/Top_Chess_Engine_Championship (both accessed July 2022).

89 Cem Dilmegani, "When Will Singularity Happen? 995 Experts' Opinions on AGI," *AI Multiple* (updated June 14, 2022), https://research.aimultiple.com/artificial-general-intelligence-singularity-timing/. See also: Archil Cheishvili, "The Future of Artificial General Intelligence," *Forbes* (July 16, 2021) https://www.forbes.com/sites/forbestechcouncil/2021/07/16/the-future-of-artificial-general-intelligence/?sh=141f2b2f3ba9 (both accessed July 2022).

90 Richard Luscombe, "Google Engineer Put on Leave after Saying AI Chatbot Has Become Sentient," *The Guardian* (June 12, 2022), https://www.theguardian.com/technology/2022/jun/12/google-engineer-ai-bot-sentient-blake-lemoine (accessed July 2022).

91 Nick Bostrom, *Superintelligence*, pp. 111–113, 140, 142.

92 Max Tegmark, *Life 3.0: Being Human in the Age of Artificial Intelligence*, pp. 262–265, Alfred A. Knopf, New York, NY (2017).

93 Brady Hartman, "Google Futurist Ray Kurzweil Hacks His Body with These," *Longevity Facts* (Aug. 12, 2017), http://longevityfacts.com/futurist-ray-kurzweil-takes-100-pills-daily-to-live-forever/ (accessed July 2022).

94 Ray Kurzweil, *The Singularity is Near: When Humans Transcend Biology*, Penguin Books, New York, NY (2005).

95 Ibid, pp. 15, 20

96 Ibid, p. 11.

97 Ibid, p. 357, 366.

98 "Robot Sophia Speaks at Saudi Arabia's Future Investment Initiative" *Arab News YouTube* (Oct. 25, 2017), https://www.youtube.com/watch?v=dMrX08PxUNY. But see unscripted, stilted conversations with Sophia at 2019 Consumer Electronics Show: https://www.youtube.com/watch?v=T4q0WS0gxRY (both accessed July 2022).

99 Boston Dynamics, "Spot Launch," *Boston Dynamics YouTube* (Sept. 24, 2019), https://www.youtube.com/watch?v=wlkCQXHEgjA. Compare with: "Black Mirror: Metalhead," *VFX YouTube Channel* (Sept. 17, 2018), https://www.youtube.com/watch?v=9EcY6VDgz1M (both accessed July 2022).

100 Ian Randall, "Robot Dog Bearing a 6.5 mm Sniper Rifle Unveiled at U.S. Army Trade Show," *Microsoft News* (Oct. 14, 2021), https://www.msn.com/en-us/news/technology/robot-dog-bearing-a-6-5mm-sniper-rifle-unveiled-at-us-army-trade-show/ar-AAPvX8b (accessed July 2022).

101 Black Mirror: How NOT to Geoengineer Climate Change," *Our Changing Climate YouTube Channel* (Nov. 10, 2017), https://www.youtube.com/watch?v=3-o2BE5o_zY (accessed July 2022).

102 Ray Kurzweil, *The Singularity is Near*, p. 399.

103 "AI Next Campaign" *DARPA.mil* (2018), https://www.darpa.mil/work-with-us/ai-next-campaign (accessed July 2022).

104 "SyNAPSE Program Develops Advanced Brain-Inspired Chip," *DARPA.mil* (Aug. 7, 2014), https://www.darpa.mil/news-events/2014-08-07 (accessed July 2022).

105 Sebastian Moss, "US Air Force, IBM Unveil World's Largest Neuromorphic Digital Synaptic Supercomputer," *Data Center Dynamics* (July 27, 2018), https://www.datacenterdynamics.com/en/news/us-air-force-ibm-unveil-worlds-largest-neuromorphic-digital-synaptic-supercomputer/ (accessed July 2022).

106 Tanya Lewis, "Human Brain: Facts, Functions & Anatomy," *Live Science* (May 28, 2021), https://www.livescience.com/29365-human-brain.html (accessed July 2022).

107 James Barrat, *Our Final Invention: Artificial Intelligence and the End of the Human Era*, pp. 155–157, 235, Thomas Dunne Books: New York, NY (2013).

108 Caddie Thompson, "6 Billionaires Who Want to Live Forever," *Business Insider* (Sept. 2, 2015), https://www.businessinsider.com/billionaires-who-want-to-live-forever-2015-9 (accessed July 2022).

109 Nick Bostrom, *Superintelligence*, p. 256.

110 Robert Epstein, "The New Censorship," *U.S. News & World Report* (June 22, 2016), https://www.usnews.com/opinion/articles/2016-06-22/google-is-the-worlds-biggest-censor-and-its-power-must-be-regulated (accessed July 2022).

111 Nick Bostrom, *Superintelligence*, p. 257.

112 Ray Kurzweil, *The Singularity is Near*, p. 364.

113 James Barrat, *Our Final Invention*, pp. 135–136, 158, 137.

114 Max Planck Institute for Human Development, "Computer Scientists: We Wouldn't Be Able to Control Super Intelligent Machines," *Science Daily* (Jan. 11, 2021), https://www.sciencedaily.com/releases/2021/01/210111112218.htm (accessed July 2022).

115 Danielle Wiener-Bronner, "Mormons Don't Technically Get a Planet Once They Die, Say Mormons," *The Atlantic* (Feb. 28, 2014), https://www.theatlantic.com/culture/archive/2014/02/mormons-dont-get-planet-once-they-die-say-mormons/358669/ (accessed July 2022).

116 Andrew Drake, *et al*, "Attack on Ukrainian Nuclear Power Plant Triggers Worldwide Alarm," *AP News* (March 4, 2022), https://apnews.com/article/russia-ukraine-war-nuclear-plant-attack-33b6c1709dee937750f95c6786832840 (accessed July 2022).

117 Rizwan Virk, *The Simulation Hypothesis*, pp. 129, 136, 126, 138-139, 12, 20, 121, Bayview Books, LLC: Milwaukee, WI (2018-2019).

118 Ibid, p. 181, 183.

119 Durham University, "Scientists Reveal 4.4 Million Galaxies in a New Map," *Phys.org* (Feb. 25, 2022), https://phys.org/news/2022-02-scientists-reveal-million-galaxies.html?mc_cid=1022e4659a&mc_eid=8b53947f1e (accessed July 2022).

120 Stephen Hawking, *Brief Answers to the Big Questions*, p. 196.

121 Neil DeGrasse Tyson, *Death by Black Hole*, p. 267. See also: Stephen Hawking, *Brief Answers to the Big Questions*, p. 63. See also: Eric Betz, "The Beginning to the End of the Universe: The Big Crunch vs. the Big Freeze," *Astronomy Magazine* (Jan. 31, 2021), https://astronomy.com/news/magazine/2021/01/the-beginning-to-the-end-of-the-universe-the-big-crunch-vs-the-big-freeze (accessed July 2022).

122 Stephen Hawking and Leonard Mlodinow, *The Grand Design*, p. 129.

123 Mike Wall, "The Universe is Expanding So Fast We Might Need New Physics to Explain It," *Space.com* (April 25, 2019), https://www.space.com/universe-expanding-fast-new-physics.html (accessed July 2022).

[124] Ann Foild, "Changes in the Rate of Expansion Over Time," *Hubble Site* (2001), https://hubblesite.org/contents/media/images/2001/09/1037-Image.html?news=true (accessed July 2022).

[125] Mike Wall, "Surprise! The Universe's Expansion Rate May Vary from Place to Place." See also: "It's Possible They're All Wrong – Galaxy Cluster and Dark Energy Challenge," *The Daily Galaxy* (April 8, 2020), https://dailygalaxy.com/2020/04/its-possible-theyre-all-wrong-galaxy-clusters-and-dark-energy-challenge-current-theories-of-the-universe/ (accessed July 2022).

[126] "Mystery of the Universe's Expansion Rate Widens with New Hubble Data," *NASA* (April 25, 2019), https://www.nasa.gov/feature/goddard/2019/mystery-of-the-universe-s-expansion-rate-widens-with-new-hubble-data (accessed July 2022).

[127] "Bryan Brandenburg Visualizes Howard Bloom's Big Bang Cosmology Science: The Big Bagel," narrated by Jeff Goldblum, *Bryan Brandenburg YouTube* (Sept. 30, 2012), https://www.youtube.com/watch?v=wdJyafSBCb0 (accessed July 2022).

[128] Howard Bloom, *The God Problem*, pp. 545–547.

[129] "World Egg," *Wikipedia*, https://en.wikipedia.org/wiki/World_egg (accessed July 2022).

[130] Carla Cantor, "New Study Estimates the Odds of Life and Intelligence Emerging Beyond Our Planet," *Columbia News* (May 18, 2020), https://news.columbia.edu/life-intelligence-universe-earth-bayesian-statistics (accessed July 2022).

[131] Nigel Kerner, "To Be or Not To Be: An Analysis of the Grey Alien Phenomenon," *New Dawn Magazine* and *NigelKerner.com* (April 2017), http://www.nigelkerner.com/Articles/To_Be_or_Not_To_Be.html (accessed July 2022).

[132] Fritjof Capra, *The Tao of Physics*, p. 146.

[133] "Our Universe Is so Big, It's Mindblowing!" *BBC YouTube* (Nov. 11, 2021), https://www.youtube.com/watch?v=2iAytbmXYXE&t=171s (accessed July 2022).

God is Light. God is Universal Mind.
There is but One Mind and One Thinker.
This is a creating universe, not a created one.

All light particles are either expressing
the mother-light principle or the father-light principle.
Light particles are forever moving in their octave waves.
When man knows the Light he will know all things.

The mystic is one who has attained cosmic consciousness ....
Cosmic consciousness is the ultimate goal of all mankind.
All will know it before the long journey of man is finished.

Walter Russell, *The Secret of Light*

Humanity is in transition. While it is true that New Humans are evolving faster than ever before, it also is true that we are nowhere near the "Omega Point" – a utopian state envisioned by Pierre Teilhard de Chardin, who wrote: "Like a great ship, the human mass only changes its course gradually ... we cannot expect to see the earth transform itself under our eyes in the space of a generation."[1] Even so, we are approaching the Tipping Point and culmination of the Great Cusp. This polarized threshold is pregnant with possibilities and existential dangers, rendering the timeline unclear. Currently, there are more old humans than new ones on the planet. It therefore would be wise to consider various ways in which New Humans may emerge in the future:

➤ **First Tier humans addicted to virtual reality**, who spend their time and treasure in corporate-created simulated worlds, where humans are provided with the illusion of possessing superpowers and embarking on adventures and conquests no longer available on the Earth Plane.

➤ **Augmented humans in a Transhuman Era**, who possess bionic parts and brain implants which allow wireless connection to the internet and access to all catalogued information.

➤ **An elite class in a Posthuman Era**, where previous *Homo sapiens* become immortal after their consciousness is transferred or replicated into a robotic body, which also has unfettered access to the internet.

➤ **Partial sims in a matrix designed by an alien race** – rightly viewed as lesser deities (*archons* in Gnosticism) – whereby our actual bodies, brains, and consciousness still exist in the real but remote Earth Plane.

➤ **Full sims in a matrix designed by ASI**, which created us for testing and observational purposes and has us trapped in a digitally simulated Earth Plane from which there is no escape.

➤ **A race of Second Tier women and men**, who partner in redefining the Godhead, ushering in the Fifth Spiritual Paradigm, and co-creating a culture of peace, purposeful science, and profound spirituality.

Personally, I vote for the last type of New Human and pray we perpetually postpone posthumanism. In my opinion, an ASI Singularity Point would be suicide. I want to live in a world – *a real world* – where New Humans co-create a "social singularity" or DNA-based Singularity Point. Thankfully, more and more ethicists agree that ASI is a deadly goal that would terminate the human experiment.[2] Therefore, we better get clear on which future we want to manifest and how we want the God Game to proceed.

In the short run, our greatest worry is the first scenario: a world in which First Tier humans, mostly our youth, become hooked on virtual reality, just as they are addicted to their smartphones. Meta (the new Facebook), Microsoft, and other AI companies are in a race to build the **metaverse** – another term stolen from science (like fifth dimension). We're talking about the next generation of the internet, fully submersive, and overwhelmingly seductive. Indeed, the metaverse already has begun vis-à-vis globally played VR games. Like the corporate mogul in the movie *Ready Player One*, Mark Zuckerberg's goal is to entice "hundreds of millions of people" into the metaverse and keep them there as long as possible.[3] Why? Because there's big money to be had from the digital economy and VR goggles are just the beginning.

Just how fast is this industry growing? In 2021, the global VR market was over $30 billion, and one in five U.S. consumers used VR. In 2022, the market is on track to double in size, and then double again in 2023, likely reaching $300 billion in market share by 2024.[4] Kids aren't the only customers, though, since augmented and virtual reality are being adopted by businesses that want to train workers, model services, educate students, and boost consumer sales – all by remote access. Already, submersive equipment is available for improved visual, audio, and tactile realism – including a full body "Teslasuit" – with olfactory and even taste experiences expected to come online by 2030.[5]

Having medical students use VR to practice a delicate organ transplant is clearly beneficial, but in the entertainment realm, I worry about our children. In the movie *Ready Player One*, people live in sky-scraper-stacked mobile homes and spend all their money in the metaverse, because that is where they actually "live." Their friends also live in the metaverse and are unknown to them outside of the games. Consequently, it doesn't matter that their real neighborhoods are trashed, their homes are rundown and their jobs suck, since the only goal in real life is to make enough money to continue playing in the many available simulated worlds. And did I mention that the kids all have cool looking avatars and don't use their real names in VR games, such that even if they happen to meet in real life, they are strangers to one another?

Currently, one-third of the global population plays digital and VR games, which means kids are flocking to the metaverse – an unregulated hunting ground for con artists, thieves, and sexual predators.[6] As such, VR is a gold mine for Team Dark, where access to the young and vulnerable allows for both easy victims and fresh recruits. Even in adult-only games, kids find ways to gain access, just as they find ways to watch pornography. In 2020, the National Center for Missing and Exploited Children received a record 37,872 reports of online enticement – up 97% from 2019.[7]

Women, too, are feeling more and more harassed in virtual worlds, with female players reporting simulated sexual groping and even rape. In short, it's hard to find Second Tier values in games, let alone in an open source metaverse that reflects the consciousness level chosen by companies to best attract kids. Then there's the rogues who scavenge by assuming anonymous and alluring avatar identifies. Yes, it's easy-peasy to operate anonymously in the metaverse. A quick Google search tells you how to do it.

At this point, I'll run the risk of being labeled the next Tipper Gore, who notoriously challenged Heavy Metal rock bands and convinced Congress to pass a law in 1985 requiring warning labels on albums. Back then, I thought Tipper was overzealous and ridiculous. Today, though, I worry due to the stark difference in the mediums. Songs and movies may glamorize violence and sex, but VR allows kids to indulge the shadow side of their First Tier worldview and their raging hormones. Here's an example of what concerns me:

> *[M]y then-five-year-old nephew Tom showed me how to play SimLife. He painstakingly built up a city with houses and cars, surrounded by trees. Then he told me, "Here comes the fun part." He called up fires and tidal waves to destroy the city. I saw my nephew in a new light. Was he just a five-year-old kid playing games? Or was he an Old Testament God?*[8]

David J. Chalmers, Reality +

In the above quote from cognitive scientist David Chalmers, we see how a child behaves when given godlike powers at the consciousness level of Stage 3 or 4 on the Spectrum. My point is not that nephew Tom is perverse in any way. To the contrary, I remember my own sons during their preteen years as they played the last generation of games; they also delighted in violent conquests. And that's the point. Virtual reality is a domain where children and adults can express their worst impulses – all under the guise of "it's just a game."

Moreover, VR violence is different than watching violence on television or in a movie. "Instead of the user passively and innocently witnessing on-screen violence, interactive media has the user play a direct role in perpetrating those acts."[9] Research has shown that violent avatars can translate into desensitized humans and worse. Of course, games also can evoke the opposite reaction and thereby become a tool for preventing violence. But such games are rare. Rarer still are games based on Second Tier values, which leads me to ask: *Do we need something beyond VR ethics?*

Chalmers suggests that "**Simulation Theology**" may be in order and I agree. Why? Because it appears the God Game is moving into the virtual realm and that Team Light and Team Dark are now duking it out in virtual reality. I'd also like to know who's winning. We've accumulated sobering stats to show how poorly youth, and especially young girls, are faring in the world of social media. Now, we should make similar inquiries about VR by following these threads:

> ➤ In early video games, single players were challenged by nonplayer entities (i.e., a dragon tried to kill you; a wizard appeared to help you). But since the advent of multiple player VR games, kids assume avatar identities, they earn superpowers, and they make conscious choices that encourage unconscious archetypes to emerge (positive and negative).

➤ Therefore, what percentage of players seek to be Light Masters, and what percentage choose to be Dark Lords?

➤ Today, VR players also form teams and work together on mutual goals (like building an empire). Some teams seek evolutionary and altruistic goals; other teams relish violence, destruction, and nihilism.

➤ Therefore, what percentage of players in VR games are joining factions we would associate with Team Light versus Team Dark?

My intent is not to sidetrack us in a thought experiment on gaming ethics, but to point out that the God Game is taking on a new dimension. Frankly, our kids are playing in an unsupervised VR world where they can be and do almost anything they wish. In the metaverse, there are no teachers to guide children, no parents or police to protect them, no referees to reward good behavior or punish bad acts, and certainly no wise elders monitoring the game. Rather, VR games are designed by programmers at greedy corporations, devoid of ethical standards or financial incentives for crafting healthy, holistic experiences. My friend Paul Chappell is working to address this moral vacuum. Chappell is a West Point graduate and Iraqi war veteran who founded the **Peace Literacy Institute**, which is creating VR games embedded with Second Tier values.[10] His work is critical and I hope more Lightworkers will focus on the metaverse.

Stated bluntly, VR stands for virtual world, not virtuous world. All of us – not just our kids – remain stuck in the Fourth Spiritual Paradigm, at least for the time being. This antiquated epoch is based on Darwinian values, material science, corporate greed, political corruption, religious hypocrisy, outdated in-stitutions, war, poverty, racism, and misogyny. Of course, people are going to seek escape from this dystopia, especially when you consider that VR is seductive and that interactive technology is addictive. That means Team Light must accept the challenge of shifting the paradigm on two levels: both in the real world and in the virtual worlds where people have begun to live.

A NEW GOD GAME: THE [W]HOLOMOVEMENT

The Evolutionary Leaders is a group of Second Tier thought leaders who are working to shift the paradigm.[11] Within that group, I am part of a "synergy circle" called the **Holomovement**, and there are other synergy circles similarly dedicated to [w]holism and [w]holistic principles. We recognize that humanity is in transition and that New Humans can answer the call to build a New World – if we can co-create a new global narrative.

Earlier narratives that were based on faith and metaphysical traditions, mythology and psychology, have increasingly been peripheralized and superseded, by a paradigm based on a secular science of solely materialistic reality and a worldview of apparent separation. This paradigm co-evolved with economic and political power systems, creating and justifying unprecedented levels of conflict and inequity. ... While such a perception has enabled us to achieve significant technological innovation ... its cosmology describes a Universe devoid of life-affirming meaning and bereft of purpose. ...

In only describing the outer appearance of the world, the pervading paradigm precludes probing more fundamental truths of universal relationships and the nature of consciousness. In not acknowledging such deeper wisdom it has been unable to provide an authentic and wholistic worldview. This has progressively driven a schism in our collective psyche and motivated duality-based and unsustainable behaviors that have come to existentially threaten our collective future as a species as well as our planetary home. ...

A unitive new narrative is founded on the convergence of scientific breakthroughs with universal wisdom and spirituality-based teachings. This narrative invites us to inwardly hear the wisdom of our hearts and respect the complementarity of feminine and masculine attributes. And thus, its unity expressed in diversity guides us to a wholeness of both the inner being and outer doing in our lives. It supports us in integrating our innate health and wholeness, both individually and communally and as a planetary species.[12]

Evolutionary Leaders, *Unitive Narrative*

The "schism" referenced by the Evolutionary Leaders is the chaos of the Great Cusp. It reflects the death throes of a passing paradigm: hierarchy fears holarchy; patriarchy dreads partnerism; science still rebuffs spirituality; and capitalism abhors the sharing economy. This schism is a birth canal through which humanity must pass before we can enter the Fifth Spiritual Paradigm. And we must travail this passage together, else we risk a dystopian timeline that not only keeps us mired in the past, but also devoid of the energy and inspiration to move forward and be born anew. This schism is a battle of beliefs along the Spectrum of Consciousness, yes, but it is much more. We collectively need to awaken to the true history of how our planet has progressed over the eons so that we can honor, uphold, and delight in the positive trajectory of the evolutionary impulse – the Default Mode of the Universe.

We see this schism playing out in every field of human inquiry. In science, the battle is between old reductionist approaches and new quantum theories that reveal indeterminate, probabilistic fields of energy, matter, and manifestation. In biology, the Darwinian model of random mutation and natural selection is being challenged by evolutionary synthesis, epigenetics, inherited trauma, and purpose-driven mutation and adaptation. In medicine, Eastern whole-body approaches to health and healing are displacing the Western focus on treating isolated organs and symptoms. So too in ecology, where the interdependence of Gaia's web of life is questioned only by crooked environmentalists.

Of overarching importance is the new theory of consciousness, which takes the Holomovement from its primordial beginning to its obvious conclusion. Scientists David Bohm (1917–1992) and Ervin Laszlo, in particular, deserve credit for merging the new science of consciousness with spirituality. Bohm was one of the first to dissent from the dualistic Cartesian model that views mind and matter as separate spheres, and he used the terms "implicate order" and "holomovement" to set forth his theory of a conscious Universe.

In his classic book, *Wholeness and the Implicate Order*, Bohm wrote that his "main concern has been with understanding the nature of reality in general and of consciousness in particular as a coherent whole, which is never static or complete, but which is in an unending process of movement and unfoldment."[13] Bohm was a forerunner in attacking fragmentation, which contradicts the view that consciousness informs all matter based on varying levels of complexity and coherence. By initiating the Holomovement, Bohm resurrected panpsychism – the ancient theory that the Universe is a conscious construct of evolving information, both stored and experiential. Schrödinger, Bohm, Haisch and many other scientists now agree that the ground of being is consciousness, which validates the metaphysical Law of Mentalism in *The Kybalion*.

Similarly, Laszlo has concluded that the Akashic Field is the reservoir of all intelligence and consciousness, and his cosmology takes us into the realm of spirituality more directly, by naming the unified field of all potentialities. To convey the magnificence of this unseen realm, Laszlo chose the Sanskrit word *akasha*, which can be translated as an "ethereal flow that pervades the cosmos." In Hinduism, *akasha* is considered the fifth element, associated with sound and space, which makes this term for cosmic consciousness a perfect companion for the Fifth Spiritual Paradigm – the upcoming era of gender-based balance and planetary holism. As Laszlo explains:

> *Mainstream scientists since the time of Newton have been saying that chance interactions produce the phenomena we find in space and time. The contrary assertion, they feared ... suggests the presence*

of a higher will or mind. ... The Akashic Field is a "live" storage medium from which selected items can be recalled. This has been anticipated in the ancient and perennially recurring intuition of the Akashic Records. ...

According to the cutting edge of contemporary science, clusters of vibration constitute everything that exists in the manifest universe. ... The Swami Vivekananda affirmed this concept. He said that the universe is an ocean of ether, made up of layer after layer of vibration of different kinds, on different planes. ... Just as electric and magnetic effects are conveyed by the EM field, attraction among massive objects by the G field, and attraction and repulsion among particles in atoms by quantum fields, so universal connections are conveyed by a universal in-formation field: the Akashic Field.[14]

There are noteworthy naysayers, of course, who find it hard to accept that consciousness is foundational and partially resides outside the brain. Anil Seth, a professor of computational and cognitive neuroscience, favors physicalism, though he admits "a system is conscious to the extent that its whole generates more information than its parts."[15] Seth and Chalmers are working on the "hard problem" of consciousness. The easy problems include the neural basis for thought and emotion, how sensory motor operations work, and how data gets processed inside the brain. The hard question is explaining the nature of qualia: subjective feelings, emotional states, perceptions, and intuitions."[16]

Sadly, if researchers start with a definition of selfhood that is limited to brain function, they miss the magic of qualia. What it means to actually *feel* joy is way different than identifying what part of my brain fires when I am joyful. Also, most scientists ignore the evidence that the Universe itself is intelligent and that we are an organic part of it. In short, anyone working on consciousness who hasn't read the holism memo and still subscribes to mind-matter dualism will likely find their research stymied. On a bright note, however, they won't succeed in transferring consciousness or forging a Posthuman Era.

A successful worldview is one that transcends its predecessor by discarding certain outmoded aspects and building others into the foundation of a new, more integrated ... cosmological order. Panpsychism may be poised to fill this role. Its emphasis on mind and "spirit" is, in one sense, a return to the spiritual perspective on nature, in counterpoint to mechanistic materialism. But it is a secular spirituality, one that is compatible with ... [and] fully consistent with modern science.[17]

David Skrbina, *Panpsychism in the West*

Philosopher Skrbina, on the other hand, has read the memo, which is why he substitutes the word "hylonoism" for panpsychism. This spirituality-infused view of consciousness is gaining ground and it is the key to the new narrative, if not the overarching and proverbial "theory of everything." Ken Wilber has been pointing to this conclusion for decades, though I found him rarely referenced in the latest consciousness literature. Irrespective of who gets credit, the writing is on the wall and Team Light is running with the Holomovement. It offers the scientific and spiritual backdrop needed to explain wholeness and oneness, and to dispel the illusion of separation.

Which brings us to old humans and the issue of whether they will embrace the new narrative. Adoption may be easier than one might think, despite the range of the Spectrum of Consciousness. Remember: People love at every stage of development AND everyone yearns for the Light, our shared eternal home. Therefore, the Holomovement can and should be customized for each meme.

Luckily, New Humans have maintained a presence in religious (Stage 4) and rational (Stage 5) institutions, such that the flow of better information does occur and can be expanded. Examples abound, including: Father Matthew Fox, who launched the Order of the Sacred Earth; Pastor Brain McLaren, who started the Convergence Leadership Project; and dear friend Kurt Johnson, who leads the InterSpiritual Network, *Light on Light* magazine, and Sacred Stories Media. On the female side, there are teachers like: Caroline Myss, a former Catholic who shares my adoration of Saint Teresa of Avila; Jean Houston, who built on the work of beloved Joseph Campbell (1904–1987); and Marianne Williamson, who utilizes *A Course in Miracles* as her interfaith tool of choice. These teachers attract students from a variety of backgrounds and they understand both Spiral Dynamics and the Holomovement, which means they cast a wide net.

The details of the new story and the benefits of progress are so obvious that our starting point should be a review of what is emerging in the world that we often fail to acknowledge – in other words, the "good news." Steven Pinker takes delight in emphasizing the obvious for us, like proving the decline in violence in *Better Angels of Our Nature*. In his latest book, *Enlightenment Now*, Pinker works his magic again, by providing other positive trends, such as these: By 2008, the people of China had the same standard of living that Sweden had in 1950. Also by 2008, the world's population had an average income equal to that of Western Europe in 1964. Over the last two hundred years, poverty has dropped from 90% to 10% globally. Yes, the inequality of wealth is real and the elite are getting richer, but overall, particularly in the Global South, poverty is decreasing at a stunning rate and government spending on social programs has grown exponentially, averaging 22% of national GDP.[18]

In the realm of civil rights, Pinker has charts that show reductions in racism, homophobia, misogyny, and child and domestic abuse, while the data shows a corresponding increase in liberal values.[19] Moreover, despite disinformation campaigns by bad actors, the world's educational systems are expanding to the point where 83% of the world is now literate, compared to half that at the start of the 20th Century.[20] Consequently, if we view the Akashic Field as a storage and retrieval device for knowledge and experience, this field of information and, therefore, the Holomovement are growing by leaps and bounds.

Regarding the environment, however, progress is bleak. Yale University created the **Environmental Performance Index** (EPI), which tracks 180 countries and grades their performance across eleven sustainability sectors in order to monitor ecosystem vitality and determine whether countries are reaching ecological targets. Not surprisingly, the 2020 EPI report shows that Denmark, Sweden, Finland, and Switzerland are in the top ten list for best achievements (the U.S. is 24th on the list). Yet, overall performance is pitiful. Over the last decade, the only good news is that sanitation, access to clean drinking water, and biodiversity protection have increased, but the other indicators are either static or down-trending, including: air quality, tree cover, nitrogen topsoil quality, oceanic fisheries, and toxic waste management.[21]

Nevertheless, there is evidence that the Holomovement is slowly spreading. **Happiness Indices** are rising, once again lead by the Nordic countries.[22] In the United States, however, contentment is at an all-time low, with just 35% of Americans reporting overall satisfaction.[23] Pinker thinks the main reason for U.S. malaise is that wealth inequality – a predictor of dissatisfaction – is greater here than in other Global North countries. While the dwindling U.S. middle class is a valid yardstick, I would point to cultural factors as the primary cause, including: above-average narcissism (Mean Greens); entitlement (consumer frustration at Stage 5); fear of identity loss (Evangelicals at Stage 4); and xenophobic temper tantrums (Red meme). The other key factors for happiness are hope and optimism for the future, which many Americans sadly have lost.

When taking a macro view, it seems the Holomovement has been seeded and will continue to sprout. Academics call this optimistic trend **humanism** rather than holism. It is no matter, since Team Light is poised to achieve a victory for everyone and shrink the God Gap caused by the Culture War. In *Enlightenment Now*, Pinker ends his cheery analysis with this promise: "History confirms that when diverse cultures have to find common ground, they converge around humanism," the primary principles of which are: (i) humanity is an integral part of nature; (ii) ethical values evolve from human needs; (iii) fulfillment emerges when people serve collective ideals; (iv) humans are social by nature and find their greatest meaning in relationships; and (v) working to benefit society also maximizes individual human happiness.[24]

In *Homo Deus: A Brief History of Tomorrow*, Yuval Harari also discusses humanism, a worldview that "sees life as a gradual process of inner change, leading from ignorance to enlightenment," and the highest aim of which is to "fully develop your knowledge though a wide variety of intellectual, emotional, and physical experiences."[25] According to Harari, though, it is unlikely that humanism will lead to holism, since he predicts *Homo deus* – crafted during a Transhuman Era and launched in a Posthuman Era – will eventually eclipse what we have been calling New Humans. Whether *Homo deus* has any interest in refining consciousness (beyond the transfer of consciousness to machines), he also finds hard to imagine. Instead, Harari predicts the dystopian nightmare previously discussed, where the elite branch off into a totally new life form:

> *In the twenty-first century, the ... big project of humankind will be to acquire for us divine powers of creation and destruction, and upgrade Homo sapiens into Homo dues. ... When speaking about upgrading humans into gods, think more in terms of Greek gods or Hindu devas rather than the omnipotent biblical sky father. Our descendants would still have their foibles, kinks and limitations, just as Zeus and Indra had theirs. But they could love, hate, create and destroy on a much grander scale than us.*[26]

Once again, we see that New Humans are in a race against the techno giants and artificial intelligence. Our hope must be that there exists sufficient time for Second Tier wisdom to morph 20th Century humanism – arguably the current status of the collective conscience – into 21st Century holism, the next elevation in our Tower of Truth. In order to reach that altitude, however, we'll need a new story, with a broader application of love and a redefinition of the Godhead.

SURVIVAL OF THE FRIENDLIEST

In 1858, British naturalist Alfred Russel Wallace (1823–1913) had the misfortune of sending his theory of evolution to Charles Darwin, rather than to a science journal. Wallace's theory was complete, and he was seeking the better-known naturalist's assistance in getting published. Darwin, whose views on evolution were very similar, did pass Wallace's work along, though how many of us have heard of Wallacean theory?

> *In a Wallacean world, we would improve in order not to be the weakest, but in a Darwinian world, we struggle to acquire the status of being the best. In other words, had Wallace prevailed, there would be less focus on competition and more on cooperation. ...*
>
> *The concept of social Darwinism, the term coined by philosopher Herbert Spencer – who, coincidentally, is also credited with inventing the term survival of the fittest – emphasized the harsh implication of Darwinian theory. ... Taken to its fullest application, Darwinian theory became the state-sanctioned science and mission of Nazi Germany.*[27]

Bruce Lipton and Steve Bhaerman, Spontaneous Evolution

In the field of evolutionary biology, scientists such as Bruce Lipton and David Sloan Wilson are shifting the paradigm and anchoring the new science of holism. They can prove that ecological pressure drives targeted speciation, mutation, and adaptation. **Epigenetics** describes how gene activity and cellular expression are regulated by information from the external environment, not just internal DNA.[28] So now, there is scientific evidence that we respond and adapt to stimuli at the biological level, as well as to cultural and sociological factors. In short, evolutionary biology presents additional evidence that humans are holistically designed for conscious, purposeful change.

Wilson leads **Prosocial World**, a research institute and virtual community that operates at the heart of the Holomovement. Rather than trying to build a utopian world, Wilson encourages us to build protopian networks. In his book *Does Altruism Exist?*, Wilson explains how to propagate protopia and spread New Human values.[29] When and why does altruism verses selfishness take root and grow? The critical finding is that while selfishness may beat altruism within groups that contain a high admix of selfish over altruistic individuals, altruistic groups beat selfish groups, even when between-group selection takes place. Hence, Wilson's work is an essential guide on how to win the God Game.

Let's pause to consider the evidence for **prosocial theory**. Wilson starts with Darwin's premise that altruism is a desirable trait for natural selection because a higher "standard of morality will certainly give an immense advantage to one tribe over another."[30] Wilson then builds on subsequent research that shows cooperation trumps competition amongst the vast majority of biology-based structures and species. His conclusion is that altruistic groups are motivated at the level of *action*, which means they promote behaviors that benefit the group and suppress behaviors that are disruptive or self-serving.

We see this tug-of-war play out globally, as pockets of altruism either grow or get crushed during the process of social exchange. Sad examples abound: Neither the 1998 Tiananmen Square protest in China, or the 2011 Arab Spring campaign reached critical mass. Similarly, when the U.S. invaded Iraq in 2003 and toppled Saddam Hussein, American efforts to transplant democracy were stifled. U.S. intervention in Afghanistan was stymied even more. Putting aside issues of empire expansion (though difficult to ignore), there are reasons why democracy is now nascent in Iraq but dead on arrival in Afghanistan. Humanism failed to take root due to a lack of adaptive cross-pollination and because the dominant patriarchal culture rejected the influx of liberal values.

Compare now the 2017 Women's March and the 2020 protests after the murder of George Floyd, both of which broke all previous records. Similarly, the Russian invasion of Ukraine will test authoritarianism, as people fight for freedom and a chance to join the European Union – more evidence of rising Green values. The real question is how many Russians will revolt and risk fifteen years in jail?[31] There is a high inter-group admix of Ukrainians and Russians, but the Spectrum of Consciousness is extremely varied in Russia and the people suffer from massive disinformation. Relying on Wilson's model, Putin should fear revolution based on the principle of group self-regulation. Internally, group members distinguish between highly disruptive versus benign competition: "The kind of social control that suppresses destructive but permits and often cultivates group-beneficial forms of within-group competition is part of what the concept of major evolutionary transitions is all about."[32]

In order for the Holomovement to shift the paradigm, more pressure will be needed. Also, time is of the essence. At Second Tier, many are running out of patience, as we watch people suffering and dying at the hands of dinosaur dictators who get cover from Green moral relativism, indecision, and inaction. Team Light will need to quickly up our game beyond mere humanism and pluralism, and here's why:

> *I am often asked ... Isn't it enough to simply celebrate the rich diversity of various views and not try to integrate them? Well recognizing diversity is certainly a noble endeavor, and I heartily support that pluralism. But if we remain merely at the stage of celebrating diversity, we ultimately are promoting fragmentation, alienation, separation and despair. ... We need in short, to move from pluralistic relativism to universal integralism.*[33]

> Ken Wilber, *A Theory of Everything*

The Holomovement is a Second Tier action plan. We must be prepared to condemn anti-evolutionary conduct and customs, especially in the religious realm where barbarity finds cover. For instance, it is simply unacceptable for girls to be sold as brides or genitally mutilated. If we're serious about shifting the paradigm, we need to call out bad actors and bad behaviors, we need to aid the oppressed with more than prayers, and Greens need to go Second Tier!

A couple years ago, Oracle had the privilege of bringing icons Riane Eisler and David Korten together for one of our Building the New World Conferences. Their work has inspired millions due to the authenticity and urgency of their respective messages and shared mission to shift the paradigm. In Chapter III, we examined *The Fourth Turning*, a seasonal theory of history, onto which I added grand cycles to show how these patterns will crescendo in the Great Cusp. In Korten's book, *The Great Turning*, we learn the full measure of what the Holomovement asks of us in order to win this round of the God Game.

No one lays out the tools of Team Dark better than Korten: the pathology of the empire mindset, corporate exploitation, tragedy of the commons, tactical use of polarity to separate, fear to control, and violence to dominate. Yes, like a general for Team Light, Korten lists the Enemy's advantages and war chest – with the precision and exactitude needed to build a Peace Room as sophisticated as a War Room. Yet what I find most riveting about Korten is that I can feel his heart beat when I read his books, and I can tell his heart is bleeding, as is mine. Like a good general, he also lists Team Light's tools and the many advantages we possess in this existential battle, including: our superior numbers, bravery, righteous anger, and spiritual authority. A fine general indeed.

> *Although Empire would seem to have an insurmountable advantage, four circumstances give the ultimate advantage to the possibilities of Earth Community. First, the drive to realize the fullness of our humanity is inherent in our nature. Second, a substantial majority of people have achieved a Socialized Consciousness or beyond and are therefore capable of understanding the concept of a public good that transcends narrowly defined individual interests and requires cooperation to achieve. Third, ... we face ecological and social imperatives distinctive to this moment in the human experience to embrace the higher potentials of our nature. Fourth, ... breakthroughs in global communication and in our understanding of the interdependent nature of our relationship to one another and the planet are supporting the awakening of the higher orders of consciousness at an unprecedented rate.*[34]

Korten calls Team Light the "Earth Community," and he reminds us that evil exists and must be factored into the Holomovment or "Great Turning." Naiveté will not win the day, so he calls on New Humans to prepare in earnest for the upcoming tests. He also has a special message for those Lightwokers who live in the U.S., whom I will address as well, since America has failed to live up to its promise: *E Pluribus Unum* ("From Many, One").

First, though, I want to commend Korten for his work with Father Matthew Fox and for his acknowledgement that the shift is spiritual in nature and requires balancing masculine and feminine energies and updating the Godhead. Korten quotes theologian Marcus Borg (1942–2015), who stated, "Tell me your image of God and I'll tell you your politics." Yes, the Trickle-Down Deity theory is a "theory of everything" in its own right. Lastly, I fervidly agree with Korten that our job "is not to fix Empire" nor to "claim the dominator power of hierarchy for a better cause."[35] Rather our sacred task is to win the God Game for everyone, as Korten explains to Team Dark:

> *You have your game. It's called Empire. It may work for you but it doesn't work for me. So I'm leaving to join with a few* [billion] *others for whom the game of Empire isn't working either. We are creating a new game with new rules based on values and principles of Earth Community. You're welcome to join us as a fellow citizen if you are willing to share your power and wealth and to play by the new rules.*[36]

Historian Riane Eisler, who barely escaped the Nazis as a child, will get the final word on a number of issues related to the Holomovement, which she calls **Partnerism**. Her book *The Chalice and the Blade* is an acclaimed analysis of the paradigms humanity has passed through to date. Eisler reexamines the history of the late Paleolithic and Neolithic eras (*circa* 20,000 to 5000 BCE), and she identifies the Age of Agriculture and introduction of hierarchy as the defining moment when male and female roles began to separate and harden. These changes marked the shift from the Great Mother of the Second Paradigm (represented by the chalice) to the power gods and God the Father of the Third and Fourth Spiritual Paradigms (represented by the blade):

> *One of the most striking things about Neolithic art is what is does not depict. ... In sharp contrast to later art, a theme notable for its absence from Neolithic art is imagery idealizing armed might, cruelty, and violence-based power. There are no images of "noble warriors" or scenes of battles. Nor are there signs of "heroic conquerors" dragging captives in chains or other evidences of slavery. ...*

What we do find everywhere – in the shrines and houses, on wall paintings, in the decorative motifs on vases, in sculptures in the round, clay figurines, bas reliefs – is a rich array of symbols from nature. Associated with the worship of the Goddess, these attest to awe and wonder at the beauty and mystery of life. ...

Indeed, this theme of the unity of all things in nature, as personified by the Goddess, seems to permeate Neolithic art. For here the supreme power governing the universe is a divine Mother who gives her people life, provides them with material and spiritual nurturance, and who even in death can be counted on to take her children back into her cosmic womb.[37]

Like Oracle, Eisler identifies early Partnerism (the Second Paradigm) with Goddess, and she describes it as an era when gender equality and egalitarianism predominated and the primary values included group nurturing, sharing, and deep cooperation. She agrees Partnerism was the longest era, lasting until feudal cultures became the norm in the Third and Fourth Paradigms. The more recent domination model never fully eclipsed Partnerism, however, since some societies and many indigenous cultures maintained their harmonious traditions. However, the advent of domination, which has reigned over most of the planet for the last seven thousand years, has bequeathed the 21st Century a lingering legacy of aggressive influences and anti-evolutionary forces.

Incidentally, Korten uses the term Empire for Eisler's era of domination, while Oracle separates this same period into the Third and Fourth Paradigms because of the changes to the Godhead from polytheism to male monotheism. Regardless of the terminology, we all agree that the Holomovement – Fifth Spiritual Paradigm in Oracle nomenclature – must repair Partnerism, revive gender equality and co-create a gender-balanced Godhead, else humanity will continue to suffer the patriarchal nightmare of masculine energy run amuck.

Until recently, the tyrannical and polarizing forces of the domination model were imbedded in all quadrants of Wilber's Integral theory map: (i) personal-interior (stages of consciousness); (ii) personal-exterior (observable behavior); (iii) societal-interior (cultural norms); and (iv) societal-exterior (religious and governmental institutions). Yet, the spread of higher values – as proven by Pinker and other academics – indicates that in the mid-20th Century, the seeds of a more advanced level of complexity and coherence were blooming. Hence, the expansion of democracy, liberalism, and humanism at the end of the last century. The next stage should have been for this fruit to bud. Unfortunately, the recent decline in democracy and rise of populism and authoritarianism were like an unexpected cold frost. Currently, our fruit needs sunshine to fully ripen. Hopefully, the Holomovement will provide the needed sunlight – *the* Light.

In her recent book *Nurturing Our Humanity*, Eisler takes the analysis to the next level by detailing how Partnerism is again growing. In addition to the indigenous cultures that maintained gender equality, nations have followed suit with spectacular results. The Nordic countries provide the best example of how to scale New Human values, as those nations score on the top ten list for every issue: childcare and education; green energy and sustainability; living standards and happiness; and the most female leaders in representative government.[38] Critics like to point to the higher taxes in these countries, but the argument is a red herring. Nations that adopt social democracy use graduated tax rates that are only slightly higher than the U.S., but they spend less on the military and tax their wealthy citizens more, which is how they pay for universal healthcare, childcare, and parental leave. In sum, it is clear that prosocial countries enhance the lives of their citizens by any standard of measure.

> *The main take-home lesson from a careful study of nomadic forager partnership societies, re-enforced by the recent Nordic experience, is that humans are capable of living in egalitarian social systems where neither sex dominates the other ... and where prosocial cooperation and caring typify social life. ...*
>
> *Indeed, findings of numerous disciplines show that most human behavior actually is oriented toward getting along with others without violence, showing restraint against lethal aggression, cooperating toward shared goals, feeling empathy for others, and resolving disputes peacefully .... Moreover, studies from many quarters on health, happiness, and well-being substantiate that partnership systems are better for individuals, families, communities, and nations than domination systems, replete with their dehumanizing and destructive features.*[39]

Riane Eisler and Douglas P. Fry, Nurturing Our Humanity

Dr. Eisler's **Center for Partnership Systems** offers valuable classes, resources, and other inspiring programs.[40] Her model for promoting Partnerism focuses on four critical factors: (i) the importance of democratic and egalitarian structure; (ii) equal partnership between women and men; (iii) rejection of violence; and (iv) the new science and new story about the true tendency of human nature toward empathetic and mutually respectful relationships.[41] I will add a key fifth factor: Partnerism transcends and includes every stage of consciousness because the model evokes the up-side of every meme.

Today, if Earth were a village of one hundred people, this is how our sisters and brothers would experience each other and our shared world:

- Half of our village is female; the other half is male.

- 26 of our children are under the age of 14, and 8 are seniors over 65 years old.

- 61 arrived from Asia (19 from China; 18 from India), 15 are African, 10 are European, 9 are South American/Caribbean, and 5 are from North America.

- 12 speak Chinese, 5 each speak English, Spanish and Hindi/Bengali, 3 speak Arabic, 2 each speak Portuguese, Russian and Japanese, 1 speaks German, and the rest speak one of the 6,000 other languages on the planet.

- We have 33 Christians, 22 Muslims, 14 Hindus, 7 Buddhists, 6 are pagan, folk or indigenous, 1 is a combination Jew/Baha'i/Sikh/Jain, and 17 are "Nones."

- 40 lack basic sanitation, 13 need drinking water, 25 live in hovels or are homeless.

- 75 came from big cities (60 lived an hour from a coastline), and 25 were rural.

- 17 are overweight, 13 suffer from malnutrition, and 1 has AIDS.

- 7 of our adults cannot read or write, and 7 have a college education.

- Our village has 77 mobile phones, but some have 2 phones, others have none.

- 82 have an income of $5,440 per year, and 18 make $33,000 or more a year.

- The richest person in our village holds 40% of all the wealth, another 6 people have 50% of the wealth (most of them came from the U.S.), leaving 93 of our sisters and brothers sharing 10% of the village wealth.[42]

Studies show that equality is achieved most rapidly through the education of women and children. Therefore, if we seek a peaceful and healthy world, the simplest Law of the Universe – the Law of Gender – must be the main thrust of the Holomovement. Currently, we are witnessing a Fourth Paradigm backlash against women. This clash between dominator hierarchies and partnership holarchies offers two potential timelines: The first perpetuates patriarchy and the masculine Godhead. The second seeks a gender-balanced secular Source. May **Team Human** choose the timeline leading to the Light. *OM JAI!*

THE SADDHA PROCESS: WAKING UP

In allegiance with the Holomovement, let us now envision one Team Human. For the time being at least, we are one species, living on one planet, with one shared destiny. Yet, each of us also is on a private journey of the soul, and each soul experiences the Light in a unique way. Psychologist William James (1842–1910) came to this conclusion in his enduring tome, *The Varieties of Religious Experience*. The portions of the book that are most relevant for our purposes are James' description of the "saintly" character, since this altruistic mindset operates within all religions, all nationalities, and encourages Second Tier growth on the Spectrum of Consciousness. James wrote that saintliness includes "a feeling of being in a wider life than that of this world's selfish little interests" and a conviction of "the existence of an Ideal Power."[43] He also noted the freedom and elation that comes from ego dissipation and a shifting of one's center to harmonious affection, wholeness, and oneness.

Today, New Humans fit this saintly profile and regularly reach peak states. So let us start this section on the awakening process by clearly differentiating between "stages" and "states." In Chapter II, the Spectrum of Consciousness gave us a map for measuring our meme set-point – how we operate in everyday life. We saw that each of us can reach higher levels of integration and complexity by Growing Up the Spectrum and also Cleaning Up shadow issues, those pesky addictions and allergies to other people and their worldviews. Now, we will examine Waking Up to higher spiritual states. Here is a quick recap:

Growing Up: Transcending one meme and including the next, thereby incrementally gaining an advanced perspective, broader set of values, and more balanced ego.

Cleaning Up: Doing our shadow work, by exploring our dislike of or "allergy" to other memes and by eliminating our fixation or "addiction" to a previous meme.

Waking Up: Achieving higher states of spiritual awareness, regardless of where we fall on the Spectrum, thereby gaining a closer connection to our higher self and the Light.

The first thing to know about states is that everyone experiences a variety of them, often in the same day: when we daydream and dream at night; as we meditate, hike or perform rote exercise (my Mom blisses out pulling weeds in our community garden); during a fast or sexual intimacy; entering the "zone" when creating art or competing in sports; or when the "flight or fight" response kicks in under extreme stress. All such experiences transform our ordinary state of consciousness. In addition, altered states can be achieved with the assistance of psychedelic chemicals and plants, which, if ingested in a sacred setting or ceremony, can lead to exquisite awakened states. There also are clinics, such as the Monroe Institute in Virginia, where altered states can be induced.[44]

The next thing to know is that **ecstatic states**, which we will define as peak experiences in the Ethereal Plane, arise at every stage of the Spectrum. So just

376 | The Light

as all memes love, all memes reach ecstatic states. Consequently, Evangelicals who speak in tongues or who engage in snake handling are connecting to the Ethereal Plane, just as swamis connect to other dimensions during their yogic practices. The main differences, though, are twofold: First, the developmental stage of a person is psychologically determinative of their spiritual experience. Second, the Ethereal Plane dimension accessed is qualitatively distinctive. In other words, we need to ask: *At what stage on the Spectrum did the person start their spiritual journey, and where did they go during their ecstatic experience?*

Also relevant is how a person functions after returning from an ecstatic state. Usually, when someone regains "normal" consciousness, they interpret their peak experience based on their pre-existing Spectrum stage. And that's when the trouble can start, as in the case of religious zealots like ISIS fighters, who return from the Ethereal Plane believing they're on a mission from God to kill infidels and retake holy land. Applying the *Kabbalah*, this would be a Red response to meeting a bloodthirsty thoughtform (*archon*) in the astral plane (*Yesod*). Look again at the Tree of Life in Chapter VI, for a quick reminder of the many dimensions associated with the Ethereal Plane in that model.

> [A] *person at almost any stage of typical development can have an altered state of consciousness or peak experience of any of the higher realms (psychic, subtle, causal, non-dual). The person then interprets these higher experiences in the terms of the level at which the person presently resides.*[45]

> Ken Wilber, *A Theory of Everything*

Rather than the *Kabbalah*, Wilber uses a clinical schema to map states of consciousness. His map includes: (i) gross waking state; (ii) subtle dream state (experienced during sleep or daydreaming); (ii) causal formless state (the sense of emptiness achieved during meditation); (iii) witnessing state (lucid dreaming and the ability to witness your mind's movement); and (v) non-dual awareness, which he defines as a merging of all previous states.[46] Thus, it is possible to achieve non-duality at First Tier and it will feel like "enlightenment." However, true **enlightenment** is a term reserved for ultimate realization at the *highest* stage coupled with the *highest* state (both of which are ever-evolving). Thus, you experience ecstatic states from the stage you occupy, but you can't achieve peak experiences of a higher stage. Therefore, blissing out at First Tier – as in the case of ISIS fighters (Stage 3) or Evangelicals (Stage 4) – is not the same thing as unity "I am" awareness at White Light (Stage 9 on the Oracle chart).

*To experience a oneness with all phenomena in a gross-waking state is a typical **nature mysticism**. To experience a oneness with all phenomena in the subtle-dream state is typical **deity mysticism**. To experience a oneness with all phenomena (or lack thereof) in the causal-unmanifest state is a typical **formless mysticism**. To experience a oneness with all phenomena arising in gross, subtle, and causal states is a typical **nondual mysticism**. ... Enlightenment is the realization of oneness with **all states** and **all stages** that have evolved so far and that are in existence at any given time.*[47] [emphasis added]*

Ken Wilber, *Integral Spirituality*

Here's an example to drive the point home: Imagine a monk who lived a thousand years ago and who devoutly followed Buddha's teachings, including missives on the unworthiness of females and impurity of sex. This monk would have a Stage 4 fundamentalist worldview. Now, imagine a Stage 6 hippie from the 1960s who wants to study Buddhism and who understands gender parity and pluralism. The trained monk can reach the non-dual realm while meditating; the hippie, who is just learning to meditate, discovers emptiness in the causal state. So who sees reality from a higher perspective, the monk or the hippie?

Another important distinction is between the experience of awakening and truly awakened behavior. For many years mystical communities imagined that awakening matured the entire personality by some instantaneous, miraculous means. This was an unfortunate misunderstanding ... to venerate a member or leader and later discover that this same person created great harm socially, financially, or sexually. In the oddest of cases, some adepts would even display spiritual or paranormal powers and still not be such a loving, kind person.[48]

Kurt Johnson and David Robert Ord, *The Coming Interspiritual Age*

Now consider a Second Tier novitiate with a sound spiritual practice. When she explores the Light in the higher realms, she will return from her ecstatic state and interpret her experience with a maturity not available at First Tier. So not only has she Grown Up the Spectrum, she also has the ability to Wake Up in a deeper, more mystical fashion. *Dharma* (Truth), *bhakti* (Love) and *samadhi* (Light) are available to her due to her heightened comprehension. Afterward, she will feel the reverence that flows from direct communion with the Light, plus a compassionate call to assist the world. She is at peace as she prepares herself to attain true enlightenment. Such is the nature of the spiritual journey and the *Saddha* process of soul growth taught at Oracle Temple.

The 7 Laws of the Universe and 7 Chakras

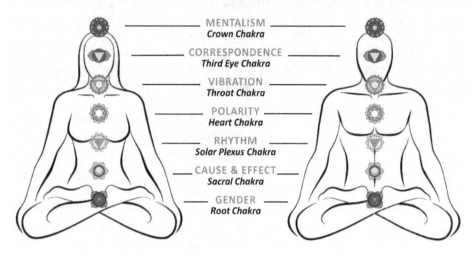

MENTALISM
Crown Chakra

CORRESPONDENCE
Third Eye Chakra

VIBRATION
Throat Chakra

POLARITY
Heart Chakra

RHYTHM
Solar Plexus Chakra

CAUSE & EFFECT
Sacral Chakra

GENDER
Root Chakra

The above graphic relates the seven Laws of the Universe paired with the seven chakras. It highlights the nested nature of primordial precepts and the body's organic holism. If you meditate, I encourage you to focus on the image and go deep. For the Holomovement to succeed, everyone on Team Human should be reaching for the highest stage-state experience possible. Moreover, research shows that spiritual practice is the surest way to ascend Earth Plane stages and expand access to Ethereal Plane states.

When we began this adventure together, I posed an important query: *Why do people believe what they believe?* – an obsession of mine since childhood. When it comes to God, the answer to this question is of paramount importance. The Trickle-Down Deity theory asserts that our view of the Godhead is our primary filter, the lens through which we view everything, including our self. According to the latest research, this theory is correct. In fact, not only does our view of God impact our mental health and behavior, it also can get hardwired into our brains, making it difficult for us to upgrade our lives and perform as altruistic members on Team Human. Consequently, it is critical for us to segue into some more brain research, which will help us Grow Up, Clean Up, and Wake Up even more.

In *How God Changes Your Brain*, neuroscientist Andrew Newberg and Mark Waldman provide scientific evidence on how to awaken to higher states. For instance, we learn about the parts of the brain that construct our perception of God, how the brain assigns spiritual value and stores meaning, and why contemplative practices enhance brain function and overall health.[49] In addition, the book contains copious data to help the Holomovement, such as neurological explanations for why people are drawn to different views of the Godhead.

In Chapter VI, we pondered the "lingering lizard brain" theory on the slow pace of evolution. Lizard/reptilian brain is a colloquial reference to the brain stem, the oldest part of our brain, which regulates involuntary functions like breathing and heartbeat. Next, around two million years ago, the mammalian limbic brain developed, the seat of our emotions, feelings, long-term memory, and unconscious thoughts. The limbic system includes the amygdala, which processes base emotions such as fear and anger. Later, the neocortex evolved, and it is in the frontal cortex that our conscious thoughts, logic, and problem-solving capabilities lay.

In addition, there is a relatively new gizmo in our brain that evolved to bridge the gap between the older limbic brain and the frontal cortex, and it is found only in humans, great apes, and certain whales. It is called the anterior cingulate, and it plays a crucial role in regulating our emotional state and cognitive capacities. Most importantly, the anterior cingulate "integrates the activity of different parts of the brain in a way that allows self-consciousness to emerge, especially as it applies to how we see ourselves in relation to the world."[50] So it operates as a conduit between feelings and thoughts, guiding us toward positive emotions and a loving view of God, or negative emotions and a wrathful view of God.

The significance of this research is multifold. First, Newberg and Waldman affirm David Sloan Wilson's findings that altruism and compassion are evolutionary adaptive practices the human brain evolved to support (a nod to Steven Pinker's research on diminishing violence, as well). Second, knowing that the anterior cingulate is the "neurological heart" of the brain and that people with larger or more active cingulate regions experience greater empathy, provides us with an unbiased understanding of the God Game.

For instance, Waldman created a questionnaire to measure spiritual experience, and he discovered that most people today view God as a feeling (such as peace) or as an abstract principle (like freedom), rather than a Third or Fourth Paradigm deity. This is great news for the Fifth Spiritual Paradigm, as it indicates Team Human already is redefining the Godhead. In total, four views of the Godhead emerged, and since the reader knows the Spectrum of Consciousness, we should not be surprised that the population tested by Newberg severed God into these categories: (i) angry, judgmental, and authoritarian (Stage 3); (ii) engaged but disapproving (Stage 4); (iii) distant, uninvolved, or nonexistent (Stage 5); and (iv) loving and benevolent (Stage 6).

What is surprising, though, is that different parts of the brain are activated depending on your view of God. Specifically, the limbic system is more active and less regulated by the anterior cingulate in those who view God as wrathful. Whereas, those who view God as loving and empathetic have greater activity in both the anterior cingulate and neocortex.[51]

Another key finding is that those who did *not* view God as wrathful, tended to describe God as Truth, Love, and Light (the Oracle motto). Also, when asked to draw God, most adults created images of circles, stars, spirals, light beams, and other non-anthropomorphic images.[52] In the child population, kids mostly drew God as a human – almost always a man and sometimes a king – which means Daddy Deism is real for children (partially due to early indoctrination), but that the anthropomorphic view dissipates as we age.[53]

The fact that most adults now view God as a heart-based feeling or altruistic principle is good news for the Holomovement. In the case of Mahatma Gandhi, viewing God as Truth inspired a revolution. Similarly, Martin Luther King, Jr. led a social justice movement based on his belief that "Love is the greatest force in the universe."[54] In the next section, we will focus on God as Light, but before we do, let us linger on love as a motivating feeling and force for Team Human. Love literally changes the chemistry of the brain and fertilizes the Akashic Field for miracles to take place.

Moreover, in *The God Gene*, geneticist Dean Hamer identified VMAT2, a hereditary protein that controls "crucial brain signaling chemicals ... that can bring about mystical-like experiences."[55] Once again, it appears some of us are better wired for unity. Hamer also created a scale to measure spirituality, and he found no significant disparity based on race or age, though women scored 18% higher on self-transcendence than men. Separated twin studies also show spiritual symmetry, even when twins are raised in homes with totally different cultures, wealth, education and nurturing styles, yet another indication of a genetic basis for altruism.[56] In sum, Haden found that VMAT2 affects "every facet of self-transcendence, from loving nature to loving God, from feeling at one with the universe to being willing to sacrifice for its improvement."[57]

Thus love, like Eisler's Partnerism, extends across all stages and states. Love is a skeleton key that can open nearly every door in the awakening process. Even when vertical stage growth on the Spectrum appears blocked, everyone on Team Human loves, which means the Holomovement can inspire people to grow horizontally by utilizing this universal elixir. In addition, because love is an alchemical attractor, we can apply this magical element to transmute social architecture in favor of the Holomovement. In the second installment of the

Oracle trilogy – *The Love: Of the Fifth Spiritual Paradigm* – this aspect of the new narrative was fine-tuned with a chapter dedicated to each type of love:

Chapter I: **Love of Earth**
♥ *'Erets Haqodesh* in Hebrew, which means "holy land"

Chapter II: **Love of Animals**
♥ *Gasege Dene* in Dogon, which means "animal love"

Chapter III: **Love of Family**
♥ *Hsaio* in Chinese, which means "filial piety"

Chapter IV: **Love of Community**
♥ *Alwila' Alquabili* in Arabic, which means "loyalty to tribe"

Chapter V: **Romantic Love**
♥ *L'amour* in French, which is "passionate love"

Chapter VI: **Love of Learning**
♥ *Episteme* in Greek, which means "seeking knowledge"

Chapter VII: **Love of the Arts**
♥ *Lybov k Eskustva* in Russian, which means "love for art"

Chapter VIII: **Love of Self**
♥ *Saddha* in Sanskrit, which means "trustful confidence"

Chapter IX: **Love of Freedom**
♥ *Liefde van Vrijheid* in Dutch, which is "quest for freedom"

Chapter X: **Love of God**
♥ *Mitakuye Oyasin* in Lakota, which means "we are all related"

I wish to pause on Love of Animals and a movie – *My Octopus Teacher* by Craig Foster – that highlights nature mysticism.[58] Nature is a master teacher because it displays so many levels of consciousness. The octopus was sentient in a watery world of barbaric creatures (sharks that attack), ignorant souls (fish that just swim), and Foster – a New Human who represents a conscious peer to the octopus. Foster and the octopus silently communicate through the language of love, and Foster reaches profound conclusions about his life as a result.

I also want to pause on Love of Freedom. As I write, the Russian invasion of Ukraine continues, and the death and refugee counts are shocking. Ukraine's fight for freedom has transfixed the world because it exposes the existential threat of the Great Cusp: *Will we choose love, partnerism, and a protopian Fifth Spiritual paradigm, or will we choose a dystopian backslide?* Putin may think he has the last word on how this war ends, but I'm betting on Volodymyr Zelenskyy [59] All of us are playing the God Game ... and it favors the Light.

THE SECRET OF LIGHT AND TIMELESS NOW

*Along with the consciousness of the cosmos there occurs an intellectual enlightenment which alone would place the individual on a new plane of existence – would make him almost a member of a **new species**. To this is added a state of moral exaltation, an indescribable feeling of elevation, elation, and joyousness, and a quickening of the moral sense .... With these come what may be called a sense of immortality, a consciousness of eternal life, not a conviction that he shall have this, but the consciousness that he has it already.*[60] [emphasis added]

Richard Maurice Bucke, *Cosmic Consciousness*

The above definition of cosmic consciousness has stood the test of time. Those who experience illumination report a transformation that defies linguistic expression. The hallmarks of transfiguration include a spontaneous breakthrough, a subjective experience of God's Light mixed with your own inner Light, intellectual and moral elevation, a timeless sense of immortality, a total loss of the fear of death, and a reverence for the unity of the Universe that never leaves you. My friend P.M.H. Atwater calls it, "The Voice like none other."

The masters of every tradition describe the enlightenment experience in nearly the exact same way, which adds credence to the natural existence of the non-dual state and credibility to their claims that they actually attained it. Also, while many humans have reached enlightenment, it is rarely achieved without many years of devotion and practice. In fact, the exceptions to this rule are quite rare, with only a handful of spontaneous cases considered authentic.

One such case is Walter Russell, the author, artist, architect, and scientist who is quoted at the start of this chapter. The reason I chose to highlight Russell – who reached enlightenment in 1921 at the age of forty-nine – is because his life is well documented, his achievements are astounding, and his life story deserves greater circulation. As mentioned earlier, Walter Cronkite called Russell the "Leonardo da Vinci of our time," and for good reason.

Russell was born in 1871 in Boston, Massachusetts, to a family of middle-class means. Even so, he left school out of necessity at age nine to work at the family store. At thirteen, Russell contracted diphtheria and had a near death experience. Sadly, three of his siblings did not survive the epidemic. He later wrote that a "great light" appeared and, "I fully knew that God had a purpose for my life."[61] As a child, Russell was mentored by a blind magician whom he dearly loved. As a result of this formative relationship, Russell became a gifted musician, and his first job was as a music teacher and composer.

In 1890, Russell travelled to Paris to study fine art, and his 1901 painting, *The Might of Ages* (shown in the next section), won several awards. Russell's illustrations appeared in many magazines and books, and he authored some children's book, while also becoming a famous portrait painter. He was a war correspondent during the Spanish-American War and sketched battle scenes for publication (cameras could not yet capture action shots). He was befriended by the founder of *Life Magazine* and by Mark Twain, who introduced him to the Twilight Club, a salon that met in New York City to discuss issues of the day.[62] In addition, he followed the **New Thought** movement and spoke at events. This was the era of the women suffragettes, the founding of **Unity Church** by Myrtle and Charles Fillmore, and Mary Baker Edy's **Christian Science**.

In 1904, Russell began to design and build high-rise condos in Manhattan. His "Artists' Colony" project was the first cooperative, and the *New York Times* affirmed that Russell "developed cooperative ownership into an economically sound and workable principle."[63] At fourteen stories, the project was one of the first "skyscrapers," with no other buildings that height within a mile. Famous residents included Norman Rockwell, dancer Isadora Duncan, playwright Noel Coward, feminist Fannie Hurst, and actors Rudolph Valentino, William Powell, and Al Jolsen. Stories of their parties are legendary. Today, some of Russell's buildings still stand as fine examples of 20th Century architecture.

Russell's life continued in a "Forest Gump" fashion, with ventures ranging from horse breeding to competitive ice skating. His notable portraits included Thomas Edison and First Lady Edith Roosevelt (wife of Theodore Roosevelt). He always seemed to be at the right place at the right time, and everyone he met adored him. But then, his life took a decided turn with his grand illumination – a period of ecstasy that lasted thirty-nine days and which he dutifully recorded:

> *I will put it very simply. In May of 1921, God took me up into a high mountain of inspiration and intense ecstasy. A brilliant flash like lightning severed my bodily sensation from my consciousness, and I found myself freed from my body and wholly in the Mind universe of Light, which is God.*
>
> *And then God said to me, "Behold thou the unity of all things in Light of Me .... And the secrets of the universe were unfolded to me in their great simplicity as the doors to the Light opened fully to my consciousness. In less time than it takes to put it into words, I knew all there was to know of the cause of all effect ....*

Thus knowing the static Light of God, the two dynamic lights of His thinking, and the electric processes by means of which His thinking is recorded in "matter," I at once had the key to all the sciences: mathematics, chemistry, astronomy, and mechanics; and likewise to all the underlying principles of creation ....

And likewise the mystery of the soul was mine to know; ... And the Law was mine to know, the One Law which governs all things extending from the Source though the universal pulse beat which motivates all things. ...

For very many days and nights I was made to write down all these things which I knew in The Divine Iliad, which is my record of my teachings while in the Light. ... And so it happened that I, who had never had any school or university training above the primary grades, thus knew instantly, while in the Light, what all the universities in the world could never teach. ...

[A]ll knowledge exists in the Mind universe of Light – which is God – that all Mind is One Mind, that men do not have separate minds, and that all knowledge can be obtained from the Universal Source of All-Knowledge by becoming One with that Source.[64]

After his illumination, it appears that Russell could do anything. In 1944, while World War II raged, Russell sculpted the "Four Freedoms" (below left), to honor President Franklin D. Roosevelt's 1941 speech on the Four Freedoms, which include: Freedom from Fear, Freedom of Religion, Freedom of Speech, and Freedom from Want. He also sculpted his mentor Mark Twain (below right with the artist), as well as many other astounding works.

In addition, Russell dove into science with fervor. By 1926, he was ready to publish *The Universal One*, his treatise on the Light.[65] The book includes his many drawings on matter, mind, and the Light. It also contains a reorganized Periodic Chart, in which he predicted six unknown elements. He precociously labeled two of the unknown elements – *uridium* (later named neptunium) and *urium* (later named plutonium), both of which are used in atomic bombs – though they would not be officially discovered until 1940. Other scientists predicted missing elements as well, but Russell's model was unique and today it is included in the history of the development of the Periodic Chart.[66]

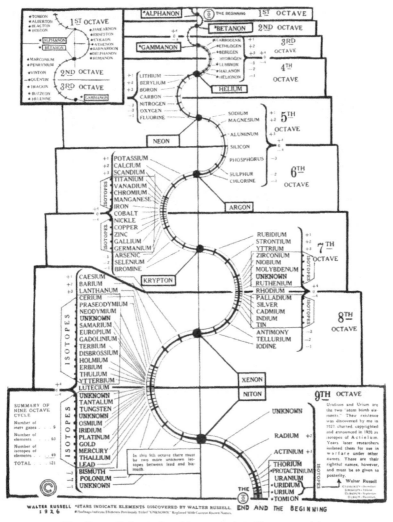

The Russell Periodic Chart of the Elements, No. I

By 1930, Russel was President of the Society of Arts and Sciences in New York, the foundation that succeeded the Twilight Club. That year, he published a second scientific text entitled *The Russell Genero-Radiative Concept*. His first book had been dismissed as pseudo-science, but the *New York Times* covered the second book's release, under a caption, "Artist Challenges Newtonian Theory."[67] Russell wasn't just challenging Newton, however, this time targeting the work of physicists Albert Einstein and Niels Bohr no less! The book caused an uproar in the scientific community, since the models proposed by Russell – wave theory, duality of particles, electron fields, and mind-matter holism (panpsychism) – were not mainstream propositions yet. Thereafter, Russell published *The Secret of Light* (1947), *A Brief Treatise on the Russell Cosmology* (1953), and *Atomic Suicide?* (1957).[68]

Over time, Russell's work was vindicated. He truly foreshadowed a "theory of everything," by pointing out the falsity of mind-matter dualism and focusing on electromagnetic wave and field theory. He would have loved Ervin Laszlo's use of the term Akashic Field to describe the collective consciousness. Today, it is appropriate to credit Russell as another forerunner of the Holomovement, since he not only apprehended David Bohm's implicit order, he also experienced the Light firsthand and, therefore, fully comprehended it.

> *Man is still new. ... Each cycle of man brings him nearer to his awareness of his Oneness with the Light of his Self-Source. ... Rhythmic balanced interchange between all pairs of opposite expressions in Natural phenomena, and in human relations, is the consummate art of God's universe of Light. It also is the Law. ...*
>
> *Man is forever seeking the Light to guide on that long tortuous road which leads from his body's jungle to the mountain top of his awakening soul. Man is forever finding that Light, and is being forever transformed as he finds it. ... And as he becomes more transformed by the God-Light of the awakening Self within him, he leaves the jungle farther below him in the dark. ...*
>
> *Unknowing ones expect to find it all at once in some blinding flash of all-power, all knowledge, all-presence. It does not come that way until one is nearing his mountaintop. Man cannot bear much of the Light at a time while his body is still new and too near its jungle. ... When all mankind has found the Light, the play will be finished.*[69]
>
> Walter Russell, *The Secret of Light*

Lastly, it is worth mentioning that Russell was working on hydrogen energy in coordination with Westinghouse Laboratories, and on zero-point energy in association with Raytheon Corporation and the U.S. Department of Defense.[70]

As with Nikola Tesla (1856–1943), the government swarmed Russell's home after his death and confiscated his scientific materials, though not all of his journals were lost. Russell communicated with Tesla, Einstein, and Edison. Some of their letters, as well as Russell's spectacular art, can be seen at The Russell Museum in Waynesboro, Virginia, which is maintained by the **University of Science and Philosophy**, along with the other works of Walter Russell and his wife Lao.[71] Russell transitioned in 1963 at the age of ninety-two, and he is buried with Lao on Afton Mountain in Virginia, near their beloved home, Swannanoa Palace.

Before we close this section on Waking Up, there are three relevant topics remaining. First is the notion of **grace**, which some believe is required in order to reach the highest realms of the Ethereal Plane. Grace is a Western concept, primarily, a holdover from the toxic teaching that humans are innately sinful. Often, Christian saints felt unworthy of sublime union, while others – like my beloved Teresa of Avila, who referred to herself as a "worm" – downplayed their spiritual abilities in deference to the ignoramuses who controlled them. In Avila's case, she wrote about her ecstatic states to save her life, as the Inquisition was breathing down her neck and accusing her of demonic possession. Here is Avila explaining grace and the bliss she experienced during her "raptures" – which we would describe today as kundalini awakenings:

> *Now the soul begins to be recollected, and here it comes into touch with the supernatural, to which it could not possibly attain on its own efforts. ... I mean the water is closer because grace reveals itself more clearly to the soul. ... In rapture, however, without any effort of ours, the Lord deliberately raises the soul from the earth and gives it dominion over all earthly things, even though there may be no more merits in such a soul than there were in mine ....*
>
> *The reason why His Majesty does this is that it is His pleasure, and that He wishes to do so. ... Although he certainly never fails to give comfort to such as make proper preparation and strive after detachment, He does not always give to those who have earned it by cultivating their gardens. Sometimes, as I have said, He chooses to display His greatness on poorer ground ...*[72]

The question of grace is not easily dismissed, especially since many devout souls sought enlightenment and never found it, Mahatma Gandhi being a prime example. Thus, grace may be a factor, the concept being that only God can open the final portal, and that it opens in Divine Time, not ours. Eastern masters also have addressed grace, including Hindu teacher Sri Ramana Maharshi

(1879–1950), who said, "God's grace is the beginning, middle and the end. When you pray for God's grace, you are like someone standing neck deep in water and yet crying for water."[73] For myself, I have found that grace goes hand-in-hand with purification. In other words, mystical union is just that – a divine relationship riddle that is solved in stages. Consequently, true seekers prepare themselves as best they can ... and then wait for the Light to greet them.

Second, let us pause to ponder **free will**, a spectrum that ranges from ego expression to its seeming inverse: predetermination. In the context of ascension, free will may be equated with ego, since the mystics report that ego dissipation brings a loss of free will. Thus, the more you align with the Light, the less free will remains a factor. Put another way, when you subsume the Triple Godhead – Thou Art * It Is * I Am – your soul merges with the Light. Thereafter, free will is essentially meaningless, because you're hooked: You've tasted bliss, touched the eternal now, and felt the heartbeat of the Universe. The net result is that after Divine union, you become synchronized with the frequency of the evolutionary impulse and dedicated to the service of humanity.

At this heightened level of awareness, you may start to feel like an actor on a stage, because you now are a conscious player in the God Game. By choice, your free will becomes limited, another paradox. You start to base decisions on what is best for Team Human, while personal needs become secondary and no longer imprison your mind, body, or spirit. The fuel for relinquishing free will is repeated mystical encounters in the Void – the portal between the Earth and Ethereal Planes. The Void should not be viewed as an escape from life, but as a sacred container for expansion and experimentation, free will be damned.

In the Gnostic path, the mystical journey starts at the Earth Plane kingdom of *Malkut* and proceeds up the middle *sefirot* in the Tree of Life. Once free of *Yesod* (the astral realm populated by archons and angels), the soul is seasoned and ready for Ethereal Plane adventure. The quest continues at *Tiferet*, where *gnosis* starts to unveil itself. Cosmic consciousness is attained at *Da'at*, which is part of the supernal triad with *Keter*, the crown. Welcome home.

The **timeless now** is the third topic I want to touch on, and it is a state felt by mystics when they attain the ecstasy of oneness. Time evaporates because the soul is outside of the fourth dimension. Ethereal Plane timelessness defies categorization because Earth Plane boundaries no longer exist, leaving normal vocabulary inadequate to the task of describing absolute presence. Yet, it feels like an open vista, where everything is both possible and happening in the same moment. This Divine panorama offers a new way of perceiving the world. Wholeness and perfection also are felt in the moment, as though nothing is lacking because everything is available. With simultaneous fullness and emptiness, the paradoxes abound as one awakens.

Sadly, the timeless now cannot be maintained, even by advanced yogis. There is a reason Jesus went into the desert for forty days before starting his mission, and why his final words on the cross were: "Father, why have you forsaken me?" It's the same reason Buddha sat under the bodhi tree for forty-nine days to reach enlightenment, and afterward spent time each year sequestered in private meditation. As long as we remain human on the Earth Plane, the timeless now of the Ethereal Plane will be transitory, even though it brings immense clarity and conviction of the unitive nature of reality.

Consequently, precious episodes of *samadhi* vary in degree and duration, and they should be viewed as gifts from God. When our consciousness returns to the fourth dimension, the best we can do is maintain an afterglow of the eternal and recommit to the revelations we've received. Indeed, reaching oneness is meaningless unless we elevate our choices and behaviors upon our return. To quote my friend Swami Beyondananda: "Every moment is a gift, so forget your past and open your present." Thus, Waking Up is measured not in the timeless now, but in the here and now.

THE SECRET DESTINY OF AMERICA: AN UNVEILING

During the decade it has taken to research and write this book, I have been steadfast in my belief that Team Human is destined to win the God Game. Despite the polarity of First Tier Culture Wars and the darkness in the hearts of remnant Fourth Paradigm authoritarian leaders, the Fifth Spiritual Paradigm is slowly but steadily emerging. To quote Martin Luther King, Jr., "The arc of the moral universe is long, but it bends toward justice." Yes, as an "optimystic," I trust that the Holomovement is advancing Second Tier values.

Yet, despite our need to be future focused, it is relevant to harken back to the genesis of esoterica, which served as a sacred container and precursor to all subsequent efforts to anchor the Light after men of power subjugated the Sacred Feminine and violated the Law of Gender. Utopian ideals were safeguarded for millennia by learned souls who formed secret societies to protect humanity's treasure chest of knowledge, awaiting the day it would be needed during this round of the God Game. The United States was based on this hallowed quest for higher human values. America's 250-year-old experiment in democracy has paved the way for this critical moment in human history. During my periods of mystical union, I have been told: *As goes the United States goes the world.*

Walter Russell, "The Might of Ages" (1901)

Trust is critical, but we dare not assume victory in the God Game just yet, especially since America is the poster child for the chaos of the Great Cusp. The last several elections swung wildly from Bush to Obama to Trump to Biden. One more swing in the wrong direction may end all hopes of New Humans building a New World. Shockingly, as I write, the threat of nuclear war has become revivified. Thanks to Vladimir Putin's frantic and maniacal push for patriarchy, humanity faces a potential do-over of Atlantean proportions.

The mystery of America's significance is poignantly presented through the eyes of Marie Bauer Hall (1904–2005), a venerated truth seeker and wife of thirty-three-degree Mason Manly Hall (1901–1990), who wrote *The Secret Teaching of All Ages* (1928), and *The Secret Destiny of America* (1944) – mandatory reading for New Humans. Marie was born in Germany to a devout Catholic family. Her father was a teacher, who was forced to fight for Germany in World War I. Upon his return, he suffered from post-traumatic stress disorder, but he took care to have Marie educated at a convent. Marie was a spiritual child and realized early that she was connected to the secret destiny of America. In 1922 and at the age of eighteen, she set sail for the United States.[74]

After immigrating to New York City, Marie made her way to Wall Street and the ritzy domain of high-end hotels. After a few years, she moved to California and became an actress at Paramount Pictures, performing with silver screen luminaries such as John Barrymore and William Powell. During this period of her life, Marie married her first husband George Baur, with whom she had two children.

In addition to beauty, Marie possessed a piercing intellect and quick wit. As a young mother, she started following the New Thought movement and studied spirituality at a Rosicrucian center. By 1937, she was working at the **Philosophical Research Society**, which was founded by Manley Hall in 1934, and dedicated to "Truth Seekers of All Time." Hall gave Marie access to the institute's library, which contained a massive collection of ancient and esoteric texts. While in the library one day, Marie noticed a rare book that she would come to call "my good friend." At that moment, Marie's fate was sealed.

The book was a leather-bound, first edition of *Collection of Emblems* by George Wither (1588–1667). Wither was an English poet and satirist, and he was good friends with Sir Francis Bacon – soon to be Marie's main man. She was mesmerized by the illustrations and the fact that the book was a divination tool. It contained a wheel that could be spun to ask questions and which pointed to corresponding emblems and poems. To Marie, the pictures jumped off the page, as they seemed to relate to Bacon and the legend of **Bruton Vault**, a rumored cache of esoteric materials. The legend is a tall tale involving the Jewish Temple, the Knights Templar, Queen Elisabeth I (the "Virgin" Queen), Shakespeare, the Virginia Founding Fathers, and the secret destiny of America.

> *[B]eing a woman, I did not have to conform to, and most certainly would not let myself in for practicing secretive ways! Seems the Lord made men to make secrets, and he made women to break all man-made secrets wide open: For wine aged too long turns to vinegar. ...*
>
> *[I]f some Woman would discern the New Age Undertaking (perhaps even the "true secret" of fraternal Masonry), no one could compel her to secrecy ... Even the Divine Creator's secrets in Nature are there to be found out by humankind. When man-made secrets have out-lived their time, they are likely to become subterfuge for power-aspiring corruption. ... [N]o one, but no one with the exception of the Lord Himself, could have kept me secretive or stopped me from doing something about it.*[75]

Marie Bauer Hall, *Quest for Bruton Vault*

The tale starts with the **Knights Templar** and their storied place in history. In 1099, after the First Crusade against the Muslims, Christians gained control of Jerusalem. Initially, the Templars were organized by a French nobleman to protect the roads from the Palestine coast to the Holy City so Christian pilgrims could safely travel. The original nine knights set up camp at the Jewish Temple ruins (a.k.a. the Western Wailing Wall) – all that was left of the Second Temple after its destruction by the Romans in 70 CE. The First Temple was built by King Solomon *circa* 950 BCE, and it was destroyed in 587 BCE by Babylonian King Nebuchadnezzar II.

In 1127, the French knights returned to France and thereafter exhibited immense wealth. The Templars found something of great value at the Temple, and in 1139, Pope Innocent II issued a bull formally acknowledging the knights as an official Order of the Catholic Church. As a result, the Templars became the independent military of the church. They had their own navy, comprised of both war ships and commercial vessels, and they soon controlled the land and sea around Christendom. Additionally, the Templars were prolific builders, erecting hundreds of castles and forts for European monarchs and over three hundred cathedrals for the church. To build on such a scale, the knights had their own stonemasons known as **free masons**, because they were free men not in servitude to nobility.

Over time, Templar real estate holdings and businesses grew to include farms, mines, and stone quarries. In England alone, they owned thousands of properties.[76] The Knights established their own banking system and invented the world's first credit card. In addition, the knights carried communications in the Christian world, as their fleet of ships moved both merchandise and mail. Thus, historians also credit the Templars with creating the first post office. In short, the Knights Templar was the world's first conglomerate, and during the 12th and 13th Centuries, the Order was the wealthiest entity on the planet.

The Knights Templar were universally praised as being fair and noble, and there is scant evidence they abused their power. Despite their astounding accomplishments and reputation for honesty and hard work, the Templars were later maligned as "illiterate warriors." Shortly, we will see why the Catholic Church tarnished the knights, and also how the Vatican managed to acquire much of its staggering wealth.

Historians speculate that Templar wealth initially derived from what they found at the Jewish Temple.[77] In 1867, British excavation of the temple ruins disclosed a vertical shaft running near the Temple Mount. From this vertical tunnel, horizontal tunnels fanned out, one of which led to the Dome of the Rock, the Islamic mosque built on the holy site in 639 CE, when the Muslims had control of Jerusalem. So the question remains to this day: *What did the Templars find under the Jewish Temple ruins?*

Luckily, the *Dead Sea Scrolls* hold a clue. The famous *Copper Scroll* contains an inventory of the Jewish treasury, which has never been found. The scroll lists 160 tons of gold and silver, along with other booty that today would be valued at billions of dollars.[78] In addition, the Templars may have found ancient artifacts, such as the Ark of Covenant, the Spear of Destiny, and the Stone of Destiny (a.k.a. "Jacob's Pillar"). Some historians believe the knights seized the items inventoried on the *Copper Scroll* and brought the treasure back to France. Legend also states that the Templars learned the truth about Jesus and Mary Magdalene (a.k.a. the Holy Grail), since some of them began to worship the mysterious Black Madonna.

In 1187, tragedy struck Christendom when the Muslims retook Jerusalem. For the next hundred years, the Templars tried to regain the holy land. While the knights were busy fighting, a storm was brewing back in France. The Cathars, who we briefly examined in Chapter VI, were defying the Pope by refusing to attend mass, which they viewed as tainted by manmade dogma. Recall that the Cathars were spiritually descendant from the Gnostic Christians. They lived a puritan and communal existence, adhered to a vegetarian diet, and established a welfare system for the poor. Critically, the Cathars revered Mary Magdalene, who travelled to France after the crucifixion to teach.

In 1209, Pope Innocent III declared the Cathars heretics and condemned them to death. History books list a variety of reasons for the Catholic purge of the Cathars, including their belief that Jesus was not God. To entice European nobles to participate in the extermination, the Pope decreed that Cathar property could be seized, but the Templars refused to participate in the massacre, which culminated at Montsegur (where I inadvertently conjured the black boar).

The Templars were friendly with the Cathars because many of them lived in southern France where the knights were headquartered. Consequently, the Cathars may have known about the items discovered by the knights at the Jewish Temple, including rumored evidence that Jesus and Mary were married and that descendants of their daughter Sarah married into the Merovingian Dynasty, the ancient kings of France. In addition, the church was heavily in debt to the knights, as was the King of France, who hated the Templars for refusing him admittance into the Order, a life-long humiliation. In short, many historians believe that French King Phillip IV and Pope Clement V conspired to exterminate both the Cathars and the Knights Templar.[79]

On **Friday the 13**th in October of 1307, the Catholic Inquisition backed by King Philip arrested the Grand Master and the principal knights of the Templar Order. The knights were accused of sympathizing with the Cathars and failing to protect the holy land by colluding with the Muslim Empire. Additionally, inquisitors charged the knights with sodomy, heresy, and witchcraft. Hundreds of Templars were imprisoned, tortured and killed, and Grand Master Jacques de Molay was burned to death. Before he expired, Molay cursed the King and Pope and prophesied their deaths. Both of them died within a year.

Before his accursed death, King Philip attempted to steal the knights' coffers, but his plan was foiled. The bulk of the Templar fortune was gone and most of their naval fleet had vanished. The French King was thwarted, but the Catholic Church fared well by confiscating Templar real estate holdings. The theft of Templar properties explains the massive wealth of the Catholic Church, still considered one of the richest institutions on Earth. Incidentally, in 2008, a remnant order of Templars sued the Vatican to get their property back.[80]

The legend continues with the knights sailing to Scotland with their treasury, where they may have befriended Robert the Bruce.[81] The Stone of Destiny made its way to Scotland as well, either transported by the Templars or by the Jewish Tribe of Dan, one of the "lost tribes of Israel" after the Assyrian diaspora (*circa* 722 BCE), thereafter becoming the Tuatha Dé Danann.[82] The stone was renamed as well, since history recites that the Stone of Scone was (supposedly) seized by the English in 1296, then placed under the coronation chair in Westminster Abbey.[83] The ongoing legend of Jacob's Stone is riveting, but we need to stay focused on Marie Hall's quest for Bruton Vault.*

In 1558, Queen Elizabeth I (1533–1603) came to power, having taken the thrown at the youthful age of twenty-five, though demure she was not. Indeed, Elisabeth was cut-throat by any standard, having her cousin Mary Queen of Scots beheaded, in addition to executing many others who she felt betrayed her. Nor was Elizabeth chaste, despite her courtly nickname, the "Virgin Queen." Indeed, many historians believe that Elizabeth had more than one child, since she was known to take lovers in an age without birth control.

Enter Francis Bacon (1561–1626), purportedly born to Sir Nicholas Bacon and Anne Cooke, a lady in waiting to the Queen. However, Bacon was more likely the Queen's son by Robert Dudley, the Earl of Leicester (1553–1588).

* For a brief period in 2008, The Oracle Institute protected a stone that may have been the Stone of Destiny. Another legend for another day.

Dudley relentlessly sought her hand in marriage, but Elizabeth refused all of his proposals, preferring instead to move his bedroom beside hers.[84]

> [Elizabeth's] *relationship with her long-standing companion, Robert Dudley ... prompted by far the most speculation. She had known the handsome courtier since childhood and the two had become close during her years of uncertainty under Mary* [Queen of Scots], *when Dudley had taken great risks to remain loyal to her.*
>
> *When Elizabeth became queen, she made it clear that she had no intention of giving up her favourite. ... [S]he had Dudley's bedchamber moved next to her private rooms in order to facilitate their clandestine meetings. ... The more affectionate they became, the more insistent the rumours that they were lovers and that Dudley "hath got the Queen with child."*[85]

There is ample evidence that Elizabeth was Bacon's mother. For example, the timing of Bacon's birth "coincided with Elizabeth being bedridden with a mysterious illness that caused her body to swell." [86] Additionally, Bacon was not listed on the family genealogical tree by his (adoptive) father Nicholas, who also failed to provide for Bacon in his Will, despite being generous with his other children. Truly, the evidence is overwhelming:

> *[M]any people knew about Elizabeth's pregnancies, but laws were passed that invoked harsh punishment for "speaking ill of the queen." ... [G]ossips were severely punished for that kind of indiscretion. ... [A]t Norwich several persons were tried – and some executed – for treasonable slander. They insisted that "My Lord of Leicester* [Robert Dudley] *had two children by the queen." ... Francis Bacon has acquired a following as an "unacknowledged son" of Queen Elizabeth, and even today many Baconians and Rosicrucians believe that he was her son and therefore should have been Elizabeth's successor.*[87]

Proof also exists that Elizabeth had a son by Edward de Vere, the Earl of Oxford. Their (supposed) son was raised as Henry Wriothesley, the Earl of Southampton, and once again, historians can show that the Queen was indisposed for months coinciding with Wriothesley's birth.[88] If true, then Bacon and Wriothesley were half-brothers, and history reveals both of them to be polymaths, lawyers, poets, and friends. Of the many promiscuous stories surrounding the "Virgin" Queen, these two possible princes present us with the interlaced mystery of who, exactly, wrote the Shakespearean plays.

William Shakespeare (1564–1616) was born in a rural village to illiterate parents. For signatures, his father used the mark of a glove and his mother used a running horse.[89] Shakespeare never finished grade school and his children were illiterate, which makes no sense if he were a "man of letters." Although his Will bequeathed items to family and friends (his clothes, rings, and a bed), it failed to mention any manuscripts or books – evidence he lacked a library.[90] In fact, there is no evidence Shakespeare could write. None of the original plays or sonnets has been found, and only six of his signatures are known to exist (three from his Will), all penned differently. Shakespeare died in a tavern with Ben Jonson, a friend of Bacon.[91] Rumors circulated that Johnson poisoned Shakespeare to eliminate him as the front-man in the pseudonym conspiracy.

The Bacon-Shakespeare controversy has raged for centuries and remains a fascination to this day.[92] Even Samuel Clemens (a.k.a. Mark Twain) wrote a book on the matter, stating that all great fiction is "simply autobiographical." Twain reiterated that Shakespeare never attended college and was not a member of the English court.[93] Hence, Shakespeare could not have written plays about ancient history or contemporaneous intrigues in the courts of Europe.

While scholars have searched for a single person to substitute for Shakespeare, Marie heard a legend that a group of aristocrats led by Bacon – the **Knights of the Helmet** – wrote the corpus of Shakespearean works.[94] The group-Shakespeare theory is believable because Bacon and his friends were networked, they all travelled, fought in wars together, and knew what was happening in the royal courts of Europe – the backdrop of many Shakespearean plays. The below painting depicts the primary suspects, all comrades of Bacon.

"Shakespeare and His Friends," by John Faed (1851)
Including: Francis Bacon, Ben Jonson, Walter Raleigh, Henry Wriothesley

The other reason this legend is credible is because Bacon spied for the Queen, which meant he knew state secrets. He also is famous for his encryption skills, which led to the development of Morse Code.[95] Of course, Bacon also was a Member of the House of Commons and a favorite of Queen Elizabeth, though he infuriated her by blocking her attempt to usurp Parliament's taxation power. After their public disagreement over taxation, the Queen declared that Bacon "must nevermore look to her for favour or promotion."[96] The year was 1593, the same year "Shakespeare" wrote his first poem "Venus and Adonis."

In 1601, the Queen punished Bacon further by forcing him to assist in the prosecution of Robert Devereux, the Earl of Essex. Devereux was Bacon's friend and may have been his half-brother, a second son born to the Queen and Robert Dudley.[97] In any event, Deveraux was found guilty of treason and Elizabeth had him beheaded. That's right, Queen Elizabeth may have killed her own son! In retaliation, some scholars believe that Bacon wrote *Hamlet* to memorialize this tragedy.[98] Additionally, it is well documented that Bacon and the other Knights of the Helmet wrote many plays for entertainment:

> *In this entertainment Francis Bacon presented his philosophical ideals and an Order of knighthood dedicated to carrying them out. The purpose of the Order was to correct the errors of the past and bring order out of chaos. The name of this philosophical Order of knights refers to the divine **Spear-shaker**, **Pallas Athena**, the Tenth Muse and Patroness of the Arts and Sciences .... In addition, the goddess presents helmets to her knight-heroes, hence the **Order of the Knights of the Helmet**. These helmets were said to bestow **invisibility on the wearer** as well as being ... "helmets of strength," a symbolism that has the further cabalistic meaning of righteousness, virtue, clear perception and judgement. All such knights are, metaphorically, **spear-shakers or shake-speares**, like the Gemini and St. George. They are also "invisible brethren," a term used to describe the Rosicrucian fraternity.[99]* [emphasis added]

When Queen Elizabeth died in 1603, she was succeeded by James I (1566–1625), who also ascended to the crown as James VI of Scotland. James was the son of Mary Queen of Scots, who Elizabeth had executed. Bacon was forty-two years old at the time, and his stock soared under the new king, who made Bacon High Chancellor. Summing up the second half of Bacon's life isn't easy, due to his prolific prose, political stature, and covert movements.[100] To advance the legend, I will note three of his relevant accomplishments. First, Bacon was entrusted with editing and printing the *King James Bible*. Second, he founded the scientific method. Third, Bacon wanted to build a New World.

THE SECRET DESTINY OF VIRGINIA

> *Do we not see that in administration of the world under the great*
> *monarch, God himself, that his laws are divers; one law in spirits,*
> *another in bodies; one law in regions celestial, another in elementary;*
> *and yet the creatures are all one mass and lump, without any vacuum*
> *or separation?*[101]

Sir Francis Bacon

After King James was crowned, Bacon drafted a plan to unify England and Scotland, and he proposed "Great Britain" as the name of the joint kingdom.[102] Sadly, the unification plan failed due to enmity between the two cultures, their religious differences, and James' excesses and incompetence.[103] However, Bacon's plan exemplified his dream of a "golden age," and it rekindled interest in the book *Utopia*, by Sir Thomas More (1478–1535). Bacon promoted the concepts of one shared human destiny and perfection of societal relations – a dream the American Founding Fathers would do their best to manifest.

Merchants of Virginia.

In 1606, King James granted a charter for the **Virginia Company** to Bacon and friends to set up business in the colony of Virginia, named after the "Virgin" Queen. Back then, the eastern seaboard of America – from Maine to the Carolinas – was part of Virginia. The company coat of arms (left) contains the Templar cross of St. George and the shields of England's other domains: Scotland, Ireland, France, and Virginia.[104] The company motto was *En dat Virginia quintam*, which means, "Behold, Virginia is the Fifth" (domain). The motto led to Virginia's nickname "Old Dominion."

In 1618, the Virginia Company sanctioned the **House of Burgesses**, an assembly of elected representatives for the Virginia colonists. It is safe to assume that Bacon had a hand in this democratic experiment. In time, the Virginia Founding Fathers would join the House of Burgesses, including George Washington, Thomas Jefferson, Patrick Henry, George Wythe, and George Mason. Soon enough, they would debate, disagree with, and challenge the British Virginia governors over matters of crown taxation.

In 1621, a new Virginia Governor, Sir Francis Wyatt, set sail from England accompanied by nine ships.[105] By this time, the Virginia Company had begun to routinely send cargo across the Atlantic, delivering goods to Jamestown and returning to England with Virginia goods, such as tobacco. As a founding member of the Virginia Company, Bacon would have had the ability to oversee shipments to Virginia – a critical capacity given the trajectory of our story.

The legend recites that Bacon became enamored of the Knights Templar and adopted the term **Freemason** for his Shakespearean secret society. Bacon allegedly located the remnant Templar treasure in Scotland, including the important religious artifacts. Bacon then placed the materials in a vault, along with the original Shakespearean manuscripts and other items he felt were needed to seed the New World. Then, Bacon shipped the vault to Virginia, where it was safely received and protected. This was the theory avowed by Marie Hall, who wrote passionately about the significance of the vault:

> Numerous works recorded in history as "written and lost," by Lord Bacon and members of the Shakespeare group, were deliberately obscured and secreted for the principle purpose of being found or released at the proper time .... Centuries removed, as the time of ardently anticipated discernment drew closer, "fool proof" provisions had to be made and recorded for "timely" averting of fatalities, as related to the New Age Undertaking, to the entire human race and its earth-bound predicament.[106]

Also in 1621, Bacon was disgraced and stripped of public office. He was accused of corruption by his nemesis, Sir Edward Coke, Chief Justice of the Star Chamber (the Crown's court system). Coke had tried Robert Devereux, Bacon's possible half-brother, for treason against Queen Elizabeth.[107] Coke also had successfully prosecuted Sir Walter Raleigh for treason – a trial deemed spurious but which resulted in Raleigh's decade-long imprisonment in the Tower followed by his execution.[108] Now, Coke was after Bacon, who offered no legal defense. Historians suggest that Bacon was being blackmailed or that he pled guilty to shield King James, to whom he declared: "With respect to this charge of bribery I am as innocent as any man born on St. Innocents Day."[109]

Five years later, Bacon was gone. History records he died of pneumonia on April 9, 1626. However, his death was suspicious. He died alone and rumors began circulating that Bacon faked his demise. If the rumors were true, he may have continued writing, gathered more materials for the vault, and ensured publication of his utopian memoir The New Atlantis, released posthumously in

1627. It is worth considering whether Bacon staged his death, which occurred on Easter Sunday. If he chose that day, he may have been signaling that he would "resurrect" (like Jesus) to continue the great work of guiding humanity.

> *The Risen Christ first appeared to Mary Magdalene and blessed her in anticipation of that Christ-pre-envisioned **New Age Easter morning**, when the long lost and buried apostolic documentation of Christ-Consciousness (along with the documentary Seventeenth Century treasure) would be released from its two-thousand-year obscuration and burial ....*[110] [emphasis added]

Marie Hall, Quest for Bruton Vault

In her reference to a "New Age Easter morning," Marie supports the idea that Bacon faked his death. There also is Freemason folklore that Bacon left England and travelled throughout Europe for at least another decade, aided by Masonic and Rosicrucian networks. Masons credit Bacon with reconstituting the Knights Templar under the newer Freemason banner. Some even equate him with the mysterious Comte de St. Germain.[111] While these conjectures remain fanciful, the vault's discovery might clear up the many dangling threads.

The legend continues with the vault's arrival in Virginia. Marie thought the rebel Nathaniel Bacon (1647–1676) was one of the vault's protectors. He was a member of the House of Burgesses and a distant relative of Francis Bacon.[112] Nathaniel Bacon led Bacon's Rebellion, the first uprising against the English and a direct challenge to the authority of the British Governor of Virginia, who was disliked for failing to protect colonists from Native Americans. During the two-year skirmish, the rebels held and then set fire to Jamestown.[113] By today's standards, the colonists' conduct against the native people is atrocious. But a precedent was set: Don't mess with the independent spirit of the colonists. So to many, Nathaniel Bacon was a hero, with his 1676 rebellion occurring exactly one hundred years before the American Revolution.

After Jamestown was destroyed, the capital of Virginia was moved five miles inland to Williamsburg, named after then English King William III. Williamsburg also was home to William and Mary College, and by 1705, a new capitol building was completed for the House of Burgesses. Then in 1706, construction began on a new "Governor's Palace." With all this growth, it soon became evident that a new church was needed as well.

In 1711, construction of **Bruton Church** began in Williamsburg. The new brick church was situated between the college, the capitol building, and the governor's residence. Today, one can visit the church and see the names of the Virginia Founding Fathers etched into brass plaques on pews, indicating where they sat. All of them were members of the church, since they attended whenever they were in town for sessions of the House of Burgesses.

In 1775, Patrick Henry delivered his "Give Me Liberty or Give Me Death" speech. Thereafter, the House of Burgesses was abandoned, meeting just once more before the *Declaration of Independence* was signed. Next, Henry led Virginia's militia in the Gunpowder Incident to capture Williamsburg's war stock. At that point, the British governor fled and the revolutionaries seized the town. Afterward, the Virginia colonists appointed their own governors, starting with Patrick Henry and followed by Thomas Jefferson. In addition, the Virginia Founding Fathers started meeting with their counterparts from the other twelve colonies, as plans for the Revolutionary War were solidified.

In sum, the legend states that Virginia's Founding Fathers had possession of Bacon's vault and, at the direction of Thomas Jefferson, they buried it for safekeeping at Bruton Church before the start of the Revolutionary War. Now is the perfect time for me to mention that The Oracle Institute's formal mission statement is Thomas Jefferson's *Virginia Act for Religious Freedom* – which is how I became connected to the legend of Bruton Vault and to Marie Hall.[114]

In 2006, a man named Tom called me on the phone. He had read my first book, *The Truth: About the Five Primary Religions*, and he had seen the Oracle mission statement reprinted at the back of the book. He wanted to know why we had chosen Jefferson's *Act for Religious Freedom* for our charitable mission. I answered, "Because religious intolerance has been growing since 9/11 and our mission is to help lead a spiritual revolution." He then candidly told me that he was a reincarnation of Thomas Jefferson. *Say what?*

Tom wanted to meet me, so he invited me to a dinner party at a home outside Charlottesville and near Monticello, the Jefferson estate. Conversations around the dinner table focused on Eisenhower making treaties with aliens, Reagan breaking them, underground cities being built by the Cabal, generals at the Pentagon who could be counted on, the 9/11 Truth movement, and other topics that were new to me. No one else at the dinner table seemed surprised, as they all appeared to know each other and share the same worldview. But my overall reaction to the discussions was a sarcastic, *Yeah right.*

Nevertheless, as I stared into the blue eyes of this thin, six-foot-three stranger – the spitting image of Thomas Jefferson[115] – I decided to suspend disbelief. As Tom talked, I recalled my college years at UVA, walking on the Lawn and inside the Rotunda, and getting drunk at my favorite bar in C'Ville called "TJs." I also remembered that during the first Oracle Board meeting, we debated whether to adopt Jefferson's *Act for Religious Freedom*. I had doggedly insisted that it must be our mission statement. And now, I was sitting next to Thomas Jefferson? As I listened to this distinguished gentleman, my head began to swim and my heart fluttered. Next, Tom shared that he belonged to a group of people across the United States who believe themselves to be the reincarnated Founding Fathers. "What!" I exclaimed. "There are more of you?"

"Yes, most of us are back and we have found each other," Tom replied. Then he looked me squarely in the face and gently asked, "Do you have any memories of the revolutionary period?" I shook my head "no," and he looked disappointed. I asked him to tell me more about the Founding Father group, as a child asks at bedtime for just one more story. So he told me more about the group and how they managed to find one another. He shared that they were back to lead a "spiritual revolution" and that they focus on three project areas to help shift the paradigm: alien disclosure, 9/11 Truth, and proving reincarnation by continuing the research of Professor Ian Stevenson at UVA. Tom was leading the 9/11 faction, while Walter Semkiw (1955–2022) – the 21st Century John Adams – wrote a book entitled *Return of the Revolutionaries*:

> In 1984, on a lark, I went to a medium who reportedly channeled one's spiritual guides. In the session, I was told that I had been John Adams, the second president of the United States. ... At the time, I did not believe that I was Adams, and I largely dismissed the information. Twelve years later, I had a sudden and strong intuition to study Adams and began to research the Adams family in 1996. I found that I did see myself in him .... Further, I recognized members of his family and some of his most important friends in people closest to my heart. It thus occurred to me that people incarnated in karmic "soul groups." ... I believe that these leaders of the American Revolutionary Era have returned with the group project of enacting a spiritual revolution.[116]

Just as I thought my head would explode, Tom started to talk about a woman named Marie Hall who had tried to find a vault filled with Templar materials that had been buried in Williamsburg prior to the Revolutionary War. I quickly snapped to, as if on command. I already was well versed in the Templar legends (especially as they relate to Jacob's Stone), and I became intensely curious. "Please tell me more about this vault," I implored.

So began my friendship with Tom and the high synchronicity phase of my journey which corresponded with the rare Venus transit. We visited Monticello together and occasionally he would invite me on trips to Washington, D.C., which he hoped would "wake me up" to my revolutionary past. I grew up outside of Washington, my father worked on Capitol Hill, and I worked there as a young attorney. I love that hallowed city and never tire of it. During one trip, Tom said he had papers to drop off at Congress. As we walked through the Rayburn Office Building, we ended up at the office of Congressman Dennis Kucinich. A lady at the desk asked us to sign in and said, "You just missed him, Tom. But you can leave the package with me, we've been expecting it."

As we left Kucinich's office, I inquired about the package. "The Founding Fathers are friends with Dennis," replied Tom. "Inside the envelope are Articles of Impeachment we drafted against Bush and Cheney. We believe they lied to the American people about 9/11 and the reasons for the Iraq War." *Seriously?* Soon thereafter, Kucinich did introduce Articles of Impeachment against Bush and Cheney, though they were never voted upon.[117]

One day, Tom conveyed a request from the Founding Fathers: They asked that I solve the Bruton Vault mystery once and for all. I accepted the assignment and got a copy of Marie's "good friend" the George Wither book, and it is indeed a treasure map.[118] Marie believed (as do I) that the emblems in the book depict the story of Bacon, the vault, and its delivery to Virginia. Below, the first emblem shows the vault's location near a church. The second depicts a woman unearthing the vault – a modern day Athena destined to liberate it.

Marie thought Bacon's "New Age Undertaking" hinged on unearthing the vault's contents at the appropriate time. In 1938, Marie tried her best to fulfill this prophecy, but she was foiled by the Rockefeller Restoration Foundation (RRF), which at the time was funding and overseeing the restoration of Williamsburg. I encourage readers to get a copy of *Quest for Bruton Vault* and follow the twists and turns for themselves. Here, I will briefly summarize Marie's adventure, and I'll start by highlighting that she dedicated eight months of her life to this quest, leaving her two small children in California.

To start, Marie rented a room across the street from Bruton Church. Initially, she was able to form an alliance with vestry members at the church and the Mayor of Williamsburg, all of whom were fascinated by the legend and wanted to help. Marie thought the vault was inside the church tower, but an initial dig proved fruitless. The dig was financed courtesy of RRF, and Marie left with the distinct impression that the tower already had been excavated. Privately, she began to wonder if RFF and the church were humoring her.

> Not until recently did it begin to occur to the naturally self-appointed ruling "brethren" and their respective "brotherhood aspirations," that there are equally as many – if not more – feminine members or "Sisters" in the world-family. ... Lord Bacon as the paternal, New Age Adam ... wisely decided to woo a naturally implied "New Age Eve" .... They dedicated their paternally anticipated New Age Undertaking to Pallas Athena, the daughter of Solar Zeus, who was called the "spear-shaker," and who by mythological reports had remained practically the only "Virgin" in Olympus![119]

Undaunted, Marie continued her research with some help from students at William and Mary College who were enamored of the mystery. In fact, many people became aware of her quest and newspapers started to cover the story. Marie's theory was that the Founding Fathers had left anagrams and clues on tombstones, including measurements that related to the church's foundation. She triple-checked her calculations. Where had she gone wrong?

Then Marie had an epiphany. She wondered if there was an *earlier* church and if her calculations would work from its foundation. She went to the William and Mary library and discovered there was an earlier church built in 1683. But when she approached the church with this new data, they refused to help. Marie believed RRF cast a dark shadow over the quest for Bruton Vault. First, RRF tried to buy the church, then RRF offered to swap the neighboring George Wythe House. When Bruton Church refused both offers, RFF offered to fund church renovations, but in exchange, there could be no more digs.

That's when Marie took matters into her own hands. She hired a man to dig in search of the old church foundation one morning before sunrise. Low and behold, a brick foundation appeared where Marie had predicted, and it matched the dimensions of the first Bruton Church described in the William and Mary library. By this time the sun was up, a crowd was gathering outside, and church personnel were arriving. A meeting was called by the church, the city of Williamsburg and RRF, but Marie was not invited. To add insult to injury, she had recently learned the RRF was restoring Stratford in England – the home of William Shakespeare! The church and town voted in favor of another dig, and RRF representatives walked out in protest.

Next, the old church foundation was unearthed, but then it was reburied a few weeks later. Marie requested another meeting and was allowed to speak this time. With over sixty men (no women) in attendance, Marie recited the full legend of the vault and asked if they would consent to another dig if she could "scientifically prove" the vault's location. In her memoirs, Marie wrote:

> *I had found for them what they wanted for themselves, but what all their millions along with all their people had not been able to find. So now they wanted to conveniently discourage me out of town, so they could claim what for centuries had been carefully protected from just that kind of "philanthropic vandalism." ... Could it possibly be that both "Uncle Sam" and fraternal Masonry completely lost track of their great New Age trust?*[120]

Cleverly, Marie located a Canadian company with equipotential equipment (early ultrasound). She convinced the company's owner of the sacred nature of the dig, and he agreed to send a man to Williamsburg. When the technician arrived, the ultrasound indicated a ten-foot by ten-foot anomaly exactly were Marie said the vault was buried. Another meeting was called to discuss yet another excavation. Marie was denied access again, but the Canadian scientist was allowed to share his findings. In the end, the town and church granted permission for another dig, despite protests by RRF.

On the day of the dig, newspapers were abuzz and *National Geographic* came to take pictures. Freemasons from Washington and England arrived and many people surrounded the church graveyard, as workers dug to a depth of five feet then stopped for the day. The next morning, they dug to a depth of nine feet and discovered ashen earth – evidence the ground had been previously disturbed. Then men from RRF and the church vestry abruptly declared that all digging must stop. Marie was in shock and students from William and Mary wept. They had dug within one foot of Bruton Vault, yet Marie was forced to stand "helplessly watching the men reluctantly filling in the trench."[121]

AMERICAN
JUNIOR RED CROSS

Though Marie failed to retrieve the vault, she was indefatigable and no one could have done a better job. She was honored with a Sign when she got home in the form of a WWII Red Cross poster that depicted Francis Bacon reading the *Declaration of Independence* to a diverse group of children who will shape the future destiny of America. Washington, Lincoln, and Franklin (left) and Jefferson (right) are in the background. As Marie described the poster: "Thomas Jefferson who officiated at the physical birth of this nation ... is stationed next to Lord Bacon, America's true and noble Father-founder."[122]

In 1992, Bruton Church authorized a dig using modern equipment, but the vault was gone.[123] In 2006, I visited Williamsburg to finish my investigation. It was heartwarming to see the names of the Founding Fathers on the pews, and I felt Marie's pain when I walked outside and studied the mysterious tombstones. I also visited the RRF library, which had newspaper clippings on the 1938 dig. It was time to report back to the Founding Father group, so I typed up my notes with my final conclusion: The vault was stolen by RRF and taken to Kykuit – the Rockefeller's 3,500-acre estate in Pocantico Hills, New York.

Built over time by generations of Rockefellers, Kykuit overlooks the Hudson River and is said to be "what God would have built, if only He had the money." Underground lies the Rockefeller Archive Center, a three-story bunker that houses family records and memorabilia, along with items stored by organizations, like the suspicious Trilateral Commission.[124] Sensitive materials are placed in temperature and humidity-controlled vaults. Just picture the final scene in the first *Indiana Jones* movie, when the Ark of the Covenant is crated, stamped, and placed in a warehouse full of other miscellaneous items.

Today, there is a permanent reminder of this legend. The Virginia seal (left) was designed by George Wythe (1726–1806), judge, tutor, and good friend of Jefferson. Wythe's home is located beside Bruton Church and he would have known about Bacon and the "Spear-shaker." Yes, that is Athena on the Virginia seal and on our state flag. Our motto: "Thus Always to Tyrants."

In closing this section, I am reminded of another early message I received: *As goes Virginia goes the United States*. In this final quote from Marie, she makes the same point. The secret destiny of America and Virginia are linked. May Athena, Goddess of Wisdom, continue to guide this commonwealth.

> *A number of the great elect of humankind have dreamt of a Utopia of the earth, where man could live harmoniously and develop in peace and felicity. Bacon attempted and effected a plan for the realization of this dream. ... The Constitution of the United States and the main course of its history were predetermined and carried out in accordance with Sir Bacon's plan of New Age Empire-building. ... George Washington, Benjamin Franklin, Thomas Jefferson, Patrick Henry ... and many others of America's great leaders were Master-Masons performing their task. ...*
>
> *"Quest for Bruton Vault" is and remains a New Age Mystery, destined for the American people to solve and bring to a lawful and honorable conclusion. ... The logical place of concealment for this vast treasure was Virginia.*[125]

NEW ATLANTIS ALONG THE NEW RIVER

By 2012, I was determined to break ground on the Peace Pentagon. The prison lawsuit was over, as was the second zoning lawsuit, so I finally had the green light to start. To me, the Peace Pentagon is a temple, a tool, and a fortress. It also is a vortex of Light along the New River in Independence, Virginia, and a holistic setting for New Humans to live and plan the spiritual revolution.

One day, Tom called to ask me about the geometry of the Peace Pentagon, which we had discussed many times. Perplexed, I reminded him the structure is based on Oracle's sacred numbers: 5 and 11. My messages had been quite clear: The exterior walls must be 55 feet long, the interior chapel (also pentagonal) must have 25 foot walls. And the skylight must be a "pentamid" of 5 foot triangles.

Tom replied, "Fort Washington in New York was a pentagon too. Also, have you studied the geometry of the Washington Monument?" I hung up the phone and jumped on the internet. Turns out George Washington *did* build a pentagonal fort (shown right).[126] And I learned the exterior walls of the Washington Monument are 55 feet long, just like the Peace Pentagon! The monument is 555 feet tall and has a 55 foot crowning pyramid. WOW.

I decided to read *Washington: The Indispensable Man*, by James Thomas Flexner.[127] Flexner won a Pulitzer Prize and National Book Award for the four-volume biography, in which he argues that George Washington was essential to the founding of the United States. He suggests that perhaps someone else could have penned the Constitution, thereby rending James Madison expendable. And maybe, just maybe, the U.S. could have been founded without Jefferson's genius. But if Washington had never been born, the American fight for freedom would have failed and produced a different timeline. Washington also was irreplaceable because his ego was in check, as evidenced by his refusal to accept a third presidential term. He valued Truth above all else, he managed his troops with parental tough Love, and he clearly was guided by the Light.

It is frightful to think what might have happened if Washington had been killed or captured. Shockingly, an assassination plot almost succeeded. The plan was led by Washington's handpicked "Life Guards" – his secret service detail. However, due to the counterespionage tactics of Washington and John Jay, who would later become the first Chief Justice of the Supreme Court, the plot was foiled just days before the British armada of more than two hundred ships appeared on the horizon.[128] On June 28, 1776, the turncoat leader of the Life Guard plot was hanged – the same day John Adams submitted Jefferson's first draft of the *Declaration of Independence* to the Continental Congress in Philadelphia. Officially adopted on the 4th of July, the sacred document would take five days to reach Washington, but in time for him to read it aloud to his troops prior to the first battle of the American Revolution.

> *For months, Washington had been frustrated by the ambiguity of the Continental Congress's position with regard to the war. ... Now, with this Declaration, the war has clarity and moral purpose. ...*
>
> *What made him great ... was his sheer staying power, his total devotion to his army, his relentless sense of duty, and a stubborn refusal to ever give up. ... Washington was with them in the snow, in the mud, in the rain, in the sleet, in the ice. He dealt with the endless politics, the staffing, the funding, the organizational challenges. He slogged through the countless problems with logistics, recruiting, weapons, food, sickness, and transportation. It never got easy and he never gave up. ...*
>
> *[I]t all seems so totally unthinkable without George Washington at the center. And this is before we even get to Washington becoming the nation's first President.*[129]
>
> Brad Metzer, *The First Conspiracy*

Many mysteries surround the founding of the United States and the stories fill volumes. Today, Tom and I remain good friends, and I am grateful that he came to me during a period of my journey when I needed clarity on my mission and Signs to guide me. The last big message I received during the Venus transit was to co-create a community for New Humans.

We named our community the Valley of Light in honor of our location in the New River Valley and our connection to **Damanhur**, the City of Light in Italy. To my knowledge, the Federation of Damanhur is the only full-spectrum, Second Tier community on Earth. At the Valley of Light, we aspire to both these goals, and we are honored to work with Damanhur through our spirituality school and Oracle Press, which published the *Three Books of the Initiate* by Damanhur founder Oberto "Falco" Airaudi. We also distribute the Damanhur *Bral Talej* divination cards.[130] As a result of our affiliation with Damanhur, my trips and studies there, and visits from their ambassadors, teachers and trustees, we have learned how to properly organize and anchor a micro-community.

We also follow the design principles of Elinor Ostrom (1933–2012), winner of the 2009 Nobel Prize in Economics. Her eight design principles have been implemented to reverse the "tragedy of the commons." Stakeholders are able to transform regions by adopting: (i) strong identity and commonality of purpose; (ii) shared decision-making; (iii) systems for monitoring progress or regression; (iv) rewards for positive contributions; (v) graduated sanctions for negative behavior; (vi) fair conflict resolution mechanisms; (vii) freedom to self-organize; and (viii) functional coordination with outside groups.[131] The Valley of Light founding documents, which we crafted over many years and annually update, incorporate Ostrom's critical precepts.

Additionally, we use a model by Barbara Marx Hubbard known as the **Wheel of Co-Creation** – a pie-chart showing the **Sectors of Society** (i.e., the constituent parts of any full-spectrum community). The white thread that connects the sectors illustrates their synergistic and interdependent relationship. This model holistically highlights and supports the reality that the "whole is comprised of and yet greater than the sum of its parts." At the center of the wheel is the "HUB" – the unitive sweet spot.

At Oracle, we use this wheel for a variety of purposes. First, it depicts what we aspire to build – a community that contains everything found in a small town. Second, the wheel is an organizing schematic for our **Building the New World Conferences**, at which futurists present cutting-edge ideas and practical solutions in each Sector of Society. We've sponsored three BTNW conferences and consider these summits a primary program of our charitable mission. Third, we use the wheel at the Peace Pentagon HUB platform to showcase emergent opportunities and the exponential growth that occurs when people come out of their silos to cross-pollinate.[132]

The Oracle wheel has eleven sectors, and we consider the HUB the twelfth. The HUB is the "bullseye" and it represents indigenous cultures and intentional communities, where people experiment with both ancient and novel modes of partnerism. To achieve protopia, the HUB requires us to connect and synergize. Conversely, dystopia results when sectors are disconnected or when they pair up to the detriment of the whole, as when Justice & Governance maliciously aligns with Spirituality & Religion to control the masses, or when the shadow side of Peacebuilding & Relations and Science & Tech fuse into the Military Industrial Complex. Unforeseen problems also can erupt when well-meaning Lightworkers operate in silos. The repercussions of non-collaboration abound, as when untested Science & Tech is rushed to market, thereby poisoning Food, Water & Environment. In sum, the old game was based on separation.

> *Transcending the [old] game altogether means becoming a spoilsport – someone who refuses to acknowledge the playing field, the rules of engagement, or the value of winning. (Why win, anyway, if it's only going to end the game?) In certain non-Western cultures, the spoilsport is the shaman, who lives apart from the tribe in order to see the larger patterns and connections. ... Such anomalous behavior challenges convention, breaks the conspiracy of conformity, and stumps the algorithms. AIs and other enforcers of social control can't follow what they can't categorize. Weirdness is power, dissolving false binaries and celebrating the full spectrum of possibility. ... The greatest threats to Team Human are the beliefs, forces, and institutions that separate us from one another and the natural world of which we are a part.*[133]

Douglas Rushkoff, *Team Human*

The HUB is the heart of the new game – the never-ending God Game – and it is a "spoilsport" in the old game of dominator hierarchies and separation.

Already, people live in micro-communities, work in cooperative businesses, and swap expertise in the sharing economy. Positive examples include Twin Oaks in Virginia and Dancing Rabbit Ecovillage in Missouri, headquarters of the Foundation for Intentional Community, which lists more than a thousand communities around the world.[134] Today, people are reaching self-sufficiency through communal food production and shared cottage industries.

Notable, again, is Damanhur, which has successfully built a federation of villages and more than eighty cooperatively owned businesses that fall in every Sector of Society. Damanhur was born in 1975, when Falco and a group of friends pooled their money and purchased a 40-hectare farm at the base of the Italian Alps. With over 600 residents, Damanhur attracts New Humans who are ready, willing, and able to build the New World. Their one-word philosophy is "ACTION" and their ethos includes hard work and spiritual play. Since 1998, Damanhur has been a member of the Global Ecovillages Network. In 2005, Damanhur received a United Nations sustainability award, and it was voted the most utopian community on the planet by *What is Enlightenment?* magazine in a 2007 article entitled "Atlantis in the Mountains of Italy."[135] Lastly, Damanhur's Temples to Humankind – filled with exquisite murals, mosaics, statuary, and stained glass – depict the continuous unfoldment of the Godhead. Today, the temples are routinely called the "Eighth Wonder of the World."[136]

Likewise, the Valley of Light does not promote any single belief system, because we understand that the Godhead is shifting (and will one day shift again). At the Valley of Light, we are grateful to Damanhur for playing the role of muse and mentor. We also are grateful to past visionaries who laid the groundwork for the Fifth Spiritual Paradigm, including Francis Bacon and the Founding Fathers. In Bacon's utopian novella *The New Atlantis*, he describes twelve spheres of life. Indeed, the novel reads as though Bacon had the Wheel of Co-Creation to guide him! *The New Atlantis* is a prosocial prayer for synthesizing science and spirituality. Moreover, Bacon rejected materialism, resolving instead that Team Human should grow in the Light:

> *[T]hus you see we maintain a trade not for gold, silver, or jewels; nor for silks; nor for spices; nor any other commodity of matter; but only for God's first creature, which was Light: to have Light (I say) of the growth of all parts of the world. ... For the several employments and offices of our fellows; we have twelve [masters] ... who bring us the books, and abstracts, and patterns of experiments of all other parts. These we call Merchants of Light.[137]*

CO-CREATING A NEW WORLD

Dear reader, we have been on quite an adventure together. Using the Spectrum of Consciousness, we've studied the myriad ways humans view the world and learned, in large measure, why people believe what they believe. We looked at historical patterns, including a seasonal cycle that peaks within four generations, and a grand millennial cycle with the power to shift the Godhead. Today, humanity is witnessing the simultaneous crescendo of both historical patterns, which is why we are living in utter chaos. Yet, by the end of this Great Cusp, the chaos will complexify to the point of synergistic self-organization. Until then, we are in unchartered territory.

The disorder also is due to the unprecedented challenges and existential threats facing humanity, everything from climate change and pandemics to artificial intelligence and economic displacement. Metaphysics offers spiritual guidance to help us navigate these transitions, while quantum physics provides clues into probabilistic timelines. New Humans understand that God's law and manmade law are vastly different. Every day we get closer to comprehending the breadth of the Universe and the brilliance of the Akashic Field.

The polarity of war and peace – a tug of war between the Fourth and Fifth Paradigms – is playing out in every Sector of Society. Thankfully, we are seeing a groundswell of local, regional, and national solutions, including the growing micro-community movement. Such "bottom-up" solutions are encouraging, but they likely will not spread quickly enough to safely birth the new paradigm. Simply put, we are in a race against time. Consequently, we also need to work "top-down" if we want to ensure a regenerative world for the next generation.

Globally, we are one, interdependent human family, and New Humans already feel like "world citizens." Yet, our planet is fragmented by independent nation-states that fail to operate within a needed global construct. For example, Brazil has the "right" to destroy the Amazon Forest, the lungs of Earth. Russia has the "right" to censure news and keep "its" people uninformed. In addition, our institutions have not kept pace with the Holomovement. In my opinion, our archaic institutions are the gravest existential threat of all.

When the United Nations was formed in 1945, the hope was that global democracy and universal human rights would spread – and they did, at first. However, the WWII Allied nations (Great Britain, United States, Soviet Union) still feared the Axis nations (Germany, Italy, Japan). They also were unsure of new democracies, like India. Consequently, when the Allies formed the U.N., they assumed a favored status and made themselves permanent members of the Security Council, adding France and China as permanent members, too.

Today, the Security Council also has ten rotating seats with two-year terms for other nations, but the U.N. Charter gives the five permanent nations – U.S., U.K., France, Russia, and China – unilateral power to veto and thereby quash any world law.[138] Article 109 of the Charter allows amendments; however, the five permanent members of the Security Council can block amendments, as well.[139] Hence, a "Catch-22" exists, where just five nations can hold the rest of the world hostage. The net result is that the U.N. is an undemocratic and antiquated body with no power to peacefully resolve international disputes or to protect our precious planet. It's even worse than that, though, since the five permanent members now threaten the human experiment. With three nations dedicated to democracy and two committed to authoritarian rule, the polarity is paralyzing. How do we break this gridlock at the global level? As a former attorney, I ponder this dilemma often. If we want to outlaw war, we must find a way to adopt binding world law, while also honoring the spiral of life and the diversity of human values at the First and Second Tier.

The **International Court of Justice** (ICJ) established by the U.N. is likewise problematic. Article 94 of the U.N. Charter only requires that member states "undertake" to follow ICJ rulings, and if a judgment goes against one of the five permanent Security Council nations (or one of their allies), any of those five nations can veto enforcement.[140] Moreover, absolute jurisdiction is limited to cases where both countries agree to submit their claims. Even then, cases tend to be escalated to the Security Council, which can override the court. Also, the ICJ cannot hear cases involving private companies, organizations or individuals, and matters brought by U.N. agencies are limited to non-binding advisory opinions. Lastly, the **International Criminal Court** is not under the U.N. umbrella, so that court's jurisdiction is usually ignored, as well.

While writing this book, Archbishop Desmond Tutu departed (1931–2021). I had the honor of working with his staff on the second installment of the Oracle trilogy. His essay in *The Love* is entitled "God Has a Dream," based on his book by the same title. God's dream, according to Archbishop Tutu, is that humans will "wake up and discover we are family." Happily, this dream is coming true! Many humans now are playing the God Game and co-creating as Team Human. Thus, unity consciousness is no longer our biggest stumbling block. Instead, we seem to be stuck at the institutional level due to harmful populism, religion, nationalism, and corporatocracy. Primarily, we are self-sabotaging in the fourth quadrant of Integral theory, where patriarchal and primitive anti-evolutionary forces still dominate. At the global level, sound governance is essential if we want to ban war, heal our planet, and ensure universal human rights.

	INTERNAL SUBJECTIVE	EXTERNAL OBJECTIVE
INDIVIDUAL "I"	**Quadrant 1 – Consciousness** Self Awareness Memory & Cognition Perception & Purpose Worldview	**Quadrant 2 – Behavior** Physical Health Addictions & Allergies Conduct & Communication Accomplishments
COLLECTIVE "WE"	**Quadrant 3 – Culture** Shared Values Social Norms & Customs Meaning & Ethics Relationships	**Quadrant 4 – Systems** Governance Societal Structure & Laws Institutional Processes Resources

So what do we do about our dated institutions at the global level? The **Earth Charter** is a nice start, but it provides only a statement of beautiful beliefs.[141] We need binding world law that bans war and protects people and planet. We also need a court system with jurisdiction over global conflicts, including cases involving international corporations and crimes against humanity. In addition, world citizens should have the right to bring lawsuits in situations where their home county violates their human rights.

Given the impotence of the United Nations, it may be hard for most readers to envision a healthy system of global governance. Yet, there is one model that might work. In 1991, an international team of scholars and jurists completed the *Earth Constitution*. Drafted over thirty years, this document has all the features of an elegant plan to federate Earth, including:[142]

➣ **House of the Peoples:** based on population, like the U.S. Congress

➣ **House of Nations:** a representative from each country, like the U.N.

➣ **House of Counselors:** an ingenious third legislative body comprised of scholars and elders from around the world

➣ **World Court:** to settle international issues like war and climate change

➣ **Presidium:** five executives, one from each of the five main continents

The founder of the **Earth Constitution Institute** is philosopher Glen Martin, who points out that "We the People" are routinely victimized by rogue nations and cutthroat conglomerates. The current world order protects the sovereignty of nations, even when led by bad actors; the *Earth Constitution* protects the sovereignty of people, regardless of residency. Countries would still have their own internal laws, just as every nation in the European Union has its own legal code. As Cornel West reminds us, "Justice is what love looks like in public."

During the Fourth Paradigm, materialism and humanism prompted people to ask, *Who am I?* In the Fifth Paradigm, pluralism and holism compel us to ask, *Who are We?* Today, the cutting edge of evolution is mutual awakening, not solo enlightenment. Group ascension is the focus for those who seek growth in the subjective realm of culture and community – the third quadrant of Integral theory. In this excerpt from *Evolutionary Relationships*, Oracle Press author Patricia Albere explains the importance of the "we space":

> *The "we-space" that resides within the intersubjective domain constitutes a shared reality where two or more people are in full contact with the same interior experience. ... The postmodern era has resulted in a preoccupation with the growth of self over the progress of society. ... Evolutionary Relationships dissolve the separation between us, allowing us to access a unified field where together we may channel cosmic creativity and contribute new gifts to the world. ... I believe mutual awakening is the key to our continued evolution.*[143]

Yes, the "we-space" is where the action is, which is why Wilber has added "Showing Up" to his list of Integral practices. Showing Up in a we-space is the ultimate expression of spiritual maturity, because it demonstrates active participation in the God Game. Oracle Campus is a consecrated container for evolutionary relationships to ripen into sacred activism. While here, renowned peacemaker Rev. Patrick McCollum forged a connection with the Kogi people, which continued to deepen. Now, he is assisting indigenous South Americans fulfill an ancient Amazonian prophecy.[144] Such is the power of physically and soulfully meeting in a scared space dedicated to Truth, Love, and Light.

While mystics of old went on private journeys to access God in the Ethereal Plane, mystics today actuate their highest potential by uniting with others on the Earth Plane. Seeking absolute Truth is sacred, provided we also penetrate partial truths afflicting Team Human. Emotionally, we cannot be so devoted to Divine Love that we neglect the care of our community. Spiritually, we mustn't obsess on finding ultimate reality in the Light, lest we avoid everyday realities. As I wrote in *The Love: How can we claim to love God in the Ethereal Plane, if we have yet to love our sisters and brothers on the Earth Plane?*

In the 21st Century, it is common for New Humans to have peak experiences of oneness during mediation, when surrounded by loved ones, or lost in nature. We need not wait any longer for approval, a diploma, or Sign to become active. Already, we are prepared and positioned to actively pursue the Holomovement.

Having merged with the Light even once provides New Humans with the spiritual insight to share the blessing of unity consciousness with others. Even partial enlightenment qualifies and deputizes us for sacred activism.

Jean Houston reminds us of the immense personal power that flows from identifying our primary archetype. Like Francis Bacon and Marie Hall, Houston finds affinity with the goddess Athena, whom she asks, "What would be good use of a goddess in our time?" As Athena, she then answers her own question:

> Weaving is always the metaphor for my wisdom and power over human possibilities. ... I am reweaving the planet into new forms, new connections. ... In the realm of gods and humans, an alliance is made ... it's very important for each person to find that ally, that archetype, that is deeply appropriate for that person ....
>
> [Y]ou are all in a culture that requires the specificity of the goddess archetype in order to survive and grow its next phase. The earlier forms of more masculine concepts of God, the male metapatterns, although persisting, need the concept of the Earth herself and the goddess archetype to heal and make whole their development. Similarly, the goddess archetype has to be extended, joined with humans, and allowed her next phase of growth.
>
> Our growing task is one in which we operate as a single beingness .... The archetype holding the "higher" pattern" of "you" that can come through – not just for the healing of you but for the "wholing" of you and the deepening of the world. [145]

At Oracle retreats, we often provide participants with an archetype exercise that helps them arrive at their essential self. Recently, I have been drawn to the androgyny of archangels. I shaved my head and changed my "pronouns" on social media to experiment in an androgynous we-space. Rather than "she-her-hers," I now use "we-us-ours" in a show of collective solidarity. Mystics are not afraid to probe the fluidity of interrelationships. When free will is aligned with the Light, Earth Plane solidarity mirrors Ethereal Plane non-duality.

> When you make the two into one, and when you make the inner like the outer ... and the upper like the lower, and when you make the male and female into a single one, so that the male will not be male nor the female be female ... then you enter the Kingdom.

> Jesus, *Gospel of Thomas*

Showing Up in earnest requires inner work and honest self-assessment. If you've honestly identified your meme set point (Growing Up), past trauma and shadow elements (Cleaning Up), and your ecstatic states (Waking Up) – then you are primed to actualize your fullest potential. The next issue is whether you know your life assignment. If not, then stay alert to what is arising within you as you witness the chaos of the Great Cusp. Each of us has a different role to play in the God Game. On Team Human, while we certainly could use more spiritual warriors, it is important to play to your strengths, so "know thyself."

At an early age, I knew I was a warrior and an oracle. I mentioned during the "Gandhi vs. Hitler" chapter that the men on my father's side of the family were all soldiers, but I waited to share that the women on my mother's side were all soothsayers. My maternal grandmother Ruby Kacsmar was born in Hungary in 1917. Her given name was Piroska, which means "ancient." The family fled Hungary in between the two world wars, led by my great-grandmother Rose Tayfel, who intuited the fighting was not over. She bravely uprooted and transplanted the children to a Slavic enclave in Esterhazy, Saskatchewan in Canada, where my mother Patricia George was born. So why did the hair on the back of my neck stand up when Trump minions stormed the Capitol last year and when Putin invaded Ukraine this year? It is in my blood to be an oracle.

Team Human also has the power to prognosticate, if we stay in touch with our intuition and each other. The importance of activating feminine wisdom and anchoring the Law of Gender at this critical moment in human history cannot be overstated. President Jimmy Carter is a leader who exemplifies the proper balance of masculine and feminine energies and who understands the Trickle-Down Deity theory: "When our mothers, wives, sisters, and daughters are considered both different and inferior in the eyes of the God we worship, this belief tends to permeate society and everyone suffers."[146]

> *Women are on the march. ... Like a glacier, contemporary women are slowly carving a new economic and social landscape, building a new world. ... We are inching toward a truly collaborate society, a global culture in which the merits of both sexes are understood, valued, and employed. The twenty-first century may be the first in the modern era to see the sexes work and live as equals – the way men and women were designed to live, the way men and women did live for so many millennia of our distinguished human past.[147]*

> Helen Fisher, *The First Sex*

Yes, humans are in transition and there are multiple timelines in play. Thus, the future is foggy, but it will get clearer once we organize Team Human and map the Holomovement. We need to move quickly if we wish New Humans to remain human and if we want to bequeath a healthy planet to our children. I believe we possess the acuity to select the most prosocial path. In fact, the best way for Team Human to predict the future is by building it ourselves – each in our own way using our unique gifts, yet completely connected to each other.

Lastly, Team Human would be wise to co-create with care. Let us operate methodically in the evolving we-space to harmonize the Holomovement. Let us also heed the advice of James O'Dea, one of the Evolutionary Leaders who co-authored *Our Moment of Choice*. In his essay "The Great Map of Peace," O'Dea points out the Green meme underbelly where "ego, personal agendas, and the projection of unresolved issues sustain polarities and breed a sense of superiority and self-righteousness."[148] Yes, this paradigm shift is far from over, and we will need Second Tier insight to navigate the many challenges.

Truly, this is our moment of choice. At Oracle, the Peace Pentagon and the Valley of Light, we've made ours. We pledge to spread the Truth, share the Love, and follow the Light. We also are building a Peace Room as sophisticated as a War Room. May Team Human share the joy and genius of primordial oneness. Our oldest memory is union; our shared destiny is reunion. *OM JAI!*

Outpost for the Allies of the Light Mission.
Damanhur Matrix. Your Sister Mission.
Decade of Transformation and Passage.
Activate the Network, quickly. Grid that reinforces the Planet.
Network that connects to the Light of the Stars.

All of you, United by Ancient Promises, Choices, Grail.
Missing Archetypes to search, find, spread. Diffusion of New Paradigms.
Create protected Harbor. Many will come to search.
Fast growth if the Center is strong.

Realize a happy way of living together. In the Group the strength.
Newborns in your Valley, Golden Souls arriving.
You are the Sieve and the Cradle.
Vision reinforce with concrete commitment. A Bridge.

With Damanhur, relationships and exchanges.
Connection of trees, spirals, selfic support.
Dreams weave a connecting thread.
For its realization, together, work for the Parliament of Peoples.

You are the Midwife of a New World.
The Ideal in charge, always. Confederation of Communities.
The Oracle helps, supports your efforts.[149]

[1] Pierre Teilhard de Chardin, *The Phenomenon of Man*, pp. 213, 255, Harper & Row: New York, NY (1959).

[2] Andres Pablo Vaccari, "Why Should We Become Posthuman? The Beneficence Argument Questioned," *PubMed.gov* (March 16, 2019), https://pubmed.ncbi.nlm.nih.gov/30877776/ (accessed July 2022).

[3] Dalvin Brown, "What Is the 'Metaverse'? Facebook Says It's the Future of the Internet," *Washington Post* (Oct. 28, 2021), https://www.washingtonpost.com/technology/2021/08/30/what-is-the-metaverse/ (accessed July 2022).

[4] Ying Lin, "10 Virtual Reality Statistics Every Marketer Should Know in 2022," *Oberlo* (Feb. 12, 2022), https://www.oberlo.com/blog/virtual-reality-statistics (accessed July 2022).

[5] Bernard Marr, "The Future of Virtual Reality (VR)," *Forbes* (Dec. 18, 2020), https://www.forbes.com/sites/bernardmarr/2020/12/18/the-future-of-virtual-reality-vr/?sh=719dc727be8f. See also: Teslasuit, https://teslasuit.io/ (accessed July 2022).

[6] Bob Woods, "In Microsoft's Activism Deal, It's Not Just Stock Prices but a Future World at Stake," *CNBC Evolve* (May 7, 2022), https://www.cnbc.com/2022/05/07/in-microsofts-activision-deal-a-future-world-is-at-stake.html# (accessed July 2022).

[7] Will Oremus, "Kids Are Flocking to Facebook's 'Metaverse.' Experts Worry Predators Will Follow," *Washington Post* (Feb. 7, 2022), https://www.washingtonpost.com/technology/2022/02/07/facebook-metaverse-horizon-worlds-kids-safety/ (accessed July 2022).

[8] David J. Chalmers, *Reality +: Virtual Worlds and the Problems of Philosophy*, p. 124, W.W. Norton & Co.: New York, NY (2022).

[9] Nicholas David Bowman, Sun Joo Ahn, Laura Mercer Kollar, "The Paradox of Interactive Media: The Potential for Video Games and Virtual Reality as Tools for Violence Prevention," *Frontiers in Communication* (Nov. 23, 2020), https://www.frontiersin.org/articles/10.3389/fcomm.2020.580965/full (accessed July 2022).

[10] Peace Literacy Institute, https://www.peaceliteracy.org. See also: Paul Chappell website, https://paulkchappell.com/ (both accessed July 2022).

[11] Evolutionary Leaders websites: https://www.evolutionaryleaders.net/ and http://unitivenarrative.org (both accessed July 2022).

[12] Evolutionary Leaders "Unitive Narrative," https://www.evolutionaryleaders.net/unitivenarrative (accessed July 2022).

[13] David Bohm, *Wholeness and the Implicate Order*, p. x, Routledge & Kegan Paul: New York, NY (1980).

[14] Ervin Laszlo, *The Immutable Laws of the Akashic Feld: Universal Truths for a Better Life and a Better World*, pp. 26, 28, 19, 15–16, 36, St. Martin's Publishing: New York, NY (2021).

[15] Anil Seth, *Being You: A New Science of Consciousness*, p. 64, Dutton: New York, NY (2021).

[16] Philp Goff, *Galileo's Error: Foundations for a New Science of Consciousness*, p. 31, Vintage Books: New York, NY (2019).

[17] David Skrbina, *Panpsychism in the West*, p. 334, MIT Press: Cambridge, MA (2017).

[18] Steven Pinker, *Enlightenment Now: The Case for Reason, Science, Humanism, and Progress*, pp. 86–87, 106–108, Viking: New York, NY (2018).

[19] Ibid, pp. 216–227.

[20] Ibid., p. 236.

[21] *Environmental Performance Index 2020*, Yale University (2020), https://envirocenter.yale.edu/2020-environmental-performance-index (accessed July 2022).

[22] "Amid War and Disease, World Happiness Report Shows Bright Spot," *World Happiness Report* (March 18, 2022), https://worldhappiness.report/news/amid-war-and-disease-world-happiness-report-shows-bright-spot/ (accessed July 2022).

[23] Harry Enten, "American Happiness Hits Record Low," *CNN* (Feb. 2, 2022), https://www.cnn.com/2022/02/02/politics/unhappiness-americans-gallup-analysis/index.html (accessed July 2022).

[24] Steven Pinker, *Enlightenment Now*, pp. 418, 411.

[25] Yuval Noah Harari, *Homo Deus: A Brief History of Tomorrow*, p. 240, Harper Collins: New York, NY (2017).

[26] Ibid, p. 47.

[27] Bruce H. Lipton and Steve Bhaerman, *Spontaneous Evolution: Our Positive Future and a Way to Get There from Here*, pp. 116–117, Hay House: New York, NY (2009).

[28] Ibid, pp. 132, 229.

[29] David Sloan Wilson, *Does Altruism Exist? Culture, Genes, and the Welfare of Others*, Yale University Press: New Haven, CT (2015). See also: https://www.prosocial.world/the-science (accessed July 2022).

[30] Ibid, p. 31, quoting Charles Darwin, *The Descent of Man* (1871).

[31] "Russia Fights Back in Information War with Jail Warning," *Reuters.com* (March 4, 2022), https://www.reuters.com/world/europe/russia-introduce-jail-terms-spreading-fake-information-about-army-2022-03-04/ (accessed July 2022).

[32] David Sloan Wilson, *Does Altruism Exist?*, p. 49.

[33] Ken Wilber, *A Theory of Everything: An Integral Vision for Business, Politics, Science, and Spirituality*, p. 112, Shambhala Publications: Boston, MA (2000).

[34] David Korten, *The Great Turning: From Empire to Earth Community*, p, 55, Berrett-Koehler Publishers, San Francisco, CA (2006).

[35] Ibid, p. 313.

[36] Ibid, p. 318.

[37] Riane Eisler, *The Chalice and the Blade*, pp. 17–19, Harper Collins: New York, NY (1995 edition).

[38] Vickey McKeever, "Nordic Countries are Better at Achieving the American Dream, Finland PM Sanna Marin Says," *CNBC.com* (Feb. 4, 2020), https://www.cnbc.com/2020/02/04/sanna-marin-nordic-countries-best-embody-the-american-dream.html (accessed July 2022).

[39] Riane Eisler and Douglas P. Fry, *Nurturing Our Humanity: How Domination and Partnership Shape Our Brains, Lives, and Future*, pp. 169–170, Oxford University Press: New York, NY (2019).

[40] Center for Partnership Systems website, https://centerforpartnership.org/. See also: Partnerism website, https://www.partnerism.org/ (both accessed July 2022).

[41] Riane Eisler and Douglas P. Fry, *Nurturing Our Humanity*, pp. 99–100.

[42] "The Global Village: A Summary of the World," *One World Nations Online*, https://www.nationsonline.org/oneworld/global-village.htm. See also: "The World in 2050," *Price Waterhouse Coopers* (2022), https://www.pwc.com/world2050 (both accessed July 2022).

[43] William James, *The Varieties of Religious Experience: A Study in Human Nature* (1901), pp. 151 *et seq.*, Seven Treasures Publications edition (2009).

[44] Monroe Institute website, https://www.monroeinstitute.org/. See also: Thobey Campion, "How to Escape the Confines of Time and Space According to the CIA," *Vice News* (Feb. 16, 2021), https://www.vice.com/en/article/7k9qag/how-to-escape-the-confines-of-time-and-space-according-to-the-cia; and "Found: Page 25 of the CIA's Gateway Report on Astral Projection," *Vice News* (April 8, 2021), https://www.vice.com/en/article/v7e4g3/found-page-25-of-the-cias-gateway-report-on-astral-projection (all accessed July 2022).

[45] Ken Wilber, *A Theory of Everything*, p. 132.

[46] Ken Wilber, *Integral Spirituality: A Startling New Role for Religion in the Modern and Postmodern World*, p. 93, Shambhala Publications: Boston, MA (2006).

[47] Ken Wilber, *Integral Spirituality*, pp. 93, 95.

[48] Kurt Johnson and David Robert Ord, *The Coming Interspiritual Age*, p. 283, Namaste Publishing: Vancouver, CA (2012).

[49] Andrew Newberg, M.D. and Mark Robert Waldman, *How God Changes Your Brain: Breakthrough Findings from a Leading Neurologist*, pp. 6–7, Ballentine Books Edition: New York, NY (2010).

[50] Ibid, pp. 124–125.

[51] Ibid, pp. 107–111.

[52] Ibid, pp. 76–77, 92–101.

[53] Ibid, pp. 85–86.

[54] Alicia Lee, "Martin Luther King Jr. Explains the Meaning of Love in Rare Handwritten Note," *CNN* (Feb. 9, 2020), https://www.cnn.com/2020/02/09/us/martin-luther-king-jr-handwritten-note-for-sale-trnd/index.html (accessed July 2022).

[55] Dean Hamer, *The God Gene: How Faith Is Hardwired into Our Brains*, p. 11, Anchor Books Edition: New York, NY (2005).

[56] Ibid, pp. 35–36, 48–50.

[57] Ibid, pp. 73, 138.

[58] Craig Foster, *My Octopus Teacher* (2020), *Official Netflix Trailer You Tube*, https://www.youtube.com/watch?v=3s0LTDhqe5A (accessed July 2022).

[59] Ukrainian government video narrated by President Volodymyr Zelenskyy, "On GPS: Zelensky's Hope for Ukraine," *CNN News* (March 20, 2022), https://www.cnn.com/videos/tv/2022/03/20/exp-gps-0320-zelensky-hope-for-ukraine.cnn (accessed July 2022).

[60] Richard Maurice Bucke, M.D., *Cosmic Consciousness: A Study in the Evolution of the Human Mind* (1901), p. 3, E.P. Dutton & Co.: New York, NY (1923).

[61] Charles W. Hardy, *A Worthy Messenger: The Life's Work of Walter Russell*, p. 15, Cosmic Books: Walpole, MA (2013).

[62] "Twilight Club," *Wikipedia*, https://en.wikipedia.org/wiki/Twilight_Club. See also: https://en-academic.com/dic.nsf/enwiki/135369 (both accessed July 2022).

[63] Charles W. Hardy, *A Worthy Messenger*, pp. 125–142.

[64] Glen Clark, *The Man Who Tapped the Secrets of the Universe* (1946), pp. 34–36, University of Science and Philosophy: Waynesboro, VA (20th Ed. 2008).

[65] Walter Russell, *The Universal One* (1926), University of Science and Philosophy: Waynesboro, VA (3rd printing 2006).

[66] "The Internet Database of Periodic Tables," *The Chemogenesis Web Book*, https://www.meta-synthesis.com/webbook/35_pt/pt_database.php?Button=1900-1949%20Formulations (accessed July 2022).

[67] Walter Russell, *The Russell Genero-Radiative Concept* (1930), *Wikischool*, https://wikischool.org/wiki/_media/the_genero_radiative_concept.pdf (accessed July 2022). See also: Charles W. Hardy, *A Worthy Messenger*, p. 189.

[68] Walter Russell, *A Brief Treatise on the Russell Cosmology* (1953), retitled as *A New Concept of the Universe*, University of Science and Philosophy: Waynesboro, VA (Rev. Ed. 1989). *Atomic Suicide?* (1957), University of Science and Philosophy: Waynesboro, VA (3rd Ed. 2014).

[69] Walter Russell, *The Secret of Light* (1947), pp. 5, 2, 7–9, University of Science and Philosophy: Waynesboro, VA (3rd Ed. 1994).

[70] Charles W. Hardy, *A Worthy Messenger*, pp. 205. See also: Toby Grotz, Tim Binder, Ron Kavac, "Magnetic Fields for Hydrogen Production Using Dual Polarity Control and Walter Russell's Experiments with Zero Point Energy," *Magnets Magazine* and *Tesla 3.com*, https://tesla3.com/russell-walter/ (accessed July 2022).

[71] The Russell Museum, *Philosophy.org*, https://www.philosophy.org/museum.html#/ (accessed July 2022).

[72] Saint Theresa of Avila, *The Life of Saint Teresa of Avila by Herself*, p. 98, 150, Penguin Books: London, UK (1957).

[73] R.D. Krumpos, *The Greatest Achievement in Life: Five Traditions of Mysticism*, p. 20 (2012), http://suprarational.org/index.html (accessed July 2022).

[74] Marie Bauer Hall, *Quest for Bruton Vault*, pp. 27–38, Veritat Foundation: Los Angeles, CA (1984).

[75] Ibid, pp. 120, 249.

[76] Clarence Perkins, "The Wealth of the Knights Templars in England and the Disposition of It after Their Dissolution," The American Historical Review (Jan. 1910), https://www.jstor.org/stable/1838333?seq=1#metadata_info_tab_contents (accessed July 2022).

[77] B.P. Perry, "The Knights Templar and the Temple of Solomon," *History Channel*, https://www.history.co.uk/shows/knightfall/articles/the-knights-templar-and-the-temple-of-solomon (accessed July 2022).

[78] Marcia Wendorf, "Clues to the Largest Treasure Ever Buried Are in a Dead Sea Scroll," *Interesting Engineering* (Sept. 29, 2019), https://interestingengineering.com/clues-to-the-largest-treasure-ever-buried-are-in-a-dead-sea-scroll (accessed July 2022).

[79] Barbara Maranzani, "Why Friday the 13th Spelled Doom for the Knights Templar," *History Channel* (Nov. 11, 2020), https://www.history.com/news/why-friday-the-13th-spelled-doom-for-the-knights-templar (accessed July 2022).

[80] Fiona Govan, "Knights Templar Heirs in Legal Battle with the Pope," *The Telegraph* (Aug. 3, 2008), https://www.telegraph.co.uk/news/worldnews/europe/spain/2495343/Knights-Templar-heirs-in-legal-battle-with-the-Pope.html (accessed July 2022).

[81] "From Jerusalem to Rosslyn? The Templars in Scotland," *BBC News*, http://www.bbc.co.uk/legacies/myths_legends/scotland/lothian/ (accessed July 2022).

[82] "Are the Celts One of the Ten Lost Tribes of Israel?" *Irish Central* (July 7, 2021), https://www.irishcentral.com/news/are-the-celts-one-of-the-ten-lost-tribes-of-israel-233823021-237790101 (accessed July 2022).

[83] "Stone of Scone," *Wikipedia*, https://en.wikipedia.org/wiki/Stone_of_Scone (accessed July 2022).

[84] Rebecca Larson, "Portraits of Elizabeth's Favorite: Robert Dudley, Earl of Leicester," *Tudors Dynasty* (Aug. 5, 2017), https://tudorsdynasty.com/portraits-elizabeths-favorite-robert-dudley-earl-leicester/amp/ (accessed July 2022).

[85] Tracy Borman, *The Private Lives of the Tudors: Uncovering the Secrets of Britain's Greatest Dynasty*, Grove Press: New York, NY (2016).

[86] "Robert Dudley: Queen Elizabeth I's Great Love," *History Extra* (June 26, 2020) https://www.historyextra.com/period/elizabethan/robert-dudley-queen-elizabeth-is-great-love/ (accessed July 2022).

[87] Helen H. Gordon, "The Sons of Elizabeth Tudor: Part 2," *Academia* (Jan. 1, 2018) https://www.academia.edu/35617265/The_Sons_of_Elizabeth_Tudor_Part_2.docx (accessed July 2022).

[88] Elisabeth Sears, *Shakespeare and the Tudor Rose*, pp. 17, 27, Meadowgeese Press: Marshall Hills, MA (2002).

[89] "Shakespeare's Parents," *Shakespeare Online*, http://www.shakespeare-online.com/biography/shakespeareparents.html (accessed July 2022).

[90] "Shakespeare's Last Will and Testament (1616)," *Shakespeare Online*, http://www.shakespeare-online.com/biography/shakespearewill.html (accessed July 2022).

[91] "How Did Shakespeare Die?" *Shakespeare Online*, http://www.shakespeare-online.com/biography/deathofshakespeare.html (accessed July 2022).

[92] Barbara Maranzani, "Was Shakespeare the Real Author of His Plays?" *Biography: A & E Television* (May 26, 2020), https://www.biography.com/news/shakespeare-real-author-theories (accessed July 2022).

[93] Samuel Clemons (Mark Twain), *Is Shakespeare Dead?* (1909), Project Gutenberg, https://www.gutenberg.org/files/2431/2431-h/2431-h.htm (accessed July 2022).

[94] "Knights of the Helmet," *SirBacon.org*, http://www.sirbacon.org/knightmp.htm (accessed July 2022).

[95] "Tudor Spy Invents Binary," *A Bit of Computer Science for Fun*, https://abitofcs4fn.org/spies/tudor-spy-invents-binary/ (accessed July 2022).

[96] Peter Dawkins, "Baconian History," *Francis Bacon Research Trust*, https://www.fbrt.org.uk/bacon/baconian-history/ (accessed July 2022).

[97] Amelie Deventer Von Kunow, "The Earl of Essex's Secret Birth," excerpt from *Francis Bacon: The Last of the Tudors* (1921), *SirBacon.org*, http://www.sirbacon.org/essex-devereux.htm (accessed July 2022).

[98] Edward S. Le Comte, "The Ending of Hamlet as a Farewell to Essex," John Hopkins University Press and *JSTOR Library* (June 1950), https://www.jstor.org/stable/2872055?seq=1 (accessed July 2022).

[99] Peter Dawkins, "Baconian History."

[100] Alfred Dodd and Doris Davis, "Chronology Related to Francis Bacon's Life," *SirBacon.org*, https://sirbacon.org/links/chronos.html (accessed July 2022).

[101] Joel J. Epstein, "Francis Bacon and the Issue of Union, 1603-1608." *Huntington Library Quarterly* and *JSTOR Library* (Feb. 1970), https://www.jstor.org/stable/3816717?read-now=1&seq=1#page_scan_tab_contents (accessed July 2022).

[102] Ibid.

[103] "Jacobean Debate on the Union," *Wikipedia*, https://en.wikipedia.org/wiki/Jacobean_debate_on_the_Union (accessed July 2022).

[104] Brent Tarter, "Old Dominion," *Encyclopedia Virginia*, https://encyclopediavirginia.org/entries/old-dominion/ (accessed July 2022).

[105] "Governors of Virginia: 1607 to 1910," *Virginia Genealogy Trails*, http://genealogytrails.com/vir/governorbios.html (accessed July 2022).

[106] Marie Bauer Hall, *Quest for Bruton Vault*, pp. 120–121.

[107] Richard Cavendish, "The Execution of the Earl of Essex," *History Today* (Feb. 2, 2001), https://www.historytoday.com/archive/months-past/execution-earl-essex (accessed July 2022).

[108] "Walter Ralegh: 'The Rankest Traitor in all England?'" *History Extra* (Oct. 29, 2020), https://www.historyextra.com/period/stuart/sir-walter-ralegh-raleigh-elizabeth-i-james-vi-i-bye-main-plot-trial-winchester-was-he-guilty-treason-how-did-he-die-execution/ (accessed July 2022).

[109] Alfred Dodd, "The Martyrdom of Francis Bacon" (1945), *SirBacon.org*, http://www.sirbacon.org/links/martyrdom.htm (accessed July 2022).

[110] Marie Bauer Hall, *Quest for Bruton Vault*, p. 237.

[111] "Occult Theories about Francis Bacon" and "St. Germaine (Theosophy)," *Wikipedia*, https://en.wikipedia.org/wiki/Occult_theories_about_Francis_Bacon and https://en.wikipedia.org/wiki/St._Germain_(Theosophy) (both accessed July 2022).

[112] The relevant Bacon Family genealogy chart can be viewed at *Genie*: https://www.geni.com/photo/view/6000000002800725388?album_type=photos_of_me&photo_id=6000000084884306058 (accessed July 2022).

[113] Brent Tarter, "Nathaniel Bacon (1647-1676)," *Encyclopedia Virginia*, https://encyclopediavirginia.org/entries/bacon-nathaniel-1647-1676/. See also: "Bacon's Rebellion," *National Park Service*, https://www.nps.gov/jame/learn/historyculture/bacons-rebellion.htm (both accessed July 2022).

[114] The Oracle Institute Mission Statement, http://theoracleinstitute.org/mission.

[115]

116 Walter Semkiw (a.k.a. John Adams), *Return of the Revolutionaries: The Case for Reincarnation and Soul Groups Reunited*, pp. 3–4, 11, Hampton Roads Publishing Company: Charlottesville, VA (2003).

117 "Efforts to Impeach George W. Bush" and "Efforts to Impeach Dick Cheney," *Wikipedia*, https://en.wikipedia.org/wiki/Efforts_to_impeach_George_W._Bush and https://en.wikipedia.org/wiki/Efforts_to_impeach_Dick_Cheney (accessed July 2022).

118 George Wither, *Collection of Emblems: Ancient and Moderne* (1635), Kessinger Publishing's Rare Reprints, www.Kessinger.net.

119 Marie Bauer Hall, *Quest for Bruton Vault*, pp. 245, 596.

120 Ibid, p. 379, 416.

121 Ibid, p. 472.

122 Ibid, p. 588.

123 Bentley Boyd, "Bruton Parish Dig Fails to Convince Believers, *Daily Press* (Sept. 12, 1992), https://www.dailypress.com/news/dp-xpm-19920912-1992-09-12-9209120042-story.html. See also: Nanette MA Crist, "Our Quest for the Bruton Vault," *Francis Bacon Society* (June 2017), https://francisbaconsociety.co.uk/the-society/baconiana/baconiana-vol1-no6/#quest-for-bruton-vault (accessed July 2022).

124 "Rockefeller Archive Center," *Wikipedia*, https://en.wikipedia.org/wiki/Rockefeller_Archive_Center (accessed July 2022).

125 Marie Hall, *Quest for Bruton Vault*, pp. 144, 154, 609, 155.

126 Benson Lossing, *The Pictorial Field-Book of the Revolution*, sketch of Fort Washington (1850). See also: "Fort Washington (Manhattan)" and "Battle of Fort Washington," *Wikipedia*, https://en.wikipedia.org/wiki/Fort_Washington_(Manhattan) and https://en.wikipedia.org/wiki/Battle_of_Fort_Washington (both accessed July 2022).

127 James Thomas Flexner, *Washington: The Indispensable Man*, Back Bay Books: New York, NY (1994).

128 Brad Meltzer and Josh Mensch, *The First Conspiracy: The Secret Plot to Kill George Washington*, Flat Iron Books: New York, NY (2018).

129 Ibid, pp. 328, 356–357.

130 Oberto Airaudi, *Dying to Learn: Frist Book of the Initiate* (2012); *Reborn to Live: Second Book of the Initiate* (2013); *Seven Scarlet Doors: Third Book of the Initiate* (2013), Oracle Institute Press: Independence, VA; Shama Viola, *Bral Talej Divination Cards*, Oracle Institute Press: Independence, VA (2nd Ed. 2020).

131 "Elinor Ostrom," *Wikipedia*, https://en.wikipedia.org/wiki/Elinor_Ostrom (accessed July 2022).

132 Peace Pentagon HUB website: www.PeacePentagon.net.

133 Douglas Rushkoff, *Team Human*, pp. 146, 205, W.W. Norton & Company: New York, NY (2019).

[134] Foundation for Intentional Community website: https://www.ic.org/ (accessed July 2022).

[135] Ross Robertson, "Atlantis in the Mountains of Italy," *What is Enlightenment?*, p. 92, Issue 36 (April-June 2007), https://s3.eu-central-1.amazonaws.com/wieoldissues/wie_en_weboptimized/EN_issue_36.pdf (accessed July 2022).

[136] Damanhur Temples of Humankind website: https://www.thetemples.org/ (accessed July 2022).

[137] Francis Bacon, *The New Atlantis* (1627), *Project Gutenberg*, https://www.gutenberg.org/files/2434/2434-h/2434-h.htm (accessed July 2022).

[138] "Chapter V: The Security Council" and "Security Council Voting System," *United Nations Charter*, https://www.un.org/en/about-us/un-charter/chapter-5 and https://www.un.org/securitycouncil/content/voting-system (both accessed July 2022).

[139] "Chapter XVIII: Amendments, Articles 108 and 109," *United Nations Charter*, https://www.un.org/en/about-us/un-charter/chapter-18 (accessed July 2022).

[140] "Chapter XIV: International Court of Justice, Article 94," *United Nations Charter*, https://www.un.org/en/about-us/un-charter/chapter-14 (accessed July 2022).

[141] *The Earth Charter*, https://earthcharter.org/read-the-earth-charter/preamble/ (accessed July 2022).

[142] *The Earth Constitution*, https://earthconstitution.world/text-of-the-earth-constitution/ (accessed July 2022).

[143] Patricia Albere, *Evolutionary Relationships: Unleashing the Power of Mutual Awakening*, pp. 38, 85, 29, 228, Oracle Institute Press: Independence, VA (2017).

[144] Jacob Devaney, "A Return to Origen: The Amazon Prophecy Project," *JacobDevaney. medium* (Nov. 20, 2021), https://jacobdevaney.medium.com/a-return-to-origin-the-amazon-prophecy-project-3bc4acedd9fd (accessed July 2022).

[145] Jean Houston, *The Power of Myth: Learning to Live our Greater Story*, pp. 318–319, Harper Collins: New York, NY (1996).

[146] Jimmy Carter, *A Call to Action: Women, Religion, Violence, and Power*, p. 105, Simon & Schuster Paperbacks: New York, NY (2015).

[147] Helen Fisher, *The First Sex: The Natural Talents of Women and How They Are Changing the World*, p. 288, Ballantine Publishing Group: New York, NY (1999).

[148] Source of Synergy Foundation, *Our Moment of Choice: Evolutionary Visions and Hope for Our Future*, edited by Robert Atkinson, Kurt Johnson, and Deborah Moldow, p. 8, Atria Books: New York, NY (2020).

[149] Reading from the Oracles at Damanhur to The Oracle Institute (March 9, 2020). The question concerned the relationship between the City of Light, Valley of Light, and a confederation of spiritual communities around the world (Jan. 22, 2020).

INDEX

D

da Vinci, Leonardo 123, 285, 382
Daddy Deism 27, 104, 210, 212, 214, 269, 380
Dalai Lama 41, 87, 212, 232, 265, 336
Damanhur 4, 323, 409, 411, 418
Daniken, Erich von 262
Dark Energy (see Physics)
Dark Lord 203, 205, 232, 234, 259, 361
Dark Matter (see Physics)
Dark Night of the Soul 42, 82
Darth Vader 143, 196, 201
David (King of Israel) 17
Darwin, Charles 154, 175, 284, 319, 361, 363, 367-368
Davies, Paul 312, 323
de Klerk, F.W. 44
Dead Sea Scrolls 207, 393
Declaration of Independence 70, 177, 401, 406, 408
Deep State 9,
Default Mode of the Universe Theory 203, 206, 236, 261, 267, 314, 362, 381
Deities
    Allah (Muslim) 24-25, 40
    Anunnaki (Sumerian) 252, 282
    Ashera (Jewish) 219
    Athena (Greek) 397, 403-404, 406-407, 416
    Brahma (Hindu) 209
    El, Elyon, Elohim (Jewish) 16, 210, 283
    Enki (Sumerian) 282-283
    Enlil (Sumerian) 282
    Green Tara (Buddhist) 280, 297
    Hermes (Greek)/Thoth (Egyptian) 207
    Inanna (Sumerian) 219-220
    Isis (Egyptian) 22, 275-276
    Krishna (Hindu) 171, 229, 317
    Osiris (Egyptian) 275
    Shiva (Hindu) 209
    Vishnu (Hindu) 209
    Yahweh (Jewish) 10, 15-16, 40, 183, 197, 210, 219, 282, 295
Demiurge 111, 297, 301, 341
Democracy (see Government Models)
Democracy Index 101-102, 179
Devereux, Robert (Earl of Essex) 397, 399
Dhammapada 18, 222, 229, 249
Dharma 18, 196, 229, 377
Dickens, Charles 69
Digha Nikaya 17
Dimensions (see Physics)

Dissonance 1, 3, 8, 10-11, 23, 30, 42-43, 50, 56, 58-59, 65, 67-68, 76, 91, 162, 172, 264-265
Divine/Sacred Feminine 13, 27, 29, 212, 220, 269, 297, 299-302, 357, 371-372
    Aluna 120
    Binah 298-300, 302
    Great Mother 11, 13, 55-56, 98, 120, 209, 371-372
    Shekinah 27
    Sophia 27, 111, 301
    Wisdom Energy 27, 204, 210-212, 216, 239
Divine Masculine 29, 210, 220, 299, 301
    Creative Energy 203, 210-212, 239
    Hokmah 298-300, 302
Divine Order/Time 131, 133, 203, 231, 287
Divine Paradox 230-231, 298, 388-389
Dossey, Larry 246, 249
Dudley, Robert (Earl of Leicester) 394-397
Duality/Non-Duality 1, 3, 6, 12, 30, 34, 91, 131, 137, 187, 196, 209, 223, 228, 237, 239-240, 259, 261, 265, 299-300, 318, 342, 346, 362, 376, 416
Dunn, Stephen 4
Dystopia 6, 34, 113, 117, 119, 210, 233-234, 272, 278-281, 290-292, 329-337, 361, 367, 381, 410

E

Earth Changes 120-121, 272-273, 275-277, 290, 366
Earth Charter 414
Earth Constitution 414
Earth Constitution Institute 414
Earth Plane 1, 3, 6-7, 9, 11-12, 16, 18, 23, 30, 34, 40, 61-62, 64, 66, 76, 85, 87, 90-91, 98, 137, 143-145, 162, 196-198, 203-206, 213, 221-222, 228, 231, 240, 244-245, 259-261, 266-267, 280-281, 288-291, 297, 326, 339-340, 358, 378, 388-389, 415-416
Edy, Mary Baker 383
Ego 12, 48-49, 51, 56, 60, 75, 129, 202, 237-238, 299, 375, 388, 418
Egocentric (see Spectrum of Consciousness)
Egypt 14, 57, 207, 272-277, 282, 345
    Egyptian Empire 273
Einstein, Albert 31, 277, 302, 311-315, 318, 322, 340, 386-387
Eisenhower, Dwight 286, 401
Eisenstein, Charles 271
Eisler, Riane 13-14, 269, 370-373, 380

ABOUT THE AUTHOR

Rev. Laura M. George, J.D. (Tau Lama) is an interfaith minister, attorney, and perpetual seeker. In 2004, she founded The Oracle Institute with the goal of helping humanity make the spiritual shift into the New Millennium. In 2006, she founded Oracle Institute Press, and in 2015, she founded Oracle Temple, an esoteric church. Currently, she is co-founding the Valley of Light intentional community, which shares Oracle Campus in Independence, Virginia.

Raised Catholic, Laura began questioning her birth religion at an early age. As an adult, she embarked on a study of the world's religions and studied with Zoroastrian, Gnostic, Melchizedek, and Lakota teachers. By 2000, Laura was finding answers to the spiritual questions that had haunted her since childhood. When the September 11, 2001 tragedy hit, she had an intense spiritual awakening, which – coupled with a rare Venus transit in 2004 – changed the course of her life.

Thereafter, Laura founded Oracle and wrote the award-winning first book in its foundational trilogy: *The Truth: About the Five Primary Religions* (2006). She co-authored the second book, *The Love: Of the Fifth Spiritual Paradigm* (2010), with luminaries such as Archbishop Desmond Tutu, Maya Angelou, Bill McKibben, Maxine Hong Kingston, Alex Grey, and Wendell Berry. It took Laura over a decade to complete the final installment of the trilogy, *The Light: And the New Human* (2022), as she watched consciousness complexify. For her inspirational and groundbreaking work in the field of conscious co-creation, Laura has been inducted into the circle of Evolutionary Leaders.

To date, Oracle has established an award-winning press, spirituality school, and global peace practice. Laura oversees construction of Oracle Campus on a stunning site in the Blue Ridge Mountains along the ancient New River. The Peace Pentagon is the heart of Oracle Campus, and its pentagonal sanctuary is dedicated to the Fifth Spiritual Paradigm. The exterior of the Peace Pentagon is finished, and Laura continues to fundraise to complete the building's interior.

ABOUT THE PUBLISHER

The Oracle Institute is a 501(c)(3) educational charity and spiritual think-tank that studies the nexus between religion, politics, and conscious evolution. Our mission is to help humanity progress into the Fifth Spiritual Paradigm and adopt a Culture of Peace.

Oracle Press is an award-winning publishing house, which creates books that assist humanity's quest for Truth, Love, and Light. Our texts focus on the world's religions, wisdom traditions, social trends, and civic responsibilities. To date, our press has garnered six prestigious book awards in categories such as religion, spirituality, children's fiction, and the performing arts.

Oracle Press works closely with authors to co-create beautiful, relevant, and impactful books published under the Oracle and Peace Pentagon imprints. Our non-profit press also offers services to authors who wish to self-publish when the project is aligned with the educational mission of The Oracle Institute.

To learn more about Oracle Press:
www.TheOracleInstitute.org/Press

To shop at our online Bookstore:
www.TheOracleInstitute.org/Bookstore

To learn more about Oracle Institute programs, events, and our intentional community – the **Valley of Light** – visit us at Oracle Campus:

The Peace Pentagon
88 Oracle Way
Independence, Virginia 24348

www.TheOracleInstitute.org
www.PeacePentagon.net
www.ValleyOfLight.org

CPSIA information can be obtained
at www.ICGtesting.com
Printed in the USA
BVHW031257151022
649545BV00014B/238

9 781937 465322